CHRIST IN THE CAMP

OR

Religion in the Confederate Army

BY

REV. J. WILLIAM JONES, D. D.

Formerly Chaplain in Army of Northern Virginia; Secretary Southern Historical
Society; Author "Personal Reminiscences, Anecdotes and Letters of
R. E. Lee;" "Army of Northern Virginia, Memorial Volume;"
"Jefferson Davis, Memorial Volume;" "School His-
tory of the United States;" "Life and
Letters of R. E. Lee;" "The Sol-
dier and the Man," etc.

WITH AN
INTRODUCTION
BY

REV. J. C. GRANBERRY, D. D.

Bishop of the Methodist Episcopal Church, South; Formerly
Chaplain in Army of Northern Virginia

Harrisonburg, Virginia
SPRINKLE PUBLICATIONS

1986

Sprinkle Publications
P. O. Box 1094
Harrisonburg, Virginia 22801

TO MY COMRADES AND TO WORKERS AMONG THE CHAPLAINS, MISSIONARIES, AND COLPORTERS, OF THE ARMY OF NORTHERN VIRGINIA, AND OF OTHER CONFEDERATE ARMIES, WHO LABORED FAITHFULLY IN THAT GREAT HARVEST FIELD OF SOULS, THIS BOOK IS AFFECTIONATELY DEDICATED BY THE AUTHOR, IN THE CONFIDENT HOPE THAT AS WE CHERISH HALLOWED MEMORIES OF THOSE DAYS OF TOIL, BUT OF PRECIOUS BLESSINGS, SO WE WILL OVER THERE ENJOY SWEET COMMUNION WITH EACH OTHER AS WE SHALL TALK OVER THE WONDERFUL MANNER IN WHICH CHRIST WAS IN OUR CAMP, TO SAVE THE PENITENT, TO STRENGTHEN THE TRUE CHRISTIAN AND TO MAKE EVEN BATTLEFIELD AND HOSPITAL BRIGHT AND GLORIOUS BY HIS PRESENCE.

LIST OF ILLUSTRATIONS

LIST OF ILLUSTRATIONS

PREFACE TO NEW EDITION.

IN PUBLISHING this new edition of "Christ in the Camp" the author would express his sincere gratification at the reception of his book as first published, the very favorable notices of the press, and especially the commendations of his old comrades among the chaplains, missionaries, and soldiers who wore the Gray.

The last edition having been out of print for some years, and there coming to him a considerable demand for copies of the book, the author counts it very fortunate that he has been able to secure a reliable and efficient Southern Publishing House to bring out a new edition.

In sending out this edition, with the notable improvements made by the Publishers, public sentiment in this section appeals to all interested in this most important chapter of the history of our grand old army, to see to it that it is put into the libraries and homes of our people that the story of how Christ was in the Camp may be read by the present generation, and handed down to our children's children.

The book is sent forth with the fervent prayer that yet more in the future than in the past, it may prove useful in showing our young people the power of religion to promote real manhood, and in leading our old soldiers to follow their Christian leaders, and comrades, "even as they, also, followed Christ."

J. WM. JONES.

RICHMOND, VA.
May 1st, 1904.

PREFACE.

THE history of the Army of Northern Virginia is yet to be written. Much concerning it has already been published—much that is valuable as "material for the future historian;" more, perhaps, that is worthless—but it remains for some master-hand to separate the wheat from the chaff and tell the true story of the heroic deeds and splendid achievements of that Grand Army which sheds lustre upon the American name and is fast becoming the pride of the whole country—North as well as South.

It will ever be a source of regret to all lovers of the truth of history that the great chieftain who led this army to so many splendid victories, who sheathed his stainless sword at Appomattox and retired to the shades of academic life at Lexington, the idol of his people and the admiration of the world, was not spared to finish the task he had begun of writing the history of his campaigns; for *the world* would have believed what he wrote as implicitly as it did those modest despatches which used to be signed, "R. E. Lee, General."

But he was called from his unfinished work to wear his glittering "crown of rejoicing," and so we must wait for the historian of the future to study the material, estimate the "overwhelming numbers and resources" against which the Army of Northern Virginia fought, and give to posterity the results of his labors.

But any history of that army which omits an account of the wonderful influence of religion upon it—which fails to tell how the courage, discipline and *morale* of the whole was influenced by the humble piety and evangelical zeal of many of its officers and men—would be incomplete and unsatisfactory. The Army of Northern Virginia has a *religious* history as distinct and as easily traced as its *military* exploits, and the material for volumes on this feature of its history is so abundant, that in attempting its portrayal one is embarrassed chiefly by the richness of the mine he is to work—the main difficulty being that of selecting from the mass of material at his disposal so as to condense the wonderful story within the limits of a single volume. For such a work I think that I may (without improper egotism) claim some special qualifications.

It was my proud privilege to follow the fortunes of that army, as private soldier or chaplain, from Harper's Ferry in '61 to Appomattox Court House in '65—to know personally many of its leading officers—to mingle freely with the private soldiers in camp, on the march, in the bivouac, on the battle-field, and in the hospital—and to labor in those glorious revivals which made nearly the whole army vocal with God's praises.

In 1865 I was solicited by many of my fellow-chaplains and old comrades, and by General Lee himself, to prepare this chapter of our history, and I collected at that time a large amount of material, to which I have since made constant additions. It will, therefore, be for me a "labor of love" to cull here and there an incident, to recall here and there a reminiscence, to paint here and there a picture which will serve to illustrate the subject, and to show beyond all cavil that "religion in Lee's army" was not a myth, but a blessed reality, a "silver lining" to the dark cloud of war, a bright spot in the gloomy picture, a solace in hardships, sufferings and afflictions, and a bright guiding star to many of our brave men when called on to "cross over the river and rest under the shade of the trees."

In the preparation of this volume I have made free use of my own diary, and of letters from the army which I wrote for the *Religious Herald* and the *Christian Index,* and especially of a series of papers recently published in the *Religious Herald,* which were very kindly received, and for the publication of which, in book form, I have received many calls from friends living in different sections of the country and representing all creeds of our evangelical Christianity.

I must also make especial acknowledgment of indebtedness to the excellent book of my friend, Rev. Dr. W. W. Bennett (late President of Randolph-Macon College), on "The Great Revival;" to war files of several religious newspapers; to a large number of letters and other documents furnished me in '65 and '66 by chaplains, missionaries, and others of our army-workers, and to a complete file of the minutes of our Chaplains' Association of the Second and Third Corps, furnished me by the courtesy of the accomplished secretary, Rev. L. C. Vass.

Nor must I fail to make due acknowledgment to my old friend and honored brother, Rev. J. C. Granberry, D. D., Bishop of the Methodist Episcopal Church South, for his admirable introduction. Bishop Granberry's zealous and efficient service as chaplain in the Army of Northern Virginia—a service which was only temporarily suspended when he was wounded and taken prisoner in the faithful discharge of his duty—gives him special qualification to speak on this subject, while his wide influence with evangelical Christians of every name gives peculiar weight to his kind words of commendation.

It may be proper to add that, while the book is written by an ardent Confederate, who does not pretend to conceal warm Confederate sympathies, everthing has been scrupulously avoided which could reasonably give offence from either sectional or sectarian bias.

The work begun twenty-two years ago is now
finished, and the author sends it forth with the earnest
hope that it may prove acceptable to many at the
North as well as at the South, with the fervent prayer
that it may be useful in leading men to Christ and in
strengthening the faith and brightening the hope of
true children of our loving Father, who, behind the
"frowning providence" of war, hid "a smiling face"
for those who trusted Him even in the storm.

J. W. J.

RICHMOND, VIRGINIA,
    May 30, 1887.

CONTENTS.

(9)

CHAPTER IV.

INFLUENCE OF CHRISTIAN OFFICERS—*Concluded.*

CHAPTER V.

BIBLE AND COLPORTAGE WORK.

CHAPTER VI.

HOSPITAL WORK.

CHAPTER VII.

WORK OF THE CHAPLAINS AND MISSIONARIES.

CHAPTER VIII.

EAGERNESS OF THE SOLDIERS TO HEAR THE GOSPEL.

CHAPTER IX.

STATE OF RELIGION IN 1861–62.

CHAPTER X.

REVIVALS IN THE LOWER VALLEY AND AROUND FREDERICKSBURG.

CHAPTER XI.

THE GREAT REVIVAL ALONG THE RAPIDAN.

CHAPTER XII.

PROGRESS OF THE WORK IN 1864–65.

CHAPTER XIII.

RESULTS OF THE WORK AND PROOFS OF ITS GENUINENESS.

APPENDIX.

APPENDIX No. 2.

INTRODUCTION.

By REV. J. C. GRANBERRY, D. D., *Bishop of the Methodist Episcopal Church South, formerly Chaplain in the Army of Northern Virginia.*

THESE annals are fresh and vivid. They read like the story of what happened yesterday. They are not less accurate for being aglow. Dr. Jones was no small part of the religious movement he narrates; a quarter of a century does not fade in the memory of an actor in such extraordinary scenes. But he has not trusted memory alone. He has preserved or collected publications of the day; he jotted down many incidents when they occurred, and this history is with him no new thought. Besides, he writes out of his heart. Add to this how he loves the Army of Northern Virginia. He is too wise and live a man to miss present duties and privileges in brooding over a lost cause, or burying himself in the grave of the Confederacy: but reconstruction did not work out of him admiration and affection for his fellow-patriots and fellow-soldiers of 1861–5; he went back into the Union with his whole heart (which, like his body, is big and strong), but the integrity of that heart includes changeless devotion to his comrades of the fiery struggle.

To us of the South, this volume possesses special interest. For the men who wore the blue we have no unkindness; we are ready to cast flowers on the neatly-kept graves of those who fell, and to clasp the hands of those who survive; but the men who wore the gray are our brothers, defenders, heroes. The ex-Confederate may now be a Democrat or a Republican; he may reside in Florida or Washington Territory: but his heart will be still and cold in death when it ceases to throb and warm at the mention of the soldiers of the South, whether they sleep as the greater part do, or yet live. How grateful then to us should be the story of what divine grace did for those brave men; how it exalted and hallowed their character, comforted

(13)

them amid all their risks and sufferings, inspired the dying, whatever may have been the issue of the day, with immortal triumph, and continues to be in peace as in war the guide and joy of those whom battle, accident and disease have spared!

But the value of this book is not restricted by sectional, partisan, or national lines. It is independent of all political and social questions involved in the civil strife. These pages do not discuss slavery, State-rights, secession; nor compare the skill of generals and prowess of troops on the opposing sides. "Christ in the Camp; or, Religion in the Army," never mind what camp or army, is a theme of deep, thrilling, world-wide significance. The only triumphs the author records are the triumphs of the cross. That so many soldiers were saved by the power of the Gospel to the praise of the riches of God's grace is the fact in which he desires all Christians to rejoice. Some narrow and prejudiced Federals may not be able to understand how it was possible for those men to be saved without repenting of "the sin of rebellion." We cannot waste time on them. Those of broader views and more generous spirit, especially godly men who followed the Stars and Stripes, will thank God for the evidence that the soldiers who opposed them with constancy and valor, many shedding their lifeblood on the field, were partakers of like precious faith with themselves. To me it is a happy thought that in the two confronting camps, often at the same hour, there rose with voice and heart the common strain,

"All hail the power of Jesus' name!"

I would add my testimony to that of Dr. Jones on the evangelical tone of the preaching and worship in our army. Chaplains and visiting ministers determined not to know anything among them save Jesus Christ, and Him crucified. It was always assumed that the cause for which they contended was righteous; on it was invoked the divine blessing, and the troops were exhorted to faithful service. But the grounds of the war were not discussed; constitutional and historical questions were passed by, except a certain local coloring, such as illustrations drawn from active military life and appeals based on the perils of war. The sermons in the camp would have suited any congregation in city or country, and with even less change might have been preached to the Union armies. Eternal things, the claims of God, the worth of the soul, the wages of sin which is death, and the gift of God which is eternal life through Jesus Christ our Lord—these were the matter of preaching. The marrow and fatness of the Gospel were set forth. The style was not controversial, speculative or curious, but eminently practical and direct; hortatory, yet also instructive. There were pathos and urgency of appeal. The hearers were besought to immediate and uncompromising action, for the time was short. The songs, prayers, lay testimonies and exhortations, in a word, all the exercises, were in the same line. There was no stirring up of bad blood; no inflaming of malice and revenge. The man of God lifted up, not the Bars and Stars, but the cross, and pressed the inquiry, "Who among you are on the Lord's side?"

"Religion in the army" was a peculiar type or phase of piety. I mean not that it differed from religion in other armies, but that it differed from religion at home and in peace; identical in essence, but modified in manifestation by the extraordinary circumstances amid which it sprang up or developed. It was a variety in the fruit of the manifold grace of God; it had its own form, color, flavor. Military discipline was not wholly unfavorable. The martial imagery of which Paul was fond shows an analogy between the life of the soldier and the life of the saint. The centurion of Capernaum and the centurion of Cesarea were patterns of faith and of a devout spirit. The soldier's habits of unquestioning obedience to orders, of trust in superior officers, and of freedom from anxiety about things for which he is not responsible, fit into the life of faith. Our men planned not for the future, but did the duty of the hour; they went when and whither they were bid, were content not to know beforehand the object of a campaign or the strategy for its accomplishment, and drew not back from any feat, however apparently impossible, or any hazards, however apparently unnecessary. Yet they were intelligent and thoughtful and full of enthusiasm in the cause for which they fought. Multitudes of them, privates as well as officers, prized not their own liberty, health or life in comparison with the honor and success of the Confederate States. They carried into their religion a profounder faith and consecration.

Certainly our soldiers were exposed to severe temptations, and deprived of many aids to pious culture. Yet grace triumphed over all those disadvantages. I have nowhere witnessed more complete, symmetrical and beautiful examples of Christian character than in the army. Some of them were boys, others mature men; some in the ranks, others officers of various grades. Away from the happy influences of neighborhood and home, they were chaste, temperate and pure. Cut off from Church and Sunday-school, often having no day of sacred rest and little communion of saints, they feared the Lord and thought upon His name. On every march they carried the well-thumbed Bible, and the hard ground on which they lay without pillow, bed or tent, often proved to them a Bethel. The lonely vigils of sentinels and picket were hallowed and cheered by sweet meditations of God. Patience had her perfect work amid the long privations and discomforts of their lot. They were kind, sympathetic and generous to their comrades in arms; and these were the only persons with whom, as a rule, they came in contact. They delighted in devotional meetings, and were not ashamed to witness for Christ. Not recklessly, but with thoughtful and prayerful solemnity, they went into fierce battle; yet the peace of God which passeth all understanding kept their hearts against alarm; and if a ball shivered a limb, or entered the body, a smile of resignation lit up the rugged faces as they were borne off to the hospital and surgeon, or with words of victory they on the field yielded up their spirit to the God in whom they trusted. To God be all the glory!   J. C. GRANBERRY.

"LEAVING HOME."

"Will my innocent boy come back a reckless, vicious man?"

(See Companion picture — "The Sequel." — See page 17.)

CHAPTER I.

ON the memorable 17th day of April, 1861—the day on which the Virginia Convention, in response to Mr. Lincoln's call for seventy-five thousand men to coerce the seceded States, passed its ordinance of secession—there occurred at the little village of Louisa Court House a scene similar to those enacted all over Virginia and the South, which none who witnessed it can ever forget. The "Louisa Blues," a volunteer company composed of the best young men of the county, were drilling at noon on the court green, when a telegram from the governor of the State ordered them to be ready to take a train of cars at sundown that evening. Immediately all was bustle and activity—couriers were sent in every direction to notify absentees—and in every household there were busy fingers and anxious hearts preparing those brave men to meet promptly the call of the sovereign power of their native State.

I remember one doting mother who wept in secret the tears she restrained in the presence of her loved boy of just sixteen summers, who had but recently risen from severe illness, but whose frame grew strong with eagerness to march with his comrades to the post of duty. When asked if she was not willing for her boy to respond to his country's call, she replied in that spirit of patriotism which characterized the women of the South throughout the war: "Certainly I am! I wish him to go, and should be ashamed of him if he were unwilling to go. But there is one thought of which I cannot rid myself, and which causes me the bitterest anguish. I have always looked upon an army as a complete 'school of vice,' and I fear that, amid the demoralizing influences of the camp, my boy (carefully nurtured though he has been) will wander far from the paths of virtue and religion, and will come back, if spared to return, not the innocent boy I send forth to my country's service but a reckless, vicious man."

2

An hour before the appointed time that splendid company—mustering considerably more than its previous roll strength, for a number of new recruits had enlisted in its ranks—marched to the depot where an immense crowd had assembled to see them off. An aged minister of the gospel (now gone to his reward) spoke words of earnest counsel, and led in a fervent prayer that the God of Jacob might go forth with these young men, keep them in the way whither they went, and bring them back to their homes in peace and safety—but, above all, that he would shield them from the vices of the camp and lead them into paths of righteousness.

The man of God is interrupted by the shrill whistle of the iron horse—the train dashes up to the depot—all are soon aboard, and, amid tender farewells and suppressed sobs of anxious friends, and the waving of handkerchiefs and vociferous cheers by the vast crowd, those patriot-soldiers hurry forth at the bidding of their loved and honored Virginia.

At Gordonsville they were met by companies from Augusta and Albemarle, and two companies of students from the University of Virginia, who marched forth from those classic shades to illustrate a bright page in the history of their *Alma Mater.*

Orange, Culpeper and other counties along the route swelled their numbers as they rushed to the capture of Harper's Ferry and the defence of the border.

The call of Virginia now echoes through the land—from seaboard to mountain-valley, from Alleghany to Chesapeake, from the Potomac to the North Carolina border, the tramp of her sons is heard. Maryland, the Carolinas, Georgia, Florida, Alabama, Mississippi, Kentucky, Tennessee, Arkansas, Louisiana, Missouri and Texas catch the sound, and her sons in every clime heed the call of their Mother State. The farmer leaves his plow in the furrow, the mechanic his job unfinished, the merchant his books unposted, the lawyer his brief unargued, the physician his patient unattended, the professor his chair unfilled, the student his classes, and the preacher his pulpit, and there rush to our northern frontier, not Hessian or Milesian mercenaries, not men bought up for so much " bounty money," but the wealth, the intelligence, the refinement and culture, the virtue and patriotism, the very flower of our Southern youth and manhood.

Thus was formed what was afterwards called the *Army of*

"THE SEQUEL."

'I trust in Jesus and am not afraid to die."

(See Companion picture, "Leaving Home.")

(Facing page 19.)

Northern Virginia—the noblest army (I hesitate not calmly to affirm, after the lapse of years) that ever marched under any banner or fought for any cause "in all the tide of time." But I do not propose, in this volume, to attempt even a sketch of the military exploits of this noble army of heroes.

I revert rather to another and far different scene from the one I have sketched. Over a year has rolled by, and that fair-haired, rosy-cheeked boy, "mother's darling," of April, 1861—now a bronzed veteran of the Army of Northern Virginia, whc has followed the "stars and bars" on many a victorious field—returns to his boyhood's home. But he comes not back with light, elastic step and erect carriage as when he marched forth so gayly at his country's call. He is borne on a litter—he has been shot through the lungs, his life-tide is ebbing away, and he has come home to die. On that memorable 27th day of June, 1862, at Cold Harbor, when "Stonewall" Jackson issued his crisp order, "Tell General Ewell to sweep the field with the bayonet," and our whole line pressed grandly forward, carried every position before it, and persuaded General McClellan that it was indeed time to "change base" from before Richmond to the shelter of his gun-boats at Harrison's Landing, our youthful hero fell in the very forefront of the battle in one of the most splendid charges of the famous old Thirteenth Virginia Infantry. The surgeons gave us no hope, but God spared him to reach home and linger for over six months to illustrate how a Christian soldier could be patient under suffering, and how, when he came to die, a smile could light up his countenance, joy could beam from his eye, and peace reign within his heart. The camp had not proven to him a "school of vice," but on the contrary he had learned there the preciousness of his mother's Bible, and had gone with simple faith to her Saviour. And as the last hour drew near he met death with calm resignation, said to the weeping loved ones who stood around: "I trust in Jesus and am not afraid to die," and left, in his triumphant death as well as in the peaceful hours of his later life, the fullest assurance that he went to join his sainted mother—for she had "gone before," a few weeks prior to his death—in that brighter, better home above, where "war's rude alarms" never disturb, and loved ones never part.

The fears of that Christian mother, as her boy left the parental roof to encounter the peculiar temptations of soldier life, were the fears of our wisest and best men. Armies had been hitherto regarded as decidedly demoralizing, and it had passed into a proverb: "The worse the man the better the soldier," against which the examples of Hedley Vickars, Havelock, Colonel Gardiner and other Christian soldiers were cited in vain. It is not for a moment denied that these fears were well-founded, and that as a rule the influence of an army is demoralizing. Its very object is to destroy life, and its scenes of carnage unquestionably tend, if not properly used, to blunt the moral perceptions, and harden in iniquity. And, then, absence from the influences of home and church, and the restraints of society, coupled with the common idea that things which would be criminal at other times are allowable in the army — all tend to raise the floodgates of immorality and vice.

I shall give no rose-colored picture in these sketches, but shall frankly admit that vices common to most armies were, alas! but too prevalent in our own, and that many of our most skilful officers and bravest men blotted their fair name by open vice or secret sin.

But I shall be able to show, on the other hand, that Jesus *was* in our camps with wonderful power, and that no army in all history — not even Cromwell's " Roundheads "— had in it as much of real, evangelical religion and devout piety as the Army of Northern Virginia.

I shall not discuss in these pages the causes of the great "War between the States," or revive any of its " buried issues." Let its stormy passions, its animosities, its bitter memories be buried forever beneath the wave of forgetfulness. And let us thank God that men who " wore the blue " and men who " wore the gray " may meet once more in friendly reunion—that older brethren, North and South, long alienated, have come to "see eye to eye," and to realize that they had only been " looking at the opposite sides of the shield "— that younger men have no alienations to reconcile, no bitter memories of a stormy past to efface — that the day is hastening when the North and the South shall be more ready to do justice to each other's motives —that the day has come when a Confederate soldier, on a Boston platform, or a Federal soldier, to a Charleston audience, may

" Shoulder his crutch
And fight his battles o'er again,"

while those who were once his enemies, now his friends, stand with uncovered head, or cheer to the echo his story of heroic deeds.

But it is due to the truth of history, as well as necessary to a correct understanding of my subject, that I should say that the Christian people of the South not only thought they were right in resisting the invasion of their soil and the coercion, by the Federal Government, of sovereign States, but that they went forth to battle, or sent their sons, in firm reliance upon "the Lord of hosts." Scarcely a company moved without some public religious service, and it was considered a most important part of each man's equipment that he should carry in his knapsack a copy of God's word.

All of our evangelical denominations were well represented in the rank and file of our army, and many of our preachers felt it their duty to go to the front, accompanied by the very flower of their young men. Of the first four companies from Georgia to arrive in Virginia, three of the captains were earnest, Christian men, and fifty of one of the companies were members of the same church. A regiment, stationed near Portsmouth in June, 1861, was reported to contain 400 of the same denomination, and another regiment had in its ranks *five* ministers of the gospel. I well remember that the first time I ever saw the famous old Rockbridge Artillery—on the 4th of July, 1861, when we were drawn up in line of battle at Darksville, in the lower Valley of Virginia, expecting an attack from General Patterson—it contained seven Masters of Arts of the University of Virginia, forty-two other college graduates, nineteen theological students, others (including a son of General R. E. Lee) who were among the noblest young men of the South, and a proportion of Christian men as surprisingly large as it was highly gratifying.

When the news of the secession of Virginia reached the quiet little town of Lexington, Virginia, nestled among the Blue mountains, some of the students of Washington College at once raised a secession flag on the dome of the college building. (They had done the same thing some days before, but the faculty had unanimously voted that it must be taken down, as Virginia was still in the Union.) The next morning, the president of the college, Rev. Dr. Junkin (the father-in-law of the afterwards famous "Stonewall" Jackson, but an ardent Union man all through the war), called a meeting of the faculty to ask what they proposed to do about the breach of discipline on the part of the students, as he regarded it, in again raising the flag on the college.

Professor White voiced the sentiments of the faculty and of the whole State when he at once said, " Virginia has now acted, and the boys are right. I say let the flag wave, and, for myself, I propose to fight under it, and to use my influence to induce our students to do the same."

Accordingly, he raised among the students and a few graduates of the college a company of seventy-two, which they called the " Liberty Hall Volunteers, " the name borne by a company of students from the same institution who did valiant service in the Revolution of 1776. They elected Professor White as their first captain, all of their officers were Christian men, more than half of the rank and file belonged to some evangelical church, and about one-fourth were candidates for the ministry.

Rev. Dr. J. M. P. Atkinson, President of Hampden-Sidney College, organized a company composed of his own students and those of the Union Theological Seminary, and nearly all of this company were professed Christians.

Not a few of our pastors had a large majority, and sometimes all of their male members in the army, and in some cases they commanded companies composed largely of members of their own churches.

I cannot better illustrate the subject of this chapter than by giving from the files of our religious newspapers copious extracts from letters from the camp, or from men in position to see and know the state of things in the army, and among the people during these early days of the war. Some of these extracts illustrate several of my chapters, but I give them as they are.

Rev. Dr. Joseph Walker thus writes from Richmond to the *Religious Herald*, under date of May 2, 1861 :

"*Messrs. Editors :* I have never understood the compatableness of Christianity with war as I see it in the present struggle for Southern independence. Never have I seen or read of greater promptness on the part of Christians, of all denominations, to shoulder the musket in defence of their homes, their families, and all that makes life desirable. I can now comprehend what is meant by the New Testament phrase, ' a devout soldier,' for I have seen the men for whom I have preached, with whom I have prayed, and whom I have seen presiding at Baptist associations, fully panoplied for the war. The self-denial of volunteers to serve in this war is unmistakably manifest in the advent among us of Southern soldiers. The gallant South Carolinians came first. Close on their rear came the Georgians; and we hear that Alabama, Mississippi and Louisiana are on the way. To cap the climax, we hope soon to see Jefferson Davis on the hills of Richmond. But my main object in penning these lines was to speak briefly of the Georgians. At least three of the companies already arrived are commanded by Christians. Captain Doyall and Captain Beall are Baptists; Captain Smith is a Methodist; Captain Hardeman, though not, I believe a professor himself, is closely connected with a religious family. All of these gentlemen occupy high social positions in their several communities, and their companies comprise the best fighting, and some of the best praying materials of this nation. With a just cause and such defenders, can the contest in favor of the South be doubtful?

This morning I had the pleasure of visiting Captain Beall's company, which is quartered in this city. A more substantial body of men cannot be found. Among them are lawyers, doctors, and deacons of churches. From forty to fifty of this company are Baptists, mostly from Irwinton, Georgia, and its vicinity; Beall, Rivers and Stanly are my personal acquaintances and friends, who have left (I hope only for a brief season) interesting families, whose hospitality I have often enjoyed. May God preserve these patriots, and return them at His good pleasure to their homes.

. . . .

JOSEPH WALKER.

RICHMOND, May 2, 1861.

The *North Carolina Presbyterian* had, about this same date, the following editorial:

" The ministers of the Gospel of Peace throughout the South seem to be fully alive to the awful issue presented to us by the Northern people, who are prepared to invade our homes, and they are meeting it like men who have as much at stake as others. Reference was made last week to the fact that there were three ministers in one of the companies of Home Guards formed in this place. In the other company there are two ministers. The last North Carolina *Christian Advocate*, referring to this subject, says: " The Rev. Messrs. Atkinson, Presbyterian; Fitzgerald and Smedes, Episcopal; James and Skinner, Baptist;

J. W. Tucker, Methodist, and one of the editors of this paper
have attached themselves to the Home Guard, a company organized in this city, under the command of Senator Bragg, for
the defence of our homes.   The other editor of this journal is
aiding in forming a similar company near his residence in the
country.   Rev. Willis L. Miller, formerly one of the editors of
the *North Carolina Presbyterian*, is the captain of the Thomas-
ville Rifles, which company has offered its services to the State."

A letter from Richmond, Virginia, states that the Rev. George
Woodbridge, D. D., pastor of the Monumental (P. E.) Church,
and a graduate of West Point, has been busily engaged for
several nights drilling two volunteer companies.   The Rev. Dr.
Wilmer, pastor of the Emanuel Church, near Richmond, is the
captain of a military company.   The Rev. Moses Hoge, D. D.,
is a member of the Home Guard."

Rev. Dr. A. E. Dickinson, who had been for several years
superintendent of the Virginia Baptist colportage board, and who
in the early days of the war saw the necessity for this work, and
promptly sent his band of trained colporters to the army and the
hospitals, thus writes in the *Religious Herald:*

"There never was a more inviting field for colportage effort
than that now afforded by the large armies that are being
stationed at various points in this State.   In a few hours a colporter may place a tract in the hands of hundreds of our most
promising young men, may urge upon them the claims of the
Gospel, and in many ways do them good.   Who can calculate
the amount of good that may be done by placing the life of
Havelock, or of Captain Vicars, or of Colonel Gardner, in the
hands of an ambitious young man.   The greater portion of the
soldier's time is now occupied by the duties of his profession.
How many leisure hours may be rescued from scenes of vice and
turned to good account by having a colporter in every regiment?   A large proportion of the volunteers are professors of
religion.   In a company of seventy-five we found twelve Baptists,
and were told of another company in which there were forty.
The flower of our churches are enlisted for this struggle, and it
is sad to think of how many temptations will beset them, and
of the probability that many will be led into the paths of vice,
and have their Christian character wrecked.   Of what immense
value would a colporter be to this class in affording them good
books and collecting them in prayer-meetings.   Having secured

the sympathy and co-operation of the pious, the colporter could through them reach even the most irreligious. We invite earnest, prayerful attention to the subject. It is one of unspeakable importance. Let our pious, self-sacrificing men be urged by the constraining love of Christ to say, 'Here I am, send me;' and let patriotism, as well as religion, afford the means for their support."

A colporter writes: "I have been visiting the volunteers in this county, and I find them very anxious to obtain pocket Bibles and Testaments. Some of these brave men have wept as I have spoken to them of the claims of the Gospel, and they have asked me to pray for them. I lose no opportunity for speaking to them of their soul's salvation, and I do think that good is being done."

A Southern Methodist bishop wrote with respect to the state of things in his vicinity: "There is more prayer among the people generally than heretofore. Prayer for the country and for brothers, sons and husbands, calls the people so often to the mercy-seat that it must almost necessarily increase the spirit of devotion among them. Hence there is a good deal of religious feeling in our congregations."

The following will illustrate a phase of Southern society and the kindly relations and sympathies between master and slave which none can appreciate who did not witness them, but illustrations of which could be indefinitely multiplied. The incident is related by the *Texas Christian Advocate:* "A Texas planter having responded in person to one of the late calls of Colonel Van Dorn for service in the West, his negroes were left in the care of the overseer. One night, at a late hour, the overseer was aroused by a noise at the 'quarter.' He immediately arose and went in the direction of the noise far enough to ascertain that it was the voice of prayer. Drawing still nearer, he discovered that the prayer-meeting was a special occasion, for the benefit of the master who had 'gone to the wars.' Earnest prayers ascended that his health and life might be spared, and that God would grant him a safe return."

The following was from a soldier on duty at Manassas Junction, who professed conversion and was baptized after he enlisted in the struggle for Southern independence: "I have received and distributed the greater portion of the tracts among my brother soldiers. May God's word be blessed to the turning of their hearts to Jesus. We feel that God's people are praying for us; and surely the poor soldier, more than any one else, needs to be remembered at the mercy-seat. Oh, that none may fall in battle till at the feet of the Crucified One they have found joy and peace! My own heart is so sinful that I often tremble lest I may be a castaway, but in the mercy of God through Jesus Christ I hope. I hope that the Christians of this land will pray that the peace of God may be sent into the hearts of all, that our rulers may rule in righteousness, and that the North may see its folly and guilt in seeking to subdue and oppress the South."

Two prayer-meetings were reported as held weekly in Jackson, Mississippi, on behalf of Southern soldiers—one, a female prayer-meeting, held in private residences on Monday; another held on Wednesday, at 5 P. M., alternately at the different churches. Members of all denominations participated in both.

A correspondent writes:

"A soldier from one of the Gulf States, whose company was stationed at Norfolk, Virginia, was very sick. A kind lady paid him a visit and found him delirious. He gazed at her a moment and said: 'Go away from me; you are not my mother.' But her heart was too full of sympathy for the mother of whom the poor soldier was thinking to leave him. She waited until the fever had abated, and then she talked to him of his absent, loved mother. Tears flowed down the sick man's cheeks, and that interview was a blessing to him, as also to the kind woman who had hunted him out.

" Whose heart does not swell with tender emotions as he looks upon the noble soldiers who are flocking to our State, and thinks of the mothers they have left behind? Oh, the anxious hearts, the tender tears, the earnest prayers of Southern mothers, as day after day and hour after hour they think of the loved ones far away on the battle-fields of the Old Dominion!

" Reader, if you know anything of a parent's heart you will sometimes think of these mothers, and your prayers will ascend with theirs for a blessing on their sons. What patriot and Christian but will thank God that an effort is being made to send colporters among the soldiers, through whose labors they may be instructed in the things that pertain to salvation. Surely such an enterprise ought to have the sympathies, prayers and contributions of every Christian among us. The colporters may rest assured that every hour in every day some pious mother will be pleading before the mercy-seat for heaven's richest blessings upon their labors. Colporters, think, I beseech you, of these mothers; make mention of them as you go among their sons. It will enable you to deliver your message with more of tenderness, and they will hear it with more of profit."

Rev. Dr. Geo. B. Taylor writes from Staunton:

"We have had a good many soldiers at this place, and I have found it very pleasant to visit them in capacity of minister and self-appointed colporter. By making a public request for small Bibles and Testaments I secured from the citizens generally some two or three bushels, which I distributed, getting from each soldier receiving one the promise that he would read it. I would suggest that brethren in the country and in towns, where there are more Bibles and Testaments than are actually needed, collect as many as possible together and forward them to some point where they may be given to the soldiers; small hymn-books are also acceptable. One brother introduced himself to me and begged for a hymn-book, saying that he would have daily worship with his company. I said that I would go home and get one, and hand it to him as the regiment passed out of town. They were then about starting. I stationed myself on the sidewalk to find my friend. There was no trouble in doing this, for a square before he reached me he held out his hand to attract my attention. I was more than repaid by his joy and gratitude when I gave him a prayer-meeting hymn-book. Nor could I help emptying my pockets to other soldiers, who seemed eager to take Testaments and hymn-books even as they were marching off. As I was talking to one soldier about the Testaments I was distributing, and referring to their small size, a comrade, partially overhearing my remarks, asked whether it was *hooks* I was speaking of. I told him, 'Yes, hooks to catch men;' and asked him if he had been caught. He told me he was a Christian." . . . . .

The following is from the pen of the venerable and beloved Rev. Dr. Robert Ryland, so long president of Richmond College, and is given in full, as illustrating the views and feelings of one of our noblest Christian ministers—one of our most widely known and honored representative Southern men—in writing in the early days of the war to his son, who had enlisted in the Confederate army:

"A Letter to a Son in Camp.

"At Home, July 17, 186ı.

"*My Dear Son:* It may have seemed strange to you that a professing Christian father so freely gave you, a Christian son, to enlist in the volunteer service. My reason was that I regarded this as a *purely defensive war.* Not only did the Southern Confederacy propose to adjust the pending difficulties by peaceful and equitable negotiations, but Virginia used again and again the most earnest and noble efforts to prevent a resort to the sword. These overtures having been proudly spurned, and our beloved South having been threatened with invasion and subjugation, it seemed to me that nothing was left us but stern resistance or abject submission to unconstitutional power. A brave and generous people could not for a moment hesitate between such alternatives. A war in defence of our homes and firesides—of our wives and children—of all that makes life worth possessing is the result. While I most deeply deplore the necessity for the sacrifice, I could not but rejoice that I had a son to offer to the service of the country, and if I had a dozen *I would most freely give them all.* As you are now cheerfully enduring the hardships of the camp, I know you will listen to a father's suggestions touching the duties of your new mode of life.

"1. Take special care of your health. More soldiers die of disease than in battle. A thin piece of damp sponge in the crown of your hat during exposure to the hot sun—the use of thick shoes and a waterproof coat in rainy weather—the practice of drinking cold water, when you are very warm, as slowly as you sip hot tea—the thorough mastication of your food—the avoiding of damp tents and damp grounds during sleep—and frequent ablutions of your person, are all the hints I can give you on this point. Should you need anything that I can supply, let me hear from you. I will do what I can to make you comfortable. After all, you must learn to endure hardness as a good soldier. Having never slept a single night in your whole life except in a pleasant bed, and never known a scarcity of good food, you doubtless find the ways of the camp rough; but never mind. The war, I trust, will soon be over, and then the remembrance of your hardships will sweeten the joy of peace.

"2. The rules of war require prompt and unquestioning obedience. You may sometimes think the command arbitrary and the officer supercilious, but *it is yours to obey*. An undisciplined army is a curse to its friends and a derision to its foes. Give your whole influence, therefore, to the maintenance of lawful authority and strict order. Let your superiors feel that whatever they intrust to *you* will be faithfully done. Composed of such soldiers, and led by skilful and brave commanders, our army, by the blessing of God, will never be defeated. It is, moreover, engaged in a holy cause, and must triumph.

"3. Try to maintain your Christian profession among your comrades. I need not caution you against strong drink as useless and hurtful, nor against profanity, so common among soldiers. Both these practices you abhor. Aim to take at once a decided stand for God. If practicable, have prayers regularly in your tent, or unite with your fellow-disciples in prayer-meetings in the camp. Should preaching be accessible, always be a hearer. Let the world know that you are a Christian. Read a chapter in the New Testament which your mother gave you, every morning and evening when you can, and engage in secret prayer to God for his Holy Spirit to guide and sustain you. I would rather hear of your death than of the shipwreck of your faith and good conscience.

"4. As you will come into habitual contact with men of every grade, make special associates of those whose influence on your character is felt to be good. Some men love to tell extravagant stories, to indulge in vulgar wit, to exult in a swaggering carriage, to pride themselves on their coarse manners, to boast of their heroism, and to give utterance to feelings of revenge against the enemy. All this is injurious to young and impressible minds. If you admire such things, you will insensibly imitate them, and imitation will work gradual but certain detriment to your character. Other men are refined without being affected. They can relax into occasional pleasantries, without violating modesty. They can be loyal to their government without indulging private hatred against her foes. They can be cool and brave in battle, and not be braggarts in the absence of danger. Above all, they can be humble, spiritual, and active Christians, and yet mingle in the stirring and perilous duties of soldier life. Let these be your companions and models. You will thus return from the dangers of camp without a blemish on your name.

"5. Should it be your lot to enter into an engagement with the enemy, lift up your heart in secret ejaculations to the ever-present and good Being, that He will protect you from sudden death; or, if you fall, that He will receive your departing spirit, cleansed in the blood of Jesus, into His kingdom. It is better to trust in the Lord than to put confidence in princes. Commit your eternal interests, therefore, to the keeping of the Almighty Saviour. You should not, even in the hour of deadly conflict, cherish personal rage against the enemy, any more than an officer of the law hates the victim of the law. How often does a victorious army tenderly care for the dead and wounded of the vanquished. War is a tremendous scourge which Providence sometimes uses to chastise proud and wicked nations. Both parties must suffer, even though one may get the advantage. There is no occasion, then, for adding to the intrinsic evils of the system the odious feature of animosity to individuals. In the ranks of the foe are thousands of plain men who do not understand the principles for which we are struggling. They are deceived by artful demagogues into a posture of hostility to those whom, knowing, they would love. It is against such men that you may perhaps be arrayed, and the laws of war do not forbid you to pity them, even in the act of destroying them. It is more important that *we* should exhibit a proper temper in this unfortunate contest, because many professed Christians and ministers of the Gospel at the North are breathing out, in their very prayers and sermons, threatenings and slaughter against us! Oh! how painful that a gray-headed pastor should publicly exclaim, '*I would hang them as soon as I would shoot a mad dog.*'

"6. Providence has placed you in the midst of thoughtless and unpardoned men. What a beautiful thing it would be if you could win some of them to the Saviour! Will you not try? You will have many opportunities of speaking a word in season. The sick, you may comfort; the wavering, you may confirm; the backslidden, you may reclaim; the weary and heavy laden, you may point to Jesus for rest to the soul. It is not presumptuous for a young man, kindly and meekly, to commend the Gospel to his brother soldiers. The hardest of them will not repel a gentle approach, made in private. And many of them would doubtless be glad to have the subject introduced to them. They desire to hear of Jesus, but they lack courage to inquire of his people. An unusually large proportion of pious men have entered the army, and I trust they will give a new complexion to military life. Let them search out each other, and establish a fraternity

GENERAL ROBERT E. LEE.

(Facing page 30.)

among all the worshippers of God. To interchange religious views and administer brotherly counsel will be mutually edifying. ' He that watereth shall be watered also himself.'

"And now, as a soldier has but little leisure, I will not occupy you longer. Be assured that every morning and evening we remember you, at the family altar, to our Father in Heaven. We pray for a ' speedy, just, and honorable peace,' and for the safe return of all the volunteers to their loved homes. All the children speak often of ' brother,' and hear your letters read with intense interest. That God Almighty may be your shield and your exceeding great reward is the constant prayer of your loving father. " Ro. RYLAND."

We clip, without comment, from files of religious newspapers, the following items as illustrating the subject of this chapter, as well as other phases of soldier-life in the early days of the war.

Hon. J. L. M. Curry, in a letter published by the *South-western Baptist*, states that for two months a weekly prayer-meeting has been kept up in Talladega, Alabama. "When the hour comes, at 9 o'clock on every Thursday morning, the doors of every business house are closed, and the house is usually filled with sincere worshippers who congregate to pray for our country. The meetings are alternately held in the three church houses."

Says the *Christian Index:* "Unconverted young men have written home that they daily read their Bibles, and are seeking preparation for the judgment. Some religious soldiers state that such is the pious influence in their companies, they believe themselves improved instead of injured by the camp. O that this could be said of all! "

Rev. Dr. Cross writes from the Walker Legion, near Fredericksburg, to the Nashville *Christian Advocate:* "A young man who, being slightly unwell, has spent a few days under the hospitable roof of Rev. Dr. Broaddus in town, returned to camp this morning happily converted to God. When I said to one of the Edgefield boys it was time for all hands to cease swearing and begin praying, he replied: ' I stopped the former when I enlisted, and am now trying to practise the latter.' Another, who had been very profane at home, has never been known to utter an oath since he left Nashville."

The *Southern Christian Advocate* thinks that there is at least one advantage for evangelical effort in the present aspect of affairs. "The only mitigating circumstance of a religious character that we find in this dreadful war, into which we have been forced, is found in what we believe to be the fact—that it has enhanced the religious sentiment in our people. The sense of trust in Divine Providence is widespread. We see it exhibited where we little thought to find it. Editors, who heretofore have manifested no great respect for religion, fiery soldiers who do not themselves serve God, writers who ordinarily would not be suspected of trusting in anything else than the 'arm of flesh,' all acknowledge God's gracious dealings in the events of the few past months. It is not unlikely that men have lately prayed to whom prayer has been heretofore unknown. And as this feeling grows more general, as we trust it will, they who have kindred exposed, or who may lose their friends in the course of the war, may be led to earnest prayer in asking protection for others or consolation for themselves."

In Colonel Ector's regiment from Georgia there are fourteen ministers: one Methodist, one Primitive Baptist and twelve Missionary Baptists.

A correspondent of the *North Carolina Presbyterian* states that after a recent sermon to the Third Regiment of North Carolina State troops, near Aquia Creek, Virginia, preached by a Methodist minister belonging to the regiment, some fifteen or twenty of the soldiers knelt to indicate anxiety for salvation.

A writer from the Second Palmetto Regiment to the *Southern Christian Advocate*, says: "God's hand was in the great achievement, and I believe that the most irreligious man in our patriot army will frankly acknowledge the fact. So evident was it, it is believed an improvement has since taken place in the morals of our troops. At least, I can say as much for this regiment. Whilst, during the campaign, we have occupied the advanced post, the post of honor and danger, and this for weeks, in the very face of the enemy, God has given us a grateful sense of security, and our religious services have gone on. Even while interrupted by the booming cannon and bursting shell, lying in our trenches, expecting every moment that the storm would break in all its fury upon us, we worshipped God."

A correspondent of the *Central Presbyterian* expresses the opinion that "every Southern Sabbath-school has one living representative at least in this war, and that most schools have many "

A minister thus writes to the *Religious Herald:*

"*Brother Editors:* For the encouragement of fathers and other friends of our soldiers, I send you the following for the *Herald:* My son, a young man of less than twenty years of age, left home early in May with his company of volunteers for the seat of war. When he left he was a stranger to God's forgiving grace, and so far as I know, was not seriously concerned about his condition. I determined to follow him with my prayers, if haply the Lord might have mercy upon him. I asked three beloved brother-ministers to pray for him. I also put the New Testament into his hand, with the request that he would read it carefully and prayerfully. He made no promise, but I felt sure he would comply with my request. I have seen him but once since—a few days after leaving. It was not long before he commenced alluding to reading the Scriptures, as he wrote to us from week to week, in such a manner as to encourage us to hope that the Lord was at work with his heart. Not long after, a dear brother—the author of the little tract, 'Are you Ready?' addressed to soldiers—sent me a number containing an affectionate address to my dear boy, in pencil lines, with a note to me, requesting me to forward it to him, which I did, accompanied by the note to me. To the almost overpowering joy of my heart, a few days since I received a letter from him containing the following extract: 'Oh! what comfort and consolation that tract afforded me; and thank God I can answer, I think, I am ready. And I am willing to die for my country. Oh! what a consolation it is to know that so many fervent prayers go up daily for me, and that they are answered! I have great reason to bless and praise the blessed God for His great goodness to me. He has preserved my life and health, and provided for me so many comforts—many more than He has provided for many others who are far more deserving than I am.' "A FATHER."

A correspondent of the *North Carolina Presbyterian* states that, as the result of prayer-meetings held every night for two or three weeks in the Third Regiment of North Carolina State Troops, seven of the soldiers have applied for membership in the Methodist and four in the Baptist Church. "We sometimes feel

2

more as if we were in a camp-meeting than in the army expecting to meet an enemy."

A soldier writes to a friend: " I will here state to you what I never have written home to E——, of the thoughts that have most affected my mind, and I hope and trust in God that the same thoughts and reflections have changed my manner of life. E—— has doubtless shown you what I call my farewell letter to my children while I was at Richmond, Virginia. The advice I thought and still think was good; but alas, where does that advice come from? It is from the best friend my children have upon earth, a father; yes, a father, who says: ' My children, read your Bibles, abstain from bad company and bad habits, the lusts of the flesh and the vanities of a wicked world,' but who says at the same time by *his own conduct and example*, '*Come along, children*'—taking them, as it were, by the hand—' I will lead you down to hell;' yes, I was leading them by my own example directly to hell as fast as I possibly could. Oh, the horrible thought of being the means of damning the souls of my children! Conviction seized upon me, and *then* and *there*, on the —th of June, I resolved, if God would spare my life, that I would reform my habits of life; or if He would permit me to return home, that I would set a different example before my children. I have prayed that He would, and that I might keep my resolution to the day of my death. I wrote you a letter on the same day, while my eyes were still wet with tears. I asked your prayers in my behalf; I know you have prayed for me. Can God in justice forgive me? I pray He may; I know my children will; may God bless them and help them to do so, save them from following my bad example, and at the same time to take my good advice and carry it out, that they may be saved from that awful hell to to which I was leading them."

A happy transformation is thus described: " There was another company whose captain was a wicked man. He exerted a bad influence over his men. He was openly profane and never attended religious services. In these days the company was known as one of the most wicked in the regiment. Months rolled away, and another man was appointed to the command. He was a consistent Christian, and a man of earnest, deep-toned piety. He sought to carry his men to church, and in the prayer-meeting strove to lead them to the throne of grace. He showed that he cared for their spiritual as well as their physical interests. Now, mark the change. In that company, once noted for wickedness, prayer-meetings were held every night. Among its members are some active, energetic Christians, and some happy converts have been made there. How responsible the position of an officer."

A correspondent of the Louisville *Courier* writes from Virginia: "To-day the Second Brigade, to which we are attached, was mustered for Divine service. The occasion reminded me more of a Baptist Association gathering than anything I have seen for a long time. A rustic pulpit was erected beneath the shade of the forest trees, and about the clergyman was gathered a force of over three thousand men. The good old songs of Zion caused the leaves to quiver with a poetic tremulousness, and the very air was redolent with heartfelt prayer and praise. Our fighting chaplain, Rev. H. A. Tupper, of the Ninth Georgia, a chaplain in the Confederate army and a Baptist minister at home, a lover and defender of civil and religious liberty everywhere, preached us a very able discourse from the advice of Eli to Joshua: 'Be ye men of good courage.' It was no war philippic, but an earnest, heartfelt, Christian discourse."

A notice of a revival, in the Nashville *Christian Gazette*, says: "Several volunteers were anxiously inquiring the way of life and salvation, and one or two of them embraced religion." A second notice: "Several members of Captain Bankhead's company, Fifteenth Regiment, Alabama Volunteers, came out on the Lord's side." A third: "Among the number converted were eight noble-hearted men who had volunteered to defend the liberties of their country. You may imagine the lovely scene which then transpired: fathers and mothers embracing their noble boys, exclaiming, with hearts all illumed by heavenly love, 'Now we can give you up better satisfied.'"

Rev. Dr. Cross writes from the Walker Legion: "The other day I visited General Holmes at his quarters. Seeing a pistol in my belt, he said: 'What! are you a soldier as well as a chaplain?' 'A soldier of Christ, general,' I replied. 'Ah,' said he, 'that is the noblest soldiership! Follow Him closely, serve Him faithfully; there is no way in which you can do so much for your country. We have plenty of men to fight, but not half enough to pray. May we never forget our dependence upon the Divine succor.' These remarks were characteristic. The general is a godly man, and frequently adverts to these matters in conversation with his officers. On the field of Manassas the chaplain of one of his regiments approached him in a dress which he deemed too military for a clergyman. ' Go back, sir,' said he, ' this is no place for you; take off that sash, retire to the grove and besiege a Throne of Grace !' "

Rev. R. W. Cole writes to *The Religious Herald*:

" CAROLINE COUNTY, September 17.

"*Messrs. Editors:* It was my privilege to spend some three or four days with the soldiers embracing Colonel Cary's regiment, a short time since, at Marlborough Point. The season was truly gloomy—being rainy—but it seemed not to detract from the energy and cheerfulness of those noble sons who are sacrificing for their country's welfare. To speak of the merit of those officers and men under Colonel Cary's command is not now my design. Suffice it to say, they all appear to be well fitted for their respective positions. It was my privilege to distribute tracts, which were thankfully received; also, to address the soldiers on the all-important concern of the soul's salvation, for three successive nights. It was truly gratifying to see the extraordinary good order maintained amongst them during religious services. On the second day after my arrival two of the soldiers, young men from Caroline, made an open profession of Christ, and were buried with Christ in baptism by your correspondent in the fair waters leading from the Potomac. Visits from our brethren in the ministry to this portion of our army will be gratifying and no doubt be hailed with pleasure by them. While they need shoes, coats and all the necessaries for bodily comfort, they also need spiritual food. May God pour out His Spirit upon our soldiers, and scores become the subjects of His salvation !   " R. W. C."

Rev. Mr. Hopkins, of Martinsburg, Virginia, sends $5.00 to be appropriated to the purchase of tracts for Captain Robert White's company, Thirteenth Regiment, Virginia Volunteers. It is a *thank-offering* from a widowed mother, whose son died of fever at Winchester, contracted at Manassas. Up to the time of leaving home he had not made a profession of faith in Christ, although she had long dedicated him to God's service in the ministry. But her cause of gratitude now is, that during his camp life he evinced so much devotion to reading his Bible, and for some time before his sickness had shown so many signs of piety, and died acknowledging his love to the Saviour, and supported by this love now " sleeps in Jesus."—*Central Presbyterian.*

Dr. Cross, chaplain of the Walker Legion, writes to one of his church papers: " It is interesting to see how they flock to our nightly prayer-meetings, frequently in greater numbers than your Sabbath congregations in some of your city churches. I preach to them twice on the Lord's day, seated around me on the ground, officers and all, in the most primitive order you can imagine. But the most interesting, probably the most useful part of my work, is the visitation of the sick. Every morning I go to the hospital, visiting the several apartments successively; in each of which I talk privately with the men, then read a passage of Scripture, make some remarks upon it, and finish with prayer. However wicked and thoughtless they are in camp they are all glad to see the chaplain when they are sick, and I have yet to meet one who is not most respectful and attentive. *I think I have never occupied a field that afforded such an opportunity for usefulness.*"

A soldier wrote for the *Southern Churchman* the following:

"A Guardian Spirit passed through a group of soldiers who lay stretched on the ground, some exchanging together in broken converse such thoughts as their situation suggested, some in the deep slumber of weariness, forgetting both danger and toil. Unchallenged by the watchful sentinel he approached one manly form extended on the ground and gazed with interest on the sunburnt features and the thoughtful, sunken eye which was fixed on the descending sun.

"*Soldier.*—That sun which is setting on us in such full glory is now smiling on my own sweet home, casting its slanting beams upon the daisy-spangled meadow where my little ones are at play; on the rich green wheat-fields and many-colored orchards; and shining on the peaceful village churchyard, where my bones may never be laid. How those dear hearts at home are thinking of us now! How many prayers are daily offered for our safety! But the bright eyes may soon be bathed in tears; the fond hearts be wrung with sorrow! O God! my God! Thou knowest that I can face death—face it firmly, fearlessly; but my soul quails at the thought of what others will suffer! Who will comfort my broken-hearted mother? Who will take care of my precious orphan babes?

" *Spirit.*—He who hath said, ' Leave thy fatherless children; I will preserve them alive; and let thy widows trust in me.'

" *Soldier.*—There is strong comfort in resting all on His prom-ises, committing all to His care. It is in an hour like this that we prove the support and solace of religion. When we look on the sinking sun with more than a doubt that we shall ever behold it rise again; when there is none of the excitement of conflict, the eager rush to the attack, the hope of triumph, the certainty of honor, to stir up all the natural ardor which glows in the breast of man—but the probability of death coming in the confusion of a night attack—then is the hour when we cling to the thought of a protecting Father and a guiding Saviour, as a drowning man clings to the one plank which supports him in a wild and stormy sea.

"*Spirit.*—And you can hold fast this confidence in your God ?

"*Soldier.*—' The Lord is my light and my salvation, whom shall I fear ?   The Lord is the strength of my life, of whom shall I be afraid ?'

"*Spirit.*—You can resign yourself into His hand, for life or for death ?

" *Soldier.*—' Whether we live, we live unto the Lord, and whether we die, we die unto the Lord; whether we live, there-fore, or die, we are the Lord's.'

"*Spirit.*—Yes, it matters little to the Christian whether, with the snows of age on his head, he descends quietly into the waters of death, accompanied to the brink by loving friends; or, in his prime, clears the deep, narrow stream with one bound, exchanging in an instant the desperate struggle, confused noises and garments rolled in blood, for the sudden hallelujah and the changeless peace of the skies!   The darker the conflict the brighter the transition.

"*Soldier.*—The bullet or the steel bears the message of God, and He sends no message to His servants that bears not on it the seal of love.

"*Spirit.*—Faith sees that love in all things. Should this night indeed be your last, you can say, ' I have fought a good fight, I have finished my course, I have kept the faith; henceforth there is laid up for me a crown of righteousness, which the Lord, the righteous judge, shall give me at that day.'

" *Soldier.*—The words of the holy apostle are not for a sinner like me. As one said of old, ' I lay both my good deeds and my evil deeds together, and flee from them to my Saviour. ' ' I know whom I have believed, and am persuaded that He is able to keep that which I have committed to Him.' Confiding in His merits, His merits alone, now in this solemn time of danger, ' I will both lay me down and sleep; for thou, Lord, only makest me to dwell in safety.' ' Yea, though I walk through the valley of the shadow of death, I will fear no evil; for thou art with me.' Waking or sleeping, living or dying, keep me, my God, for I am thine!

"Darkness shrouded the earth; the heavy eyelids closed, and on that hard, rude couch slumber, calm and peaceful as an infant's, fell on the weary man."

An officer in the army of the Rappahannock, writes from Camp Anderson (Caroline): "I am happy to state that we hold prayer-meetings every night, when the weather permits; and that the sweet incense of prayer and the voice of praise rise up to the Father of spirits and wielder of nations' destinies. It is particularly soul-cheering to me, in the midst of the profanity and blasphemy of the camp, to find so many fervent Christians, whose faith, hope and charity, being tested, are more fully developed. There are, perhaps, a dozen officers, out of about thirty, who have named the name of Jesus; and they and hundreds of the men bow down together at the same altar and cry unto our common Father."

Says the *Southern Presbyterian:* "It was remarked by a distinguished son of Georgia, lately a member of Congress, now an officer in our army, in a public address to the citizens of a neighboring town, that when the war commenced he had many fears respecting the demoralizing effect on our young men of a life in the camp, but that personal observation in some of the camps had greatly relieved his anxiety on that score, and that he knew of many instances in which our soldiers had been converted since they had gone into the army."

D. W. Chambers writes to the *Biblical Recorder* that seven weeks ago a religious association for the promotion of morality and piety was formed in the Thirty-seventh Regiment, North Carolina troops, at the instance of the chaplain and with the aid of the colonel. It numbers 132 members, belonging to some seven or eight denominations. Fifty-five soldiers have asked the prayers of their believing associates, and five have found relief in the Saviour's blood. "Our chaplain and colonel," he says, "are, with many good brethren, ministering spirits throughout our camp."

A writer in the *Southern Presbyterian* says: "When Lincoln's war-cry rang along our valleys and our mountains, the students of this college, with their Greek professor for their captain, exchanged those classic walls for the tented field. On the day of the Manassas battle, they were forty-five in number—of these five fell slain upon the field, two more were mortally wounded, and others slightly. About the same time others died from disease. Thus, in one vacation, this college has cheerfully sacrificed one-fifth of its fighting force in defence of its country."

"Of the North Carolina soldiers now in Virginia, some thirty were baptized recently by Rev. W. F. Broaddus, D. D., of Fredericksburg, and six by Brother Bagby, chaplain of the Fortieth Virginia Regiment."

A correspondent writes to the *Southern Churchman* from Headquarters Artillery, Camp Pendleton, near Centreville: "Our chapel is completed, and last Sunday was well filled. Colonel Pendleton preached on prayer, a most useful sermon. In the afternoon a general prayer-meeting was held. There are many pious and influential Christian men in this corps, who I trust will make their lives tell powerfully for Christ and His religion. Many of God's people enjoy religion now as they never did before, because the Holy Spirit draws manifestly near, and is preparing, I hope, a great blessing for us. Some of the officers pray with their men at morning roll-call; others meet with them in the cabin at night. Doubt not but, when the fierce struggle for liberty and life is renewed upon this famous ground, many will go forth from the closet of communion with God, strengthened from on high. The vices which, alas, too commonly hang upon our armies, such as Sabbath-breaking, profanity, drunkenness and gambling, are, I can with candor and gratitude say, the exception in this corps."

A soldier writes as follows:

"I belonged to a Virginia regiment, engaged in active service in the mountains, far away from friends and home. I was surrounded by wicked and thoughtless companions, who spent their time in gaming, drinking, and frivolous conversations. I had, in by-gone years, been impressed with the necessity and importance of religion, but my serious impressions were gone, and I was now ashamed to acknowledge they had ever existed. Early Sabbath morning I was sent out with a scouting party many miles from camp, and, ere we were aware of their approach, we were surrounded by a large body of Federal troops. A desperate battle ensued, during which I was cut off from my comrades and badly wounded in my hip. I concealed myself under a rock, and there lay for several hours meditating upon my sad and hapless fate. Wearied and exhausted by loss of blood, I fell asleep and was soon in the land of dreams. I thought myself again at my humble home in the East. But to my sorrow and inexpressible grief, my dear mother, during my absence, had been taken sick, and, after a brief illness, died. My only sister and two little brothers were left alone, in the care of two faithful old negroes, and all were clothed in mourning. My sister told me that mother spent her last moments in talking about and praying for me. She said that our dear mother told her to tell me, should I ever live to reach home, ' that all of us were poor sinners and rebels against God—that we were justly condemned to die, for we had sinned against our Heavenly Father, who was our constant friend and benefactor, and had never done us an injury; but, on the other hand, had given His Son Jesus Christ to die, that we might be justified, pardoned, and saved. And if I would only believe that God would save me for His Son's sake, and would love that Son, that God would love me, forgive all my sins, make me happy ; and, though I would never again see her face on earth, I would meet her in heaven.'

" I was so affected by this narrative that I awoke, sobbing like a child, and the first expression which burst from my full heart was : ' O God! give me faith in Thy promises, love for Thy dear Son, and an obedient heart, that I may meet Thee and my dear mother in Heaven.' I felt at once that I was willing to give up all the world for the love of God, that I could trust Him and serve Him forever. My heart was light; I saw God reconciled through His Son, and was so *happy*. I hobbled away to the distant camp. I told my comrades what the Lord had done for me, and many a hardened sinner wept and gave his heart to Christ, and we made the Western mountains ring with shouts of joy to God."

These extracts might be almost indefinitely multiplied, but the above must suffice.

CHAPTER II.

INFLUENCE OF CHRISTIAN OFFICERS.

NO army, with whose history I am acquainted, at least, was ever blessed with so large a proportion of high officers who were earnest Christian men, as the Army of Northern Virginia.

We had at first such specimens of the Christian soldier as R. E. Lee, Stonewall Jackson, D. H. Hill, T. R. Cobb, A. H. Colquitt, Kirby Smith, J. E. B. Stuart, W. N. Pendleton, John B. Gordon, C. A. Evans, A. M. Scales, "Willie" Pegram, Lewis Minor Coleman, Thos. H. Carter, Carter Braxton, Charles S. Venable, and a host of others too numerous to mention. And during the war Generals Ewell, Pender, Hood, R. H. Anderson, Rodes, Paxton, W. H. S. Baylor, Colonel Lamar, and a number of others of our best officers professed faith in Christ.

Nor was the example of these noble men merely *negative*—many of them were *active* workers for the Master, and did not hesitate, upon all proper occasions, to " stand up for Jesus."

OUR CHRISTIAN PRESIDENT, JEFFERSON DAVIS, was always outspoken on the side of evangelical religion, and manifested the deepest interest in all efforts for the spiritual good of the soldiers. His fast-day and thanksgiving-day proclamations were not only beautiful specimens of the chaste style and classic English for which this great man is remarkable, but they also breathed a spirit of humble, devout piety, which did not fail to have its influence on the armies of the Confederacy.

He said to Rev. A. E. Dickinson, who was then superintendent of the Virginia Baptist Colportage Board, which resolved in June, 1861, to send to labor in the army its band of nearly one hundred trained colporters : " I most cordially sympathize with this movement. We have but little to hope for, if we do not realize our dependence upon heaven's blessing and seek the guidance of God's truth."

In his message under date of April 29, 1861, President Davis

(42)

used this language, as expressive of his sentiments and his feelings:

" We feel that our cause is just and holy; we protest solemnly in the face of mankind that we desire peace at any sacrifice save that of honor and independence; we ask no conquest, no aggrandizement, no concession of any kind from the States with which we were lately confederated; all we ask is to be let alone; that those who never held power over us shall not now attempt our subjugation by arms. This we must resist to the direst extremity. The moment that this pretension is abandoned the sword will drop from our grasp, and we shall be ready to enter into treaties of amity and commerce that cannot but be mutually beneficial. So long as this pretension is maintained, with a firm reliance on that Power which covers with its protection the just cause, we will continue to struggle for our inherent right to freedom, independence and self-government.

" JEFFERSON DAVIS."

From his proclamations, which always had the right ring, I select the following, which may be taken as specimens of the whole:

"*To the People of the Confederate States:* The termination of the Provisional Government offers a fitting occasion again to present ourselves in humiliation, prayer and thanksgiving before that God who has safely conducted us through our first year of national existence. We have been enabled to lay anew the foundations of free government, and to repel the efforts of enemies to destroy us. Law has everywhere reigned supreme, and throughout our wide-spread limits personal liberty and private right have been duly honored. A tone of earnest piety has pervaded our people, and the victories which we have obtained over our enemies have been justly ascribed to Him who ruleth the universe. We had hoped that the year would have closed upon a scene of continued prosperity, but it has pleased the Supreme Disposer of events to order it otherwise. We are not permitted to furnish an exception to the rule of Divine government, which has prescribed affliction as the discipline of nations as well as of individuals. Our faith and perseverance must be tested, and the chastening, which seemeth grievous, will, if rightly received, bring forth its appropriate fruit. It is meet and right, therefore, that we should repair to the only Giver of all victory and, humbling ourselves before Him, should pray that He may strengthen our confidence in His mighty power and righteous judgments. Then may we surely trust in Him that He will perform His promise and encompass us as with a shield. In this trust and to this end, I, Jefferson Davis, President of the Confederate States, do hereby set apart Friday, the 28th day of February instant, as a day of fasting, humiliation and prayer; and I do hereby invite the reverend clergy and the people of the Confederate States to repair to their respective places of public worship, to humble themselves before Almighty God, and pray for His protection and favor for our beloved country, and that we may be saved from our enemies, and from the hand of all that hate us."

"*To the People of the Confederate States:* Once more upon the plains of Manassas have our armies been blessed by the Lord of Hosts with a triumph over our enemies. It is my privilege to invite you once more to His footstool; not now in the garb of fasting and sorrow, but with joy and gladness, to render thanks for the great mercies received at His hands. A few months since and our enemies poured forth their invading legions upon our soil. They laid waste our fields, polluted our altars and violated the sanctity of our homes. Around our capital they gathered their forces, and, with boasting threats, claimed it as already their prize. The brave troops which rallied to its defence have extinguished these vain hopes, and under the guidance of the same Almighty hand, have scattered our enemies and driven them back in dismay. Uniting these defeated forces and the various armies which had been ravaging our coasts with the army of invasion in Northern Virginia, our enemies have renewed their attempts to subjugate us at the very place where their first effort was defeated, and the vengeance of retributive justice has overtaken the entire host in a second and complete overthrow. To this signal success accorded to our arms in the East has been graciously added another equally brilliant in the West. On the very day on which our forces were led to victory on the plains of Manassas, in Virginia, the same Almighty arm assisted us to overcome our enemies at Richmond, in Kentucky. Thus, at one and the same time, have the two great hostile armies been

JEFFERSON DAVIS.

stricken down and the wicked designs of our enemies set at naught.   In such circumstances it is meet and right that as a people we should bow down in adoring thankfulness to that gracious God who has been our bulwark and defence, and offer unto Him the tribute of thanksgiving and praise.   In His hand is the issue of all events, and to Him should we in an especial manner ascribe the honor of this great deliverance : Now, therefore, I, Jefferson Davis, President of the Confederate States, do issue this, my proclamation, setting apart Thursday, the 18th of September instant, as a day of thanksgiving to Almighty God, for the great mercies vouchsafed to our people, and more especially for the triumph of our arms at Richmond and Manassas, in Virginia, and at Richmond, in Kentucky ; and I do hereby invite the people of the Confederate States to meet on that day at their respective places of public worship, and to unite in rendering thanks and praise to God for these great mercies, and to implore Him to conduct our country safely through the perils which surround us to the final attainment of the blessings of peace and security.   " JEFFERSON DAVIS."

"March 5, 1863.

" It is meet that, as a people who acknowledge the supremacy of the living God, we should be ever mindful of our dependence on Him ; should remember that to Him alone can we trust for our deliverance ; that to Him is due devout thankfulness for the signal mercies bestowed on us, and that by prayer alone can we hope to secure the continued manifestation of that protecting care which has hitherto shielded us in the midst of trials and dangers.   In obedience to His precepts, we have from time to time been gathered together with prayers and thanksgiving, and He has been graciously pleased to hear our supplications, and to grant abundant exhibitions of His favor to our armies and our people.   Through many conflicts we have now attained a place among the nations which commands their respect, and to the enemies who encompass us around about and seek our destruction the Lord of Hosts has again taught the lesson of his inspired word : ' That the battle is not to the strong, but to whomsoever He willeth to exalt.'   Again our enemy, with loud boasting of the power of their armed men and mailed ships, threaten us with subjugation, and with evil machinations seek, even in our own homes and at our own firesides, to pervert our men-servants and our maid-servants into accomplices of their wicked designs. Under these circumstances it is my privilege to invite you once more to meet together, and to prostrate yourselves in humble supplication to Him who has been our constant and never-failing support in the past, and to whose protection and guidance we trust for the future.

"To this end I, Jefferson Davis, President of the Confederate States of America, do issue this, my proclamation, setting apart Friday, the 27th day of March, as a day of fasting, humiliation and prayer; and I do invite the people of the said States to repair on that day to their usual places of worship, and to join in prayer to Almighty God, that He will graciously restore to our beloved country the blessings of peace and security.

"In faith whereof I have hereunto set my hand at the city of Richmond on the twenty-seventh day of February, in the year of our Lord one thousand eight hundred and sixty-three.

" JEFFERSON DAVIS."

"Again do I call the people of the Confederacy—a people who believe that the Lord reigneth, and that His overruling Providence ordereth all things—to unite in prayer and humble submission under His chastening hand, and to beseech His favor on our suffering country. It is meet that when trials and reverses befall us, we should seek to take home to our hearts and consciences the lessons which they teach, and profit by the self-examination for which they prepare us. Had not our successes on land and sea made us self-confident and forgetful of our reliance on Him? Had not the love of lucre eaten like a gangrene into the very heart of the land, converting too many among us into worshippers of gain and rendering them unmindful of their duty to their country, to their fellow-men, and to their God? Who, then, will presume to complain that we have been chastened or to despair of our just cause and the protection of our Heavenly Father? Let us rather receive in humble thankfulness the lesson which He has taught in our recent reverses, devoutly acknowledging that to Him, and not to our feeble arms, are due the honor and the glory of victory; that from Him, in His paternal providence, comes the anguish of defeat, and that, whether in victory or defeat, our humble supplications are due at His footstool. Now, therefore, I, Jefferson Davis, President of these Confederate States, do issue this, my proclamation, setting apart Friday, the

21st day of August ensuing, as a day of fasting, humiliation and prayer; and I do hereby invite the people of the Confederate States to repair on that day to their respective places of public worship, and to unite in supplication for the favor and protection of that God who has hitherto conducted us safely through all the dangers that environed us. "JEFFERSON DAVIS."

" The Senate and House of Representatives of the Confederate States of America have signified their desire that a day may be set apart and observed as a day of humiliation, fasting and prayer, in the following language, to wit: ' Reverently recognizing the Providence of God in the affairs of man, and gratefully remembering the guidance, support and deliverance granted to our patriot fathers in the memorable war which resulted in the independence of the American Colonies, and now reposing in Him our supreme confidence and hope in the present struggle for civil and religious freedom, and for the right to live under a government of our own choice, and deeply impressed with the conviction that without Him nothing is strong, nothing wise and nothing enduring; in order that the people of this Confederacy may have the opportunity, at the same time, of offering their adoration to the great Sovereign of the Universe, of penitently confessing their sins and strengthening their vows and purposes of amendment in humble reliance upon His gracious and almighty power: *The Congress of the Confederate States of America do resolve*, That Friday, the 8th day of April next, be set apart and observed as a day of humiliation, fasting and prayer, that Almighty God would so preside over our public counsels and authorities; that He would inspire our armies and their leaders with wisdom, courage and perseverance; and so manifest Himself in the greatness of His goodness and majesty of His power, that we may be safely and successfully led, through the chastening to which we are being subjected, to the attainment of an honorable peace; so that while we enjoy the blessings of a free and happy government we may ascribe to Him the honor and the glory of our independence and prosperity.' A recommendation so congenial to the feelings of the people will receive their hearty concurrence; and it is a grateful duty to the Executive to unite with their representatives in inviting them to meet in the courts of the Most High. Recent events awaken fresh gratitude to the Supreme Ruler of nations. Our enemies have suffered repeated defeats, and their nefarious scheme to burn and plunder our capital, and to destroy our civil government by putting to death the chosen servants of the people, has been baffled and set at naught. Our armies have been strengthened; our finances promise rapid progress to a satisfactory condition, and our whole country is animated with a hopeful spirit and a fixed determination to achieve independence. In these circumstances it becomes us, with thankful hearts, to bow ourselves before the throne of the Most High, and while gratefully acknowledging so many mercies, confess that our sins as a people have justly exposed us to His chastisement. Let us recognize the sufferings which we have been called upon to endure as administered by a Fatherly hand for our improvement, and, with resolute courage and patient endurance, let us wait on Him for our deliverance. In furtherance of these objects, now, therefore, I, Jefferson Davis, President of the Confederate States of America, do issue this, my proclamation, calling upon the people of the said States, in conformity with the desire expressed by their representatives, to set apart Friday, the 8th day of April, as a day of humiliation, fasting and prayer, and I do hereby invite them on that day to repair to their several places of public worship, and beseech Almighty God ' to preside over our public counsels, and so inspire our armies and leaders with wisdom, courage and perseverance; and so to manifest Himself in the greatness of His goodness, and in the majesty of His power, that we may secure the blessings of an honorable peace, and of free government; and that we, as a people, may ascribe all to the honor and glory of His name.'

"JEFFERSON DAVIS."

Not simply in his official station, but in his private life and influence as well, Mr. Davis was pronounced in his Christian character, and no one who has seen him, as it has been my privilege to do, in the freedom of his beautiful home at Beauvoir, and heard him talk of the struggles of the past, the trials of the present, and the hopes of the future, can doubt for a moment that his faith is built on "the rock Christ Jesus," and that he has for years taken Jesus as "the man of his counsel" and the guide of his life.

GENERAL R. E. LEE, the great commander of the Army of Northern Virginia from June, 1862, to the surrender at Appomattox Court House, was one of the noblest specimens of the Christian soldier that the world ever saw.

In this age of hero-worship there is a tendency to exalt unduly the virtues of great men, to magnify the religious character of one professing to be a Christian, and even to manufacture "Christians" out of those of notoriously irreligious lives. This is so well understood that there may be with those who never came in contact with this great man a lingering doubt as to the genuineness of his piety—a fear that with him, as with so many others, his profession of religion was merely nominal. A few incidents, culled from the many that might be given, will serve to dissipate any such impression, and to show beyond all cavil that with General Lee *vital godliness* was a precious reality.

I can never forget my first interview and conversation with General Lee on religious matters. It was in February, 1864, while our army was resting along the Rapidan, Rev. B. T. Lacy and myself went, as a committee of our Chaplains' Association, to consult him in reference to the better observance of the Sabbath in the army, and especially to urge that something be done to prevent irreligious officers from converting Sunday into a grand gala day for inspections, reviews, etc. It was a delicate mission. We did not wish to appear as either informers or officious intermeddlers, and yet we were very anxious to do something to further the wishes of those who sent us, and to put a stop to what was then a growing evil and, in some commands, a serious obstacle to the efficient work of the chaplain. The cordial greeting which he gave us, the marked courtesy and respect with which he listened to what we had to say and expressed his warm sympathy with the object of our mission, soon put us at our ease. But as we presently began to answer his questions concerning the spiritual interests of the army, and to tell of that great revival which was then extending through the camps, and bringing thousands of our noble men to Christ, we saw his eye brighten and his whole countenance glow with pleasure; and as, in his simple, feeling words, he expressed his delight, we forgot the great warrior, and only remembered that we were communing with an humble, earnest Christian.

In July, 1862, he had issued a general order to the army in which he said: "Habitually all duties except those of inspection will be suspended during Sunday, to afford the troops rest and to enable them to attend religious services."

The day after our interview he issued the following:

4

"HEAD-QUARTERS, ARMY OF ⎱
NORTHERN VIRGINIA, February 7, 1864. ⎰
"*General Order* No. 15.

"I. The attention of the army has already been called to the obligation of a proper observance of the Sabbath; but the sense of its importance, not only as a moral and religious duty, but as contributing to the personal health and well-being of the troops, induces the commanding general to repeat the orders on that subject. He has learned with great pleasure that in many brigades convenient houses of worship have been erected, and earnestly desires that every facility consistent with the requirements of discipline shall be afforded the men to assemble themselves together for the purpose of devotion.

"II. To this end he directs that none but duties strictly necessary shall be required to be performed on Sunday, and that the labor, both of men and animals, which it is practicable to anticipate or postpone, or the immediate performance of which is not essential to the safety, health or comfort of the army, shall be suspended on that day.

"III. Commanding officers will require the usual inspections on Sunday to be held at such time as not to interfere with the attendance of the men on divine service at the customary hour in the morning.

"They will also give their attention to the maintenance of order and quiet around the place of worship, and prohibit anything that may tend to disturb or interrupt religious exercises.

"R. E. LEE, General."

As we were about to leave his tent, Mr. Lacy said: "I think it right that I should say to you, general, that the chaplains of this army have a deep interest in your welfare, and that some of the most fervent prayers we offer are in your behalf." The old hero's face flushed, tears started in his eyes, and he replied, with choked utterance and deep emotion: "Please thank them for that, sir—I warmly appreciate it. And I can only say that I am nothing but a poor sinner, trusting in Christ alone for salvation, and need all of the prayers they can offer for me."

He never failed to attend preaching when his duties did not absolutely preclude his doing so. Nor was he a mere listless attendant. The simple truths of the Gospel had no more attentive listener than General Lee; and his eye would kindle and

GENERAL LEE AT THE SOLDIERS' PRAYER-MEETING.

(See page 51.)

his face glow under the more tender doctrines of grace. He used frequently to attend preaching at Jackson's head-quarters; and it was a scene which a master-hand might have delighted to paint—those two great warriors, surrounded by hundreds of their officers and men, bowed in humble worship before the God and Saviour in whom they trusted.

General Lee always took the deepest interest in the work of his chaplains and the spiritual welfare of his men. He was a frequent visitor at the chaplains' meetings, and a deeply interested observer of their proceedings; and the faithful chaplain, who stuck to his post and did his duty, could be always assured of a warm friend at head-quarters.

While the Army of Northern Virginia confronted General Meade at Mine Run, near the end of November, 1863, and a battle was momentarily expected, General Lee, with a number of general and staff officers, was riding down his line of battle, when, just in rear of General A. P. Hill's position, the cavalcade suddenly came upon a party of soldiers engaged in one of those prayer-meetings which they so often held on the eve of battle. An attack from the enemy seemed imminent—already the sharp-shooting along the skirmish-line had begun—the artillery was belching forth its hoarse thunder, and the mind and heart of the great chieftain were full of the expected combat. Yet, as he saw those ragged veterans bowed in prayer, he instantly dismounted, uncovered his head and devoutly joined in the simple worship. The rest of the party at once followed his example, and those humble privates found themselves leading the devotions of their loved and honored chieftain.

It is related that as his army was crossing the James, in 1864, and hurrying on to the defence of Petersburg, General Lee turned aside from the road and, kneeling in the dust, devoutly joined a minister present in earnest prayer that God would give him wisdom and grace in the new stage of the campaign upon which he was then entering.

Rev. Dr. T. V. Moore gave the following in his memorial sermon:

"About the middle of the war, when the horizon looked very dark, I spent an evening with him, at the house of a friend, and he was evidently, in spite of his habitual self-command, deeply depressed. Happening to be alone with him, as we parted for the night, I endeavored to cheer him with the fact that so many

Christian people were praying for him. I shall never forget the emphasis with which he grasped my hand as, with a voice and eye that betrayed deep emotion, he assured me that it was not only his comfort, but his only comfort, and declared the simple and absolute trust that he had in God, and God alone, as his helper in that terrible struggle. Another incident impressed me still more, because it brought out a most beautiful trait in his character. No one ever rendered him a service, however humble, that was not instantly and gratefully acknowledged, however lowly the person might be. During the summer of 1864, after he had been holding at bay the tremendous forces of General Grant for long weeks, retreating step by step, as he was outflanked by overwhelming numbers, until he reached the neighborhood of Cold Harbor, I had occasion to render him a slight service, so slight that, knowing at the time that he was sick, and overburdened with the great responsibilities of his arduous and continually menaced position, I never expected it to be acknowledged at all; but, to my surprise, I received a letter thanking me for this trivial service, and adding: ' I thank you especially that I have a place in your prayers. No human power can avail us without the blessing of God, and I rejoice to know that, in this crisis of our affairs, good men everywhere are supplicating Him for His favor and protection.' He then added a postscript, which most touchingly exhibited his thoughtful and tender recollection of the troubles of others, even in that hour when all his thoughts might be supposed to be absorbed by his vast responsibilities as the leader of the Army of Northern Virginia."

Not long before the evacuation of Petersburg, I was one day on the lines not far above Hatcher's Run, busily engaged in distributing tracts and religious newspapers, which the soldiers were eagerly crowding around to get, when I saw a large cavalcade approaching. As they drew near I recognized Generals Lee, A. P. Hill, Gordon, Heth and several other generals, who, accompanied by a large staff, were inspecting the lines. I stepped aside to let the cavalcade pass, but the keen eye of Gordon recognized and his cordial grasp detained me while he eagerly inquired about my work. General Lee reined in his noble steed ("Traveller," whom we all remember so well) and joined in the conversation, the rest all gathered around, and the humble tract distributer found himself the centre of a group whose names and deeds shine on the brightest pages of the history they contributed so much to make.

My old colonel, now Lieutenant-General A. P. Hill, and one of the most accomplished soldiers, as well as one of the most high-toned gentlemen whom the war produced, pleasantly asked of me, as he gave me a hearty greeting, " John " (as he always familiarly called me), " don't you think the boys would prefer ' hard-tack ' to tracts just now ? "

" I have no doubt that many of them would," I replied; " but they crowd around and take the tracts as eagerly as they surround the commissary, when he has anything to ' issue,' and, besides other advantages, the tracts certainly help them to bear the lack of ' hard-tack.' "

" I have no doubt of it," he said, " and I am glad you are able to supply the tracts more abundantly than we can the rations."

General Lee asked me if I ever had calls for prayer-books among the soldiers. I told him that I frequently had, and he replied : "Well, you would greatly oblige me if you would call at my quarters and get and distribute a few which I have. I bought a new one when in Richmond the other day, and upon my saying that I would give my old one, which I had carried through the Mexican war and had kept ever since, to some soldier, the bookseller offered to give me a dozen new prayer-books for the old one. I, of course, accepted so good an offer; and now I have a dozen to give away instead of one."

I called at the appointed hour; the general had been called away from his quarters on some important matter, but he had (even amid his pressing cares and responsibilities) left the prayer-books with a member of his staff, with directions concerning them. In each one he had written, in his own well-known handwriting, " Presented to ———— by R. E. Lee." Had *I* been disposed to speculate, I am quite sure that I could easily have traded each one of these books containing the autograph of our great chieftain for a dozen others, and I know that the soldiers to whom I gave them have treasured them as precious mementos, or handed them down as priceless heirlooms. (I saw one of these books several years ago in the hands of a son whose father was killed on the retreat. *It was not for sale.* Indeed, money could not buy it.)

General Lee's orders and reports always gratefully recognized

the " Lord of Hosts " as the " Giver of victory," and expressed
an humble dependence upon and trust in Him.

He thus began his dispatch to the President the evening of
his great victory at Cold Harbor and Gaines's Mill.

" HEAD-QUARTERS, June 27, 1862.
" HIS EXCELLENCY, PRESIDENT, DAVIS :

"*Mr. President:* Profoundly grateful to Almighty God for the
signal victory granted to us, it is my pleasing task to announce
to you the success achieved by this army to-day."

His beautiful general order of congratulation to the troops on
their series of splendid victories during the seven days' battles
opened with these memorable words :

" HEAD-QUARTERS IN THE FIELD, July 7, 1862.
" *General Order* No. 75.

" The commanding general, profoundly grateful to the Giver
of all victory for the signal success with which He has blessed
our arms, tenders his warmest thanks and congratulations to the
army, by whose valor such splendid results have been achieved."

His dispatch announcing his great victory at Fredericksburg
contains the brief, but significant sentence—" *Thanks be to God.*"

The following extracts from an order which he issued to the
troops not long after the battle of Fredericksburg show the
same spirit :

" HEAD-QUARTERS, A. N. VA., December 31, 1862.
"*General Order* No. 132.

" The general commanding takes this occasion to express to
the officers and soldiers of the army his high appreciation of
the fortitude, valor and devotion displayed by them, which, under the blessing of Almighty God, have added the victory of
Fredericksburg to the long list of their triumphs.

. . . . . .

" That this great result was achieved with a loss small in
point of numbers only augments the admiration with which the
commanding general regards the prowess of the troops, and increases his gratitude to Him who hath given us the victory.

. . . .

"The signal manifestations of Divine mercy that have distinguished the eventful and glorious campaign of the year just closing give assurance of hope that under the guidance of the same Almighty hand the coming year will be no less fruitful of events that will insure the safety, peace and happiness of our beloved country, and add new lustre to the already imperishable name of the Army of Northern Virginia.

"R. E. LEE, General."

In his dispatch to President Davis, after Chancellorsville, he said: "We have again to thank Almighty God for a great victory."

And in his general orders to his troops he holds this significant language: . . . . "While this glorious victory entitles you to the praise and gratitude of the nation, we are especially called upon to return our grateful thanks to the only Giver of victory, for the signal deliverance He has wrought.

"It is, therefore, earnestly recommended that the troops unite, on Sunday next, in ascribing unto the Lord of hosts the glory due unto His name."

In closing his general order for the observance of the fast-day appointed by President Davis in the spring of 1863, he makes the following earnest appeal: "Soldiers! No portion of our people have greater cause to be thankful to Almighty God than yourselves. He has preserved your lives amidst countless dangers. He has been with you in all your trials. He has given you fortitude under hardships, and courage in the shock of battle. He has cheered you by the example and by the deeds of your martyred comrades. He has enabled you to defend your country successfully against the assaults of a powerful oppressor. Devoutly thankful for signal mercies, let us bow before the Lord of hosts, and join our hearts with millions in our land in prayer that He will continue His merciful protection over our cause; that He will scatter our enemies and set at naught their evil designs, and that He will graciously restore to our country the blessings of peace and security."

He announced the victory at Winchester in the following dispatch:

"To HIS EXCELLENCY, JEFFERSON DAVIS:

"June 15, 1863.—God has again crowned the valor of our

troops with success. Early's Division stormed the enemy's in-trenchments at Winchester, capturing their artillery, etc.

"R. E. Lee."

His order requiring the observance of the fast-day appointed by President Davis in August, 1863, was as follows:

"Head-quarters, A. N. Va., August 13, 1863.
"*General Order* No. 83.

"The President of the Confederate States has, in the name of the people, appointed the 21st day of August as a day of fasting, humiliation and prayer. A strict observance of the day is en-joined upon the officers and soldiers of this army. All military duties, except such as are absolutely necessary, will be suspended. The commanding officers of brigades and regiments are re-quested to cause divine service, suitable to the occasion, to be performed in their respective commands. Soldiers! we have sinned against Almighty God. We have forgotten His signal mercies, and have cultivated a revengeful, haughty, and boastful spirit. We have not remembered that the defenders of a just cause should be pure in His eyes; that 'our times are in His hands;' and we have relied too much on our own arms for the achievement of our independence. God is our only refuge and our strength. Let us humble ourselves before Him. Let us confess our many sins, and beseech Him to give us a higher courage, a purer patriotism and more determined will; that He will convert the hearts of our enemies; that He will hasten the time when war, with its sorrows and sufferings, shall cease, and that He will give us a name and place among the nations of the earth. "R. E. Lee, General."

I can never forget the effect produced by the reading of this order at the solemn services of that memorable fast-day. A precious revival was already in progress in many of the com-mands—the day was almost universally observed—the attend-ance upon preaching and other services was very large—the solemn attention and starting tear attested the deep interest felt—and the work of grace among the troops widened and deepened and went gloriously on until there had been thousands of professions of faith in Christ as a personal Saviour. How far these grand results were due to this fast-day, or to the quiet influence and fervent prayers of the commanding general, eternity along shall reveal.

When General Meade crossed the Rapidan in November, 1863, the troops were stirred by the following address:

" HEAD-QUARTERS, ARMY NORTHERN VIRGINIA,
" November 26, 1863.
"*General Order* No. 102.

" The enemy is again advancing upon our capital, and the country once more looks to this army for protection. Under the blessings of God your valor has repelled every previous attempt, and invoking the continuance of His favor we cheerfully commit to Him the issue of the coming conflict.

" A cruel enemy seeks to reduce our fathers and our mothers, our wives and our children to abject slavery; to strip them of their property and drive them from their homes. Upon you these helpless ones rely to avert these terrible calamities, and secure them the blessings of liberty and safety. Your past history gives them the assurance that their trust will not be in vain. Let every man remember that all he holds dear depends upon the faithful discharge of his duty, and resolve to fight and, if need be, to die in defence of a cause so sacred, and worthy the name won by this army on so many bloody fields.

" (Signed) R. E. LEE, General."

I give the following as illustrating not only his trust in God, but also his tender solicitude for his soldiers:

" HEAD-QUARTERS, A. N. VA., January 22, 1864.
"*General Order* No. 7.

" The commanding general considers it due to the army to state that the temporary reduction of rations has been caused by circumstances beyond the control of those charged with its support. Its welfare and comfort are the objects of his constant and earnest solicitude ; and no effort has been spared to provide for its wants. It is hoped that the exertions now being made will render the necessity of short duration: but the history of the army has shown that the country can require no sacrifice too great for its patriotic devotion.

" Soldiers ! you tread with no unequal steps the road by which your fathers marched through suffering, privation and blood to independence !

"Continue to emulate in the future, as you have in the past, their valor in arms, their patient endurance of hardships, their high resolve to be free, which no trial could shake, no bribe seduce, no danger appall: and be assured that the just God, who crowned their efforts with success, will, in His own good time, send down His blessing upon yours.

"(Signed) R. E. LEE, General."

The following was his order for the observance of the fast-day appointed for April, 1864:

"HEAD-QUARTERS, A. N. VA., March 30, 1864.
"*General Order* No. 23.

"In compliance with the recommendation of the Senate and House of Representatives, His Excellency the President has issued his proclamation calling upon the people to set apart Friday, the 8th of April, as a day of fasting, humiliation and prayer. The commanding general invites the army to join in the observance of the day. He directs due preparation to be made in all departments to anticipate the wants of the several commands, so that it may be strictly observed. All military duties, except such as are absolutely necessary, will be suspended. The chaplains are desired to hold services in their regiments and brigades. The officers and men are requested to attend.

"Soldiers! let us humble ourselves before the Lord our God, asking through Christ the forgiveness of our sins, beseeching the aid of the God of our forefathers in the defence of our homes and our liberties, thanking Him for His past blessings, and imploring their continuance upon our cause and our people.

"R. E. LEE, General."

In his dispatch announcing the result of the first day's battle in the Wilderness he says: .... "By the blessing of God we maintained our position against every effort until night, when the contest closed." .... And in his dispatch concerning the advance of the enemy on the next day he says: .... "Every advance on his part, thanks to a merciful God, has been repulsed." ....

He closed his dispatch concerning the first day at Spottsylvania by saying: "I am most thankful to the Giver of all victory that our loss is small." And that concerning the action of June

3, 1864, with: "Our loss to-day has been small, and our success under the blessing of God all that we could expect." . . . .

He closed his announcement of A. P. Hill's brilliant victory at Reams's Station, in August, 1864, by saying: . . . "Our profound gratitude is due the Giver of all victory, and our thanks to the brave men and officers engaged."

In his order assuming the chief command of all of the Confederate forces he said: . . . . "Deeply impressed with the difficulties and responsibility of the position, and humbly invoking the guidance of Almighty God, I rely for success upon the courage and fortitude of the army, sustained by the patriotism and firmness of the people, confident that their united efforts under the blessing of Heaven will secure peace and independence." . . . .

I give the above only as specimens of his dispatches and general orders, which all recognized in the most emphatic manner his sense of dependence upon and trust in God.

With the close of the war and the afflictions which came upon his loved land, the piety of this great man seems to have mellowed and deepened, and I could fill pages concerning his life at Lexington and the bright evidences he gave of vital, active godliness.

He was a most regular attendant upon all of the services of his own church, his seat in the college chapel was never vacant unless he was kept away by sickness, and if there was a union prayer-meeting, or a service of general interest in any of the churches of Lexington, General Lee was sure to be among the most devout attendants.

His pew in his own church was immediately in front of the chancel, his seat in the chapel was the second from the pulpit, and he seemed always to prefer a seat near the preacher's stand. He always devoutly knelt during prayer, and his attitude during the entire service was that of an interested listener or a reverential participant.

He was not accustomed to indulge in carping criticisms of sermons, but was a most intelligent judge of what a sermon ought to be, and always expressed his preference for those sermons which presented most simply and earnestly the soul-saving truths of the Gospel. I heard him remark in reference to the Baccalaureate sermon preached at the college by Rev. Dr. J. A. Broadus: "It was a noble sermon—one of the very best I ever heard—and the beauty of it was that the preacher gave our young men the very marrow of the Gospel, and with a simple earnestness that must have reached their hearts and done them good."

Upon another occasion a distinguished minister had addressed the Young Men's Christian Association of the college, and on the next night delivered a popular lecture. Speaking of the last, General Lee said: "It was a very fine lecture and I enjoyed it. But I did not like it as much as I did the one before our Christian Association. *That* touched our hearts, and did us all good."

He had also a most intelligent appreciation of the adaptation of religious services to particular occasions, and of the appropriateness of prayers to the time and place in which they were offered.

He once said to one of the faculty: "I want you to go with me to call upon Mr. ——, the new minister who has just come to town. I want to pay my respects to him, and to invite him to take his turn in the conduct of our chapel exercises, and to do what he can for the spiritual interests of our young men.

"And do you think that it would be any harm for me to delicately hint to Mr. —— that we would be glad if he would make his morning prayers *a little short?* You know our friend —— —— is accustomed to make his prayers too long. He prays for the Jews, the Turks, the heathen, the Chinese and everybody else, and makes his prayers run into the regular hour for our college recitations. Would it be wrong for me to suggest to Mr. —— that he *confine his morning prayers to us poor sinners at the college, and pray for the Turks, the Jews, the Chinese and the other heathen some other time?*"

The suggestion is one which those who lead in public prayer would do well to ponder.

General Lee was emphatically a *man of prayer*. He was accustomed to pray in his family and to have his seasons of secret prayer which he allowed nothing else—however pressing—to interrupt. He was also a constant reader and a diligent student of the Bible, and had his regular seasons for this delightful exercise. Even amid his most active campaigns he found time to read every day some portion of God's word.

As I watched alone by his body the day after his death, I picked up from the table a well-used pocket Bible, in which was

J. WILLIAM JONES, WHEN CHAPLAIN OF 13th VIRGINIA
REGIMENT, C. S. A.

(Facing page 60.)

written, in his characteristic chirography, " R. E. Lee, Lieuten-ant-Colonel United States Army." How he took this blessed book as the man of his counsel and the light of his pathway—how its precious promises cheered him amid the afflictions and trials of his eventful life—how its glorious hopes illumined for him "the dark valley and shadow of death," eternity alone will fully reveal.

And he always manifested the liveliest interest in giving to others the precious Bible. During the war he was an active promoter of Bible distribution among his soldiers, and soon after coming to Lexington he accepted the presidency of the Rock-bridge Bible Society, and continued to discharge its duties up to the time of his death. I give his letter accepting this office :

"*Gentlemen:* I have delayed replying to your letter informing me of having been elected President of the ' Rockbridge Bible Society,' not for want of interest in the subject, but from an ap-prehension that I should not be able to perform the duties of the position in such manner as to advance the high object proposed. Having, however, been encouraged by your kind assurances, and being desirous of co-operating, in any way I can, in extending the inestimable knowledge of the priceless truths of the Bible, I accept the position assigned me.

" With many thanks to the society for the high compliment paid me by their selection as their president, I am, with great respect, Your obedient servant,

" R. E. LEE.

" REV. DR. PENDLETON,   ⎫
  COL. J. T. L. PRESTON,   ⎬ Committee."
  MR. WM. WHITE,   ⎭

The following paper may be appropriately introduced here :

"At the meeting of the Board of Managers of the Rockbridge County Bible Society, on the 12th inst., for the purpose of im-parting to the organization greater efficiency—in addition to other important measures adopted and in substance since published—the undersigned were appointed a committee to prepare and publish a minute, expressing the deep sense which the managers and members of this Society have of the exalted worth of their last president, the illustrious General R. E. Lee; of the blessed influence which he exerted as a Christian man and in his official relation to this cause, and of the grievous loss to us in his removal, even to celestial joy.

"The duty is to us most grateful. World-wide and enduring as must be the renown of our honored friend for great abilities, grandeur of character and achievements, perhaps, in proportion to appliances, never surpassed—his crowning glory was, in our view, the sublime simplicity of his Christian faith and life. To the inviolable dignity of a soul among the noblest of all history was in him thoroughly united that guileless, unpretending, gentle and yet earnest spirit of a little child, so emphatically designated by our Lord as the essential characteristic of his chosen ones. These were the traits which, while they justly endeared him to children, and friends, and all the people, rendered him prompt to every, even the humblest duty, and caused him, although burdened with weighty cares, to accept the quietly useful task of presiding over so inconspicuous a good work as that of the Rockbridge County Bible Society. Of the judicious zeal with which he undertook this service, evidence conclusive was at once given in the wisely simple yet stirring appeal, which he penned and sent forth to the several ministers and congregations of the county, urging them to renewed energy in remedying Bible destitution throughout our borders. Well may the friends of this cause mourn the loss of such a leader, and record on the tablets of their hearts an example so good, as an incentive to their own efficiency for the future !

"In connection with this testimonial of the society's loving estimate of their last president, the undersigned were instructed to cause to be published the *Appeal* above referred to, written by General Lee's own hand, of which copies were at the time sent to all the ministers and congregations of the county. The original remains, a precious memento, in the archives of the society. To it, as hereunto subjoined in print, we ask the attentive consideration due alike to its great author and to the important cause for which he pleads. Facts and principles bearing on the question are to-day very much as they were five years ago, when the mind of this great and good man was moved so impressively to put them forth in the following circular.

"Although now resting from his labors, his works do follow him ! Shall they not, in this and in other forms, effectually plead with all to be alive to Christian privilege in this matter, and faithful to duty therein and in all things?

"W. N. PENDLETON, ⎫
J. L. CLARKE,   ⎬ Committee."
J. W. PRATT.   ⎭

"LEXINGTON, VA., January 14, 1869.

"The Rockbridge County Bible Society, whose operations were interrupted and records lost during the war, was reorganized on the 5th of last October by representatives of different churches of the county, in pursuance of a notice given through the *Lexington Gazette*. A new constitution was adopted which provides for the reorganization of a Board of Managers, composed of the ministers of each church and one representative from each congregation, appointed by them, to meet at least once a year, on the first Saturday in October; and that the officers of the society shall be a President, a Vice-President, Secretary and Treasurer, and Librarian, who shall constitute the Executive Committee of the society.

"At the meeting mentioned, the officers elected were:

"R. E. LEE, President.

"J. T. L. PRESTON, Vice-President.

"WM. G. WHITE, Secretary and Treasurer.

"JOHN S. WHITE, Librarian.

"In compliance with a resolution of the meeting requesting the Executive Committee to take measures to procure a supply of Bibles, and to obtain from the congregations of the county funds for the purpose, it is respectfully requested that you will make, at the earliest and most suitable occasion, a collection in your congregation for this object, and cause the amount to be transmitted to the treasurer, Mr. Wm. G. White, at Lexington, and inform him at the same time, as far as practicable, how many copies of the Bible will be required to meet the wants of the congregation, as the constitution provides that each congregation shall mainly conduct the work of their distribution within their respective spheres.

"The revival of the time-honored organization of the Rockbridge Bible Society, it is believed, will fill with pleasure the hearts of all good citizens in the county, and the Executive Committee earnestly appeal to the churches, their members, and all persons interested in the great work of the society, to unite cordially and promptly with them for its accomplishment. The first object is to supply every family with a copy of the Bible that is without it, and as many years have elapsed since there has been a distribution of the Holy Scriptures among us, it is feared, for reasons that are apparent, that there is at this time a great destitution among the people. The united and zealous efforts of all the denominations in the county are therefore earnestly solicited in aid of this good work.

" Respectfully submitted,

" R. E. LEE,

" President Rockbridge Bible Society.

" To the Ministers and Churches of the County of Rockbridge, Virginia."

General Lee was also deeply interested in the Virginia Bible Society and their noble work of giving the word of God to the people.

He wrote as follows to the president of that society:

" LEXINGTON, VIRGINIA, April 5, 1869.

"*Rev. and Dear Sir :* Your letter of first instant was only received this morning.

" To reach Richmond by to-morrow evening, the anniversary of the Bible Society, I should have to ride all to-night to take the cars at Staunton to-morrow morning. I am suffering with a cold now, and fear the journey would lay me up.

" I would, however, make the trial, did I think I could be of any service to the great object of the society. If the managers could suggest any plan, in addition to the abundant distribution of the Holy Scriptures, to cause the mass of the people to meditate on their simple truths, and, in the language of Wilberforce, ' to read the Bible—read the Bible,' so as to become acquainted with the experience and realities of religion, the greatest good would be accomplished. Wishing the society all success and continued advancement in its work,

" I am, with great respect, most truly yours,

" R. E. LEE."

" REV. GEO. WOODBRIDGE, President Virginia Bible Society."

The following graceful acknowledgment of a copy of the Scriptures sent him by some English ladies may be appropriately introduced at this point:

" LEXINGTON, VIRGINIA, April 16, 1866.
" HON. A. W. BERESFORD HOPE,
    " BEDGEBURY PARK, KENT, ENGLAND:
    "*Sir:* I have received within a few days your letter of the
14th of November, 1864, and had hoped that by this time it
would have been followed by the copy of the Holy Scriptures
to which you refer, that I might have known the generous
donors, whose names you state are inscribed upon its pages.

    " Its failure to reach me will, I fear, deprive me of that pleas-
ure! and I must ask the favor of you to thank them most
heartily for their kindness in providing me with a book, in comparison with which all others in my eyes are of minor importance; and which in all my perplexities and distresses has never
failed to give me light and strength. Your assurance of the
esteem in which I am held by a large portion of the British nation, as well as by those for whom you speak, is most grateful
to my feelings; though I am aware that I am indebted to their
generous natures, and not to my own merit, for their good
opinion.

    " I beg, sir, that you will accept my sincere thanks for the
kind sentiments which you have expressed towards me, and my
unfeigned admiration of your exalted character.

    " I am, with great respect, your most obedient servant,
                                    " (Signed) R. E. LEE."

General Lee was a most active promoter of the interests of
his church, and of the cause of Christ in the community; and
all of the pastors felt that they had in him a warm friend.

He was a most liberal contributer to his church and to other
objects of benevolence. At the vestry meeting, which he attended and over which he presided the evening he was taken
with his fatal illness, an effort was being made to raise a certain
sum for an important object. General Lee had already made an
exceedingly liberal contribution, but when it was ascertained
that $55 were still lacking, he quietly said, " I will give the bal-
ance." These were the last words he spoke in the meeting—
his contribution, his last public act. I happen to know that,
within the last twelve months of his life he gave $100 to the edu-
cation of soldiers' orphans, $100 to the Young Men's Christian
Association of the college and smaller sums to a number of
similar objects—making, in the aggregate, a most liberal contri-

5

bution. And then, his manner of giving was so modest and unostentatious. In giving me a very handsome contribution to the Lexington Baptist Church, he quietly said: "Will you do me the kindness to hand this to your treasurer, and save me the trouble of hunting him up? I am getting old now, and you young men must help me." And his whole manner was that of one receiving instead of bestowing a favor.

General Lee was not accustomed to talk of anything that concerned himself, and did not often speak freely of his inner religious feelings. Yet he would, when occasion offered, speak most decidedly of his reliance for salvation upon the merits of his personal Redeemer, and none who heard him thus talk could doubt for a moment that his faith was built on the " Rock of Ages."

He one day said to a friend in speaking of the duty of laboring for the good of others: "Ah! Mrs. P——, I find it so hard to keep one poor sinner's heart in the right way, that it seems presumptuous to try to help others." And yet he did, quietly and unostentatiously, speak "a word in season" and exert influences potent for good in directing others in the path to heaven. He was a "son of consolation" to the afflicted, and his letter-book contains some touching illustrations of this. We give the following extract from a letter written to an afflicted mother on the death, by drowning, of her son (then a student at the college):

" LEXINGTON, VIRGINIA, April 6, 1868.

"*My Dear Madam:* It grieves me to address you on a subject which has already been announced to you in all of its woe, and which has brought to your heart such heavy affliction.

" But I beg to be permitted to sympathize in your great sorrow, and to express to you on the part of the faculty of the college their deep grief at the calamity which has befallen you. It may be some consolation in your bereavement to know that your son was highly esteemed by the officers and students of the college, and that this whole community unite in sorrow at his untimely death. May God in His mercy support you under this grievous trial, and give you that peace which, as it passeth all understanding, so nothing in this world can diminish or destroy it."

On the death of Bishop Elliott, of Georgia, he wrote the following letter to his wife:

"LEXINGTON, VIRGINIA, February 21, 1867.

"*My Dear Mrs. Elliott:* It would be in vain for me to attempt to express my grief at your great affliction. In common with the whole country, I mourn the death of him whom for more than a quarter of a century I have admired, loved and venerated, and whose loss to the church and society, where his good offices were so important, I can never expect to see supplied.

"You have my deepest sympathy, and my earnest prayers are offered to Almighty God that He may be graciously pleased to comfort you in your great sorrow, and to bring you in His own good time to rejoice with Him whom in His all-wise Providence He has called before you to heaven.

"With great respect, most truly yours,
"R. E. LEE."

The following, to the widow of his cherished friend, General Geo. W. Randolph (for a time Confederate Secretary of War), will be read with mournful pleasure by the large circle of admirers and friends of this gifted and widely lamented Virginian :

"LEXINGTON, VIRGINIA, April 11, 1867.

"*My Dear Mrs. Randolph:* The letter I received this morning from your niece offers me an opportunity of writing to you on a subject over which I deeply mourn. But it is the survivors of the sad event whom I commiserate, and not him whom a gracious God has called to Himself; and whose tender heart and domestic virtues make the pang of parting the more bitter to those who are left behind. I deferred writing, for I knew the hopelessness of offering you consolation ; and yet for what other purpose can a righteous man be summoned into the presence of a merciful God than to receive his reward ? However, then, we lament, we ought not to deplore him or wish him back from his peaceful, happy home. I had hoped to have seen him once more in this world, and had been pleasing myself with the prospect of paying him a special visit this summer. But God in mercy to him has ordered otherwise, and I submit.

"The recollection of his esteem and friendship will always be dear to me, and his kind remembrance in his long and painful illness will be gratefully cherished. His worth and truth, his unselfish devotion to right, and his exalted patriotism, will cause all men to mourn the country's loss in his death, while his gentle, manly courtesy, dignified conduct, and Christian charity, must intensely endear him to those who knew him.

"Mrs. Lee and my daughters, while they join in unfeigned sorrow for your bereavement, unite with me in sincere regards and fervent prayers to Him, who can alone afford relief, for His gracious support and continued protection to you. May His abundant mercies be showered upon you, and may His almighty arm guide and uphold you.

"Please thank Miss Randolph for writing to me.

"With great respect and true affection, your obedient servant,

"(Signed)   R. E. LEE."

The following expresses a great deal in brief compass:

"LEXINGTON, February 28, 1870.
"MR. SAMUEL R. GEORGE,
    "71 Mt. Vernon Place, BALTIMORE, MARYLAND:
"*My Dear Sir;* I have learned with deep regret the great sorrow that has befallen you, and sincerely sympathize in your overwhelming grief. But the great God of heaven takes us at the period when it is best for us to go, and we can only gratefully acknowledge His mercy and try to be resigned to His will. Every beat of our hearts marks our progress through life and admonishes us of the steps we make towards the grave. We are thus every moment reminded to prepare for our summons. With my earnest sympathy for yourself and kindest regards to your children, in which Mrs. Lee and my daughters unite,

"I am most truly yours,
"R. E. LEE."

The friendship between General Lee and the venerable Bishop Meade, of Virginia (whose efficient labors in the cause of evangelical piety were widely known and appreciated even outside of his own communion), was touchingly beautiful, and the following letter will be read with peculiar interest:

"LEXINGTON, VIRGINIA, March 7, 1866.
"RT. REV. JOHN JOHNS, Bishop of Virginia,
    "Theological Seminary, near ALEXANDRIA, VIRGINIA:
"*Rt. Rev. and Dear Sir:* I am very glad to learn, from your note of the 27th ult., that you have consented to write a memoir

of our good and beloved Bishop Meade. Of all the men I have ever known, I consider him the purest; and a history of his character and life will prove a benefit to mankind. No one can portray that character, or illustrate that life better than yourself; and I rejoice that the sacred duty has devolved upon you.

"In compliance with your request, I will state as far as my recollection enables me, the substance of what occurred in the short interview I had with him the evening before his death; and I do so the more readily, as you were present and can correct the inaccuracies of my memory. I received a message about dark that the bishop was very ill, and desired to see me. On entering his room he recognized me at once, and extending his hand said, that his earthly pilgrimage was nearly finished, and that before the light of another day he should have passed from this world. That he had known me in childhood, when I recited to him the church catechism taught me by my mother before I could read; that his affection and interest began at that time and strengthened by my marriage with his godchild, and continued to the present. Invoking upon me the guidance and protection of Almighty God, he bade me a last farewell.

"With kindest regards to Mrs. Johns and your daughters, I am most truly yours,

"(Signed) R. E. Lee."

A clergyman present, in describing the last interview, states that the bishop said to the great soldier: "God bless you! God bless you, Robert, and fit you for your high and responsible duties. I can't call you 'General,' I must call you 'Robert;' I have heard you your catechism too often."

General Lee was deeply affected by the interview, and when he turned to leave the room, the bishop, much exhausted and with great emotion, took him by the hand and said: "Heaven bless you! Heaven bless you! and give you wisdom for your important and arduous duties."

On the death of Randolph Fairfax, who fell at Fredericksburg, General Lee, who highly appreciated the manly virtues of this young soldier of the cross, wrote the following letter to his bereaved father:

"Camp Fredericksburg, December 28, 1862.

"*My Dear Doctor:* I have grieved most deeply at the death of your noble son. I have watched his conduct from the commencement of the war, and have pointed with pride to the patriotism, self-denial and manliness of character he has exhibited. I had hoped an opportunity would occur for the promotion he deserved; not that it would have elevated him, but have shown that his devotion to duty was appreciated by his country.

"Such an opportunity would undoubtedly have occurred; but he has been translated to a better world, for which his purity and piety eminently fitted him. You do not require to be told how great is his gain. It is the living for whom I sorrow. I beg you will offer to Mrs. Fairfax and your daughters my heartfelt sympathy, for I know the depth of their grief. That God may give you and them strength to bear this great affliction, is the earnest prayer of your early friend,

"R. E. LEE.

"Dr. ORLANDO FAIRFAX, RICHMOND."

On the death of his personal friend, George Peabody, General Lee wrote the following to Mr. Peabody Russell:

"LEXINGTON, VIRGINIA, November 10, 1869.

"*My Dear Mr. Russell:* The announcement of the death of your uncle, Mr. George Peabody, has been received with the deepest regret wherever his name and benevolence are known: and nowhere have his generous deeds, restricted to no country, section, or sect, elicited more heartfelt admiration than at the South.

"He stands alone in history for the benevolent use and judicious distribution of his great wealth, and his memory has become justly entwined in the affections of millions of his fellow-citizens in both hemispheres.

"I beg in my own behalf, and in behalf of the trustees and faculty of Washington College, Virginia, which has not been forgotten by him in his acts of generosity, to tender our unfeigned sorrow at his death. With great respect, your obedient servant,

"R. E. LEE."

Upon the death of Professor Frank Preston, of William and Mary College, General Lee issued the following announcement:

"WASHINGTON COLLEGE, November 23, 1869.

"The death of Professor Frank Preston, a distinguished graduate and late assistant professor of Greek in this college, has caused the deepest sorrow in the hearts of the faculty and members of the institution.

" Endowed with a mind of rare capacity, which had been enriched by diligent study and careful cultivation, he stood among the first in the State in his pursuit in life.

" We who so long and so intimately possessed his acquaintance, and so fully enjoyed the privilege of his companionship, feel especially his loss and grieve profoundly at his death ; and we heartily sympathize with his parents and relatives in their great affliction, and truly participate in the deep sorrow that has befallen them.

" With a view of testifying the esteem felt for his character and the respect due to his memory, all academic exercises will be suspended for the day ; and the faculty and students are requested to attend, in their respective bodies, his funeral services at the Presbyterian Church, at 11 o'clock, to pay the last sad tribute of respect to his earthly remains, while cherishing in their hearts his many virtues.

" R. E. LEE, President."

The above was written, *currente calamo*, immediately on his hearing of the death of Professor Preston, whom he most highly esteemed, not only as an accomplished scholar and high-toned gentleman, but as one who had been a gallant Confederate soldier and wore till his death a badge of honor in the " empty sleeve " that hung at his side.

We also give the following extracts from a letter to Rev. Dr. Moses D. Hoge, of the Presbyterian Church, Richmond, soon after the death of his wife. After writing of a number of matters connected with the interests of the Viriginia Bible Society, he concludes as follows :

" And now, my dear sir, though perhaps inappropriate to the occasion, you must allow me to refer to a subject which has caused me great distress and concerning which I have desired to write ever since its occurrence ; but, to tell the truth, I have not had the heart to do so. I knew how powerless I was to give any relief and how utterly inadequate was any language that I could use even to mitigate your suffering.

" I could, therefore, only offer up my silent prayers to Him

who alone can heal your bleeding heart, that in His infinite
mercy He would be ever present with you—to dry your tears
and staunch your wounds; to sustain you by His grace and support you by His strength.

"I hope you felt assured that in this heavy calamity you and
your children had the heartfelt sympathy of Mrs. Lee and myself, and that you were daily remembered in our prayers.

"With our best wishes and sincere affection, I am very truly
yours,

" R. E. Lee."

The date of the following letter gives it additional interest.
The movements of Burnside were developing themselves, and the
battle of Fredericksburg about to open; but the charger of the
great captain must " wait at his tent door " while from a heart as
tender as that of the gentlest woman he sends these lines of
affectionate sympathy to a bereaved mother:

"Camp Fredericksburg, December 10, 1862.

" I heard yesterday, my dear daughter, with the deepest sorrow
of the death of your infant. I was so grateful at her birth. I
felt that she would be such a comfort to you, such a pleasure
to my dear Fitzhugh, and would fill so full the void still aching
in your hearts. But you have now two sweet angels in heaven.
What joy there is in the thought. What relief to your grief.
What suffering and sorrow they have escaped. I can say nothing to soften the anguish you must feel, and I know you are
assured of my deep and affectionate sympathy. May God give
you strength to bear the affliction He has imposed and produce future joy out of present misery, is my earnest prayer.

" I saw F—— yesterday. He is well and wants much to see
you. When you are strong enough, cannot you come up to
Hickory Hill, or your grandpa's, on a little visit, where he could
ride down and see you? My horse is waiting at my tent door,
but I could not refrain from sending these few lines to recall to
you the thought and love of your devoted father,

" R. E. Lee.

" Mrs. Wm. H. Fitzhugh Lee."

Colonel Walter H. Taylor, of his staff, relates (in his admirable
book, " Four Years With Lee ") that he carried him the letter

which told of the death of his daughter Annie, along with important official papers, and that the stern soldier suppressed his emotion until he could dispatch the business that was then most pressing; but that on going into the tent not long after he found him with the letter in his hand, weeping tears of loving sorrow.

In a letter written not long after, he thus alludes to his great affliction: "The death of my dear Annie was indeed to me a bitter pang. But the Lord gave, and the Lord has taken away; blessed be the name of the Lord. In the hours of night, when there is nothing to lighten the full weight of my grief, I feel as if I should be overwhelmed. I had always counted, if God should spare me a few days of peace after this cruel war was ended, that I should have her with me. But year after year my hopes go out, and I must be resigned."

The daughter whose death is so touchingly alluded to in the above letter was Miss Annie Carter Lee, who died at Warren, White Sulphur Springs, North Carolina, the 20th of October, 1862. At the close of the war the citizens of the county erected over her grave a handsome monument, which was unveiled with appropriate ceremonies. In response to an invitation to be present, General Lee wrote the following:

"ROCKBRIDGE BATHS, July 25, 1866.
"*Ladies:* I have read with deep emotion your letter of the 17th instant, inviting myself and family to witness the erection of a monument over the remains of my daughter, at Warren, White Sulphur Springs, on the 8th of next month.

"I do not know how to express to you my thanks for your great kindness to her while living, and for your affectionate remembrance of her since dead.

"My gratitude for your attention and consideration will continue through life, and my prayers will be daily offered to the throne of the Most High for His boundless blessings upon you.

"I have always cherished the intention of visiting the tomb of her who never gave me aught but pleasure; but to afford me the satisfaction which I crave, it must be attended with more privacy than I can hope for on the occasion you propose.

"But there are more controlling considerations which will prevent my being present. Her mother, who for years has been afflicted with a painful disease, which has reduced her to a state of helplessness, is this far on her way to the mineral springs, which are considered the best calculated to afford her relief. My attendance is necessary to her in her journey, and the few weeks I have now at my disposal is the only time which can be devoted to this purpose.

"Though absent in person, my heart will be with you, and my sorrow and devotions will be mingled with yours.

"I hope my eldest son and daughter may be able to be present with you, but, as they are distant from me, I cannot tell under what circumstances your invitation may find them. I feel certain, however, that nothing but necessity will prevent their attendance.

"I enclose, according to your request, the date of my daughter's birth, and the inscription proposed for the monument over her tomb. The latter are the last lines of the hymn which she asked for just before her death.

"I am, with great respect, your obedient servant,

"R. E. LEE.

"Mrs. Joseph S. Jones,
Mrs. Thomas Carroll,
Miss Brownlow,
Miss M. Alston,
Mrs. J. M. Heck,
Mrs. Lucinda Jones,
    } Committee."

His son's wife, to whom he was deeply attached, and to whom he wrote many touchingly beautiful letters, full of the consolations and hopes of the Gospel, died while her husband (General W. H. F. Lee) was in a Northern prison, and on his return General Lee wrote him the following:

"Camp, Orange County, April 24, 1864.

"I received last night, my dear son, your letter of the 22d. It has given me great comfort. God knows how I loved your dear, dear wife, how sweet her memory is to me, and how I mourn her loss. My grief could not be greater if you had been taken from me. You were both equally dear to me. My heart is too full to speak on this subject, nor can I write. But my grief is for ourselves, not for her. She is brighter and happier than ever—safe from all evil, and awaiting us in her heavenly abode. May God in His mercy enable us to join her in eternal praise to our Lord and Saviour. Let us humbly bow ourselves before Him, and offer perpetual prayer for pardon and forgiveness. But we cannot indulge in grief, however mournfully pleasing. Our country demands all our strength, all our energies. To resist the powerful combination now forming against us will require every man at his place. If victorious, we have everything to hope for in the future. If defeated, nothing will be left us to live for. I have not heard what action has been taken by the department in reference to my recommendations concerning the organization of the cavalry. But we have no time to wait, and you had better join your brigade. This week will, in all probability, bring us active work, and we must strike fast and strong. My whole trust is in God, and I am ready for whatever He may ordain. May He guide, guard and strengthen us, is my constant prayer.   Your devoted father,

"R. E. LEE.

"GENERAL W. H. F. LEE."

His affection for Jackson and Jackson's love for him were very touching. To Jackson's note informing him that he was wounded General Lee replied: "I cannot express my regret at the occurrence. Could I have directed events I should have chosen for the good of the country to have been disabled in your stead. I congratulate you on the victory which is due to your skill and energy." It was on the reception of these touching words that the wounded chieftain exclaimed: "Better that ten Jacksons should fall than one Lee."

Several days afterwards, when his great lieutenant was reported to be doing well, Lee playfully sent him word: "You are better off than I am; for, while you have only lost your *left*, I have lost my *right* arm."

Hearing soon after that Jackson was growing worse, he expressed the deepest concern and said: "Tell him that I am praying for him as I believe I have never prayed for myself."

The 10th of May, 1863, was a beautiful Sabbath day, and Rev. B. T. Lacy, at the special request of the dying chieftain, left his bedside to hold his usual services at the head-quarters of the Second Corps. General Lee was present at the service, and at its conclusion he took Mr. Lacy aside to inquire particularly after Jackson's condition. Upon being told that he would not probably live through the day, he exclaimed: "Oh! sir, he must not die. Surely God will not visit us with such a calamity. If I have ever prayed in my life I have pleaded with the Lord that Jackson might be spared to us." And then his heart swelled with emotion too deep for utterance, and he turned away to weep like a child.

He thus announced the death of Jackson:

"HEAD-QUARTERS, A. N. VA., May 11, 1863.
"*General Order*, No. 61.

"With deep grief the commanding general announces to the army the death of Lieutenant-General T. J. Jackson, who expired on the 10th inst., at a quarter past 3 P. M. The daring, skill and energy of this great and good soldier are now, by the decrees of an all-wise Providence, lost to us. But while we mourn his death, we feel that his spirit still lives, and will inspire the whole army with his indomitable courage and unshaken confidence in God as our hope and strength. Let his name be a watchword to his corps, who have followed him to victory on so many fields. Let his officers and soldiers emulate his invincible determination to do everything in the defence of our beloved country. "R. E. LEE, General."

In a private letter to his wife General, Lee wrote:

"CAMP NEAR FREDERICKSBURG, May 11, 1863.
"In addition to the death of officers and friends consequent upon the late battle, you will see that we have to mourn the loss of the great and good Jackson. Any victory would be dear at such a price. His remains go to Richmond to-day. I know not how to replace him; but God's will be done! I trust He will raise up some one in his place."

General Lee manifested the deepest concern for the spiritual welfare of the young men under his care. Soon after becoming president of Washington College, he said, with deep feeling, to Rev. Dr. White—then the venerable pastor of the Lexington Presbyterian Church—"I shall be disappointed, sir; I shall fail in the leading object that brought me here, unless these young men become real Christians; and I wish you and others of your sacred profession to do all you can to accomplish this."

Rev. Dr. Brown, editor of the *Central Presbyterian*, and one of the trustees of Washington and Lee University, says in his paper: "The crowning excellence of such men as Jackson and Lee was their sincere Christian piety." The remark made by General Lee to the Rev. Dr. White was made to us upon another occasion in a form even more emphatic. "I dread," said he, "the thought of any student going away from the college without becoming a sincere Christian."

At the beginning of each session of the college he was accus-tomed to address an autograph letter to the pastors of Lexington inviting them to arrange for conducting in turn the regular chapel services of the college, asking them to induce the students to at-tend their several churches, Bible-classes, etc., and urging them to do all in their power for the spiritual good of the students. Not content with this general request, he was accustomed to prepare lists of students who belonged themselves, or whose families were connected with particular churches, and to hand these to the several pastors with the earnestly expressed wish that they would consider these young men under their especial watchcare, and give them every attention in their power. And he would frequently ask a pastor after individual students— whether they belonged to his Bible-class, were regular in their attendance at church, etc.

General Lee did not believe in *enforced* religion, and never re-quired the students by any collge law to attend chapel or church, but he did everything in his power to influence them to do so, and with the largest success.

At the "Concert of Prayer for Colleges," in Lexington, in 1869, I made an address in which I urged that the great need of our colleges was a genuine, pervasive revival—that this could only come from God; and that inasmuch as He has promised His Holy Spirit to those who ask Him, we should make special prayer for a revival in the colleges of the country, and more particularly in Washington College and the Virginia Military Institute. At the close of the meeting General Lee came to me and said, with more than his usual warmth: "I wish, sir, to thank you for your address; it was just what we needed. Our great want is a revival which shall bring these young men to Christ."

During the great revival in the Virginia Military Institute in 1869 he said to his pastor, with deep emotion: "That is the best news I have heard since I have been in Lexington. Would that we could have such a revival in all our colleges!" Rev. Dr. Kirkpatrick, professor of moral philosophy in Washington College, relates the following concerning a conversation he had with General Lee just a short time previous to his fatal illness: "We had been conversing for some time respecting the religious welfare of the students. General Lee's feelings soon became so intense that for a time his utterance was choked; but, recovering himself, with his eyes overflowed with tears, his lips quivering with emotion and both hands raised, he exclaimed: 'Oh, doctor! if I could only know that all the young men in the college were good Christians, I should have nothing more to desire.'"

General Lee was deeply interested in the Young Men's Christian Association of the college, and seemed highly gratified at its large measure of success.

His letter in reply to one making him an honorary member of the association was as follows:

"*My Dear Sir:* I have received your letter announcing my election as an honorary member of the Young Men's Christian Association of Washington College—a society in whose prosperity I take the deepest interest and for the welfare of whose members my prayers are daily offered. Please present my grateful thanks to your association for the honor conferred on me and believe me,

"Very respectfully, your obedient servant,

"R. E. LE

"MR. A. N. GORDON, Corresponding Secretary Young Men's Christian Association."

Rev. Dr. Brantly, of Baltimore, and Bishop Marvin, of Missouri who stayed at his house during the college commencement of 1870, both speak of the warm gratification which General Lee expressed at the encouraging report of the religious interest among the students.

General Lee was a member of the Episcopal Church, and was sincerely attached to the church of his choice; but his large heart took in Christians of every name; he treated ministers of all denominations with the most marked courtesy and respect; and it may be truly said of him that he had a heart and hand "ready to *every* good work." When once asked his opinion of a certain theological question, which was exciting considerable discussion, he replied: "Oh! I never trouble myself about such questions; my chief concern is to try to be an humble, earnest Christian myself."

An application of a Jewish soldier for permission to attend certain ceremonies of his synagogue in Richmond was endorsed by his captain: "Disapproved. If such applications were granted the whole army would turn Jews or Shaking Quakers." When the paper came to General Lee he endorsed on it: "Approved, and respectfully returned to Captain ——, with the advice that he should always respect the religious views and feelings of others."

The following letters, addressed to a prominent rabbi of Richmond (to whom I am indebted for copies), will serve to illustrate the broad charity of this model Christian:

"HEAD-QUARTERS, VALLEY MOUNTAIN, August 29, 1861.
" RABBI M. J. MICHELBACHER, Preacher Hebrew Congregation,
      House of Love, RICHMOND, VIRGINIA:

"*Reverend Sir:* I have just received your letter of the 23d inst., requesting that a furlough from the 2d to the 15th of September be granted to the soldiers of the Jewish persuasion in the Confederate States Army, that they may participate in the approaching holy service of the synagogue. It would give me great pleasure to comply with a request so earnestly urged by you, and which, I know, would be so highly appreciated by that class of soldiers. But the necessities of war admit of no relaxation of the efforts requisite for its success, nor can it be known on what day the presence of every man may be required. I feel assured that neither you nor any member of the Jewish Congregation would wish to jeopardize a cause you have so much at heart by the withdrawal even for a season of its defenders. I cannot, therefore, grant the general furlough you desire, but must leave it to individuals to make their own applications to their several commanders, in the hope that many will be able to enjoy the privilege you seek for them. Should any be deprived of the opportunity of offering up their prayers according to the rites of their church, I trust that their penitence may nevertheless be accepted by the Most High, and their petitions answered. That your prayers for the success and welfare of our cause may be answered by the Great Ruler of the Universe is my ardent wish.

" I have the honor to be, with high esteem,
      " Your obedient servant,
            " R. E. LEE, General Commanding."

" HEAD-QUARTERS, A. N. VA., April 2, 1863.
" M. J. MICHELBACHER, Minister of Hebrew Congregation,
   RICHMOND, VIRGINIA:
"*Sir:* It will give me pleasure to comply with the request
contained in your letter of the 30th ult., as far as the public interest will permit. But, I think it more than probable that the
army will be engaged in active operations, when, of course, no
one would wish to be absent from its ranks, nor could they in
that event be spared. The reports from all quarters show that
General Hooker's army is prepared to cross the Rappahannock,
and only awaits favorable weather and roads.

" The sentence in the case of Isaac Arnoldh as been suspended
until the decision of the President shall be known. Thanking
you very sincerely for your good wishes in behalf of our country,

" I remain, with great respect,   " Your obedient servant,

                                              " R. E. LEE."

" HEAD-QUARTERS, A. N. VA., September 20, 1864.
" REV. M. J. MICHELBACHER, RICHMOND:
"*Sir:* I have received your letter of the 15th inst., asking that
furloughs may be granted to the Israelites in the army from
September 30 to October 11, to enable them to repair to Richmond to observe the holy days appointed by the Jewish
religion.

" It would afford me much pleasure to comply with your request did the interests of the service permit, but it is impossible
to grant a general furlough to one class of our soldiers without
recognizing the claims of others to a like indulgence. I can
only grant furloughs on applications setting forth special grounds
for them, or in accordance with the general orders on that subject applicable to all the army alike.

" I will gladly do all in my power to facilitate the observance
of the duties of their religion by the Israelites in the army, and I
will allow them every indulgence consistent with safety and discipline. If their applications be forwarded to me in the usual
way, and it appears that they can be spared, I will be glad to
approve as many of them as circumstances will permit. Accept
my thanks for your kind wishes for myself, and believe me to
be, with great respect,

                        " Your obedient servant,

                                              " R. E. LEE."

GENERAL "STONEWALL" JACKSON, C. S. A.

(Facing page 80.)

This characteristic was noted by all who came in contact with him, and not a few will cordially echo the remark of the venerable Dr. White, who said, with deep feeling, during the memorial services, " He belonged to one branch of the Church and I to another; yet, in my intercourse with him—an intercourse rendered far more frequent and intimate by the tender sympathy he felt in my ill health—the thought never occurred to me that we belonged to different churches. His love for the truth, and for all that is good and useful, was such as to render his brotherly kindness and charity as boundless as were the wants and sorrows of his race."

It were an easy task to write pages more in illustration of the Christian character of our great leader; but the above must suffice.

If I have ever come in contact with a sincere, devout Christian —one who, seeing himself to be a sinner, trusted alone in the merits of Christ—who humbly tried to walk the path of duty, " looking unto Jesus " as the author and finisher of his faith— and whose piety constantly exhibited itself in his daily life—that man was GENERAL R. E. LEE.

6

CHAPTER III.

THE piety of STONEWALL JACKSON has become as historic as his wonderful military career. But, as it was my privilege to see a good deal of him, and to learn from those intimate with him much of his inner life; and as his Christian character is well worthy of earnest study, and of admiring imitation, I give a somewhat extended sketch of it.

I first came into personal contact with him on the 4th of July, 1861, while our army was drawn up in line of battle at Darkesville, to meet General Patterson. The skill and tact with which he had reduced the high-spirited young men who rushed to Harper's Ferry at the first tap of the drum into the respectable "Army of the Shenandoah," which he turned over to General Johnston on the 23d of May, 1861, and the ability and stern courage with which he had checked Patterson's advance at Falling Waters, had won for him some reputation, and I was anxious to see him.

A colporter (good brother C. F. Fry) had sent me word that he desired permission to enter our lines to distribute Bibles and tracts. With the freedom with which in our army the humblest private could approach the highest officer I at once went to General Jackson for the permit. I have a vivid recollection of how he impressed me. Dressed in a simple Virginia uniform, apparently about thirty-seven years old, six feet high, medium size, grey eyes that seemed to look through you, light brown hair and a countenance in which deep benevolence seemed mingled with uncompromising sternness, he seemed to me to have about him nothing at all of the "pomp and circumstance of war," but every element which enters into the skilful leader, and the indomitable, energetic soldier who was always ready for the fight. Stating to him my mission, he at once replied in pleasant tones and with a smile of peculiar sweetness: "Certainly, sir; it will give me great pleasure to grant all such per-

(82)

mits. I am glad that you came to me, and I shall be glad to be introduced to the colporter."

Afterward introducing my friend, Jackson said to him: "You are more than welcome to my camp, and it will give me great pleasure to help you in your work in every way in my power. I am more anxious than I can express that my men should be not only good soldiers of their country, but also good soldiers of the Cross." We lingered for some time in an exceedingly pleasant conversation about the religious welfare of the army, and when I turned away, with a very courteous invitation to call on him again, I felt that I had met a man of deep-toned piety, who carried his religion into every affair of life, and who was destined to make his mark in the war.

Jackson had become a Christian some time before; but it was not until the 22d of November, 1851, that he made public profession of religion and united with the Presbyterian Church in Lexington, then under the care of the venerable and beloved Rev. Dr. W. S. White, whose death in 1871 was so widely lamented.

The following incident, which was given me by Dr. White, not only illustrates his Christian character, but gives the key-note to his whole life.

Not very long after his connection with the church the pastor preached a sermon on prayer, in which it was urged that *every male church-member* ought, when occasion required, to lead in public prayer. The next day, a faithful elder of the church asked "Major Jackson" what he thought of the doctrine of the sermon, and if he was not convinced that he ought to lead in public prayer. "I do not think it my duty," he replied, and went on to assign as his reason that he hesitated in his speech to such an extent when excited that he did not think he could "pray to edification" in public. "Have you made the matter a subject of secret prayer?" persisted the elder. "No, sir; but I will do so to-night." The elder then advised him also to consult his pastor, and he went at once to Dr. White's study and went over with him the arguments and passages of Scripture by which he supported his position. The next day the elder saw him walking rapidly by his place of business, and fearing that he wished to avoid the subject of their previous conversation he called him back and asked, "Have you made that matter a subject of prayerful investigation, major?" "Yes, sir, and I was just on my way to ask Dr. White to call on me to lead in prayer at the meeting to-night." Soon after he was called on, and made such a stammering effort that the pastor felt badly for him, and he was greatly mortified. Several subsequent efforts resulted in little better results, and the pastor began to think that, perhaps, Major Jackson was right—that he really could not "pray to edification"—and that he was, perhaps, an exception to the general rule that male members of the church ought to lead in public prayer. Accordingly he said to him one day: "Major, we do not wish to make our prayer-meetings uncomfortable to you, and if you prefer it, I will not call on you to lead in prayer again."

The prompt and emphatic reply was: "My comfort has nothing in the world to do with it, sir; you, as my pastor, think that it is my duty to lead in public prayer—I think so too—and *by God's grace I mean to do it. I wish you would please be so good as to call on me more frequently.*" Dr. White says that he saw from Jackson's reply and manner that *he meant to succeed*—that he did call on him more frequently—and that he gradually improved until he became one of the most gifted men in prayer whom he had in his church. It was my privilege to hear him pray several times in the army, and if I ever heard a "fervent, effectual prayer," it was offered by this stern soldier.

He was a "deacon" (not an "elder," as has been frequently asserted) in the church, and was untiring in the discharge of all the duties of the position. On one occasion he went at the appointed hour to attend a "deacons' meeting" at which there was important business to be transacted, and after waiting *five minutes* for several absentees (pacing back and forth, watch in hand), he asked to be excused for awhile, and darted off to the residence of one of them. Ringing the door-bell violently the gentleman came out, and Jackson accosted him with "Mr. ——, it is eight minutes after 8 o'clock" (the hour appointed for the meeting). "Yes, major, I am aware of that, but I didn't have time to go out to-night." "Didn't have time?" retorted the deacon; "why, sir, I should not suppose that you *had time for anything else.* Did we not set apart this hour (only one in the month) for the service of the church? How then can you put aside your obligations in the matter?" With this he abruptly started back to the meeting, and his brother deacon felt so keenly his rebuke that he immediately followed. There was no difficulty in the finances of that church as long as "Deacon" Jackson managed them.

The venerable pastor said to me with deep emotion: "Oh, sir, when Jackson fell I lost not only a warm personal friend, a consistent, active church-member, but the best deacon I ever saw!"

He was once collector for the Rockbridge Bible Society, and when the time came to report (to the surprise of his colleagues) he reported contributions from a number of negroes, remarking in explanation: "They are poor, but ought not on that account to be denied the sweet privilege of helping so good a cause." He also reported: "I have a contribution from every person in my district except one lady. She has been away ever since I was appointed collector, but she will return home at 12 to-day, and I will see her at 1 o'clock." The next day he reported a contribution from her also.

He frequently sought the counsel and instruction of his pastor, upon whom he looked as his "superior officer," and to whom he would sometimes "report for orders." He was never blessed with large pecuniary means, but was always a most liberal contributor to every charitable object, and ever ready "to visit the fatherless and the widow in their distress."

Jackson was one of the most thoroughly conscientious masters who ever lived. He not only treated his negroes kindly, but he devoted himself most assiduously to their religious instruction. He was not only accustomed (as were Christian masters generally at the South) to invite his servants in to family prayers, but he also had a special meeting with them every Sunday afternoon in order to teach them the Scriptures. He made this exercise so interesting to them that other negroes of the town craved the privilege of attending, and he soon had his room full to overflowing of eager pupils. 'This suggested to him the idea of organizing a negro Sunday-school, which he did several years before the war, and to which he devoted all of the energies of his mind and all the zeal of his large, Christian heart.

He was accustomed to prepare himself for the exercises of this school by the most careful study of the lessons. The day before he left home for the war was Saturday, and he was very busy all day long making every preparation to leave at a moment's warning. He paid all outstanding accounts, and settled up as far as possible his worldly affairs, while his devoted wife was busily plying the needle to prepare him for the field.

At the supper-table Mrs. Jackson made some remark about the preparations for his expected departure, when he said, with a bright smile: "My dear, to-morrow is the blessed Sabbath day. It is also the regular communion season at our church. I hope I shall not be called to leave until Monday. Let us then dismiss from our conversation and our thoughts everything pertaining to the war, and have together one more quiet evening of preparation for our loved Sabbath duties."

Accordingly the dark cloud of war was pushed aside. He read aloud to her for awhile from religious magazines and news-papers, and then they went to their accustomed study of the Bible lesson, which was to be taught on the morrow to the colored Sunday-school. It was such a bright, happy Saturday evening as is only known in the well-regulated Christian home. Alas! it proved the last which he ever spent under his own roof tree. Early the next morning a telegram from the governor of the Commonwealth ordered him to march the corps of cadets for Richmond at 12.30 o'clock that day. Not waiting for his breakfast he hurried to the institute, and spent the morning in making necessary preparations for the departure of the cadets, not forgetting to send a request to his pastor that he should be present to hold with them a brief service before they marched forth at the call of their sovereign State.

At 11 o'clock he came home to take a hurried breakfast and make a few personal arrangements, and the last thing he did before leaving home was to retire with his wife into their cham-ber, read a part of the fifth chapter of Second Corinthians—beginning, "For we know that if the earthly house of this taber-nacle were dissolved, we have a building of God, an house not made with hands, eternal in the heavens"—and then made an humble, tender, fervent prayer, in which he begged that the dark cloud of war might even then be dissipated; that the God of Peace might calm the storm and avert the calamity of war, or that He might at least go forth with him and with the young men under his command to guide, guard, help and bless them.

At 12 o'clock the venerable pastor was present to make to the corps an appropriate address of Christian counsel, and lead in a fervent, tender prayer.

At the appointed hour, to the exact minute, Major Jackson gave the order: "Attention! Forward! March!"

And thus the loving husband bade adieu to his home, the

faithful church-member turned away from his communion service, the earnest Sunday-school teacher left his lesson untaught,
and the peerless soldier marched forth from the parade-ground
to win immortal fame, to come not back again until his body
was borne to its burial in the beautiful cemetery at " Lexington,
in the Valley of Virginia," and two continents were bursting with
the fame of " Stonewall " Jackson.

Jackson gave a great deal of time to his colored Sunday-
school. He was accustomed to carry around himself the most
carefully prepared reports of the conduct and progress of each
pupil, and to do everything in his power to interest the whites
of the community in the school.

Soon after one of the great battles, a large crowd gathered one
day at the post-office in Lexington, anxiously awaiting the opening of the mail, that they might get the particulars concerning
the great battle which they had heard had been fought. The
venerable pastor of the Presbyterian Church (Rev. Dr. W. S.
White, from whom I received the incident) was of the company,
and soon had handed him a letter which he recognized as directed
in Jackson's well-known handwriting. " Now," said he, " we
will have the news! Here is a letter from General Jackson
himself." The crowd eagerly gathered around, but heard to
their very great disappointment a letter which made not the most
remote allusion to the battle or the war, but which enclosed a
check for fifty dollars with which to buy books for his colored
Sunday-school, and was filled with inquiries after the interests
of the school and the church. He had no time or inclination to
write of the great victory and the imperishable laurels he was
winning; but he found time to remember his noble work among
God's poor, and to contribute further to the good of the negro
children whose true friend and benefactor he had always been.
And he was accustomed to say that one of the very greatest
privations to him which the war brought, was that he was taken
away from his loved work in the colored Sunday-school.

Jackson thus acquired a wonderful influence over the colored
people of that whole region, and to this day his memory is
warmly cherished by them. When Hunter's army was marching
into Lexington, the Confederate flag which floated over Jackson's
grave was hauled down and concealed by some of the citizens.
A lady who stole into the cemetery one morning while the
Federal army was occupying the town, bearing fresh flowers

with which to decorate the hero's grave, was surprised to find a miniature Confederate flag planted on the grave with a verse of a familiar hymn pinned to it.   Upon inquiry she found that a colored boy, who had belonged to Jackson's Sunday-school, had procured the flag, gotten some one to copy a stanza of a favorite hymn which Jackson had taught him, and had gone in the night to plant the flag on the grave of his loved teacher.

It will be gratifying to many of our readers to add that this school is still kept up, and is in a most flourishing condition under the management of Colonel J. L. T. Preston, of the Virginia Military Institute, Professor J. J. White, of Washington and Lee University, and others of the best people in Lexington.

Jackson was equally scrupulous in attending to all his religious duties.   " Lord, what wilt Thou have me to do?" seemed the motto of his life.   Regular in meeting all of his religious obligations, he walked straight along the path of duty, doing with his might whatsoever his hands found to do.   In the army his piety, despite all obstacles, seemed to brighten as the pure gold is refined by the furnace.   He beautifully illustrated in his life the lesson of the great apostle: " Not slothful in business, fervent in spirit, serving the Lord."   He was a man of prayer, accustomed in all he did to ask the Divine blessing and guidance.   His old body-servant said that he "could always tell when a battle was near at hand by seeing the general get up a great many times in the night to pray."   He was frequently observed in the beginning and in the midst of the battle to lift up his hands towards heaven, and those near could hear his ejaculatory prayers.   Just before the battle of Fredericksburg he rode out in front of his line of battle and offered earnest prayer for the success of his arms that day.   The morning of the opening of the campaign of Chancellorsville he spent a long time in prayer before mounting to ride to the field.

A writer in the Richmond *Whig* thus describes a scene enacted soon after the battle of McDowell: "General Jackson addressed his troops in a few terse and pointed remarks, thanking them for the courage, endurance and soldierly conduct displayed at the battle of McDowell on the 8th inst., and closed by appointing 10 o'clock of that day as an occasion of prayer and thanksgiving throughout the army for the victory which followed that bloody engagement.   There, in the beautiful little valley of the South Branch, with the blue and towering mountains covered with the verdure of spring, the green sward smiling a welcome to the season of flowers, and the bright sun, unclouded, lending a genial, refreshing warmth, that army, equipped for the stern conflict of war, bent in humble praise and thanksgiving to the God of Battles for the success vouchsafed to our arms in the recent sanguinary encounter of the two armies. While this solemn ceremony was progressing in every regiment, the minds of the soldiery drawn off from the bayonet and sabre, the enemy's artillery was occasionally belching forth its leaden death; yet all unmoved stood that worshipping army, acknowledging the supremacy of the will of Him who controls the destinies of men and nations, and chooses the weaker things of earth to confound the mighty."

Rev. Dr. Wm. Brown, former editor of the *Central Presbyterian*, relates a characteristic anecdote of this " man of prayer." During a visit to the army around Centreville, in 1861, a friend remarked to Dr. Brown, in speaking of General Jackson in the strain in which many of his old acquaintances were accustomed to disparage him, " The truth is, sir, that ' old Jack ' is *crazy*. I can account for his conduct in no other way. Why, I frequently meet him out in the woods walking back and forth muttering to himself incoherent sentences and gesticulating wildly, and at such times he seems utterly oblivious of my presence and of everything else." Dr. Brown happened the next night to share Jackson's blanket, and in a long and tender conversation on his favorite theme—the means of promoting personal holiness in camp—the great soldier said to him : " I find that it greatly helps me in fixing my mind and quickening my devotions to give articulate utterance to my prayers, and hence I am in the habit of going off into the woods, where I can be alone and speak audibly to myself the prayers I would pour out to my God. I was at first annoyed that I was compelled to keep my eyes open to avoid running against the trees and stumps ; but upon investigating the matter I do not find that the Scriptures require us to close our eyes in prayer, and the exercise has proven to me very delightful and profitable."

And thus Dr. Brown got the explanation of the conduct which his friend had cited to prove that " old Jack is crazy."

A friend was once conversing with him about the difficulty of obeying the Scripture injunction, " pray without ceasing," and Jackson insisted that we could so accustom ourselves to it that it could be easily obeyed. " When we take our meals there is the grace. When I take a draught of water I always pause, as my palate receives the refreshment, to lift up my heart to God in thanks and prayer for the water of life. Whenever I drop a letter into the box at the post-office I send a petition along with it for God's blessing upon its mission and upon the person to whom it is sent. When I break the seal of a letter just received I stop to pray to God that He may prepare me for its contents and make it a messenger of good. When I go to my class-room and await the arrangement of the cadets in their places, that is my time to intercede with God for them. And so of every other familiar act of the day."

" But," said his friend, " do you not often forget these seasons, coming so frequently ? "

" No ! " said he. " I have made the practice habitual to me ; and I can no more forget it than forget to drink when I am thirsty. The habit has become as delightful as regular."

Jackson had a firm and unshaken trust in the promises of God and His superintending Providence under *all* circumstances, and it was his habitual practice to pray for and trust in Divine guidance under every circumstance of trial.

His friend, Elder Lyle—one of the noblest specimens of a faithful Christian that ever lived—used to question him very closely on his Christian experience, and one day asked him if he *really believed* the promise: "All things work together for good to them that love God, to them who are the called according to his purpose." He said that he did, and the elder asked: " If you were to lose your *health*, would you believe it then ? " " Yes ! I think I should." " How if you were to become entirely blind ? " " I should still believe it." " But suppose, in addition to your loss of health and sight, you should become utterly dependent upon the cold charities of the world ? " He thought for a moment and then replied with emphasis: " If it were the will of God to place me there, He would enable me to lie there peacefully a hundred years." He nobly stood this test when called on to cross the Jordan of Death.

Soon after he was wounded he said to Rev. B. T. Lacy—who exclaimed, on seeing him : " Oh, general, what a calamity ! " " You see me severely wounded, but not depressed—not unhappy. I believe it has been done according to God's holy will, and I acquiesce entirely in it. You may think it strange ; but you never saw me more perfectly contented than I am to-day; for I am sure that my Heavenly Father designs this affliction for my good. I am perfectly satisfied that either in this life, or in that which is to come, I shall discover that what is now regarded as a calamity is a blessing. And if it appears a great calamity (as it surely will be a great inconvenience) to be deprived of my arm, it will result in a great blessing. I can wait until God, in His own time, shall make known to me the object He has in thus afflicting me. But why should I not rather rejoice in it as a blessing, and not look on it as a calamity at all? If it were in my power to replace my arm, I would not dare do it unless I could know that it was the will of my Heavenly Father."

His dispatches and official reports all breathed this spirit of trust in and dependence upon God. His simple " God blessed our arms with victory at McDowell yesterday," was but a type of the character and spirit of his dispatches.

After his capture of Winchester in 1862 he issued the following order:

" HEAD-QUARTERS, VALLEY DISTRICT.
WINCHESTER, May 26, 1862.
"*General Order* No. 53.

" Within four weeks this army has made long and rapid marches, fought six combats and two battles, signally defeating the enemy in each one, captured several stands of colors and pieces of artillery, with numerous prisoners and vast medical, ordnance and army stores, and finally driven the boastful host, which was ravaging our beautiful country, into utter rout. The general commanding would warmly express to the officers and men under his command his joy in their achievements, and his thanks for their brilliant gallantry in action, and their patient obedience under the hardships of forced marches, often more painful to the brave soldier than the dangers of battle. The explanation of the severe exertions to which the commanding general called the army, which were endured by them with such cheerful confidence in him, is now given in the victory of yesterday. He receives this proof of their confidence in the past with pride and gratitude, and asks only a similar confidence in the future. But his chief duty to-day, and that of the army, is to recognize devoutly the hand of a protecting Providence in the brilliant successes of the last three days, which have given us the results of a great victory without great losses, and to make the oblation of our thanks to God for His mercies to us and our country in heartfelt acts of religious worship. For this purpose the troops will remain in camp to-day, suspending, as far as practicable, all military exercises, and the chaplains of regiments will hold Divine service in their several charges at 4 o'clock P. M. to-day."

A correspondent, as quoted in Dr. Bennett's "Great Revival," says: "I saw something to-day which affected me more than anything I ever saw or read on religion. While the battle was raging and the bullets were flying, Jackson rode by, calm as if he were at home, but his head was raised toward heaven, and his lips were moving, evidently in prayer. Meeting a chaplain near the front in the heat of a battle, the general said to him, 'The rear is your place, sir, now, and prayer your business.' He said to a colonel who wanted worship, 'All right, colonel, but don't forget to drill.'

"This incident is related by one of his staff. Entering the general's room at midnight, Major —— found him at prayer. After half an hour the major stepped to the door and asked of the aid if he did not think the general had fallen asleep on his knees from excessive fatigue. 'Oh, no; you know the general is an old Presbyterian, and they all make long prayers.' The major returned, and after waiting an hour the general rose from his knees."

Another writer says: "General Jackson never enters a battle without invoking God's blessing and protection. The dependence of this strange man upon the Deity seems never to be absent from his mind, and whatever he says or does, it is always prefaced, 'by God's blessing.' 'By God's blessing we have defeated the enemy,' is his laconic and pious announcement of a victory. One of his officers said to him, 'Well, general, another candidate is waiting your attention.' 'So I observe,' was the quiet reply, 'and by God's blessing he shall receive it to his full satisfaction.'

"After a battle has been fought the same rigid remembrance of Divine power is observed. The army is drawn up in line, the general dismounts from his horse, and then, in the presence of his rough, bronzed-faced troops, with head uncovered and bent awe-stricken to the ground, the voice of the good man, which but a few hours before was ringing out in quick, fiery intonations, is now heard subdued and calm, as if overcome by the presence of the Supreme Being, in holy appeal to the 'sapphire throne.'

" Few such spectacles have been witnessed in modern times, and it is needless to add that few such examples have ever told with such wondrous power upon the hearts of men. Is it surprising that ' Stonewall ' Jackson is invincible, and that he can lead his army to certain victory, whenever God's blessing precedes the act ? "

Jackson delighted in religious conversation and frequently engaged in it with his whole soul at times least expected by those who did not know him. During one of his battles, while he was waiting in the rear of a part of his command, which he had put in position to engage the attention of the enemy while another division had been sent to flank them, a young officer on his staff gave him a copy of the sketch of " Captain Dabney Carr Harrison," a young Presbyterian minister, widely known and loved in Virginia, who had been killed at Fort Donelson. He expressed himself highly gratified at getting the sketch, and entered into an earnest conversation on the power of Christian example. He was interrupted by an officer, who reported " the enemy advancing," but paused only long enough to give the laconic order, " Open on them," and then resumed the conversation, which he continued for some time, only pausing now and then to receive dispatches and give necessary orders. A chaplain relates that on the eve of the battle of Fredericksburg he saw an officer wrapped in his overcoat, so that his marks of rank could not be seen, lying just in the rear of a battery quietly reading his Bible. He approached and entered into conversation on the prospects of the impending battle, but the officer soon changed the conversation to religious topics, and the chaplain was led to ask, " What regiment are you chaplain of ? " What was his astonishment to find that the quiet Bible-reader and fluent talker upon religious subjects was none other than the famous " Stonewall " Jackson.

He did everything in his power to encourage his chaplains and help them in their work, was a regular and deeply interested attendant on religious services, and was largely instrumental in the organization of our Chaplains' Association. He was accustomed to say, when hearing accounts of religious matters in the army which pleased him : " That is good—very good—we ought to thank God for that."

I remember one day, when walking over from near Hamilton's Crossing to a meeting of our Chaplains' Association, that General Jackson overtook me (riding alone, as was his frequent habit), and, inquiring where I was going, he promptly dismounted, and throwing his bridle over his arm walked with me several miles, engaged in earnest conversation about the religious interests of his men, and how best to promote them.

He was especially anxious to have his regiments supplied with chaplains, and his corps with missionaries, and it was largely due to his exertions that his corps was better supplied than any other part of the army.

In a letter to the Southern Presbyterian General Assembly he said :

" My views are summed up in a few words :

" Each branch of the Christian Church should send into the army some of its most prominent ministers who are distinguished for their piety, talents and zeal ; and such ministers should labor to produce concert of action among chaplains and Christians in the army. These ministers should give special attention to preaching to regiments which are without chaplains, and induce them to take steps to get chaplains, to let the regiments name the denominations from which they desire chaplains selected, and then to see that suitable chaplains are secured.

"A bad selection of a chaplain may prove a curse instead of a blessing. If the few prominent ministers thus connected with each army would cordially co-operate, I believe that glorious fruits would be the result. Denominational distinctions should be kept out of view, and not touched upon. And, as a general rule, I do not think that a chaplain who would preach denominational sermons should be in the army. His congregation is his regiment, and it is composed of various denominations. I would like to see no question asked in the army of what denomination a chaplain belongs to ; but let the question be, Does he preach the Gospel ?

" The neglect of the spiritual interests of the army may be seen from the fact that not one-half of the regiments have chaplains.

.   .   .   .

"Among the wants of the church in the army are some ministers of such acknowledged superiority and zeal as, under God, to be the means of giving concert of action. Our chaplains, at least in the same military organization encamped in the same neighborhood, should have their meetings, and through God's blessing devise successful plans for spiritual conquests. All the other departments of the army have system, and such system exists in any other department of the service that no one of its officers can neglect his duty without diminishing the efficiency of his branch of the service.   And it appears to me that when men see what attention is bestowed secularly in comparison with what is religiously, they naturally underestimate the importance of religion.   From what I have said, you may think I am despondent; but, thanks to an ever kind Providence, such is not the case.   I do not know where so many men, brought together without any religious test, exhibit so much religious feeling.   The striking feature is that so much that is hopeful should exist, when so little human instrumentality has been employed for its accomplishment.   In civil life, ministers have regular meetings to devise means for co-operation in advancing the interests of the church.   This can be done in the army, and I am persuaded it should be done. . . .

   "Some ministers ask for leave of absence for such trivial objects, in comparison with the salvation of the soul, that I fear they give occasion to others to think that such ministers do not believe that the salvation of the soul is as important as they preach.   It is the special province of the chaplains to look after the spiritual interests of the army, and I greatly desire to see them evincing a rational zeal proportional to the importance of their mission.   Do not believe that I think the chaplains are the only delinquents.   I do not believe, but know, that I am a great delinquent, and I do not design saying what I have said respecting the laxness of chaplains to apply to all of them.   I would like to see each Christian denomination send one of its great lights into the army.   By this arrangement I trust that, if any should have denominational feelings, they will not be in the way of advancing a common and glorious cause."

   Let us go some bright Sabbath morning to that cluster of tents in the grove across the Massaponax, not far from Hamilton's Crossing.   Seated on the rude logs, or on the ground, may be seen fifteen hundred or two thousand men, with upturned faces, eagerly drinking in the truths of the Gospel.   That reverent worshipper that kneels in the dust during prayer, or listens with sharpened attention and moist eyes as the preacher delivers his message, is our loved Commander-in-Chief, General R. E. Lee; that devout worshipper who sits at his side, gives his personal attention to the seating of the multitude, looks so supremely happy as

he sees the soldiers thronging to hear the Gospel, and listens
so attentively to the preaching, is " Stonewall" Jackson; those
" wreaths and stars " which cluster around are worn by some of
the most illustrious generals of that army; and all through the
congregation the "stars" and "bars" mingle with the rough garb
of the " unknown heroes " of the rank and file who never quail
amid the leaden and iron hail of battle, but are not ashamed to
" tremble" under the power of God's truth.   I need not say that
this is Jackson's head-quarters, and the scene I have pictured one
of frequent occurrence.

General Jackson had Rev. B. T. Lacy commissioned chaplain
(not " corps chaplain," as he has been improperly called, for there
was no such rank; and, indeed, Confederate chaplains had no
military rank whatever, but were all on the same footing of
equality as simply preachers and spiritual leaders of their commands), and ordered to report to him for duty, and he assigned
him to preach at his head-quarters and labor in the more destitute
commands of the corps.   Dr. Lacy was a genial gentleman, an
indefatigable worker, and a powerful and effective preacher, and
his association with General Jackson gave him special influence
and a wide field of usefulness.   Some of the services at Jackson's
head-quarters were of deep interest and wide-reaching in their
blessed results.

Upon one occasion, I called at Jackson's head-quarters and
found him just going in to a prayer meeting which he was accustomed to hold.   I gladly accepted his invitation to attend, and
shall never forget the power, comprehensiveness, and tender
pathos of the prayer he made during that delightful prayer-
meeting.   Only a few days before the battle of Chancellorsville,
I had the privilege (in company with several brother-chaplains)
of dining with him at his mess, and of lingering for an hour of
most delightful converse in his tent.   Military matters were
scarcely alluded to, and then he would quickly change the topic;
but we fully discussed questions pertaining to the promotion of
religion in the camps—how to secure more chaplains and to
induce pastors to come as missionaries to the soldiers, and kindred topics.   And then we got on the subject of personal piety,
the obstacles to growth in grace in the army, the best means of
promoting it, etc., and as the great soldier talked earnestly and
eloquently from a full heart, I had to lay aside my office as
teacher in Israel and be content to " sit at the feet " of this able

"STONEWALL JACKSON PREPARING FOR BATTLE."

Gen'l Ewell.—"If that is religion, I must have it."

(See page 97.)

theologian, this humble, earnest Christian, and learn of him lessons in the Divine life.   More than almost any man I ever met, he accepted fully the precious promises of God's word, walked by a living faith in Jesus, and was guided by the star of hope as he trod firmly the path of duty.   How far the glorious revivals with which we were favored were in answer to the prayers, and in blessing on the efforts of "Stonewall" Jackson, and to what extent his influence was blessed to individuals, eternity alone can reveal.   I have it from a well-authenticated source that the conversion of Lieutenant-General Ewell, Jackson's able lieutenant, was on this wise: At a council of war, one night, Jackson had listened very attentively to the views of his subordinates, and asked until the next morning to present his own.   As they came away, A. P. Hill laughingly said to Ewell, "Well! I suppose Jackson wants time to pray over it."   Having occasion to return to his quarters again a short time after, Ewell found Jackson on his knees and heard his ejaculatory prayers for God's guidance in the perplexing movements then before him.   The sturdy veteran Ewell was so deeply impressed by this incident and by Jackson's general religious character, that he said: "If that is religion, I must have it;" and in making a profession of faith not long afterwards he attributed his conviction to the influence of Jackson's piety.

Since he lived such a life, it was to be expected that he would die a glorious death.   In the full tide of his splendid career, just as he was completing what he regarded as the most successful military movement of his life, with high ambition and bright hopes for the future, he was shot down by the fire of his own men, who would gladly have yielded up their own lives to have saved their loved chieftain one single pang.

He bore his sufferings, and the amputation of his arm with the utmost Christian fortitude, saying repeatedly that he was perfectly resigned to God's will and would not, if he could, restore the arm, unless assured that it was his Heavenly Father's will.

When he seemed better and expected to recover, he spoke freely of being so near death when first wounded, and expecting fully to die before a surgeon could reach him, and said that he "gave himself up to the hands of his Heavenly Father, and was in the possession of perfect peace."

Rev. Dr. B. T. Lacy relates that, alluding to this period of

7

expected death, he said: "It has been a precious experience to me that I was brought face to face with death, and found all was well. I then learned an important lesson: that one who has been the subject of converting grace and is the child of God can, in the midst of the severest sufferings, fix his thoughts upon God and heavenly things, and derive great comfort and peace; but that one who had never made his peace with God would be unable to control his mind, under such sufferings, so as to understand properly the way of salvation, and repent and believe on Christ. I felt that if I had neglected the salvation of my soul before, it would have been too late then."

He dictated a letter to General Lee, in which he congratulated him on "the great victory which God has vouchsafed to your arms."

But before this note was sent, the following came to him from General Lee, in response to a previous note which had been sent by Jackson:

"General: I have just received your note informing me that you were wounded. I cannot express my regret at the occurrence. Could I have directed events, I should have chosen, for the good of the country, to have been disabled in your stead. I congratulate you upon the victory which is due to your skill and energy.   Most truly yours,
                              "R. E. LEE, General."

Jackson seemed deeply touched at the generous letter from his chief, but said, after a brief pause: "General Lee is very kind: but he should give the glory to God."

Afterwards, in talking about this great victory, he said: "Our movement yesterday was a great success; I think the most successful military movement of my life. But I expect to receive far more credit for it than I deserve. Most men will think I had planned it all from the first; but it was not so—I simply took advantage of circumstances as they were presented to me in the Providence of God. I feel that His hand led me: let us give Him all the glory."

When he had been removed to the house of Mr. Chandler, near Guinea's Station, and had so far rallied as to feel confident of his recovery, he talked very freely on his favorite religious topics. Dr. Dabney says (in his admirable biography of Jackson, to which I am indebted for several incidents given above): " He requested his chaplain to visit him at 10 o'clock each morning for reading the Scriptures and prayer. These seasons were the occasions of much religious conversation, in which he unbosomed himself with unusual freedom and candor. He declared that his faith and hope in his Redeemer were clear. He said he was perfectly willing to die at that time; but believed that his time was not yet come, that his Heavenly Father still had a work for him to do in defence of his beloved country, and that until that was completed he should be spared. During these morning hours he delighted to enlarge on his favorite topics of practical religion, which were such as these: The Christian should carry his religion into everything. Christianity makes man better in any lawful calling; it equally makes the general a better commander, and the shoemaker a better mechanic. In the case of the cobbler, or the tailor, for instance, religion will produce more care in promising work, more punctuality, and more fidelity in executing it, from conscientious motives; and these homely examples were fair illustrations of its value in more exalted functions. So prayer aids any man, in any lawful business, not only by bringing down the Divine blessing, which is its direct and prime object, but by harmonizing his own mind and heart. In the commander of an army at the critical hour, it calmed his perplexities, moderated his anxieties, steadied the scales of judgment, and thus preserved him from exaggerated and rash conclusions. Again he urged that every act of man's life should be a religious act. He recited with much pleasure the ideas of Doddridge, where he pictured himself as spiritualizing every act of his daily life; as thinking when he washed himself, of the cleansing blood of Calvary; as praying while he put on his garments, that he might be clothed with the righteousness of the saints; as endeavoring, while he was eating, to feed upon the Bread of heaven. General Jackson now also enforced his favorite dogma, that the Bible furnished men with rules for everything. If they would search, he said, they would find a precept, an example, or a general principle, applicable to every possible emergency of duty, no matter what was a man's calling. There the military man might find guidance for every exigency. Then, turning to Lieutenant Smith, he asked him, smiling: 'Can you tell me where the Bible gives generals a model for their official reports of battles?' He answered, laughing, that it never entered his mind to think of looking for such a thing in the Scriptures. 'Nevertheless,' said the general, 'there are such, and excellent models, too. Look, for instance, at the narrative of Joshua's battle with the Amalekites; there you have one. It has clearness, brevity, fairness, modesty; and it traces the victory to its right source, the blessing of God.'"

As he gradually grew worse, and his physicians and friends became alarmed about his condition, he was calm, resigned, even joyous, at the prospect.

Noticing the sadness of his loving wife, he said to her, tenderly: "I know you would gladly give your life for me, but I am perfectly resigned. Do not be sad. I hope I may yet recover. Pray for me, but always remember in your prayers to use the petition, 'Thy will be done.'"

When he saw the number of surgeons who were called in, he said to his medical director, Dr. Hunter McGuire: "I see from the number of physicians that you consider my condition dangerous, but I thank God that, if it is His will, I am ready to go."

When his wife informed him that the doctors thought his recovery very doubtful, he was silent for a moment, and then said: "It will be infinite gain to be translated to heaven." When later, on that beautiful Sabbath day, he was informed that he could scarcely live till night, he engaged for a moment in intense thought, and then replied: "Very good, very good; it is all right."

Dr. McGuire thus concludes a deeply interesting paper on the wounding and death of Jackson: "He tried to comfort his almost heart-broken wife, and told her he had a good deal to say to her, but he was too weak. Colonel Pendleton came into the room about 1 o'clock, and he asked him: 'Who is preaching at headquarters to-day?' When told that the whole army was praying for him, he replied: 'Thank God—they are very kind.' He said, 'It is the Lord's day; my wish is fulfilled. I have always desired to die on Sunday.'

"His mind now began to fail and wander, and he frequently talked as if in command upon the field, giving orders in his old way; then the scene shifted, and he was at the mess-table in conversation with members of his staff; now with his wife and child; now at prayers with his military family. Occasionally intervals of return of his mind would appear, and during one of them I offered him some brandy and water; but he declined it, saying: 'It will only delay my departure and do no good; I want to preserve my mind, if possible, to the last.' About half-past one he was told that he had but two hours to live, and he answered again feebly, but firmly : 'Very good; it is all right.'

"A few moments before he died he cried out, in his delirium : 'Order A. P. Hill to prepare for action! Pass the infantry to the front rapidly! Tell Major Hawks'—then stopped, leaving the sentence unfinished. Presently a smile of ineffable sweetness spread over his pale face, and he said quietly, and with an expression as if of relief, 'Let us cross over the river and rest under the shade of the trees;' and then, without pain, or the the least struggle, his spirit passed from earth to the God who gave it."

In fine, Jackson took Jesus as his Saviour, his Guide, his great Exemplar, "the Captain of his salvation," whom he followed with the unquestioning obedience of the true soldier. And having thus *lived*, it is not surprising that he died the glorious death which has been described. Nay, it was not death; the weary, worn, battle-scarred veteran only received an "*honorable discharge.*" He had won the victory, he only went to wear the "crown of rejoicing;"

> " That crown with peerless glories bright,
>   Which shall new lustre boast
> When victors' wreaths and monarchs' gems
>   Shall blend in common dust."

CHAPTER IV.

INFLUENCE OF CHRISTIAN OFFICERS—*Concluded.*

THE number and influence of Christian officers in our army is a chapter which expands so widely as one comes to write it, that I find myself compelled to condense much of the material that it may be brought within proper limits; but there are other facts which must not be omitted.

GENERAL J. E. B. STUART, Chief of Cavalry, Army of Northern Virginia, has been called "the flower of cavaliers," the "Prince Rupert" of the Confederacy, and "Harry of Navarre," and he has been described as a gay, rollicksome, laughing soldier, "always ready for a dance or a fight." And yet Stuart was an humble, earnest Christian, who took Christ as his personal Saviour, lived a stainless life, and died a triumphant death. He used to attend our Chaplains' Association when he could, took a deep interest in its proceedings, and manifested the liveliest concern for the spiritual welfare of his men.

Not long before his lamented death he sought a personal interview with me, and discussed with great interest and intelligent zeal plans for the better supply of the cavalry with chaplains and religious reading. He spoke of the active life the cavalry were compelled to lead, as at the same time a serious obstacle to regular services among them and an increased necessity for having men of God who would follow them on their rapid marches, or carry the bread of life to them on the outposts. He was especially anxious to get an efficient man at his head-quarters, who could always be found when a preacher was needed, and made a very liberal offer for the comfort and support of such an one. But he was very emphatic in saying: "I do not want a man who is not both able and willing to endure hardness as a good soldier. The man who cannot endure the fatigues, hardships and privations of our rough riding and hard service, and be in place when needed, would be of no earthly use to us, and is not wanted at my head-quarters.'

(102)

He fell in battle at Yellow Tavern, in a heroic and successful effort to save Richmond from Sheridan's raid in May, 1864, and in the full tide of a brilliant career. But though thus cut down when full of life and hope, he said, when the surgeon expressed the belief that he would ultimately recover : " Well, I don't know how this will turn out; but if it is God's will that I shall die, I am ready."

He reached the house of his brother-in-law, Dr. Brewer, in Richmond, and began to sink so rapidly that it was very evident to his friends and to himself that he must soon pass away. He calmly made disposition of his effects, and gave necessary directions. Hearing the sound of artillery, he said to his gallant and trusted adjutant, Major H. B. McClellan, who was with him, and whose valuable services in the field he so highly appreciated : " Major, Fitz. Lee may need you," and expressed interest in how the battle was going.

But he quickly added, with a sigh : " But I must be preparing for another world."

About noon President Davis visited his bedside, and tenderly taking the hand of his great cavalry-man, asked him how he felt. " Easy, but willing to die, if God and my country think I have fulfilled my destiny and done my duty." To the surgeon later in the afternoon he replied, when told that he could not live long: " I am resigned if it be God's will. I would like to see my wife. But God's will be done."

His noble wife had been sent for, and was hastening to him, but she did not arrive until after his death.

To the doctor, who was holding his wrist and counting his pulse, he said : " Doctor, I suppose I am going fast now. It will soon be over. But God's will be done. I hope I have fulfilled my destiny to my country and my duty to God." Turning to Rev. Dr. Joshua Peterkin, of the Episcopal Church, of which General Stuart had long been a consistent member, he asked him to sing :

> " Rock of Ages, cleft for me,
> Let me hide myself in Thee,"

and he himself joined in the song with all the strength he could summon.

He joined with fervor in prayer with the ministers present, and again said, just before he passed away : " I am going fast now; I am resigned; God's will be done." And thus the dashing soldier quietly "fell on sleep," and left behind the record of a noble life, and a simple trust in Christ—the prophecy of a blissful immortality, where charging squadrons and clashing sabres never disturb the "rest that remaineth for the people of God."

GENERAL JOHN B. GORDON, of Georgia (now governor of that grand old Commonwealth), who rose from the captaincy of a company to command the remnant of the old "Stonewall" corps, and to win a reputation as one of the most brilliant soldiers which the war produced, was one of the most active of our Christian workers, and exerted a fine influence in the army.

He was accustomed to lead prayer-meetings in his command, and during seasons of special revival I have heard him, with eloquent words and tearful eyes, make powerful appeals to his men to come to Christ, and have seen him go off into the woods with his arms about some ragged private, that he might point him to "the Lamb of God that taketh away the sin of the world."

He was always the active friend and helper of his chaplains, and did everything in his power to promote the spiritual welfare of his men.

He wrote Dr. A. E. Dickinson, Superintendent of Army Colportage, the following stirring appeal, which was published in the *Religious Herald* at the time and is well worth preserving, not only as illustrating his character and influence, but as showing also the condition of things in the army:

"CAMP NEAR ORANGE COURT HOUSE, VIRGINIA, September 6, 1863.

"*Brother Dickinson :* Why is it that our good people at home, of the various denominations, are not sending more missionaries to the army? Every effort is made to supply the soldiers with 'creature comforts,' and I believe you find little difficulty in raising money to furnish religious reading to the army—but why is it so few preachers are sent us? They have either concluded that soldiers are so 'demoralized' that it is useless to preach to them, or else there is criminal indifference on this subject. They cannot, after all that has been written on this point, be ignorant of the fact that there is a great lack of ministers in the army—that many whole brigades of one or two thousand men are without a chaplain and rarely hear a sermon. But, suppose I tell these *good Christians*, who think preaching to

GENERAL JOHN B. GORDON, C. S. A.
(Taken while representing Georgia in the United States Senate.)
(Facing page 104.)

a body of soldiers is 'casting pearls before swine,' that these men, exposed as they are to temptations on every side, are more eager to listen to the Gospel than are the people at home; that the few missionaries they have been kind and generous enough to *lend* us for a *few* weeks are preaching—not in magnificent temples, it is true, and from gorgeous pulpits on Sabbath days, to empty benches, but daily, in the great temple of nature, and at night, by heaven's chandeliers—to audiences of from one to two thousand men, anxious to hear of the way of life. Suppose I tell them that many men of this army, neglected, as I *must* say they have been by Christians at home, are daily professing religion—that men, grown old in sin, and who never blanched in the presence of the foe, are made to tremble under the sense of guilt, and here in the forests and the fields are being converted to God—that young men, over whose departure from the paternal roof and pious influences have been shed so many and bitter tears, have been enabled under the preaching of a few faithful ministers to give to parents and friends at home such assurances as to change those *bitter* tears into tears of rejoicing. Suppose I tell them these things and assure them of the great encouragement afforded every missionary now laboring in this field, will it arouse them to act? or will each church admit the necessity of action, and yet conclude that ' our brethren of the neighboring church ought to send their preacher, but really we can't give ours, even for a month? '

" Let them beware lest, while they look upon the soldiers as too '*demoralized*' to be benefited by preaching, the soldiers ascertain that they are the ' demoralized ' portion of the army of the Cross.

" I close by telling you, that in the last few weeks nearly two hundred in this single brigade have been added to the different churches.   Yours, etc.,
                    " J. B. GORDON."

Let us hope that this gallant and accomplished soldier, whom Georgia has honored with a seat in the United States Senate and now as governor of the Commonwealth, may be in this high position as outspoken for Christ, and may exert as decided a religious influence as he used to do among his ragged boys in the camp!

General **D. H. Hill,** and General Ewell, after his profession of conversion, and others of our higher officers, were equally as pronounced, and just as ready to " stand up for Jesus."

But I have space for only a few illustrations of the Christian character and influence of officers of less rank.

COLONEL LEWIS MINOR COLEMAN, Professor of Latin in the University of Virginia, was one of the noblest sacrifices which the old Commonwealth laid on the altar during those terrible years of trial, and his death was widely mourned, especially by the large circle of his old pupils and army comrades who will, I am sure, be glad to have reproduced here the following sketch of him as a *Christian soldier*, taken from an address delivered before his old command by Rev. Dr. J. L. Burrows, of Richmond, and widely circulated, in tract form, in the army. I only regret that I have not space to insert the whole of the eloquent sketch of "The Christian Scholar and Soldier." But the following extract gives his record as a peerless soldier, and an account of his glorious death:

"The portentous clouds threatening the rushing tempest of war threw their gloomy shadows over these serene and happy scenes. Professor Coleman promptly settled for himself the course to be pursued in the issues that were forced upon us. ' He believed in the sovereignty of his native State; he believed that the rights and privileges guaranteed to us in the Constitution had been disregarded by our Northern foes; and he earnestly believed that nothing remained for the South but the exercise of the right of secession or revolution. Virginia was invaded; his allegiance was due to Virginia, and was only subordinate to his allegiance to his God. God and the State alike demanded that Virginia's sons should defend her borders.' He deemed it his duty to remain at his post in the university until the close of the session. Even under the impulses of his fervent patriotism, he would not abandon duties to which he considered himself pledged. With the close of the term he tendered his resignation to the Board of Visitors. The board refused to accept it, keeping the place vacant for his return at the termination of the war.

"When the early expedition to Harper's Ferry was determined on, many of the students at the university volunteered for that enterprise. A younger brother asked Professor Coleman's advice concerning his joining the company. ' It is your

OR. RELIGION IN LEE'S ARMY.   **107**

duty, Malcolm,' said he, 'to decide for yourself.' Shortly after
his decision was made, he said to his wife: 'Malcolm has determined to go, and I am much pleased. I wanted him to go,
but felt that I ought not to influence him.'

" He remained with the gathering students at the depot till a
late hour, encouraging and cheering them until the cars bore
them away. Then throwing himself upon his sleepless bed, he
exclaimed: 'I am so sorry I did not make a speech to those noble boys. The poor fellows called me out, too. Some of them
I may never see again, and, upon the verge of so important a
step, I failed to urge upon them the performance of their whole
duty in this matter, and especially to remind them of their accountability to God. How I regret that I did not speak to
them.'

" Mr. Coleman loved his profession. He was admirably
fitted for it. He had reached the most prominent position to
which intellectual ambition can aspire in this country, for there
is no literary height to which any man can climb from a profes-
sorship in the University of Virginia. He is there upon the
summit of his profession—there are no peaks above.

" On the other hand, he had no predilection, no training, no
taste for a soldier's life, no aspirations for military renown.
Personally such a life was intensely distasteful. He anticipated
the service with shrinking repugnance. It severed him from his
dear family. It broke up his loved habits of study. It took
him from his books, which were his delight. It dispelled the
serenity and calm in which he found his highest enjoyment.

" Nor was there any compulsion to drive him to the army.
He was beyond the reach of all conscription laws. He was
specially exempted. His friends urged upon him the importance of his position in the university. Some of the faculty
protested against his resignation. Many argued with him that
he could do more good to the country by remaining to aid in
the education of the neglected youth. Every dissuasive that
affection and prudence could suggest was employed to turn
him from his purpose.

" But in this, as in everything else, he was earnestly conscientious. He felt sad because of the necessity, yet, impelled by a
fervent patriotism, he would not shrink from the duty which he
felt he owed to his country.

" A cherished friend has well said: ' In the hour of his country's trial, when the call was made for her children, he relinquished his cherished pursuits, his high and well-merited position, fortune, comfort, home, all—and at last, even life itself—and freely chose to stand, where his unfailing perception of the right pointed him, by his country's standard in the battle for freedom. Few, even in these days of sacrifice, have placed a richer gift on the altar of liberty.'

"Immediately after the first battle of Manassas, he returned to his native county, enlisted in the service and received authority to raise an artillery company. Some discouraged the attempt by representing that most, who could be induced to volunteer, had already entered the army—that attempts of a similar kind had been made and failed. But he listened to no discouragements, and entered upon the work with characteristic energy. He appointed meetings and made speeches which roused the patriotic ardor of the people like a trumpet-blast. His graphic pictures of the perils of the country, and of the methods by which it might be delivered from oppression, and rendered free and prosperous, often drew tears from eyes unaccustomed to weep.

"In beating up recruits, he visited the house of a poor, aged woman, who resided on his farm, inquiring after her son. The son was already in the service. In speaking of his visit, the old lady said: 'Captain Coleman looked about and found my Bible; he read to me, and then we knelt down, nobody but him and me, and such a beautiful prayer as he offered I never heard in all my life. Just to think! that he should take so much interest in a poor old woman like me! He certainly must be the best man in the world.'

"Such incidents illustrate the predominating spiritual-mindedness of the man.

"By such influences and energies a very large company was speedily recruited, which was mustered into service, under Mr. Coleman as captain, in August, 1861.

"He now devoted himself with characteristic energy and perseverance to the acquisition of the military knowledge necessary for his position. He soon learned all that the books could teach him. I visited him in camp on one occasion, by his invitation, to preach for his company, and found him drawn up in line, with a few of his brother-officers, receiving instructions in practical sword exercises. He omitted nothing that promised to promote his intelligence and efficiency as an officer. The friend to whom I am indebted for so much that is interesting in this sketch says : ' By study and continued practice he made himself one of the best artillery officers in the service, and his company also became one of the most thoroughly drilled and efficient in the army. Here, again, his power in controlling men was strikingly exhibited. Strict in discipline and in every requirement of duty, he was just and impartial, sedulous to supply all the wants of his men, furnishing them, when necessary, with shoes and clothing from his own purse, nursing them personally when sick— kind and affable at all times. He set the example of duty himself and required all to come up to the standard.' He soon gained the confidence and affection of his men. He made them feel that he relied upon them, and that they might depend upon him.

"Captain Dance, of Powhatan, was preparing a company at the same time and place for the field, and was consequently thrown into close intercourse with Captain Coleman. He says : ' I was struck, upon my first acquaintance with him, with his genial temperament and fine social qualities, rendering him at all times a most agreeable companion; but I soon learned to admire still more his untiring energy, perseverance and industry, as exhibited in his endeavors to equip and drill his company, and perfect himself and them in the necessary knowledge of tactics and military science. The first attempts at drilling his company excited a smile among those who had longer experience; but in a very short time his company was well drilled. His was a spirit never satisfied with mediocrity. Whatever he undertook he desired to do well and he always succeeded. Although his company was mustered in after mine,' continues Captain Dance, ' yet he succeeded in getting all ready and starting before me.'

"In this relation, too, he manifested an earnest, practical Christian spirit. He provided, so far as possible, for the religious instruction and culture of his men. Upon every suitable opportunity he solicited ministers of the Gospel to preach for them. He conversed with them personally concerning their need of piety toward God, and trust in Him as a preparation for the trials of life and for death.

"Regularly, when the bugle sounded the *reveille* in early dawning, and the tattoo in the evening, he was among the first to come from his tent, and taking his position in front of the line with uncovered head and raised hands, like a father at his family altar, he solemnly and in clear tones, that reached the extremity of the line, implored the favor and blessing of Almighty God upon his men.   This, it is true, was not required by the regulations.   It was seen and felt to be the sincere and voluntary devotion of a pious heart.

" In speaking of these religious exercises held at the head of his company, Captain Kirkpatrick characterizes them as 'those direct, earnest, deeply fervent prayers for which he was remarkable,' and then says : ' Indeed, he had to a degree that few have, the real gift of prayer.   I shall never forget the prayer he offered on the sad and memorable Sabbath morning when we commenced our retreat from Centreville.   His heart was very tender and very full, and it seemed to unburden itself into the sympathizing ear of that Saviour who is God over all, blessed forever, and who yearns over all His troubled children with such unspeakable tenderness.'

" 'I have listened on some of these occasions,' says another brother-officer, 'when his prayers, giving evidence of a highly cultivated intellect, yet marked by deep humility and fervent sincerity, left the impression that he would have been a most efficient minister of the Gospel, had he been called to that holy office.'

"Another says : ' Though I always had a high opinion of his power and felicity of expression, yet in these *extempore* prayers I was frequently struck with the force and eloquence, and always with the earnestness and fervor of his petitions.'

" Oh ! if such concern were generally exhibited by officers, nominally pious, for the higher, the spiritual welfare of their men, how much more easily would they be controlled; how effectively restrained from wrong and encouraged in right.   Do such exhibitions of solicitous piety weaken discipline ?   Rather do they strengthen it, by superadding a sense of obligation to the army regulations.   Do they diminish courage ?   He is the bravest fighter, other things being equal, who has the firmest trust in God.   Even infidelity can see that such a spirit must make heroes of an army.

" Under such influences and energies it is not wonderful that his company became one of the best disciplined and most efficient in the service.   At a trial of skill between several rival companies, soon after reaching Manassas, his command was pronounced, by competent judges, to be the second, if not the best in the corps.

"Especially was this company distinguished at the bloody battle of Sharpsburg, where, in the heat of the conflict and amid severe suffering, it gallantly maintained its position, and nobly aided in the defeat of the enemy.

"The day before his company was ordered to the field his aged grandmother visited him at Richmond. They were together at the residence of a mutual friend. Captain Coleman went into her room just before she retired and, kneeling at the dear old lady's feet, said: 'Grandma, I shall leave in the morning before you are up, and I may never see you again in this world, for this is a serious, earnest work which I have undertaken, and I want you to bless your child before he parts from you.' And placing the hand of this aged saint upon his head he received from her, who for more than fifty years has been a bright and shining light in the Church of God, the patriarchal blessing. In imitating this beautiful ancient and oriental custom is evinced Mr. Coleman's familiarity and reverence for the old Bible. When a child of six years old, for so early he could read readily, that old grandmother would spread the family Bible upon a chair, and Lewis, drawing his little stool before it, would sit and pore over its narratives for hours together. It was not unnatural, then, that the association of childhood strengthened in youth and manhood; that his whole spirit, imbued with the fitness and beauty of the old customs, should have led him to feel 'that his heart would be lightened and encouraged in the discharge of a sacred though dangerous duty by receiving from the eldest of the family' the formal patriarchal blessing.

"His company was ordered to Manassas and formed a part of General Pendleton's reserve corps of artillery. Time will not permit us to do more than follow the track of the company in the retreat from Manassas, the march to Yorktown and the withdrawal from the Peninsula, the battles around Richmond and the marches to the Rappahannock and to Maryland, in all of which it honorably participated.

"At the reorganization of the army, in 1862, Captain Coleman was appointed major of artillery and soon after was elected Lieutenant-Colonel of the First Regiment of Virginia Artillery.

"Colonel Coleman was always to be found in his place, never

absenting himself from the post of duty except from necessity, and once, for several weeks, from sickness.

"During the battles around Richmond he was, by a mistake of position, for a short time in the hands of the enemy. But he managed, by his coolness and presence of mind, to extricate himself. Speaking of the terrible storm of battle he said, that while beyond conception it was awful, yet a relying trust in God gave him perfect confidence and peace. One of his fellow-officers remarked that the earnestness and sincerity of his ejaculatory prayers upon the battle-field convinced him 'that the soul of Colonel Coleman was always fixed upon the one sure hope and source of strength.'

"'We were drawn up in line of battle,' says Captain Kirk-patrick, 'on the eastern bank of the Chickahominy, with the advancing enemy in front, on a Sabbath morning in April or May, 1862. Captain Coleman approached where I was lying, took from my hands the Bible I had been reading and turning to the Eighty-fourth Psalm read it and commented upon its beautiful verses. I can now recall the earnest, longing tones in which he repeated, "How amiable are Thy tabernacles, O Lord of Hosts! My soul longeth, yea, even fainteth for the courts of the Lord; my heart and my flesh crieth out for the living God!" He drew a parallel between David's condition when he composed that psalm and ours as we had been driven by our enemies, and spoke of the wonderful adaptedness of God's word, when even such circumstances as those around us only the more forcibly impressed its truths and beauties upon the soul. He then went on to speak in glowing words of the sweet privileges of God's house, the solemn assemblies of His saints, their blissful communion with Him in all the ordinances of His worship. The impression made upon me by that reading and those running comments will never be effaced from my memory, and while my soul retains its powers the Eighty-fourth Psalm will be associated in my mind with Lewis Minor Coleman and that beautiful but anxious Sabbath morning.'

"He was prevented by severe illness from accompanying the army into Maryland in 1862. Even then his active spirit chafed under the necessary restraint. He requested a brother-officer to send for him if there was any prospect of a battle. In the dead hour of night he heard a rap at the door. ''Tis a message for me,' said he, 'and I must go.' Said his wife, 'you cannot go;

you have not strength to walk across the room.' 'No matter,' he replied, 'I will go; God will give me strength.' Fortunately the message related to some other matter.

"A short time before the battle of Fredericksburg he resumed his command. Three days before that fatal battle, while riding with a friend towards Port Royal, his friend remarked: 'In the seven days' fight around Richmond I fought literally over my father's grave; my gun being but a few yards from it. If I should fall in this war I should prefer to fall upon such, to me, sacred ground.' Colonel Coleman replied, 'If I am killed in this war I should prefer to fall here, for hard by my father lies buried.' Three days after, not far distant, he received his mortal wound.

"I am permitted to make a few extracts from letters written during his services in the army, which allow us a glance into his inner life, and reveal to us a little of his pure and loving heart.

"In immediate expectation of a battle near Yorktown, April 27, 1862, he thus writes:

"'*My Dearest Mother:* I have a little time this Sabbath afternoon, and will write a few lines to tell you how strongly, at this last moment, when no one knows what an hour may bring forth, the thought of all the love and tenderness and fostering care bestowed in my childhood comes over your loving son. If I have ever caused you needless trouble, let me now ask your forgiveness. All that I am, all the happiness I have ever enjoyed, is, I believe, due to you, and from you in great measure, under Providence, comes my hope of immortal life. I thank God that I can and do love, from my heart of hearts, all who are near to me—father, mother, grandma (God bless her), brothers, sisters, wife, children, all. . . . . .

"'I pray and hope that I may be spared to see you all in peace and happiness again. No one can tell what his fate may be in the bloody struggle which impends, and if I fall I want you all to know how dearly I love you, and to know further that my only hope and confidence is in God, through Jesus Christ our Lord.'

"In writing of his beloved wife, who, while visiting her sick father, had been surprised and detained within the enemy's lines,

8

and separated from her children, after expressing his pain and regret, he says: 'But it was right for her to go and see her dying father, notwithstanding the suffering it involves. Suffering encountered in the path of duty can never do harm.'

"Upon the death of the youngest brother of the family he thus writes, just a month before his own death-summons:

"'*My Dearest Mother:* It is with heartfelt anguish that I have just learned of dear Willie's death. I know your heart is bowed down with grief at the loss of your youngest born—so sweet, so gentle, so lovely in all respects. I always regarded him as the lamb of the flock. . . . . Can you not, my dear mother, in this dark hour, put your whole trust and confidence in our Heavenly Father, who doeth all things well? God grant that we may all strive to be little children, as our dear Willie was.'

"After speaking of the grief of two young brothers who were with him in the service, he adds:

"'I trust that this great affliction, which for the present seemeth so very grievous, may bring to them a far more exceeding and eternal weight of glory. I trust, too, that I shall be stirred up to be a better guide, both by example and precept, to my two young brothers so strangely associated with me, after so many years of separation.'

"But I must hasten to the sad close of this sketch. Colonel Coleman was on duty with his regiment at the battle of Fredericksburg, on the 13th of December, under General Jackson, and, with unflinching courage and entire self-possession, maintained his position on that bloody field.

"'He might,' says Captain Dance, 'without any dereliction of duty, have kept out of that battle altogether, for when his regiment was brought up other artillery had already occupied the position. But he was anxious to render some service, and sought out the general commanding that part of the line, and obtained leave to place some of his guns in position, and two guns of my battery were all he could find room for, and it was at one of these that he received the wound which finally proved mortal. His horse had been killed, and, though on foot and wounded, he still insisted upon remaining on the. ground, and even offered his assistance in filling up a ditch, that my guns might be carried over to advance on the enemy.'

"Late in the day he was struck by a ball in the leg, just below the knee. He deemed the wound a slight one, and, as we have seen, refused to leave the field until by increasing faintness he was compelled to do so, but not until the victory had been decided for our arms. When his wound was dressed, he playfully remarked that it would be a 'good furlough' for awhile. He was borne to the house of Mr. Yerby, in Spotsylvania county. Here, when found by his uncle, Rev. James D. Coleman, he was surrounded by the wounded and dying, to whom, in his benevolent self-forgetfulness, he was striving to administer such aid and consolation as was in his power. He spoke more of his suffering comrades than of himself, and especially expressed his sympathy and sorrow for a terribly mutilated young officer who was lying by his side. He was removed to Edge Hill, Caroline county, the residence of his brother-in-law, Mr. Samuel Schooler. Soon his wound assumed a threatening and dangerous character. Virulent erysipelas supervened, and he suffered intense agony. By profuse discharges from his wound, and by constant, severe pain, his frame became emaciated and reduced to little more than a skeleton. Every attention which the skill of physicians and the affectionate care and nursing of the assembled family could render could only retard, but could not overcome the steady approaches of coming death. His friends were unwilling to believe that one for whom they so ministered, for whose recovery they so fervently prayed, upon whose continued life so many hopes and interests were depending, must be taken from them. But the gravest fears were soon excited, and before long Colonel Coleman himself began to anticipate his speedy departure from earth. He endured with marvellous patience and uncomplaining cheerfulness the most excruciating agonies of body. His faith in the rectitude and benevolence of his covenant God never wavered, rather steadily increased as death approached nearer and still nearer. And now the beautiful light of his pious spirit, like the glories of a clear autumn sunset, illumed the chamber in which he was gasping away his life, and lighted up, with sweet resignation and hope, the hearts of his lamenting kindred. In the early stages of his disease he hoped—expected to recover. He had much for which to live, and few men could better enjoy or adorn life, or render it more useful than he. He now decided, what before he had often pondered, that, with recovered health, he would devote his life and talents to the more direct service of

God in the work of the Gospel ministry. 'At the close of the war,' said he, 'more than ever will laborers be needed to reap in the harvest-field of the Gospel. I may do some good in that sphere of labor.' But a higher ministry, in a brighter sphere, had been appointed for him. 'I hope I shall live,' said he to a friend; 'I think I can do good—be of some use; but God knows best and His will be done.' In the solitary night, when a troubled sleep could be induced only by means of powerful opiates, his mind would wander fitfully over the scenes of the past. Now he would imagine himself in presence of a class of pupils teaching, and he would recite rapidly in Latin and French, and then he seemed at the head of his company in the battle and uttered the stern word of command. Then the names of distant friends, as in cheerful and social converse, passed his lips; then the dear names of 'wife,' 'mother,' 'child,' in loving murmurs proved whither his restless thoughts were turning, and always the devotional ejaculation of praise to God and of fervent prayer for grace and strength would mingle with his wildest wanderings.

"In one of these restless hours, shortly before he died, he roused himself up and turning to his brother said: 'Malcolm, did I die as a Christian soldier ought to die?'—then entirely recovering consciousness, he smiled and said: 'I thought I had died on the battle-field.'

"For ninety-eight weary days he endured physical agonies, relieved by only occasional respites from pain, such as probably few men have ever been called to bear. The incurable erysipelas, the inflammation involving the whole limb, and extending by sympathy to his whole frame, the frequent incisions and probings, the drain from incessant suppuration, the inaccessible ulcers originating in his changeless position on the couch, all combined to produce excruciating pain. Yet all was borne with a patience, resignation, even cheerfulness, that has, perhaps, never been surpassed. When convinced that there was no rational hope of his recovery, he fixed the eye of his faith steadily upon the bright home in heaven, and seeming to enter already into communion with the beloved ones who had gone before, looked beyond the interval over which he must pass, and lived as though already in the light of his Redeemer's glory. He was more than patient; he was exultant, at times enraptured.

"Referring to the fact that he was in the neighborhood where much of his youth had been spent, he said: 'Here were most of the sins of my early life committed, and here do I come to die, and to find them all forgiven through the mercy and love of Jesus.'

"'Why, it is but a short trip,' said he to his weeping friends. 'It is only taking a little journey, and then safe and happy forever. It is but a trip; we shall all meet again soon, and I want to start and be with Christ.'

"'I had hoped,' said he, 'to do good, living as a minister of the Gospel, but perhaps God will make my death a ministry for the conversion of those dear ones who are yet out of Christ. I may do more good by dying than by living.' These hopes have not been in vain. One of his brothers has already united with the Church of Christ. Another dear friend, to whom he had appealed in a former serious illness, and to whom, later, he sent this message: 'Tell Charles M—— that I once before knocked at the door of his heart, and that he must strive to meet me in heaven,' writes me, 'his warning from the deathbed, I trust, has not been in vain. I feel that, under God, I now have a hope of a better life.' He called all the household, even the servants, to his bedside, and tenderly gave them his dying counsels and bade them loving farewells. He asked them what messages he should bear for them to the ransomed loved ones who had gone before.

" Referring to the recent death of his youngest brother, he said, with a sweet smile, to his brother, Dr. Coleman: 'Dear little Willie! I shall be more fortunate than you were, Robert; you went to Lexington to see him and were disappointed, but I shall not be disappointed. I shall certainly see him.'

" Turning to his beloved wife, who had been an unwearied watcher and ministrant during his lingering illness, says Rev. Mr. Coleman, 'he pronounced upon her character and life a most tender and beautiful eulogy, and in words that seemed to gush from the depths of his soul, praised, and thanked, and blessed her, for the happiness and joy which her love had brought to his heart and life.'

" He charged those who ministered to him with pious messages to the absent. 'Tell General Jackson and General Lee,' said he, 'they know how Christian soldiers can fight, and I wish they could see now how a Christian soldier can die.'

" In communicating this message to General Jackson, Dr. Coleman wrote: 'I doubt not, general, that the intimate acquaintance

with yourself which my brother desired on earth, will be vouchsafed to him in heaven, and that when your career of usefulness
here is ended, " in the green pastures and beside the still waters "
of a brighter sphere you and he will meet in sweet communion
and fellowship, and that your earthly acquaintance will be purified and perfected into an eternal friendship.'

" General Jackson's response was characteristic.   He writes:

" ' Had your brother lived, it was my purpose to become better acquainted with him.   I saw much less of him than I desired.   I look beyond this life to an existence where I hope to
know him better.

" 'Very truly, your friend,
" ' T. J. JACKSON.'

" When scarcely five weeks had passed, these anticipations were
realized, and these sainted spirits met, where no sounds nor perils of war will evermore disturb the holy repose and bliss of
their communion.

" As Arnold had been his model as a teacher, so Havelock was
his model as a Christian soldier.   And almost the words of
Havelock were those which he transmitted in his dying message to his own beloved generals.

" Once only, when writhing in agony intense, did his faith for a
brief space seem to fail, and he expressed a dread that God's
face was hid from him.   A few days after, he recalled this expression of doubt to mind, and said : ' Doctor, you remember I
said I did not feel God's presence with me.   I could not hear
the rustling of the angels' pinions.   Now I *know* that he is near
me, and I feel the breath of the angels' wings.'

" He exacted from his younger brother, Dr. Malcolm Fleming,
who watched constantly at his bedside, a promise that he would
let him know when his end was approaching.   When his feeble,
sinking pulse indicated the speedy termination of his sufferings,
Malcolm said to him, with throbbing heart and streaming eyes,
' Brother Lewis, you remember my promise.'   ' Yes, Malcolm ;
do you think I am dying ? '   He could only bow his head in
answer.   Immediately, with as much composure as he had ever
given a lecture to a class, he dictated his last will and then fell
asleep as calmly as in childhood.   When he awoke he expressed surprise that he still lived.   He had fallen asleep amid

the farewells of loving lips and the suppressed wailings of bleeding hearts. He had hoped to waken in heaven. 'Come, Lord Jesus, come quickly, O come quickly,' was his frequent prayer. He was asked, 'Would you not prefer to stay with us?' 'No! no!' he replied; 'I prefer to go.' They sang, at his request, such hymns as—

> 'Jesus, and shall it ever be,
> A mortal man ashamed of Thee;'

and—

> 'How firm a foundation, ye saints of the Lord,
> Is laid for your faith in His excellent word.'

And in feeble tones he joined in the sacred songs. Late in the night he asked them to sing the hymn commencing—" Jesus, I love Thy charming name," and the last verse he sung with them in faltering, dying tones—

> 'I'll speak the honors of thy name
> With my last laboring breath—
> And dying, clasp Thee in my arms,
> The antidote of death.'

"Some one said to him, 'You will soon be in heaven; are you willing to go?' 'Perfectly willing; certainly I am.' They were his last words, and soon, in the early dawn of the morning, on the 21st of March, 1863, he fell asleep in Jesus.

"When the summons of death comes to us, may we each be ready to say—'Perfectly willing; certainly I am.'

"Young men! we have thus presented, for your contemplation, an imperfect survey of the life of a Christian scholar and soldier. The extraordinary deeds of some world-worshipped hero or fabulous demigod might, perhaps, have better amused or entertained the multitude. But such a sketch as this cannot fail to be more useful, in so far as it is practical and imitable. Here are excellencies you may attain, a character you may emulate, a life you may copy.

"'If no faults shade the picture,' to quote the beautiful sentiment of Rev. Dr. Hoge, in speaking of another of Virginia's noble sons fallen in battle, 'it is not because I have hidden them from my readers, but because grace has hidden them from me.'

"It may be true that Colonel Coleman's natural mental endowments, his original physical capabilities were of a higher order than God has given to most. But as a practical life I have endeavored to sketch one that is plainly imitable.

"Perhaps the most prominent characteristic of his moral nature was his conscientiousness. In little matters, as in those more important, he was accustomed to ask, and to act upon the answer, what is duty?

"'His conceptions of duty,' says Major Venable, one of his earliest and latest friends, 'were as true and direct as his performance of it was thorough and exact.' This is imitable by all.

"Persevering industry, including earnest attention to little things, was another marked feature of Lewis Coleman's life. In his studies, earlier and later, in all the practical routine of daily requirements, in the study and lecture-room, on the farm and in the camp, whatever service devolved upon him was promptly performed. He seldom had arrearages of business to bring up. He pushed his work steadily before him, rarely needing to drag it along after its appropriate hours. Such an example may be wisely copied.

"He was uniformly cheerful and social. He always had a pleasant word for all he met, even for servants. His lively wit, without a shade of malice or ill-nature; his honest ringing laugh, the wonderful sprightliness, felicity and tact of his ordinary conversation, drawing as from a perennial spring sparkling rills of facts, fancies and illustrations, made him a most genial and instructive companion.

"He evinced in all his life the most unselfish benevolence of spirit. He sought to promote the happiness of others rather than his own. He lived for others rather than for himself. No friend ever asked him for a favor who did not meet a cheerful and ready response, if the bestowment was within the compass of his means and the approval of his conscience.

"And for the happiness and welfare of the loved ones of his own family circle, no sacrifice was deemed too severe. There seemed only one earthly love that could surpass that of mother, father, brothers, sisters, wife and children for him, and that was his love for them.

"And this trait of heart, too, is imitable.

"Throwing its soft light over all these excellencies was his beautiful humility. He rarely made himself, or anything that he did, the theme of conversation. 'He was a man of few professions,' says Major Venable, 'and his Christianity found more expression in action than words; yet it was not difficult to read the clear simplicity of his life and character.'

" He never seemed himself aware that there was anything especially meritorious or unusual in his sweet, genial, benevolent life. He never seemed conscious, even upon his death-bed, that he had made any notable sacrifice in resigning his elevated position at the university for his humble position in the army. He often spoke in desponding tones of the little he had accomplished as a student and a Christian, and ever longed and struggled for higher attainments and higher usefulness.

" Is not this temper worthy of imitation?

" The supreme, fostering, originating principle of all these excellencies of life and heart was his piety. Early he learned that 'beginning of wisdom—the fear of the Lord.' His piety was not the mere coloring that ornamented life; it entered into the warp and woof of his inner nature. He loved God, and lived in daily communion with the Redeemer, and thus became 'a living epistle of Jesus Christ, known and read of all men.'

" Have I not well said that his was an imitable life, and therefore well worthy of delineation for the study of young men who are aiming at something beyond mere personal, selfish enjoyment—at an honorable, beneficent life?

" One who knew him well and loved him dearly has beautifully said: 'As the dew, falling silently, refreshing and rendering fruitful the earth, and crystalizing upon the spires of grass and in the calyxs of flowers, crowns, as with diamonds, the brow of morning, so the unostentatious virtues of Lewis Minor Coleman refreshed the hearts, gladdened and made fruitful in good deeds the lives of others; and when the Sun of Righteousness shall arise, those virtues will shine more resplendently as gems in that crown which the Righteous Judge shall give to him on that day.' "

In 1871 Rev. John Lipscomb Johnson, B. A., of the University of Virginia (for the past fourteen years professor of English in the University of Mississippi), published a volume of 765 pages, containing sketches of nearly two hundred alumni of the University of Virginia who fell in the " War between the States," and even then a number of names were omitted for lack of proper information. In eagerly reading these pages, in which Dr. Johnson has done a graceful service to his *Alma Mater*, which should be gratefully remembered, I have been struck with the fact that a very large proportion of these men were humble, useful Christians; and I might appropriately transfer to this book a number of these sketches as beautifully illustrating "Christ in the Camp." The same may be said of the "Virginia Military Institute Memorial" volume prepared by Rev. C. D. Walker, and containing sketches of one hundred and seventy of its alumni who fell in the struggle for Southern independence. And no doubt the same would be true of the colleges of the South generally. But I have space for only a part of the sketch of my old friend and brother, REV. DABNEY CARR HARRISON, who was chaplain at the university when I was a student there, and of whose stainless life and efficient labors I could testify in strongest terms. I should insert the sketch prepared by the gifted and lamented Rev. Dr. Wm. J. Hoge, but, while I circulated thousands of copies in the army, I have been unable to secure a copy for my present use.

I am fortunate, however, in being able to present the following extracts from the sketch prepared for "The University Memorial" by the graceful pen of my honored and distinguished brother, Rev. Dr. M. D. Hoge, of Richmond, whom I first knew as an able and eloquent preacher in the camps, and whose "abundant labors" seem to increase as the years go on.

"REV. DABNEY CARR HARRISON,

"Captain, Company K, Fifty-sixth Virginia Infantry.

"To furnish a brief sketch of this faithful minister of Christ, this noble gentleman and valiant officer, who fell at Fort Donelson while cheering on his men and striking for the honor and independence of the young Confederacy, is to me an easy task, for I need only to abridge the carefully prepared memoir of him, written by my brother, the Rev. William J. Hoge, D. D., about a year before his own death. Short as was that memoir, it was composed so conscientiously, and was such a labor of love on the part of the writer, that I have little to add or supply, and need only say that the calmest review, after the lapse of years, only confirms my estimate of the fidelity and truthful beauty of that tribute to the memory of one so deserving of our love, and so worthy of a place among those whose names, embalmed with 'our praises and our tears,' we transmit to those who come after us, in the pages of 'The University Memorial.'"

After an exceedingly interesting sketch of Mr. Harrison's early life, education, and services as a minister (especially as chaplain at the University of Virginia), which I regret I am not able to reproduce, Dr. Hoge says:

"But after many months of fruitful toil (in a new pastorate), his peaceful life was disturbed by the coming of our national troubles. Dark shadows soon became darker realities. This sovereign Commonwealth was required to aid in beating down into degradation, and whipping back into servility, her free sisters of the further South, or join with them in their just independence, and throw her generous breast before them to receive the first blow of the tyrant's rod, and bear the brunt of his wrath. She obeyed her heart, exercised her right, and stood in the breach.

"In the battle of Bull Run he lost his gallant cousin, Major Carter H. Harrison. Three days later, at Manassas, his native soil was wet again by the blood of the only nephews of his mother, the only sons of their mother, Holmes and Tucker Conrad, and by the blood of his own pure and beautiful brother, Lieutenant Peyton Randolph Harrison. These four young men were all faithful servants of God. Their lives were lovely and useful. In His fear they fought. They were sustained by His grace when they fell. The Conrads were shot at the same moment, and falling side by side, lay, as in the sleep of childhood, almost in each other's arms. The younger of them was a student of theology, and was nearly ready, with glowing heart, to enter on the higher service of his Lord, in the ministry of the Gospel.

"The noble deaths of these young men stirred the soul of Dabney Harrison to its lowest depths. From the beginning of the war he had longed to share the hardships and dangers of his compatriots. Nothing but his sacred office held him back for a moment. But now he hesitated no longer. His mind was made up. ' I must take my brother's place,' he calmly said, and nothing could turn him from that resolve. He left 'the quiet and still air of delightful studies,' left his loving people and sweet little home in Hanover, and, having raised a company by great personal exertions, entered the service.

"Even then he would not have taken up the sword if he had been compelled to lay down the Bible; he would not have become a captain, if he could not have remained a minister. He entered the army believing that his usefulness, even as a preacher of God's word, would be increased in that new and hazardous field.

"And after he became fully enlisted in his work as a soldier, no one ever saw him even for a moment give way to a bitter spirit, or heard him speak a word unbecoming a minister of Christ. Several months after he entered the service, he said, with thankfulness and joy, that he had not been conscious of one revengeful feeling toward our enemies. No: he would fight for his country; but he would not hate. He durst die, but not sin. Conscience, not passion, made him a soldier; but who does not know that conscience is mightier than passion! His valor was, through the grace of God, without fierceness: but like steel whose heat has been quenched in cold water, it was, therefore, all the firmer and keener, of higher polish and more fatal stroke.

" He spent the first three months after the organization of his company, in the Camp of Instruction, near Richmond, where I was in daily intercourse with him. In addition to my pastoral duties in the city, I served as chaplain in that camp during the years 1862 and 1863. Captain Harrison was with me longer than any other minister in the service, and delighted to avail himself of every opportunity of aiding me in my arduous work.

" Whenever I was prevented by any cause from meeting my engagements, he was always ready to take my place; and I had the most abundant evidence of the efficiency of his labors, and of the gratitude of the men for his efforts to promote their temporal and spiritual welfare.

" During his stay, at one time several thousand troops were stationed at our camp, and Captain Harrison was, of course, brought into contact with a large number of officers. Over these he exercised the most happy influence.

" While no man was more inflexible in his adherence to his convictions of duty, or more prompt to rebuke whatever he believed to be wrong in principle or in conduct, yet his manner was so conciliating, such was the candor and kindness of his disposition, such his scrupulous respect for the rights and regard for the feelings of others, that he rarely gave offence, even when he attempted to repress what he deemed culpable. The very presence of one so frank and fearless in his bearing, so delicate and refined in his tastes, so pure and elevated in his principles, was ordinarily sufficient to check any exhibitions of profanity or vulgarity; and, withal, he was so genial in his nature, so entertaining in his conversation, and so obliging in his disposition, that his presence was never regarded as imposing an irksome restraint, even in a company of the irreligious.

"If others have shown

'How awful goodness is,'

it was Dabney Harrison's happy province to show how amiable and attractive it may appear, when thus illustrated in the life of a Christian gentleman and soldier. While he remained in our camp, he moved about as one whose superiority was tacitly acknowledged without exciting ill-will or envy; and when he left us, he was regretted as one whose place was not to be filled again.

"While Captain Harrison's good work extended to the surrounding multitudes, his first anxiety was, of course, for his own men. He had gathered them and given them to the service. They were to follow him, it might be, to the death. They, of all others, would see what he actually was, as a servant of his country, as a servant of his God.

"Therefore he sought to be, every day and in every thing, an example to them. He shared their hardships, and all so cheerfully, that the most despondent could hardly fail to catch some quickening ray from his sunny spirit. As far as was possible, too, he made them share any comfort pertaining to his position. The inexperienced found in him a faithful guardian, the perplexed went to him freely for counsel, and all the company felt that in him they had not only a brave and gallant commander, but a true friend. His usefulness was like a continual dew. He gave to his soldiers new impressions of the power and sweetness of the religion of Christ, when they saw how beautifully innocence could blend with wisdom; how the very purity of woman could consist with the valor of man, just as whiteness and enduring substance are combined in marble; and how the most uncompromising godliness could be interwoven with the elegance of the gentleman, while the devoutest piety but gave new fire to the ardor of the patriot.

"It is unnecessary to dwell on the hardships of Captain Harrison's winter campaign in the West—hard fare and harder lodging, and constant exposure to the wet and cold. Whatever he bore, many thousands bore with him; and there are multitudes of whom that may be said which is so true of him—no one ever saw him falter, no one ever heard him murmur. A brief extract from one of his letters may serve to show the pleasant spirit in which all these privations and annoyances were met:

"'BOWLING GREEN, KENTUCKY, January 18, 1862.

"'*My Dear Father :* I have been forcibly reminded to-day of an incident in Ruxton's travels. Out on a prairie he found a wretched-looking man, all alone in a pouring rain, stooping over a few smouldering embers, and singing:

> "'How happy are we,
> Who from care are free.
> Oh! why are not all
> Contented like me?'

"'My tent is on a hill-side, and has a flue instead of a chimney. It rained hard all last night, has rained all of to-day, and is raining yet. The water has risen in my tent, the fire has been drowned out, the floor is nearly all mud, and I have been writing all the morning in a chair stuck deep in this mud. My bed is kept out of it by some fence rails, and my larder is a basket on the ground at the bed's head, containing a piece of pork and a bag of flour. There is not a negro in Virginia that would not despise such lodgings, but I am " contented." I sleep soundly, work hard, eat heartily, and am fattening.'

"A day or two later he writes: 'I have just finished a large stone chimney to my tent, and shall have it floored with poles to-morrow; then I shall be in great state.'

"On Monday night, February 10, six days before his death, he thus closes a long letter from the camp before Fort Donelson: ' Oh, how all these adventures, with their perils and deliverances, their privations and blessings, do drive us to our God! I want no other strength than the Lord Jehovah; no other Redeemer than our blessed Saviour; no other Comforter than His Holy Spirit. I believe that when we do our duty the Lord will fight for us. I feel a constant, bright and cheery trust in Him. I think of my precious wife and little ones, and long for their society and caresses; but I am satisfied that it is right that I should be here, and I await the development of His will. I think His mercy in making us His children, in spite of all our ill-desert, ought to make us willing meekly to bear all that He chooses to lay upon us.'

"Mightily as many earthly loves drew upon his soul, his Lord's love for *him* was more than all. He had 'prepared a place' for him 'in His Father's House,' and now he desired his coming. Beyond the river, and before the throne, His voice was heard saying, 'Father, I will that they whom Thou hast given me be with me where I am, that they may behold my glory.' And then from Mount Zion, which is above, came words which once sounded in thunder from Mount Sinai; but now they came softly, and were unheard by any mortal ear. They were words of discharge and blessing, breathed in music that night over the pillow of the sleeping soldier: 'Six days shalt thou labor and do all thy work; but the seventh is the Sabbath of the Lord thy God.'

"Six days for earth and labor; only six. Then his eternal Sabbath would begin; rest and worship and joy forever!

"The battle of Fort Donelson began on Wednesday. That night was spent in throwing up breastworks. His men say that no man in the company worked harder, or did more in this heavy labor, than 'the captain.' Thursday night was cold and stormy. The rain fell in torrents on the weary watchers in the trenches, and, soon changing into sleet, their clothes froze upon them. By Friday evening, Captain Harrison's frame, never robust, gave way for a time, and he was compelled to retire to the hospital, where he lay quite sick all that night. Yet on Saturday morning, a great while before day, and against the remonstrances of his friends, he rose and returned to his command.

"The officer who commanded the Fifty-sixth Regiment at this time, gave several instances of such zeal and daring on the part of Captain Harrison, that one cannot refrain from applying to him what Clarendon says of 'that incomparable young man, Lord Falkland,' in his touching account of his death: 'He had a courage of the most clear and keen temper, and so far from fear, that he seemed not without some appetite of danger.'

"'You *ought* to be braver than the rest of us,' said some of his brother-officers to Captain Harrison one day, after witnessing some exhibition of his serene fearlessness in danger.

"'Why so?' said he, pleasantly.

"'Because,' said they, 'you have everything settled for eternity. You have nothing to fear after death.'

"'Well, gentlemen,' said he, solemnly, after a moment's pause, 'you are right. Everything *is* settled, I trust, for eternity, and I have nothing to fear.'

"As the sun rose on the morning of Saturday, it saw him enter the thick of the battle and wrestle valiantly with the foe. With dauntless heart he cheered on his men. They eagerly followed wherever he led. Their testimony is, that he never said, 'Go on,' but always, 'Come on,' while ever before them flashed his waving sword. At length, with fear and pain, they saw his firm step faltering, his erect form wavering. He fell, and the fierce tide of battle swept on. It was impossible for his most devoted men to pause. And they best did his will by passing over his prostrate body, throwing themselves on the foe, and leaving him to die. 'He had warred a good warfare, ever holding faith and a good conscience.'

"Three balls had passed through his hat, without harming him; a fourth cut his temple; a fifth passed through his right lung; and this was the fatal wound.

"Two incidents of his dying hours are yet to be recorded. Calling, about noon, for one of his manuscript books, he took a pencil, and, with a trembling hand, feebly wrote these words:

"'February 16, 1862.—Sunday.

"'I die content and happy; trusting in the merits of my Saviour Jesus; committing my wife and children to their Father and mine.   "'DABNEY CARR HARRISON.'

"Precious legacy of love and prayer! Precious testimony of faith and blessedness!

"A little while before he died, he slept quietly for a few minutes. In dreams his soul wandered back to yesterday's conflict. He was again in the battle. The company for which he had toiled and prayed and suffered so much was before him, and he was wounded—dying on the field. But even in dreams he had not lost

'th' unconquerable will,
And courage never to submit or yield.'

Starting out of sleep, he sat once more erect, and exclaimed: 'Company K, you have no captain now; but never give up! never surrender!'

"The arms of his faithful attendant received him as he rose, and now supported him tenderly as his drooping form grew heavier. With his head pillowed on a soldier's breast, he sank, peacefully as a babe, into that sleep which no visions of strife shall ever disturb. Thus he died, as he was born, on the Sabbath. Thus was his life bounded on either hand by the Day of God. Care and conflict came between, but a Sabbath blessing was on it all, and then he entered on the higher 'Sabbath of the Lord his God, eternal in the heavens.'"

As an appropriate appendix to this sketch, and to show that neither of the brothers concerned in its preparation held Captain Harrison in higher regard than any others who knew him well, I append the following eloquent tribute to his memory, from the pen of the Rev. Joseph M. Atkinson, of Raleigh, North Carolina. It is taken from a Southern periodical, in which it was published in 1863:

"While our church or our country shall survive; while freedom, or religion, or learning, the noblest gifts of nature, or the brightest instincts of personal or hereditary worth, shall be treasured among men, never will the name and the memory of the Rev. Dabney Carr Harrison be forgotten; a gentleman, a scholar, a Christian, a minister, a martyr to his conscientious conviction of public duty and his uncalculating devotion to his country. Among the illustrious worthies of ancient story, among the deified heroes of ancient song, in the golden records of Grecian fame, in the glowing chronicles of mediæval knighthood, in the ranks of war, in the halls of learning, in the temple of religion, a nobler name is not registered than his, nor a nobler spirit mourned."

CAPTAIN HUGH A. WHITE, who graduated at Washington College, and was a student at Union Theological Seminary when the war broke out, was a specimen of the Christian officer well worthy of a full sketch in this chapter; but space can be found for only brief extracts from the memoir of him written in 1864 by his venerable father, Rev. Dr. W. S. White, then pastor of the Presbyterian Church in Lexington, Virginia.

The sketch of his leaving home for the army is given in full, as it well illustrates the spirit not only of this noble young man, but of thousands of others of our "Boys in Gray:"

"He remained at the seminary until his second session closed. He stood his examinations, attended the marriage of a friend, and reached home about the middle of May, 1861. He was then twenty years and eight months of age. His appearance, though not indicative of serious disease, was such as to awaken some uneasiness in the minds of his friends. The professors

9

said he had confined himself too closely to his room and his books during the winter. His father feared that the privations and exposure of the camp might be fatal to his health, and held a full interview with him, in which he sought to convince him, that considering his age, his acquisitions, his tastes and habits, he could more effectually serve both God and his country by spending the summer as a colporter, than by entering the army at that time. He also urged, that after spending the summer in that way, he might then, in eight months more, complete his course in the seminary, obtain license to preach, and enter the army as a chaplain. A commission had already been sent to him from the Board of Publication, at Philadelphia, inviting and empowering him to labor in their service for such time and in such a field as he might prefer. But the war had already begun, and this commission, of course, could not be accepted. There was a good supply of books, however, in the depository at Lexington, and he was urged to use these in the service of the committee of Lexington Presbytery. But, having listened to his father, as he always did, with the most deferential attention, he replied substantially as follows:

" ' Father, what you say has much force. But this is to be no ordinary war, and for young men like me to hold back will have a very bad moral effect. The superior numbers and resources of the North will make it necessary for every man in the South, not disabled by age or infirmity, to take part in the work of resistance. I have thought and prayed much over this question for the last two months. To be entirely candid, I observed a day of fasting and prayer at the seminary, with a view to learn what the will of the Lord is, and the result is as firm a conviction that I ought at once to take part in the defence of my native State, and especially of you and mother, as I ever felt that I ought to preach the Gospel.' His appearance, manner and thoughts impressed the memory and heart of his father in a way never to be forgotten, and under the impression thus made, he said: ' Go, my son, and the blessing of God go with you.' And although he fell, the blessing of God did go with him.

" The students of Washington College had formed themselves into a volunteer company, with the title of the Liberty Hall Volunteers, and chosen their professor of Greek, James J. White, their captain. Hugh at once enrolled himself as a private in the ranks of this company, under the command of his eldest brother, whom he had always loved and reverenced, almost as he did his father. This company was composed almost exclusively of those then connected with the college, or who were recent graduates of the college. It consisted of seventy-two in the aggregate, more than half of whom were professors of religion, and about one-fourth of whom were candidates for the ministry. It embraced an amount of intellectual and moral worth rarely equalled in any military company. On the morning of the 8th of June, 1861, they were formed in front of the Court House in Lexington. The Court House square, the main street, the windows of the houses, were crowded with the citizens of the town and of the surrounding country. They were well drilled, handsomely equipped, and made a very imposing appearance. A beautiful Confederate flag, wrought by the hands of the ladies of Falling Spring congregation, was presented in very appropriate terms by the Rev. John Miller, and received in a few pertinent words by Captain White. A brief address was then made to them, and prayer offered for them and their invaded State, by the father of the captain; after which the command was given, and with solemn step they marched away amidst the sighs and tears of the whole community. A large number in carriages, on horseback, and on foot, followed in their rear to the river, a mile below the town; then returning entered the Presbyterian Church, where prayer and praise were offered to the God of grace, who is also the God of battles.

"In the first battle of Manassas, such was the gallantry displayed by this company, that they won from General Jackson the designation of 'more than brave young men.' Twelve of them have fallen in battle. Seven have died of disease contracted in camp. Fourteen have been wounded in action. They have been in thirteen pitched battles, and many combats, in a period of eighteen months; and on no occasion have they failed to evince a high order of courage. From the casualties of battle and disease they are now commanded by their fourth captain.

"As they awaited orders at Staunton, Hugh wrote to his father:

"'Some hearts, it may be, are now swelling with the desire for military distinction, and some heads becoming dizzy with anticipations of earthly glory. But I confess I am either too cowardly or too stupid to belong to either class. They may win the laurels, provided only that our cause triumphs.'

"Under date of June 24, he wrote from Manasses:

"'Yesterday we heard two sermons and attended a prayer-meeting. This gave the appearance, at least, of holiness to the day, but still, if you had looked into our camp you would have thought it the busiest day of the week. Some were cooking, others cutting wood, and others pitching their tents. It is painful but necessary to spend the Sabbath in this way. Our religious privations are what we feel most keenly. We seek to remedy this by a brief prayer-meeting held every night after roll-call. Nearly all the members of our company attend with becoming seriousness. May the trials of our country work in it a great moral reformation. If so, we may hope for true and lasting prosperity when peace shall again come. If not, God will overturn in the future as He is doing now. May He speedily redeem our world from sin and ruin.'

"In his letters describing the battle of Manasses, July 21, 1861, he said:

"'It was an awful Sabbath. How often I longed to be with you, enjoying the privileges of the Sabbath. Even one hour would have been delightful. But God ordered otherwise. We are all in His hands. He casts down and He keeps alive. May He speedily crown our cause with complete success! If it please Him, may I again see my father and mother in peace, and spend my life in preaching His Gospel. The scenes in which I am now engaged are very sad; yet the taste of victory, though bought by precious blood, is sweet. But to preach would be far better.'

.   .   .   .

"'Brother James and I heartily unite with you in praising the Grace which has spared our lives in this bloody battle. He and I joined in the pursuit beyond the Stone Bridge. We saw the enemy as they passed through the woods a mile ahead of us, and we returned to attend to our wounded and dead. Night soon closed the scene. The next day we buried our dead. It rained the whole day, and that night we sat up around our fires. Brother James had religious service over their graves.

"'It is a great victory; but may I never pass through such a scene again. Death and hell may rejoice on the battle-field, but let man be silent. May God, who has won this victory for us, now give us peace. My best love to sister, Willie and the children.   Your affectionate brother,

                                        ' HUGH.'

"Writing from Centreville to his mother, he says: 'How much I would give to be permitted to spend the Sabbath day in Lexington. We have no house of worship here, and are thus deprived of the delights of the sanctuary. One day of sacred rest, like hundreds which have passed away, uncared for and unimproved, would be at this time a feast of fat things to my soul. We are almost entirely cut off here from the reviving influences of social worship. A prayer-meeting every night is in part a substitute. Mother, in your anxiety for my bodily comfort and welfare, I hope you will not forget my soul. The atmosphere surrounding that is as cold as that which surrounds my body. How much I wish that the power of Divine grace was more at work within me. But though cast down, I will not despair, but still trust in God.'

"Of the death of a fellow-soldier, another of the ' more than brave' Liberty Hall Volunteers—a native and resident of Rock- bridge, he says: ' You have doubtless heard before this of the death of another of our company; I refer to W. J. Thompson. His body, I suppose, passed through Lexington this morning, to reach his widowed mother to-day. He was cut down almost in a day. No one here was aware of his danger until the night before he was taken to the Junction. The next news from him told us of his death. He died of typhoid fever, rendered more incurable by some disease of the stomach. He was a professing Christian, honoring the name by a character which was above reproach, and by a conduct which evinced the sincerity of his profession. He was delirious much of the time after he became ill, but was permitted to enjoy an hour or two of consciousness a short time before he died. These hours he spent in making some necessary arrangements of a secular nature, and in reading his Bible, accompanied by audible prayer. We have therefore good grounds to hope that he has entered his home in heaven, though his remains may now cast sorrow over his home on earth. He is the tenth of our company who has fallen. Surely the hand of the Lord is heavy upon us. But how little apparent good results. I greatly fear that, as His chastisements have not softened our hearts and thus been made a savor of life unto life, they will prove a savor of death unto death, in hardening them, and thus rendering us vessels of wrath fitted for destruction. How shall we remedy this? How shall we avert God's anger, which seems daily to gather strength? Oh that all hearts would turn unto the Lord, and by penitence and faith seek the only refuge from His wrath. "Turn Thou us, O Lord, and we shall be turned." This must be our prayer, for God alone can help us. Father, you urge me to seek to be useful. Would it be proper for me to conduct religious services whenever an opportunity offers? And should I connect the other parts of the service with a short address? If you approve of this, I will seek such opportunities.'

"In March, 1862, he writes:

"'Let me hear how the seminary prospers. I cannot be there, but still I am anxious to hear how many are there. The war has put a great barrier across my path, but one which cannot be avoided. It must be crossed. If I get through safely, I shall enter upon the work of the ministry with unspeakable delight. I long to spend my life in the work of saving souls; and to be kept back now, when just on the verge of commencing my work, is like being kept from home when it is just in sight. But I may do more good here than in the ministry. I bear my delay therefore with patience.

"'Your letter was a treat to me. The expressions of affection, and the accompanying prayers for me, are grateful to the heart. You expect us to move forward very soon, either to another great battle on our own soil, or to invade that of our enemies. Of course, I cannot tell what a day may bring forth, but I see no reason to expect a great battle so soon. I am ready, I hope, for anything. I do not feel like turning my face homeward, however, until all at home are relieved from fear of the enemy. I wish to return to enjoy with you the pleasures of home in peace, and not to share the anxieties which now distress you. Let us only bear up with Christian firmness, and fight with courage, trusting in God, and we may hope for a speedy close to the war.

"'Thank T—— for the prayer with which he closes his letter to me. Oh! if he were a Christian, how much more willing I should be to die!

"'Mrs. General Jackson arrived yesterday. She came to headquarters just as Bishop Johns was about to begin evening worship. Her arrival occasioned some excitement. She looks very well. I had the pleasure of speaking to her after the service had ended. Her face, as always, seemed like sunshine.

"'Bishop Johns preached for us two very good sermons. They were simple, earnest, faithful proposals of Christ to his hearers. I enjoyed them both very much, and hope they did good to all.

"'Much love to one and all, but especially to you, my devoted mother. From your son,

"'HUGH.'

"On his election to the captaincy of his company he wrote to his father as follows:

"'The result surprised me greatly. I had hoped for nothing higher than the lieutenancy, and was not confident of that. But the question was decided in my favor, and with much fear I accept the position. I do not expect any increase of happiness, but an increase of responsibility, leading to much perplexity and toil. The care, the kindness, the ceaseless effort called for, will greatly increase my need of help from the grace of God. To this source I look, praying that by example and by effort the men may become good soldiers and good Christians. I ask that all at home will pray that I may be fitted for the position I now hold.'

"On the same subject he writes to his brother Henry:

"'Promotion in itself brings neither peace nor happiness, and unless it increases one's usefulness it is a curse. An opportunity is now afforded for exerting a wider influence for good, and if enabled to improve this aright I shall then be happier than before. My life is now given to the army, and will be spent in it, even to the end of the war. But if my life is spared to see the end, and we are successful in our struggle, it will be the delight of my heart to spend the remainder of it in the work of the ministry. I am not fond of the army. Indeed many things in it are hateful to me; but nothing is so much so as the invader of my native soil.'

"To a sister he writes:

"'Our life at present is so much better than it has been for several months that we are having a delightful time. It is true the sky is our roof and the earth our bed, but then it don't rain, and we are not marching; and when a box comes in from home, we live and feel like princes. I am sorry that father could not visit us, but hope he will still do so. He will feel quite at home at General Jackson's head-quarters with the general and Dr. Dabney. The latter is very busy, but preaches whenever he has an opportunity. I heard him last Saturday, then twice on the Sabbath, when about two hundred soldiers received the sacrament of the Lord's Supper at his hands. This was a spiritual feast indeed. The religious element in our company is very strong; sufficient, I hope, to control all other elements and give tone to the whole body. We hold a brief meeting every night, just after roll-call. The man whose turn it is stands up, while the rest stand around him. He reads a chapter, sometimes sings a hymn, then leads in prayer. There is some profanity, but this is lessening. Why should not the army be a school for the reformation of the wicked? Such it has proved to J. W. and J. R. They are now perfectly sober men and good soldiers. I am much gratified at the accounts I receive of your prayer-meetings held in our behalf. The prayers of those at home greatly strengthen and encourage us in the army. I will endeavor to remember you all at your hours of prayer. Yet we are so drawn about from one place and employment to another that I have scarcely a moment for connected, sober thought.'

" To a brother in the pastorate he writes:

"'Rest satisfied therefore that duty bids you stay at home; mine is to remain in the army, and I am willing to do it for the glorious cause in which our young Confederacy is engaged. If we give up, everything is lost. If we struggle on, endure hardships, exert our utmost strength, and put our trust in God, who has so far been very gracious to us, we may hope after awhile to taste the most blessed fruits from these present distresses.

"'My chief source of sorrow is, that I can do so little, or rather that I do so little for the cause of my Saviour. Father seems to think the army a glorious field for usefulness. To him, doubtless, it would be. But what have I done? I hope my influence for good has been felt in our own company—but to how little extent! I can only look to God to give me the heart to work, and then open up paths of usefulness for me. If I really wish to do good in the world, it must become a subject of constant study, followed by ceaseless effort. I am very glad to hear that you are so comfortably situated. You have nothing now to hinder you from doing much good. May God grant you this great privilege. It is a pleasing subject of thought to me, espe-cially on the Sabbath, that father, two brothers and a cousin are all preaching the gospel. I do not forget to pray for you. May I soon be permitted to join the number, and give my energies to the same good work.'

"He was ever considerate, in a remarkable degree, of his mother's comfort. One of his chief sources of anxiety at the approach of a battle was that she might be prepared for her sad share in its results. He would write to her beforehand to pre-pare her for it. On the eve of one of the most desperate of the eight battles in which he bore an active part, he wrote her a letter full of the tenderest filial love, and expressive of the strongest faith. He concludes this letter in these words: 'Mother, don't be anxious about me. I have a sweet assurance that my soul is safe; and as to my body, that is only dust.'

"And then, when the battle was over his first effort was to find time to communicate the intelligence of his safety to all at home; and a form of expression he used on such occasions was this, 'May the anxious heart of my devoted mother now be com-forted.' Truly his was the heart, and the tongue, and the life, of a devoted son.

"The mother of a young man belonging to the army called at the Lexington parsonage to inform her pastor that her son seemed much interested about his soul, and, indeed, she hoped he was a Christian and would embrace the first opportunity to connect himself with the Church; and then, weeping as she spoke, added: 'Your son Hugh has been very kind and faithful to him. As he did not belong to his company, and as he could not easily see him, he wrote to him; and soon after he went over to his camp, and asked him to walk with him. They went together into a grove, a considerable distance from the camp; and, after conversing fully with him, he proposed that they should unite in prayer; then, kneeling at the root of a tree, he prayed for the soul of my son, and now I hope he is a Christian.'"

This is but a specimen of his active work for Christ.

In the last letter he ever penned, dated "Banks of the Rappa-hanock, August 24, 1862," and addressed to his father, he said:

"This has been very little like the Sabbath. With spirits saddened by hunger and fretted by the constant roar of artillery, we have been kept in an uncomfortable frame of mind. The busy preparations for to-morrow prevent any enjoyment of the Sabbath.   However, Dr. Stiles is to preach to the brigade this afternoon, and I hope to hear him.   It requires a great struggle to keep the busy scenes around me from driving all devotion from my heart.   They ought to have a contrary effect.   I ought now more than ever to seek my strength, my happiness, my all, in God.   How could I live without Him?   With Him no storm can disturb my peace, no danger can come nigh, no harm can befall which will not do me good.

 . . . .

"I send you three hundred dollars.   Of this I wish you to appropriate one hundred dollars for T——'s outfit for the cavalry, one hundred to be held subject to my order, and one hundred as a donation to the Confederate States Bible Society and our committee for the publication of religious tracts and books.

"Give my warmest love to all at home.   You are constantly in my mind and firmly engraved upon my heart.   Write when you can to your devoted son.   "Hugh."

Leaving, for the moment, the narrative of the afflicted father, I will describe the death of Captain White and Colonel Baylor as I received and wrote it at the time from the lips of eye-witnesses.

On the night before the last day's battle at Second Manassas, Friday, August 29, 1862, Colonel W. S. H. Baylor (I ought really to call him *general*, for "Stonewall" Jackson and R. E. Lee had both recommended his promotion, and his commission had actually been made out when news of his lamented death reached Richmond), one of the most widely known and loved young men in the State, was in command of the famous old "Stonewall Brigade," which had the year before won its name and immortal fame on these historic plains.   Sending for his friend, Captain Hugh White—son of the venerable Dr. Wm. S. White, of Lexington, "Stonewall" Jackson's old pastor, and himself a theological student—who commanded one of the companies in the brigade, "Will" Baylor (as we used familiarly to call him) said to him: "I know the men are very much wearied out by the battle to-day, and that they need all of the rest they can get to fit them for the impending struggle of to-morrow.   But I cannot consent that we shall sleep to-night until we have had a brief season of prayer to thank God for the victory and preservation of the day, and to beseech His protection and blessing during the continuance of this terrible conflict." Hugh White entered at once into the proposal. Rev. A. C. Hopkins (then chaplain of the Second Virginia Infantry, now pastor of the Presbyterian Church at Charlestown, West Virginia, and one of those faithful chaplains who was always found at the post of duty, even when it was the post of hardship or of danger) was found in the bivouac near by and gladly consented to lead the meeting. The men were quietly notified that there would be a prayer-meeting at brigade headquarters as soon as they could assemble, and nearly the whole of this brigade and many from other brigades promptly gathered at the appointed spot. It was a tender, precious season of worship, there in line of battle and in full hearing of the enemy. Colonel Baylor entered into it with the burning zeal of the young convert—he had found Christ in the camp only a short time before—and Captain Hugh White, with the ripened experience of the Christian of long-standing, and many of the participants, realized, with Jacob of old, that the place was "none other than the house of God and the gate of heaven." In the great battle which followed the next day, when the Confederate line was pressing grandly forward and driving everything before it, Will Baylor, with the flag of the Thirty-third Virginia in his hands and the shout of victory on his lips, fell in the very forefront of the battle and gave his brave, noble, young life to the land and cause he loved so well and served so faithfully.

As the flag fell from the nerveless grasp of Baylor, Captain Hugh White sprang forward, caught the falling colors, waved them in the view of the veterans of the old "Stonewall Brigade," and rushing to the front called on them to follow him to victory. The smoke of battle soon concealed the young hero from his comrades, but when the line swept irresistably forward to drive the enemy before them and add "Second Manassas" to the long series of Confederate victories, it was found that Hugh White, too, had been killed, and those two young men who mingled so lovingly in the prayer-meeting of the night before had entered through the pearly gates, were walking the golden streets, and were wearing fadeless crowns of victory.

Mrs. Margaret J. Preston (whose graceful verse has adorned so many bright pages of Southern literature, and who has sung so tenderly from the depths of a full heart concerning the heroes of the Confederacy) thus wrote to Captain White's afflicted mother:

"May the tender Jesus, who said 'Weep not' to His own mother in the extremity of her sufferings, say the same to you, dear friend. What need have we to look away from the surroundings of our dear ones' deaths, to forget the battle and the blood, and all the awful circumstances through which they passed into the pure presence of God. Think of it—the exchange of the boom of cannon for 'the harpers, harping with their harps' —the shrieks of furious enemies for the hallelujahs of angels— the fierce onset for the 'Come, ye blessed of my Father'—the madness of war for the boundless peace of heaven! These were the exchanges your precious boy made when he breathed out his life into the hands of his Saviour. For himself he felt nothing but a holy joy, as our Willie* did, and if he turned his thoughts to the anguish of his father and mother at his loss, it must have been with the triumphant assurance that the trust in Jesus which they had taught him, and *which was strong enough for him to die by, was also strong enough for them to live by.*

"You are an honored mother to have reared such a son for immortality. He did not need long years to fit him for a life with God, and if he has gotten home the soonest, without the toilsome march, you will not think *that* cause of sorrow, dear friend. If he could lean from the heavenly heights to-day, would he not say something like this: 'Precious mother, there is no need of tears for me. I had all the happiness earth can give. I had a sweet, beautiful life with you all, and without the trial of any grief am translated now to the full possession of the bliss of God's redeemed. Rejoice in my joy.'

"* Wm. C. Preston, son of Colonel J. T. L. Preston, of Lexington, Virginia, who fell in the same battle.

"The following extract is taken from a sketch of his life and death, published in the *Central Presbyterian :*

"'"Don't distress yourselves about me, boys; I am not afraid to die," he said to his comrades, as they pressed anxiously around him. There spoke the considerate friend—the chivalrous young soldier—the fearless Christian. Of the few remaining hours of his life little is known. Thus much we are permitted to know. His beloved captain, Hugh A. White, was with him on the morning preceding his death. Turning to the surgeon, Willie asked if it was possible for him to survive; he received a negative answer. "Could you get a letter to my father?" he asked of Captain White. Upon being reminded of the difficulty, he acquiesced and said: "Then I will deliver my messages to you." These undelivered messages are forever sealed up in the bosom of the noble young leader, who fell, instantly killed, a few hours later.'

"Thus let the names of these martyrs in the cause of their country go down to posterity together."

" His dear father and you have my tears and prayers. What have I else to give ?

"Yours in like faith and sufferings,

"M. J. P."

" From a large number of letters written to his family and friends, it is deemed advisable to insert extracts from only three. All these relate chiefly to the time and manner of his death. As to the slight discrepancy which appears in two of these accounts of the posture in which he was found, it is sufficient to remark, that one saw him before and the other after he had been turned from the posture in which he fell.

" The first of these extracts is from a letter of General Thomas J. Jackson to Rev. Dr. Dabney. The general says:

" ' In the second battle of Manassas I lost more than one personal friend. Among the number was Captain Hugh A. White. We were members of the same church, and had been co-laborers in the same Sabbath-school. His Christian labors were not confined to times of peace. In the army he adorned the doctrine of Christ his Saviour. When Testaments or other religious works were to be distributed, I found him ready for the work. Though his loss must be mourned, yet it is gratifying to know that he has left us a bright example, and that he fell, sword in hand, gallantly cheering on his men, and leading them to victory in repelling the last attack of the enemy upon that bloody field.

" 'Very truly, your friend,

" ' T. J. JACKSON.'

" The following extract is from a letter to his brother from one who served with him as first lieutenant, and who succeeded him as captain, and who was wounded on the previous day:

" ' *Dear Sir :* I have endeavored to procure all the particulars of your brother's fall, but have only partially succeeded. Many saw him just previous to his death, and several very soon afterward, but I can find no one who saw him in the interval between the time when he was struck and when he expired, if there was any. The reason seems to be this : Immediately before he was shot the brigade had been ordered to charge, but had not proceeded far before it was thrown into considerable confusion, partly by obstructions in the line of march, but principally by the fierce resistance of the enemy; and it was just at this juncture, when companies were separated from their regiments, and officers from their companies, that your brother, eager to meet the foe, and undismayed by the circumstances which had produced a temporary confusion in his regiment, having advanced far to the front, with his sword in one hand and his hat in the other, calling on his men to follow him, *fell* unobserved near the spot already hallowed by the blood of the gallant Colonel Baylor. Before his fall, and probably at the moment the fatal missile entered his noble bosom, he was bearing the standard with which Colonel Baylor fell while leading the brigade to the charge.

" ' But although, on account of the confusion, his death was unobserved, his presence was soon missed and a member of his company, fearing he had been injured, proceeded to look for him, and soon found his body. He was lying on his face, resting it in his hands, and his pistol and his unsheathed sword lay by his side.

" ' He was afterwards " buried on the field " by a few of his little band, assisted by some friends from other companies.

" ' Thus fell our beloved captain, mourned not only by the company that had followed him so long, but by every soldier who knew him. We loved him not only as a soldier, but also and especially as a Christian gentleman. As a soldier and officer he was a model; to his company he was exceedingly kind, but his kindness never assumed the form of partiality. He was just. In the camp he devoted himself exclusively to the promotion of its interests, temporal and eternal. In action he was perfectly fearless, yet his courage was controlled by a sound discretion. On such occasions he was possessed with a peculiar enthusiasm—an unconquerable zeal and determination to meet the foe—and consequently he was always seen among those gallant spirits who go farthest in the direction of the foe. His command never was " *go on*," but always " come on."

" 'As a Christian gentleman he was also a model. Such earnestness of disposition—such nobility of soul—such sublimity of purpose—such humility—such devotion to Christ's cause; not inducing noisy demonstrations, but those quiet, irresistible movements, which are like the silent flow of deep streams.

How rare are such characters! I have never known one as young as he so faultless. His piety was active—a real living principle, whose movements and influences were seen and felt, not only by his fellow-Christians, but also by all who came in contact with him. His efforts to secure the salvation of his company were unceasing, and to compass this end he was much in prayer, and abounded in good works. As often as circumstances permitted, he distributed religious reading—tracts, newspapers, memoirs, etc.—among his company and sometimes in the regiment. It was also his custom, as occasion offered, to assemble his company nightly before the door of his tent for religious services.

"'We deeply mourn his loss, and feel that his place can never be filled. But,

"Though lost to sight, to memory ever dear."

"'It gives me unspeakable pleasure thus to bear testimony to the inestimable worth of your noble brother.

"'Your friend,
"'*G. B. S.'

"The last extract is from a letter to Rev. Dr. Brown, of Richmond, from one who, at the time, belonged to the Rockbridge Artillery, but who was soon after promoted to a place on General Jackson's staff. Dr. Brown published this extract in the *Central Presbyterian*. The writer says:

"'The "Stonewall Brigade" received the attack well; was flanked by a strong body of the enemy, fell back a few rods, changed front and, again advancing, drove the enemy with great slaughter from the field and the cover which they sought. The result to our dear old brigade was fearful. Colonel Baylor, commanding, was mortally wounded, and O! how sad I am to tell you, that our dear friend, Captain Hugh A. White, of Lexington, the noblest of soldiers, fell pierced through his body, when in advance of the brigade, with hat and sword in hand, calling to his men, "come on, come on." I have seen no one myself who saw him fall. Just after this success of our brigade we advanced with our battery to cover their advancing columns. The ground was strewn around with the gallant, dearly loved

---

* Now Rev. Dr. Geo. B. Strickler, of Atlanta, Georgia.

veterans of our old " Stonewall Brigade." Beyond was the long
line of blue-coated hirelings, who paid for their crime with their
life's blood.

" ' I stood leaning against my gun, waiting for orders and
watching the tide of battle as it steadily receded from me. Soon
one of the Liberty Hall Volunteers came up, and, with tears
rolling down his cheeks, told us his brave captain was lying
there in front of us.

" ' I ran forward, and there, *too true*, was my best, my noblest
friend, with his sweet, lovely face upturned, his eyes gazing upon
that world where his spirit had gone, and his body in its last,
long sleep.

" ' His sword had been already taken away. I found and
took off his Bible and several letters. It was indeed heart-
rending as we gathered around. Dear, *dear* Hugh, the purest,
the truest, the best of us all. May we of his companions who
are spared live to love and serve our God more and better, and
die to meet him in our home above. What a blessed ministry
did we anticipate in his! How full of the promise of usefulness were his amiable, attractive qualities, his accurate and increasing attainments, and his quiet, yet earnest, active piety.
But I must say no more, though of this subject my heart and
head are full. Our victory is great. Again let us turn to God
—may His goodness lead us to new repentance and obedience.

" ' * J. P. S.'

" God was good in giving this son, good in making him
what he was, and no less good in taking him away, just when
and as He did. The belief is sincerely entertained that neither
vanity nor ostentation prompts to this effort to perpetuate his
memory. But as it was the ruling desire of his heart to make
this bad world better, and as the bitterest grief of his parents on
account of his early death flows from the consideration that he
did not accomplish this by living, this effort is made so to perpetuate his existence on earth that, being dead, he may yet
speak. Well may the old ask, why are we feeble, withered,
fruitless branches spared, and they, so young, so fresh, so fruitful, taken away? God's ways are not our ways, neither are His
thoughts ours. He may enable a youth like this, who dies at

---

* Now Rev. James P. Smith, of Fredericksburg, Virginia.

twenty-two, to accomplish far more for man's good and His own glory than they who live to threescore and ten years.

"The young are not likely to find a more striking illustration of the truth, that 'the ways of wisdom are ways of pleasantness, and all her paths are peace,' than his life furnishes. He was habitually cheerful and happy. Seeking to enjoy everything in God, he enjoyed God in everything, and thus even the vicissitudes of life ministered to his comfort. His life was beautiful, and his death safe, honorable and useful."

It is no exaggeration to say that volumes could be filled with sketches of other officers and men, worthy to take their places beside those given above; but these must suffice.

Rev. Dr. J. A. Broadus, while preaching in the army, thus wrote, in the *Religious Herald*, on the "Influence of Officers:"

"I recently became acquainted, in the Army of Northern Virginia, with Brigadier-General ——, from one of the Gulf States, who is a Baptist, and a very interesting man. He is said to be an admirable officer, having taken charge of a brigade which had been in very bad condition, and made it one of the finest in the army, and having gained, by his skilful and gallant leadership in the field, the entire confidence and warm affection of his command. He struck me at once by his pleasing address, and his cordial greeting to a Christian brother. He would listen, with a glowing countenance and not without tears, to the more affecting truths of the Gospel, and in all our intercourse seemed to me an unusually zealous, devout and humble Christian. I hear that he is always ready to pray and exhort in the prayer-meetings. His conversation showed an absorbing anxiety for the spiritual welfare of his men. And in mentioning incidentally an occasion on which he had tried to gather them into a special meeting for prayer, and the good results, he spoke with humble gratitude of the joy with which he found it possible to exert a marked religious influence over his officers and men. May God bless him in all his efforts to do good.

"Every civilian who goes into the army will be struck with the wonderful influence possessed by the officers. Everything is arranged so as to give them authority and secure them respect—a thing necessary to the efficiency and the very existence of an army. And you very soon feel the effect upon

10

yourself. You did not care any more for officers than privates—
not you. But stay in camp awhile, and you catch the feeling.
You will go with a friend who is introducing you—will perhaps
see a rather indifferent-looking youngster, eating his dinner, and
care very little for him; but when he looks up and you see three
stars on his collar, and your friend says, 'Colonel ——,' you
take off your hat.

"And let any officer, from the highest to the lowest, be a
decidedly religious or a decidedly irreligious man, and the influence diffuses itself throughout his entire command. These men
sought distinction, and delight in authority. Alas! many of
them little think of the weighty responsibilities which always
pertain to any position of influence. They cannot divest themselves of this responsibility, not merely to the nation for the
military efficiency of their command, but to God for the religious
influence exerted upon these their fellow-men. Of course, no
one wants them to do anything officially to constrain the men
into anything like religion. But their example, and their
ways of talking, produce an effect that is positively astonishing.

"Have you a friend who is an officer? Urge him not to
neglect the solemn responsibility of his position. If he is a
Christian, let him try to be such a specimen of the Christian
officer as the general above described, and he may do incalculable good. If still unconverted, ask if he has a right not only to
slight his own soul, but by his example and influence to be
ruining the souls of others.

"Are you an officer yourself? Has Providence placed you as
a leader to your fellow-men, and shall you lead them to perdi-
tion? Parents ought to become Christians for the sake of their
children, besides personal considerations; and so ought officers
to become Christians for the sake of their men.

" J. A. B.

" Orange Court House."

A correspondent of another paper writes:
" The brigade, the regiment, or the company, which has
enjoyed the influence of a real Christian commander, stands out
in bold and bright relief. I have seen enough of this to make
every Christian proud, yes, boastfully, most joyfully proud, of his
blessed, his wonder-working religion. I have seen companies,
composed of the same material, encamped very near each other,

yet steadily travelling different roads, and constantly developing the most contrary characteristics. In one you would see gambling, drinking, disorder and discontent; in the other everything would go on very much as in any well-regulated Christian household, In other words, I was never so well satisfied as I am now, that the religion of Christ is essential to the existence— not to say the efficiency—of a *volunteer* army. It *may be* that in the regular army, where the common soldier is hardly better than a brute—a mere machine—men may be trained to the arts of war, and may become most efficient soldiers without the restraints of religion; but, in an army like ours, I believe that religion is absolutely indispensable in order to make it fit to accomplish the mighty results dependent on its efforts."

The following incident well illustrates the influence of Christian officers:

"When General Havelock, as colonel of his regiment, was travelling through India, he always took with him a Bethel tent, in which he preached the Gospel; and when Sunday came in India he hoisted the Bethel flag, and invited all men to come and hear the Gospel; in fact, he even baptized some. He was reported for this at head-quarters, for acting in a non-military and disorderly manner; and the commander-in-chief, General Lord Gough, entertained the charge, but, with the true spirit of a generous military man, he caused the state of Colonel Havelock's regiment to be examined. He caused the reports of the moral state of the various regiments to be read for some time back, and he found that Colonel Havelock's stood at the head of the list; there was less drunkenness, less flogging, less imprisonment in it, than in any other. When that was done, the commander-in-chief said: 'Go and tell Colonel Havelock, with my compliments, to baptize the whole army.'"

Thank God that we had in the Confederate armies so many Christian officers—men worthy to take their places beside Havelock, Colonel Gardiner, Captain Headley Vickars, General George H. Gordon, and all of the Christian soldiers of history, and to exhibit the power of the Gospel in making men truer patriots, braver soldiers, and more influential leaders of their fellows.

CHAPTER V.

THE world's history has never presented a wider field of usefulness to the humble colporter who tries to do his duty than the camps and hospitals of the Confederate armies, and rarely have Christian workers more fully improved their golden opportunities.

When the war broke out, nearly all of the great publishing houses were located at the North, our people generally did their Bible and tract work in connection with societies whose headquarters were in Northern cities, and our facilities for publishing were very scant. The great societies at the North generally declared Bibles and Testaments "contraband of war," and we had at once to face the problem of securing supplies through the blockade, or manufacturing them with our poor facilities.

The first Confederate Bible printed, so far as I can ascertain, was from the presses of the South-western Publishing House, at Nashville, 1861. A copy of this edition was sent to President Davis, who replied: "The Bible is a beautiful specimen of Southern workmanship, and if I live to be inaugurated the first President of the Confederacy, on the 22d of February, my lips shall press the sacred volume which your kindness has bestowed upon me."

The British and Foreign Bible Society gave to the Confederate Bible Society unlimited credit in the purchase of supplies, and made liberal donations of Bibles and Testaments for our soldiers, as the following statement of Dr. Bennett will show:

"Finding that for the main supply they must rely on importations from abroad, the Confederate Bible Society directed its corresponding secretary, Rev. Dr. E. H. Myers, to communicate with the British and Foreign Bible Society, with the view of securing such occasional supplies as might be lucky enough to escape the dangers of the blockade and reach our ports.

"Dr. Myers, after detailing the operations of the society, said:

(148)

'The proposition is simply that we be allowed a credit with your society for the Scriptures we need—say to the value of £1,000—until such time as sterling exchange is reduced to about its usual cost—we paying *interest* on our purchase until the debt is liquidated.'

"To this letter the following noble response was sent, granting the society three times the amount they asked, free of interest:

"'LONDON, 10 Earl Street, Blackfriars, October 10, 1862.
"'THE REV. DR. MYERS:

"'*Dear Sir:* I beg leave to acknowledge the receipt of your letter of the 19th of August, which did not, however, reach us until the 3d of this month. The request which it contains was immediately submitted to our committee for their consideration and decision, and I have much pleasure in informing you that it was unanimously agreed that your request should be complied with, and that the Scriptures should be sent as directed, to Messrs. Fraser, Trenholm & Co. The only portion of your letter to which the committee demurred was that in which you proposed that interest should be paid upon the debt until it was liquidated. We could not, for a moment, entertain such a proposition. We are only too thankful that God has in his Providence put in our hands the means of supplying your wants. Into the political question which now agitates the States of America it is not our province to enter. We hear of multitudes wounded and bleeding, and we cannot pass by on the other side, when it is in our power to do something towards stauching the wounds and to pour into them some few drops of the Balm of Gilead. May He who sitteth above the water-floods speedily command peace, and as Jesus in the days of His flesh trod the boisterous waves of the Sea of Galilee into stillness, so may He walk upon the rough waters of political strife and fierce contention, which now desolate your country, with such majesty and mercy that immediately there may be a great calm.

"'You will, then, understand, my dear sir, that a credit has been granted by our society to the Bible Society of the Confederate States to the amount of £3,000, free of interest, and that the books will be forwarded as directed to Messrs. Fraser, Trenholm & Co. The first order, which has already reached us, will be executed with as little delay as possible. It will be gratifying to our committee to receive any account of the work of God within the district which your society embraces with which you may be pleased to favor us.

" ' I am, my dear sir, yours very sincerely,

" ' CHARLES JACKSON, Secretary.'

" This venerable institution gave another illustration of the principles on which it is founded by granting to Rev. Dr. M. D. Hoge, of Virginia, who went abroad during the war to procure religious reading-matter for our soldiers, 10,000 Bibles, 50,000 New Testaments, and 250,000 portions of the Scriptures, ' mainly for distribution among the soldiers of the Confederate army.'

" With the portion of these grants that passed in to us through the blockade, the New Testaments printed within our limits, and, we are happy to say, several donations from the American Bible Society—one of 20,000 Testaments to the Baptist Sunday-school Board, and others through the Bible Society of the city of Memphis—our camps were kept partially supplied with the Divine word. We say partially, for often the distribution would be limited to a single copy of the Bible or Testament for a mess of five or six men."

The visit of Rev. Dr. Moses D. Hoge, of Richmond, to England was not only very useful in securing the large donations of Bibles and Testaments noted above, but his eloquent statement of the religious work in the Confederate armies, in which he was so able and efficient a helper, elicited the sympathies and prayers of many Christians in Great Britain.

He brought over also many very valuable books and tracts, some of which were republished for use in our armies.

One of my most cherished mementos of the war is a portable Bible, commentary and concordance, which were brought over by Dr. Hoge, and copies of which were presented to many of the chaplains by that accomplished Christian woman and noble worker, Mrs. E. H. Brown (of the *Central Presbyterian*), who was appropriately called "The chaplains' friend," and whose untiring labors in the hospitals won her the warm love of the soldiers, and doubtless many "stars" in the "crown of rejoicing" she now wears.

Unfortunately, however, only a part of the Bibles and other supplies secured by Dr. Hoge succeeded in "running the blockade," and many copies of God's word intended for our suffering soldiers were captured and scattered through the North as "souvenirs."

I must not forget to say that the "American Bible Society" made liberal donations of their publications, and did it with a Christian courtesy and charity which arose above the passions of the hour, and which our Southern people should gratefully remember, even if they had not continued, after the war, to make grants, amounting to considerably over $100,000, to circulate God's word among the needy of our Southern land.

I find this item in a file of the *Religious Herald* for 1864:

"On an application by Rev. Levi Thorne, of North Carolina, approved by Governor Vance, 100,000 Bibles and Testaments, principally for North Carolina troops in the Confederate service, were granted by the American Bible Society, New York, at its meeting in December. For the South-west 50,000 were granted at the same time."

If other societies at the North made any such donations, I am not aware of it, and should be glad to be informed that I may give them due credit.

But with all the copies we could import or print, there was a great scarcity of Bibles and Testaments, and we appealed through the papers for extra copies that might be in the homes of the people or in the Sunday-schools. Some of the responses to these appeals were very touching.

One lady wrote: "This Bible was the property of my dear son H——, who died three years ago; it was given him by his only sister, about the time he was taken sick. For this reason I have kept it back, but seeing the earnest request in the papers, and as I can no longer read its sacred pages, after dropping a tear at parting with it, I send it for the use of the soldiers. I had given away long since all I could find about the house, and now send you this, hoping that, with God's blessing, it may save some soul."

In response to one of my appeals, I received from Miss Chapin, his aunt, the pocket-Bible which E. Garland Sydnor (son of our honored brother, Rev. Dr. T. W. Sydnor) carried in his pocket when he gave his noble young life to "the land he loved." It was stained with the blood of the patriot-soldier, and his aunt wrote that while she prized it above all price, she could not withhold it from some poor soldier who needed it, and sent it bedewed with her tears and carrying with it her prayers. I wrote on a fly-leaf a statement of these circumstances, and requested its return to me if it should survive the war. I carried it for a noble fellow in Wright's Georgia Brigade, who had recently found Christ in the camp, and to whom I had promised a Bible, but found that he had been killed on the skirmish-line that morning, and had gone to study God's truth with clearer vision and in the clearer light of heaven.

I gave it to another, and ten days after his messmate brought me back the Bible, saying that his comrade had fallen in the forefront of the battle, and had died in the hospital in the full assurance of the Christian faith, and with warm expressions concerning the comfort and joy which that Bible had given him. I then gave it to my old university friend and brother, Edwin Bowie, of Westmoreland county, who was badly wounded, but survived the war, and only last year the book, around which so many hallowed associations and precious memories cluster, was returned to Dr. Sydnor.

Garland Sydnor was a cousin of Captain Hugh A. White, whose death has been described in the previous chapter, and there are some interesting coincidences in their lives, and the circumstances attending their death, which seem worthy of record :

1. They were near the same age—Hugh born in September, 1840, and Garland in March, 1843.

2. They were sons of ministers of the Gospel.

3. Like Timothy, they knew the Scriptures from childhood, each having been taught by a pious mother and a pious grandmother.

4. Each made a public profession of religion when about fifteen years of age.

5. Each decided shortly after his conversion to devote himself to the ministry, and had entered upon a course of study preparatory to that great work—Hugh at Union Theological Seminary, and Garland at Columbian College.

6. Their studies were interrupted by the war, and each returned to his home and volunteered as a soldier in the Confederate army.

7. They proved themselves brave and patriotic soldiers, and through all their military career maintained an elevated and consistent Christian character.

8. Both lost their lives in battle—Hugh in the second battle

of Manassas, and Garland just two weeks after, in the battle of Sharpsburg.

9. Each was slain while bearing aloft the flag of his regiment.

Reared in different parts of the State, these young men were never brought together except on the field of battle, and had no personal acquaintance with each other. They were taught to know and to love each other by their fathers, who were very intimate. " Their hopes, their fears, their aims were one." " Lovely and pleasant in their lives, in their death they were not divided."

As showing the desire of the men to procure Bibles, and the expedients to which we resorted to supply them, I give the following clippings from the newspapers of the day:

March 17, 1864.

" Last summer," says a letter in a Southern Baptist paper, " a chaplain arrived in Staunton with several large packages of Testaments and tracts, which he was anxious to get to Winchester, but had despaired of doing so as he had to walk, when a party of several soldiers volunteered to lug them the whole distance—ninety-two miles—so anxious were they that their comrades should have the precious messengers of salvation."

Rev. B. T. Lacy, in the *Central Presbyterian*, says : " The New Testament is the most popular book, the Scriptures of Divine truth the most acceptable reading, in our army."

Rev. W. R. Gaultney writes to the *Biblical Recorder*, that, during the battle at Fredericksburg, he saw a large number of soldiers reading their Testaments with the deepest interest, while lying in the entrenchments awaiting orders. He witnesses the same every day in camp.

" We were present not long since," says the *Soldier's Visitor*, " when a chaplain, at the close of a public service, announced that he had a prospect of being able to get a supply of Testaments for the portion of the men still destitute, and that those who wished a copy could give him their names after the benediction was pronounced. Scarcely had the ' Amen ' died on the minis-ter's lips before the war-worn heroes charged on the chaplain almost as furiously as if storming the enemy's breastworks."

Another narrates the following: "As some of the Confederate troops were marching through Fredericksburg, Virginia, with bristling bayonets and rumbling artillery, a fair lady appeared

---

on the steps of a dark brown mansion, her arms filled with Testaments, which with gracious kindness and gentle courtesy she distributed to the passing soldiers. The eagerness with which they were received, the pressing throng, the outstretched hands, the earnest thanks, the unspoken blessings upon the giver, thus dispensing the word of life to the armed multitude, to whom death might come at any moment, all made up a picture as beautiful as any that ever shone out amid the dark scenes of war. As a rough Texan said, ' If it was not for the ladies, God bless them, there would be no use of fighting this war.' "

During a skirmish some of our men were ordered to the front as sharp-shooters, and directed to lie on the ground and load and fire as rapidly as possible. After a short time the ammunition of one of these men was expended, and though his position was very dangerous as it was, it would have been certain death to procure a fresh supply. " In this condition," says an eye-witness, " this soldier drew from his pocket his Bible, and while the balls were whizzing about him and cutting the grass at his side, quietly read its precious pages for a few minutes, and then closed his eyes as if engaged in prayer."

CAMP NEAR PETERSBURG, November 10.

There is a general demand in the army for small Bibles. I have daily applications from soldiers so eager to get them that they frequently say they will give several months' wages for one. But the supply at all of the depositories and book-stores has long since been exhausted and there seems little prospect of a replenishment. Our brave boys must beg in vain for Bibles, unless the good people at home, who have hitherto contributed so liberally to the spiritual and temporal welfare of the army, will also come to the rescue in this matter. Almost every family might (by a little sacrifice) spare one or more small Bibles. A lady sent me the other day a Bible, owned by her nephew, a noble Christian soldier, who carried it in nine battles, and had it in his pocket when he fell at Sharpsburg. It was to her a precious relic, and yet she was willing to give it up, that its glorious light might illumine the pathway of some other soldier. I have given it to a gallant fellow, who says that he has been trying for twelve months to procure a Bible. Are there not others who will and can aid in this way ?

J. WM. JONES, Army Evangelist.

"I THANK GOD THAT I HAVE ONE ARM LEFT, AND AN
OPPORTUNITY OF USING IT FOR THE SUP-
PORT OF THOSE I LOVE."

(See page 464.)

I have an old memorandum-book filled with names of soldiers from every State of the Confederacy who had applied to me for Bibles and Testaments, and some of the scenes I witnessed in my work of Bible and tract distribution are as fresh in my memory as if they had occurred on yesterday.   I had a pair of large " saddle-bags " which I used to pack with tracts and religious newspapers, and with Bibles and Testaments when I had them, and besides this I would strap packages behind my saddle and on the pommel.   Thus equipped I would sally forth, and as I drew near the camp some one would raise the cry, " Yonder comes the Bible and tract man," and such crowds would rush out to meet me, that frequently I would sit on my horse and distribute my supply before I could even get into the camp.   But if I had Bibles or Testaments to distribute, the poor fellows would crowd around and beg for them as earnestly as if they were golden guineas for free distribution.   Yes, the word of God seemed to these brave men " more precious than gold—yea than much fine gold."   The men were accustomed to form " reading clubs," not to read the light literature of the day, but to read God's word, and not unfrequently have I seen groups of twenty-five or thirty gather around some good reader, who for several hours would read with clear voice selected portions of the Scriptures.

I have never seen more diligent Bible-readers than we had in the Army of Northern Virginia.

The efforts made by our Confederate people to supply our armies with Bibles and religious reading were worthy of all praise, and a whole volume would not suffice to give even a meagre record of the labors of the different societies formed for the purpose.

Dr. W. W. Bennett, who was himself Superintendent of the Soldiers' Tract Association, and a most efficient chaplain, has given in his " Great Revival " so admirable a summary of the work of these agencies, that I quote him, as follows :

" So important was the work of colportage in promoting religion among the soldiers, that we feel constrained to devote to it a separate chapter.   And the pious laborers in this depart-ment are eminently worthy of a place by the side of the most devoted chaplains and missionaries that toiled in the army re-vival.   Receiving but a pittance from the societies that employed them, subsisting on the coarse and scanty fare of the soldiers, often sleeping on the wet ground, following the march of the armies through cold or heat, through dust or mud, everywhere were these devoted men to be seen scattering the leaves of the Tree of Life. Among the sick, the wounded, and the dying, on the battle-fields, and in the hospitals they moved, consoling them with tender words, and pointing their drooping spirits to the hopes of the Gospel. The record of their labors is the record of the army revival; they fanned its flame and spread it on every side by their prayers, their conversations, their books, and their preaching. They went out from all the churches, and labored together in a spirit worthy of the purest days of our holy religion. The aim of them all was to turn the thoughts of the soldiers not to a sect, but to Christ, to bring them into the great spiritual temple, and to show them the wonders of salvation. If any man among us can look back with pleasure on his labors in the army, it is the Christian colporter.

" The number of religious tracts and books distributed by the colporters, chaplains, and missionaries in the army, we can never know. But as all the churches were engaged in the work of printing and circulating, it is not an overestimate to say that hundreds of millions of pages were sent out by the different societies. And, considering the facilities for printing in the South during the war, we may safely assert that never were the soldiers of a Christian nation better supplied with such reading as maketh wise unto salvation; and certainly, never amidst circumstances so unpropitious to human view, did fruits so ripe, so rich, so abundant, spring up so quickly from the labors of God's servants.

" Earliest in the important work of colportage was the Baptist Church, one of the most powerful denominations in the South. In May, 1861, at the General Association of the Baptist Churches in Virginia, vigorous measures were adopted for supplying the religious wants of the army.

" The Sunday-school and Publication Board, in their report on colportage, said : ' The presence of large armies in our State affords a fine opportunity for colportage effort among the soldiers. These are exposed to peculiar temptations, and in no way can we better aid them in resisting these than by affording them good books. To this department of our operations we ask the special, earnest attention of the General Association. Shall we enter this wide and inviting field, place good books in the hands of our soldiers, and surround them by pious influences? or shall we remain indifferent to the spiritual dangers and temptations of those who are flocking hither to defend all we hold dear ? '

" The association cordially responded, and ' recommended to the board to appoint at once, if practicable, a sufficient number of colporters to occupy all the important points of rendezvous, and promptly to reach all the soldiers in service in the State; that during the war as many colporters as could be profitably employed, and as the means of the board would admit, be kept in service; that special contributions to colportage should be raised from the Baptist Churches, from the community, and even from such persons in other of the Confederate States as may feel interested in the welfare of the soldiers who are gathered from the various Southern States to fight their common battles on the soil of Virginia; that steps should be taken to secure the issue of a tract or tracts specially adapted to general circulation among the soldiers.'

" The work was put in charge of Rev. A. E. Dickinson, who had already acquired a valuable experience and a high reputation as the Superintendent of Colportage under the direction of the General Association. He sent forth his well-trained band of colporters into this new field, which they cultivated with the happiest results, and with a zeal and self-denial worthy of the cause of Christ.

" One year after these labors were commenced, Mr. Dickinson said, in his annual report:

" ' We have collected $24,000, with which forty tracts have been published, 6,187,000 pages of which have been distributed, besides 6,095 Testaments, 13,845 copies of the little volume called " Camp Hymns," and a large number of religious books. Our policy has been to seek the co-operation of chaplains and other pious men in the army, and, as far as possible, to work through them. How pleasant to think of the thousands who, far from their loved ones, are, every hour in the day, in the loneliness and gloom of the hospital, and in the bustle and mirth of the camp, reading some of these millions of pages which have been distributed, and thus have been led to turn unto the Lord.'

" In his report for 1863, in the midst of the war, he says:

" ' Modern history presents no example of armies so nearly converted into churches as the armies of Southern defence. On the crest of this flood of war, which threatens to engulf our freedom, rides a pure Christianity; the Gospel of the grace of

God shines through the smoke of battle with the light that leads to heaven; and the camp becomes a school of Christ. From the very first day of the unhappy contest to the present time, religious influences have been spreading among the soldiers, until now, in camp and hospital, throughout every portion of the army, revivals display their precious, saving power. In one of these revivals over three hundred are known as having professed conversion, while, doubtless, there are hundreds of others equally blessed, whose names, unrecorded here, find a place in the " Lamb's book of life."'

"And in 1865, in reviewing the blessed work of saving souls amid the bloody scenes of four gloomy years, the board said:

"' Millions of pages of tracts have been put in circulation, and thousands of sermons delivered by the sixty missionaries whom we have sent to our brave armies. If it could be known by us here and now how many souls have been saved by this agency, doubtless the announcement would fill us with surprise and rejoicing. Hundreds and thousands, we verily believe, have in this way obtained the Christian's hope, and are now occupying some place in the great vineyard of the Lord, or have gone up from the strife and sorrow of earth to the peaceful enjoyments of the heavenly home."

"The Evangelical Tract Society, organized in the city of Petersburg, Virginia, in July, 1861, by Christians of the different denominations, was a most efficient auxiliary in the great work of saving souls. It was ably officered, and worked with great success in the publication and circulation of some of the best tract-reading that appeared during the war. More than a hundred different tracts were issued; and in less than one year after the organization of the society, it had sent among the soldiers more than a million pages of these little messengers of truth. *The Army and Navy Messenger*, a most excellent religious paper, was also published by this society, and circulated widely and with the best results among the soldiers. Holding a position similar to that of the American Tract Society, this association was liberally sustained by all denominations, and had ample means for supplying the armies with every form of religious reading, from the Holy Scriptures to the smallest one-page tract. Its officers, editors, agents, and colporters were among the most faithful, zealous, and successful laborers in all departments of the army.

During the period of its operations, it has been estimated that 50,000,000 pages of tracts were put in circulation by it.

" The Presbyterian Board of Publication, under the direction of Rev. Dr. Leyburn and other ministers of that Church, entered the field and did faithful service in the good cause. The regular journals of that denomination, a monthly paper—*The Soldier's Visitor*—specially adapted to the wants of the army, Bibles, Testaments, and most excellent tracts in vast numbers, were freely sent forth to all the camps and hospitals from their centre of operations.

" The Virginia Episcopal Mission Committee heartily united in the work, and spent thousands of dollars per annum in sending missionaries to the army, and in printing and circulating tracts. Rev. Messrs. Gatewood and Kepler, of the Protestant Episcopal Church, were the zealous directors of operations in Virginia, while in other States such men as Bishop Elliott, of Georgia, Doctor, now Bishop, Quintard, of Tennessee, and the lamented General Polk gave the weight of their influence and the power of their eloquence, written and oral, to promote the cause of religion among our soldiers.

"At Raleigh, North Carolina, early in the war, Rev. W. J. W. Crowder commenced the publication of tracts, encouraged and assisted by contributions from all classes of persons. In less than a year he reported: ' We have published, of thirty different tracts, over 5,000,000 pages, more than half of which we have given away, and the other half we have sold at about the cost of publication—1,500 pages for one dollar.' This gentleman continued his labors in this good work throughout the war, and furnished millions of pages of the best tracts for army circulation.

" ' The Soldiers' Tract Association ' of the Methodist Episcopal Church, South, was organized and went into operation in March, 1862, and became a valuable auxiliary in the work of colportage and tract distribution. By midsummer it had put in circulation nearly 800,000 pages of tracts, and had ten efficient colporters in the field. Its operations steadily increased to the close of the war; and besides the dissemination of millions of pages of excellent religious reading, with thousands of Bibles and Testaments, two semi-monthly papers were issued, *The Soldier's Paper*, at Richmond, Virginia, and *The Army and Navy Herald*, at Macon, Georgia, 40,000 copies of which were circulated every month throughout the armies.

" In addition to these, there were other associations of a like character successfully at work in this wide and inviting field.

" The Georgia Bible and Colportage Society, Rev. F. M. Haygood, agent, was actively engaged in the work of printing and circulating tracts in the armies of the South-west.

" The South Carolina Tract Society was an earnest ally in the holy cause, and sent out its share of tracts to swell the vast number scattered like leaves of the Tree of Life all over the land.

" The presses in every great commercial centre were busy in throwing off religious reading of every description, and yet so great was the demand that the supply was unequal to it during the whole of the war. At Richmond, Raleigh, Columbia, Charleston, Augusta, Mobile, Macon, Atlanta, and other cities, good men labored day and night to give our gallant soldiers the bread of life; and still the cry from the army was, 'Send us more good books.' At one period of the war the Baptist Board alone circulated 200,000 pages of tracts weekly, besides Testaments and hymn-books; and, with the joint labors of other societies, we may estimate that when the work was at its height not less than 1,000,000 pages a week were put into the hands of our soldiers."

Rev. Dr. C. H. Ryland, who was a colporter in the army during the first year (sustained by his own church, Bruington, King and Queen county), and afterwards depositary, agent and treasurer of the army colportage work of the Virginia Baptist Sunday-school and Publication Board, has kindly furnished me the following additional facts and figures.

The Bible Board, in its report for 1861, said: " We earnestly suggest to the association the importance of making prompt and adequate provision for supplying our soldiery with the Bible. While in aid of what we all esteem a noble and sacred cause, the protection of our homes, our firesides, our altars, our mothers, sisters, wives and little ones from desecration and outrage by wicked and cruel invaders, we put into the hands of our brave defenders appropriate weapons; let us not fail to supply them with the means of waging an even higher and holier, because a spiritual and Divine, warfare. Let us give every man not already armed with it 'the sword of the Spirit, which is the word of God.'"

At the meeting of the same body in 1863, this board was "instructed to correspond with pastors suited to the work and endeavor to engage them to labor as voluntary evangelists in the army, and that the board defray their expenses."

"*Resolved:* That this board be instructed, in connection with other boards which may deem such a measure important for their interests, to inquire into the expediency of deputing some suitable brother to visit Europe, for the purpose of procuring Bibles, books, tracts and any other appliances that may aid the general usefulness of such boards; and, if deemed expedient, be authorized to make arrangements therefor."

During 1862 and 1863 alone this Sunday-school and Publication Board collected for army colportage $84,000. It published and distributed in the army 30,187,000 pages of tracts, 31,000 Bibles and Testaments, 14,000 "Camp Hymns," and thousands upon thousands of religious books sent by the people from their homes, and religious papers without number.

During 1864 sixty colporters were kept at work in the army. These were kept supplied with tracts, Bibles and Testaments, but for this year the exact records have been lost.

I regret that I have been unable to obtain fuller and more exact reports of the other Bible and tract societies; but the following clippings from war files of the religious newspapers give the most interesting details of the spirit with which our people engaged in the work, and the wonderful success which crowned their efforts.

"The annual report of the Southern Methodist Episcopal Soldiers' Tract Association for 1863 shows a receipt during the year of $95,456.71, and a disbursement of $64,470.60. The association has issued for circulation 7,000,000 pages of tracts, 45,000 soldiers' hymn books, 15,000 soldiers' almanacs, 15,000 Bible readings for soldiers; and has circulated 15,000 copies of the Holy Scriptures—Bibles, Testaments and Gospels separately bound, 50,000 copies of *The Soldier's Paper* and 20,000 copies of *The Army and Navy Herald.*"

The *Petersburg Express* says: "When the war commenced, the Baptists of Virginia were extensively engaged in the work of colportage. They were soon impressed with the importance of employing this powerful agency in circulating the Scriptures and religious books in the army. After a few months' labor it was found that the colporters were highly esteemed by the soldiers, and Rev. A. E. Dickinson was instructed by the General Associa-

11

tion of Virginia to appeal to the Christians of the South for means to publish and circulate Testaments and tracts. These appeals, made through secular and religious papers, were liberally responded to by men of all denominations. The board intrusted with the management of this immense work is composed of men of intelligence. They have sought distinction neither for themselves nor the society they represent. It has a history that will survive the present revolution—a place in the affections and a claim to the esteem of the public that time cannot shake. All of its numerous publications are said to be highly evangelical, and commend themselves to members of all denominations. We have no means at present of estimating the number of pages this society has printed and circulated. It has done much—and much remains to be done. The army is large and is daily growing larger. The demand for the Scriptures and tracts continues to be as great, if not greater than at any former period."

Rev. A. E. Dickinson, the general superintendent of this board, gives the following incidents illustrating the feeling of our people generally at the beginning of this work:

"When in Augusta, Georgia, some months ago, I made a public appeal in behalf of the soldiers then in Virginia. After the services were concluded a bright and beautiful little girl of four summers came up with a dime, and said, 'Tell my brother Johnnie howdie, and buy him some good little tracts with this.' She thought, of course, everybody knew *her* brother, and that there would not be any difficulty in finding *him*. With a glad heart she went away smiling at the thought that she had given her all. The next morning an old negro man came through the drenching rain to my place of abode, and made the following remark: 'My heart was so sorry when I heard you tell of dem poor soldiers in Virginia—how dey starving for de Gospel; and to think dat here I hab de preached word all de time, and there dey is fighting for me. My heart is monstrous 'flicted when I think of my young massa out in de army, and I wants to send him de Gospel.' So saying, he placed a gold dollar in my hand and expressed his regret that it was 'so little.' Several persons gave large sums; but of all the hundreds thrown into the treasury it seemed to me that this little girl and this gray-haired African were the most liberal—they gave of their poverty. God grant that 'brother Johnnie' and the 'young massa' may become savingly interested in the great salvation!

"A. E. DICKINSON."

Mr. Dickinson wisely secured the influence and help of our best men, as the following will show. Hon. John Randolph Tucker has been for years a member of the Presbyterian Church, and one of those public men who never hesitates " to show his colors "—to speak out for Christ.

"*Messrs. Editors:* The following letter from John Randolph Tucker, Esq., Attorney-General of Virginia, will be of service to the cause I have the honor to represent. Mr. Tucker evinces the depth and sincerity of his conviction in this matter by his deeds, as, in addition to former gifts, this letter enclosed a handsome donation.

"A. E. DICKINSON."

" RICHMOND, June 19, 1862.

"*Dear Sir:* In compliance with your request I take great pleasure in expressing the conviction of my mind, that the scheme of colportage for the army under your charge is worthy of the support of every Christian and every patriot. Our cause, under God, is committed to the keeping of our noble army. That cause rises far above all secular objects; for it involves within it our religion in its purity and in its successful dissemination throughout our whole Southern country. The enemy has not only invaded our homes, but has desecrated our churches and stifled the voice of prayer in the temples of God, and seized His ministers clinging to the very horns of the altar. Freedom to worship God has ceased wherever the legions of the foe have advanced; and the conscience of an outraged people, forbidden to utter its voice in public devotion, can only breathe its prayers for the rescue of our land from the enemies of our country and the despisers of our religion. But shall the defenders of a free faith and of our hearthstones be without the word of God and the means of personal salvation? The scheme of colportage answers the question. By it religion noiselessly walks through the camp, sowing the precious seed among the soldiers of the South. It enters the hospitals and speaks peace to the sick and the dying, and lifts the broken and wounded spirit to the hope

which anchors the soul in the haven of eternal rest.   What may
we not hope to accomplish in filling the ranks of our host with
the true soldiers of the Lord of battles?   Shall we not rob
war of much of its horror, when thousands of men, loyal to their
country, but in disloyal opposition to the King of kings, shall
be brought to acknowledge the sceptre of His power and yield
obedience to His law?

"The word of God—the tract which conveys little by little portions of that word to the mind of the soldier on duty; the book,
or paper or pamphlet, which leads him to the fountain of all
truth—these are the means you use to make the citizen-in-arms
a better, because a Christian patriot.   The labors of the colporter,
however humble and simple, thus become the instruments of the
largest benefit to the army, to the country and to the kingdom
of the Redeemer.   To the sick, the wounded and the dying,
stilling the noise and tumult of the battle with the gentle whis-
pers of a Saviour's love, his presence is an incalculable blessing.
The fruits of his toil are presented in a rich harvest already perceptible all through our army.   Let him go on in the discharge
of his duty; let men everywhere sustain him by counsel and
contribution, and we will see the work crowned with temporal
benefits, which can scarcely be estimated, and with eternal blessings, which shall be full of glory.

" I am, dear sir, yours, very truly,
"J. R. TUCKER."

And the following report of a grand mass-meeting held in
Richmond in the same interest will show the general co-operation of our people.

"*Messrs. Editors:* Will you be kind enough to transfer to your
columns, from the *Richmond Whig*, the enclosed account of the
meeting held in the First Baptist Church on Sunday night,
February 23?

" A. E. D."

" Last Sabbath evening, at the First Baptist Church of this
city, an unusually enthusiastic meeting was held, in behalf of
army colportage.   Every seat was occupied, while many went
away unable to find admission.   After singing and prayer, Rev.
A. E. Dickinson made some statements, giving an account of

what had been effected by colportage labors among the soldiers.

"Rev. Robert Ryland, D. D., colporter for the hospitals of this city gave a deeply interesting narrative of his labors. He had found the inmates of our hospitals eager to receive instruction. Sometimes they had professed to be greatly benefited by the tracts, and often sent for him to come again. An invalid remarked to him, that prior to his entering the army he had enjoyed religion, and had been a member of the Presbyterian Church; but, surrounded by the vices of the camp, he had become a backslider and lost all religious enjoyment. After frequent conversations he became much interested in his soul's salvation, sent for the colporter again and again, and before his death expressed himself perfectly resigned to the will of God. Other facts and incidents of much interest were narrated.

"He was followed by John Randolph Tucker, Esq., in a speech of great power and eloquence. Mr. Tucker thought it augured well for the country that such an immense audience had assembled, notwithstanding the inclemency of the weather, to consider the spiritual wants of our army. We are passing through the most momentous era in the history of this country. The year 1861 was filled with victories and covered Southern arms with imperishable glory; but from the beginning of this year we have met with nothing but disaster. Every message brought over the telegraph but tells of some new defeat. Why is this? Up to the battle of Manassas our whole people were prostrate before God in prayer. The speaker had met with many on the street with prayer trembling on their lips, while tears of penitence filled their eyes. Now, those men have upon their lips blasphemous oaths, and their eyes are never turned to God for His blessing. After the great victory of Manassas we ceased to realize our dependence on heaven; and nothing was more common than to hear such expressions as, 'We can whip the Yankees any way.' Greed and avarice have taken possession of the hearts of many, while in every portion of the Confederacy distilleries have been springing up, until now the whole land groans under the liquid poison which is sweeping so many of our soldiers into the grave. Our streets are blocked up with men made drunk by the distilleries. How dare we expect the blessing of God when such things are tolerated? It is the decree of heaven that 'righteousness exalteth a nation, but sin is a reproach to any people.' It is vain to speak of the justice of our cause, unless we seek upon that cause the blessing of heaven, and use the instrumentality which Providence places in our hands. The speaker believed that piety will make a man a truer patriot and a braver soldier. It assures him that God is his friend; that 'all things work together for his good,' and that when he falls into the icy grasp of death, his soul will rise up to the unfading bliss of heaven. It is not necessary to refer to Cromwell, Havelock and other pious generals, to illustrate this great principle. We have illustrations in every division of our own army. Where can we look for a braver soldier than Stonewall Jackson; and yet never had the speaker known a more humble and earnest Christian than this noble man. What will become of these hundreds of thousands of soldiers when they return? If religious influences are not now brought to bear upon them, we may expect at the close of this war to have the country overrun with the most desperate, lawless men ever known in the South. In view of all these considerations, the speaker argued that this work has the most weighty claims upon all classes of the community. Mr. Tucker closed with an eloquent tribute to President Davis. In all his reading he had never known of a state paper closing, as the President's inaugural address, with an earnest prayer to the God of heaven, for His blessing upon himself and his country.

" Colonel Wright, member of Congress from Georgia, followed in an able speech. Nothing is more powerful than words, and the pen is mightier than the sword. From experience in command, he was prepared to commend this work. There is no better way to insure success in this great struggle than by surrounding our men with religious influences. It is difficult to get the soldier to attend regular preaching, but he will read a tract, and in the tedium of camp-life nothing is more acceptable. Colonel Wright closed with an eloquent appeal in behalf of the soldiers' spiritual culture.

" Hon. J. L. M. Curry said that he had made no promise to speak, but his love for the cause would not permit him to be silent when called out, if any words of his would advance its interests. He had no hope of success in establishing a free government unless Christian principle permeates all classes. There must be in high and low station a Christian conscience. We need a conservative element. This point was elaborated with power, and with that high order of eloquence so characteristic of this distinguished gentleman. Mr. Curry narrated some thrilling incidents in illustration of the good that may be done by circulating Testaments and tracts among the soldiers.

" Judge Chilton, representative of the Montgomery District (Alabama) in Congress, said it was too late for him to enter upon any lengthy remarks, but that with all his heart he endorsed the cause. He believed it one of the holiest and most glorious to which a good man can aspire. He had given to it the previous Sabbath, but was willing to give again, and to *continue* to give as long as he had a dollar and as any soldier's soul needed to be cared for. While the devil's colporters are going from camp to camp destroying the souls of our dear boys, he felt that the Christian community must do all in their power to counteract their ruinous influence. A collection was made, amounting to $1,250, after which the congregation was dismissed, all feeling that the entertainment was an " over-pay " for going out on such an inclement evening."

Rev. Dr. A. E. Dickinson, of Richmond, now editor of the *Religious Herald,* has had a career of great usefulness in the varied stations he has occupied, but the assertion is ventured that he never had four years of more abundant evidence of God's richest blessing upon his labors than during the years he superintended the grand work of his board in the camps and hospitals of the Confederacy, and pushed it forward with a zeal and consecrated tact which entitles him to a high place on the record of our army work.

The same may be said also of Dr. Bennett and others who had charge of army colportage.

Dr. Dickinson, however, kept his work constantly and so prominently before the public, through both the religious and secular press, that our newspaper-files abound with most interesting details of the labors of his colporters, 100 of whom he turned into the camps and hospitals at the very beginning of the war, and it is a very easy task to cull from his reports all the material necessary to further illustrate this chapter. I only regret that the material for a sketch of the labors of the other boards and societies is not so accessible. But none of these evangelical societies published sectarian tracts or engaged in sectarian labors during the war, and in giving, therefore, the work of one, I really give but a specimen of that of them all.

I quote, then, *in extenso*, from the reports of Dr. Dickinson, and along with these such reports of others as I have been able to find.

"A few weeks ago a soldier in the service of the Confederate States professed faith in Christ, united with a Baptist Church, and went on his way rejoicing. I have now before me a letter which this young soldier of the Cross has addressed to a member of the Sunday-school and Publication Board. 'Please find enclosed,' he writes, 'ten dollars, in return for which please send me some good religious tracts, such as you may think best to distribute among the unconverted soldiers. I do hope and trust that the Lord is with us.' It is said that the angels of the Lord encamp round about those who love Him and hope in His mercy. Who will not aid in supplying this dear disciple with books and tracts, that he may distribute hundreds of dollars' worth of these silent preachers to his comrades? There are scores of pious men in the army who will become voluntary colporters if we can supply them with books. What a field of usefulness this war has opened! May it not be that this is one of the ways in which God makes the wrath of men to praise Him? Let all who can imitate the example of this pious soldier, and very soon the tree of life will be placed within reach of the tens of thousands of brave men who are now congregated within the limits of our State.

"A. E. D."

Brother J. W. Williams, Mathews county: "Our soldiers are all well. I have morning and evening services, weekly prayer-meetings, and preaching every Sunday. I have no tracts. Do send me some, that I may be placing them in the hands of the soldiers."

Brother H. Madison, Richmond: "I have been laboring three weeks in the various encampments around Richmond, and so much have I been prospered that I feel like thanking God and taking courage. I find that, almost without exception, the soldiers are religiously inclined, and hundreds of times have those who are not members of any church said to me that their only hope of success in this struggle is in God—that from their cradles they have been taught to believe in the Bible and to trust in the Saviour it reveals. There are many Methodists, Baptists, Presbyterians and Episcopalians here, and some of them have public prayers morning and night, as they have been accustomed to do at home around the family altar.   One young man looked over my books and selected 'Attractions of Heaven' and 'The Gift of Mourners' to send as a present to his sister in Mississippi. A few days ago a pious soldier said to me, as I entered an encampment: 'Your labors have not been in vain here, for two of the young men have professed to be converted.'   I have circulated a great many copies of sermons which were given to me, and they have been read with unusual interest, so much so that numbers inquire of me as soon as I go among them: 'Have you any more of those sermons?'   My sales have been considerable; they buy Bibles, Testaments, hymn-books, and books on almost every religious subject, though my grants are much larger than my sales."

Rev. R. Lewis, Smythe county: "Though my sales have been small, I have been constantly at work visiting encampments, conversing with our soldiers, holding prayer-meetings and distributing books.   I sell 'Baxter's Call,' 'Alliene's Alarm,' 'Anxious Inquirer,' and many such books to soldiers.   I was much pressed to stay with the companies I have visited, but am now about to start for the Abingdon encampment.   I believe I can do more good among the volunteers than anywhere else."

Rev. R. W. Cridlin, Matthias Point: "I have disposed of all my Testaments.   You can hardly conceive of the anxiety of soldiers for books.   One said to me: 'If I am spared to return to my home, I shall ever love the colportage cause, since it has done so much for me.'   I could distribute 1,000 Testaments to great advantage.   I have begged a goodly number from the families around, but you must send me a large number.   While urging the importance of Divine things on a company the other day, some wept freely, thus evincing their concern.   Oh, let us labor for these dear souls!   Many of them may be won to Christ."

Brother C. F. Fry, Winchester: "I have been laboring in this place nearly two weeks.   The most of my time has been spent in visiting the sick.   Last Sunday I visited the hospital, talked with the inmates about the great salvation, and distributed among them tracts and Testaments.   Two young men asked me to pray for them, and never can I forget how they wept and thanked me for searching them out.   How I rejoice at being allowed to labor for the souls of these dear soldiers."

" Last Thursday evening the Sunday-school and Publication Board of the Baptist General Association determined to have 10,-000 copies of the New Testament printed in Richmond. This, if we mistake not, is the first time the New Testament has ever been published south of Mason and Dixon's line. It is surely an important move, and should be encouraged by all who feel interested in the effort to secure Southern independence. . . .

"A. E. DICKINSON,
" General Superintendent."

" Several young men in the Alabama regiments have been converted by reading the tract, ' Come to Jesus,' and the works, ' Persuasives to Early Piety ' and ' Baxter's Call.' On another occasion I gave books and tracts to a young man who had been in several engagements since he left home, though he had up to that time escaped injury, speaking to him at the same time of the importance of being prepared to die. Shortly after I had a letter from him, stating that my advice had caused him to reflect on his past life; that he had exercised faith in Christ, and now felt himself prepared for death. I often visit the sick in the hospitals with books. Among others, I conversed several times with the son of a Baptist minister, and on one visit was rejoiced to hear from him that he intended soon to write to his father (being, of seven, the only child not a member of the church) that he had taken Christ for his Captain, and felt better prepared for the great responsibilities before him. In one room, of five who were sick, two died. I embraced the opportunity of urging on the survivors, who were much affected, the possibility of death and the necessity of being born again. One of them then and there resolved to trifle no longer, and on the Sunday following I found him rejoicing in the Lord. I could multiply facts, but these may suffice for the present. My stock of Bibles and Testaments, which was unusually large, is nearly exhausted, and I therefore hail with pleasure the proposition of our board to print the latter. I trust that all friends of the Bible will respond liberally to the call made, and may the blessing of God attend the enterprise.

" E. C."

Rev. W. J. W. Crowder, who did so noble a work in printing and circulating tracts, gives the following statement concerning his work:

"*Messrs. Editors:* I hope that a few facts about colportage among the soldiers will not be unacceptable to your readers. Though I have been acting as agent for the American Tract Society in Norfolk, Portsmouth and the vicinity seven years, my labors have never been so blessed as from the 19th of April to the present time. I have distributed $300 worth of Bibles and tracts, and in all instances they have been gladly received by both religious and irreligious.

"Since June 1st, under the approval of all the pastors of this city, we have reprinted especially for the soldiers over 81,000 pages of each of the following appropriate tracts: 'A Voice from Heaven;' 'Don't Put it Off;' 'All-sufficiency of Christ;' 'Self-dedication to God;' 'Private Devotion;' 'The Act of Faith;' 'The Sentinel' and 'Motives to Early Piety'—in all of these over 618,000 pages; and of the excellent tract, 'Come to Jesus,' 17,280 copies, or 545,280 pages—making in all reprinted, 1,163,-520 pages; in value, $930.56. These we have got out at the prices heretofore paid to the American Tract Society, New York —1,500 pages for one dollar, and 'Come to Jesus' for three cents a copy. Nearly all of these have been sent to the soldiers, more or less, of all the Confederate States, most of whom receive them gladly, saying: 'This is the kind of reading we want to help us fulfil the promises we made to our wives, parents, sisters, ministers and loved ones on leaving home, that we would seek the Lord.' Such expressions I have frequently heard from a great many of the more than seven thousand soldiers with whom I have talked on personal religion.

"Recently a soldier of intelligence came to me in Richmond, Virginia, to express his thanks for the saving influence of the tracts he had received since being in camp. He believes they were sent to him in answer to a pious mother's prayers. He stated that before leaving home he felt but little interest in religion, but now it is his delight and comfort. Another soldier in a Mississippi regiment writes that the tract 'Come to Jesus' has been the means of leading him to Christ since being in Virginia. A prominent officer in one of the regiments in Virginia writes: 'I feel it my duty to say that the good influence exerted upon the minds and actions of our men by the Bibles, books and tracts you have sent us is incalculable; and to my knowledge they have been blessed of God in producing a spirit of religious inquiry with many of a most encouraging character. I trust you

and Christian friends at home will continue to supply all our
soldiers with this means of grace, which is so well adapted to
our spiritual wants, and can be diffused among us as perhaps no
other can so effectually.'

"An efficient colporter, who has been laboring as such many
years about Charlottesville, Virginia, writes: 'I am devoting
almost my whole time to the soldiers, and especially to the hospitals, in which there is a large number of sick and wounded
here, and about as many at Culpeper Court House. This is
one of the best fields for usefulness, as they have so much time
for reading and thought. Over half of them are well enough to
read, and most of them are very thankful for religious reading.
I furnish many of them with Bibles and larger books to use
while here, and tracts and smaller books to take with them when
they leave. Yesterday I was conversing with quite a sick soldier, who told me he embraced religion since being in camp at
Harper's Ferry, while engaged in prayer alone with his cousin.
I want 1,000 copies of 'Come to Jesus,' and a great many more
of the other kinds you publish.' As Christians, we ought to improve every means possible for doing good to the souls and
bodies of these soldiers; and this is one of the most effective
religious instrumentalities. The colporter should be kept well
supplied with religious reading to distribute in his labors of
mercy and love. . . .

"W. J. W. CROWDER, Tract Agent.

" RALEIGH, NORTH CAROLINA,
      "September, 1861."

"A pious lady who has been for some time acting as nurse
among the sick soldiers at Culpeper Court House, writes to us
as follows: 'I would be very much obliged to you if you could
send a package of tracts. The poor soldiers are really begging
for something good to read. This is true especially of the
wounded. I hope that you will pray that the divine blessing
may be bestowed on these afflicted ones who are so far from
their loved ones, and that I may be a blessing to them. There
is nothing I desire so much as, by nursing, to do good to those
who have given up all for their country. There is great room
for usefulness open to pious females now in ministering to the
temporal and spiritual wants of our sick soldiers. I have lost
four of my patients; three died rejoicing in Jesus. They were

intelligent, noble, godly young men. One from Virginia said to me as he was dying, "Sing me a hymn;" I repeated, "Jesus lover of my soul." He remarked, "Where else but in Jesus can a poor sinner trust?" Just as he passed away, he looked up to heaven and said, "*Heaven is so sweet to me*," and to the presence of Jesus he went. Another from South Carolina sang with joy, " Happy day, when Jesus washed my sins away." Young B——, of Virginia, was resigned and even rejoiced at the near prospect of death. He repeated the lines, " How firm a foundation, ye saints of the Lord." His end was peace. One of these young men had determined to enter the Christian ministry. I close by asking that you will send the tracts as soon as possible.' . . .

"A. E. DICKINSON."

"LYNCHBURG, VIRGINIA, September.

" The tracts and Testaments and small Bibles I have given to the sick in the hospitals and in private families, a few to soldiers in camp, and to others passing through the city. There have been at times as many as 10,000 soldiers in the encampment here. There have been, and are now, a large number of sick soldiers here. Many soldiers have the Bible or Testament, and love to read it. A good many are members of churches. Far away from home and kindred, they are delighted to receive the visits of a brother-Christian, and to get something to read. So also on the part of the unconverted there is a strong desire for something to read. All receive the tracts and read them with delight. The Lord has blessed the work. I believe He has poured out His Spirit upon many. They have been awakened and have been led to hope in the Saviour; so they seem to give evidence. One soldier who died a week ago said, in a whisper, a short time before he breathed his last, when his nurse held up the tract, ' Come to Jesus,' and pointing to the heading, ' I can't see.' He was told it was the tract ' Come to Jesus,' and that Jesus says, ' Him that cometh unto me I will in nowise cast out.' ' Thank the Lord for that,' he replied. ' Have you come to Him, and do you find Him precious?' ' Precious, thank the Lord.' And so he would say of all the promises quoted. On the same day I visited, in two different hospitals, two young men sick of typhoid fever. They both seemed concerned about their souls, and listened with apparent interest to invitations of the Saviour to come to Him. After a few days I visited them again; both were improving and rejoicing in the Saviour. Now they say they love Him more and more. Several tell me they delight to read the Bible now, and that since they became soldiers they have been led to seek the Saviour, and some hope they have found Him. Yesterday one told me, to whom I had given a tract, that at home he was a steady man, never swore, but that, becoming a soldier, he did as many others do—threw off restraint and did wickedly; ' but now,' said he, ' I have done swearing; I will seek the salvation of my soul.' . . .

"A lieutenant in the Southern Army writes from Monterey to Rev. A. M. Poindexter:

"' The soldiers here are *starving* for reading matter. They will read anything. I frequently see a piece of newspaper no larger than my hand going the rounds among them. If the bread of life were now offered them through the printed page, how readily they might be led to Christ. I have never seen a more appropriate and effective means of doing good than the distribution of tracts among the soldiers of the Confederate army.'

"Such appeals as the above are almost daily placed in our hands, and frequently they are accompanied with funds from the meagre earnings of our soldiers. Our soldiers are literally *starving* for the bread of life. If we believe the teaching of the Word of God, how eagerly ought we to strive to aid in a work which proposes to seek out all the starving souls, and tell them of the things pertaining to salvation.

"A. E. DICKINSON, General Superintendent."

" ROCKBRIDGE ALUM SPRINGS HOSPITAL.

" . . . Imagine 600 men, used at home to comforts, many of them well educated and piously trained, cut off for nearly four months from preaching, books and newspapers; and then remember that many of them have languished for weeks in their tents, lonely and depressed, having no way to pass the time; and remember too that these deprivations still exist in this hospital, and you can form some idea of the eagerness with which I am welcomed into every room. ' Yes, and thank you for it; I haven't had any good reading for a long time,' is the almost invariable reply when I ask a man to receive a tract. In the absence of a better supply I preached for the men yesterday morn-

ing. For the want of a better place the services were held on
the lawn, and in spite of the cold wind quite a good number
attended. Their interest plainly told that they enjoyed the opportunity to hear the truth, and several told me it was the first
sermon they had heard for several months. There should by
all means be a regular chaplain here. I gave away several
pocket-Testaments and all the 'Hymns for Camp' I had with
me, and as I walked out about sunset I found the men gathered
in squads for the delightful exercise. Many are very tender
about their souls, and seek rather than avoid conversation. On
Saturday night I went to a room in which there were five men,
all just rallying from the fever, and while there read, sung and
prayed with them. None of them were Christians, but all
seemed deeply affected, and during prayer one man sobbed
aloud.

"These little incidents greatly encourage me, and give promise of speedy and lasting good. . . .

"C. H. RYLAND."

The following is from Rev. J. C. Hiden, who was laboring as
chaplain in the Wise Legion: "Can't you send me some Testaments and tracts? They are greatly needed in the army.
Vast numbers of our soldiers have none. I was walking along
near camp the other day, with some tracts under my arm, when
a man on horseback said to me: 'Give me one of those to read,
so as to keep me out of devilment.' 'Twas a rough way of expressing a good idea, I thought. Of course I gave him one,
and immediately the soldiers were swarming around me, desiring to be furnished, and were sadly disappointed when they saw
that my supply was exhausted. I turned away with a sad heart
to see so many hungering in vain for that which was able to
make them wise unto salvation."

A chaplain—Rev. W. B. Owen—thus writes from Leesburg,
Virginia: "A package of tracts sent to Captain Ivey, Seventeenth Mississippi Regiment, came to hand, and I am glad of
the opportunity to thank you for them. I assure you, had you
been present as I passed up and down every company in our
regiment distributing them, and seen how eagerly they were
read by the soldiers, you would be stimulated to put forth every
exertion to scatter such blessings continually among the soldiers. We have had considerable religious interest in our regi-

ment; some have been converted, and others are seeking Jesus. If you can, do send us more tracts of different kinds, and 100 copies or more of that excellent tract, ' Come to Jesus.' "

A surgeon writes:

" Several interesting cases of conversion among the soldiers had occurred before the arrival of Brother Clopton at this post (Rockbridge Alum Springs). One of those cases it may be interesting to relate. A young man, who, from his own account, had been very ungodly, was brought to the hospital in a very enfeebled condition. He was confined to his bed for several weeks, gradually declining. I frequently conversed with him upon the great subject of his soul's salvation, and urged him to seek, by diligent and importunate prayer, the mercy of God and the pardon of sins. Some days before his death he told me, with a joyful expression of countenance, that he had found peace in believing in the Lord Jesus Christ. His evidences of pardon and acceptance with God were Scriptural, clear and satisfactory. Said he: ' Doctor, I bless God that you ever taught me the way of life and salvation. I have been a poor blind sinner all my life; but now I feel an assurance of happiness in heaven through Christ my Redeemer. Oh, I hope to meet you in heaven, and bless you there for the interest you have taken in my soul's salvation!' He died in full assurance of a blessed immortality. Other cases of interest might be related; but let this suffice to show that it is not in vain in the Lord to labor for the conversion of the most reckless soldier. I will just add, that I accepted the appointment of assistant surgeon in the hospital at this post that I might have an opportunity of preaching the Gospel to our soldiers, and I bless God that he permits me to labor in such a ield of usefulness.
                                        " N. W. CALHOUN."

Brother J. C. Clopton, one of our colporters, writes:

" During my stay among the forces under General Jackson I heard little profanity. There are many pious, Christian men in this division of the army, and among others the general himself. I am told that he keeps on hand a supply of tracts, and occasionally goes among his men as a tract distributer. One of his aids inquired of me where tracts could be obtained, and gave me $5 to help on the cause."

"RICHMOND.

" Though there are interesting letters from several gentlemen who are employed at this post, we will give extracts from but one. Rev. Mr. C—— says : 'I have been a month laboring in this city, during which I have distributed 41,000 pages of tracts, besides many copies of God's inspired word. I preach frequently (almost daily) in the hospitals or camps. A notice of a few minutes will suffice to bring together a large congregation, and never in my life have I witnessed such earnest, solemn attention to the preached word. Oftentimes I meet with soldiers who tell me that they have become Christians since they entered the army, and not unfrequently I am asked by anxious inquirers what they must do to be saved. The soldiers, almost without exception, have received me with great kindness, and have appeared very thankful for reading matter. " Oh, how encouraging to a soldier is a word of sympathy ! " said one of these sick men to me.' We have been enabled to bring out some 10,000 copies of the New Testament, and to publish over 5,000,-000 pages of tracts ; and to-day have not less than twelve depositories in the different States and 150 tract distributers at work.

"A. E. DICKINSON."

" LYNCHBURG, VIRGINIA, May 8.

" There are about 3,000 in the hospitals of this city, and others are being brought here from more exposed points. It is the purpose of the authorities to establish hospitals at Liberty and Farmville. Several hundred sick soldiers are already in these two towns. The hospitals afford a most inviting field for religious effort. The solemn quiet and the serious reflections which pervade the soul of the sick soldier, who, far away from home and friends, spends so many hours in communing with his own heart, is very conducive to religious improvement. An invalid remarked that during the month he had been in the hospital he had read through the New Testament and the Psalms, though he was not a professor of religion. Last Monday, at an early hour, I walked through the hospital at Staunton, and found not a few of the inmates reading diligently their Bibles. There is, without doubt, considerable religious feeling in the *camps*. Take the following as one of many facts corroborative of this statement. After several days of long, weary marches, General Jackson's command came into Staunton Sunday and Monday.

12

The first regiments which arrived were literally overcome with fatigue and hunger; and yet, when marched into the yard of the Blind and Deaf Asylum, though it was nearly sunset, and they had not had their dinner, as they fell down upon the green grass to rest their wearied limbs, many took from their pockets copies of God's word, which, with the utmost eagerness and solemnity, they perused. A soldier said of his Testament: 'I would not take anything in the world for this book. It was given me by a pious lady.' In hundreds of instances the reading of *tracts* has been blessed to the spiritual good of our men. Major-General Jackson is a pious deacon in the Presbyterian Church, and Major Dabney, one of his aids, is a Presbyterian Doctor of Divinity. 'I wish, instead of two, you had a dozen colporters in my army,' said General Jackson; 'and I am ready to do anything I can to aid you in so good a work.' There is reason to hope that in a few weeks fully a dozen colporters will be operating among the soldiers in the valley. General Edward Johnson, though not a professor of religion, encourages colporters to visit his command. On one occasion, when orders had been given that no one was to be permitted to enter the lines, a colporter came, and no sooner was the object of his mission made known than the general gave him a cordial welcome. 'We are always glad to see you; stay with us, and do all the good you can.' He then took the good man to his own tent, and shared with him his blankets. We have now more than 100 engaged in these labors of love among the soldiers, and hope that the day is not distant when the number shall be more than doubled. The fields are white unto the harvest.

"A. E. DICKINSON."

"A few days since a colporter was distributing tracts among a number of soldiers. He gave to an officer of high grade a tract, entitled, 'A Mother's Parting Words to her Soldier Boy.' Turning to the colporter, he said: 'Oh, sir, I can never thank you enough for this tract! The title itself is a most affecting sermon to me. My mother spoke words of tenderness and love to me as I was about to leave her for the army, and everything that reminds me of those words affects my heart.' Tears rolled down his cheeks while he spoke, so that a bystander afterwards remarked that he had never seen a man more perfectly subdued.

" Thus it is that a mere sentence is often blessed of God to the good of souls. A one-page tract, headed ' Eternity,' was handed to a wild young man, and the word eternity filled him with alarm and was instrumental in leading him to Christ. ' God hath chosen the foolish things of the world to confound the wise ; and God hath chosen the weak things of the world and things that are despised, yea, and things that are not, to bring to nought the things that are, that no flesh should glory in His presence.' 'A Mother's Parting Words,' etc., is a most interesting and touching tract of eight pages, written by one of the best writers in the Southern Confederacy. Let every mother buy a copy (price one cent) and send it to her ' soldier boy.'

Brother M. D. Anderson, Richmond, Virginia : "A short time ago I met a young man from one of the upper counties of this State, who had been wounded. When I commenced talking with him on the subject of religion, he said, ' Oh, sir, don't you remember that at the camp-meeting in —— you spoke with me on this subject? Do pray for me.' He has since been con- verted and raised up from his bed of suffering, and is actively engaged distributing tracts in the army, and in many other ways seeking to glorify his Saviour. An old marine, who had weathered many a storm, who was lying sick in the hospital, seemed astonished that I should urge upon his attention the claims of the Gospel. ' How is it that you, a young man, should be so concerned about me, a poor sailor ?' He said that rarely, if ever before in his life, had any one spoken to him about his soul. From day to day I visited him, and his interest in Divine things grew until, I think, he became a true Christian. He certainly died a most happy death. To-day a soldier, after receiving from me a few tracts and a book, handed me five dollars as a donation to the board."

Rev. W. L. Fitcher, Petersburg, Virginia : " The work of the Lord is progressing in Petersburg. We scarcely ever go to the hospital without finding some one concerned about the salvation of his soul. The tracts are very kindly received and read with soul-saving interest by many."

" The following report of Dr. R. Ryland's labors will be read with interest.—A. E. D."

" With an interruption of ten days' sickness, and a short trip to Lynchburg with a view to restore my strength, I have labored regularly in the hospitals for the last eight months. Wherever

I found the most destitution there I made the most frequent visits. I have usually conversed with each patient, or made an address and prayer in the hearing of all the inmates of the ward. I have distributed thousands of tracts, hymn-books, spelling-books and religious newspapers. These last have been particularly acceptable to the soldiers. The proprietors of the *Religious Herald*, *Central Presbyterian*, *Southern Churchman* and *Christian Observer* have shown a cheerful liberality in furnishing me with their papers for distribution; and, as they all conduct their journals with ability and with a catholic spirit, I have thankfully received them and distributed them widely among the soldiers. They are more appreciated than tracts, because they afford more variety of matter. I take this method of suggesting to those subscribers to all these papers who have been within the enemy's line during part of the year, and who consequently have not received all their numbers, that they would do well to pay, for the *whole year*, inasmuch as all the copies which failed to find them —and many more—were generously circulated among the convalescents in the hospitals, and among the several camps.

"The *result* of my labors I must leave to the final day to disclose. Many cases of deep and thrilling interest have come under my observation. Some were fervent disciples of Jesus, who, during the war, having maintained their integrity, gave me a cordial welcome to their bedside. Others were rejoicing in a recent hope of eternal life. And many others exhibited marked anxiety about their salvation, and received with a docile spirit every suggestion made for their benefit. I cannot begin to particularize. Suffice it to say, that since the battle of Seven Pines I have conversed with probably 500, who, having passed through the recent bloody scenes either unhurt or wounded, have told me, with different degrees of emphasis, that they have resolved to lead a better life. They ascribe their deliverance to the special providence of God, and felt obliged to requite Him with love and obedience. I shall be disappointed if very many soldiers do not seek fellowship with the churches of Christ immediately after their return home. Let pastors look out for them. All these battles, with their hair-breadth escapes and their terrible sufferings, have produced a softened state of mind which harmonizes well with our efforts to evangelize.

"If all the colporters and chaplains of posts in and near Richmond could have a meeting and agree on some plan of *distribut-*

ing their labors, the benefits of those labors would be more equalized. By the present arrangement some hospitals may be visited by several brethren during the same week, while others might not be visited by any one for several weeks. It seems to me that *you* would be a suitable person to attend to this matter.

" Yours, etc.,
" R. RYLAND."

At the late anniversary meeting of one of our district associations Dr. R. Ryland made the following remarks : " I have, from almost the beginning of the war, been laboring as colporter in the hospitals of Richmond, and my impression is that the results of this work are infinitely greater and more glorious than many believe. As to myself, every week's observation would have enabled me to write out facts and incidents of the most cheering character, enough to fill up half of the *Religious Herald,* and yet I have written but a few lines, leaving unpublished this great mass of facts, illustrative of the good this work is doing."

Rev. Wm. M. Young said, as chaplain in the field as well as in the hospital, he had seen scores of instances in which the reading of tracts had been instrumental in the conversion of souls. The following is one of the incidents he relates : " Yesterday, going up Main street, I was hailed by a soldier sitting on the pavement : ' Parson, don't you know me ? Under God I owe everything to you. While languishing in the hospital you gave me a tract which has brought joy and peace to my soul. If God spares me to go home, I expect to devote my life to the public proclamation of the Gospel.' "

"At present a revival of religion is in progress at Camp Winder, near this city, and thirty-five have professed conversion. At Chimborazo a meeting of equal interest is in progress. Rev. R. W. Cridlin informs me that frequently from thirty to forty come up for prayer. Many have professed conversion. An old man, who happened to be present a few evenings ago at these meetings, professed conversion, and said: ' Thank God, to-morrow I leave for Georgia to meet my wife and children, to tell them what great things the Lord hath done for me.'

" Brother McVeigh, post chaplain at Farmville, writes me that a good work is going on in the hospitals in that town, and several have obtained ' a good hope ' through Christ. For two months there has been unusual religious interest among the soldiers in the hospitals at Lynchburg, and many have made the good profession.

" Rev. J. B. Hardwick, post chaplain, favors us with a deeply interesting account of a work of grace among the hospitals of Petersburg, where 100 profess to have found the Saviour since they have been brought to that city. . . .

"A. E. D."

" 'A Mother's Parting Words,' etc. This is the title of one of the most popular tracts ever published on this continent. It has been but a year since the first edition of 50,000 copies was issued. Recently we have been induced, by the frequent applications for this tract, to issue the third edition of 50,000. Thus, within one year, 150,000 copies have been issued. But this is not all. The tract has been reprinted by the Methodist Tract Society located in Petersburg, and it may be by others. I suppose, in all, at least 250,000 copies have been issued. Hundreds have professed conversion from the reading of this tract, while thousands have felt their hearts moved to noble resolve by its appeals. 'Do you know anything about my personal history,' inquired a soldier of a colporter, 'that you should give me *this* tract? Had you seen me part with my loving mother, and heard those "parting words" which she uttered, *then* it would not seem strange that you should select this tract for me. I thank you, sir; the mere title has done me good. I expect a rich treat from reading it.' An anxious mother, after many days of fatiguing travel, reached one of our Virginia hospitals just in time to witness the death of her noble soldier boy. All the sad, long days she had spent coming from her home in the far South, her heart was bleeding at the thought that her son was unprepared to die. 'Oh, if he were only a Christian, then I could give him up,' and then tears, such as none but loving mothers ever shed, would tell how deeply the heart was wrung with crushing sorrow. She reached the couch of her sick boy just in time to hear one sentence, but that was enough: 'Mother, I have found the Saviour. Oh, that dear tract, "A Mother's Parting Words." ' God only knows how many such sons have passed from the hospitals and battle-fields of the South to the peaceful mansions above. I think it highly probable that never, in the history of tract literature, has as much been accomplished in so short a period by one tract.

"At the annual session of the Strawberry Association, a little more than a year ago, while the claims of colportage were before that body, Rev. J. C. Clopton, of Lynchburg, made some affecting remarks in reference to his son, who had recently entered the service, and spoke of the solicitude his wife felt, and of some of the efforts she had made in his behalf. Rev. J. B. Jeter publicly thanked Brother Clopton for his speech, and remarked that he had promised the superintendent of colportage a tract, and that Brother Clopton had furnished him with a theme, 'A Mother's Parting Words to her Soldier Boy.' And in a few days the tract was written and printed.

"A. E. D."

Elder J. A. Doll writes:

" SCOTTSVILLE, October 2.

" We have a gracious revival here, going on among the soldiers and citizens. One service is held during the day in one of our hospitals, and another at night in the church. A goodly number of soldiers and citizens have already professed conversion, and the prospect is cheering."

A private letter from a soldier who was in the Maryland campaign, published in the *South-western Baptist*, says: " I had my Bible in my right breast-pocket, and a ball struck it and bounced back. It would have made a severe wound but for the Bible."

Brother H. Madison writes: " I have seen much of the goodness of God since coming to the army. Many and warm thanks I receive from the soldier. Oh, it is a sad and yet glorious thing to see a Christian soldier. They are so happy, so powerfully sustained of the Lord as, far from home, they go through the dark valley. I might tell you the particulars of two such cases."

Rev. M. D. Anderson : " I met with a young man some time ago, who said to me : ' Parson, you gave me a book (" Baxter's Call "), which I have been reading, and it has made me very unhappy ; I feel that my condition is awful, and desire to find peace.' I pointed him to the Lord Jesus. His regiment was ordered off, and therefore I have not seen him of late, but have written to him. While in a hospital with my tracts, one poor afflicted soldier wept piteously and said : ' Sir, I cannot read ; will you be good enough to read some of those tracts to me ? ' I read several, and among them, 'A Mother's Parting Words to her Soldier Boy.' 'Oh,' said he, 'that reminds me so much of my poor old mother, who has faded from earth since I joined the army.' He wept and seemed greatly affected."

Rev. J. B. Hardwick: "God is blessing the distribution of tracts and the labors of chaplains and colporters here (Petersburg). More than a hundred soldiers have been converted since April. I never knew a work of grace so powerful, quiet, and deep. It seems at times, that the hospital is a Bethel. But we need more assistance—I call for reinforcements, and you must furnish them immediately, if possible. Send us at least two colporters, one for the hospitals and the other for the camps."

Rev. J. C. Hiden: "Can't you send us a colporter here (Charlottesville). There is a most encouraging state of things at present. I am holding a protracted meeting. Crowds attend the preaching, and some have professed a change of heart, while others are interested. It is an interesting sight to see men, wounded in every variety of way, sitting attentive to the story of the Cross."

Rev. T. J. McVeigh, chaplain at Farmville: "My supply of tracts has been distributed, and the soldiers ask for more. I administered the ordinance of baptism (for the first time) a few Sabbaths since, in the Appomattox river, to a young soldier from Alabama. It was the most deeply interesting and beautiful scene I ever witnessed. All of the soldiers who were able to leave their rooms gathered upon the banks of the river, and seemed to have a high appreciation of the ordinance."

Rev. Wm. Huff, Marion, Virginia: "Our colporters now in the Western army are laboring with encouraging prospects. Rev. J. H. Harris is visiting General Marshall's command. He finds them destitute, and anxious for something to read. He says: 'After the labors of the day it is truly gratifying to see them grouped together, reading aloud to each other such portions of their tracts as interest them most, and speaking in the highest praise of the little camp hymn-books.'" . . .

Rev. M. D. Anderson: "I formed the acquaintance of a noble young man, the nephew of a most useful Baptist minister. Found him interested in reference to his soul, and endeavored to explain to him the Gospel. He urged me to come to see him again, as he was quite sick. When I went again and found him sinking, on being asked how he was he replied, 'I know in whom I have believed, and am persuaded that He is able to keep that which I have committed unto Him.' At my next visit I found him unable to speak above a whisper. I stooped down to his ear and inquired how it was with him. He replied, 'I had rather depart and be with Christ, which is far better;' and in this delightful frame of mind he passed to his heavenly home."

Rev. A. L. Strough, chaplain Thirty-seventh North Carolina Regiment: " In our retreat from Newberne, North Carolina, when overpowered by the superior force of the enemy, we lost nearly all the Testaments, etc., we had, and have not since been able to secure anything to read except fifteen small volumes presented to us by Kingston Baptist Church. Our regiment is now in four different directions, hence the chaplain cannot be with them all. Before we left North Carolina there were 137 in the regiment penitently inquiring after the Saviour."

Rev. W. G. Margrave: " Besides laboring here and there in the camps and hospitals, I have paid special attention to the sick in Lewisburg. Just before I left home, I visited a sick soldier and read to him the fourteenth chapter of the Gospel of John. He said, 'I have but one more step to take, and I shall be over the Jordan of death,' and soon, in perfect peace, he passed away. I commit all into the hands of my Father in Heaven, and go forth to tell of Jesus' dying love. We must return to God and restore that of which we are robbing Him, if we would be blessed. Say to our Congress, restore to God His Sabbath by stopping the transportation and opening of the mails on the day of the Lord."

Rev. A. M. Grimsley writes, from Culpeper county: " God is blessing us up here. Many of our brave boys have professed conversion. God grant that the work may spread."

Rev. C. F. Fry: " The past month I have spent in Winchester, Woodstock, and Staunton. Several have expressed themselves as being anxiously concerned about the great salvation. It was, of course, a delightful work to point them to the sinner's Friend. I also found many truly devoted Christians, who seemed rejoiced to have a colporter come among them. They are eager to secure reading matter. An officer remarked to me that he believed that the men would read more of a religious character now than during all their former lives, from the fact that they cannot obtain any other reading than that which the colporter carries them, and they are compelled to read to relieve the tedium of the camp and hospital."

Brother Henry Madison, near Winchester: " Every night, for some time, I have had prayer-meetings in the tent of Captain S——, which is filled even to overflowing. My own heart has been made to rejoice at seeing how gladly the word is received, and how deep and sincere the interest seems to be. I have been kindly received by officers and privates. I visited a wounded soldier, who told me that before the war he enjoyed the presence and blessing of God, but that the temptations and vices of the camp had swept him on in sin. Since the wound was received he has had time to repent of his backslidings, and seems now to have returned to his first love. 'Oh,' said he, 'it was a great mercy in God to send upon me this affliction, and I can truly say, with the apostle, that these light afflictions, which are but for a moment, are working out for me a far more exceeding and eternal weight of glory.'"

Rev. J. M. B. Roach, chaplain of Tenth Alabama Regiment, writes ; " Just before the battle of Williamsburg, a lieutenant asked me for a copy of each of my tracts. He compressed them into as small a space as possible, and placed them in his pocket. During the battle he was struck by a ball which, in all probability, would have deprived him of life had it not lodged in the tracts, which were just over his heart. He seems solemnly affected, and I trust will soon be at the feet of Jesus."

Brother J. C. Clopton: " Passing along to the hospital and handing tracts to numbers of soldiers on the way, as I was approaching a man the evil one tempted me, suggesting that it was hardly worth while to give *him* one ; but, going up to him and inquiring whether he was a Christian, I found instantly that he was under deep conviction of sin. 'Can you stop awhile with me ? I wish to speak with you,' he said. Then, as we sat together, with tears and sobbings he told me of his sin-burdened heart, and asked to be directed to Jesus. Another, nigh unto death, said to me, 'I am nearly to my journey's end, and, oh, sir, I would give worlds if I had them for the Christian's hope.' He seemed deeply moved, and I tried to explain to him the way. He has since passed to the spirit land."

Rev. G. C. Trevillian : " The revival is still progressing among the soldiers at this place (Lynchburg), and many are inquiring after the Saviour. I go from one to another, distributing tracts in the day, and at night we have a prayer-meeting. About fifty have professed conversion in connection with the meetings at the

Baptist Church. I have also spent a week at Liberty, where I found a deep interest as to religious matters among the soldiers. Many of them begged me to hold a protracted meeting there."

"RICHMOND, VIRGINIA, December 19.

"*Messrs. Editors:* It was my privilege to attend a meeting for soldiers on last Sabbath, in one of the hospitals in Staunton, at which some twenty-five asked for the prayers of God's people, and all seemed to be serious in regard to the things which make for their peace. I was assured by the post chaplain (Rev. G. B. Taylor), that a great and blessed reformation had been effected in the hospitals. He said that in the early stages of the war it was very difficult to secure the attention of the men to the preached word. Many would sit with hats on during religious services, engage in conversation, smoke, walk about, etc. But now the room is filled with earnest, solemn, and often weeping listeners, while multitudes eagerly embrace any and every opportunity for securing the prayers of God's people. What is stated by this chaplain of his hospitals is substantially true of almost every hospital (and of many camps) throughout the Confederacy. Brother Taylor, with the aid of the Sunday-school and Publication Board, has established two large libraries for the soldiers at Staunton. The books are loaned out to such as will appreciate and return them. You would be surprised to see how admirably this plan is working. As I walked through the hospital, I found almost every man poring over a book, presenting very much the appearance of a college or university. Among the books selected for one of the libraries were "Bunyan's Practical Works;" and in a day or so after the enterprise began nine volumes of Bunyan had been taken out.

"A. E. D."

Rev. W. L. Fitcher, Petersburg: "There is still much religious interest here among the soldiers. I handed, this morning, to an aged soldier, the tract, 'The Sick and the Physician.' 'That means the Saviour,' said he; 'Oh, that he were my Saviour!' 'Many of my company have become Christians,' said another, 'and I too wish to learn what I must do to be saved.' He requested me to visit him, and aid him in securing life everlasting."

"February 17, 1863.

"After getting my tracts, hymn-books, etc., I supplied the Sixty-third, Fifty-first and Fifty-eighth Regiments, and also Derrick's and Clarke's Battalions and Brian's Battery. The brave men received the tracts eagerly and thankfully, and were always pleased with an appointment for preaching or prayer. We held meetings in Monroe, and at the narrows of New river, and at Thorn Spring, near Dublin, where four artillery companies are now in camp. Never have I met with more patient and attentive audiences. One and another would inquire for Testaments, and express a resolution to lead a new life. With the batteries we held repeated meetings, and there is evidently an increasing interest in religion. Wherever I have gone among our troops, I have found a cheering proportion of pious men—soldiers of Christ. I have found young brethren who stand firm in their Christian integrity despite of temptation. Among these there are many who boldly advocate the cause of truth.

"I have distributed 30,000 pages of religious matter, and humbly trust the Divine blessing has accompanied this labor of love.

"J. T. TABLER."

March 5, 1863.

"Our Sunday-school and Publication Board has brought out recently a number of tracts, which will add not a little to the usefulness and reputation of its issues. We give their names: 'The Evils of Gaming; a Letter to a Friend in the Army,' by Rev. J. B. Jeter, D. D.—'Swearing,' by Hon. J. L. M. Curry—'God's Providence, a Source of Comfort and Courage to Christians,' by Rev. A. M. Poindexter, D. D.—'For the Confederate Army,' by Hon. M. J. Wellborn.—'David,' by Professor Geo. E. Dabney—and 'We Pray for You at Home,' by Rev. John A. Broadus, D. D. Besides these, the board has issued, in conjunction with the Georgia Bible and Colportage Society, editions of the following excellent new tracts:

"'Woman's Words to the Soldiers,' by Mrs. L. N. Boykin—'To Arms! To Arms!' by Rev. C. D. Mallory—'The Mourner,' by Mrs. M. M. M'Crimmon—and 'A Proclamation of Peace,' by Rev. J. L. Dagg, D. D. The board has also succeeded at last in getting through the press 'The Soldiers' Almanac for 1863,' prepared by Rev. George B. Taylor. In its selections, this bears the marks of the editor's usual piety, judgment and taste."

The following is from one of the most useful ministers we ever had in Virginia:

"PETERSBURG, February, 1863.

"*Dear Brother Dickinson:* I do not know whether regular re-ports are required of your colporters, but I have thought it would be well to forward to you a brief statement concerning my labors here during the past month.   There are several hos-pitals in this place, all, except one, capable of accommodating a large number of patients.   They are generally well filled, but at this time the number of patients is considerably reduced.   The officers and patients have warmly welcomed me in my visits among them.   Tracts and other religious publications are eagerly received, and seem to be read with great interest. ' Come again, soon, with your tracts and papers,' is the repeated request, as I have been about to leave them.   I have aimed to engage every man in the hospitals in special conversation on the subject of religion.   Frequently, these have been very profitable seasons to me, and I trust have been beneficial in many cases. Often I find a tract a valuable help in conversation, suggesting some important train of thought, and affording me the oppor-tunity to urge the reading of it with a serious and prayerful spirit.   A day or two since an instance occurred which I trust betokens a good connection with such a course.   I gave a young man Brother Shaver's tract, ' You Must Labor for Salvation,' tell-ing him there were many things in it he would not receive un-less God should influence his heart, and urging him, while he read it, to pray that he might be made willing to believe and re-ceive whatever is true in reference to his soul's salvation.   At the period above referred to I saw him, and inquired of him if he had read the tract as I requested.   He could only answer with his tears, while I felt encouraged to press on him the claims of the Gospel, and commend to him its preciousness. Some conversation then ensued which gave me hope that he had been graciously enlightened through the instrumentality of the printed message placed in his hands.   There are many ' refugees ' here from the country below, to whom I have felt it my duty to direct my labors.   Such of these as appear to be strangers I have given particular attention to, especially if they were in needy circumstances. On many accounts, this has been arduous service; but I have felt in my soul a recompense, as these have generally evinced great interest in my visits among them. The three chaplains on duty here are very attentive to the hospitals, and co-operate with me heartily. Another large hospital will be opened here very soon. There are also some regiments quartered around us, which I intend to visit. I feel that this is a great work in which I am engaged. Pray for me.

"Yours truly,
" T. Hume."

March 12, 1863.

Brother M. D. Anderson: " I have for some time been aiding in a revival now in progress at Fredericksburg, at which upwards of *sixty* soldiers have professed conversion. Last night about *one hundred* asked for the prayers of Christians. A great work is going on."

Brother G. C. Trevillian, Lynchburg, Virginia: "We have a soldiers' reading room here, which is well supplied with religious papers. Our hospitals are very much thinned out. A few days since I was sent for to be with a dying man, who desired to see a minister of the Gospel. I found him rejoicing in a hope of strengthened faith. Our prayer-meetings continue with increasing interest. We have also an interesting Bible-class, which meets every Sunday morning."

Brother Bagby, besides his labors as colporter, renders valuable service by occasionally taking an agency tour for us. He recently spent a few weeks in the Rappahannock Association, and returned with $850. We would like to appoint a few more such laborers. Rev. J. H. Campbell writes, from Savannah: " Last Sunday, at a meeting held at this place, at least *three hundred* soldiers came forward for prayer."

Brother Campbell writes most imploringly for reading matter, and says : " The soldiers manifest more anxiety for reading matter of late than ever before."

Three of the most useful Baptist ministers in Georgia, Elders J. H. Campbell, S. Landrum and D. G. Daniel, are now acting as tract distributers for us at Savannah.

Rev. W. L. Fitcher writes, from Petersburg, Virginia: "I have enjoyed many interesting seasons among the soldiers since I've been in your employ. Have always been kindly received by officers and men, and the kind thanks that I have received from them have fully repaid me for all my labors." Rev. John H. Taylor writes, from near Guinea's Depot, Caroline county: "A very interesting meeting is in progress here, conducted by the chaplains of the different regiments in this brigade. Oh that there may be an abundant outpouring of the Holy Spirit! I find the men very anxious for something to read, and there is a prospect of effecting good among them."

Rev. J. N. Fox, Culpeper Court House: "I was greatly impressed, yesterday, with the magnitude and importance of my work, when for hours I was besieged by the soldiers for the Word of God, and saw, too, how ready they were to be advised with in regard to the great concerns of the soul. At my meetings there is good attention to the word spoken. Oh that the Lord will prepare me to be faithful to souls!" Rev. M. D. Anderson furnishes us with an interesting account of the great revival which for weeks has been progressing in Fredericksburg among the soldiers. Scores there have become "obedient to the faith."—A. E. D.

April 30, 1863.

Rev. Perry Hawkins, writing to the *Confederate Baptist*, gives the following account of a conversion among the soldiers at Pocotalio, as related by the subject of it: "When I entered the army, I was the chief of sinners. I did not love God, nor my own soul, but pursued the ways of unrighteousness with ardor, without ever counting the cost. I studiously shunned preaching and our faithful chaplain, lest he should reprove me; and when he was preaching in the camp I would be in my tent gambling with my wicked companions. One day he presented me a tract, entitled, 'The Wrath to Come,' and so politely requested me to read it that I promised him I would, and immediately went to my tent to give it a hasty perusal. I had not finished it before I felt that I was exposed to that 'wrath;' and that I deserved to be damned. It showed me so plainly where and what I was that I should have felt lost without remedy had it not pointed me to that glorious "Refuge," which I trust has indeed been a refuge to me from the storm; for I now feel that I can hope and trust in Christ."

Rev. W. G. Margrave, who is alluded to in the following letter, was spared to continue his work until some years after the war, when, full of labors and ripe for heaven, he "went up higher:"

" For more than forty years this venerable brother has been travelling the mountains and valleys of Western Virginia as a colporter. He is probably the oldest tract man in the South. Hardly a day for twoscore years, except when hindered by sickness, but has found him in the lowly cabin comforting the sad, arousing the careless, kneeling in prayer with those who scarcely ever before had heard the voice of prayer, distributing tracts, and directing all to the ' sinner's Friend.' Hundreds, it may be thousands, have professed faith in Christ in connection with his labors. Some time since, when entering a public conveyance, Brother Margrave was embraced by one, a stranger to him, who, with the deepest emotion, remarked : ' I thank God for the privilege of once more meeting with you. Thirty years ago, when I was a child, you gave me a book, which under God has made me all I am.' Thus it is with many others who now occupy positions in Church and State. All they are, and all they hope to be, is traceable to the influence which this brother exerted upon them. From the very first of the war Brother Margrave has been following our armies in Western Virginia like a ministering angel, pointing to heaven and leading the way. Recently his aged companion was removed from earth to heaven ; but, though greatly crushed in spirit, he falters not in his devotion to the great cause to which his life has been given. Mr. Samuel Price, of Greenbrier, so well known in Eastern as well as Western Virginia, and a Presbyterian, pays Brother Margrave a handsome tribute in a private letter just received. ' I desire to say,' writes Mr. Price, ' that he has been indefatigable in his labors, in visiting the sick, attending the camps, distributing tracts, etc. ; and, indeed, in doing everything that an industrious, pious Christian minister could do. We should feel his loss in this section most seriously. It would be positively irreparable. He is the most efficient colporter that I remember ever to have known.' What an example have we here for those who have a heart to do good in the colportage work ! If one will only *continue* at these labors, instead of growing weary of them, as so many do after a few months, he will, as the years pass away, see rich clusters of fruit ripening around him, and then, when called home to heaven, he will be ' held in everlasting remembrance ' by those whom he has won for Christ."— A. E. D.

A few days since, a lady said to Elder William G. Margrave :

"My husband, before he became a soldier, rarely ever read the word of God, but now he delights in perusing its blessed pages. He hopes that his sins are forgiven, and that he is a child of God." Through what instrumentality was this soldier converted? A lady in Fincastle, who from the beginning of the war has been a tract distributer, furnished the printed page which, under God, brought about this change. Thus does the Divine Spirit honor those who seek to honor the Master by saving precious souls. We know not what word, what page, what sermon is thus to be honored, and hence, "Blessed are they that sow beside all waters." "In the morning sow thy seed, and in the evening withhold not thine hand, for thou knowest not whether shall prosper either this or that, or whether they both shall be alike good."—A. E. D.

The following from the *Christian Advocate*, communicated by a chaplain, is suggestive: "A young man in my company," said a lieutenant in one of our regiments, "came out before his comrades and openly embraced religion to the surprise of us all. One day he happened in my tent, and I inquired by what means his mind was awakened so suddenly to the subject of religion. He took from his pocket a letter from his mother, saying, 'There is something in that letter which affected me as it had never done before.' The letter said: 'We have sent you a box of nice clothes, and a fine variety of cakes and fruits, and other luxuries and comforts, and many good times we hope you will have enjoying those nice things with your friends.' Near the close of the letter were these words: '*We are praying for you, Charlie, that you may become a Christian.*' 'That's the sentence,' said the grateful boy, and the tears gushed from his eyes. 'When I was eating those dainties, I thought, mother is praying for me. I knew where she used to go to pray, and I could almost hear the words, "We are all praying for you, Charlie, that you may become a Christian." Now, I thank God for a praying mother, for her prayer is answered, and I am happy.'"

"The amount contributed during July and August for the Sunday-School and Publication Board will not fall short of *twenty thousand dollars*. Never have the churches responded more liberally to the claims of this board than of late. A church in Pittsylvania county (Shockoe) has this year given $2,400—one member leading the list with $900—a larger amount than a few years ago was contributed by all the churches in Virginia to

13

Baptist colportage. Berea Church, in Louisa county, instead of giving us about $100 as formerly, has already raised in the neighborhood of $1,000 as its contribution for this year. The churches of the James River Association sent up to their annual meeting an average of more than $200 apiece without a word being said to any one of them by an agent." . . .—A. E. D.

"Brother E. Steadman, of Georgia, authorized Elder A. E. Dickinson to draw on him for $25,000 for army colportage. This is in addition to the $6,000 recently paid by him to our board for the same purpose."

"A wounded Confederate captain was recently baptized at Shelby, North Carolina, who was awakened and led to Jesus while in camp by a "fragment of a religious tract" which he picked up in an adjoining grove."

"A missionary in the Army of Northern Virginia mentions the case of a lady at home who attributed her conviction and subsequent conversion to a tract which her cousin in the army procured from our depository at Orange Court House, and sent to her last winter."

"ORANGE COURT HOUSE, VIRGINIA.

"I have conversed with soldiers daily since I have been stationed at this place, and have heard much to encourage me in my labors of love. A young man, a few days ago, gave me an account of the state of his company about a year ago. Brother M. D. Anderson visited them, commenced a series of meetings, a number professed conversion and now they have a company of praying men—a year ago they had a company of gamblers. In visiting the hospitals of this place, I have conversed with many who were anxious about their souls' salvation, and seemed much gratified at my visiting and praying for them. I have been very busy this week, receiving and sending books and tracts to chaplains, and to Christians in regiments where they have no chaplains. Please send all the books you can, Testaments, Bibles, etc.; the soldiers are anxious for something to read. I wish you could be here and see what a perfect rush there is for books and tracts. I could give many interesting incidents, as related to me, of the good results from reading your publications, but must close.

"C. F. FRY."

The above details might be almost indefinitely multiplied, and the work of the colporters described up to the very close of the war; for they carried the "bread of life" to the trenches at Petersburg, and did not cease their labors until the dissolution of the army at Appomattox. But want of space forbids further details, and besides, the labors of the colporters soon mingled with those of the chaplains and missionaries, and will be further described as we tell the story of the great revivals which resulted from God's blessing on these combined labors.

CHAPTER VI.

THE work of colportage and the work in the hospitals run into each other so naturally that it is really difficult to separate them into chapters, and much written about the one will apply equally to the other. Eternity alone will reveal the amount, character and results of work in the Confederate hospitals.

"Wayside hospitals," where the sick and worn-out were cared for—"field hospitals," in rear of the line of battle—"receiving hospitals," from which the sick and wounded were distributed—and large hospitals in the cities, towns or other suitable places—all had their peculiar features, presented fields of great usefulness, and were scenes of self-sacrificing labors and touching incidents.

I want to bear testimony to the fact that (while, of course, there were some incompetents and a few brutes in the service) our Confederate surgeons were as able, skilful and humane men as have ever been seen in this noble profession.

They labored under great disadvantages in their lack of suitable medicines and appliances, and their lack of hospital stores, proper rations, etc.; but they did their best and had almost miraculous success in their treatment of the sick and wounded.

But even more than to the surgeons the credit of any comfort or sunshine in the hospital was due to our noble women, who were indeed "ministering angels" to our boys, and ready at all times to sacrifice themselves for the welfare of the humblest private who marched to the music of Dixie, or yielded to the bullet or to disease.

That noble young "heroine of Winchester," who sat all night on the battle-field of Kernstown holding the head of an unconscious youth of whom she knew nothing save that he was a Confederate soldier, and who saved his life at the imminent risk of her own, was but a type of those Confederate "Florence Nightin-

(196)

gales" who were found in every hamlet, and came to serve in every hospital.

A gifted Southern lady, who was herself an "angel of mercy" to many a sick and wounded soldier, has thus described these "wayside hospitals:"

" These wayside hospitals are located, generally, at the depot of some railroad, where the sick and wounded soldier immediately, as he leaves the cars, exhausted, weary and faint, finds a grateful shelter; where surgical aid, refreshments and attention are immediately tendered him. These institutions are generally supported entirely by voluntary contributions, and refreshing and delightful it is to see the unstinted supplies coming daily in and always equalling the demand. Much faith and prayer have been put in exercise for these tarrying-places for the war-worn soldier, so that their 'bread and water' have never failed; nor do we believe they ever shall while the people of a covenant-keeping God claim His exceeding great and precious promises.

" There are many cases of pathetic interest to be met with at these hospitals. One I will relate, as an incentive to early piety, and as another testimony to the power of our holy religion:

"After I had ministered to several of the wounded I drew near to the couch of one whose case was considered one of the worst there, but who appeared, since his wounds had been dressed and refreshments administered to him, much relieved. After conversing some time with him he asked my name. I told him, and that I was the wife of the gentleman who had just given him his breakfast (for he had to be fed as an infant). I told him, moreover, that the gentleman was a preacher—a Methodist preacher. 'I am a member of the Methodist Church,' said he. 'Would he be kind enough to pray for me now? for I have not heard the voice of prayer for many months.'

"After the prayer was ended the subject of religion continued to be our theme. He said he was quite resigned to God's will concerning him, and that he was not afraid to die; and while dwelling on the goodness of God his countenance assumed that serene and beautiful expression indicative of peace within and joy in the Holy Ghost. Well was it for him that he had strength from on high, and that the everlasting arms of God's love were his support, for in a few hours from the time we conversed together it was found amputation of his arm would be necessary, from which he suffered excruciatingly until death came to his relief. But all the time of his mortal agony his faith remained firm and unshaken, and he pillowed his sinking head on the bosom of Jesus, and 'breathed his life out sweetly there' while, to all around, witnessing a good confession of Christ's power to save to the uttermost all those that put their trust in Him."

At Richmond, Virginia, there was a little model hospital known as the "Samaritan," presided over by a lady who gave it her undivided attention, and greatly endeared herself to the soldiers who were fortunate enough to be sent there. "Through my son, a young soldier of eighteen," writes a father, "I have become acquainted with this lady superintendent, whose memory will live in many hearts when our present struggle shall have ended. But for her motherly care and skilful attention my son, and many others, must have died. One case of her attention deserves special notice: a young man, who had been previously with her, was taken sick in camp near Richmond. The surgeon being absent, he lay for two weeks in his tent without medical aid. She sent several requests to his captain to send him to her, but he would not in the absence of the surgeon. She then hired a wagon and went for him herself; the captain allowed her to take him away, and he was soon convalescent. She says she feels that not their bodies only, but their souls are committed to her charge. Thus, as soon as they are comfortably fixed in a good, clean bed, she inquires of every one if he has chosen the good part; and through her instruction and prayers several have been converted. Her house can easily accommodate twenty, all in one room, which is made comfortable in winter with carpet and stove, and adorned with wreaths of evergreen and paper flowers; and in summer well ventilated, and the windows and yard filled with green-house plants.

"A library of religious books is in the room, and pictures are hung round the walls. Attached is a dining-room for the convalescent patients, supplied by private families, except the tea and coffee, which are made in the room; and there is also a dressing-room, where they keep their knapsacks, etc. The rooms are kept in order by the convalescents, who serve under her direction, and learn to love their respective duties. The sick are supplied with everything that can make them comfortable. Morning and evening services are held, consisting of reading the Scriptures, singing and prayer; and she is her own chaplain, except when she can procure a substitute. Thus has she been engaged since April, 1861, with uninterrupted health and unparalleled success, making soldiers and mothers and wives glad, and heaven rejoice over repenting sinners."

Here is another sketch of a soldiers' friend who labored in some of our largest hospitals.

"She is a character," writes a soldier, "a Napoleon of her department; with the firmness and courage of Andrew, she possesses all the energy and independence of "Stonewall" Jackson. The officials hate her; the soldiers adore her. The former name her 'The Great Eastern,' and steer wide of her track; the latter go to her in all their wants and troubles, and know her by the name of 'Miss Sally.' She joined the army in one of the regiments from Alabama, about the time of the battle of Manassas, and never shrunk from the stern privations of the soldier's life from the moment of leaving camp to follow her wounded and sick Alabamians to the hospitals of Richmond. Her services are not confined, however, to the sick and wounded from Alabama. Every sick soldier has now a claim on her sympathy. Why, but yesterday, my system having succumbed to the prevailing malaria of the hospital, she came to my room, though a stranger, with my ward nurse, and in the kindest manner offered me her services, and soon after leaving returned to present me with a pillow of feathers, with case as tidy as the driven snow. The very sight of it was soothing to an aching brow, and I blessed her from heart and lips as well. I must not omit to tell why 'Miss Sally' is so disliked by many of the officials. Like all women of energy, she has eyes whose penetration few things escape, and a sagacity fearful or admirable, as the case may be, to all interested. If any abuse is pending, or in progress in the hospital, she is quickly on the track, and if not abated, off 'The Great Eastern' sails to head-quarters. A few days ago, one of the officials of the division sent a soldier to inform her that she must vacate her room instantly. 'Who sent you with that message to me?' she asked him, turning suddenly around. 'Dr. ——,' the soldier answered. 'Pish!' she replied, and swept on in ineffable contempt to the bedside, perhaps, of some sick soldier.

"She always has plenty of money to expend in her charitable enterprises, and when not attending in the wards, or at the cooking-stove, dresses with care in the neatest black silk. Such a woman merits an honorable fame."

A lady, writing from the hospital at Culpeper Court House, says: "I have lost four of my patients. Three of them died rejoicing in Jesus. They were intelligent, noble, godly young men. One from Virginia said to me as he was dying: 'Sing me a hymn.' I repeated, 'Jesus, lover of my soul.' He remarked, 'Where else but in Jesus can a poor sinner trust?' Just as he passed away, he looked up and said, 'Heaven is so sweet to me;' and to the presence of Jesus he went.

"Another from South Carolina seemed very happy, and sung with great delight, 'Happy day, when Jesus washed my sins away.' Young B——, of Virginia, was resigned and even rejoiced at the near prospect of death. He repeated the line, 'How firm a foundation, ye saints of the Lord.' His end was peace.

"One of these young men had determined to enter the Christian ministry."

The scene described by Rev. Mr. Crumley, as he distributed among the soldiers, after one of the Maryland campaigns, the supplies sent forward by the Georgia Relief Association, one of the noblest institutions of the war, is truthful and touching:

"After leaving Warrenton, I visited the wounded in private houses around the battle-field, where I very narrowly escaped being taken prisoner by the Yankees. In Winchester I found thousands of the wounded from Maryland crowded into churches, hotels, private houses and tents, in every imaginable state of suffering and destitution. Though kind words and prayers are good and cheering to the suffering, they could not relieve the terrible destitution. At length my anxious suspense was relieved by the coming of Mr. Selkirk, Dr. Camak and Rev. Mr. Potter, bringing supplies from the Georgia Relief and Hospital Association, which were in advance of anything from the Government. Their coming was clothing to the naked, medicine to the sick, and life to the dying. Could that little girl have been with us as we distributed the gifts of the association, and have seen the pleasure with which the heroic youth, who had made the Maryland campaign barefooted, drew on his rough and bruised feet the soft socks which she knit, no doubt she would knit another pair. Could that young lady have seen the grateful expression upon the face of that noble warrior, as, with lips parched with fever, he sipped the wine or tasted the pickles her hand had prepared, whispering, 'God bless the ladies of Georgia;' or that other, as he exchanged his soiled and blood-stained garments for those sent by the association, ejaculating, ' Yes, we will suffer, and die, if need be, in defence of such noble women '—fresh vigor would have been added to her zeal in providing comforts for our suffering 'braves.' How much more comfortable and sweet would have been the slumber of that mother could she have seen her 'patriot boy,' who had lain upon the bare ground, warmly wrapped in the coverlet or carpet-blanket she had sent for the suffering soldiers.

"After the battle of Sharpsburg we passed over a line of railroad in Central Georgia. The disabled soldiers from General Lee's army were returning to their homes. At every station the wives and daughters of the farmers came on the cars and distributed food and wine and bandages among the sick and wounded. We shall never forget how very like an angel was a little girl; how blushingly and modestly she went to a great, rude, bearded soldier, who had carved a crutch from a rough plank to replace a lost leg; how this little girl asked him if he was hungry, and how he ate like a famished wolf. She asked if his wound was painful, and in a voice of soft, mellow accents, ' Can I do more for you? I am sorry that you are so badly hurt. Have you a little daughter, and wont she cry when she sees you?' The rude soldier's heart was touched, and tears of love and gratitude filled his eyes. He only answered, ' I have three little children. God grant they may be such angels as you.' With an evident effort he repressed a desire to kiss the fair brow of the little girl. He took her little hand between his own and bade her ' Good-bye, God bless you.' The child will always be a better woman because of these lessons of practical charity stamped ineffaceably upon her young heart."

"As we were on our way to Manassas on the 19th of July, 1861," said an officer of the Virginia troops, " on a crowded train of flats, the people along the route of the Manassas Gap Railroad turned out in large bodies, bringing baskets full of provisions and luxuries for the soldiers. Everybody was full of joy, and we rushed on to battle with railroad speed amid the waving of handkerchiefs and the loud huzzahs of a loyal people— little thinking that many of the hearts that beat high for praise would ' soon feel that pulse no more.' Not far from one of the depots, which we had just left in great glee, on an eminence by the road, there stood a lady of more than womanly stature, but of womanly face, with hands uplifted and eyes upturned to heaven in reverential prayer for us and our country. And there she stood with outstretched arms until the train carried us out of sight. I thought of Miriam the prophetess—only the hands of one were lifted in praise, of the other in prayer to God. I never shall forget that scene and the deep impression it made upon all. The shout of reckless joy was turned into serious thought, and blessed, I believe, was the influence of that sight on many a brave heart."

A correspondent writes:

"LYNCHBURG, June 19, 1862.

"The last fortnight, during which I have been visiting among the sick and wounded in this place and Liberty, has been spent most agreeably, and I trust most profitably. It is indeed a grateful task to labor for the spiritual and physical good of our brave soldiers who are suffering in the defence of our country—to smooth their pillows, fan their fevered brows and, while thus promoting their bodily comfort, to speak with them of Him who alone can give peace to the soul. The thoughts of the sick are naturally turned to religion, under any circumstances, but a soldier in a hospital, away from home, surrounded by many sick, and seeing men die daily around him, is peculiarly susceptible of good impressions. At least such I have found to be the case. I have never had a proffered tract refused, or an inquiry or remark on the subject of religion ungraciously received. On the contrary, great interest was universally manifested in the theme of which I spoke, and in many instances I was invited to 'come again.' Especially by professors of religion was I welcomed. They did not stop to ask me to what denomination I belonged, but they hailed me as one who loved the same Saviour as themselves, and therefore, a friend and brother. More than once these have taken from beneath their pillows copies of God's word, given them by our colporters, and spoken of them as their 'best friend and only true counsellor.' In view of all that I have seen, it seems to me, that with the thousands of pale and emaciated forms in the hospitals, with the tens of thousands of sin-sick souls in our camps, a vast responsibility is resting upon the Christians of our State and country. If a surgeon should be filled with remorse to see his patient die for want of attention from himself, how should each Christian, who has not done all he could, feel at each announcement of a soldier's death? And with what pangs of remorse must he behold each mound in the soldiers' graveyard."

"RICHMOND, July 22, 1862.

"Having spent some time recently in visiting the largest hospitals in several of the States and seen and heard much of the soldiers, I have a pretty good opportunity of ascertaining something of the religious status of the army. It is, beyond doubt, true that many have had their morals ruined by the seductive temptations of the camp. But it is equally true that others have been benefited spiritually, and in many cases savingly converted! The solemn stillness, the suffering of body and spirit, the absence of loved ones and the pleasures of home are well calculated to win the soul to a contemplation of the 'rest' which 'remaineth.' Said a soldier to me as we were journeying together: ' But for this book (the Bible) I should long since have gone beside myself. When I think of my poor little motherless children far away, sadness and sorrow fill my heart, and in despair I am ready to sink; but at such times I always betake myself to the reading of God's word, and it has never failed to comfort, sustain and even to fill me with joy. But for this, to-day, sir, I would be a raving maniac.'

"While going south on the cars with the sick and wounded, I noticed that quite a number would take from their pocket tracts which I had given them, weeks and months before, and with much interest read them again. On taking from my pocket a few packages of tracts, one and another would inquire, ' Have you tracts to dispose of?' Then came a captain with $2 and said, ' Give me the worth of this in tracts for my men.' Another soldier said, ' I want to help on this work; will you accept this?' handing $1. After while an elderly gentleman handed a $5 bill, saying that he 'was delighted to see how eagerly the soldiers had read what was given them.' A soldier took from his pocket several tracts tied up in a roll—said he had read them repeatedly and hoped often to peruse them in days to come. They had been sent to him through the mail by his wife, to whom they were given by a colporter.

"Since he had been in the army his wife had sickened and died, and this was one of the last gifts she had sent him. The above illustrates, though but feebly, how vast and inviting is the field now appealing for our sympathy and toil. Untold good may be effected by means so simple, that in the eyes of many they seem as foolishness.   The look of love, the tear of sympathy, the word of entreaty, the printed page of Gospel truth, are now, as much as ever before, the 'power and wisdom of God,' and are mighty for pulling down the strongholds of wickedness.

"A. E. D."

A young soldier, while dying very happily, sung the following stanza :

"Great Jehovah, we adore Thee,
God the Father, God the Son,
God the Spirit, joined in glory
On the same eternal throne ;
Endless praises
To Jehovah, three in one."

The chaplain then asked him if he had any message to send to his friends.   " Yes, " said he.   " Tell my father I have tried to eat my meals with thanksgiving."   " Tell him that I have tried to pray as we used to do at home."   " Tell him that Christ is now all my hope, all my trust, and that He is precious to my soul."   " Tell him that I believe Christ will take me to Himself, and to my dear sister, who is in heaven."   The voice of the dying boy faltered in the intervals between these precious sentences.   When the hymn, commencing, " Nearer, my God, to Thee," was read to him, at the end of each stanza he exclaimed, with striking energy, " O Lord Jesus, thou art coming *nearer to me.*"   Also, at the end of each stanza of the hymn commencing—

"Just as I am—without one plea,
But that Thy blood was shed for me,"

he exclaimed—"*I come! O Lamb of God, I come !*"   Speaking again of his friends, he said, " Tell my father that I *died happy.*"   His last words were, " Father, I'm coming to Thee ! "   Then the Christian soldier sweetly and calmly fell " asleep in Jesus."

This was witnessed by about twenty fellow-soldiers and the effect upon the feelings of all was very marked.   Said a Roman Catholic, who lay near the dying one, with tears in his eyes, and strong emotion, " I never want to die happier than that man did."   Said another, " I never prayed until last night; but when I saw that man die so happy, I determined to seek religion too."

A colporter writes from " Seabrooks " hospital, Richmond, to Rev. N. B. Cobb, North Carolina : " We had a very interesting young man in our hospital, who made a profession of faith after he entered the army. He told me that soon after he enlisted in the army he began to study about the horrors of war, and was led to feel his need of a Saviour, and felt under deep conviction. There were in his company three pious, praying men. He requested them to accompany him to the woods every day to pray for him, which they did. They had some very happy meetings, at one of which he found Jesus precious to his soul. I think he is the most devoted young man I ever saw. He is badly wounded, but spends every day in prayer and praise to God for the great mercy shown him."

W. R. Gualtney writes from Richmond to the *Biblical Recorder*: "The Lord is with us at the 'Seabrooks' hospital. We have a great revival of religion here. A greater one I scarcely ever witnessed. Rarely a day passes but I find one or more new converts. The number in our hospital is being rapidly reduced, many being transferred to other places, and many having died. But the religious element in our midst is by no means dying out. A large number are yet inquiring, 'What must we do to be saved?' Those who have professed a hope in Christ seem to be in the full enjoyment of faith."

The *Petersburg Express* says: "We are gratified to learn that the state of religious feeling at the hospitals in this city is very encouraging. Within the last three and a half months there have been eighty conversions, and a large number manifest interest in the subject of religion. The chaplains (Rev. Messrs. Young and Hardwick) acknowledge that they have received valuable assistance from the colporters. Tracts have been extensively distributed, and are highly valued by the soldiers. If we can make good Christians of our fighting men, our armies will be invincible against all the hosts that can be brought against them."

A correspondent of the *Religious Herald* writes: "Not long since it was my privilege to stand by the bedside of one of the heroes who are daily offering themselves as sacrifices upon the altar of their country. He was an officer of the gallant Fifty-sixth Virginia, with which he had been at Donelson, had borne his part in the hardships and glories of that memorable place, had been in the battles around Richmond, had been wounded in the battle of Sharpsburg, and now had come home—to die. As I entered his room he raised his emaciated hand and kindly welcomed me; spoke to me of his sufferings, and conversed with so much cheerfulness that I could not help expressing the hope that he might yet weather the storm. I was particularly struck with his eye. There was a brightness and fire about it I had never noticed before; but its lustre was of heaven, not of earth; it was soon to close on earthly things, and to gaze on the 'King in His beauty.' He told me he had no fear of death, his trust had been firmly fixed on Christ for seventeen years, and for him the last enemy had no terrors. He requested me to read the Fifty-first Psalm, and pray with him.

"Jesus, who has said, 'Where two or three are gathered together in my name, there am I in the midst of them,' fulfilled His promise, for as I rose from my knees and wiped away the blinding tears from my eyes, my full heart said, 'Surely this is none other than the house of God and the very gate of heaven.'

"This interview has taught me a lesson of humility which I shall not soon forget; for as I gazed upon the thin, emaciated form, confined to one position, the humble soldier's cot on which he lay, I thought, 'Jesus, the King of kings, dwells here, and I had rather be this poor soldier than to be the tenant of a palace.' I bade him 'good-bye,' and promised to call soon and see him again, but death came sooner than I expected, for when I heard from him again he had fallen asleep in Jesus; earth bore another grave, but heaven had won a sweeter strain of praise to Him who doeth all things well. Oh, blessed Jesus! Oh, thou divine Redeemer! when we see our friends treading the verge of Jordan, free from fear because Thou art with them, we would raise our hearts and our voices in adoration, and praise, and thankfulness to Thee,

> "'Who captive leads captivity
> And takes the sting from death.'

"TYREE GLENN."

Rev. C. F. Fry writes, from Staunton, Virginia: "While I was preaching at the hospital a young man, confined to his bed, wept most bitterly. After the service was over he said to me, 'I have been thinking a great deal about my condition, but never, until now, could get the consent of my mind to trust the Saviour. God being my helper, I shall never cease looking unto Jesus for life, joy, and peace.'"

"*Brother Editors :* I should have written of our hospitals before this, but have been twice anticipated by 'A. E. D.' Besides, I have been deterred, observing the tendency to put these subjects in a rose-colored light. But, on the other hand, it is but proper for me to contribute my mite of experience, as I have certainly derived benefit from the letters of others. For instance, I had not made any attempt to stop the card-playing among the convalescents until I read what a brother chaplain had done. His success emboldened me. So, one day, approaching a group who were busily 'throwing the spotted leaf,' but who desisted when they saw me, I did not content myself with proposing to give them some of my cards, but urged them to give up theirs. 'We mean no harm, sir,' said a bright youth—'we do not play for money, only for pastime. It is dull here.' 'Yes,' I replied, 'it must be dull, and I do not wonder you wish some recreation; but then you have books and papers in abundance, and I would not resort to cards.' 'I do not think it is wrong, sir.' 'The mere act of throwing cards may not be, but it is connected closely with gambling. Besides, it does seem an inappropriate employment in a room filled with sick and dying men, and for those who have just been raised up from death's door. But I will give you a simple argument. Have you a mother?' 'I have.' 'Do you think she would be willing for you to play cards, even for fun?' 'I know she would not.' 'Well, at what age is a man justifiable in violating his mother's wishes?' The cards were thrown aside—I hope, permanently. The group scattered, and the youth who had been the principal speaker followed me, and sat by my side while I read and prayed with a dying Christian. Possibly this piece may strike the eye of some card-playing soldier. To such an one, I put the question, 'Would your mother approve of it?'

"Encouraged by this success, I made a similar attempt in one other hospital, with like results; and subsequently coming into the same room, I asked an elderly, one-legged soldier what had become of the cards? He replied, 'I have not seen them since you talked to the boys the other day.' I feel the more free to speak against cards because we have large and well-selected libraries of both religious and secular volumes, and because I am constantly distributing papers in abundance. I have also lately queried within myself whether we ought not to supply our convalescent soldiers with other innocent means of recreation. There are thousands in our hospitals, not able to go to camp, who are well enough to find confinement very wearisome. Some of them are readers. Those who are can't read all the time. I have thought of instituting clubs—of introducing a draught-board, grace-hoops, etc. To some, this would seem very queer work for a chaplain; but I am sure these things would help to make the hospital a pleasant home, and I know that in a late convalescence, on the rainy days, I did not despise such ministrations. Tell me if you think I am wrong. This is certain, that I find frequent religious meetings very acceptable to the men—acceptable, if for no other reason, because such services break in upon the monotony of their lives. I have lately, in connection with Brother Walton, held several extra meetings, and I never in my life saw more earnest attention. These meetings are held in a large room, partly filled with patients. To them especially are the services acceptable. As we ask one and another, ' Will the service disturb you ? ' the reply is, ' If it did, I would wish to have it.' Very solemn is a meeting in such a place, where the preaching is sometimes not interrupted, so much as rendered more impressive, by the cough or hollow groan of a sufferer. I think if the minister who was so severe on colporters and chaplains, could have seen the convalescents gathering, the cripples hobbling in, one dear little North Carolina boy, who lost both legs at Sharpsburg, brought in and placed in the broad window-sill on cushions —could have seen how happy some Christians looked, and how solemn some sinners appeared, he would have altered his mind and concluded, perhaps we were doing some good after all. Many bedside visits, many sermons, tracts, and papers may fail to do good in the army. But is not this true of our work in the pastorate ? Is it not true of the expenditure of ammunition in a battle ? Ordinarily, a man's weight in lead is expended for every one that is killed. I have not told the half that I designed when I began, but thinking only short pieces appropriate for the *Herald*, in its present limited dimensions, I close.

" Yours truly,

" GEO. B. TAYLOR.

" STAUNTON, February 24, 1863."

" HUGUENOT SPRINGS HOSPITAL, June 8th.
"*Messrs. Editors:* On the third Sabbath in May we commenced a series of meetings at this hospital, which continued till the first Sabbath of June. The Lord's blessing rested upon the meeting,

from twenty-five to thirty making a public profession of faith in Christ. Fifteen have been baptized, and others are awaiting the ordinance. . . .

"G. W. HYDE, Chaplain of the Post."

" Last week, while in Lynchburg, I had the pleasure of seeing from fifteen to twenty soldiers present themselves for prayer and religious instruction. Rev. Jno. L. Johnson had just baptized eight. Brother Johnson has succeeded in establishing a soldiers' library, by means of which papers, religious and secular, magazines and books are placed in the hands of every soldier who desires reading matter. We have two efficient colporters in Lynchburg, Elders G. C. Trevillian and C. A. Miles. The latter was severely wounded at the battle of Seven Pines. One of these brethren is in the library-room certain hours of each day, lending out books, etc., to those who come for them. During the moments I was in the depository, many came to return books which they had read and to secure others. Some came for papers. One would say, ' I am from Alabama, and want an Alabama paper,' and he would be presented with the *South-west Baptist.* Another would say, ' Can't you let me have the *Christian Index* ? That's the paper I read at home.' Others would desire the *Confederate Baptist*, others the *Herald*, etc. You may judge of the desire for religious papers, when I assure you that hundreds of applicants daily supply themselves at this depository. When a sick man walks as far as from the hospital to this reading-room to solicit a paper, we may be assured that he will make a good use of it, reading and pondering almost every word.

" I also spent a Sabbath in Charlottesville and, with Dr. W. F. Broaddus, attended services at the hospital, where a large and attentive congregation listened to a sermon from the text, ' Come unto me, all ye that labor and are heavy laden, and I will give you rest.' Many an eye was moistened as the preacher urged the acceptance of the blessed invitation. Dr. Broaddus is doing a grand work among the sick and wounded at this point. I was astonished to see how many soldiers he was acquainted with, knowing their names, where they came from, etc. The greater part of his time is spent among them. I feel assured that the Church will, as far as possible, release Brother Broaddus from pastoral visits, as he can be so much more useful in the hospitals,

14

It will be gratifying to them to know that their loss in this matter is the gain of those to whom, under God, they owe everything—men who are far from home and friends, sad and afflicted, and many of them nigh unto death. Who would not give up everything for the comfort and salvation of a poor wounded soldier as he pines upon his cot, away from the fond endearments of home? Rev. J. C. Hiden is laboring efficiently here as chaplain. Gordonsville now affords a fine field for doing good. Besides the hospitals, the encampments in this vicinity contain many who have both the time and the desire to attend religious services. I am informed that within a few weeks over thirty soldiers here have made a profession of religion. Rev. D. B. Ewing, of the Presbyterian Church, is the post chaplain. He is eminently adapted to such labors, and finds much encouragement in the work. Brother Ewing, assisted by several of the chaplains, is now holding a protracted meeting."—A. E. D.

"July 2, 1863.

" We have now a noble band of laborers in the hospitals, ministering to the spiritual wants of our suffering soldiers. In Richmond, we have Elders R. Ryland, D. Shaver, B. Philips, J. W. Williams, and others; at Petersburg, Elder Thos. Hume, Sr.; at Charlottesville, Elder W. F. Broaddus; at Lynchburg, Elders G. C. Trevillian and C. A. Miles; at Liberty, Elder Jas. A. Davis; at Scottsville, J. C. Clopton; at Culpeper Court House, Elder J. N. Fox; at the hospitals in the upper part of the Valley, Elders A. M. Grimsley and H. Madison; at Emory, Henry College, and other hospitals on the Virginia and Tennessee Railroad, Elders R. Lewis, J. D. Chambers, and W. Buckels; and at Danville we have Elder Jno. C. Long. Besides, many of the chaplains at these several points are likewise acting as our agents, and receiving their supplies from our depositories. What vast good will be effected by these men of God, if the Holy Ghost deigns to attend the message which they, almost every hour, are delivering to some soul heavy-laden with a sense of its sins and sorrows. . . .

"A. E. D."

Says an exchange: "A friend in Danville told us that, out of 2,000 letters he had opened, from friends of deceased soldiers, not more than a dozen were found that did not contain religious advice." Perhaps some of the writers never gave religious advice until those to whom they wrote were in the grave. . . .

"CHARLOTTESVILLE, July 25.
" The interest of our soldiers in the hospitals here, in the great things of eternity, is exceedingly encouraging. Several have professed conversion, while many others are evidently asking, 'What must I do to be saved?' Brother Hiden, chaplain of the Delavan, at this post, is preaching with me, in a series of meetings, in the Charlottesville church, and crowds of the convalescent attend, while those who are still confined to their sick beds are, in many instances, eager to have preaching in their wards. What a luxury, to press the cup of salvation to one who is physically unable to inquire for it by going to the Lord's house!
"W. F. BROADDUS."

"At the protracted meeting at the First Church, Richmond, seventeen soldiers professed conversion. A number professed at a similar meeting held in the hospital, and several are obtaining the good hope at a meeting now in progress at the Second Baptist Church. There have been fully *seventy-five* conversions since the first of last October. Quite a number of soldiers are being taught to read. Some commence with the alphabet. One man fifty years old commenced with his letters, and now reads. The chaplains are doing a good work here."

"RICHMOND COLLEGE, March 19.
" On the 14th instant I finished my second month of colportage work in the hospitals. I could fill a large sheet with interesting details, but they would only be repetitions of what you constantly receive from those in your employment. Suffice it to say, that I have conversed with, addressed and prayed for, many hundreds of invalid soldiers during the month, and given to each a tract or a New Testament, and have received from *all* great respect, and from *many* the most tender expressions of gratitude. I have found about forty-five men who could not read. To these I have given some such books as ' McGuffey's First Reader,' after demanding and obtaining the promise from the recipients that they would *try to learn*, and requesting their comrades to teach them. I have also distributed a small num-

ber of French and German Testaments to such as could read only these languages. These books and the elementary readers have been purchased by funds solicited of a few generous persons, amounting to $27, and not yet exhausted. The editors of the *Religious Herald* have given me some two hundred papers for distribution, all which have been eagerly sought by the soldiers. The editors of the two Presbyterian papers have given me each a bundle, and I shall call on the Methodist paper soon for a similar favor. I have also received and disbursed Sunday pamphlets, magazines and books of a miscellaneous character. In fine, the work is full of encouragement, and worthy of far more piety, learning and talents than I possess.

" R. RYLAND."

Rev. J. C. Hiden, post chaplain, writes to us from Charlottesville: "In a stay of nearly a month, I have not heard three oaths, nor seen but one man under the influence of intoxicating liquor. We have preaching or prayer-meeting almost every day, and the attendance is large, and there is evidently considerable interest among the men. Many of them want Testaments and hymn-books, and eagerly seek after them, and *all* seem approachable on the subject of religion."

The Richmond *Dispatch*, of April 11, states that a revival of religion has been in progress, at Camp Winder, near this city, for about two weeks. At that date twenty soldiers had professed conversion and many others had asked an interest in the prayers of their pious comrades.

Brother J. C. Clopton furnishes the following in reference to the Rockbridge Hospitals:

"As I go along among the hospitals my heart is pained at seeing so much to be done and so few laborers. Sometimes I see several physicians going around together to consult about the physical man—to see if the body can be saved from the power of disease, while scarcely any one seems to be concerned about the disease of sin or the death which never dies. Every hospital ought to have at least one colporter. A poor, sick soldier, fifty-four years of age, was deeply affected by my visit to his couch and exclaimed, '*Thank God, a minister has come to pray with me.*' Oh, I assure you, that to go to these sick men and to read to them the promises of the Gospel, and to invoke upon them the blessing of God, is the next thing to a visit of an angel. It relieves them from the sad gloom of the sick-room, and sends sunshine into their sorrowing hearts—the sunshine of heaven."

Rev. J. G. Skinner, Manassas: "I have met with very great success during the past month. There is a great demand for reading matter among the soldiers. If you have any tracts, do send them, for I assure you that there never was a time nor a place where such things were more needed than here. I have been preaching and holding prayer-meetings whenever an opportunity presented itself."

Rev. J. B. Taylor, Jr., Winchester: "This morning I went through one hospital to the couch of every man. They thankfully received my tracts and words of sympathy and advice; some calling out to me, before I reached them, to bring them a tract."

Rev. H. G. Crews writes, from Winchester: "A young man in the hospital, upon being asked if he was a Christian, replied: 'I have been one, but have gone astray.' I urged him to repent of his backsliding and to return unto God. He seemed deeply moved, and, with moistened eyes, asked that I would visit him again. All the sick seem comforted by having religious conversation; many who make no pretensions to piety listen with solemn attention. A lieutenant desired to be supplied with tracts, that he might distribute them among his men. The same request had been made by others. In the hotels and saloons I have distributed tracts, as well as on the streets, to the hundreds who come in from the camps around. Oh, it is a blessed work to care for the souls of our brave boys. If I could reach the ear of every Christian in the Confederacy I would cry, 'Men of Israel! help!'"

Mr. J. C. Clopton, who has been laboring at the hospitals in Staunton, and at the Rockbridge Alum Springs, writes: "Oftentimes I see the soldiers reading the tracts for days after they have been received, and manifesting the most eager desire to be benefited by them. Passing along to the hospital, I saw a group of convalescents, and at once I was tempted to be ashamed of the work, and was about to pass them without giving any tracts; but it appeared to me that this might be a temptation of the evil one, and I determined to overlook no one. Going up to a soldier, I asked if he was a Christian. He was deeply moved, and replied, 'I wish to have some conversation with you; can you sit down with me awhile?' He told me that he had been a professor of religion; had enjoyed the smile of God on his soul; but that temptation and vice had led him astray, until now he was almost ready to despair. Weeping and sobbing he confessed his sin. I urged him to seek again the smile and favor of God. A very sick man said to me, 'Oh, sir, I would give worlds for an interest in salvation, and the pardon of sin.' He has since passed away."

A chaplain writes from Williamsburg: "I know twelve men in my regiment, who have professed conversion from reading your tracts. One came to me with a tract in his hand, and tears flowing down his cheeks, and said, 'I would not take thousands for this tract. My parents have prayed for me, and wept over me; but it was left for this tract to bring me, a poor convicted sinner, to the feet of Jesus. Oh, sir, I feel to-day that I am a new man, and have set out for heaven.'"

Another chaplain, whose regiment is near Yorktown, says: "For three months I have not preached a sermon. We have no preaching place, and I do not know when we shall have one. The most that I can do is by colportage work, from camp to camp, distributing the pages of Divine truth. The soldiers are anxious for Testaments and tracts, and read them most eagerly."

Rev. Dr. James B. Taylor writes:

"It has been my privilege recently to spend a few days in the town of Winchester, visiting the camps, but more especially the hospitals. Until the sick and stores were removed, with reference to an evacuation of the place, three or four of us were busily engaged in spiritual labors among the soldiers. During my whole stay only two men refused tracts from me—one a Roman Catholic, and the other unable to read. As I would go from cot to cot, leaving a tract or a Testament and speaking of Jesus, it was not uncommon for some sufferer in another part of the room to call out, 'Bring me one.' I shall never forget my first visit to one of these hospitals. There, stretched out before me, on coarse, hard beds, lay perhaps a hundred sick soldiers, mostly young men, some of them the flower of the land. They were my brothers—far from happy homes—lonely, despairing, sick—some of them sick unto death. How cheering the sight of any friend! What an opportunity for the child of God! Christian reader, your Saviour 'went about doing good.' He went where there was sickness and misery and death. This was

His great concern, His meat and drink. He never faltered, nor wearied, nor turned aside. Are you one of His? Then here is work for you; and if you cannot *personally* engage in it, then help to send others out into this field, so vast and so inviting. Thus shall you win souls who shall deck the diadem of your Redeemer—who shall be stars to glitter in your crown of rejoicing for ever and ever. At the union prayer-meeting (of all denominations) one afternoon, that gallant soldier and pious man, General 'Stonewall' Jackson, was present, and led in prayer. At the supper-table, some professing Christians, when told of it, expressed regret at not having been present. Had they known 'that *General Jackson* was to have been there,' they would certainly have gone. Alas! they forgot that a greater than Jackson, or any other mere man, had promised to meet with His people, even the Lord of life and glory.

"It is certainly a gratifying fact that General Jackson is an active, humble, consistent Christian—restraining profanity and Sabbath-breaking—welcoming army colporters, distributing tracts, and anxious to have every regiment in his army supplied with a chaplain. Indeed, our officers generally seem disposed to favor efforts for the moral and religious improvement of the soldiers. I am told that a general in command of an important post, a man notoriously cross and profane, welcomed a colporter to his division with words something like these: 'Sir, you have come, I hope, to do all the good you can.' He then invited the colporter to his head-quarters, to mess at his table and to share his blankets.

"It is proper I should refer to the little time I have employed in visiting the hospitals in Culpeper and Staunton during the last fortnight. In accordance with your request I proceeded at once to Culpeper Court House, where, by the kindness of the gentleman who had charge of the hospital, I continued day after day to call upon and, as far as possible, to converse with the sick soldiers, numbering in all about 400. In no instance did I meet with repulsive treatment. Generally they received my approaches respectfully, and many of them conversed freely on their spiritual condition. At Staunton, in like manner, I found about 320 confined in the hospital. I was permitted without hindrance to visit the different wards, which I did several days in succession. I attended, also, two meetings in the large chapel, and preached once to the convalescent soldiers. In this hospital,

also, I made it my business to converse individually with most
of those to whom I had access. To each one at Culpeper Court
House and Staunton I gave tracts or Testaments, and in some
instances both. These were received with special interest. In
performing this work I found it growing in magnitude, and my
own heart more and more interested in it. Some of the cases
were particularly touching. One man from south-western
Georgia, with deep feeling, told me that out of ninety-eight composing his company twenty-four were buried in western Virginia. I pressed upon him the claims of the Gospel, and he
seemed thankful and penitent. Another, far from home, seemed
near the grave. The tears flowed from his languid eyes when I
asked him about his spiritual condition, and with trembling lips
he replied, 'No hope.' He gazed at me wistfully, as I pointed
him to the ' Lamb of God that taketh away the sin of the world.'
Another, a young man, was much moved, as he told of his
desertion of the Saviour, having been thrown with evil associates
far away from the privileges of the house of prayer. Here and
there I found a faithful one cleaving to the Lord and maintaining with consistency his Christian character. One young man
seemed much interested in all I said, and promised me to give
heed to the truths I had been urging upon his attention. I was
specially affected by the remarks of a soldier, who said: ' Oh, sir,
you know not how difficult it is to stem the tide of corruption
in the army. Many of our officers drink and swear, and dis-
courage all manifestations of religious feeling.' One of the soldiers in Staunton, on seeing one of the pastors pass along the
street, said: 'There is the man who gave me a Bible; I never
read it before, but I have now read it through several times, and
wonder at the things it contains.' I could mention other incidents, but these will suffice.

" JAS. B. TAYLOR, SR."

" The field of labor opened here for the accomplishment of good
is beyond measure. An angel might covet it. True; and we
are not surprised that Rev. Dr. Ryland, President of Richmond
College, should accept the position of colporter in the hospitals
of the city tendered him by the ladies of the First Baptist Church.
The time thus spent will not be esteemed the least honorable
portion of his life in the last day."

A writer in one of the papers gives the following touching description of religious services in a military hospital: "At 3 o'clock services were held in the main hall of the hospital. It was to me a most imposing spectacle, to witness that large assembly of men in all stages of sickness—some sitting upon their beds, while others were lying down listening to the word of God—many of them probably for the last time. The subject of the sermon was ' Peace in Christ,' and a most timely and instructive discourse it was. I do not think that I ever saw a more attentive audience. They seemed to drink in the word of life at every breath."

"A series a meetings held in the First Baptist Church, Petersburg, during the absence of the pastor, Rev. T. G. Keen, D. D., by Elders W. M. Young and T. Hume, Jr., has resulted in the conversion of four of the citizens and from twelve to fifteen of the soldiers in the hospitals of that city."

The colporters of the Soldiers' Book and Tract Society of the Southern Methodist Church report favorably as to the fruit of their labors in the hospital. Rev. J. E. McSparran reports four conversions in the hospitals at Lynchburg, and many seriously and anxiously inquiring the way of life. Rev. J. E. Martin reports sixteen conversions in the Chimborazo Hospital, Richmond. He has found only twelve men who could not read, and they were mostly foreigners. " One young man was very anxious to learn to read. I procured a spelling-book, and in a few days he learned so as to be able to read the Bible. He has since professed conversion."

Rev. A. D. Cohen writes from the camp near Goldsboro', North Carolina, to the *Biblical Recorder:* " I have more opportunity to do good than at any other time of my pastoral life. Every tent is the habitation of a family of from six to eight men, each one of whom feels constrained to pay at least respectful attention to the kind counsel and good advice of their chaplain."

Rev. J. H. Campbell, army evangelist, Georgia, relates the following incident: " Noticing on the cars a soldier who looked sick and sad I offered him certain tracts which I hoped might suit his case. This led to a conversation, from which I learned that he had been dangerously ill in camp for many weeks, during which he had received intelligence of the death of his wife, who, he said, was ' one of the best women,' and that he was returning, broken in health, to his three little motherless children. But for the comforts of religion he thinks he would have lost his mind; his fellow-soldiers came frequently into his tent, and read the Scriptures and sang and prayed with him. 'One text,' said he, 'was in my mind day and night, awake and asleep: "*Though He slay me, yet will I trust in Him.*"' I concluded the poor fellow knew more about religion than myself, and felt comforted while trying to comfort him."

Rev. Mr. Hume writes:

" PETERSBURG.

" I have been for some weeks devoting my time to the hospitals in the city, and find myself becoming more and more absorbed in the work. The noble men are so fond of having one to talk with them about Jesus, that my heart is made to rejoice with theirs. The other day I was reading a few tracts to a sick soldier, and while reading one on the ' Blood of Christ ' he became so enthused that he shouted aloud, 'Glory to God!' and it was some time before he could be quieted. Another said to me: ' When I first came into the hospital I was sad and dissatisfied, but since I have been here I have learned of Jesus, and thank God even for tribulations.' There is great need of Testaments, as many are destitute of them. . . .

"A. E. DICKINSON."

Rev. Joseph E. Martin, from Chimborazo Hospital at Richmond, writes: " We have had lately sixteen conversions. One young man was very anxious to learn to read. I procured him a spelling-book, and in a few days he learned so rapidly as to be able to read the Testament. He has since professed religion. A middle-aged man from Georgia has learned to read since he joined the army, and has committed to memory almost all the New Testament, with the book of Job."

Rev. George Pearcy, writing from Lynchburg, Virginia, says: " I collected from Sunday-schools and individuals above a hundred Testaments, a few Bibles, and some books and tracts—these were placed in three large hospitals for the sick soldiers. There have been as many as 10,000 soldiers in the encampment here, hence it is a most interesting field for usefulness. Many soldiers have the Bible or Testament, and love to read it. A good number are members of Churches. Far away from home and kindred, they are delighted to receive the visits of brother Christians, and get something to read. All receive the tracts, and read them with delight. The Lord has blessed the work.

He has poured out His Spirit upon many. Several have died in the triumphs of faith. It was a great pleasure and privilege to speak to them of the Saviour, and witness their trust in Him during the trying hour. One who died a week ago said, in a whisper, a short time before he breathed his last, when the nurse held up the tract, ' Come to Jesus,' ' I can't see.' He was told it was the tract, ' Come to Jesus,' and that Jesus says, ' Him that cometh unto me I will in nowise cast out.' ' Thank the Lord for that,' he replied. ' Have you come to Him ? and do you find Him precious ? ' ' Precious, thank the Lord.' ' He has promised never to leave nor forsake His people.' ' Thank the Lord for that; ' and so he would say of all the promises quoted. One young man, to whom I gave a tract, told me that at home he was a steady, sober man; never swore ; but that becoming a soldier he did as many others did—threw off restraint, and did wickedly. ' But now,' said he, ' I have done swearing, and will seek the salvation of my soul.' "

"When I joined the army," said a soldier to a colporter, " I was a member of the Church, and enjoyed religion, but since I came into camp I have been without anything of a religious character to read, and assailed on every side by such temptations as have caused me to dishonor my religious profession. Oh, sir, if you had been with me, and extended such aid as you now bestow, I might have been kept from all the sin and sorrow which, as a poor backslider, I have known."

One who had visited the hospitals at Richmond wrote : " The field of labor opened here for the accomplishment of good is beyond measure. An angel might covet it. At 3 o'clock services were held in the main hall of the hospital. It was a most imposing spectacle to see men in all stages of sickness—some sitting upon their beds listening to the word of God—many of them probably for the last time. I do not think I ever saw a more attentive audience. They seemed to drink in the word of life at every breath."

"Some time since," says Rev. A. E. Dickinson, " it was my pleasure to stand up in the presence of a large company of convalescent soldiers in one of our hospitals to proclaim salvation. During the reading of a portion of Scripture tears began to flow. I then announced that dear old hymn—

" ' There is a fountain filled with blood,
   Drawn from Immanuel's veins,' etc.,

the reading of which seemed to melt every heart, and the entire audience was in tears before God. Every word in reference to spiritual truth fell with a soft, subduing fervor on their chastened hearts."

Rev. J. T. Carpenter, post chaplain at Castle Thunder, Richmond, in a letter to the *Army and Navy Messenger*, reports 131 professions of conversion among our soldiers in confinement there.

" CHARLOTTESVILLE, VIRGINIA.

"Brother Clopton seemed very much interested for Imboden's men, and if he received your approval has, perhaps, started in that direction.

"There is much interest in the hospitals here. My last visit was one of the most delightful hours of my life. It is such a precious privilege to point the deeply anxious soldiers, languishing in the hospitals, to the blessed Jesus—even in the imperfect way that I can do it. I did not find a man who did not seem very grateful for the privilege of conversing on the subject of personal religion. How brightly and beautifully the impressions made on youthful hearts by pious parents come out amid the darkness of trouble and suffering in the hospital! God be praised for these sanctifying influences on the heart of the soldier! One noble soldier said to me: ' Thank God for the tract you gave me. It was blest to my conversion. I may die from this wound (he was shot through the breast), but I feel that Jesus is my trust. I fear not to die.'

"A. P. ABELL."

A lady, living at the North, writes to a Southern friend, after visiting the hospital for Confederate prisoners on David's island: " Oh! I felt proud as a queen to see how beautifully they behave —grave, thoughtful, dignified, uncomplaining, cheerful, grateful for kindness, courteous—gentlemen to the backbone. They received me with as much ease (flat on their backs, in shirt and drawers, bunked up all kinds of ways) as if they had been doing the hospitality in their far-off homes. Every man had his Bible, and I heard from one of the carpenters, who rowed us over to the island, that a profane word was never heard from them."

Brother Luther Broaddus writes from Charlottesville: " In compliance with your request I have put myself under the direction of my cousin, Dr. W. F. Broaddus, and have been doing what I could in the way of tract distribution, etc. I find it a very pleasant work, indeed; the soldiers all seem anxious to secure reading matter, and some are concerned about their souls."

This noble young man was then just beginning that career of usefulness in which he walked so worthily in the footsteps of illustrious sires, and made himself a warm place in the hearts of his brethren and a prospect for still larger success, which his recent death has cut off.

"HUGUENOT SPRINGS, August 10th.

"I am glad to announce that the Lord has been good to us at this post. For some time past deep seriousness has pervaded the minds of the masses of the soldiers congregated here. Profound attention has been given to the preached word, and your unworthy brother has never been more encouraged in 'holding forth the word of life.' Brother H. Hatcher recently aided in a series of meetings, and, as the result, the writer baptized sixteen noble soldiers, who henceforth purpose to be soldiers of the Cross and followers of the Lamb. I am happy to say that at least one of these noble young men, a Virginian, has solemnly determined, should God spare his life through this war, to give himself to God in the ministry. And may we not expect many recruits to the ministry from the ranks of our Christian army after the close of this war? As for myself, I have high expectations from this quarter. Let Christians at home continue in supplication for the Divine blessing to rest upon our army, and upon Christ's ambassadors who preach to them the glorious Gospel.

"GEO. W. HYDE, Post Chaplain."

"CHARLOTTESVILLE HOSPITAL.

"*Dear Brother Dickinson :* The number of sick and wounded soldiers has somewhat increased of late at the hospitals here; not, as I suppose, on account of a general increase of sickness in our armies, but on account of the location of Charlottesville in relation to the present movement of our forces. I am more and more impressed with the importance of furnishing our soldiers in the hospitals with our religious newspapers. I could distribute profitably ten times the number I receive. Every State in the Confederacy is represented here. Why cannot every State, not cut off from us by the enemy, furnish papers for this hospital?

The *Biblical Recorder* and *Confederate Baptist,* once sent here, have ceased to come. Why is this ? *The Christian Index, Religious Herald* and *Southern Baptist* come with tolerable regularity ; but never in sufficient numbers to supply the demand. Every Georgian wants the *Index*—and so of other soldiers; each wants to see a paper from his *own dear State.* There are some signs of religious awakening among the soldiers here. A few are decidedly interested, and I am not without hope that we are about to be favored with an ingathering of souls to the Lord. Let our soldiers be remembered in all the prayers of the disciples of Jesus. May thousands of them soon become soldiers of the Cross !

"Yours truly,
"W. F. BROADDUS."

I might multiply at great length incidents illustrating the great value of this colportage work, but I must now content myself with adding only the following :

A father sent to his son in the army the tract, "Are you Ready ? " and was soon after rejoiced by the reply : " Yes, sir ! I can now say that *I am ready.* The tract you sent awakened me. I have gone to Jesus for salvation, and am prepared now for whatever may await me."

A mother sent her son Dr. J. A. Broadus's tract—" We are Praying for You at Home "—and added the simple words : "Yes ! we are praying for you, Charley, that you may become a Christian." That boy saw no peace until he found Christ and experienced sweet " peace in believing." A soldier once asked me for a copy of the tract, " You Must Labor for Salvation," saying that it had been blessed to his own conversion—that he had given it to a comrade, and he, too, had been converted—and that he now wanted to distribute all of the copies he could get.

CHAPTER VII.

WORK OF THE CHAPLAINS AND MISSIONARIES.

UNQUESTIONABLY one of the most potent factors in the grand success of our work was the union of hearts and hands on the part of chaplains and missionaries, and indeed of all Christian workers of the evangelical denominations.

The gifted and lamented Dr. Wm. J. Hoge thus wrote of a visit he made to Fredericksburg in the spring of 1863, during the great revival in Barksdale's Mississippi Brigade: "The Rev. Dr. Burrows, of the First Baptist Church, Richmond, was to have preached that night, but as he would remain some days and I could only stay a day, he courteously insisted on my preaching. And so we had a Presbyterian sermon, introduced by Baptist services, under the direction of a Methodist chaplain, in an Episcopal church. Was not that a beautiful solution of the vexed problem of Christian union?"

This was but a type of what was usual all through the army. No one was asked or expected to compromise in the least the peculiar tenets of the denomination to which he belonged; but, instead of spending our time in fierce polemics over disputed points, we found common ground upon which we could stand shoulder to shoulder and labor for the cause of our common Master. Bound together by the sacred ties of a common faith in Jesus, a common hope of an inheritance beyond the skies, and a common desire to bring our brave men to Christ and to do all within our power to promote their spiritual interests, we mingled together in freest intercourse, took sweet counsel together, preached and prayed and labored together, and formed ties of friendship—nay, of brotherhood—which time can never sever, and which, we firmly believe, eternity will only purify and strengthen. It was our custom, when men professed faith in Christ, to take their names and ask what Church they desired to join, and, if there was no minister present of that denomination, we would promptly send for one.

(223)

Some of my most cherished war mementos are notes from Rev. Dr. T. D. Witherspoon (then chaplain of the Forty-second Mississippi Regiment, now pastor of one of the Presbyterian Churches in Louisville, and one of the noblest Christian gentlemen I ever knew) and Rev. W. S. Lacy (of the Twenty-seventh North Carolina, one of the truest and most efficient of the many noble workers whom our Presbyterian brethren sent to the army), and a number of others of my Pedobaptist brethren, asking me to come and baptize men who had professed conversion in their meetings and wanted to unite with the Baptists.

And I did not hesitate to reciprocate the courtesy, when men of my command wanted to unite with other denominations on a profession of " repentance towards God and faith towards the Lord Jesus Christ."   I remember that my good Brother Witherspoon told me, one day, that he had " a good joke on Brother Jones," which was to the following effect: I had gone over to Davis's Mississippi Brigade, at Brother Witherspoon's invitation, and had cut the ice on a mill-pond, at Madison Run Station, Orange county, Virginia, and baptized a number of men.   In the service I had read, without note or comment, some of the passages of Scripture bearing on the ordinance.   The next day, one of the men, who had been active in the revival meetings, went to Chaplain Witherspoon and said : " I do not think that you ought to invite Brother Jones to come over here any more."

" Why not ?   What has Brother Jones done that is wrong ? "

" Well, you know that, while there is no law or rule on the subject, it is generally understood that, inasmuch as we have all of the evangelical denominations represented in our brigades, no man ought to present *his own peculiar doctrines."*

" Yes," said the chaplain, " that is true ; but Brother Jones has in no way violated this tacit agreement.   He has not preached his peculiar doctrines."

" Well, no ; he has not exactly *preached* them," was the reply; " but then he read to the crowd *all of them Baptist Scriptures."*

Of course, my good Brother Witherspoon replied : " Why, I do not admit that those *are 'Baptist Scriptures.'* "

Rev. W. S. Lacy, in a series of admirable papers on the " Religious Interest in Lee's Army," written in the *New York Watchman* soon after the war (a series of such rare merit, that I have urged him to put them into more permanent form), tells a joke which his Methodist Brother Webb, chaplain in the same brigade, got off on him.   It so happened that Brother Lacy's regiment came from a strong Baptist community, and that a large proportion of the converts insisted upon "going down into the water," and he never failed to send for me or some other Baptist chaplain, and to show every Christian courtesy in the premises. He would go with us to the water's edge, join heartily in the service of song, and be the first one to greet the young converts as they "came up out of the water."   And so Brother Webb said to him : "Brother Lacy, you remind me of a hen setting on duck eggs.   She carefully nurses the eggs until the little ducks appear, and diligently watches over and cares for them.   But some day she goes near the water and the whole brood of little ducks plunge in, while she has to stand clucking on the bank." "Yes," said Brother Lacy, "I cannot follow them in ; but I go with them to the water's edge, I receive them with open arms when they come out, and I am ever ready to hail them as my spiritual children, and to do all in my power to help them serve our common Master and reach the home of our common Father above."

And when we Baptist chaplains were called on to assist young converts of our charges to unite with other denominations, I trust we were not wanting in like Christian spirit and courtesy.

This cordial co-operation of the chaplains and missionaries of the different evangelical denominations had the very happiest effect on our work.   And I am glad to believe that the fraternal spirit which has so largely prevailed for some years among evangelical Christians at the South is in no small degree due to the habit of co-operation which so generally prevailed during the war.

I was sent once to stop the firing of one of our own batteries, which was, by mistake, firing into our own men ; and I shall never forget the eagerness with which I put spurs to my horse and galloped across the field, crying at the top of my voice, as I waved a white handkerchief: "Cease firing!   Cease firing!   You are firing into your friends !"   And so I never see bitter controversies between evangelical Christians that I do not feel like crying with all of my feeble powers: "Cease firing into the ranks of your brethren, and trail your guns on the mighty hosts of the enemies of our common Lord."

This spirit of fraternity and co-operation was largely promoted by the organization of the Chaplains' Associations of the Second

15

and Third Corps, and the intercourse between the chaplains thus brought about.

It was my privilege to know personally nearly all of the chaplains of that army, and I do not hesitate to say that, while there were in the number a few who were utterly worthless, I never knew a more zealous, laborious, self-sacrificing corps of Christian ministers than most of these chaplains were.

Rev. Dr. J. C. Stiles, of the Presbyterian Church, who, though seventy years old, gave himself to "the work of an evangelist" in the army with an ability and zeal which younger men might well have imitated, thus speaks of the work of the faithful chaplain as it came under his observation :

" These men not only give themselves laboriously to ordinary duties of the Christian ministry in their peculiar position, but their earnest love of Christ and the soldiers' life prompts them to a course of extraordinary self-denying service, admirably adapted to revive and extend the interest of the Christian Church in the army.

" They form Camp Churches of all the Christians of every denomination in their regiments.   The members are expected to practise all the duties of brotherly love, Christian watchfulness and Christian discipline.   Indeed, they are taught to feel themselves under every obligation of strict membership.   The chaplain writes to every minister or Church with which the member may have been connected, or the young convert desires to be united, and giving the name of the person, solicits the prayers of the said Church, both for the individual and the whole Camp Church, and by correspondence keeps them apprised of the history of the party.   These chaplains keep a minute record, not only of the names of the whole regiment, but of all that may assist them either to save the sinner or sanctify the believer. Some of them have ten or twelve columns opposite the names of different companies of the regiment, so headed as to supply all that personal knowledge of the party which might be serviceable in promoting their spiritual welfare.   These columns they fill up gradually with such intelligence as they may be able to obtain in their pastoral visitations—when sick, wounded or slain; when awakened, convicted, converted—all important information is conveyed by the chaplain to the family and the Church. These things must necessarily follow—the work of the faithful chaplain is most laborious ; he is held in the very highest and warmest estimation by every man in the regiment—saint and sinner. He possesses a power to sanctify and save them which nothing but earnest and hard-working devotion could finally secure."

Rev. Dr. George B. Taylor, who served so faithfully as chaplain of the Twenty-fifth Virginia Regiment, and afterwards as post chaplain in Staunton, and whose useful labors in these positions were but the prophecy of his subsequent success as missionary to Rome, Italy, wrote a letter on the chaplaincy so just and discriminating that I give it in full, as follows:

"The men generally want chaplains, and appreciate them, even if only moderately good and faithful. I believe this is largely true of officers, too, though there are some notable exceptions. A certain brigadier said chaplains were 'the scourge of the army.' Some colonels have objected that even faithful ministers, by awakening men's fears of retribution, have unfitted them for battle. And it is quite notorious that some field-officers object to chaplains, who might be a restraint on their drinking and profanity. But, after all, I believe most officers desire chaplains, and wish them to be good, earnest men. Certainly my observation and pleasant experience has been, that from officers, high and low, chaplains receive generally the most courteous and even kind treatment. In short, I believe that a minister in the army, as elsewhere, will find his true status, and in proportion to his soberness, purity and zeal, be loved and respected by those who receive his ministrations. Let none suppose that a chaplain's post is a *sinecure*. True, he may shirk his duties and not be court-martialed. True, he has some facilities for locomotion and 'foraging,' not enjoyed by either officers or men. In fact, I believe his place is the most pleasant as well as the highest in the army. Specially may he, with brother chaplains, with Christians of all Churches, and with cultivated men in the ranks or in office, enjoy Christian intercourse, often more extensive and unreserved than could be in an ordinary pastorate. But, after all, as I said, his post is no sinecure. If he sticks to the men as he ought, he must learn to say, ' 'Tis home where'er my oil-cloth is,' and may often be seen at dewy eve, selecting a clean place or smooth rail for his bivouac. He, too, must learn to eat once a day, to live on crackers, and may often be seen broiling his fat bacon on the coals, or making rye coffee in a tin-cup. Above all, he must forego domestic joys, and even when a furlough is practicable, forbear to use it, that he may stay at his post and labor for his men. I do not believe public sentiment in the army requires chaplains to 'take the sword.' In a battle, the chaplain's place is with his ambulance, and then at the hospitals. But to be thus just in the rear is often to encounter the hottest fire of cannon-balls and shells.

"The material of his congregation is the best, and his preaching is constantly backed by most solemn providences. Then, as a general thing, except on forced marches, he may preach almost whenever he pleases. He must learn, however, to be 'instant out of season.' At 'Cross Keys' I felt that a battle was imminent during the day, and preached about half-past 7 o'clock A. M. Soon the distant cannon was heard, and ere I reached 'thirdly,' the colonel asked me to close as soon as I could, as he had orders to 'fall in.' It was the last message some poor fellows ever heard. Two weeks thereafter we marched nearly all day, and it was not until the setting of the sun that we could gather for praise and prayer.

"Last Monday was the hottest and most airless day I ever felt. About 3 P. M. a brother-chaplain said to me, 'Go preach for my regiment.' 'What! Monday, and such a warm day, too?' 'Yes. I will give you a good crowd, and take care of you.' I went. In ten minutes we were gathered. What Richmond pastor has such an advantage? After preaching I was hospitably entertained to supper by the colonel, who kindly asked me to preach for his regiment when I could. *En passant*, I doubt whether a man is ever truly grateful until he enters the army. Before, he may be thankful in the abstract, but then he learns to be thankful for each hour of slumber, and each individual cracker or cup of water. In conclusion, I think, among the many evils of war, we should not forget such a benefit as this, that it corrects the growing tendency to effeminacy. How desirable, if many of our young preachers in this school shall learn to 'endure hardness.' Then they can preach as the pioneers did, and not be concerned what they shall eat, or where they shall sleep; nor need to be coddled by the mothers in Israel, or have eggs and brandy mixed for their throats by the pretty daughters in Israel.

"CHAPLAIN.

"CAMP IN CHARLES CITY, July 9, 1862."

I heartily endorse the views expressed above by Dr. Taylor, and I desire to testify especially that the officers of the army generally were disposed to extend to the faithful chaplain every courtesy, and to give him every facility for the prosecution of his work.

Certainly, I received nothing but kindness from the officers with whom I came in contact.

As showing my appreciation at the time of the office of chaplain, and the men fitted for it, I append a card which I published in the *Religious Herald.*

The Men We Want.

Messrs. Editors: As my name has been mentioned as one of the " committee of correspondence to facilitate the introduction of chaplains into the various regiments of our corps," perhaps I ought to say a word with reference to the matter.   In private letters to brethren I have said, " Send us the names of *good men ; "* and I here repeat, we want *none others*—our object being not merely to fill up the regiments with nominal chaplains, but to fill the vacancies with *efficient, working* men.   We want *effective Gospel preachers,* whose burden shall be Christ and Him crucified.   It is a common mistake that *anybody* will do to preach to soldiers; and hence the chaplaincies are generally filled by young and inexperienced men.   But a moment's reflection will suffice to convince, that since we have in the army the flower of the country, so we ought to have the best preaching·· talent of the country.   I call upon our city and country pastors earnestly to consider whether it is not their duty to enter this wide field of usefulness.   It is a field worthy the attention of our most experienced, most useful ministers, and if they cannot get their consent to enter regularly upon it, I call upon them to at least give us occasional visits.   We want men who will *stick to their posts.*   I am persuaded that a great deal of harm has been done by chaplains resigning, or absenting themselves for long periods from their commands, on " detail to collect clothing," or some such pretext.   The great business of the chaplain is to *preach Christ* publicly, and from tent to tent, and the temporal welfare of the soldiers should be made subordinate to this.   We want men *physically able as well as willing to endure hardships and privations.*   If a chaplain would live up to the full measure of his usefulness, he must be with his regiment on the weary march (frequently resigning his horse to some foot-sore soldier), lie with them around the bivouac-fire after evening prayers are over; be drenched on the outposts, or face the pelting snow-storm; divide with some hungry soldier his last hard cracker, and, in a word, share with his regiment whatever hardships they may be called on to endure. Now, if a brother is physically unable to endure these hardships, he had best not enter the work, but there is no question that many a delicate brother would have his health permanently improved, if he would thus learn to "endure hardness as a good soldier."

I trust that brethren in sending testimonials will remember these points. And if the committee should feel called on to decline recommending any one, of course they will not be understood as deciding who shall be denied chaplaincies, but simply *their own unwillingness to act in the matter*. Thus much I felt it due to myself and the cause to say.

J. Wm. Jones, Chaplain Thirteenth Virginia Infantry.

Our Chaplains' Association was organized in March, 1863, at old "Round Oak" church, in Caroline county, and our first care was to seek to increase the numbers and efficiency of the chaplains in the corps.

A report of this first meeting, which I wrote for the *Religious Herald* at the time, will give the facts more accurately than I could now recall them:

NEAR HAMILTON'S CROSSING, March 19.

Dear Brethren: We had, on last Monday, a meeting of the chaplains of our corps (Jackson's) which proved exceedingly interesting, and resulted, I trust, in much good. It was a meeting for general consultation and prayer, and there were points elicited which I am sure would prove of interest to the readers of the *Herald*.

General Jackson has taken especial pains to have his command supplied with chaplains, and yet a little over half of the regiments in our corps are still destitute. There are several entire brigades without a single chaplain. This destitution was made a special topic of discussion, and it was resolved that we will make every effort to get chaplains for all of the regiments; and in the meantime, that we will each preach as often as we can to those that are destitute. Rev. Dr. Lacy has been requested by the general to labor as a missionary in the regiments of his corps that are without chaplains, and to recommend ministers of the different denominations to fill the vacancies. Brethren desirous of obtaining chaplaincies for themselves or friends would do well, therefore, to write at once to Dr. Lacy, at General Jackson's head-quarters, or to some one of the chaplains of our corps. And are there not brethren now in the pastorate who might be spared for this most important work? "The harvest is plenteous, and the laborers are few." I suppose that in the other army corps there is greater destitution than in ours.

Another point discussed was the *general efficiency* of chaplains. One brother was disposed to coincide with the very harsh opinions that have been expressed so frequently concerning chaplains; but the general expression of opinion was, that while we all have to mourn that we have come far short of our duty, and there are some sad examples of inefficiency, *as a class* army chaplains are as attentive to their duties and as efficient as the same number of pastors at home. In my own personal observation, during the *twenty-two months* I have been in the army, I have met with several chaplains who shamefully desert their posts on the slightest pretexts; but, *as a general rule*, I have found them faithfully discharging their duty. Let the chaplain who is nearly always absent from his post, and shirks duty when there, be held up *by name* to public censure, but let not the man who is constantly at the post of duty be made to share *his* shame. This is as manifestly unjust as it would be to hold up the "shirker," the coward, or the "straggler" as a type of the noble soldiery that compose our Southern army. It is as fair as it would be to take some of the lazy, good-for-nothing preachers at home as types of our Southern ministry. But I find that I am making this notice rather lengthy, and must pass on. We found the meeting so exceedingly pleasant that we determined to hold another next Tuesday, and to have them as frequently as circumstances would permit.

A committee (consisting of Rev. B. T. Lacy, Rev. W. C. Power, of South Carolina, and J. Wm. Jones) was appointed at this meeting to issue an address to the Churches of the Confederacy on the needs of the army. The following paper, written by Mr. Lacy, was adopted by the association, and is reproduced here as showing the views and feelings of the chaplains at the time:

Dear Brethren: The relations which we sustain to the various branches of the Church of Christ in our country, and the position which we hold in the Army of the Confederate States, induces us to address you upon the important subject of the religious instruction of the soldiers engaged in the sacred cause of defending our rights, our liberties, and our homes. The one universal subject of thought and of feeling is the war. The hearts of the people, with singular unanimity, are enlisted in the common cause. The object of special interest to all is the army. The political and social interests involved excite the patriotism, and move the affection of all. There is little necessity for exhortation to love of country, or love to our sons and brothers, who are fighting and falling in our defence. These emotions, strong in the beginning, have become more intense from the heroic fortitude of our noble army, and from the wicked designs and infamous conduct of our enemies. The history of the past two years of the war has amazingly developed and magnified the issues, and strengthened and deepened the convictions under which the conflict began. Base, beyond all conception, must that heart be which does not swell with patriotic devotion to our dear and suffering country, which is not stirred with deep and righteous indignation against our cruel and guilty foes, and which is not melted with profound and tender sympathy for the privations of our soldiers and the afflictions of our oppressed fellow-citizens in the invaded districts. While these emotions may exist in some adequate measure, is the religious interest commensurate with the demand of the times? Is the Church as much alive to its duty as the State? Is the Christian as active and as earnest as the citizen? Duties never conflict. Our patriotism will be all the stronger and purer when sanctified by religion. The natural sympathies require the controlling influence and the plastic power of the love of Christ for their proper regulation. To the political and social must be added the religious element. To patriotism must be added the mightier principle of faith. Let love of country be joined to love of God —let the love of our suffering brother be associated with the love of our crucified Saviour—let the temporal interests be connected with the eternal. One duty should not be allowed to exclude another, nor one emotion crowd from the heart the holier presence of another. The Church should clearly understand and fully estimate the relation which it sustains to the war, and the duty which it owes to the army. In an important sense, the

cause of the country is the cause of the Church. The principles
involved are those of right, of truth, and of humanity, as well as
of law, of constitutional liberty, and of national independence.
In a sense equally as true, and even more important, is the fact,
that the Church, to the full extent of its ability and opportunity,
is responsible for the souls of those who fall in this conflict.
Has she realized this solemn responsibility? Has she discharged
her sacred duty? With the opportunities which we have for
estimating the work to be done, and of observing what has been
accomplished, we are constrained to say that she has not. Surely
her whole duty has not been done. We tremble when we contemplate the results which may follow from such delinquency.
To estimate correctly the work which the Church is called to
perform, we must consider the vast number of our citizens who
now compose the armies. All the men of the country, below
the age of forty, are in the field. To these must be added many
manly boys below, and many patriotic men above the prescribed
ages. The intellectual and physical strength of the entire
country is assembled in martial array. The ratio of religious
instructors assigned by the bill for the appointment of chaplains
(a bill in some important respects still defective), is one chaplain
for every regiment. How has this arrangement been seconded
by the Church and the ministry? How many of the five or six
hundred regiments are now supplied with faithful pastors? We
have not the means of determining the number engaged in the
whole service, but we give you the result as to our own corps—
a body of troops commanded by that sincere Christian, Lieutenant-General T. J. Jackson, who has given special encouragement to the work of supplying the corps with chaplains—not
one-half of the regiments of infantry are supplied. Some entire
brigades have no chaplain at all. In the artillery attached to
the corps the destitution is still greater. With these facts before
us, is it too much to affirm that there are not two hundred chaplains now in the field in all our armies? At the same time, will
not the statistics of the different Churches in the Confederate
States show an aggregate of five or six thousand ministers of
the Gospel?

Ministerial brethren, ought this thing so to be? Church of
the living God, awake from your lethargy and arouse to your
duty! We are well aware of the pure and lofty patriotism of
the Southern ministry. We know that your hearts are as truly

and deeply enlisted in the cause of the country as ours; and we are also aware of the fact that a large number of chaplains are stationed at posts and laboring faithfully in hospitals, and many ministers of the Gospel are serving as officers and as privates in the army. But how great is the destitution in the field? And how many of our soldiers are perishing without the bread of life?

There are no great difficulties in the way of obtaining an appointment for any suitable minister in any denomination of Christians. God has opened a wide and effectual door of access to the work. In the work itself there are no difficulties which zeal and faith cannot readily overcome. The chief obstructions are those which exist everywhere in the conflict between sin and holiness. There are no vices or prejudices peculiar to the army which are any greater hindrances to the work of grace than those which are to be encountered in the cities and throughout the country. Our work is a hard work, and there are privations which must be endured. The fare of the chaplain is that of the soldier. The exposures and discomforts to be encountered are in striking contrast with the previous lives of most ministers of the Gospel. The health of some has failed in the service, and some, indeed, have laid down their lives for their brethren, but to many the change of habits has been beneficial, and the feeble have come to endure hardness as good soldiers. The chaplain, however faithful, will at times be discouraged. Men will seem to take little interest in his preaching; profanity, card-playing, and Sabbath-breaking will be on the increase; his presence often will be no restraint upon vice, and when he has faithfully discharged his duty he may meet with censure and ridicule. In camp-life there is an indolence of mind produced, and an aversion to serious thought. There is also a disposition to seek entertainment in all manner of foolish talking and jesting. On the march, and on an active campaign, the attention is much absorbed, and time is often wanting for religious duties. The carelessness and open apostasy of professors of religion are here—as well as everywhere else—a great hindrance to the success of the Gospel. The readiness with which chaplains have resigned their places, or absented themselves from their regiments, is a source of discouragement to the soldiers and to their brethren who remain. In the hasty opinions and sweeping judgments of many, in and out of the army, the deficiencies of some have been unjustly attributed to others, and the failure of a few regarded as the failure of all. But these, you perceive, brethren, are essentially the same difficulties, in a different form, which the minister of God must encounter everywhere in this sinful world. Our chief ground of discouragement, however, is in ourselves. With more faith in God, and more love for the souls of men, with more of the spirit of our blessed Lord, we should behold greater and more precious results.

If there are discouragements peculiar to our work, there are peculiar encouragements also. We believe that God is with us, not only to own and bless His word to the salvation of men, but that His blessing rests upon our cause and attends our armies. It is a high privilege and great satisfaction to preach to soldiers to whom God has given such signal victories. The moral influence of a just and righteous cause is a happy introduction to, and a good preparation for the holier cause of religion. The objects for which our soldiers are fighting possess incalculable power in controlling the naturally demoralizing influence of war. We are thankful to God for the large number of Christian officers who command our armies and aid us in our work. The presence of so many pious men in the ranks gives us a Church in almost every regiment to begin with. The intercourse and communion of Christian brethren in the army is as intimate and precious as anywhere upon earth. It is an interesting fact, that by this work ministers of the different denominations are brought into closer and more harmonious co-operation, thus promoting the unity and charity of the whole Church, and greatly encouraging each other. Many of the greatest temptations to vice are excluded from the army. There is much time for profitable reflection. The near approach of death excites to serious thought. Religious reading is sought and appreciated. Many opportunities for personal kindness to the sick and the wounded, on the battle-field and in the camp, bind grateful hearts to faithful chaplains. In preaching the word, conducting prayer-meetings and Bible-classes, by circulating the Scriptures and other religious reading, and by frequent conversations in private, we have ample opportunity for doing our Master's work and laboring for immortal souls. Our greatest encouragement, however, has been from the presence and power of the Holy Spirit among us. He who has led our armies to victory, conducting them like the hosts of Israel with the pillar of cloud and of fire by night and by day, has also encamped round about us, and the tabernacle of the Lord has been in the midst of our tents. We believe there have been more powerful and blessed revivals of religion *in* the army than *out* of it during the last two years. We know of a large Church in which almost all the additions for more than a year have been of young men visiting their homes on furloughs from the army. At this very time a most interesting and extensive work of grace is in progress amongst the troops stationed in and around the desolated city of Fredericksburg. The evidences of God's love and mercy are thus brought into immediate and striking contrast with the marks of the cruelty and barbarity of men.

Brethren, do not these movements of the Holy Ghost indicate where God's ministers should follow, and in what work they should engage ? Our work, though hard, is a pleasant work, and we feel it to be a precious and glorious work. Much more has been accomplished than has been made known abroad. Comparatively few publications have been sent out by the chaplains, but many earnest and faithful sermons have been preached, many copies of the Holy Scriptures have been put into the hands of the soldiers by chaplains and colporters, and much printed matter in the form of religious newspapers and tracts has been circulated and eagerly read ; precious communions have been held, and souls have been added to the Church of Christ, of such as, we believe, shall be saved. Eternity alone can disclose the extent of the blessed work which faithful chaplains have accomplished in our armies.

We have told you these things, brethren, that your interest might be increased in this cause, and in ourselves as identified with the cause. If we have only mentioned what was before familiar to you, we desire to stir up your pure minds by way of remembrance. We would respectfully, and in Christian love, submit the following suggestions for your consideration, earnestly beseeching your co-operation, your sympathy and your prayers :

Let the Church humble herself before her Lord—let all Christians, of every name in our land, engage in acts of humiliation and of prayer. The frequent calls of our excellent and pious President to this duty have been attended by evident tokens of the Divine favor. May the observance of the appointed day, which is now at hand, be followed by the signal blessing of Almighty God, and the solemn day be kept holy unto the Lord by the army and by all the people.   I fever a nation was called to prostrate itself at the foot of the Cross, and to suplicate the mercy of God with strong crying and tears, it is this.   God, we believe, will deliver us from our enemies, but that deliverance must come in answer to prayer.

In order that our prayers may be heard, and our solemn days be not an abomination unto the Lord, we must put away sin from among us.   There are sins, both of a national and individual character, which are rapidly engendered in a time like this— a spirit of recklessness and profanity—a disregard of the laws of life and of property—too great a reliance upon an arm of flesh— and it may be, under peculiar aggravations, a sinful feeling of malignant and bloodthirsty revenge has been indulged.   But, more than all, a spirit of unhallowed greed, of unrighteous extortion.   Ill-gotten gains will prove a curse to the individual, and injurious to the country.   It is no time for amassing wealth. Can the true patriot, can the true Christian grow rich in the hour of his country's peril?   If in any proper and legitimate manner, without injury to others, money is accumulated, give it to your country, give it to the poor, give it to the suffering families of the soldiers, send a chaplain to the army, and assist in the support of his family while he is engaged in the work.   Let the Church of Jesus Christ clear herself of this sin, and let not the hidden wedge and the Babylonish garment be found in her tents.   By precept and example let the Church seek to foster a generous and self-sacrificing spirit among all classes of the people.

Brethren, send us more chaplains.   The harvest truly is great, the laborers are few.   We send abroad to the Churches the Macedonian cry, Come and help us.   The work is an earnest, a pressing work.   Now is emphatically the accepted time for the army.   The cause will not brook delay.   A series of battles, which may speedily follow the opening of the campaign, will sweep away thousands of our brave comrades and friends— thousands of your own sons and brothers.   Then come while it is called to-day.   Come up to the help of the Lord, to the help of the Lord against the mighty, and escape the curse of Meroz.

We especially appeal to the Churches in their organized capacity, and ask of conventions, conferences, presbyteries and associations, to set apart men of the best talent and largest experience unto this work.   Such a call. coming with the potential authority of a Church of God, would doubtless decide many of the ablest ministers in the country to cast in their lots with us. We cordially and earnestly invite the venerable fathers of the church to visit the army and preach for a few days or weeks in the regiments. Such voluntary labors, in many instances, have been signally blessed. The Churches should be willing to spare their pastors for this work, and seek temporary supplies from neighboring ministers; or, at least, all congregations might allow their ministers to visit the army for a time and labor for those who have gone forth in their defence. Have not the soldiers, who are away from their homes and Churches, the right to claim a part of the time of their own pastors? But especially do we call upon the younger men in the ministry—and we call upon you, young men, because you are strong—come, take part in this sacred cause and this holy fellowship with us.

If the ministers of the Gospel, below the age of forty, are exempted from ordinary military duty, are they not bound to serve their country and the army in the capacity of chaplains? Have you a right to stay away while this destitution exists? We urge no extreme or fanatical view; let all the regiments be supplied, and still the vast majority of ministers will remain at home with their congregations. We plead only for that which is just and equal. And we feel that we but do this when we maintain that congregations should assist in the support of the families of chaplains while laboring in the army. Such an arrangement would give hundreds of excellent men to the work.

Brethren, pray for us. To know that we are constantly remembered at a throne of grace—in the Churches and in the families—in the public and in the private devotions of the people of God—will greatly encourage our hearts and strengthen our hands. Prayer should be made without ceasing to the God and Father of our Lord and Saviour Jesus Christ in behalf of our cause, our country, our officers and our soldiers. Pray for us, that we may be faithful, and that our labors may be blessed in the conversion of souls.

We ask these things of you, dear brethren, because we believe that the final success of our arms is intimately connected with the fidelity of the Church in fulfilling its duty to the army, and closely related to the religious character of the army itself. It was remarked by one of our distinguished and Christian generals, that " the only ground of apprehension to be felt is from the want of piety in the army. Were all the soldiers sincere Christians and praying men, in a cause like ours, they would be invincible." In such an army there would be two distinct sources of success in addition to the ordinary elements of military power —the loftier courage derived from Christian faith, and the direct blessing of God in answer to prayer. If the want of faithfulness on the part of the Church, the impiety of the army and the people, should prevent God's blessing, then the unfaithfulness of the Church will have blasted our hopes, destroyed our country, and left a continent in ruins.

There should be no separation made between the army and the country, between the soldier and the citizen. The army is composed of the people, and the soldiers are citizens. At this very time the soldiers in the field are the only electors of representatives for many of the congressional and legislative districts. Those who achieve our independence are the same who must maintain it. The sole governors of the country, for one generation at least, will be the survivors of the army. Those who win the battles, must make, administer, enforce and obey the laws. If these be depraved and godless through the neglect of the Church, and their want of moral integrity and elevation destroy the government, and bring upon the land the curse of God, then in vain the mighty sacrifice of treasure and of blood —in vain the army of our martyred dead—in vain the sacred gift bequeathed from bleeding sires to sons. Better never to have fought and won the victory, than afterwards to forfeit it and lose the blessing. This may be the last struggle for constitutional liberty which will be made on this continent. The progress of the race, the happiness of millions, are involved. A grand responsibility rests upon our young republic, and a mighty work lies before it. Baptized in its infancy in blood, may it receive the baptism of the Holy Ghost, and be consecrated to its high and holy mission among the nations of the earth.

This, we fondly hope, will be the last year of this bloody war. But of that no one can certainly know. How ardently is a permanent and honorable peace desired! For this object united prayers should go up continually to the throne of God by night and by day. Weeping between the porch and the altar, Zion should lift up her voice without ceasing unto her Saviour and her God. This war must be regarded by all Christian men as a chastisement from the hand of God on account of our sins.

The object of all chastening is purification.   War, pestilence and famine, when they came upon God's ancient people, were designed to turn them from their sins, and to bring them back to his love and service.   When that result was accomplished the chastisement was removed. Has the Church in our afflicted land learned aright the chastening lessons of her God?   Have the rulers and the people, like those of Nineveh, repented before the judgments of the Lord?   In some hopeful measure this undoubtedly has been the result.   We believe that in humility, in sincerity of faith, in thankfulness for mercies, and in prayerfulness, there has been improvement.   Men have been called to sacrifice self for principle, and freely has the sacrifice been made by millions.   A tenderer charity, and a larger benevolence than ever before, open the hands and fill the hearts of many.

A higher estimate has been placed upon *truth* and upon *right* by a people resisting unto blood, striving against sin.   We may indulge the hope that the results which God designed are following from the war.   And when they are accomplished the war will cease.   The coming of peace will be insured, and will be hastened by our fidelity in duty and our devotion in prayer.

But, brethren, our great argument with you is the salvation of the souls of men, the salvation of our sons and brothers, the salvation of our dear soldiers.   We plead for those who are ready to lay down the life that now is.   Shall they lose also the life which is to come?   If the sacrifice of the body is demanded, shall that of the soul be made?   If time is forfeited, must eternity be lost?

The great object for which the Church of God was instituted upon earth is the same as that for which the Son of God died upon the Cross—THE GLORY OF GOD IN THE SALVATION OF MEN.

We urge you, then, by this last and greatest of all considerations, to aid us in this blessed work by your presence, your sympathies, your contributions, and your prayers.

March 24, 1863.

The address and the efforts put forth were very effective, and the number of chaplains and missionaries was greatly increased, and the estimate put upon the value of the services of a faithful missionary was greatly enhanced, until even the most irreligious officers of the army were anxious to have the services of the faithful chaplain or missionary.

Dr. Leyburn gives the following from the letter of a distinguished gentleman: "There is a marked and perceptible difference between the *morale* of a regiment furnished with a good chaplain and one which has none. The men are more orderly, better contented, and really more efficient. Now and then I meet with an officer who appreciates all this, and even some irreligious colonels seek the co-operation of a good chaplain in their desire to render their regiments as efficient as possible."

The denominations generally appointed some of their best men to enter the army as missionaries, and supplemented the scant salaries of the chaplains.

It was reported in 1864 that "The Old School Presbyterians employed, the past Assembly-year, 130 missionaries and chaplains in our different armies; and contributions to that work fell little short of $80,000. These laborers reported, at the General Assembly, in its meeting at Charlotte, the conversion of 12,000 soldiers during the year."

But the work of the chaplains and missionaries will further appear as our narrative proceeds, and it will be seen that we had an earnest, zealous, and faithful corps of laborers.

16

CHAPTER VIII.

BUT, in pointing out the instrumentalities which God blessed to the spiritual good of our brave men, their own *eagerness to hear the Gospel* must not be overlooked. Indeed I believe that the desire of these men to listen to the Gospel and to receive religious instruction has never been surpassed. Let us visit some of these camps, and mingle in some of these scenes of worship, and if I shall be able to picture them as I saw them, I can give a far more vivid idea of them than by the recital of the detailed facts and figures.

It matters not what day in the week it may be, or what hour of the day, you have only to pass the word around that there will be preaching at such a point, and there will promptly assemble a large crowd of eager listeners. No appointment for weeks, or days, or hours ahead is necessary. No church-bell summons, to gorgeous houses of worship, elegant ladies or fashionably attired men. But a few taps of the drum, a few strains of the bugle, or, better still, the singing of some old, familiar hymn, serves as a " church call " well understood, and from every part of the camp weather-beaten soldiers, in faded and tattered uniforms, hasten to the selected spot and gather close around the preacher, who, with " Nature's great temple " for his church, and the blue canopy of heaven for his " sounding board," is fortunate if he have so much as a barrel or well-rounded stump for a pulpit.

But I proposed to take you, kind reader, to some of our meetings. Let us first visit the battered old town of Fredericksburg in the early weeks of 1863. We enter at sundown, just as the regiments of Barksdale's Brigade of heroic Missisippians are returning to their quarters from " dress parade," and we pause to gaze with admiration on the men who, on that bleak December morning, held the town with such tenacity against Burnside's mighty hosts until " Marse Robert " had formed on the hills beyond his lines of Gray, against which the waves of Blue surged in vain.

Soon we hear the familiar command, " Break ranks," and immediately the streets are filled with soldiers eagerly running in a given direction.

"What does this mean?" a stranger would inquire. "Is ' Old John Robinson' about to have a performance of his circus? Has 'Wyman, the great magician,' come to town? Are the 'Negro Minstrels' about to exhibit? What means this eager running?" Ask one of the men, and he will scarcely pause as he replies: "We are trying to get into the church before all of the seats are taken."·

Yes! the house of God is the goal they seek, and long before the appointed hour the spacious Episcopal church, kindly tendered for the purpose by its rector, is filled—nay, *packed*—to its utmost capacity—lower floor, galleries, aisles, chancel, pulpit-steps and vestibule—while hundreds turn disappointed away, unable to find even standing-room. The great revival has begun, and this brigade and all of the surrounding brigades are stirred with a desire to hear the Gospel, rarely equalled.

Enter, if you can make your way through the crowd, and mingle with that vast congregation of worshippers. They do not spend their time while waiting for the coming of the preacher in idle gossip, or a listless staring at every new comer, but a clear voice strikes some familiar hymn, around which cluster hallowed memories of home, and of the dear old church far away—the whole congregation join in the hymn, and there arises a volume of sacred song that seems almost ready to take the roof off of the house. I may be an " old fogy," but I declare I would not give one of those old songs which "the boys" used to sing "with the spirit and the understanding," and into which they threw their souls, for all of the "classic music" which grand organ and "quartette choir" ever rendered.

The song ceases, and one of the men leads in prayer. *And he prays.* He does not tell the Lord the news of the day, or recount to him the history of the country. He does not make "a stump-speech to the Lord" on the war—its causes, its progress, or its prospects. But, from the depths of a heart that feels its needs, he tells of present wants, asks for present blessings, and begs for the Holy Spirit in His convicting, converting power. I have rarely, if ever, heard such prayers as some of these men used to make. I remember that Brother Owen, the Methodist chaplain who had the general conduct of these meetings, used to keep an accurate list of the men who professed conversion in the brigade, and from this list they were called on to lead in prayer.

I never heard of one who refused, and as a rule they made tender, earnest, appropriate prayers.

But presently some man in a tattered jacket gets up to speak, and the stranger might ask : " What business has he to speak in one of these meetings ? " Listen, and you will soon see. As in simple, earnest style, he tells something of his own experience, or exhorts his comrades to come to Chirst, you hear indeed

> " Words that breathe
> And thoughts that burn,"

and you feel that if eloquence is " logic set on fire," then that soldier is eloquent beyond almost any man you ever heard. The crowd seems thrilled by the power of his burning words and the momentous truth he utters.

But, after a while, the preacher comes in and the pulpit-service begins. It may be Dr. J. C. Stiles, the able expounder of the Gospel, who preached very frequently in these meetings, and whose untiring labors in the army were so richly blessed—it may be that gifted pulpit-orator, the lamented Dr. William J. Hoge—it may be " the golden-mouthed orator of the Virginia pulpit," Dr. James A. Duncan, in whose death his denomination and the State sustained an irreparable loss—it may be the peerless Dr. J. L. Burrows, whose self-sacrificing labors for the temporal and spiritual welfare of the soldiers were so greatly blessed, and gave him so warm a place in the affections of " the boys " and of our whole Confederate people—it may be our earnest evangelist, Brother Carroll—it may be one of the chaplains, or it may be Brother J. L. Pettigrew, of Mississippi, or some other private soldier. But, whoever it is, *he preaches the Gospel.* He does not discuss the " Relation of Science to Religion," or the slavery question, or the causes which led to the war, or the war itself. He does not indulge in abusive epithets of the invaders of our soil, or seek to fire his hearers with hatred or vindictiveness towards the enemy. He has no use for any theology that is *newer than the New Testament,* and he indulges in no fierce polemics against Christians of other denominations. He is looking in the eyes of heroes of many a battle, and knows that the "long roll" may beat ere he closes—that these brave fellows may be summoned at once to new fields of carnage—and that he may be delivering then the last message of salvation that some of them may ever hear.

I remember that I preached to this vast congregation the very night before Hooker crossed the river, bringing on the battles of Second Fredericksburg and Chancellorsville—that, in my closing appeal, I urged them to accept Christ then and there, because they did not know but that they were hearing their "last invitation," and that sure enough we were aroused before day the next morning by the crossing of the enemy, and in the battles which followed, many of these noble fellows *were* called to the judgment-bar of God. And so, when the preacher stood up before these congregations of veterans, his very soul was stirred within him, and he "determined to know nothing among them save Jesus Christ and Him crucified." If the personal allusions may be pardoned, I do not believe that Dr. Burrows, Dr. Stiles, Dr. Hoge, Dr. Dabney, Dr. Pryor, Dr. Lacy, Dr. Moore, Dr. Read, Dr. Duncan, Dr. Granberry, Dr. Rosser, Dr. Doggett, Dr. Edwards, Dr. John A. Broadus, Dr. Pritchard, Dr. Wingate, Dr. Andrew Broaddus, Dr. Jeter, Dr. A. B. Brown, or any of the missionaries or chaplains were ever able, before or since, to preach sermons of such power as they were stirred up to preach in the army. If a man had any capacity whatever to preach, it would be developed under circumstances which would have stirred an angel's heart; and if he knew anything about the Gospel at all, he would tell it to these congregations.

And so our preacher, whoever he may be, tells "the old, old story of Jesus and His love." He has throughout the undivided attention of the crowd; there are tears in eyes "unused to the melting mood;" and when at the close of the sermon the invitation is given, and some stirring hymn is sung, there will be 20, 50, 100, or even as many as 200, to ask an interest in the prayers of God's people, or profess their faith in Jesus.

There were over 500 professions of conversion in these meetings at Fredericksburg, and the good work extended out into the neighboring brigades, and went graciously on—only temporarily interrupted by the battle of Chancellorsville—until we took up the line of march for Gettysburg. Indeed, it did not cease even on that active campaign, but culminated in the great revival along the Rapidan in August, 1863, which reached nearly the

whole army, and really did not cease until the surrender at
Appomattox.

On Sunday evening, September 6, 1863, I had an engagement
to preach for Brother J. J. D. Renfroe, chaplain of the Tenth
Alabama, in the great revival in Wilcox's Brigade, camped near
the Rapidan, not far from Orange Court House. As further
illustrating the character of our work, I may mention that I
preached to a large congregation in my own brigade at 6 o'clock
that morning. At 11 o'clock I went to the Baptist church at
Orange Court House, and assisted in the ordination of Brother
W. G. Curry, of the Third Alabama Regiment, who had been gallantly serving in the ranks, but who had been appointed chaplain
of his regiment, and whose Church had called for his ordination.

In the afternoon I witnessed a most interesting baptismal
scene in a creek near the railroad, about a mile and a half north
of Orange Court House, where Dr. Andrew Broaddus, of Caroline county (acting for Chaplain Hilary E. Hatcher, of Mahone's
Brigade, who was sick), and Chaplain Renfroe baptized eighty-
two soldiers belonging to Mahone's Virginia and Wilcox's Alabama Brigades. About five thousand soldiers, from the general
to the private, lined the banks. There was deep solemnity
pervading the vast throng, and a more impressive scene is rarely
witnessed.

About dusk that evening I went with Brother Renfroe to his
place of worship. The men came from every direction, not only
from this, but from all of the neighboring brigades, until, when
I got up to preach, the light of the fire-stands revealed at least
5,000 men seated on the rude logs, or on the ground, and with
upturned, eager faces, ready to drink in every word the preacher
had to say. My text was: " The blood of Jesus Christ His Son
cleanseth us from all sin ; " and as I tried to tell in simple, earnest
words

> " The old, old story,
> Of Jesus and His love,"

I could see in the dim light the intense interest and the starting
tear. At the close of the service, those interested in their souls'
salvation and desiring an interest in the prayers of God's people
were invited to come and give us their hand, and they continued
to press forward until we had counted over 600, of whom about
200 professed conversion.

I remember that, after our service was over, I went by

Mahone's Brigade, a short distance off, and found Dr. J. A. Broadus and Brother Hatcher still instructing a large number of inquirers who lingered at their place of preaching, loath to depart.

Immense congregations assembled at this period in almost any brigade at which we had preaching, and some of the scenes are as vividly impressed upon me as if they had been yesterday. Dr. John A. Broadus, Dr. Andrew Broaddus, Rev. Andrew Broaddus (of Kentucky), Dr. Burrows, Dr. Thos. H. Pritchard, Dr. Jeter, Dr. Dickinson, Rev. F. M. Barker, Rev. L. J. Haley, Dr. J. A. Duncan, Dr. Rosser, Dr. Doggett, Dr. J. E. Edwards, Dr. Hoge, Dr. Stiles, Dr. Bocock, Dr. Pryor, Dr. Bennett, and others, came to preach in the camps, and the chaplains had no sort of difficulty in giving them constant work and very large congregations. I vividly recall dear old Brother Andrew Broaddus (who had been acting as agent for army missions, but often "took a furlough" to come to the army, where his labors were greatly blessed) as he rode up to my quarters, near old Pisgah Church, one day, and to my invitation to dismount, replied: "No! I was ordered by '*General Dickinson*' to report to you for duty; but I must know where I am to preach to-night before I can get off my horse, for if you have no place for me, I must at once proceed to find one for myself." "Oh!" I replied, "there are a planty of places at which you can preach, but I have just received a note from Brother Cridlin, of Armistead's Brigade, saying that he is in the midst of a great revival, is sick, and greatly needs help." "All right," responded the veteran; "now I will dismount. I will eat some of your rations and go at once to help Brother Cridlin."

On fast-day of that autumn I had Dr. John A. Broadus to preach *four times*, at different points; and while all of the services were of deep interest, I particularly recall the service at sundown, held at General Gordon's head-quarters. The general, who had conducted a prayer-meeting himself in the morning, and made a stirring address to his brigade, had sent out the notices and exerted himself to have a congregation, and a large crowd, especially of officers, attended. I recall the text—"Her ways are ways of pleasantness and all her paths are peace"—and the sermon as clearly as if it had been last week, instead of twenty-three years ago, and the profound impression which it produced lingers in my memory as "a sweet savor." At times there was scarcely a dry eye in the vast throng, and the tears of generals, colonels and captains mingled freely with those of the rank and file. I never heard Dr. Broadus preach with more power, and I do not believe that he ever did.

In an appeal for more preachers to come to the army, published in the *Religious Herald* about the 1st of September, 1863, Dr. Broadus thus writes: " It is impossible to convey any just idea of the wide and effectual door that is now opened for preaching in the Army of Northern Virginia. . . . In every command that I visit, or hear from, a large proportion of the soldiers will attend preaching and listen well; and in many cases the interest is really wonderful. . . . A much larger proportion of the soldiers attend preaching in camp than used to attend at home; and when any interest is awakened the homogeneity and fellow-feeling which exists among them may be a powerful means, as used by the Divine Spirit, of diffusing that interest through the whole mass. Brethren, there is far more religious interest in this army than at home. The Holy Spirit seems everywhere moving among us. These widespread camps are a magnificent collection of camp-meetings. Brethren, it is the noblest opportunity for protracted meetings you ever saw. The rich, ripe harvest stands waiting. Come, brother, thrust in your sickle, and, by God's blessing, you shall reap golden sheaves that shall be your rejoicing in time and eternity."

We made it a rule to preach at least once every day during this period, and many of us for weeks together averaged two sermons a day to congregations of from one to three thousand listeners. I remember that at one and the same time I had the general conduct of *four* protracted meetings in four brigades (Gordon's Georgia, Hays's Louisiana, Hoke's North Carolina, and Smith's Virginia), and attended a service in each every day; and that on several occasions I baptized two, three and four times (at different points) without changing my clothes. (The plain truth was that I *had* only *one* change, and considered myself fortunate in having that.)

As illustrating how men would come out to preaching under difficulties, one of the chaplains reported that one Sunday in the early winter of 1863 there came a fall of snow, which he supposed would entirely break up his Sunday service, as they had no chapel; but, at the appointed hour, he heard singing at their usual place of worship, and looking out he saw that a large congregation had assembled. He, of course, went at once to the place and preached to deeply interested men, who stood in snow several inches deep, and among the number he counted *fourteen barefooted men*, besides scores whose shoes afforded very little protection from the snow. Many times have I seen barefooted men attending prayer-meeting or preaching in the snow or during the coldest weather of winter.

I went one day to meet an appointment in Davis's Mississippi Brigade, which had lost their winter-quarters and comfortable chapel, south of Orange Court House, by being ordered on picket-duty near the Rapidan. A steady rain was falling, and I went with no idea of being able to preach, but hoping to meet a few of the inquirers under their rude shelters, that I might point them to "the Lamb of God that taketh away the sin of the world." To my surprise, as I rode up, I heard a volume of sacred song ascending from the usual place of worship, and found a large congregation assembled on the rude logs. I told them that while I was willing to preach to them, I would not ask them to remain in the rain—that I would take it as no discourtesy if they left, and rather thought that they *ought* to do so. Not a man stirred, and I preached forty minutes in a constant rain to as attentive a congregation as I ever addressed. The men used to say: "We go on picket; we march and fight, and do all other military duty in any weather that comes, and we cannot see why we should allow the weather to interrupt our religious privileges."

Our brethren who in these days are accustomed to stay from church if it rains or snows, *or looks like it might do so in the course of a week*, would do well to study the example and catch the spirit of these soldiers.

At first the popular impression, even among the chaplains, was that but little could be done during an active campaign except in the hospitals. But it soon appeared that the faithful chaplain who would stick to his post and watch for opportunities—who was ready to resign his horse to some poor fellow with bare and blistered feet while he marched in the column as it hurried forward—who went with his men on picket—who bivouacked with them in the pelting storm—and who went with them into the leaden and iron hail of battle—who, in a word, was ready to share their hardships and dangers—such a man had, during the most active campaign, golden opportunities of pointing the sick and wounded to the great Physician ; the hungry to " the bread of life ; " the thirsty to " the water of life ; " the weary to the " rest that remaineth for the people of God," and the dying to " the resurrection and the life." The largest congregations I ever addressed were on the eve of some great battle, when men would throw away their cards, cease their profanity, and be in a most tender frame of mind to hear the Gospel. And some of the most precious seasons I ever enjoyed were in some of our meetings on the eve of battle. I can recall, as if it were last night, some of those scenes on that famous " Valley campaign," which won for our brave boys the sobriquet of " Jackson's Foot Cavalry."

Starting at " early dawn " (a favorite hour, by the way, with our great chief, of whom " the boys " used to say : " He always marches at early dawn, except when he *starts the night before* "), it was tramp, tramp, tramp all day along the hard turnpike, the only orders being, " Press forward ! " " Press forward ! "

As the evening shadows began to gather on the mountain tops some of the best men would fall out of ranks and declare that they could go no further, and it did seem that even " the Foot Cavalry " could do no more. But presently the word is passed back along the line, " The head of the column is going into camp." Immediately the weak grow strong again, the weary become fresh, the laggard hastens forward, and there upon some green sward on the banks of the beautiful Shenandoah—though like Jacob of old we had but the hard ground for our couch, rocks for our pillows, and the blue canopy of heaven for our covering—we lay us down to rest, oh ! so sweet after a hard day's march. But before the bivouac is quiet for the night there assembles a little group at some convenient spot hard by, who strike up some dear old hymn which recalls hallowed memories of home and loved ones, and of the dear old church far away, and which serves now as a prayer-call well understood. From all parts of the bivouac men hasten to the spot; the song grows clearer and louder, and in a few moments a very large congregation has assembled. And as the chaplain reads some appropriate Scripture, leads in fervent prayer, and speaks words of earnest counsel, faithful admonition or solemn warning,

> " Something on the soldier's cheek
> Washes off the stain of powder."

A SERVICE INTERRUPTED.

(See page 251.)

Ah! I can recall, even after this lapse of twenty-five years, not a few bright faces who used to join in those precious meetings, who were soon after striking golden harps as they joined the celestial choir.

I recollect that we had very large congregations at Winchester, after Banks had been driven across the Potomac, on the call of our Christian leader to the "thanksgiving" service which he was accustomed to appoint after each victory—that we had a very large gathering at Strasburg, while Ewell's Division was in line of battle to keep back Fremont until all of Jackson's troops could pass the threatened point—and that on that whole campaign I never found the men too weary to assemble promptly for the evening service. Indeed, we accustomed ourselves to make sermons on the march to preach when we should go into bivouac in the evening, and, while in some respects it was sermonizing under difficulties, I doubt if we ever made better sermons than under the inspiration of the circumstances which surrounded us and the consciousness that we were preparing to deliver the last message of salvation which many of those brave fellows would ever hear.

The morning of the battle of Cross Keys a large part of Ezley's Brigade assembled at *half-past seven* A. M. to hear a sermon from the efficient chaplain of the Twenty-fifth Virginia Regiment (my honored brother, Dr. George B. Taylor), who, being satisfied that a battle was imminent, determined to deliver one more message for his Master.

In the midst of his sermon the preacher was interrupted by the colonel of his regiment, who told him that the enemy was advancing and the battle about to open. Soon the shock of battle succeeded the invitations of the Gospel, and men were summoned from that season of worship into the presence of their Judge.

After the battle of Port Republic, while we were resting in the beautiful valley preparatory to marching to "Seven Days around Richmond," we had some delightful meetings, and on the march we had frequent seasons of worship. I preached in a grove near Louisa Court House, and again at Ashland, I well remember, to deeply interested congregations, and as I mingled among our wounded at Cold Harbor (where on the 27th of June, 1862, my regiment, the Thirteenth Virginia, carried into action 306 men and lost 175, killed and wounded), I found a number who referred to those meetings and expressed themselves as deeply affected by them.

Rev. Dr. R. L. Dabney was a gallant and efficient officer on Jackson's staff, and often preached to the men at head-quarters, and in their camps and bivouacs as opportunity offered. On this march he preached a very able sermon on " Special Providence," in the course of which he used this emphatic language: " Men, you need not be trying to dodge shot or shell or minnie. Every one of these strikes *just where the Lord permits it to strike, and nowhere else,* and you are perfectly safe where the missiles of death fly thickest until Jehovah permits you to be stricken."

Major Nelson, of General Ewell's staff, one of the bravest of the'brave and an humble Christian and devout churchman, heard that sermon and did not fully endorse what he called its " extreme Calvinism."

Dr. Dabney rode with General Jackson into the very thickest of the fight, on many a hard fought field. The men used to say of their soldier-preacher " He does not mind it any more than we do." The gallant Major Nelson frequently met Dr. Dabney and discussed with him his doctrine of " Special Providence," and when upon one occasion he heard him directing the men who were under heavy fire to shield themselves as far as possible behind trees, and a convenient stone wall he rode up to him and with a graceful military salute said: " Major Dabney, every shot and shell and minnie *strikes just where the Lord permits.* And you must excuse me, sir, for expressing my surprise that you are directing the men to shelter themselves behind trees and a stone wall, and to *put such things between themselves and ' Special Providence.'* " But Dr. Dabney promptly replied: " Why, Major, you do not understand the doctrine of 'Special Providence.' I believe it, and teach it with all my heart, but *I look* upon those trees *and that stone wall as a very ' special providence' for the men at this time,* and I am simply acting on the doctrine when I direct them to *avail themselves of these ' Special Providences.'* " Major Nelson was convinced, and accepted the doctrine of " Special Providence " as Dr. Dabney expounded it.

I remember that, remaining for a season with the wounded in the field hospitals after Cold Harbor and Gaines's Mill, I rejoined the command just after the line of battle was formed in front of General McClellan's position at Harrison's Landing (Westover), and General Ewell said to me pleasantly: " I have not seen you preaching, or heard the songs of your prayer-meetings for several days, and I have missed them." I explained that I had been back in our hospitals looking after our wounded, and that my regiment had more men back there than in front just then, but that I was going to have a service as soon as I could assemble the men. And so we soon had a very tender, precious service in full hearing of the enemy's lines.

Some of the meetings we held around Richmond when we came back from Harrison's Landing—around Gordonsville when Jackson went to meet Pope—in line of battle at Cedar Run—and on the march to Second Manassas—were of deep solemnity and great interest, but I must pass them by at present.

The morning that Early's Brigade was relieved from its perilous position on the north bank of the Rappahannock near the Fauquier White Sulphur Springs, where for twenty-four hours we faced the whole of Pope's army with an impassable river, swollen by a sudden storm, in our rear, one of the largest congregations I ever saw promptly assembled on an intimation that there would be preaching. I never saw the army massed within as small a space as at that point. General Lee had purposed crossing his whole army over at the Springs, and by a rapid march on Warrenton and the railroad to plant himself firmly on General Pope's line of retreat. General Early was thrown across as the advance guard, but the severe storm made the river unfordable, and as we had no pontoon-bridges the movement had to be abandoned. So men from many other commands as well as our own came to our service until, when I stood up to preach, I seemed to look on *a solid acre* of eager listeners.

An artillery duel was going on across the river and an occasional shell would shriek overhead or fall near by, but the service went on, regardless of that strange church music until, as we were singing the last hymn before the service, an immense rifle-shell fell in the centre of the congregation, a few feet from where the preacher was standing. It fell just between Colonel (afterwards General) James A. Walker and Captain Lewis N. Huck, of the Thirteenth Virginia, and found just space enough to wedge its way in between their legs without striking either. It was a "cap shell," the reverse end struck, and it simply buried itself in the soft ground, threw dirt on all around, but did not explode. There was, of course, a moving back from that spot, as it was supposed that the shell would explode, but the leader of the singing lost no note, his clear, ringing voice did not tremble, the song was sung through, the preacher announced his text, and the service would have gone on despite the interruption. But Colonel Walker stepped up to the chaplain and told him if he would suspend the service he would move the brigade back under the hill where it would be more sheltered. Accordingly the announcement was made to the congregation, the benediction was pronounced, and we moved back under cover. As we moved out a shell exploded in an artillery company in our rear and killed or wounded five men. The service was resumed. I preached ·(from the text, "*Except ye repent ye shall all likewise perish*") as plainly and earnestly as I could. At "early dawn" the next morning we started on that famous flank march of "Jackson's Foot Cavalry," which culminated in the battle of Second Manassas, and many of our poor fellows heard their last sermon that day on the Rappahannock.

I went back that afternoon to the spot where we had our service, and found that after we moved at least twenty shells had fallen and exploded in the space occupied by that congregation.

When the orders for moving came to A. P. Hill's Corps near Fredericksburg in June, 1863, and put the column in motion for Gettysburg, they found Chaplains J. J. Hyman and E. B. Barrett, of Georgia, engaged in baptizing in Massaponax Creek some of the converts in the revival which had begun in their regiments, and which did not cease during the bloody campaign which followed, and as the result of which a memorable scene was enacted near Hagerstown, Maryland, on Sunday, June 29, 1863.

The banks of the historic Antietam were lined with an immense crowd of Confederate soldiers. But they came not in "battle array"—no opposing host confronted them—no cannon belched its hoarse thunder—and the shriek of shell and the whistle of the minnie were unheard. Instead of these, sweet strains of the songs of Zion were wafted on the breeze, and the deepest solemnity pervaded the gathered host as one of the chaplains led down into the historic stream fourteen veterans who a few months before had fought at Sharpsburg, and were now enlisting under the banner of the Cross.

Several times during the revival in Gordon's Georgia Brigade in the autumn of 1863, Rev. T. H. Pritchard, of North Carolina, or Rev. Andrew Broaddus, of Kentucky, who were laboring in this brigade, administered the ordinance of baptism in the

Rapidan in full view and easy range of the pickets on the opposite side. Not many of the men were permitted to attend for
fear of attracting the fire of the enemy. But General Gordon
himself was always present—his tall form presenting a tempting
target to the sharpshooters on the north bank of the river. To
the credit of "the men in blue," let it be said, however, they
never fired at this time upon any of these baptismal parties, but
contented themselves with looking on in mute wonder while the
solemn ordinance was administered. Upon two occasions at the
same period I baptized in the Rapidan in full view of the pickets
on the other side, and with no apprehension of interruption from
them.

On the bloody campaign from the Rapidan to Cold Harbor in
1864, when the army was constantly in the trenches or on the
march, and fought almost daily, Bryan's Georgia Brigade had a
season of comparative repose, while held in reserve, when they
had from three to five meetings a day, which resulted in about
fifty professions of conversion, most of whom Rev. W. L. Curry,
the efficient chaplain of the Fiftieth Georgia Regiment, baptized
in a pond which was exposed to the enemy's fire, and where
several men were wounded while the ordinance was being
administered.

Major Robert Stiles, of Richmond, in an address delivered in
1869 before the Male Orphan Asylum of Richmond, related an
incident which illustrates the point I am making, and which I
will not mar by condensing, but give in his own eloquent words:

"One of the batteries of our own battalion was composed
chiefly of Irishmen from a Southern city—gallant fellows, but
wild and reckless. The captaincy becoming vacant, a backwoods
Georgia preacher, named C——, was sent to command them. The
men, at first half-amused, half-insulted, soon learned to idolize
as well as fear their preacher captain, who proved to be, all in
all, such a man as one seldom sees, a combination of Praise-God
Barebones and Sir Philip Sidney, with a dash of Hedley Vicars
about him. He had all the stern grit of the Puritan, with much
of the chivalry of the Cavalier, and the zeal of the Apostle.
There was at this time but one other Christian in his battery, a
gunner named Allan Moore, also a backwoods Georgian, and a
noble, enthusiastic man and soldier. The only other living
member of Moore's family was with him, a boy of not more than
twelve or thirteen years, and the devotion of the elder brother to

the younger was as tender as a mother's. The little fellow was a strange, sad, prematurely old child, who seldom talked and never smiled. He used to wear a red zouave fez that ill-befitted that peculiar, sallow, pallid complexion of the piney-woods Georgian; but he was a perfect hero in a fight. 'Twas at Cold Harbor in 1864. We had been all day shelling a working party of the enemy, and about sunset, as adjutant of the battalion, I was visiting the batteries to arrange the guns for night-firing. As I approached C——'s position, the sharpshooting had almost ceased, and down the line I could see the figures of the cannon-eers standing out boldly against the sky. Moore was at the trail, adjusting his piece for the night's work. His gunnery had been superb during the evening, and his blood was up. I descended into a little valley and lost sight of the group, but heard C——'s stern voice: 'Sit down, Moore, your gun is well enough; the sharpshooting isn't over yet. Get down.' I rode to the hill. 'One moment, captain. My trail's a hair's-breadth too much to the right;' and the gunner bent eagerly over the handspike. A sharp report—that unmistakable crash of the bullet against the skull, and all was over. 'Twas the last rifle-shot on the lines that night. The rushing together of the de-tachment obstructed my view; but as I came up, the sergeant stepped aside and said, 'Look there, adjutant.' Moore had fallen over on the trail, the blood gushing from his wound all over his face. His little brother was at his side instantly. No wildness, no tumult of grief. He knelt on the earth, and lifting Moore's head onto his knees, wiped the blood from his forehead with the cuff of his own tattered shirt-sleeve, and kissed the pale face again and again, but very quietly. Moore was evidently dead, and none of us cared to disturb the child. Presently he rose—quiet still, tearless still—gazed down on his dead brother, then around at us, and, breathing the saddest sigh I ever heard, said just these words: 'Well, I am alone in the world.' The preacher-captain instantly sprang forward, and placing his hand on the poor boy's shoulder, said solemnly, but cheerfully: 'No, my child, you are not alone, for the Bible says, "When my father and mother forsake me, then the Lord will take me up," and Allan was both father and mother to you: besides, I'm going to take you up, too; you shall sleep under my blanket to-night.' There was not a dry eye in the group; and when, months afterwards, the whole battalion gathered on a quiet Sabbath evening on the banks of the Appomattox, to witness a baptism, and C—— at the water's edge tenderly handed this child to the officiating minister and, receiving him again when the ceremony was over, threw a blanket about the little shivering form, carried him into the bushes, changed his clothing, and then reappeared, carrying the bundle of wet clothes, and he and the child walked away hand in hand to camp—then there were more tears, manly, noble, purifying tears; and I heard the sergeant say, 'Faith! the captain has fulfilled his pledge to that boy.' My friends, hear the plea of the orphan: 'I am alone in the world.' How will you answer it? What will you do with it? Will you pass my noble Georgian's pledge to 'take him up?' Will you keep it as he kept it?"

A missionary to Featherston's Mississippi Brigade writes of conducting religious services while the pickets were fighting heavily six hundred yards in front, and with balls falling all around. Preaching was heard with eagerness, penitents were numerous, and seventeen young converts were baptized.

I knew of several instances on the Petersburg lines where men were wounded in congregations which remained quiet while the preacher continued his sermon.

We were blessed with a comparatively quiet Sabbath at Cold Harbor in June, 1864, and the chaplains generally availed themselves of the opportunity to hold frequent services. I preached *four* times that day to very large and deeply solemn congregations. The service at sundown was especially impressive. It was held on the very ground over which the grand charge of the Confederates was made on the memorable 27th of June, 1862, and was attended by an immense crowd. It was a beautiful Sabbath eve, and all nature seemed to invite to peace and repose. But the firing of the pickets in front—the long rows of stacked muskets—the tattered battle-flags which rippled in the evening breeze—and the very countenances of those stern veterans of an hundred battles, who now gathered to hear the Gospel of Peace on the very ground where two years before they had joyfully obeyed the order of their iron chief to "sweep the field with the bayonet"—all told of past conflicts, betokened impending battle and stirred the soul of preacher and hearer to an earnestness seldom attained. There were earnest faces and glistening tears, and when at the close of the sermon those desiring the prayers of God's people were invited to come forward, there were over

17

200 who promptly responded, a number of whom professed faith
in Christ before leaving the ground.

In that long line of nearly forty miles of entrenchments extending from north and west of Richmond to Hatcher's Run
and Five Forks below Petersburg, the opportunities for preaching and other religious services were varied. Some parts of the
line were subjected to almost constant fire from the enemy, and
the men could never assemble outside of the "bomb-proofs"—
but other parts were sufficiently distant from the enemy's lines
to allow the men to assemble even outside of the trenches. A
large number of comfortable chapels were erected—more would
have been built but for the scarcity of timber—and where the
men could not assemble in crowds there were precious seasons
of prayer and praise and worship in the "bomb-proofs."

Let me try to picture several scenes as specimens of our daily
work along the Petersburg lines. One day I went to Wise's
Brigade, stationed in the trenches near the Appomattox, at a
point where the lines of the enemy were so close that it was
almost certain death to show your head above the parapet. As
I went into the lines I saw what I frequently witnessed. An
immense mortar shell (the men used to call them "lamp-posts")
would fly overhead, and some ragged "gray-jacket" would exclaim, "That is my shell! That is my shell!" and would
scarcely wait for the smoke from its explosion to clear away before rushing forward to gather the scattered fragments, which he
would sell to the ordnance officer for a few cents a pound (Confederate money), to help eke out his scant rations. Entering
the trenches I soon joined my gallant friend, Major John R.
Bagby, of the Thirty-Fourth Virginia Regiment, who accompanied me down the lines as we distributed tracts and religious
newspapers, and talked with the men concerning the great salvation. There was a good deal of picket-firing going on at the
time, the minnie-balls would whistle by our ears, and (forgetful
of Dr. Dabney's application of the doctrine of "Special Providence") I found myself constantly *dodging* to the no small
amusement of the men. At last we came to a man who was the
fortunate possessor of a frying-pan, and the still more fortunate
possessor of something to fry in it. As we stood near, a minnie
struck in the centre of his fire and threw ashes all around. He
moved about as much as I should have done to avoid smoke,
and went on with his culinary operations, coolly remarking:

DISTRIBUTING TRACTS IN THE TRENCHES.

(See page 258.)

" Plague take them fellows. I 'spect they'll spile my grease yet before they stop their foolishness." Soon after, the major looked at his watch and proposed that we should go into one of the "bomb-proofs" and join in the noonday prayer-meeting. I am afraid that some other feeling besides a devotional spirit prompted me to acquiesce at once. But when we went in we found the large "bomb-proof" filled with devout worshippers, and it proved one of the most tender, precious meetings I ever attended. If I mistake not Rev. John W. Ryland (then orderly sergeant of the King and Queen Company) led the singing, and they sang, with tender pathos which touched every heart, some of those old songs which dear old " Uncle Sam Ryland " used to sing, and which were fragrant with hallowed memories of " Bruington." (I wonder if " Uncle Sam " is not now singing, with Richard Hugh Bagby and other loved ones, some of those same old songs, for surely they were sweet enough for even the heavenly choir.)

I might write columns about those services in the trenches, but I can find space now for only one other incident. In the summer of 1864 I preached a good deal in Wright's Georgia Brigade, where we had a precious revival, and a large number of professions of conversion. The brigade was stationed at a point where the opposing lines were some distance apart, and I used to stand on a plat of grass in front of the trenches while the men would gather close around me, or sit on the parapet before me. One night, with a full moon shedding its light upon us, we had an unusually large congregation and a service of more than ordinary interest and power. A large number came forward for prayer, there were a number of professions of faith in Christ, and at the close of the service I received nine for baptism, and had just announced that I would administer the ordinance in a pond near by at 9 o'clock the next morning, when the "long roll" beat, the brigade formed at once, and in a few minutes were on the march to one of the series of bloody battles which we had that summer. Several days later the brigade returned to its quarters, and I went back to resume my meetings, and look up my candidates for baptism. I found, alas! that out of the nine received three had been killed, two were wounded and one was a prisoner, so that there were only three left for me to baptize.

The alacrity with which the men went to work to build chapels may be cited as an illustration of their eagerness to hear the Gospel.

When we went into winter-quarters along the Manassas lines in the winter of 1861–62, a few of the commands had well constructed chapels. I think the first one was built in the Seventeenth Virginia Regiment, of which my old university friend, Rev. John L. Johnson (now the distinguished Professor of English in the University of Mississippi), was chaplain. There was one also in the Tenth Virginia Infantry, of which Rev. S. S. Lambeth, of the Virginia Methodist Conference, was chaplain. In the Thirteenth Virginia Infantry we had a chapel and "parsonage" under the same roof, and a well-selected circulating library, which proved a great comfort and blessing to the men. Down on the Rappahannock the next winter there were a still larger number of chapels. I remember especially a large and very comfortable one in the "Stonewall" Brigade, which General Jackson was accustomed to attend, and where I had the privilege of preaching one Sunday to a deeply attentive congregation, and of watching with great interest the world-famous chief as he "played usher" until the men were all seated, and then listened with glistening eyes to the old-fashioned Gospel in which he so greatly delighted.

But the chapel-building reached its climax along the Rapidan in the winter of 1863–64, and along the Richmond and Petersburg lines in the winter of 1864–65.

The great revival which swept through our camps on the return of the army from the Gettysburg campaign, and which resulted in the professed conversion of thousands and the quickened zeal of Christians generally, naturally produced a desire to have houses of worship during the winter. As soon as we went into winter-quarters the cry was raised in wellnigh every command: "We must have a chapel." No sooner said than done. The men did not wait to finish their own quarters before they went to work on "the church." They did not take months, weeks, days, or even hours, to discuss "plans and specifications." They held no "fairs" or "feasts"—a scanty feast their larders would have afforded—and they sent out no agents to collect money from "friends at a distance." Better than all this, they divided into suitable parties, and, with strong arms and glad hearts, they went to work themselves. Their axes rang through the woods—some cut logs for the body of the building—others "rove" slabs, some provided "ridge poles," and "weight poles,"—and there were parties to do the hauling, put up the house and undertake "the finer work." Never since the days of Nehemiah have men had a better "mind to work" on the walls of Zion, and in from two to six days the chapel was finished, and the men were worshipping God in a temple dedicated to his name. These chapels were not, of course, quite equal in architectural design or finish to the splendid edifices of some of our city churches. No frescoed ceilings delighted the eye—no brilliant gas-jets illuminated the house—no lofty spire pointed heavenward—no clear-sounding bell summoned to cushioned seats elegantly attired ladies or fashionably dressed men—and no pealing notes of the grand organ led the music. But rude as they were, the completion of these chapels was hailed with the liveliest manifestations of joy on the part of those who had helped to build them, and each one of them proved, indeed, "none other than the house of God and the gate of heaven."

Rev. W. S. Lacy, of the Forty-Seventh North Carolina, thus writes of an evening service in his chapel: "It was a solemn sight to see one of those earnest, crowded congregations by our feeble light in that rude chapel. We had no brilliant gas-jets, softened by shaded or stained glass. The light was reflected from no polished surface or snowy wall; one or two rough-looking specimens of candles (we thought them magnificent) adorned the pulpit, and, perhaps, three others were in the room, subject to the caprices of the wind.

"A few torches in the fireplace filled the complement of light, and fully served to render the darkness visible. But there was a sort of spell in the flicker of those lights and the solemn stillness of the vast crowds, and as they would flare the lurid gleam would reveal many an earnest face and brimming eye."

There were forty chapels built along the Rapidan in the winter of 1863–64, and over sixty the next winter along the Richmond and Petersburg lines, notwithstanding the fact that at this last period timber was very scarce and transportation hard to obtain on a large part of the lines, and the men had to bring the lumber at great distances on their shoulders.

In many of these chapels there were circulating libraries and daily prayer-meetings, Sunday-schools, literary societies, Young Men's Christian Association meetings, etc. And many of them answered the double purpose of church and school. Some few were taught to read and write. I remember one poor fellow, who said to me: "Oh! chaplain, if you will just teach me how to read, so that I can read God's word, and how to write, so that I can write to my wife, there is nothing in this world I will not do for you," and I shall never forget what a proud fellow he was when in a very short time he had learned both to read his Bible and write to his wife. But I met during the four years of the war very few Confederate soldiers who could not read and write, and the schools established were generally for the study of Latin, Greek, mathematics, French, German, etc. There was, at the University of Virginia, during the session of 1865–66, probably the most brilliant set of students ever gathered there at one time, and many of them were prepared to enter advanced classes by the schools taught in these army chapels by some of the best teachers ever sent out from this grand old university. The witty editor of the Richmond *Christian Advocate* (Dr. Lafferty) once said of a certain State: "They already have there *twelve* ' universities ;' and at our latest advices they were *cutting poles* for another." We did not "cut poles" for "universities;" but we had in our log chapels schools which, in the extent and thoroughness of their teaching, were greatly superior to many of the so-called "universities" of the land to-day.

I might write very fully of some of the glorious meetings we held in these chapels, but I have space for only one characteristic incident of that noble old soldier of the Cross, Rev. Andrew Broaddus ("Kentucky Andrew"). He went to labor in one of the brigade chapels in the winter of 1863, when he was told that he could accomplish nothing, as the large theatre which had been erected in the centre of the brigade was "drawing" large crowds, and would seriously diminish his congregations. But, with his accustomed zeal and pluck, the old man went to work, the Lord blessed his labors, and soon the chapel was crowded and the theatre deserted. In the great revival that followed, the owners of the theatre and some of the actors, professed conversion, the "plays" were suspended, and Brother Broaddus was invited to hold his services in the theatre, as that was a larger and more comfortable building than the chapel. He readily consented to do so, and begun his first service by saying, in his own quaint way: "My friends, I am only a plain old country Baptist preacher, and have been opposing theatres all of my life.

I never was in one before, and if any one had told me that the time would come, in my old age, when I should myself *go upon the stage*, I should have taken it as a personal insult. But the times change, and we change with them, and so I am here to-night, ready to occupy *even this position* for the glory of God and the good of souls." It is scarcely necessary to add that the work went graciously and gloriously on, and that *this* theatre, at least, proved " a school of virtue," and ? means of grace to many who attended on " the acting " of this grand old preacher of the Gospel.

CHAPTER IX.

HAVING brought out, in previous chapters, the various instrumentalities and influences which were so potential in promoting religious influences in the army, it remains to give a chronological outline of the results upon the men, which have been already indicated, but need to be more distinctly related.

During the first months of the war, the influences of home and church were decidedly felt, and made their impress upon the soldiers at the front. Nearly every community had its weekly union prayer-meeting. The pastors made frequent visits to the camps. Father and mother, and gentle sister, wrote frequent letters to the soldier-boy, breathing a spirit of humble piety, and urging him to read his Bible, observe his hours of secret prayer, and attend regularly such religious services as were within his reach. The army was flooded with religious tracts, newspapers, and books, nearly every regiment had its prayer-meeting, and the large number of Christian officers and men made themselves felt in the moral and religious status of the army. There were, at this period, not a large number of professions of conversion, though a few found Jesus in the camp or in the hospital, and there were a few sad cases of men making shipwreck of their faith; but it may be said that the Christian element fairly held its own and made some advance, and that there was at least as much religious zeal in the camps as among the Churches at home.

I select only a few extracts from newspaper reports, which illustrate the condition of things during the summer and autumn of 1861.

A writer, speaking of the religious services in the Fourth North Carolina Regiment, says:

" There are four ministers of the Gospel attached to this regiment. Sabbath before last a most solemn service was held at Garysburg. The sacrament of the Lord's Supper was adminis-

(264)

Rev. Jno. A. Broadus, D. D.,
Army Evangelist.

Rev. M. D. Hoge, D. D.

Rev. A. E. Dickinson, D. D.,
Gen. Supt. Army Colportage.

Rev. A. J. Duncan, D. D.

Rev. J. B. Jeter, D. D.,
Grace St. Baptist Ch., Richmond, Va.

(Facing page 264.)

Rev. J. L. Burrows, D. D.,
First Baptist Ch., Richmond, Va.

Rev. John A. Broadus, D. D., LL. D., was graduated as Master of Arts of the University of Virginia in 1850, was for several years Assistant Professor of Greek at the University, and was pastor of the Baptist Church in Charlottesville, and Chaplain at the University of Virginia, until on the organization of the Southern Baptist Theological Seminary in 1859, he became Professor of "Homoletics," and of "New Testament Interpretation" (English and Greek) in that great "School of the Prophets" — a position which he continued to hold despite of the most tempting offers to him to go elsewhere. He rose to the very forefront of biblical scholars, writers, and preachers, and has a reputation second to none on this Continent. But he never did grander preaching, or more effective service than when he thrilled the crowds of Confederate veterans who flocked to hear him when he was preaching in the camps of Lee's army.

Rev. M. D. Hoge, D. D., was never Pastor of but one church, but for over fifty years charmed, thrilled and instructed the crowds who waited on his ministry at the Second Presbyterian Church, Richmond. During the war he preached to large numbers of officers and soldiers in his church, was a frequent visitor to the camps and hospitals, and was untiring in his labors for the spiritual good of the men. He ran the blockade and went to England where he secured large grants of Bibles, and evangelical books for distribution in the camps and hospitals, and his name was a household word throughout the Confederacy. He is recognized to-day in Europe as well as in America as one of the greatest pulpit orators of the age, and he seemed to be renewing his youth in the vigor with which he preached three times every Sunday and had heart and hand "ready for every good word and work."

Rev. A. E. Dickinson, D. D., was the efficient General Superintendent of the Virginia Baptist Colportage Work when the war gathered on the soil of the Old Dominion the large Confederate armies which were maintained there throughout the struggle. He at once put to work in the camps and hospitals his band of nearly one hundred trained colporters, and by his untiring zeal, wise management, and real ability he enlisted in his work the sympathies, prayers and contributions of our highest officials and our people generally, so that to the end of the war he was enabled to maintain and increase his force of colporters, and army evangelists, to publish many millions of pages of tracts, and to do a work which eternity alone can reveal. He did most successful preaching, and other personal work in the camps and hospitals, and no man was more abundant in labors or more useful than he. Since the war as Pastor of the Leigh Street Baptist Church, Richmond, editor and proprietor of the *Religious Herald* (whose splendid success is due more to his talents as a first-class newspaper man than to any other cause), agent for Richmond College, and leader in well-nigh every good enterprise, Dr. Dickinson has had, and is still having, a splendid career of usefulness and success.

Rev. James A. Duncan, D. D., of the Virginia Methodist Conference (South) was called "the golden-mouthed orator of the Virginia pulpit." During the war he was Pastor of the Broad Street Methodist Church, Richmond, Va., and large crowds of Confederate officials, senators, congressmen, and soldiers waited with delight on his ministry. He was also a frequent visitor to the camps and the hospitals, and contributed no little to the success of our work. Soon after the war he was made President of Randolph Macon College, which position he held at the time of his lamented death, and his clarion voice and eloquent words were heard all over Virginia advocating the cause of Christian Education. He declined to be Bishop of his church in order to continue at the head of his college.

Rev. J. B. Jeter, D. D., of the Grace Street Baptist Church was one of the most useful Pastors in Richmond, and one of the most untiring and successful workers among the soldiers. For many years he was one of the ablest and most influential leaders in his denomination, and soon after the war he became one of the editors of the *Religious Herald*, and died, recognized by all as one of the ablest thinkers, soundest theologians, clearest writers, wisest leaders, and most influential men in his denomination, or among evangelical Christians.

Rev. J. L. Burrows, D. D., was during the war Pastor of the First Baptist Church, Richmond, member of the "Richmond Ambulance Corps," and general worker for the physical and spiritual wants of the soldiers. Crowds waited with delight on his ministry. He probably received more soldiers into the membership of his church than any other Pastor in the South, and the soldiers used to say: "We are always glad to see that short, fat preacher come on the battlefield or into the hospital because we know that he will take off his coat, and go to work." He would work all night in the hospitals, and preach in the camps three, four or five times the next day, and he always preached the simple, soul-saving truths of the Gospel with wonderful earnestness, pathos and power. Twenty years Pastor of the First Baptist Church, Richmond, five years in charge of the Broadway Church, Louisville, Ky., and for seven years Pastor of the Free-Mason Street, Norfolk, Dr. Burrows' activity and influence seemed to grow with his advancing years, and he continued to hold the place he long ago won as a leader in Israel.

tered to the Christian professors of the regiment. The services were conducted by Rev. Captain Miller, aided by several other clergymen. The thought that it would probably be the last time in which some would participate in the ordinance, and that before another opportunity occurred they might be on the field of battle, affected every mind, and gave great tenderness to the meeting."

"I have spent," says Rev. W. J. W. Crowder, "most of the time for several weeks among the soldiers, to whom I gave about 200,000 pages of tracts, and had conversations on personal religion with over 2,300 in their camps and hospitals. I find many of them pious, daily reading the Bible and praying to God. But by far the largest portion of them are irreligious. In three companies, of about three hundred men, only seven were professors of religion, and there were but few Bibles and Testaments among them. A lady requested me to give for her all I had of the excellent tract, 'Come to Jesus,' $10.76 worth; a copy of which I gave to a soldier one Sunday morning, on which I marked the Ninety-first Psalm. The Sunday following, he wished me to sit with him in his tent. He stated that the tract caused him to get his Bible and read the psalm. On opening to it he was surprised to find a piece of paper pinned to this psalm, upon which was written in a beautiful hand, by his sister Emma, these lines:

'When from home receding,
And from hearts that ache to bleeding,
Think of those behind who love thee;
Think how long the night will be
To the eyes that weep for thee.'
'God bless thee and keep thee.'

"The melting tenderness before God in that tent cannot be expressed. Some of his mates were religious and ready to encourage him in seeking salvation."

The same useful man says that when he handed his tracts to the soldiers they would say: "This is the kind of reading we want, to help us fulfil the promises we made to our wives, parents, sisters, ministers, and loved ones on leaving home, that we would seek God to be our guide and refuge."

"Such expressions," he says, "I have frequently heard from a great many of the more than 7,000 soldiers with whom I have talked on personal religion."

A prominent officer came to Mr. C———, and said: "I feel it my duty to say that the good influence exerted upon the minds and actions of our men by the Bibles, books and tracts you have sent us, is incalculable; and, to my knowledge, they have been blessed of God in producing a spirit of religious inquiry with many of a most encouraging character. I trust you and Christian friends at home will continue to supply all our soldiers with this means of grace, which is so well adapted to our spiritual wants, and can be diffused among us as perhaps no other can so effectually."

"A soldier," he says, "came to express his thanks for the saving influence of the tracts he had received since being in camp. He believes they were sent to him in answer to a pious mother's prayers. He stated that before leaving home he felt but little interest in religion, but now it is his delight and comfort."

"Another soldier, in a Mississippi regiment, writes that the tract, 'Come to Jesus,' has been the means of leading him to Christ, since being in Virginia."

"Many persons," says a writer from the Nineteenth Virginia Regiment, "having relatives and friends in the army, are concerned about the religious privileges which we enjoy. A brief sketch of this feature of camp-life in the Nineteenth Regiment will doubtless be gratifying to them. Every night the voice of prayer and praise is heard in one or more of the tents, and on the Sabbath mornings and evenings, and on Wednesday nights, sermons are preached in a church in the immediate vicinity of the camp by the chaplain, the Rev. P. Slaughter, assisted by the Rev. Mr. Griffin. The interest of these services was much enhanced on last Sunday by the celebration of the sacraments of Baptism and the Lord's Supper, and by the admission of three officers to their first communion. Many hearty prayers were offered that they may manfully fight under the banner of the Cross, and continue Christ's faithful soldiers until their lives end. It is encouraging to see the disposition of those in command to furnish facilities for public worship, and the alacrity of the men in responding to every call, marching to church sometimes in double-quick time, lest they should fail to get seats. Let those who remain in their pleasant homes remember the soldier on the tented field. He needs the grace of God to enable him to bear patiently the toils and sufferings of the campaign, even more than to face the enemy in the field."

Good tidings came from many other portions of the army. Scenes like the following became more frequent every week:

"For more than a week a revival has been in progress among the soldiers stationed at Ashland. Services are held every night in the Baptist church, and the seats set apart for the anxious are frequently wellnigh filled by the soldiers, who are asking for the prayers of God's people. Rev. W. E. Hatcher, of Manchester, preaches every night. At Aquia creek thirty have professed conversion within a few weeks, a number of whom were baptized in the Potomac by Rev. Geo. F. Bagby, a chaplain. The entire regiment with which the converts were connected turned out to witness the ceremony. Our informant says he has never looked upon a more lovely and impressive scene. We understand that a protracted meeting is in progress in Colonel Cary's regiment, and that Rev. Andrew Broaddus, of Caroline, is officiating. We hear of another revival in which twelve soldiers professed conversion, five of whom united with the Methodists, four with the Baptists, and the remainder with the Presbyterians. The religious community of the Confederate States ought to feel encouraged by these tokens of the Divine power to put forth still greater efforts in behalf of the spiritual welfare of our army. Fully *one-third* of the soldiers are destitute of a copy of the New Testament, and of all other religious reading."

From Fairfax Court House, Rev. J. M. Carlisle wrote, to a religious paper at Richmond:

"As chaplain of the Seventh Regiment, South Carolina Volunteers, I desire to return thanks to certain unknown parties, in your city, for a donation of religious books and tracts forwarded to me for distribution among the soldiers. They were gladly received, and are being generally read, and I trust will be a positive good. May the blessing of God be upon those whose gift they are."

But there came, soon after the first battle of Manassas, and during the long inactivity which followed it, a period of demoralization which was unequalled by any witnessed during the war. Our people generally thought that this great victory had virtually ended the war—that before the spring England and France would recognize the Confederacy, and the North be forced to acknowledge our independence. Many people at home quit praying and went to speculating in the necessaries of life, coining money out of the sufferings of soldiers and people, and the demoralization soon extended to the army. The vices common to most armies ran riot through our camps. Drunkenness became so common as to scarcely excite remark, and many who were temperate, and some who were even total abstinence leaders at home, fell into the delusion that drinking was excusable, if not necessary, in the army.

The drunken brawls of even high officers were the common talk around the camp-fires, and the men of the rank and file claimed the privilege of imitating their leaders.

In a debate in the Confederate Senate on the proposition to cashier every officer found to be drunk, either on or off duty, Hon. Wm. L. Yancey, of Alabama, said: That, from his observation, he had come to the conclusion that drunkenness was not only *the* vice of the army, but of the *country*. Drinking from 12 M. to 12 midnight was habitual, and among those who called themselves gentlemen the vice was extensive. Ours is a popular army, and if we find drunkenness in it, nothing more can be expected when the vice is so extensive among the people. Abroad, he had read the unvarnished statement of a Richmond paper, which brought the blush of shame to the friends of the country. He doubted its truth, but after travelling the length of the country he was convinced of its truth, and had arrived at the conclusion that drunkenness was the vice of the country.

An army surgeon, writing to the Richmond *Dispatch* respecting the prevalence of drunkenness in the army, says: " I was greatly astonished to find soldiers in Virginia, whom I had known in Georgia as sober, discreet citizens, members of different Churches, some deacons and official members, even preachers, in the daily and constant habit of drinking whiskey for their health."

The chaplain of the Twenty-third North Carolina Regiment writes from the camp between Union Mills and Centreville to the *Biblical Recorder :* . . . " If we ever meet with a defeat in this army, it will be in consequence of drunkenness. Young men that never drank at home are using spirits freely in camp. I fear that while Lincoln may slay his thousands, the *liquor-maker at home will slay his tens of thousands."*

A Southern editor wrote, on this subject: " The prevalence of vice, of drunkenness and profanity in our camps on the Potomac and elsewhere is attributable to the officers themselves. A large number of the officers of our Southern army are both profane and hard drinkers, where they are not drunkards. It has been prophesied that the South will lose the next battle on the

Potomac, and lose it by drunken officers. We are satisfied that God alone can prevent it. If the battle soon to transpire near Manassas is lost, we shall be satisfied that *whiskey whipped our men*."

Another correspondent writes from Centreville to the *Central Presbyterian:* " There is an appalling amount of drunkenness in our army. Not, I believe, so much among the common soldiers as with the officers, high as well as low. Too many of our generals, and colonels, and majors, and captains, lieutenants and surgeons (I am tempted to say *especially the surgeons*) are notorious drunkards. During the bad weather of winter, the army lying idle, the temptation to excessive drink is a hundredfold greater than in the summer months."

Another correspondent writes of the condition of things at this period:

"A general officer fell from his horse while reviewing his troops, and lay drunk in his quarters for weeks, without losing his command. ' I speak that which I do know, and testify to that whereof I have seen,' in reference to this matter; for many a weary hour did I pace the sentinel's beat in front of those headquarters, my only orders being ' to prevent any one from disturbing the general '—*i. e.*, in his drunken slumbers.

" I remember one night, about 2 o'clock, I was impatiently pacing my beat with a feeling of profound disgust that my bright anticipations of 'the pomp and circumstance of glorious war' had degenerated into the mean avocation of guarding a drunken general, when there came along a huge six-footer, belonging to an artillery company, who had aboard enough ' apple-jack ' to make him merry. When he drew near he yelled out an invitation to the general to come out and take a drink with him. I rushed up, musket in hand, commanded him to be silent, and threatened to call the sergeant of the guard and send him to the guard-house, if he repeated the offence. He proceeded to argue the case with me, saying that he had in his canteen some of the best ' apple-jack ' that had ever been produced, and that I knew, as well as he did, that if ' General —— ' ever got a taste of that, he would not allow the man that brought it to be molested. Seeing that I was inexorable, he sadly said: ' Now, sentinel, I leave it to you if this is not a hard case. A brigadier-general, with all his high responsibilities, gets drunk on duty, falls off his horse, and lies drunk in his quarters with a sentinel to keep anybody from disturbing him; but, if a poor private gets a drop too much, you talk about sending him to the guard-house. Is this fair? Is it justice? Is it in accord with the great principles of constitutional freedom, for which we are fighting?'

"I told him that I could not answer his argument—that, in fact, I fully agreed with him—but that, inasmuch as I would be sent to the guard-house if I did not obey my instructions, I hoped he would see that I must enforce order, and would go peaceably to his quarters. He finally went, but muttering as he went: 'I certainly would like to have an opportunity of giving old —— a swig at my canteen, for I think he would promote me to a place on his staff after he found out what nectar I can bring in after a forage.'"

At this period the ear was greeted on all sides with the most horrid profanity, and "the army in Flanders" could surely not have beaten the army at Manassas in this senseless vice.

Gambling became so common, so open, and so unrebuked, that men wearing "the bars," and even "the stars," of rank would win from the private soldier his scant pay, which he ought to have sent home to his suffering family.

I remember that some men in one of the companies of my own regiment captured at the battle of Manassas a regular "faro bank" with all its appurtenances, and not long after opened it in one of the tents. It had been doing for some time a thriving business, attracting officers and men from all of the surrounding commands, when one day Colonel A. P. Hill sent for the officer of the guard, and ordered him to take a file of men, surround the tent, capture "the bank," and arrest and bring before him all of the players. I happened to be on the detail, and it fell to my lot to stand at the door of the tent and arrest all who attempted to escape. The first man who tried to pass me was a prominent politician, who was known also to be "fond of a little game," and was said to be remarkably successful in "fighting the tiger," and who, being in camp on a visit to his son, could not resist the temptation of "taking a hand." It was reported that he was at the moment of our raid a large winner, and insisted that the officer of the guard should wait until the dealer could "cash his chips," but this being refused he hustled up to the door and started to pass out, saying: "I am a citizen, sir, and a member of the Legislature. You have no right to molest me."

"I cannot help what your position is, sir," I replied, " but more's the pity if you are violating the law against gambling which you helped to make, or at least are sworn to support. My orders are imperative, and you cannot pass."

"I will do so, sir; you have no right to arrest a citizen," he retorted, as he attempted to push by me.

But when I brought my gun to a "charge bayonets,', and threatened to put my bayonet in him if he attempted to "force the guard," he desisted with loud protests and imprecations, and we marched the whole party up to Colonel Hill's quarters, the Hon. Mr. Law-maker (and law-breaker) heading the column.

Oh! for one day of A. P. Hill—the chivalrous soldier who *always* did his duty—in our towns and cities now, that he might close the vile gambling dens which our city authorities *can never find*, but which (unless they are shamefully slandered) some of our law-makers (and *law-breakers*) *do find*, to their shame and ruin.

At this period the sanctity of the Sabbath was recognized by but few—many professed Christians made shipwreck of their faith and became ringleaders in every species of vice—and wickedness of every description held high carnival in our camps.

Comparatively little was done to counteract these evil influences. There were at this time but few chaplains in the army, and it must be confessed that some of these were utterly worthless, and that but few of them appreciated the importance or the fruitfulness of the field if properly cultivated. There were exceptions to this, and here and there faithful labors were crowned with some measure of success. But the general moral picture of the army during the autumn of 1861, and the winter of 1861–62, was dark indeed.

A faithful chaplain thus put it, in a letter to the *Religious Herald*:

"But, O! brethren, the great trial of being in the army is not its hard bread, its weary marches, its cheerless bivouacs, or even its absence from the loved ones at home. It is the having to see and hear, all the time, such abounding wickedness. One constantly has his blood curdled by oaths you can't conceive, or hears foul language that makes him blush for his common humanity. Often, though not so 'righteous' as Lot, like Lot, he has his 'soul vexed' at the wickedness of those around him, and like the patriarch cries, 'O that I had wings like a dove, that I might fly away and be at rest.' He learns to feel that the sweetest element of that 'rest' which 'remaineth for the people of God,' next to freedom from personal sin, is the being where 'the wicked cease from troubling.' He realizes the necessity, for the happiness of the good, that 'the wicked shall be driven away in his wickedness;' he feels that sin itself, in its last results, will itself be a hell.

"Do not think I exaggerate the sin of the army, or intimate that there are not many men there who are good, aye, better for being there. But in the army many wicked men are massed together, and many of the restraints to sin—such as the family, the society of children and females, the Sunday-school and Church— are largely removed, so that the sin which was in the heart before, which is in the hearts of those at home, is simply *developed*. If the world is the theatre where God is showing the universe what sin is, war is one of the scenes where the illustration is most perfect. It is frequently said that the war will end when the nation is better, as if the ungodly were at least to be partially purified and raised to a higher moral status. Is not this a false view? Do not the bad ever (*i. e.*, while impenitent) 'wax worse and worse?' Is there any way for any society to improve but for men to be converted and for Christians to 'grow in grace?' *Outside of this*, is not the morality of society getting worse? This war is like any affliction, in that it makes those who suffer from it better or worse. This is realized with reference to the soldier, but I fear not with reference to the loved ones at home, and by them. They are sufferers, too. Are they thinking more of the war's ending, or of being made better by it? God help the man or woman who comes out of it no better! God have mercy on him who turns God's very rod into a lever by which to improve his earthly condition and pamper his lusts. Ah! I have seen some hardened by this war, and I fear God will say of them: 'I tried to make them better, and they transmuted my very discipline into a means of indulgence. They have their choice. I will "let them alone."' O reader! is the war making you better?

"CHAPLAIN."

The Confederate disasters of the early part of 1862 brought our people once more to their knees, and the active campaign which followed very decidedly improved the religious tone of the army. As men stood amid the leaden and iron hail of battle, saw comrades fall thick and fast around them, and were made to feel, " There is but a step between me and death," they were brought to serious reflection and solemn resolve.   Earnest men and noble women were untiring in the hospitals in pointing the sick and wounded to the Great Physician, and God richly blessed their efforts.

Some of the more incompetent chaplains were *sloughed off* when they found that there was real work to be done and hardship and danger to be met.   Some noble, self-sacrificing workers were added to our number, and all were stirred up to their duty by the solemn scenes in which they were called to minister.

We had some precious seasons of worship from the day that old " Stonewall " electrified the Confederacy with his famous dispatch : " God blessed our arms with victory at McDowell;" all through the Valley campaign; Seven Days around Richmond; Cedar Run; Second Manassas, and The first Maryland campaign; and there were a number of professions of conversion, while backsliders were reclaimed and careless professors awakened to their duty.

But when we came back from Sharpsburg to rest for a season amid the green fields and beautiful groves, and beside the clear streams of the lower Valley of Virginia, there began that series of revivals which went graciously and gloriously on until there had been over fifteen thousand professions of conversion in Lee's Army, and there had been wrought a moral and religious revolution which those who did not witness it can scarcely appreciate.

A South Carolina chaplain writes, from camp near Richmond, to the *Southern Presbyterian :* " I am both astonished and I trust grateful to see how attentively officers and men listen to the preached word, and how eagerly they read the tracts which I have been able to supply.   It would gladden the heart of many a pious friend at home if they could be permitted to listen to the chorus of manly voices which blend in singing the sweet songs of Zion amid the green trees of our bivouac. The tone of morality is much higher than I dared to hope."

The *Richmond Christian Advocate* speaks hopefully of the state of religion in the army and the country.   Of the former it says that numbers, including several prominent officers, are reported both from hospitals and camps as brought from death unto life.

18

It believes that religion among the people generally is increasing.

A correspondent of the *Christian Observer* says: "It is a common opinion that our young men in the army are very wicked, but, judging from what I have seen in various camps, the charge is utterly unfounded. It would seem that their privations and sufferings have been greatly sanctified to them; and no doubt much is due to the labor of chaplains and colporters."

A writer to the *Southern Presbyterian*, from the camp of the Sixth Regiment of South Carolina Volunteers, near Richmond, says: "I am happy to report to you the manifest tokens of the presence of the Spirit among us, even in these times of strife and battle. I do believe that these solemn visitations of Providence have been His chosen way of touching many a heart. There are earnest desires awakened in many a bosom, which I trust will lead them to the Cross. I believe there are many of our brave men lying on their hard pallets in the hospitals who are now secretly indulging a hope in Jesus; and I console myself with the sweet thought that others, who have never told it, have died on the battle-field looking to their Saviour. I know there are dreadful exhibitions of deliberate wickedness, but Satan ever delights in placing his abominations in the porch of God's temple."

Another writer, from Richmond, in the *Southern Presbyterian*, gives the following thrilling account of his experience in the recent battles near this city: "In the battle of the Seven Pines, in which we lost one-third of our regiment in about twenty minutes amid the most terrific shower of shot and shell of this whole war, the Lord not only so far sustained me as to enable me to stand up and do my duty to my country, but to do it without the least fear of anything that man could do unto me. Nor did I, as many men seem to do, lose sight of my personal danger. My mood was so calm that my calculations were perfectly rational. I felt that the Lord's hand was with me; that His shield was over me, and that whatever befell me would be by His agency or permission, and therefore it would all be well with me. It was a period of positive religious enjoyment, and yet of the most vigorous discharge of my duties as a soldier. Again, at the battle of Gaines's Mill, or Cold Harbor, on Friday, June 27, the most furious of the whole series, and in which one-third of our regiment was reported as killed and wounded, I was visited with the same peace of mind and the same resolute composure. The two battles leave me with nine perforations in my clothing, made by at least six balls; a slight contusion from a piece of bomb, and a severe wound in my left thigh, a large ball passing clear through, ranging between the bone and the femoral artery. Upon receiving it, I looked down and discovered the hemorrhage to be very copious. I was not only not afraid to die, but death seemed to me a welcome messenger. Immediately there came over my soul such a burst of the glories of heaven, such a foretaste of its joys, as I have never before experienced. It was rapturous and ecstatic beyond expression. The New Jerusalem seemed to rise up before me in all its beauty and attractiveness. I could almost hear the songs of the angels. My all-absorbing thought, however, was about my Redeemer, whose arms were stretched out to receive me. So completely overwhelming and exclusive was the thought of heaven, that I was wholly unconscious of any tie that bound me to earth. I was still standing within a few steps of where I was wounded, and yet I utterly forgot my danger and thought of no means of preserving my life. There I stood in the midst of men, and where deadly missiles were flying thick and fast, and yet my thoughts were completely abstracted from everything around me. So fully was God's love shed abroad in my heart, and so delightful was the contemplation of the offices of the blessed Saviour, that I could think of nothing else. Now, how gracious it was in the Lord thus to grant me an experience which has made me thank Him a thousand times since for what has befallen me! I will not call it an *affliction*, nor even a 'blessing in *disguise*,' but the most clear, open, manifest *blessing* I have ever enjoyed. The intent, no doubt, was to let me know where my heart lay, and by unveiling the reward that awaits the faithful to stimulate me to renewed and ever-increasing obedience. The Lord has permitted me to live, and I bless Him for it. I bless Him for anything, everything, He may choose to allot me. Our enthusiasm about earthly objects must, of course, be far less intense than when heaven, with all its glories and beatitudes, is the subject of our contemplation."

A few days since, a chaplain at Gordonsville said to Brother J. C. Clopton : " One hundred of the men in my regiment have professed conversion since we have been in the service, and the greater number spoke of your tracts as having been instrumental in leading them to Christ." Rev. W. L. Fitcher, our colporter in

Petersburg, writes that over 300 have professed conversion in the hospitals of that city. A revival of religion is in progress in Lynchburg, and twenty were received into the Baptist Church of that city on Friday evening, on profession of faith in Christ. A pious man writes to us: " God is in the army. Many in my regiment have passed from death unto life." These things being so, should not Christians at home be encouraged to redouble their efforts in this direction! Our fathers never enjoyed such facilities for doing good as are now presented us in the camps and hospitals, nor will those who come after, for centuries, see such an inviting field.—A. E. D.

The following, dated Richmond, August 10, 1862, is from the pen of " Personal," army correspondent of the *Charleston Courier :*

" Probably at no period of the war has the religious element in the army been more predominant than it is at present. In many instances, chaplains, army missionaries, colporters and tracts have accomplished great things; but by far the most cogent influences that have operated upon and subdued the reckless spirit of the soldiery, are those which are born in the heart itself, upon the field of battle. There is something irresistible in the appeal which the Almighty makes when he strikes from your side, in the twinkling of an eye, your friend and comrade, and few natures are so utterly depraved as to entirely disregard the whisperings of the " still, small voice," which themselves so vividly heard at such a moment. Every man unconsciously asks himself, ' Whose turn will come next?' and when, at the termination of the conflict, he finds himself exempted from the awful fiat that has brought death to his very side and all around him, his gratitude to his Creator is alloyed, though it may be but dimly, with a holier emotion, which, for the time, renders him a wiser and a better man. In this aspect, the recent battles have done more to make converts than all the homilies and exhortations ever uttered from the pulpit. A man who has stood upon the threshold of eternity while in the din and carnage of the fight, has listened to eloquence more fiery and impressive than ever came from mortal lips.

" It is not strange, therefore, as you go through various camps, even on a week day, that your ears are here and there saluted with the melody of a choir of voices, rich, round and full, sung with all the seriousness and earnestness of true devotion; or,

that, before the lights are out in the evening, manly tones are
heard in thanksgiving for the blessings of the day; or, that the
Bible and prayer-book are common books upon the mess-table;
or, that when Sunday comes, the little stand from which the
chaplain is wont to discourse, is the centre of a cluster of interested and pious listeners.

"In many of the regiments much of this kindly influence is
due to the pure and elevated character of the officers.   Wherever 'hese are found, you invariably also find a neat, well-disci-
plined, orderly, quiet command, as prompt in the camp as they
are brave upon the field.   Now and then you may hear a taunt
about 'our praying captain,' or 'colonel;' but even these
thoughtless expressions come from men who venerate their
officers and would follow them to the death.   As you know,
some of our ablest generals are men who have dropped the
gown of the Christian for the apparel of the soldier.   Polk was
a bishop, Pendleton a clergyman, D. H. Hill a religious author,
Jackson a dignitary of the Church, while scores of others occupying subordinate positions, are equally well known for their devotion at the shrine of Christianity.   All of these gentlemen
have been eminently successful in whatever they have undertaken, have passed unharmed through the dangers by which
they have been frequently environed, and are living illustrations
of the truth that a fighting Christian is as terrible to his enemies as he is gentle to his friends.

"General Jackson never enters a fight without first invoking
God's blessing and protection.   The dependence of this strange
man upon the Deity seems never to be absent from his mind,
and whatever he does or says, it is always prefaced, 'by God's
blessing.'   In one of his official dispatches, he commences—'By
God's blessing we have to-day defeated the enemy.'   Said one
of his officers to him the other day—"Well, general, another
candidate (referring to Pope) is waiting your attentions.'   'So I
observe,' was the quiet reply; 'and by God's blessing he shall
receive them to his full satisfaction.'

"After a battle has been fought, the same rigid remembrance
of Divine Power is observed.   The army is drawn up in line, the
general dismounts from his horse, and there in the presence of
his rough, bronzed-face troops, with heads uncovered and bent
awe-stricken to the ground, the voice of the good man, which
but a few hours before was ringing out in quick and fiery into-

nations, is now heard, subdued and calm, as if overcome by the presence of the Supreme Being, in holy appeal to 'the sapphire throne.' Few such spectacles have been witnessed in modern times, and it is needless to add that few such examples have ever told with more wondrous power upon the hearts of men. Are you surprised, after this recital, that 'Stonewall' Jackson is invincible, and that he can lead his army to certain victory whenever God's blessing precedes the act?"

Rev. G. T. Gray, chaplain of a regiment stationed in western Virginia, writes to the Bristol *Advocate* that, several Sabbaths since, "the sacrament was administered to all the field officers and staff except one, and to eight captains, and to upwards of one hundred other officers and privates. I doubt," he adds, "if the annals of war ever witnessed such another solemn scene."

"LYNCHBURG, August 21, 1862.

"*Messrs. Editors :* For two weeks meetings have been held in the Baptist church here, and many indications of the Divine presence and blessing have been enjoyed. Thus far seven have been received into the Church. Rev. J. L. Johnson is one of the chaplains at this post, and is laboring with great zeal and efficiency. Brother G. C. Trevillian has been for some months our regular colporter to the hospitals here. There are at least 4,000 sick and wounded, and a few weeks may bring as many more, as this is one of the principal points to which the wounded of the great army near Gordonsville are brought.

"At Lovingston, in Nelson, the government is establishing hospitals ; there are now about a thousand at that point. At Scottsville are several hundred sick and wounded, and about as many at Hillsborough, in Albemarle. I would like to have several additional tract distributers at these several points.

"Rev. J. C. Hiden, chaplain at Charlottesville, gave me some interesting facts in reference to the hospitals in that town. He represents the men as being very eager to hear the Gospel and to secure religious reading-matter.

"In Staunton, I found Brother Fry, our colporter, earnestly engaged. His labors have, indeed, been greatly blessed here and elsewhere. He gave me an interesting account of some conversations he had with General T. J. Jackson. On one occasion the general told him of several prominent officers who were sick, and urged him to go and converse with them on personal religion just as he would with the humblest private, adding that it was 'sad to see so many officers regardless of their eternal interests.' . . .

"A. E. D."

The chaplain of the Ninth Georgia Regiment, in a letter from Richmond, July 8, to his parents, says: "We have a delightful religious revival progressing in our camps—in our regiment especially."

Rev. A. D. Cohen, chaplain of the Forty-sixth North Carolina Regiment, writes:

. . . "At 4 o'clock we had another meeting. Our dear visiting brother preached a very appropriate sermon, very short, but comprehensive. I made a few remarks, and invited all who felt their need of a Saviour to manifest it by kneeling. Now, dear brother, I know that your heart would have been filled with gratitude, and your eyes would have run rivulets of tears of joy, to have seen so many of our brave and dauntless soldier-boys there, overpowered by the strength of their convictions, humbly and *tearfully* bowing their knees upon the bare ground, asking for prayer. At night we had a prayer-meeting, which our brother concluded by asking ' all those who were determined to *try* to meet him in heaven, to come up and shake his hand; and oh, how my heart burned when men (almost every man) came up with the big tears coursing down their cheeks, and their manly bosoms heaving with sobs of true repentance, I trust, and grasped our hands.

"And then the sobs were audible as the man of God poured forth his fervent prayers for their conversion and their reunion in heaven. That brother, as well as every one present, will never forget our last Sabbath at that camp."

Elder J. J. Hyman, army chaplain, in a letter to the *Christian Index*, gives the following account of religious exercises in his regiment (Forty-ninth Georgia, in " Stonewall " Jackson's command) the second week after the battle at Cedar Run: " On the following Monday night, after all became quiet, I opened a meeting, as usual, in one of the companies, to have what we call family prayer before retiring to rest. Seeing so many making their way towards where we were singing, after singing one hymn we called on one brother, and then another, to lead in prayer. We had what might be called an old-fashioned prayer-meeting, with about six hundred soldiers present. After several prayers had been offered, for a few moments all was silent. I must say, I never had such feelings before; such crying I never heard—not aloud, but with deep sobbing. The stoutest and hardest hearts were softened—not a word of exhortation was given—all was the effect of singing and prayer. I gave an invitation to anxious ones to come forward for prayer, and probably 300 responded!

"After prayer the meeting closed; but still the soldiers remained for some time about the place where God was blessing their souls. The impression that our soldiers are becoming greatly demoralized is false. I will only add, we have had many more such meetings. The night of the 8th inst. will long be remembered by many. I have seen the seeker weep; I have seen the new-born soul rejoice; fifteen have been converted in my company in a short time."

During the spring of 1862 two faithful chaplains, Rev. J. W. Timberlake, of the Second Florida, and Rev. W. H. C. Cone, of the Nineteenth Georgia, died from disease contracted in the service, and two, Rev. Geo. W. Harris, of Upperville, and Rev. Dr. J. C. Granberry (then chaplain of the Eleventh Virginia Regiment), were wounded in the faithful discharge of their duty.

The chaplains, missionaries, colporters and Christian workers generally were stirred up to renewed diligence by the scenes through which they were called on to pass, but, as a wounded soldier put it, "God preached to us as all of the preachers on earth could not do."

The testimony to the blessed fact of God's presence among the soldiers is most abundant. "God is in the army," wrote a pious man; "many in my regiment have passed from death unto life." "One hundred of my regiment," said a chaplain, "have professed conversion since we have been in the service."

Rev. J. M. Stokes, chaplain in Wright's Georgia Brigade, says of the religious condition of the troops:

"I am happy to state that the health of our troops seems to be much better than it was a few months since. It will be a source of delight to Christians and all thinking people to know that the religious element among our troops is much greater now than at any time previous since the war began. I believe sincerely that *there is less profanity in a week now, than there was in a day six months ago.* And I am quite sure *there are ten who*

attend religious services now to one who attended six months ago.
I speak principally with reference to our own regiment, but I
have been informed by those who have travelled among the
different parts of the army in Virginia that such is the case
everywhere."

"Strange as it may appear to some," writes an experienced
post chaplain, " scores of men are converted immediately after
great battles. This has become so common that I as confidently
look for the arrival of such patients as I do for the wounded. It
is not very strange, if we remember that before they went into
battle they had been serious and thoughtful. Here God covered
their heads, and their preservation was a manifestation of His
power and goodness that humbled their souls. ' What cause
for gratitude to God that I was not cut down when my comrades
fell at my side.' ' But for God I would have been slain.' ' I do
not see how I escaped. I know that I am under renewed obligations to love Him, and am resolved to serve Him.' 'After the
battle at Malvern Hill, I was enabled to give my soul to Christ—
this war has made me a believer in religion, sir,' said a wounded
soldier. These and other expressions show how God is working out His purposes of grace and wisdom in these times of
darkness and distress."

Among the many thousands of wounded that filled the Richmond hospitals, the work of salvation was deep and general.
" The Lord is with us at Seabrooks' Hospital," wrote Rev. W. R.
Gualtney ; " we have a great revival of religion here. A greater
one I scarcely ever witnessed. Rarely a day passes but I find
one or more new converts. The number in our hospital is being
rapidly reduced, many being transferred to other places, and
many having died ; but the religious element in our midst is by
no means dying out. A large number are yet inquiring, ' What
must we do to be saved ? ' Those who have professed a hope in
Christ seem to be in the full enjoyment of faith."

" I am happy," says another minister, " to report the manifest
tokens of the presence of the Spirit among us, even in these
times of strife and battle. I do believe that these solemn visitations of Providence have been His chosen way of touching many
a heart. There are earnest desires awakened in many a bosom,
which I trust will lead them to the Cross. I believe there are
many of our brave men lying on their hard pallets in the hospitals
who are now secretly indulging a hope in Jesus."

My own experience and observation fully confirm what is said above, and I have some very clear illustrations of the fact that Christ was *on the battle-field* as well as " in the camp," and that He manifested His saving power to not a few of our brave boys during that bloody campaign of 1862.

CHAPTER X.

EVEN the brief season of comparative quiet which we enjoyed in the Lower Valley of Virginia, after our return from the first Maryland campaign, developed very decided indications of revivals in a number of the brigades.

So far as I have been able to learn, the first revival of much interest which occurred in the army at this time was in Trimble's Brigade, and especially in the Twelfth and Forty-fourth Georgia Regiments. Rev. A. M. Marshall, who had been a gallant private in the Twelfth Georgia, had been a short time before commissioned chaplain in his regiment, and, like other chaplains promoted from the ranks, proved himself as faithful in the chaplaincy as he had been as a soldier, and as he has been as a pastor since the war.

As soon as the army went into camp, near Bunker Hill, in the Lower Valley of Virginia, Mr. Marshall began a series of special services, which at once developed decided interest. He called Rev. James Nelson, of the Forty-fourth Virginia, and myself to his aid, and was especially fortunate in having Dr. Joseph C. Stiles, who was then preaching in Lawton's Georgia Brigade, to preach for him once every day. Large crowds attended the meetings, numbers presented themselves for prayer, there were a number of professions of conversion, and the work had developed into a revival of increasing power, when it was interrupted by the active campaign which culminated in the great victory of First Fredericksburg.

Dr. Stiles thus wrote of his labors at this time:

"At his earnest request, I preached to General Pryor's Brigade last Sabbath. Upon one hour's notice, he marched up 1,500 men, who listened with so much interest to a long sermon that I was not surprised to hear of such a beginning of religious interest in various regiments of the brigade as issued in a half-way promise on my part to fall in with the proposal of the general to

(283)

preach very early to his soldiers for a succession of nights. In General Lawton's Brigade there is a more decided state of religious excitement. The great body of the soldiers in some of the regiments meet for prayer and exhortation every night, exhibit the deepest solemnity, and present themselves numerously for the prayers of the chaplains and the Church. Quite a number express hope in Christ. In all other portions of Early's Division a similar religious sensibility prevails.

"In General Trimble's, and the immediately neighboring brigades, there is in progress, at this hour, one of the most glorious revivals I ever witnessed. Some days ago a young chaplain took a long ride to solicit my co-operation, stating that a promising seriousness had sprung up within their diocese. I have now been with him three days and nights, preaching and laboring constantly with the soldiers when not on drill.

"The audiences and the interest have grown to glorious dimensions. It would rejoice you over-deeply to glance for one instant on our night-meeting in the wildwoods, under a full moon, aided by the light of our side-stands. You would behold a mass of men seated on the earth all around you (I was going to say for the space of half an acre), fringed in all its circumference by a line of standing officers and soldiers—two or three deep—all exhibiting the most solemn and respectful earnestness that a Christian assembly ever displayed. An officer said to me, last night, on returning from worship, he never had witnessed such a scene, though a Presbyterian elder; especially such an abiding solemnity and delight in the services as prevented all whisperings in the outskirts, leaving of the congregation, or restless change of position.

"I suppose at the close of the service we had about sixty or seventy men and officers come forward and publicly solicit an interest in our prayers, and there may have been as many more who, from the press, could not reach the stand. I have already conversed with quite a number, who seem to give pleasant evidence of return to God, and all things seem to be rapidly developing for the best.

"The officers, especially Generals Jackson and Early, have modified military rules for our accommodation. I have just learned that General A. P. Hill's Division enjoys as rich a dispensation of God's Spirit as General Early's. In General Pickett's Division, also, there are said to be revivals of religion."

I give also the closing part of one of my own letters to the *Religious Herald*, written at this time:

"But I have saved the best for the last. There is a very inter-esting revival in our corps. Soon after the return of our army from Maryland, Brother Marshall, chaplain of the Twelfth Georgia Regiment, assisted by Brother Nelson, of the Forty-fourth Virginia, and other brethren, began a series of meetings which soon became very interesting—the attendance from the entire brigade being very large, and many coming forward for prayer. The Rev. Dr. Stiles came to our aid, and his able sermons and earnest labors were attended with the happiest results. The meetings were providentially brought to a close, and up to that time there had been forty-five professions of conversion and there were still from seventy-five to a hundred inquirers. At the same time, Dr. Stiles was aiding the chaplains in Lawton's Brigade in a very interesting revival. There has also been, under the same efficient labors, an interesting revival in Jackson's old brigade ("Stonewall"), and in Taliaferro's. A meeting was begun in our brigade (Early's) two weeks ago, and, despite our frequent moves and the bad weather, we are still keeping up the meetings, and the Lord is blessing our efforts. Several have professed conversion, there are a number deeply interested about their souls, the congregations are large and attentive, and the interest is daily increasing.

"Brethren, pray for us, that the word of the Lord may have free course in our midst. Our meetings at night present a scene of vivid interest. The large fire-stands (built camp-meeting style), and the crowd of upturned, anxious faces, with the camp-fires far and near, all combine to form a scene which a master-hand might delight to paint. We were favored the other day by a visit from Brother C. F. Fry, who brought a large supply of Testaments, 'camp-hymns,' and tracts, which were in great demand amongst us. I wish we had a colporter for every brigade in the army. No one who has not seen the eagerness with which our soldiers receive and read these 'messengers of love,' can begin to appreciate the noble work in which Brother Dickinson and his band of colporters are engaged, in thus carrying to the soldier's tent and bivouac the printed page that tells of Jesus.

"Our soldiers are not heathen (as some seem to suppose), and, despite the varied temptations of camp-life, are usually thankful for a kind word of advice, whether spoken or written.

" OCCASIONAL."

Captain Thos. J. Kirkpatrick writes, from the Army of the Potomac, to the *Central Presbyterian*, that within three weeks between forty and fifty members of his company have been hopefully converted, and that out of the whole number in it (115), there is hardly a single man who is not a professor of faith in Jesus, or in some degree an inquirer for the way of life. He states also that " some seventeen have been baptized, not into communion with any particular denomination, but with Christ's people."

The revival alluded to by Captain Kirkpatrick was one of the most powerful enjoyed in the army at this time. The meetings were conducted by Rev. Hugh Roy Scott, an Episcopal clergyman of King George county, who described the work of grace in a tract which was published by the " Evangelical Tract Society," of Petersburg, and which contains so many details of interest that I insert it in full, as follows :

" CAMP NINEVEH.

"By Rev. Hugh Roy Scott.

" ' Not by might, nor by power, but by my Spirit, saith the Lord of hosts.'— *Zech.* iv. 6.

" During the month of October, 1862, it was my privilege to witness one of the most remarkable spiritual awakenings that has ever occurred in this country.

" I joined our army near Winchester, just as it returned from Maryland, after the battle of Sharpsburg, for the purpose of spending a few weeks with friends, and to avail myself of an opportunity to preach the Gospel to our soldiers. For four months our brave troops had been marching and fighting. About one dozen terrible battles had been fought, and several hundred miles of wearisome marching, under a burning summer's sun, had been endured. During this period nearly all religious services had been necessarily suspended. But their minds had been most forcibly turned to the subject by the many sad scenes through which they had passed. They had seen field after field strewn with their dead and dying comrades. This, and the uncertainty of the future to themselves, produced a serious, thoughtful frame of mind, which pervaded nearly the whole army. Nearly all seemed disposed to converse on the subject of religion, and freely admitted that it was a matter of the deepest importance.

" On the 4th day of October, the reserved artillery, under command of Brigadier-General Pendleton, moved to Camp Nineveh, about twelve miles from Winchester, on the road to Front Royal. Here they halted for four weeks, in one of the most beautiful regions of the State. Besides the natural beauties of the place, it was rendered more attractive to us from the fact of General Muhlenburg, of the Revolutionary War, having offi-ciated as a clergyman in a church in the immediate vicinity.

" On the first evening after our arrival here, I held the first of a series of services, that were kept up, when the weather per-mitted it, every evening during the stay of the army in this region. These services were held after dark, in the open air, around a blazing camp-fire. They commenced always with sing-ing, which quickly attracted a congregation, and were followed by prayer, and a plain, practical sermon, in which the great doctrines of justification by faith, evangelical repentance, and the new birth were set forth in the simplest language. When the sermon closed, after singing and prayer, generally an earnest exhortation was made by Captain K——, a man who, while most efficiently discharging the duties of a soldier of his country, has never forgotten that he is a soldier of Christ.

" From the beginning of these services it was evident that God's Spirit was working in many hearts. The men listened with the deepest attention, and seemed very reluctant to leave the ground when the benediction was pronounced—sometimes spending hours in singing hymns, and earnest religious con-versation. On one of these occasions Captain K—— went to them and said : ' What a blessed thing it would be, if all of you who are here present could agree to give yourselves to God from this hour.' And after an earnest exhortation to flee at once to Jesus for righteousness, sanctification and redemption, he asked them what their views were on the great subject; and, to his surprise, six out of seven who were sitting together declared their determination to seek at once an interest in the atoning blood of Jesus.

" This was the beginning of the great and glorious work of grace that followed. Every night a deeper and deeper anxiety was manifested. There was little or no excitement, and no extraordinary means to promote deep feeling were resorted to. The Spirit of God went with the preached word and earnest, pointed conversation, and the heads of many of the most hardened sinners were bowed down, as 'they became convicted of sin, of righteousness, and of a judgment to come.' A deeper sense of sin, or more childlike faith, I have never seen manifested. Another striking characteristic was the eagerness which was manifested by all for the sincere milk of the word. The Bible was the book to which they continually resorted; and those who had tasted of the love of Christ showed the greatest eagerness to lead others to the same precious fountain.

"After the services had been continued for a week, a number of the young converts manifested a desire to dedicate themselves to the Lord in baptism. And, though the weather was inclement, it was thought advisable not to postpone the service, as it then seemed probable that the army would move speedily. The service was one of the most solemn and deeply interesting I ever witnessed. The six soldiers to be baptized stood in a line near the blazing camp-fire, surrounded by a large congregation of attentive and interested spectators. The deep darkness of the night, and slight fall of rain, added much to the solemnity of the occasion.

"Among the six soldiers who came forward to enlist under the banner of the great Captain of their salvation there was a great variety of character. The first was a poor, weak man, who had given much trouble to the officers of his company; the next, a man of remarkable bravery, had been one of the most notorious sinners in the company. His evidence of conversion was strikingly clear. His sorrow for sin was very deep, and his faith simple and ardent. Then came forward one who had been regarded as one of the most unpromising men in his company—whose previous life had been anything else than religious. He seemed now to be thoroughly in earnest, and manifested the spirit of a genuine penitent. The next was an amiable and moral young man, who had been long seeking the Saviour. The last two were among the bravest and best men in the army. Having nobly struggled as good soldiers of their country, they came forward to enlist zealously in the service of their Redeemer.

" When these six were baptized, a very interesting youth, who had been deeply concerned for several days, expressed a desire to follow their example. He said he felt himself to be a guilty, helpless sinner, but he had given his soul to Jesus to be His forever, and desired at once to enlist as His soldier. Believing him to be a genuine convert, we at once administered to him the ordinance of baptism.

"This was an evening never to be forgotten by any who were present. The Holy Spirit was evidently with us, working with power in many hearts; and Jesus was also there, manifesting His power and willingness to save. Besides the little band of seven who put on the Christian armor, there were many hearts moved that evening, and tears flowed from many eyes unused to weeping. From that solemn hour we have reason to believe that a goodly number resolved to spend their lives in the service of their Lord and Saviour.

"From this time our services increased in interest, the number of anxious inquirers increased steadily, and many backsliders were led to repentance. When four weeks had passed by, during which time the meetings were kept up every evening, except when interrupted by bad weather, nineteen men had been baptized, thirty-six admitted, for the first time, to the communion of the Lord's Supper, and about sixty had professed a hope in the Lord Jesus.

"A few of the most striking cases of awakening are worthy of being specially noticed. Among the first persons awakened was a notorious card-player and swearer. He was one evening standing guard near enough to the camp-fire to hear what passed. Upon hearing an old friend, who had long been his companion in sinful practices, confess a determination to renounce his sins, and seek an interest in the atoning blood of Jesus, he, too, became powerfully convicted. He realized, as never before, that he was a wretched sinner, standing on the verge of an awful hell. He became more and more alarmed, and, at last, became so powerfully excited—to use his own words—he felt as if some one was after him with a bayonet, and soon found himself almost on a run, as he moved backwards and forwards on his beat. After a time he succeeded in driving off his serious feelings, but in a few days they returned with renewed violence, and he found no rest until he laid hold of Jesus. Well do I remember the earnest, happy expression of this man's face as he sat, night after night, by the camp-fire, eagerly devouring the preached word. From

19

the day he found peace in believing he went forth as a genuine missionary. He preached the Gospel in season and out of season; day by day he warned his ungodly companions to flee from the wrath to come. On one occasion he visited a neighboring camp, and earnestly exhorted the men to come to our meetings. As he walked across a field near the camp, he met a man who was swearing in a terrible manner. After gently reproving him, he asked him if he would not attend the evening meetings, and told him that there had been a great visitation of the Spirit in his camp. The man replied that he did not know that he had any visitation except from the Yankees. 'Yes,' says he, 'God has poured out his Spirit upon many in my camp, who were hardened in sin, and they are now happy Christians.'

"'Are you a Christian, too?' asked the stranger.

"'Yes, I was like yourself, going on hardened in sin, and a few evenings since the Lord led me to see and feel my sins, and I now have a hope in Jesus.'

"After a short pause, with much feeling he said, 'Will you pray for me?'

"'Yes, I will pray for you, and all like you, that you be brought to Jesus as I have been. But you must, at the same time, pray for yourself.'

"Then they parted. After a few days they met again, and the reader can imagine the joy it gave our young convert to find that his appeal had gone to the heart of a stranger; that he had sought the Saviour, and found peace to his troubled soul.

"Another case I will describe, of peculiar interest. An ungodly young man came to our meetings, and became convicted. And, as is too often the case, he earnestly strove to drive off all serious feeling. While all around him attended the services, he staid away, fearing that he might be forced to yield his heart to the movings of the Spirit. One night, when nearly all in his tent had gone to the meeting, a young friend, who had once been a professing Christian, persuaded him to accompany him. They came within hearing distance, and sat down on a pile of hay. During the sermon he became powerfully awakened, and as soon as it closed a cousin of his came and asked me to go to him. I found him in great distress of mind. As soon as he saw me, he clasped my hand, and said: 'I have sent for you to know what I must do.'

" I replied: ' You have nothing to do. Everything has been done for you. If you feel yourself to be a sinner, you may rest assured that the Lord is willing and ready to bless you now.' And without a moment's delay he took hold of Christ, and found peace in believing.

" He then, in an earnest tone, said : ' Where is W., who brought me here ? He is a backslider ; go and talk to him.'

" The next Sunday was a very stormy day. Not being able to hold a public service, I went from tent to tent, conversing and praying with the men. While in the tent occupied by these two young men, I asked, ' Are all in this tent Christian soldiers ? ' When I asked this question, I observed that young W. seemed depressed, though he said nothing. That night was exceedingly stormy, and fearing that my tent would blow down, I went to a neighboring house. Just before reaching the house I heard some one address me, it being too dark to see distinctly. I turned around, and discovered it was young W. He had followed me from the tent, that he might open his heart to me. He said : ' When you asked in my tent to-day, if all were Christian soldiers, and some one replied, "All except one," I felt that that was not exactly true. I was once a professing Christian, but have recently been very wicked ; and, while living an ungodly life, have led my sisters to believe that I was still a Christian. I now feel as never before. I trust I have truly repented of my sins, and believe that I am pardoned.'

" I exhorted him to confess all to his family, and to make a fresh consecration of himself to his Saviour. And as I thought of his experience, and that of his friend, I could not but be impressed by the mysterious way in which God works. He had here made use of a backslider to lead a wicked companion to Jesus, and then used the converted man to lead the backslider to repentance.

" One other interesting incident, in like manner illustrating God's gracious and mysterious Providence, I will mention. One evening, just before night, a large body of troops marched by our camp. In one of the regiments was a very intelligent young man, from Norfolk, who, not being able, on account of sickness, to keep up with his regiment, stopped at our camp to rest, about the usual hour for service. He listened with the deepest interest to the preached word. I dwelt, in my sermon, on God's mysterious dealings with His people, and endeavored to show His faithfulness in afflicting us, and that He leads all His people 'by the right way' into His heavenly kingdom.   When the service closed, observing him very thoughtful, I asked him if he was a professing Christian.   He said he was not, but trusted he could from that hour give his heart to the Saviour.   He said he came to the meeting in a bad humor, being displeased at his regiment moving so rapidly; but he then saw why he had been left behind, and believed he would be able to praise the Lord through eternity for having brought him to our service that evening.

" The sixty men who professed a hope in Jesus within these four weeks were from three or four different companies.   But the larger portion of them belonged to the company of Captain K——. When this company entered the service, one year before, it was made up, for the most part, of the most wicked men to be met with.   The larger portion of the men were grossly addicted to gambling, drinking, and profanity.   The captain labored unceasingly to overcome these vices, and continually pressed upon his men the great truths of the Gospel.   He had the satisfaction of seeing a steady improvement in the deportment of all, and he was especially gratified to see profanity almost entirely abandoned.   And now, after one year of faithful, persevering labor, he was rewarded by this gracious and most abundant outpouring of the Spirit.   The seed, which he had diligently sown, now took root, sprang up, and brought forth abundant fruit.   Of the eighty odd members of his company present during these services, seventeen were professing Christians when they commenced, forty-three more expressed a hope in Christ before they closed, fourteen were more or less anxious on account of their souls, and not more than six, if so many, were indifferent.

" The following extract from a letter I recently received from Captain K——, written about six months after the great awakening, will show how the young communicants in his company have held out:

" ' The young Christians in my company,' he says, ' have held out, I think, with remarkable consistency; only two or three have been otherwise.   We have regular preaching, prayer-meeting, and Bible-class, which are well attended, everything considered.   The religious interest, though nothing like it was at Camp Nineveh, still continues.'

" Does not the experience of this company show what may be expected when the officers of our army strive to promote the moral and spiritual welfare of their men ? Would to God we could see all among our soldiers, who profess the name of Christ, laboring as Christian soldiers. Then, doubtless, such scenes as were witnessed at Camp Nineveh would often be repeated, and our armies, instead of being schools of vice, would become most valuable training-schools for the kingdom of Heaven."

There was every reason to hope that we were on the eve of a general revival throughout Jackson's Corps at this time. The chaplains were aroused to their duty, and Christian soldiers were working and praying as I had not seen them before. General Jackson himself was a frequent attendant at our meetings, and manifested the deepest concern for the salvation of his men, and the liveliest hope that we were about to be blessed with a general revival.

But soon tidings came that Burnside had relieved McClellan and was moving on Fredericksburg—that Lee, with Longstreet's Corps, was hastening to confront him—and that Jackson was needed on the Rappahannock.

The order to move is at once given, and "the foot cavalry" march, with their swinging stride, through the mountains and down through Madison, Orange, Spottsylvania, and Caroline counties, to take their appropriate place on the line of the Rappahannock, and bear their heroic part in the great battle of Fredericksburg on the memorable 13th of December.

We had some precious seasons of worship on that march, and while awaiting the opening of the battle of Fredericksburg, and in laboring among the wounded of the battle, we found a number who had recently found Jesus. But, of course, the active campaign, the battle, and the severe winter weather which was now upon us, seriously hindered regular preaching and out-door service, and it was some time before any of the brigades had chapels, while several changes of camp prevented some of us from having chapels at all this winter. But the revival spirit manifested itself in a number of the brigades during the winter and following spring.

" STAUNTON, VIRGINIA, October 28.

" I have for six days been aiding in a protracted meeting at this place. Hundreds of soldiers pass here every day, returning to the army, while quite as many sick are coming in to take the cars. Besides, there are here several large hospitals, well filled.

Thus our meetings were well attended by soldiers—the church filled every night. Quite a number asked for prayer, a few of whom found the Saviour; but having to go right on to the army, they were not received into the Church. Never have I known such eagerness to hear and to read the Gospel as is manifested by the convalescent soldiers here. Rev. George B. Taylor and Rev. Mr. Smith are the chaplains at this post. Brother Taylor has recently collected more than $300, with which to buy a circulating library for the hospitals. This is a good move, and deserves the consideration of all chaplains who are stationed at hospitals. Brother C. F. Fry is laboring here, in the employment of our board, and is doing a vast amount of good. We need at least a hundred more to act as colporters in the camps and hospitals. Have we earnest-hearted men who are ready to enter this service, constrained by love to Christ and to souls? I am persuaded that the post of colporter in the army is one worthy of our very best ministers. At least this is the opinion of Rev. Ro. Ryland, who for a year has been giving himself to the work.   "A. E. D."

"I have recently closed a protracted meeting in my regiment, which resulted in about ten conversions.
        "F. McCarthy, Chaplain Seventh Virginia Regiment."

A correspondent of one of our exchanges says: "I have never heard tenderer, more fervent or more importunate prayers, than in the tent, or rough bivouac, or in the woods."
        Elder A. B. Campbell, chaplain of the Ninth Georgia Regiment, writes from camp near Orange Court House, Virginia, November 10, to his parents: "From the time we left the Peninsula until now, we have never suffered an opportunity to hold meetings to pass unimproved. Many souls have been converted, and Christians in the army have been greatly revived, and many who had fearfully backslidden have been reclaimed. Two of these young men have fallen in battle. As one of them fell at Manassas, he turned his dying eyes to his companions, and said: 'Write to mother, and tell all the family to meet me in heaven, for I am going there.' The other was wounded there also, and subsequently died—declaring to the last that he was 'willing to depart and be with Christ.' Others of the young converts are with us, battling nobly for the cause of Christ. It is no longer

a question whether the work of God can be carried on in an army."

I have alluded to the great revival in Barksdale's Mississippi Brigade, stationed in the battered old town of Fredericksburg—a work which, begun not long after the battle of the 13th of December, was interrupted, but not seriously retarded, by the battle of Chancellorsville, and went gloriously on until the line of march was taken for Gettysburg. Indeed that active and bloody campaign only interfered with "gathering in the sheaves," but did not stop the work, which still went graciously on.

Rev. W. B. Owen (Methodist), chaplain of the Seventeenth Mississippi, had the general conduct of the meetings, and was assisted at different times by Rev. Dr. J. C. Stiles, Rev. Dr. William J. Hoge, Rev. James D. Coulling, Rev. Dr. J. A. Duncan, Rev. Dr. J. L. Burrows, Rev. Dr. A. E. Dickinson, Rev. W. H. Carroll, and others, and the constant help of Rev. J. L. Pettigrew and other earnest workers in the brigade.

Dr. Stiles began his labors there the latter part of February, and not long after wrote as follows:

"After my arrival we held three meetings a day—a morning and afternoon prayer-meeting and a preaching service at night. We could scarcely ask of delightful religious interest more than we received. Our sanctuary has been crowded—lower floor and gallery. Loud, animated singing always hailed our approach to the house of God; and a closely packed audience of men, amongst whom you might have searched in vain for one white hair, were leaning upon the voice of the preacher, as if God Himself had called them together to hear of life and death eternal. At every call for the anxious, the entire altar, the front six seats of the five blocks of pews surrounding the pulpit, and all the spaces thereabouts ever so closely packed, could scarcely accommodate the supplicants; while daily public conversions gave peculiar interest to the sanctuary services. Of this class we have numbered during the week say some forty or fifty souls. Officers are beginning to bow for prayer, and our house to be too strait for worshippers. The audience, the interest, the converted, the fidelity of the Church, and the expectations of the ministry, are all steadily and most hopefully increasing."

The above was written by Dr. Stiles a few days after he got there. In later communications he was enabled to speak still more strongly of the progress and results of the great revival.

The meetings were first held in the Presbyterian and then in the Methodist church (the Baptist church had been so injured by the bombardment that it could not be used), but these houses were soon overflowed, and the meetings moved to the more spacious Episcopal church, which the rector offered for the purpose.

One present at this time thus writes concerning the gracious work: " Last evening there were fully 100 penitents at the altar. [I saw fully 200 one night]. So great is the work, and so interested are the soldiers, that the Methodist Episcopal church has been found inadequate for the accommodation of the congregations, and the Episcopal church having been kindly tendered by its pastor, Rev. Mr. Randolph, who is now here, the services have been removed to that edifice, where meetings are held as often as three times a day. This work is widening and deepening, and ere it closes, it may permeate the whole Army of Northern Virginia, and bring forth fruits in the building up and strengthening in a pure faith and a true Christianity the best army the world ever saw."

It was my own privilege to go frequently into Fredericksburg (especially when my regiment would be on picket below the town) and to labor in this great revival, and I can endorse fully what has been said of its extent and power.

Rev. W. B. Owen sent the following letter to the *Religious Herald:*

" March 26, 1863.

" *Messrs. Editors:* Will you permit me to inform the readers of your paper and the friends of Jesus that we have a glorious revival in our brigade (Barksdale's)? This is the twenty-first day of the meeting, and the interest is still on the increase. About one hundred have professed faith in Jesus. Dr. J. C. Stiles and Rev. Mr. Coulling have been with us, and Rev. Dr. Burrows is with us at present. Rev. M. D. Anderson, colporter in the army, an employé of Brother A. E. Dickinson, has been with us for several days. In the early part of the meeting he supplied me with a variety of tracts, which I was much in need of, and which I trust have exerted a good influence in this brigade. He also gave me a number of Testaments, which the soldiers truly were glad to obtain. Brother W. H. Carroll, of Selma, Alabama, who is also a colporter in the army, has rendered us good service. The brethren in the brigade have

been very faithful. We ask an interest in the prayers of our Christian friends, and earnestly desire that the convicting and converting power of the Holy Spirit may be felt throughout our army.   " W. B. OWEN,
          " Chaplain Seventeenth Mississippi Regiment."

Rev. Mr. Owen was unquestionably one of the most devoted, laborious and efficient chaplains whom we had in the army, and held a warm place in the hearts of the soldiers.

The following extract from one of my letters written at this time will give my impressions of this great work as I came into personal contact with it :

It was my privilege on last Tuesday to visit Fredericksburg and participate in the exercises of the glorious revival they have been having there for the past month. I went in with the hope of meeting with Dr. Burrows, who had been preaching there for the past week, but he had just left that morning, and the brethren pressed me into service to preach for them that night. I have never preached under more impressive circumstances. The Episcopal church—capable of seating about twelve hundred— was well filled with attentive listeners ; and I felt while speaking that it was, perhaps, the last message of salvation that some of the poor fellows would ever receive. When, at the close of the sermon, Brother Owen, chaplain of the Seventeenth Mississippi, made a few earnest remarks and invited inquirers to come forward, there was a simultaneous move of about seventy-five deeply penitent men. It was a touching scene to see the stern veteran of many a hard-fought field, who would not hesitate to enter the deadly breach or charge the heaviest battery, trembling under the power of Divine truth, and weeping tears of bitter penitence over a misspent life. This was the thirty-first day of the meeting, and up to this time there had been *one hundred and twelve* public professions of conversion, while there were upwards of a hundred still seeking the way of life. Brother Carroll, of Alabama—missionary of our Domestic Mission Board—has been assisting in the meetings, and has baptized already about *twentyfive*, while others are awaiting the ordinance. Most of the rest have connected themselves with other denominations. Brother Owen, under whose direction the meetings have been conducted, is a real, whole-souled, working chaplain, and I only wish we had many more such. That night the brigade (Barksdale's) received

marching orders, but Brother Owen persisted that "the Lord
would not let them leave while the interest in the meeting continued so deep." The next morning the orders were counter-
manded, and the meeting is still progressing—claiming the warm
sympathies and fervent prayers of all who love to see the progress of the Master's cause. My brigade moved its camp about
ten days ago, and as I thereby lost the use of my chapel, and the
weather has been too inclement for outdoor exercises, I am
endeavoring now to "preach the Gospel from house to house"
by holding nightly prayer-meetings, alternating from hut to hut.
They are exceedingly pleasant, and are not without fruit.

Rev. Dr. Stiles reports to the *Christian Observer* that "there
are revivals of religion, or a state of promising preparation,
amongst others, in the following brigades: Barksdale's, Stonewall, Lawton's, Walker's, Paxton's, Hoke's, Cobb's, Jones's,
Posey's, Wilcox's and Kershaw's."

The following letter gives a better account of the condition of
things at the time I wrote it than I can give now, and so I insert
it in full:

"CAMP NEAR HAMILTON'S CROSSING, April 10, 1863.

"*Dear Brethren:* I have no 'stirring news from the seat of
war,' but can furnish a few items which will be of interest to
the lovers of Zion's prosperity. We have had, since my last,
two meetings of the chaplains of our corps, which were even
more interesting than the first. The 'appeal to the Churches'
(written by Rev. B. T. Lacy, as chairman of the committee) was
read, cordially approved and adopted, after a few unimportant
alterations. A 'committee of correspondence,' consisting of
two chaplains from each division of the corps, and representing
the several denominations, was raised for the purpose of facilitat-
ing the introduction of chaplains into the destitute regiments,
and the general subject of the scarcity of chaplains was again
freely remarked on. It was agreed that each one would aid the
committee in the discharge of their duties by every means in his
power, and that the appointment of the committee did not at all
release individuals from the discharge of their duty in the premises. And it was understood that the object of the committee
was not to assume any dictatorial power in the matter, but merely
to facilitate the supplying of chaplains for the vacant regiments,
by finding suitable men and obtaining their appointments by the

colonels. The duty of personal conversation with soldiers on the subject of religion, its difficulties, and how they may be overcome, etc., was another topic of remark; and it was agreed by all that this most potent and much neglected means of usefulness had accomplished a vast amount of good in the army. As to its difficulties it was urged that they may be overcome by a man whose heart burns with the love of Christ and love for the souls of our brave soldiers—that the sentinel's beat, the weary march, the outpost, the battle-field, the bivouac and the hospital, afford ample time and place to press upon our charges the duty of personal religion. The fast-day was mentioned, and it was agreed that by a division of labor we would have services in as many of the regiments as possible, and that, in addition to prayer for the country, we would make the religious condition of our corps a subject of special prayer—that the Lord would grant us a general revival of His work. During this meeting we were highly entertained by remarks from Colonel Faulkner, chief of General Jackson's staff, and Colonel Battle, of the Third Alabama Infantry. It is a most gratifying fact that many of the officers of our corps are earnest Christian men; and it affords me pleasure to say that of those who are not professors of religion I have never met with one who threw obstacles in the way of my work. At General Jackson's head-quarters they have daily prayers and frequent prayer-meetings, attended by the staff, couriers, etc., and when there is no minister present the general is in the habit of conducting the exercises himself. O that this were so at all of our head-quarters!

"Our last meeting was opened with a sermon at 11 o'clock by Rev. A. D. Betts, of the Thirtieth North Carolina, our moderator; and a most excellent discourse it was—earnest, fervent and practical. We spent an hour or more very pleasantly in hearing reports of the religious feeling, etc., in the different regiments. Brother Cameron, of Rodes's Alabama Brigade, reported that he was having an interesting revival—*twenty* had already made public professions of religion, and there were a large number of other inquirers. Brethren Vass and Grandin reported a very interesting state of things in the "Stonewall Brigade"—they were holding nightly meetings in their brigade chapel, at which there had been about fifty inquirers, twenty-five of whom had joined the different Churches. The interest in the meetings was daily increasing. Brother Smith, of the Sixtieth Georgia Regiment, reported a number of conversions, four received for baptism, and a large number of inquirers. The brethren generally reported unusual interest in their fast-day exercises—immense congregations and the deepest interest manifested. I am persuaded that the day was very generally observed throughout the army—even the negro cooks observed it in my regiment—and its good results are already apparent.

"The subject of religious reading for our soldiers next came up, and I wish that the brother who thought colporters of no use could have been present to hear what chaplains think of the matter. By the way, a new name was suggested by some brother for the colporter—that of ' spiritual commissary '—and tracts and religious papers were called ' spiritual rations.' Visitation of the sick was discussed—its importance, best methods of accomplishing it, etc.

"Arrangements were made to supply the ' receiving hospital ' of our corps at Guinea's Depot with the labors of a chaplain, by each of us spending alternate weeks there. These meetings are interspersed with devotional exercises, and I am sure that they have been of spiritual benefit to us. And then, they have warmed our sympathies, aroused our zeal, and given a system to our labors, which must result in lasting good. The only wonder is, that we did not begin to hold them long before we did.

" It was my privilege to be in Fredericksburg again about a week ago (while my regiment was on picket just below the town) and participate in the glorious meeting in progress there. Up to that time *one hundred and ninety* had joined the different Churches, a number of others had professed conversion, and the altar was still crowded with penitents. I like the way they do there in reference to young converts. Every day or so ' the doors of the Church are opened,' and an opportunity given to all to join the Church of their choice by relating their experience and being baptized (if they desire it).

" But I must hasten to a close—not, however, before relating a pleasing little incident that occurred in our brigade the other day. Rev. John McGill, the efficient chaplain of the Fifty-second Virginia Regiment, had the misfortune to lose his horse a few weeks ago. The members of his regiment quietly got up a subscription, amounting to four or five hundred dollars, bought him a fine horse a few days since, and had it presented to him by Captain Bumgardiner, in the presence of the regiment. Should not such incidents as this shame the Churches at home? If soldiers can spare from their scanty allowance of $11.00 per month enough to make such a handsome manifestation of their appreciation of a chaplain's services, should not Church members at home, who are *coining money* out of the war, see to it that at least the small pittance they *promise* their pastor is *promptly paid?*

"OCCASIONAL."

I will only add this further concerning the great revival in Fredericksburg:

I remember that the night before the enemy crossed the river, bringing on the battles of Second Fredericksburg and Chancellorsville, I preached to a packed house, and in appealing to the men to accept Christ as their personal Saviour *then and there*, I said: "How know you but that ere to-morrow's sun shall rise the long roll may beat, and this brigade be called to meet the enemy? It may be that some of these brave men *are hearing now their last message of salvation.*"

A number accepted the invitation and came to confess Christ, or to ask an interest in the prayers of God's people, and after the meeting I went back to the "reserve" of our picket-line just below the town.

Before day the next morning we were aroused by some of the pickets on the line below rushing in to tell us that the enemy had crossed the river. Line of battle was at once formed, and in the battles which followed a number of Barksdale's veterans fell bravely doing their duty. Poor fellows, they *had* heard their last message of salvation; but it was sweet to believe that many of them were trusting in Christ, and that for them "sudden death was only sudden glory."

There were in this revival in Barksdale's Brigade at least 500 professions of conversion—many of the converts coming from other commands—and the precious influences of the meeting went out all through the army.

Rev. Dr. Stiles, in his report as army missionary to the Board of Missions of the New School Presbyterian Synod, says: "So deep and enduring was the religious interest awakened by the Fredericksburg revival, that in an artillery company two souls, probably made anxious by the zealous piety of a comrade who had enjoyed himself abundantly at the Fredericksburg meeting, were converted in the midst of the severest fighting in the late battle;

while others felt that they were almost in heaven, and could hardly suppress their exultant religious shouts amid the loudest roar and din of the conflict, the slaughter of the cannoneers of their own guns, and the palpable peril of their own lives."

" In the Third Georgia Regiment, Army of Northern Virginia, fourteen converted soldiers have joined the Methodist and eleven the Baptist Church. There are still a hundred earnest inquirers for the way of life."

Rev. Dr. Wm. J. Hoge wrote the *Central Presbyterian*, so graceful and vivid a description of his visit to the camps about Fredericksburg, that I give it in full, although I have already made a brief quotation from it, as I am unwilling to mar its beauty:

" RELIGION IN THE ARMY.

"*Dear Doctor Brown:* As I have no great fondness for letter-writing, I am afraid that when you asked me privately to send you a sketch of my visit to camp I meant to give you the slip. But now that I am publicly challenged in leaded type and editorial columns, what can I do?

" Yet what are the terms of the challenge? 'A brief and spirited communication.' My dear sir, I compromise. I consent to be ' brief,' but to be ' spirited' is more than I dare engage.

" By special invitation from an officer in the Second Virginia Regiment, I once before set out to preach to the Stonewall Brigade; but General Jackson was up too early for me. I arrived at noon to learn that he had marched at dawn. So I returned to Charlottesville, and in a few days met in the hospital some to whom I had hoped to preach in camp, while others, alas! had passed forever beyond the reach of any earthly ministry!

" In my late visit, it was my high privilege to preach six times to crowds of men eager to hear the Gospel. Five of these sermons were to the Stonewall Brigade; the first, Saturday night. The camp was muddy, the air harsh, the night dark—just the night to chill the preacher with forebodings of empty seats and cheerless services. But as I made my way through the streets of the tented city to the substantial church erected by this enterprising brigade, I was suddenly greeted by a burst of sacred song which lifted my heart. It sounded over the camp like a bell. A prayer-meeting had been appointed for the half hour before public worship, and the house was already full: so full that it was not without difficulty that I made my way to the pulpit; so full that when General Jackson and General Paxton came to the door, they modestly retired, least they should displace some already within; so full that one of the men aptly compared the close packing to that of ' herrings in a barrel.'

"One could not sit in that pulpit and meet the concentrated gaze of those men, without deep emotion. I remembered that they were veterans of many a bloody field. The eyes which looked into mine, waiting for the Gospel of peace, had looked as steadfastly into eyes which burned with deadly hate, and upon whatever is terrible in war. The voices which now poured out their strength in singing the songs of ' Zion' had shouted in the charge and the victory. I thought of their privations and their perils, of the cause for which they had suffered, of the service they had rendered the country, the Church of God, and whatever I hold personally dear, and what could I do but honor them, love them, and count it all joy to serve them in the Gospel?

"I missed, indeed, some faces which would have beamed their welcome upon me; some voices with which, in other days, mine had joined in family worship and ' in the great congregation.' But I remembered how they lived, how they fought, how they died—in faith, the blessed faith of Christ; that 'all the ends they aimed at were their country's, their God's, and truth's,' and that they are now enrolled in 'the noble army of martyrs.' I remembered, too, with just gratification, that their rallying, charging and dying at the very crisis of our fate, at Manassas, contributed not a little towards earning for their brigade its immortal name, ' Stonewall.'

"While we were singing, one thought frequently came to me: If such meetings were common throughout the army, what a school of sacred music it would be! Surely men thus trained, returning to their homes, would break up that slothful and wicked habit, so prevalent in our Churches, of the *men* remaining stupidly mute while God's praises are sung.

"While preaching to these men, their *earnestness* of aspect constantly impressed me; the absence of that rather comfortable and well-satisfied air which often pervades our congregations, as if mere custom or prospect of entertainment had assembled us. These men looked as if they had come on business, and a very important business; and the preacher could scarcely do otherwise than feel that he too, had business of moment there!

"On Sunday we had three sermons; the third was from the

Rev. B. T. Lacy. Although the weather was excessively raw, he had already preached twice that day in the open air to large congregations in another brigade. And here, Mr. Editor, as you have called *me* out, let me call *him* out. I think a fuller and more accurate statement than I could give of the position he now holds and the work he has undertaken would be useful. I will only say that, in my judgment, he has now before him, if the Church gives him her prayers, and God His blessing, the most important field he was ever called to occupy; yea, such a field, that no man, who is free to enter it and whom God has fitted for it, need wish for one wider or more promising.

" These nightly meetings were in progress before my arrival, and were to continue after my departure. May the Spirit of grace and power make them a means of unmeasured blessing!

" On Wednesday morning I set out in company with the Rev. B. T. Lacy to visit Fredericksburg and its battle-ground. When General Jackson heard of our intention, he added to his many kindnesses that of sending us over on his horses. During part of my stay in camp I had been his guest. I will not do violence to the sacredness of private intercourse by publishing any account of the hours I was permitted to enjoy in his society. But I am sure that it ought not to wound his delicacy that I give utterance once more to the sentiment which fills his soul; his sense of the necessity and power of prayer; prayer in the army; prayer for the army; prayer by the whole country. I am sure it makes him glad and strong to know how many of the best people in the world pray for him without ceasing; and not for him merely, but for the great and just cause for which God has raised him up. I am sure that his whole expectation of success—and that he expects to succeed, who that looks into his firm and hopeful face, who that sees the placid diligence of his daily toils, can for a moment doubt?—his whole expectation of success hangs upon two things which God has joined together, and which no man can safely put asunder: natural means earnestly used, and God's blessing earnestly sought. Fanaticism scorns the use of the natural means, and presumptuously claims the blessing of God. Atheism scoffs at the blessing of God, and presumptuously depends on mere natural means. The profoundest wisdom, which is but another name for the simplest faith, fixes its humble trust in God's promised blessing *on* the means He Himself has put within our reach. Espousing a righteous cause, it prays for it with strong supplication, and works and fights for it with might and main.

" Let it cheer and stimulate every godly woman in our land to know that our beloved general, whom God has so often made victorious, has expressed it as his belief that our great successes are due not more to the prowess of our men on the battle-field, than to the prayers of our women at the mercy-seat.

" We found our soldiers at Fredericksburg all alive with religious animation. A rich blessing had been poured upon the zealous labors of the Rev. Mr. Owen, Methodist chaplain in Barksdale's Brigade. The Rev. Dr. Burrows, of the Baptist Church, Richmond, had just arrived, expecting to labor with him for some days. As I was to stay but one night, Dr. Burrows courteously insisted on my preaching. So we had a Presbyterian sermon, introduced by Baptist services, under the direction of a Methodist chaplain, in an Episcopal church! Was not that a beautiful solution of the vexed problem of Christian union?

" The large edifice was crowded with soldiers. They filled the chancel, and covered the pulpit stairs. After the sermon, some fifty or sixty of them, I should think, came forward with soldierly promptness, at the invitation of the chaplain, for conversation and prayer. An inquiry-meeting is held for them every morning. At that time it had been attended by about one hundred persons.

" There are several incidents connected with our visit to Fredericksburg on which I would like to dwell, if time served. We spent hours in riding over its great battle-field and through its melancholy streets. We stood at the spot made memorable by the fall of General Thomas R. R. Cobb—lawyer, statesman, author, orator, gentleman, Christian and Presbyterian elder. He was struck by a shell from the heights beyond the river. A few hundred yards from the tree by which he fell stands the house in which his mother was born. As she looked out of those windows, in the days of her girlhood, over this fatal field, she knew not what a tragical interest it was one day to have for her.

" In the evening, while pausing in my walk to enjoy an admirable military band attached to Barksdale's noble Mississippi Brigade, I was introduced to the general. He said his men were never more comfortable, never in such health, and never so eager for the fray as now.

"A little before sunset I ascended the spire of the Episcopal

20

church, which still gapes with many an honorable wound received as the tempest of shells swept over it. There I had a fine view of the Federal camp, the dress parade, the hills whitened as far as the eye could reach by their tents, the heights malignant with cannon menacing yet more wrath to this quiet old town, lately so rich in happy homes and pleasant citizens, in social refinement and elegant hospitality.

"But from these suggestive topics I must turn away. If any are disposed to charge me with having already forgotten my pledge to be 'brief,' I must remind them 'that this is wholly a relative term, having no prescribed limits, and therefore, fairly subject to 'private interpretation.'

"WILLIAM J. HOGE."

I have not now space to give details of revivals reported at this period in Anderson's Brigade of Hood's Division, in the Eighth Georgia Regiment, the Sixtieth Georgia Regiment, of Gordon's Brigade, the Twenty-first South Carolina Regiment, the Thirteenth Mississippi Regiment, the Twenty-eighth North Carolina Regiment, the Third Alabama Regiment, the Stonewall Brigade, J. M. Jones's Virginia Brigade, Kershaw's Brigade, Early's Brigade, Chimborazo and Camp Winder Hospitals, in Richmond, Harris's Mississippi Brigade, Wilcox's Alabama Brigade, Doles's Georgia Brigade, Thirteenth Alabama Regiment, Twenty-sixth Alabama, Wright's Georgia Brigade, and other commands.

One of the most powerful revivals at this period was in Thomas's Georgia Brigade, which began about the 1st of February, 1863, under the labors of Rev. J. J. Hyman, chaplain of the Forty-ninth Georgia Regiment, who preached from four to six times every day (to meet the demands of the scattered regiments of his brigade), and was about to break down, when Rev. E. B. Barrett came to his help and was soon after commissioned chaplain of the Forty-fifth Georgia Regiment. There were a large number of professions of conversion; Brother Hyman (and Brother Barrett, after he came) administered the ordinance of baptism almost daily, and when orders came for the command to march on the Gettysburg campaign, Brother Hyman was in the water baptizing forty-eight converts. I have told how the work went on, and have described the touching baptismal scene in the Antietam near Hagerstown.

I may say here that Brother Hyman, who was commissioned chaplain on the 1st of May, 1862, after serving for a time as private in the ranks of the Forty-ninth Georgia Regiment, was one of the most faithful and successful men we had, and though laid aside for a time by sickness (brought on by over-work), had the privilege of baptizing 238 soldiers, seeing 500 others profess conversion in connection with his labors, preaching about 500 sermons, besides many exhortations, lectures, etc., and distributing thousands of pages of tracts, and many Bibles and Testaments, and performing much other labor which may not be written here, but " whose record is on high."

Carefully compiled statistics show that, in the fall and winter of 1862–63, and spring of 1863, there were, at the very lowest estimate, at least 1,500 professions of conversion in Lee's army.

I must omit a vast amount of material which I had collected concerning this period, and insert only the following:

" HEAD-QUARTERS, FORTY-FOURTH VIRGINIA REGIMENT, April 15.

" Revivals of religion are contagious. There are times in the history of the Church when God seems to be more willing to give His Holy Spirit to them that ask Him than at others; therefore sinners are commanded to repent, that their sins may be blotted out, 'when the times of refreshing shall come from the presence of the Lord.' The same gracious Heavenly Father that has owned and revived His work at Fredericksburg, and in other portions of the army, has at last poured out upon us refreshing showers of His grace. Though the meeting is in its infancy, Christians have been mightily revived and strengthened, and sinners savingly converted. The chaplains of this brigade (General Jones's, Paxton's old division) waited on Major-General Trimble about a week ago, and requested him to suspend the customary two hours' battalion drill in the morning, that we might devote the time to religious services, which he did without a moment's hesitation. I may remark here, that our generals usually take great interest in our work, and are willing to do anything to promote our efficiency and the spiritual welfare of our soldiers. I had secured the services of Brother F. L. Kregel, whose kind and courteous manners and able sermons, replete with practical thought and Gospel truth, and delivered with unusual unction and warmth, soon won the confidence and hearts of the noble veterans whom he addressed. Would that we had a good many more such as Brother Kregel, who would spend a portion of their time in visiting the army. I was with our Christian hero, General Jackson, at his head-quarters about two weeks ago, and he urged us to write and secure the services of our ministering brethren in the country during our protracted efforts. I remember turning to a brother-chaplain in company with me; he remarked: 'Urge the bishop to come; tell him he can preach to larger congregations here than he can at Ashland.' He is very anxious that Dr. Broadus, of Greenville Seminary, should visit the army during the spring and summer. Oh! cannot the congregations of our ablest men spare them for a short time, and cannot they forego the comforts and luxuries of home, to be instrumental in saving precious, immortal souls, now imperilled in their country's cause? We will welcome you, brethren of the ministry, most cordially, if you will come, while the soldiers will call you blessed. Come, we beseech you, in behalf of our blood-drenched and wailing country, in behalf of the Church militant, and the sad, sick hearts of weeping mothers and surviving sisters, we implore you to come and labor that the souls of our noble defenders may not be sacrificed, if their bodies are, in this stupendous struggle for constitutional freedom and national independence.

"The soldiers are anxious to hear preaching. They are not—as some think—impervious to moral impressions. Their moral sensibility is not so stupefied that the *Cross of Christ* will not *convince* them, *move* them, and *save* them. During the last week twelve young men in my regiment have professed a saving faith in Christ, and are candidates for admission into the different branches of the Christian Church. Most of them have asked for baptism by immersion, and want to join the Baptist Church. Those that wish to join other Churches I have turned over to chaplains representing the several denominations of Christians in the army. There are scores concerned, and anxiously inquiring the way of life. Other regiments in the brigade are also blessed with God's presence. In my next communication I will give a full account of the interesting work of grace going on in this brigade. My tent was besieged the most of last week by men anxiously inquiring, 'What must I do to be saved?' We earnestly ask an interest in the prayers of God's people. The last meeting of the chaplains, which came off yesterday, was one of the most delightful I have ever attended. General Pendleton—who is also the Rev. Dr. Pendleton, of the Episcopal Church—was present. The feeling remarks of this aged Christian hero moved to tears eyes unused to weep ; and the tears that glistened in his eyes told that his burning words came from a heart touched with a deep sympathy in this grand work. After transacting a great deal of important business appertaining to our work, the meeting closed by passing a resolution, a solemn act of worship to Almighty God, pledging ourselves to pray for each other and the success of our labors, each day at sunset. The eternal clock, far up in the everlasting belfry of the skies, as it strikes the departure of each successive day, will remind us of our pledge to our brethren and our God. Will not the Christian Church, at this noted and impressive hour—an hour so forcibly reminding us of the ebbing away of life—unite with us in asking God's blessing upon those who are to be the future pillars of *Church* and *State ?*

" JAMES NELSON,
"Chaplain Forty-fourth Virginia Regiment."

Rev. W. H. Carroll, in an account of a visit to Cobb's Brigade, in the *Biblical Recorder*, says : "A regimental prayer-meeting was to be held just after ' tattoo,' and at the appointed time I started to it, in company with some officers. It was so dark that we could not see the stumps, but after stumbling over a few we reached the place of prayer. A part of the time it was raining and blowing too much for tallow candles, but we found a large crowd assembled—some sitting, others standing. In the thick darkness, that sweet old hymn, ' When I can read my title clear,' with the chorus, ' Remember, Lord, thy dying groans,' was sung. The services were then continued, and were interesting through-out. It was, indeed, a solemn and impressive occasion."

" RICHMOND, VIRGINIA, May 30, 1863.

" I have within a few days received the most cheering accounts from the Army of Northern Virginia. In almost every regiment protracted meetings are in progress, and souls are being born into the kingdom. Last Sabbath, Rev. N. B. Cobb, of North Carolina, baptized *five* in Ransom's Brigade, Rev. Mr. Betts *two*, and the chaplain of the Fourteenth North Carolina *five*. The meetings in this brigade are becoming more and more interesting every day, and Brother Cobb informs me that ' quite a number have been converted since last Sabbath.' In Wright's Brigade, a great work of grace is going on. Last Thursday, Brethren Hyman and Marshall, chaplains of the Twelfth and Forty-ninth Georgia Regiments, baptized *twenty-six*. The chaplain of the Fortieth Virginia reports thirty penitents in Heth's Brigade. Brother Barrett, chaplain Forty-fifth Georgia, Thomas's Brigade, reports from fifty to one hundred who are seeking the Saviour. Since the battle of Chancellorsville, he has received seven for church-membership. In the Twelfth South Carolina, twenty-five are reported as having made their peace with God. A quarter-master in Armistead's Brigade writes me that a good work has commenced there, and that nothing is so much needed as men to preach Jesus. A Baptist minister from Pickett's Division says that in 'every brigade in that division protracted meetings are being held, and a solemn and deep religious influence pervades many hearts.' Rev. Bernard Phillips, our colporter at Winder Hospital, informs me that a 'precious revival is being enjoyed at that post. Two were received for baptism last night.' Brother Phillips is assisting in a protracted meeting, at which many are crying to God for mercy. The cry is for the Gospel. In some of these protracted meetings, the voice of a minister has scarcely been heard. Will not fifty of our pastors throw themselves, for a few months, into this great work? 'Send us tracts, colporters, and evangelists.' Will not the Churches give with a munificent liberality, of their possessions, that the board may meet these pressing demands?

"A. E. Dickinson, Superintendent, etc."

"*Dear Brethren:* Our brigade has just moved, and suspended the protracted meeting which I told you in my last Dr. Pryor had commenced, in conjunction with the regimental chaplains. There have been about twenty-five conversions, and the meeting closed with about the same number of mourners at the anxious seat. We did not experience such blessings as have descended in other parts of the army, but have abundant reason for grati-tude, and to thank God and take courage. About thirteen of these conversions were in my regiment.

" F. McCarthy,
" Chaplain Seventh Virginia Infantry."

The chaplain of the Second Georgia Battalion, Army of

Northern Virginia, writes, to the *Southern Christian Advocate*: " The late battles and the recent glorious victory have tended greatly to effect a moral reformation in the army.   Many of the soldiers in the hour of danger formed good resolutions, which I am happy to state, they have not forgotten in this time of comparative safety.   We have been having some delightful refreshings from the Lord.   The glorious work is going on throughout the entire brigade."

Chaplain J. M. Cline states, in North Carolina *Christian Advocate*, that his regiment, the Fifty-second North Carolina. has been experiencing " the most glorious revival of religion he ever witnessed."   Up to the date of his letter, June 5, thirty-four had been converted.

CHAPTER XI.

THE march to Gettysburg, the great battle and fearful loss of many of our noblest and best officers and men, very seriously interfered with our regular meetings, but by no means suppressed the spirit of revival, which really deepened until, when we came back to rest for a season along the Rapidan, the "Great Revival" began with all of its power and made wellnigh every camp vocal with the praises of our God.

A large number of our most efficient chaplains felt it to be their duty to remain with our wounded at Gettysburg, and were (contrary to the "cartel" and the usage of civilized warfare) thrown into prison, thus depriving their men of their services at a most important juncture. But the different denominations sent to the army a number of missionaries and colporters, many of the pastors came on visits to the camp, the chaplains present were stirred up to double diligence by the circumstances which surrounded us, and invaluable coworkers were found among Christian officers and men.

At Winchester, as the army was returning from the Gettysburg campaign, my regiment acted as provost-guard and I had opportunity, in the hospitals and in some special services which we held in several of the Churches, of coming in contact with representatives of nearly every brigade, and of learning that there was a very decidedly hopeful religious feeling throughout the army.

We were exceedingly fortunate in having as preachers in our meetings and workers among the soldiers at Winchester, besides our chaplains, such men as Drs. Wm. J. Hoge, Wm. F. Broaddus, J. A. Broadus, J. L. Burrows, etc., and there was every prospect of a general revival among the troops around Winchester, when we took up the line of march across the mountains. [It was on this march that our honored brother, Dr. J. L. Burrows, walked the ninety-two miles from Winchester to Staunton, and, putting his coat in one of the ambulances, had it stolen from him by some

"DR. BURROWS PREACHING IN HIS SHIRT SLEEVES."

"Well, if you and your people can stand my filling your pulpit in this garb, I
reckon I can."

(See page 313.)

miscreant. Arriving in Harrisonburg on Sunday morning in his shirt-sleeves, with his suspenders strapped over his blue worsted shirt, he thought he would quietly slip into the Presbyterian church and, preserving his incog., hear a sermon from the pastor. But some one recognized and reported him, the pastor insisted upon his preaching, and at last the good doctor (who never knew how to say " No! " when anybody wants work out of him) yielded his objections—saying: " Well! if you and your people can stand my filling your pulpit in this garb, I reckon *I* can"—and, mounting the pulpit, preached what some of his friends pronounced the most powerful sermon they ever heard from him. By the way, our gifted and loved brother, who has done so much in every way to endear himself to Christian people of every name, has no brighter record of a faithful, useful service than that made by his self-sacrificing labors among our soldiers, and will have no brighter stars in his " crown of rejoicing " than those won to Christ by his efforts among " the boys in gray."]

A few days after his arrival in Winchester, Rev. Dr. J. A. Broadus thus wrote to Superintendent Dickinson :

" I am very glad I came to Virginia and came to Winchester. Though there are not such opportunities for preaching as there were some months ago at Fredericksburg, yet I meet a hearty welcome and rejoice in the work. My heart warms towards the soldiers. How they do listen to preaching. The Lord be thanked for the privilege of telling them about Jesus ; the Lord prosper all who labor to save them."

Two weeks later he wrote as follows :

" WINCHESTER, VIRGINIA, July 21.

" *Dear Brother Dickinson :* I have been preaching here for more than two weeks—the first week, every night at the Lutheran church ; the second, every afternoon at the New School Presbyterian (Dr. Boyd's). For the last few days there were some troops near, and I could preach in their camps, particularly in Corse's Brigade, where I was heartily welcomed by some old friends. The services at the churches were attended by a good many soldiers and citizens ; indeed, a large number, if one considers the almost uninterrupted rainy weather, and the confused whirl in which everybody has been living since the wounded at Gettysburg began to pour in,

"After preaching on Sunday morning, 12th inst., at Dr. Boyd's church, and watching, when we came out, the passage along the street of nearly 400 prisoners, I stopped to speak to a wounded soldier. They were occupying the basement of the church as a hospital, and the men, disliking the close room, were lying everywhere, in the enclosure before the church, and on the steps, and in the vestibule. So it is at all churches, and one never goes in or out among these poor fellows, lying on their pallets or blankets, wounded or sick, without thinking of the Pool of Bethesda. The one mentioned I simply happened, as we say, to pass by and notice. He was from Georgia. In response to my inquiry, he said he was not a Christian, but wished he was. His parents were pious, but mighty hard '(Hard Shells);' for his part, he liked to hear all denominations preach, and he had for a long time been trying and laboring to be a Christian. I sought to explain to him the way of salvation, and he listened most earnestly. Presently I was interrupted a moment by one of the ladies who were waiting on the wounded, and then turning to this man, I gave him my hand to take leave. But he held my hand hard, and said: 'Stop a little. Pray for me, won't you? I want to be a Christian. My dear mother died two years ago, after I entered the army. She had six sons that enlisted; four of them are dead, a fifth was wounded at second Manassas, and is a cripple at home; and here am I, and I remember the last words my father spoke to me: he said, " My son, I want you to be a praying boy." I've tried to do it, but I'm very wicked, and deserve God's wrath. You seem to care something for me—now pray for me, won't you?' He sat up on his blanket, drawing his wounded foot toward him, and I sat by his side. There were soldiers lying all around, and people passing in every direction, and noisy confusion in the street close by, but I never in my life felt more deeply that prayer is a living and precious reality. And when I arose, he took my hand himself, and said, 'Now you have prayed for me once—won't you remember me and pray for me still?' There had been nothing remarkable in this man's appearance; he was a hale, hearty-looking soldier; and I walked away thinking how many there doubtless are of these poor fellows whom one sees everywhere by hundreds, that would in like manner reveal to an enquirer an anxious concern for their salvation, retained in some cases for months and years. There is no mistake about it that a large proportion of these soldiers are deeply interested in the subject of religion. Any experienced preacher would see it, from the way they listen to preaching; and in private, not only are all respectful, but many cordially welcome religious conversation, and avow, without the slightest hesitation, their desire to be Christians.

"'THE CONVALESCENT CAMP.'

" The Yankees have, at various times, obtained materials for furnishing their camp from the once beautiful residence of Senator Mason, on the edge of town, and there is now nothing left but some half demolished walls. A camp, for convalescent soldiers on their way to the army, was established near there last week, and I went out to preach on Tuesday morning. Some 200 men assembled under the trees in what was Mr. Mason's yard, and it was moving to see with what fixed attention they listened. Men were there from almost every State in the Confederacy, but we had a common interest in God's worship and word. At the close of the sermon, some twenty or twenty-five readily knelt for special prayer. My appointments here having closed on Saturday, I intended to go down to Bunker Hill on Monday, and get into the army proper; but it became so clear that they were about to be in rapid motion, that I saw there would be no opportunity to preach just now, and I should simply be in the way. So I propose to fall back to Charlottesville, and wait until the army is quiet again. By the way, when at the camp of Corse's Brigade the other day, Major C. and Lieutenant F. of the Fifteenth Virginia, two Baptist brethren whom I had not met before, made me a present of a hat, which cost them $20 here, and would have cost twice as much in Richmond. I take this as a token that your army evangelists will not lack for friends. I have been treated with great kindness by Rev. Messrs. Graham and Dosh, and Rev. Dr. Boyd, pastors in Winchester, and have received much pleasure and valuable aid in the common work from the presence here of my cherished friend, Rev. J. Wm. Jones, chaplain Thirteenth Virginia, who is surely one of the most useful men in the service.

" Very truly yours,
" JOHN A. BROADUS."

The meetings which we held in Winchester and in the camps

around, and our labors in the crowded hospitals were a fit preparation for the grand work which followed when we reached
the line of the Rapidan, and the deep interest shown by the
soldiers was a prophecy of the "season of refreshing from the
presence of the Lord" which was just ahead of us.

"A writer in the *Central Presbyterian* mentions a revival progressing in the Rockbridge Artillery, with twenty-four additions
to various churches on a profession of faith. He says: 'Many
ascribe the first turnings of their attention to the subject to
*the earnest, prayerful letters from home, urging them to turn to
Christ.*' Remember this, Christian, when you write next to
your friends in camp; and so *write that God may bless your
letters; and ask Him to do so.* A revival is in progress in
Corse's Brigade, Pickett's Division, Army of Northern Virginia,
and about 200 have shared in the outpouring of God's Spirit."

" Rev. S. W. Howerton, chaplain of the Fifteenth North Caro-
linia Regiment, reports seventy hopeful conversions and many
anxious inquirers in it. . 'Every company has prayers, nightly,
immediately after roll-call, and nearly all attend and are respectful; the officers, in some instances, conducting the exercises
and leading in prayer.'—Rev. G. W. Camp, army missionary
at Kingston, North Carolina, baptized five converts, August 2,
in the river Neuse."

The special correspondent of the *Richmond Enquirer*, under
date August 12, writes: "Yesterday the chaplains of the Second
and Third Corps held their regular meeting, and after a very excellent sermon from Rev. B. T. Lacy, formerly of Fredericksburg,
most interesting reports were made, showing that a high state
of religious feeling pervades these two corps. General Ewell
was present at the meeting, and manifested much interest in the
proceedings."

Rev. John J. Hyman writes, from Orange: "We are holding a
protracted meeting of very great interest in Thomas's Brigade.
Large numbers are seeking the Saviour, and there are many
who are asking for tracts and hymn-books. If you can spare
an army missionary to us, he would be gladly welcomed. We
would say to such an one, 'Come over and help us.'"

Rev. J. H. Harris writes, from Mercer county, Virginia: "I
feel much encouraged by the anxiety which is manifested by the
troops for the printed page. They press around me so eagerly
as soon as the benediction is pronounced, and *beg* for tracts and

Testaments. I have been aiding Elder M. Bibb, who is carrying on a fine meeting in his regiment. Ten have professed conversion while many more are seeking after the Saviour."—A. E. D.

" During the whole effort, from last spring, 185 persons came forward for prayer, and 104 made a profession of faith. Of this number I have baptized forty-six, and I know of three or four others who expect to unite with us. Those who have joined the Methodists number forty-nine. I desire to feel profoundly grateful to God that our labors have been so extensively blessed. Out of about 1,500 men, we thus have 100 who, if they are not made *better* soldiers, we know they are not made *worse*—and in respect to their morals, we know they are greatly elevated; and, what is of no mean importance, they are prepared for life or death; and should they be permitted to return home, it will be to bless their friends and build up the Redeemer's Kingdom among them. I would I could say this of all, both officers and men, throughout the Confederacy.

" M. Bibb, Chaplain Sixtieth Virginia Regiment."

A writer from the army says: " I wish all the members of our Churches could be here and hear how fervently the soldiers pray that the revival of religion in the army may reach the Churches at home; that their brethren at home may be turned from the sins of extortion and speculation; and that all may be brought to humble themselves before God."

" There are great demands for evangelists in the army. Some have recently entered upon this service, and are enjoying the Divine blessing. A delightful revival is in progress near Drewry's Bluff, in which Elder A. Broaddus, Sr., has been engaged from the beginning of the meeting. There have been eighty professions of conversion; forty backsliders have been reclaimed, and and twenty-four persons baptized. We are very anxious to secure the services of several ministers adapted to this kind of labor. The brethren engaged in the revival at Drewry's Bluff are almost broken down, and need *instant* help.

"A. E. Dickinson, Superintendent.

" Richmond, Virginia."

"A majority of the Thirty-second Mississippi Regiment are Church-members."

"*Messrs. Editors:* The meeting held with the Twenty-sixth Regiment, Wise's Brigade, which commenced more than four weeks ago, is still in progress. About 175 have professed religion, among whom are a number of what are called *backsliders.* I have reason to believe that a majority of the backsliders were never converted until since the commencement of our meeting. The Lord give them grace to *slide forward* the balance of their lives! Brother Wiatt has baptized sixty-four, and about an equal number have united with a Methodist class, lately organized in camp. Major Garrett, a Methodist preacher, baptized nine the other day in the James river.   In haste,

"A. Broaddus."

" Richmond, July 23.

"I have only time to say to your readers that the meeting with the Twenty-sixth Virginia Regiment, Wise's Brigade, is still deeply interesting; that I left this morning to attend to some domestic affairs in Bedford; that Dr. Jeter has just promised to go down to-morrow and assist the chaplain the balance of the week; that Brother Wiatt has baptized seventy-two up to this time; that 185 have professed religion; that the exercises throughout have been characterized by deep *heart excitement,* without any noise or confusion; that I expect to return in eight or ten days; that I fondly hope that many others will be converted; and that I am still yours affectionately,

"A. Broaddus."

" Kingston, North Carolina, July 28.

" I am now assisting the chaplain of the Forty-second North Carolina Regiment, General Martin's Brigade, in a series of meetings every night when the weather permits. The congregations are very large and attentive. Many come forward and ask God's people to pray for them. I am very much pleased with my new field of labor thus far. The soldiers appreciate kindness.

" G. W. Camp."

By the first of August General Lee's army was camped along the line of the Rapidan (from Liberty Mills, above Orange Court House, to Raccoon Ford, below), and God blessed us with " seasons of refreshing from the presence of the Lord " in nearly every camp.

A large volume would scarcely suffice to record the details of this great revival, and I can only give here a few illustrations as specimens of the whole character of the work.

From the 1st of August to the 1st of October I averaged two sermons every day, besides other work, and other chaplains were even more laborious, so pressing were the demands upon us; and I witnessed the professed conversion of hundreds of our brave men.

My own brigade (Smith's, formerly Early's Virginia) was fortunately camped near Mt. Pisgah Baptist Church and a Methodist church in the lower part of Orange county, and Rev. J. P. Garland, of the Forty-ninth Virginia, Rev. Mr. Slaughter, of the Fifty-eighth Virginia, and myself united in holding meetings in both of these houses.   We were fortunate in having at different times Rev. Dr. J. A. Broadus, Rev. F. M. Barker (the gifted, eloquent and lamented preacher who took in my tent the cold which resulted in his death), Rev. L. J. Haley and others to help us, and the work went graciously on until interrupted, but not stopped, by the "Bristoe campaign."   There were 250 professions of conversion, and a revival among Christians, of the highest value.

During this period I had also the general conduct of revival meetings in Hoke's North Carolina Brigade, Gordon's Georgia Brigade, and Hays's Louisiana Brigade—having services at different hours and providing other preachers as I was able—and helped brother-chaplains in a number of other brigades.

I had a beautiful baptistery made at the foot of the hill near our camp, and had some of the most impressive baptisms there which I have ever witnessed.

My readers will, I trust, pardon me for so frequently reproducing my own letters from the army, but having been written at the time they give a much more accurate picture of the scenes they describe than I could now produce.   The following notices the beginning of our work on the Rapidan:

"MT. PISGAH CHURCH, ORANGE COUNTY, VIRGINIA,
"August 5, 1863.

"*Dear Brethren:* When it was my pleasure, nine years ago, to hear, from the pulpit of this church, a sermon from good Brother Herndon Frazer, I little dreamed that I was ever to witness the scene which now surrounds me. *Then* I came on a quiet Sab-

bath to hear an earnest proclamation of the ' Gospel of peace '—
now I see, on every side, the implements of deadly strife, and
hear the busy hum of the camp. Yet the scene shall not be
wholly changed; for the manly voices of war-worn veterans shall
chant at morn and eve the same good old hymns wh˙ *then*
echoed through this temple of the living God. The ' Gospel of
peace' shall still be proclaimed to those who strive for their
country's weal, and the voice of prayer shall still ascend to the
God who then met with His people. So much has occurred since
I last wrote that I scarce know where to begin or stop. Our
sojourn in Winchester was rendered most delightful by the
warm-hearted hospitality of the people—they threw open to us
their churches, their homes and their hearts—and we left there
with many bitter regrets that we were compelled to leave such a
people to the ' tender mercies' of such a foe. Brother John A.
Broadus preached every day (twice a day, sometimes) for two
weeks, and despite the bad weather and other adverse circumstances the congregations were large and attentive, and many
' precious seed' were sown which shall, in due season, bring
forth their fruit. We were especially indebted to the pastors
who were present (Rev. Dr. Boyd, Rev. Mr. Graham, Rev. Mr.
Dosh and Rev. Mr. Brooke) for the tender of their churches, as
also for many personal kindnesses—they were Christian brethren
with whom it was pleasant to hold intercourse. Dr. Burrows,
of Richmond, was also there with the ' ambulance committee,'
and preached us several sermons, which were none the less acceptable because the preacher was constantly seen on the street
with coat off and hard at work amongst the wounded, and did
not have on exactly his ' t'other clothes' when he entered the
pulpit, as some rascal had lightened his wardrobe on the route.
Rev. Dr. William J. Hoge also preached several sermons to large
and attentive congregations. I must not omit either to mention
the labors of Brother M. D. Anderson, who was untiring in the
hospitals, and whose ' silent preachers' could be seen in every
ward. By the way, the 'Ambulance Committee,' of Richmond,
are now an *institution*—they do noble work after every battle,
and their arrival is always hailed with joy by the poor sufferers
whom they come to relieve. And the ladies of Winchester will
not be soon forgotten by the thousands who received their bene-
factions. Their praise is in the mouths of all who had an opportunity of witnessing their entire devotion to the comfort of the

wounded. I was in the hospitals every day, and I never witnessed more constant attention to our wounded than was shown by these noble women, who were at the side of our poor fellows from morning until night. And besides their attention in the hospitals they threw open their houses—in a word, they did *their whole duty* to our brave boys who fell fighting to relieve them from the return of the foe. Our march from Winchester was a tedious one, and many fell out by the way, though most of them have since come up. Yet, notwithstanding the weariness of the men, I found frequent opportunities for religious services, and deeply interested listeners. And the tracts and papers I was enabled to distribute were eagerly read. Since we reached this camp the opportunities for religious services have been very fine. I have two appointments a day for preaching—shall have three after to-day, and might find opportunities for preaching even more frequently to large and attentive congregations. Now is the time for our brethren to comply with the resolutions of the General Association, and ' spend part of their time in visiting and preaching in the army.' We may move from this line if the movements of the enemy render it necessary, but shall not, probably, go far, or have a battle very soon. So, if brethren really desire to *work* in this wide field of usefulness, let them come on at once, and they shall find plenty to do. I expect to administer the ordinance of baptism to-morrow, and trust that it will not be the last time while we are enjoying this brief season of repose. Brother J. A. Broadus was compelled, by hoarseness, to leave us the other day, but we hope he may be able to return again in a few days. Our army is rapidly increasing in numbers, the weary are becoming rested, and the general *efficiency* improved. We have very few *croakers*—they are found chiefly amongst those who stay at home, and have done nothing for our cause ; but, on the contrary, our boys are cheerful and confident—longing for peace and a return to the sweets of their homes, yet willing to spend and be spent to protect their loved ones. I rejoice to see that our Christian President has again called the nation to humiliation and prayer, and shall be greatly disappointed if it is not universally observed. Our country Churches ought, by all means, to have prayer-meetings where they cannot have the services of their pastors ; and let me suggest that the *spiritual wants* of our army should form a subject of prayer on the occasion.   " OCCASIONAL."

21

Rev. L. J. Haley, in a private note, says: "There is a great religious interest and revival in the army. It has been my pleasure recently to spend a week with Smith's Brigade, Early's Division. I preached every day while I was with them, and was greatly delighted with my trip. There are religious revivals all over the army. Many are turning to God, and the good work is largely on the increase. The army is undoubtedly the great field for successful labor."

"On last evening fifteen were buried with Christ in baptism. And still the good work goes on. Our meetings are increasing in interest, and each evening scores of soldiers are inquiring, 'What shall we do to be saved?' Brother Kitzmiller has been laboring with us with a zeal and earnestness characteristic of a true Christian.

"JOHN H. TOMKIES, Chaplain Seventh Florida Regiment."

"CAMP NEAR FREDERICKSBURG, LAW'S BRIGADE, August 17.
"*Messrs. Editors :* I write to inform you of an interesting meeting which has been in progress for several days in this brigade. Brother W. H. Carroll, of Alabama, is with us, laboring earnestly and zealously for the conversion of souls, persuading men to be Christians. His services are very acceptable to us, and I verily believe well-pleasing in the sight of God. I have for a long time wished to see the power of God made manifest in our camp. Some of the regiments, particularly the Fourth Alabama, have been without a chaplain the most of the time since they entered the service. It has seemed to me that we have been neglected, and that none cared for our spiritual welfare ; that we were abandoned, each one to pursue his own course down the road to sin and destruction, without any spiritual adviser to tell us of our duties, and warn us of impending danger. But thanks be to God, He who rules and watches over us, and is ever mindful of the welfare of poor erring man, has in His good Providence directed the steps of Brother Carroll, and is manifesting His love and presence in our midst in the conviction and conversion of souls. A deep and powerful conviction of sin prevails, and religion has become the chief topic of conversation with many. Many of the noble sons of Alabama, who have stemmed the tide of many battles in defence of civil liberty, are now bowing humbly at the Cross, endeavoring to throw off the shackles of sin, and seeking liberty

from the thraldom of Satan. How many parents' hearts will be gladdened when the glorious news of a revival in our camp reaches them! We feel assured that we have the prayers of the parents and friends of these noble soldier boys, and we ask an interest in your prayers and the prayers of all true lovers of religion, that God will carry on the good work he has so graciously begun until this entire brigade and entire army shall become the followers of the meek and lowly Jesus, and our every heart shall be attuned to His praise. O, for an humble, Christian army! We can never obtain liberty and peace until we humble ourselves in the dust before God. Should we not strive earnestly and faithfully for this end? Let us all strive faithfully for this glorious result, and peace will wreathe our banners here, and unalloyed happiness be our portion in the life to come.

"J. W. H."

"CHAFFIN'S BLUFF, August 22.

"*Dear Brother Dickinson:* God has seen fit, in His mercy, greatly to bless the labors of His servants in this (General Wise's) brigade. We have recently closed a meeting in the Twenty-sixth Regiment, which resulted in the hopeful conversion of 150 souls; while forty or fifty more, many of them scarcely recognized as the followers of Christ, have been strengthened and encouraged to take a more positive stand for their Saviour and His cause. Rev. Mr. Miller, of Forty-sixth Regiment, has been laboring faithfully with those under his care, with occasional help, and as the result about two hundred have been brought, as we trust, from darkness to light. Brother A. Broaddus, Sr., and myself are now laboring in a meeting at the Bluff. Two have professed conversion, and several have been built up and strengthened in the faith.

"P. S.—*Monday.* Since writing the above, our meeting at the Bluff has greatly increased in interest. Brother Broaddus was taken sick on Saturday. Yesterday I labored almost alone. Preached twice; conducted two prayer-meetings, exhorting five or six times. Six have professed conversion, and last night thirty presented themselves for prayer. The Lord is with us.

"G. F. BAGBY."

Rev. J. J. D. Renfroe, chaplain Tenth Alabama Regiment,

writes as follows: "We have a splendid protracted meeting in progress in the brigade. About twenty-five have been baptized, and others have joined other Churches and the interest is increasing. I believe that 100 anxious souls presented themselves for prayer last night after the sermon."

Brother R. W. Cridlin, chaplain Thirty-eighth Virginia Regiment, writes me an interesting account of a work of grace in his brigade. In almost every part of the army God is at work winning souls to Himself. The cry is, "Send us tracts, hymns and Testaments." Colporters and evangelists are also in great demand. It cannot be that the people at home will withhold money when it is needed for this work of saving souls—the souls of our brave soldiers.—A. E. D.

"CAMP NEAR HAMILTON'S CROSSING, August 27, 1863.

"A glorious revival is going on in Major Henry's Battalion, Captain Riley's Battery. I have been laboring with them several days, meeting twice a day. The men are deeply interested in the meetings. Four have professed a hope in Christ and many are seriously concerned. Last night twelve came forward for prayer. Dr. W. F. Broaddus has promised to preach for us to-night. Will not some of our brethren come and assist us in this glorious work? The brethren in the company take a lively interest in it. I have been distributing a great many copies of the *Herald* among them, and find they are eagerly sought after. Pray for us, dear brethren, that this work may continue until all of this company shall become faithful and happy Christians.

"M. D. ANDERSON,

"Colporter A. N. Va."

A writer from the Army of Northern Virginia to the *Biblical Recorder* says: "I have often heard complaints about the hardships of a soldier's life, but is there a Christian who would not willingly suffer for years all the toils and hardships which a world can heap on the mortal frame, provided he could enjoy again the blessedness of his first moments with Jesus? It does seem to me that the joy of the Christian with an army in the field approaches nearer the essence of true religion than that exhibited under any other circumstances of the present day, when persecution is unknown."

"CHAPLAINS' ASSOCIATION OF THE SECOND AND THIRD ARMY CORPS.

"This association was formed in the Second or Jackson's Corps, March 16, 1863, and has held weekly meetings ever since, unless prevented by providential circumstances. We meet on each Tuesday, and first hear a sermon by the last chairman. Our doors are open to the public. The state of religious interest before and after the battle of Chancellorsville has been reported as most encouraging. Many openly assumed the armor of the Christian and numbers were inquiring the way to Jesus. Sweet communion seasons were held, where new-born souls first feasted on the shed blood and the broken body of the Lamb. Some of these never ate again on earth, for they were summoned to go up higher and sit with Jesus Himself. Our glorious Christian hero, leader and friend, fell in that fight, and our hearts mourned. The army felt deeply the blow. We trust the affliction has been blessed to us all. A new corps was formed for General A. P. Hill, and a part of General Jackson's corps was taken to fill it. Our association was then extended to both corps.

"We met first, since the battle of Gettysburg, in the Baptist church at Orange Court House, on Tuesday, August 11, 1863. Rev. B. T. Lacy preached from 2 Cor. iv. 14: 'The love of Christ constraineth us.' Rev. A. M. Marshall, of the Baptist Church and chaplain of the Twelfth Georgia Infantry, was chosen chairman. After receiving new members, we had a free conversation about the state of religion in our army. A wonderful change had passed over the army from the quiet and regular meetings at Hamilton's Crossing to the bustle and activity of an invasive campaign. The chaplains had been diligent in holding services with their regiments. Some had prayed with and exhorted them while lying in the trenches in line of battle. And though some had feared the results of this campaign upon the moral and spiritual welfare of the soldiers, and there were some excesses to be deeply regretted, yet there were many conversations on the march or in the *tumult of battle*. Now that we are quiet in camp an intense interest in spiritual things is found to pervade the army. Perhaps there is a more hopeful and blessed reviving of God's work here now than ever before. In Ramseur's, Doles's, Smith's, Gordon's, Wright's, Thomas's, Posey's and Scales's Brigades God was working wonderfully. In some, officers and men were together bowed under the heavy burden of their sins; in all,

many were earnestly seeking their souls' salvation, and many
were rejoicing in hope of reconciliation to God through His Son
Jesus. In Hays's Brigade, in which there is no Protestant chaplain, in a little prayer-meeting, five persons had professed conversion and wish to join some Church. A neighboring chaplain, on
application, went over to assist them. The prayer-meeting was
now a great congregation and the interest was growing. Wilcox's Brigade is now blessed for the first time by an outpouring
of God's Spirit. There have been some thirty conversions therein
during the week, ending August 18th. It is harvest time
with the army. Jesus is the Husbandman, and angels are
singing over the rich harvest. Laborers are needed here.
Who will come to help, Lord? Who will pray for richer
blessings on this noble army? Rev. Theo. Pryor, D. D., now
missionary in Longstreet's or First Corps, said that though he
had been a pastor for thirty-one years, he felt thankful to God
for opening the way for him to labor in the army. He had never
enjoyed the sense of God's presence in preaching as here. At
his last meeting many had requested prayer for their souls. Rev.
J. A. Broadus testified similarly. He had been deceived as to
preaching among the soldiers; for not *half* had been told him.
He had no idea of the state of religious feeling here, though he
had had more opportunities than many out of the army to know
the truth of the matter. *He had never enjoyed preaching so
much.* A far larger proportion of men attend divine services
here than at home. They come because they *choose* here. Rev.
D. B. Ewing, chaplain of the post at Gordonsville, had been much
blessed in his labors in the hospital. He never met with a re-
pulse in presenting Christ. Many were converted. Judging the
religious sentiment of the army from cases sent to the hospital,
he pronounced it better than that of the Church at home. The
scarred veteran would meet with a *religious chill* on returning to
his Church.

"This is a brief account of the results of our meeting on August
11th and on August 18th, when the conference was continued.
At this latter meeting Rev. J. A. Broadus preached from 2 Cor.
ii. 16: 'And who is sufficient for these things.' He presented the
apostle's example as worthy of our imitation amid all discouragements; and tenderly stated and forcibly illustrated the grounds
of St. Paul's confidence. After some further business, the association adjourned to meet on Tuesday, August 25th, at the same

place. We left feeling how blessed it was to work for God at such a time as this.

"L. C. VASS, Secretary."

"CAMP NEAR ORANGE COURT HOUSE, September 1.

"For nearly a week I have been aiding Rev. J. J. D. Renfroe, chaplain Tenth Alabama, in a protracted meeting. I found Brother Renfroe nearly broken down, having been for three weeks preaching daily. Our congregations have been very large; for some distance the entire grove being crowded with deeply interested listeners. Never in my life have I seen men so eager to hear and be profited by the word spoken. Though I have preached nine times I have not seen one listless hearer among all the hundreds who have been in attendance. Not a word has been spoken during the services, and, so far as I could see, every man has seemed profoundly impressed with the solemnity and importance of the occasion. It is impossible to say how many have asked to be prayed for. On several nights not less than from 150 to 200 made this request of us. Many have professed conversion—not less, I should think, than 175. Last night our congregation was considerably larger than on any previous night, and the interest is evidently on the increase. Brother Renfroe is receiving many for baptism. While *our* meeting has been going on so pleasantly, just on the opposite hill, about a hundred yards distant, in the same brigade, is another of equal interest. It is being conducted by a Baptist minister, a lieutenant and a Methodist chaplain. Fifty have professed conversion. I will give a few facts, by way of illustrating the character of this work of grace. I announced at one of the meetings that there was an assortment of tracts in the chaplain's tent. In a few moments after I found numbers crowding around the tent and helping themselves. Each man looked over the packages and selected such as he wanted, and consequently *every tract which explained the plan of salvation, or which treated of Christ, was taken, and the others left.* As the soldier's eye would glance over the titles, when he came to 'The Great Question Answered,' by A. Fuller, or, 'Come to Jesus,' his face beamed with joy. No one seemed to feel that he had time to read of anything else except the way to be saved. Another interesting feature in the meeting is the deep solicitude which all seem to have that they may be genuinely converted. The young converts often come

to us privately deeply affected, in many cases weeping and trembling, to ask for further instruction as to what constitutes conversion.   They have an unspeakable dread of being deceived on
this point.   One young man, the son of a Baptist minister, said
to me : ' Oh, sir, I have a *little hope*, but I am afraid to confess it,
for fear it may not be well founded.'   Another said that for
months he had been hoping that he was a Christian, but that he
was 'so *afraid* that he might backslide and dishonor his Master.'
It is interesting, too, to see how long the work of grace has been
in progress in many hearts.   Several have for more than a year
been under deep conviction and been seeking the Saviour.   Not
a few have received their first religious impressions on the battle-
field.   I think eight or ten spoke of having been convicted at the
Chancellorsville fight, while an interesting young man assured
us that during the battle of Seven Pines, while his comrades
were falling around him, he promised the Lord that he would
love and serve Him ; from that day to this he has been trying to
make good his vow.   Without doubt, in hundreds of instances,
the shock of battle has been sanctified to the saving of souls.
It is worthy of record that this meeting is greatly developing the
gifts of Christians.   Many a brother is aroused to his duty to
put forth active efforts for the salvation of sinners.   Two of the
young men, members of the Tenth Alabama, are now holding a
protracted meeting in a neighboring camp.   They go over every
evening and preach the Gospel, comforting and encouraging
Christians and warning sinners.   A revival has sprung up under
their labors.   A chaplain of a Virginia regiment remarked, yesterday, that the Master intends honoring many of these young
men by putting them in the ministry.   We have, from the beginning of the war, been pleading with the Churches to send
preachers to the army, and with some little success.   It seems,
now, that the army itself is to produce a supply.   I beg that all
through the land earnest and constant prayer be made that scores
and hundreds of Christian men in the army may be called of
God to the work of the ministry.   How refreshing is the thought
of hundreds of such ministers returning, after the war is over, to
aid in establishing Churches and in preaching the Gospel to
' every creature.'   Rev. J. J. D. Renfroe, a laborious and successful chaplain, was for a brief period in the employ of the Sunday-school and Publication Board.   When he made known the
fact that he had arrived at the conclusion that it was his duty to

give himself to the army, his churches were very unwilling to give him up. At one church, after several had spoken against his leaving, three of the sisters remarked, that while they valued as highly as any Brother Renfroe's services, they could cheerfully give him up to labor in the army, for they had sons there for whose conversion they felt very deeply. Each of these three sisters has received a great blessing. The sons of two of them have professed conversion, and the son of the third has been restored to the fellowship of God's people, from whom he had wandered. I cite this incident with the hope of encouraging the churches to give their pastors, at least for a few months, to this work. Your own son, or brother or father, may be converted through the preaching of your minister in camp. And if this may not be, some one else may be reached and saved. Then encourage your pastor to go, and send on what funds you may be able to contribute, with which to publish camp hymns, Testaments and tracts for our brave soldiers.

"A. E. DICKINSON."

I have already described the scene in this same brigade several weeks later, when at one service 610 came forward for prayer and over 200 professed conversion. I shall continue, instead of a connected narrative, to give letters written at the time, giving accounts of this wonderful work.

The chaplain of the Twelfth Tennessee Regiment states "that the lieutenant-colonel, adjutant, surgeon, seven captains and thirteen lieutenants are professors of religion; that not a single officer was addicted to profane swearing, card-playing or drunkenness; that a very large proportion of the men as well as officers pray in public, and heartily second any efforts for good; that the regiment has in it the largest Sabbath-school he ever saw; that the number of the faithful has been greatly multiplied, and that there are almost daily accessions to their number."

"*Dear Brethren Editors:* Grant me a small space to report what the Lord has done and is doing for us in Mahone's Brigade. This brigade has five Virginia regiments (2,000 men), and there is not a chaplain in it. The men tell me, that until recently, they had not heard a sermon for *six* months. Although deprived of this privilege, they forsook not the assembling of themselves for prayer. And God, who ever hears the earnest prayers of

His chosen, is now pouring out upon them His gracious Spirit. For the last two weeks they have been supplied with preaching twice a day, morning and night. During this time about eighty have made a profession of faith in Christ, and large numbers come forward nightly and ask us to pray for them. The interest seems to be rather increasing than diminishing. Brother J. A. Broadus and myself are still trying to point them to the Saviour. My dear brethren, we are realizing here all the primitive simplicity with which we are accustomed to think of John the Baptist, of Christ, and of the apostles, as standing in the midst of dense crowds and speaking to as many as could get near enough to hear them. I cannot fully describe the work and its peculiar joys; *you* must come and see. I freely confess, that it far surpasses anything I ever expected to realize. There is no confusion or disorder, as you might suppose; but, on the contrary, the attention is earnest and constant. Brethren, do come and help us, for we are very few.

"Hilary E. Hatcher."

"Orange Court House, Virginia, September 10.

"*Dear Brethren :* It gives me pleasure to report more definitely this week, the state of religious interest in Mahone's Brigade, where we have been holding a series of meetings for three weeks. On last Sabbath, Brother Andrew Broaddus, Jr., at my request, baptized thirty-one candidates for admission into the Baptist Church; nineteen others are awaiting to be baptized, and I learn that others will report themselves in a few days. At present 146 are reported to have found peace in Christ, and have asked for membership among some one of the evangelical denominations. The interest is unabated. Scores and hundreds are asking, 'What must we do to be saved?'

"H. E. H., Army Evangelist."

Rev. B. T. Lacy writes to the *Central Presbyterian* from the Army of Northern Virginia: "Since the arrival of the army at its present location, about 1,000 have professed faith in Christ, and more than 2,000 are earnestly inquiring the way of salvation."

"Camp, Twenty-sixth Virginia, September 12.

"*Dear Brother Dickinson :* Find enclosed the sum of $186.98, subscribed by this regiment to aid in circulating Bibles, Testa-

ment, tracts, etc., in the army. We have been very much indebted to you for about two years, and we very cheerfully contribute the above amount. Many in this regiment, no doubt,
will, in the great day, thank you and those co-operating with
you, for sending and bringing them the 'glorious Gospel of the
blessed God' in so many forms. Thousands of pages of your
tracts have been distributed and read with pleasure and profit.
Hundreds of your Bibles and Testaments have been presented to
us and most highly prized, I assure you. And your ministers
have come to us and most faithfully preached the 'word of life.'

.   .   .   .   .   .

"We have been holding prayer-meetings constantly in the
chapel for weeks, and we scarcely ever fail, how tired soever the
men may be, to have a large congregation. It is a glorious
sight to behold a hundred or two of young Christians mingling their voices in praise to their Saviour. Many of them
exhort and pray in public, and there is quite a development of
piety and of gifts. We have inquirers still, and some are giving
their hearts to the Saviour. I have already baptized seventy-
one in this regiment, and there are others to be baptized. Nearly
as many have united with the Methodist Episcopal Church, and
quite a number with the Presbyterian Church. I have also baptized thirty-six in the Thirty-fourth and Forty-sixth, some of
who mprofessed conversion at our meeting, and others in their
own regiments.   Your brother in Christ,

"WM. E. WIATT, Chaplain Twenty-sixth Virginia."

A writer in the *Southern Presbyterian,* from the Army of
Northern Virginia, states that since the forces reached their
present location, the conversions reported in the Second and
Third Corps alone, are at the rate of 200 a week, "and the work
is widening and deepening, so far as man can judge."

"ORANGE COURT HOUSE, September 20.
"*Dear Brother Dickinson:* After receiving my commission as
evangelist, I proceeded to Fredericksburg, where I labored with
the Eighth and Ninth Georgia Regiments, who were quartered
in the city. There was then, and had been for some time, a deep
religious feeling throughout the whole brigade—Anderson's—
and at the instance of Brother Burnham, Chaplain of the Ninth
Georgia Regiment, I made an appointment to baptize some

fifteen or twenty the following Sabbath. But before the next Sabbath the entire corps had been ordered South.   Thus broken up in my plans in that region, I *changed my base*, and came to Orange Court House, where there were thousands of soldiers eager to hear the Gospel.   In connection with Brother Gwin, of Rome, Georgia, I preached first in Wright's Brigade, but orders came for this brigade to move to the front, and again was I forced to seek a new field of labor.   For the past four or five days I have been preaching in Lane's North Carolina Brigade, with great pleasure, by reason of interest manifested by the soldiers in the important subject of personal salvation.   There have been as many as twenty-five and thirty forward for prayer at a time.   Three were baptized last Thursday, and others have connected themselves with other denominations.   On yesterday I aided in ordination of Brother Eatman, of North Carolina, a chaplain in this brigade, and for four years past an acceptable Methodist preacher.   I am to-day going to Pegram's battalion of artillery, and if the prospects are encouraging, will remain with them several days.   Nearly the entire army is on the Rapidan, with the enemy full in front, and a battle imminent; there is, therefore, but little opportunity for holding protracted meetings.

                                        " T. H. PRITCHARD."

        " NEAR ORANGE COURT HOUSE, September 25.
   "*Messrs. Editors:* You will be gratified, and the hearts of many of your readers will be much encouraged, to know that, during our long inactivity, the Spirit of God has been working in our midst, and that many sinners have professed conversion, and many more have offered themselves as fit subjects for prayer.   A glorious meeting was closed in this brigade (Walker's) about two weeks ago, having been exceedingly successful in its design; for more than thirty sinners appeared happily converted to God, through our Redeemer.   Prayer-meetings were held constantly from night to night, and we have cause to think that they have resulted in some good.   It is indeed a great privilege for the followers of Christ to meet frequently and unite in singing the songs of Zion.   Religious men in camp have many trials and temptations to contend with, but we have the blessed consolation of knowing that the word of God contains many cheering promises; and though we are

much tempted, we know that if we approach the *Throne of Grace* in an humble and sincere manner, our prayers will be heard and answered, and that we will be sufficiently strengthened to overcome all temptations, and to go on our way rejoicing. Brother Anderson is now conducting a protracted meeting in the Fortieth Virginia Regiment (Walker's Brigade), with a bright prospect of happy results. Rev. Mr. Anderson has been an instrument in God's hand of doing great good, both in his own regiment (Fortieth Virginia) and in the Fifty-fifth Virginia.

"BAPTIST."

"*Brethren Editors:* . . . Reaching Orange Court House late in the afternoon, I walked out about two miles to Doles's Brigade, and was almost immediately put to work. On reaching the preaching place, I was agreeably surprised at the arrangements. While I was in the field we were always moving, and nothing better than the ground was ever used by either preacher or people, and when I preached at night, some brother would hold a torch or candle while I read hymn or chapter. But here I found a large amphitheatre of log-seats, with a pulpit in the centre, covered with an arbor, and flanked on either hand by a platform, whose blazing lightwood illuminated every face in the vast congregation. The sea of upturned, earnest faces, and the songs swelling from hundreds of manly voices and making the forests resound, I was, from the accounts received, prepared for. But they were none the less impressive, and I felt it indeed a luxury to preach under such circumstances. I could not help wishing Dr. Jeter were there to stir those masses with his trumpet tones; and O! how Reynoldson would have revelled in such labors! How he would have charmed those crowds! To the last the interest increased. Every morning inquirers came to the inquiry-meeting, while at night scores and scores came forward for prayer. In the adjoining brigade, also, an interesting meeting was in progress. On Sabbath, Brother Marshall baptized twenty candidates, and appropriate Scripture was read to an immense concourse covering the adjoining hillside. Some half a dozen other baptizings were going on at the same hour in the neighborhood.

.   .   .   .

" I feared this move to the front would interfere with my operations, instead of which it facilitated them. On Monday, I preached to nearly all of Johnson's Division, which was bivouaced in a large plain. Lying as they thus were, close together, and without their usual resources, a larger audience was secured than would be possible in camp. In this division I met my old regiment, and also another containing many men from my town. On Tuesday I moved to the front. Here I met Brother J. Wm. Jones, who insisted on my preaching in his brigade. As they were right on the Rapidan, in sight and hearing of both the cannonading and sharp-shooting, which, of course, greatly interested the men, leading them to rush in crowds to a point commanding a view of what was going on, I expressed a doubt as to whether preaching was expedient. A soldier lying on the ground said, 'As soon as you begin, they will stop looking and come to hear you, and none will leave, either.' I found this literally true. In this brigade, as well as in a neighboring battalion of artillery where I preached, I found several of the members of my Church, who seemed so glad to see me, and gave such good accounts of themselves, that I felt sorry I had not sooner paid them a pastoral visit. My friends at home feared I would make myself sick in the army. Instead of this, I returned home invigorated in every respect. Preaching principally at night, I staid mainly in camp or bivouacs. But whenever I desired the refreshment of a good *home*-meal or bed, they were heartily afforded by Brother Hiden and Brother Scott, who, with their wives, think they cannot be too kind and hospitable to preachers, even in these hard times, and in the trying circumstances in which they are placed, surrounded by a large army. I should not omit to mention the cordial greeting and hospitality extended by officers of various denominations, and of none, and their testimony to the improvement in our army. I could not help noticing how many were reading their Testaments, even when they were lying on the roadside, and how they would gather in knots to spend a short leisure in singing. I tried once or twice to carry tracts, but in vain, as crowds of soldiers would gather around and humbly, but earnestly beg to relieve me. It was pleasant every day or two to meet Brothers Pritchard, Broaddus, Sr., and others, and compare notes. They will, doubtless, give you their impressions and experiences.

"Affectionately,

" GEO. B. TAYLOR.

" STAUNTON, September 23."

"CUMBERLAND, September 23.

"*Dear Brother Dickinson :* I wish to give you a short account of a prayer-meeting to which I was invited, the 8th inst. This meeting was held with Captain Massey's Company (Company C), Nelson's Battalion, stationed near Gordonsville. When I arrived I found the brethren earnestly engaged in prayer. They were without preachers, but God had given them hearts to pray, and, in answer to their prayers, five of their comrades had professed faith in Christ. We continued the meetings six nights, with preaching, exhortation and prayer, at which time they were broken up by the demonstration made by the enemy at Culpeper Court House. Twenty-two professed conversion, and about twenty-five were anxiously inquiring the way of life. In fact, the entire company, with three or four exceptions, seemed seriously impressed; also many others, from other companies of the battalion. Now that the reaping time has come, should not all God-fearing men be engaged, that the good Lord may send out more laborers to gather in the ripe harvest? I have heard much of the wickedness of the camp, but at this time the Spirit of God has so far subdued the power of sin in the soul, that I heard but *one oath*, and did not see any immoral conduct during my sojourn. To God's name be all the glory.

"J. C. PERKINS."

Rev. Dr. J. C. Granberry, who had at this time been appointed by his Church as one of their missionaries to the army, and whose able sermons and untiring labors were greatly blessed and made for him a warm place in the hearts of the soldiers, thus wrote to the *Richmond Christian Advocate*, early in September, 1863 :

"I have been employed one month in my new position as a missionary to the army. Brother Evans having been compelled by ill health to resign his appointment, Bishop Early transferred me, at my request, from Ewell's to Longstreet's Corps. I naturally felt a preference to remain with those troops among whom I had labored as a chaplain from almost the commencement of the war. The last four weeks I have been preaching daily, and sometimes twice a day, in the brigades of Pickett's Division. I have never before witnessed such a widespread and powerful religious interest among the soldiers. They crowd eagerly to hear the Gospel, and listen with profound attention. Many hearts have been opened to receive the word of the Lord in every brigade.

It would delight your heart to mark the seriousness, order, and deep feeling which characterize all our meetings. In Armistead's Brigade, where I have been most constantly working in co-operation with Brother Cridlin, a Baptist, and chaplain of the Thirty-eighth Virginia, and with other ministers, there have been some seventy professions of conversion, and the altar is filled morning and night with penitents. The change is manifest in the whole camp. Men have put away their cards; instead of blasphemy, the voice of prayer and the sweet songs of Zion are heard at all hours. There is little gambling, but all seem contented and interested. We have many proofs that it is a genuine and mighty work of grace. Yesterday reminded me of Sabbath at camp-meeting. There reigned here a deeper quiet. Divine services began at an early hour of the morning, and continued into the night with brief intervals. At 9 A. M. Sabbath-school was held under the auspices of the Christian Association. At 10 A. M., 4 and 7 P. M., the congregation met for preaching and other exercises. It was a happy day—a season of refreshing from the presence of the Lord. Brother August is conducting an excellent meeting in his regiment. Already there have been forty-two professions of faith, and the work deepens and widens. I have enjoyed the privilege of being with him frequently, and have never seen a revival progress in a more satisfactory and promising manner. The Christian Associations which have recently been organized in the different brigades will, I doubt not, accomplish great good. They furnish an opportunity for the public confession of Christ and the enjoyment of the friendship of saints. They are a nucleus for lay co-operation with the chaplains, or lay labors in the absence of chaplains. In Kemper's Brigade the revival, which began last spring, still goes on, chiefly under the ministry of Rev. Dr. Pryor, of the Presbyterian Church. He is a most laborious and efficient workman."

In a circular sent out to the Churches and people by the Chaplains' Association of the first and second corps of General Lee's army, urging hearty co-operation in the work of saving souls, most cheering accounts of the revival were given:

"The Lord is doing wonderful things for Zion in the ranks of our army. Christians are daily growing in grace and fidelity. Sinners are turning by hundreds to the King of Righteousness and finding that peace which comes by faith; while many are yet seeking the Prince of Life. We believe that, under God's direction, much of this work has been done by the fraternal inter-course secured by our organization. May the Lord bless you with His Spirit, and give His word prosperity through your in-strumentality."

The religious, and even the secular papers, often filled columns with the news of God's work among the soldiers. The *Richmond Christian Advocate* said:

" Not for years has such a revival prevailed in the Confederate States. Its records gladden the columns of every religious journal. Its progress in the army is a spectacle of moral sub-limity over which men and angels can rejoice. Such camp-meetings were never seen before in America. The bivouac of the soldier never witnessed such nights of glory and days of splendor. The Pentecostal fire lights the camp, and the hosts of armed men sleep beneath the wings of angels rejoicing over many sinners that have repented.

" The people at home are beginning to feel the kindling of the same grace in their hearts. It is inspiring to read the corres-pondence, now, between converts in camp and friends at home, and to hear parents praise God for tidings from their absent sons who have lately given their hearts to the Lord.

" ' Father is converted,' says a bright-faced child of twelve years; ' Mamma got a letter to-day, and father says that there is a great revival in his regiment.' The child is too happy to keep her joy to herself. What glorious news from the army is this! This is victory—triumph—peace! This is the token of good which the great King gives to cheer His people. It is the best evidence that prayer is heard, and that the Lord is with us. Let us show ourselves grateful for such grace and ' walk worthy of God, who has called us to His kingdom and glory.' Let fervent prayer continue, and patient faith wait on God, ' who is able to do exceeding abundantly above all that we ask or think.'

The letters from the converted soldiers were often the means, under God, of awakening an interest in the Churches at home. And back to the army went letters telling how hearts were touched and made truly penitent by reason of the tidings sent from the boys in the tents and trenches.*

Soldiers were converted by thousands every week. From Virginia, Rev. G. R. Talley wrote:

---

* Dr. Bennett's " Great Revival."

"God is wonderfully reviving his work here, and throughout the army. Congregations large—interest almost universal. In our chaplains' meeting it was thought, with imperfect statistics, that about five hundred were converted every week. We greatly need chaplains—men of experience and ministerial influence. Our Regimental Christian Association, as a kind of substitute for a Church, and our Bible-classes, are doing well."

Under the powerful stimulus of such a revival, the Churches at home redoubled their efforts to supply preachers.

In General G. T. Anderson's Georgia Brigade, composed of the Seventh, Eighth, Ninth, Eleventh, and Fifty-ninth Regiments, the influence of a Soldiers' Christian Association was most powerful for good.

"It has drawn out and developed," says a soldier of the brigade, "all the religious element among us. It has created a very pleasant, social feeling among the regiments, and has blended them into one congregation. The three chaplains of the brigade work together, and thus lighten the burdens of each other, and also extend help to the two regiments that are without chaplains. The association now numbers over four hundred members. We recently broke up a camp where, for four weeks, we have enjoyed an unbroken rest; and it has been one long ' camp-meeting '—a great revival season—during which we held divine services daily. It has been a time of great joy with us, reviving pure, evangelical religion, and converting many souls. Above eighty members have been added to the association as the fruit of our meeting. A great revolution has been wrought in the moral tone of the brigade. During a part of this time we were assisted by Rev. Mr. Gwin, of Rome, Georgia, of the Baptist Church, and by Rev. Dr. Baird, of Mississippi, of the Presbyterian Church. Their labors were highly appreciated, and were very valuable. The Eighth, Ninth, and Eleventh Regiments each have Sabbath-schools, which are a new and interesting feature in the religious teachings of the army. Much interest is taken in it. Full one-third of my regiment are members of my school."

In Law's Brigade the work was equally deep and powerful.

"Last March," says a soldier, "I was quite sick, and was sent to the hospital in Richmond, Virginia. At that time my regi- ment (the gallant Fourth Alabama) was extremely wicked. You could scarcely meet with any one who did not use God's name in vain. You could see groups assembled almost in every direction gambling. I obtained a furlough and returned home to my dear wife and children, who live not far from your city. I returned to my command some two weeks since, and to my surprise and delight I found at least three-fourths of my company not only members of the Church of the living God, but professors of religion. This state of affairs is not limited to my company, but it extends throughout the entire regiment, and I might say the whole brigade (Law's Brigade). God grant that this good work may continue to flourish throughout the entire army."

Of the work which came under his eye in Ewell's Corps Rev. Dr. Rosser wrote:

" My plan is, to visit and preach to this corps, division by division, and brigade by brigade—stopping longest where I can do most good, noticing vacancies in the chaplaincy, circulating religious reading as it reaches me, and sympathizing with the sick and wounded soldiers. A nobler work cannot engage the heart of the preacher, or the attention of the Church and nation. I can but glance at the work at this time.

" The whole army is a vast field, ready and ripe to the harvest, and all the reapers have to do is to go in and reap from end to end. The susceptibility of the soldiery to the Gospel is wonderful, and, doubtful as the remark may appear, the military camp is most favorable to the work of revival. The soldiers, with the simplicity of little children, listen to and embrace the truth. Already over two thousand have professed conversion, and over two thousand more are penitent. The hope of the Church and the country is in our armies, and religion in the army should be a subject of the most serious concern to the Church. That Church that does most for religion during the war will do most for religion when the war is over. Let our Church have an eye to this, and with a holy faith and zeal grasp both the present and the future. Oh, let the shepherds come and gather the lambs in the wilderness!

" We want our best men here—men of courage, faith, experience—holy men—hard-working men—sympathizing men—self-denying men—men baptized afresh every day by the Holy Ghost for the work. No place here for slow men, mere reasoners and expositors, however learned or eloquent; war has no time to wait for such men—the soldier has no time to wait for such men—he may die to-morrow. The few men now with us in this corps—and noble men they are—can do but a tithe of the work required—some of them have the work of a brigade. We want more and the best. Let our Churches be content to spare them.

"We want vastly more religious reading. Oh, it is affecting to see the soldiers crowd and press about the preacher for what of tracts, etc., he has to distribute, and it is sad to see hundreds retiring without being supplied! One wishes to give himself away to meet the want. While the country is expending hundreds of millions of dollars, and pouring out its blood like water on the altar of patriotism, let the Church be as prominent in devotion and zeal to religion in the army. Let religion rival patriotism in activity. Light up the great camp of war with celestial fire."

Rev. J. M. Stokes, chaplain Third Georgia, reported to the *Southern Christian Advocate:*

"Zion is flourishing again in this army. There are as many as twenty chapels. We have had a meeting in progress two weeks, and the interest is increasing daily. We have had several conversions, and there were, I reckon, fifty mourners at the altar for prayer last evening. Our chapel seats between 300 and 400, and is full every night unless the weather is very inclement.

"Rev. B. T. Lacy, chaplain in General Ewell's Corps, visited and preached for us about a week ago. He preached us a most excellent sermon, and gave us much advice and encouragement privately. His visits to the different brigades can but have the most gratifying effect both upon the chaplains and their congregations. I wish we had just such a man to every division to superintend its spiritual matters.

"There is a great harvest here, which ought to be reaped at once, and if it should pass this season we fear that much of it will be gathered by the enemy of souls."

Rev. J. O. A. Cook, chaplain Second Georgia Battalion, Wright's Brigade, wrote:

"It would do your heart good to witness our camp-services, to see the immense throngs that crowd our rude chapels, to listen to the soul-stirring music, as with one voice and one heart they unite in singing the sweet songs of Zion, and to note the deep interest and solemn earnestness with which they listen to the preaching of the word. I have never seen anything like it. I can but believe that the blessing of God is upon us, and that He is preparing us for a speedy and glorious peace.

Rev. A. B. Woodfin, D. D., of Virginia, was the efficient Chaplain of the 61st Ga. Regiment, and was greatly blessed in his labors. Since the war he has been the successful Pastor of the St. Francis Street Baptist Church, Mobile, the First Church, Montgomery, Alabama, at Columbia, S. C., and at Hampton, Va., and for two years the popular and efficient Chaplain at the University of Va.

Rev. J. E. Edwards, D. D., of the Virginia Conference, was Pastor in Richmond during the war, and one of the most popular preachers and effective workers among the soldiers. He was long one of the most prominent leaders among his people, and occupied pulpits in Richmond, Petersburg, and Danville.

Rev. D. S. Doggett, D. D., Bishop of the M. E. Church, South, was Pastor of the Centenary Methodist Church, Richmond, during the war and was unquestionably one of the ablest preachers, and most efficient workers of the Southern pulpit. He was a man of mighty influence among his people, and "a Prince in Israel" fell when God called him from his labors on earth to his glittering crown on high.

Rev. J. B. McFerrin, D. D., of Nashville, Tenn., was an evangelist in the Army of Tennessee, and a man of rare gifts, wonderful popular power, and great success as a preacher. As "Book Agent" of the M. E. Church, South, he exerted a wide influence, accomplished a grand work, and was greatly lamented when "the Lord of the vineyard" called him to "come up higher."

Rev. W. C. Power, of South Carolina, was one of our most faithful, efficient, and popular Chaplains, and has been since the war one of the most influential and useful ministers in the S. C. M. E. Conference.

Rev. R. L. Dabney, D. D., LL. D., for many years Professor in Union Theological Seminary, Virginia, and Professor in the University of Texas, stood in the very forefront of ripe scholars, able theologians, and distinguished logicians. During the war he served gallantly and efficiently as Adjutant General on the Staff of Stonewall Jackson, and frequently preached to the soldiers, sermons of great ability. As author of the "Life of Stonewall Jackson," and several theological works — as a writer of review articles — as a preacher, a professor, and a leader among Southern Presbyterians he had no superior.

Rev. A. B. Woodfin,
Chaplain 61st Ga. Regt.

Rev. J. E. Edwards, D. D.

Bishop D. S. Doggett.

Rev. J. B. McFerin, D. D.

Rev. W. C. Power.

Rev. R. L. Dabney, D. D.
(Facing page 341.)

" Bible-classes and Sabbath-schools have been organized in many of the brigades. The soldiers are taking great interest in them. We organized our Sabbath-school a few evenings since, beginning with seventy members. There is, however, a want of Bibles. If every family would furnish one of the several Bibles lying about the house the army would be very well supplied."

" CAMP OF NINTH VIRGINIA CAVALRY, near RACCOON FORD,
" September 30.

" There has been for several weeks past a most glorious revival going on in our regiment, conducted by our respected and highly esteemed chaplain, Rev. C. H. Boggs. By the blessing of God his efforts have been crowned with great success, and many souls have been brought to realize the inestimable value of a Saviour's love. We wish this good work to continue. It is still going on, but we wish to increase it—to extend its influence, if possible, until *every man* in the regiment is convinced of his lost and ruined condition, is brought to see his danger, and persuaded to fly for safety to Him who alone can save. There is already a marked change in the moral deportment of the whole regiment. But, in order to carry on this work as it should be done, it was necessary that all the Christians in the regiment should be *united*, and contend side by side and shoulder to shoulder in the cause of Christ. Therefore we (all the professors of the religion of Christ, who are members of the Ninth, without regard to denomination or sect, and only aiming at one great end, viz., ' the immortal welfare of our fellow-men ') have united ourselves in an association known as the ' Soldiers' Christian Association of the Ninth Virginia Calvary.' We wish to take immediate steps to provide the regiment with religious reading matter of every kind, but particularly papers and tracts. . . . . .
" H. B. RICHARDS, Cor. Sec. S. C. A.
" Ninth Va. Cav., W. H. F. Lee's Brigade."

" CAMP, GORDON'S BRIGADE, September 28.
" Brother Thos. H. Pritchard and myself commenced preaching about a week ago to the soldiers in General Wright's Brigade about a mile distant, and are now preaching to Gordon's Brigade. There is some interest in the former, and a great deal in the latter. Last night fifty or sixty came forward for prayer, many of them deeply affected. Yesterday evening Brother Pritchard

baptized seventeen in the Rapidan, in sight of the enemy's pickets, who looked on as though they took some interest in the proceeding. Brother Pritchard is enjoying his work very much. May his banishment from Baltimore contribute largely to the salvation of Confederate soldiers.

"A. BROADDUS, SR."

"CAMP OF THIRTIETH VIRGINIA REGIMENT, CORSE'S BRIGADE,
        NEAR CARTER'S STATION, TENNESSEE, September 29.

"In these times of sorrow and affliction how delightful it is to see the manifestation of the presence and power of God in the conviction and conversion of sinners! Every day we are called upon to record the loving-kindness of God in the conversion of those who are dear to us. It has been my privilege recently to bear testimony to the work of grace which has been going on in this brigade. Many of the dear soldiers, who have enlisted in their country's cause, are now enlisted under the bright banner of the Cross. Upon my arrival here I was pleased to learn that a glorious revival of religion was going on; and although the meetings had not been held regularly, in consequence of the continued moving from one position to another, yet the interest is still on the increase. The meetings are conducted by the Rev. Mr. August, the faithful chaplain of the Fifteenth Virginia, assisted by Captain Willis of the same regiment. A large number have professed faith in Christ, while many others are deeply concerned on account of sin. To-day Brother Willis baptized fourteen, seven of whom are from his regiment. Although this regiment has been without a chaplain for some time, I am glad to inform you that there seems to be a feeling of awakening existing among them. On last evening I held a meeting, and gave an invitation for any one to come forward for prayer; and while we were singing eight came forward, four of whom were converted. I only hold services as circumstances will permit, and distribute such reading matter as I can procure, and look to God for His blessing on these feeble instrumentalities. I have met with a cordial reception, both from the officers and men of this regiment, and am earnestly entreated to remain with this brigade.

"M. D. ANDERSON, Army Evangelist."

"Elder J. E. King, chaplain of the Fourteenth Tennessee Regiment, within two and a half months, has baptized ninety persons in various divisions of the Army of Northern Virginia."

At a meeting of the First Baptist Church, Richmond, the following resolutions were unanimously adopted:

" 1. *Resolved*, That this Church has received with great joy the tidings of God's merciful dealings with the armies of our country, in bringing many of our soldiers to repentance and salvation; and that we will earnestly pray for the continued success and enlargement of the good work amongst them.

" 2. *Resolved*, That we regard this gracious dispensation as the voice of God to His slumbering Churches, calling them to renewed zeal and consecration to His cause; and that we will labor and pray that its influence may not be lost upon ourselves or upon those within our reach."

A minister in the army writes: " Our meetings are assuming a new and interesting phase. All the recent converts meet twice a day by themselves, and pray and talk over their wants and necessities to each other, and every one who attends must lead in prayer. It is refreshing to see so many young converts, all in their freshness and vigor, serving the Lord and full of redeeming love."

Rev. N. B. Cobb, in an account of his visit to the Army of Northern Virginia, gives the following description of a convert whom he met in camp:

" One of the most wicked and desperate men in camp had been melted down into the gentleness of a little child. Before the Spirit of the Lord touched his heart, his name had been incorporated into a proverb for wickedness. He seemed to be beyond human control. Whenever he got out of camp he would get drunk, and come back or be brought back perfectly furious. When the guard would arrest him he would draw out his bowie knife and endeavor to cut his way through them; and even after he was overpowered and taken to the guard-house he had to be tied down, to keep him from rushing out over the sentinels. But the grace of God had taken hold of him, and entirely changed his nature. The roaring lion had been subdued into the gentle lamb; and it was remarkable that every man in the regiment had perfect confidence in his conversion."

Elder W. N. Chaudoin, in a letter to the *Baptist Banner*, from the Army of Northern Virginia, describing his first day in camp, says: " The quiet and order of the camp astonished me. I have

344   CHRIST IN THE CAMP;

seen and heard more confusion on Sabbath, at camp-meeting, than I heard and saw last Sunday in three brigades of soldiers."

"CAMP NEAR PISGAH CHURCH, ORANGE COUNTY, VA.,
"October 3, 1863.

.... "But the chief design of this is to let our friends know, through your paper, of the *continuance* of the glorious state of things in our regiment. Several more have professed an interest in the great salvation. On Saturday last five were 'buried with Christ in baptism' by Brother J. W. Jones, of the Thirteenth Virginia Infantry, and another on Tuesday—all of whom, we hope, arose to 'walk in newness of life.' A number are still waiting to join other denominations. . . . .

"Oh, what a contrast is there in our regiment, when compared with last year this time. Now, instead of the songs of revelry and mirth to which we used to listen, at night the forest is made to resound with songs which arise like sweet incense from new-born souls, to the Captain of their salvation—the stately steppings of Jesus are heard in our camps—the Holy Spirit is wooing hearts in our army—soldiers are enlisting under the unfurled banner of King Immanuel. . . . .

"Yours truly,
"WALLACE."

"RICHMOND COLLEGE, October 6.

"I spent four days of last week with Kemper's Brigade, stationed at Taylorsville. Brother Jno. W. Ward, chaplain of the Third Regiment, baptized eight persons the day before my arrival. Five had also been received by the Methodist chaplain of the Eleventh Regiment, Rev. Thos. C. Jennings. Two others joined the Episcopal Church. Meetings are still in progress at night, conducted by the excellent brethren above-named. Christians in this brigade seem to be active and united, and I trust they will receive a great blessing. The previous week I spent at the same place, with Cook's Brigade, and had the pleasure of baptizing six soldiers. About the same number had solicited the ordinance at my hands, and would have been baptized on Saturday, but, on the previous night, the remainder of the brigade was removed to Gordonsville, whither a part of it had gone previously. Brother Howerton is a chaplain in this bri-

gade. I also spent a week with Wofford's Brigade early in
September. Here I found only one chaplain, Rev. Mr. Flinn,
of the Presbyterian Church. I was received cordially and
treated affectionately, by both officers and men of all these brigades. During each visit I was impressed with the conviction,
that the army is an inviting field of labor, and is always ready to
welcome the evangelist.

" R. Ryland."

"Camp near Orange Court House, October 7.
" The work of the Lord is still on the increase in this army.
In every direction meetings are in progress, at which hundreds
are anxiously inquiring after the Saviour of sinners. Even where
it has been deemed best to suspend the regular series of services
prayer-meetings are held several times a day, conducted for the
most part by those who have themselves recently chosen the
service of God. These young converts sing, pray and exhort,
and their labors are made instrumental in the conversion of their
comrades. A Baptist chaplain told me yesterday, that every day
or two he was called on to baptize soldiers, brought to him by
the young converts, the fruits of their prayer-meetings. To-day
I rode twelve miles. All along the way, regiments, battalions
and brigades were encamped, and here and there on the wayside
I saw men sitting down reading their Testaments and tracts.
Brother Renfroe expects, this week, to baptize thirty-five.
Brother Cundy has baptized sixty. I suppose that fully 500
have united with the Baptist Church since the army has been
here. At Gordonsville I found a precious revival in progress.
I preached twice to large congregations at that place, and in the
afternoon witnessed the baptism of eleven, making thirty-seven
baptized by Brother Howerton, of Cook's Brigade. Permit me
to say, that I find our evangelists and colporters are greatly
encouraged. Almost every sermon they preach is being blessed
to the spiritual good of some soul, while the pages of truth they
distribute are eagerly read. We need, however, funds to support
those engaged in this good work. I beg that the pastors and
Churches at home will keep us provided with the needed contributions, the 'sinews of war.'

"A. E. D."

"Richmond, October 10.
"*Brother Dickinson:* I herewith furnish you a short statement

of my labors for the four weeks ending to-day, that I have labored as the representative of your board. I have preached twenty-one sermons, distributed 7,000 pages of tracts, witnessed thirty-six immersions, and aided in the examination of twenty-nine candidates for admission into our Church ; besides, quite a number gave their names, wishing to join other denominations. My labors were in Cobb's Legion of Cavalry, Colonel Cutt's Artillery Battalion, and the brigades of Daniel, Ramseur, Battle and Doles, but mostly in the last-named, which is composed of Georgia troops. I found a great work of grace in progress in General Doles' Brigade, which had been increasing in interest for several weeks, under the preaching and labors of Brother A. M. Marshall, of Georgia, aided by such help as he could get from other chaplains and visiting ministers. I remained with him *as a recruit* for two weeks, preaching once and sometimes twice a day in Doles' Brigade, and others in camps near by. I found in General Battle's Brigade, for which I preached twice, a precious revival spirit. Large and attentive crowds came to listen to preaching, and by fifties would flock around us for prayers. I can't forbear to mention, as one blessed feature of the work, *the reclaiming of backsliders.* Quite a number of cases came under my notice. Then again, many good, pious brethren, who had not fallen into gross sins, but had been backward in expressing themselves, feel as if a great pressure had been taken off them, and they not only *breathe* easier, but can now *speak* out for the Saviour. But I forbear making further comment now, as I have many I could make, and will perhaps offer them for the public eye, in some of our religious papers. My excuse for not doing more this month is, that I was indisposed a few days the first week, so as not to be able to work.

" W. N. CHAUDOIN."

A lady from the vicinity of Gettysburg, whose letter, describing the sufferings of the Confederate wounded left on that field of blood, appears in the *Albion*, Liverpool, England, says: "There were two brothers, one a colonel, the other a captain, lying side by side, and both wounded. They had a Bible between them."

Rev. J. J. D. Renfroe, in a private letter from the Army of Northern Virginia, to a member of his Church, Talladega, Alabama, says: " Were it not for separation from my dear family, I never was so happily situated in my life. I would rather be in the army than anywhere else. O, it is transporting to see the earnestness with which men enter upon the cause of religion, and the primitive familiarity and simplicity with which they approach each other and the preachers on the subject. And then there is scarcely an hour, but some poor inquiring soul comes to my tent to get instruction. I never saw the like of it before!"

"*Messrs. Editors:* Having spent several months in preaching to our soldiers, I have reluctantly yielded to the wish of the board, and resumed the work of collecting funds for army colportage. It is not because I love the work of an agency *less*, but because I love that of preaching *more*. Never have I realized so much pleasure in a summer's work before. Never have I seen any class of persons so appreciative of the Gospel as the Confederate soldiers generally. So far as my observation has extended, it is only necessary for a few sermons to be preached, in any regiment or brigade, to secure the conviction and conversion of sinners. A general predisposition to religion is everywhere apparent. Thousands, who, in the beginning of the war, were not only thoughtless, but profane and reckless, are now either happy Christians or trembling inquirers. It is impossible for those who have not been in the army to form a correct idea of the amount of interest manifested throughout the ranks. If many of the pastors of Churches would 'steal awhile away' from their home labors, and go to the army, they would feel amply repaid for any little sacrifice of comfort incident to camp life, by seeing that their 'work of faith was not in vain in the Lord.' Brethren and sisters of the Churches, send your pastors for a few weeks, at least, to publish salvation to perishing sinners in the army. They will return to you far better qualified to promote *your* spiritual interests, by reason of their sojourn among the soldiers. I have witnessed, during the summer, the hopeful conversion of some hundreds of souls, although I have preached to comparatively few brigades of the army. It is estimated that more than 2,000 soldiers have professed religion in General Lee's army since their return from Maryland. The army is now moving, but will soon be at rest again. Immediately after a battle, when men's minds are impressed with God's goodness in sparing their lives, is a most favorable time for presenting the claims of the Gospel. Our board still desires to employ missionaries. Who will go at once? Before I close, allow me to say, that officers generally, and General Gordon, of Early's Division, particularly, treated me kindly and respectfully. General Gordon is a man after my own heart. Should this 'cruel war' continue, and his life be spared, I predict for him a high place among the leaders of our hosts. May he receive from his country and his God, all that his true courage and rare Christian virtues so richly deserve!

"Affectionately,
"A. Broaddus."

.   .   .   .   .   .

" Recent movements have, of course, been (humanly speaking) rather unfavorable to the religious interests of the army. But up to the time of the move, the interest was unabated, and I doubt not is as great now really, though there is not quite so good an opportunity for developing it, as the nights are almost too cool for lengthy outdoor exercises, and the men are generally pretty busy in the day building huts, etc. Yet a good deal of preaching is being done, many prayer-meetings, Bible-classes, etc., are held, and the work of the Lord is prospering in our midst. I expect to baptize twenty-eight to-morrow in Hazel river. . . . I see every day increased evidences of the genuineness of this work in the army. I have been particularly struck with the fact, that out of scores I have called on to lead in prayer, *not one has refused*—and this is the testimony of chaplains generally. Many of them, too, lead the meetings, exhort, etc. And may we not hope that God in His providence designs *in the army* to answer the question that now wells up from many an anxious heart, 'Where are the preachers of the next generation to come from?' that He designs that there shall go forth from the ranks of our noble army, many who shall be useful heralds of the Gospel of peace. Let this be the subject of special prayer throughout the land. It is rejoicing our hearts that the Lord is in some measure visiting the Churches at home with outpourings of His Spirit. This will operate reciprocally upon the army. A chaplain gave me a beautiful illustration of it this morning. On a list which he handed me of those who wished to join the Baptist Church, there were eight or ten who desired to connect themselves with a single Church in North Carolina, and upon inquiry he found *that that Church had recently enjoyed a precious season of revival.* Thus it operates—the prayer of the soldier for his loved ones at home is heard, and the prayer for the absent soldier boy is not unheeded.   But I must close, as I fear I'll make your readers rejoice that my lengthy communications are only

"OCCASIONAL."

Rev. W. N. Chaudoin reports that during a recent visit to our forces at Franklin, Virginia, he baptized eight persons.   Up to the time of his leaving there were nearly fifty professions of conversion.

Rev. J. L. Truman says: "I spent the greater part of September in protracted meetings, in concert with other ministers. These meetings were attended with great good.   At one there were 140 converts, and seventy were baptized.   There were converts in all of these meetings.   A religious feeling of no ordinary character now prevails in the Army of Northern Virginia."

"We have had some precious seasons with the soldiers, who have thronged the house of the Lord, that they might be taught the way of life.   Take the following as a specimen of the cases of interest among this class of our hearers: At the prayer-meeting one afternoon, after the congregation was dismissed, a soldier came up and spoke to us, but believing him to be a member of the Church, we said nothing to him about his soul, until he remarked, 'I came here this evening, hoping that you would speak to me about the Saviour, and though you have dismissed the congregation, I must beg you to wait a few minutes and give me some instruction.'   The next day he united with the Church, and whenever called upon he has led in prayer, besides speaking a word, now and then, of exhortation. Another soldier, concerned about his soul, cried aloud, 'O that my mother were here!' 'Why do you want her here?' 'Because she has so long been praying for me, and now I have found the Saviour.'   The effect cannot be described.   Every eye was filled with tears, for all knew something of a mother's love.   The praying mother, away off in the far South, seemed to stand before us rejoicing over her penitent boy, now a fellow-pilgrim with her to the better land.   On another occasion a trooper, who had that day reached the city with prisoners from the valley, was present.   He was convicted of sin, found peace in believing, and was the most happy man that I have seen since the war has

been in progress. His love for the people of God was such that
he went around among them, giving to each the hand of fellowship and Christian affection : ' I will go back to the valley a new
man,' said he; 'the love of God burns in my heart, and I desire
now to speak for Jesus among my comrades.'

"A. E. DICKINSON."

" There is a good degree of religious interest felt in Beckham's
Battalion of Artillery, of which I am a member. We have no
chaplain, but the brethren of the different denominations keep up
a prayer-meeting and Sabbath-school. There have been some
twenty-five who have professed conversion in the battalion this
fall."

The revival in Hays's Brigade was one of very great power and
happiest results, and originated under circumstances of peculiar
interest.

A youth of the Ninth Louisiana Regiment named Bledsoe
professed conversion in hospital at Charlottesville, under the instructions of Post Chaplain J. C. Hiden, and returned to his
brigade; with the burning zeal of the young convert determined
to do something for the spiritual good of his comrades.

It is no harm to say that Hays' Brigade, though as gallant
fellows as ever kept step to the music of " Dixie," were noted
for their irreligion. They had had no chaplains except two
Romish priests, who, no doubt, did their duty as they understood
it, but were, of course, entirely out of sympathy with evangelical
religion as we understand it, and up to this period there had
been few, if any, efforts made for the conversion of these brave
fellows to the simple faith of the Lord Jesus Christ.

Bledsoe hunted diligently through the camp for men who
would unite with him in a prayer-meeting, and at last found five
others who would agree to do so.

These six young soldiers, afraid to begin their meeting in the
camp lest they should be interrupted by the jibes and jeers of
wicked comrades, went out into a clover field beyond the hearing
of their comrades, and began to pray for God's blessing upon
themselves and the brigade. The meeting grew nightly in numbers and interest until in about a week Bledsoe came to tell me
that a number of men had professed conversion, and they wanted
me to go up and take charge of the meeting. I found some 100
in attendance, fifteen professing conversion, and a number of in-

quirers after the way of life. The meetings grew in interest, we moved them into the centre of the brigade, and the work went graciously and gloriously on until over 200 professed to find "peace in believing."

Our Chaplains' Association at this period was a continued season of rejoicing, as nearly every chaplain and missionary reported that the Lord was with him in his work.

I may not now recall even the names of all the brigades in which revivals were reported, and can enter into very few details in the space at my command. But in August, September, October and November, 1863, revivals were reported in Smith's Virginia, Gordon's Georgia, Mahone's Virginia, Hays's Louisiana, Wright's Georgia, Wilcox's Alabama, Posey's Mississippi, Ramseur's North Carolina, Doles's Georgia, Scales's North Carolina, Thomas's Georgia, J. M. Jones's Virginia, Battle's Alabama, Kemper's Virginia, Armistead's Virginia, Corse's Virginia, Garnett's Virginia, Hoke's North Carolina, Benning's Georgia, Kershaw's South Carolina, Lane's North Carolina, Daniel's North Carolina, Davis's Mississippi, Kirkland's North Carolina, Semmes's Georgia, Barksdale's Mississippi, Jenkins's South Carolina, Law's Alabama, Anderson's Georgia, Steuart's Virginia, "Stonewall" (Virginia), Iverson's North Carolina, Cooke's North Carolina, H. H. Walker's Virginia and Tennessee, McGowan's South Carolina, and a number of the artillery battalions and cavalry regiments.

This revival work went graciously on, and though the "Bristoe" campaign, Longstreet's move to the battle of Chickamauga and his East Tennessee campaign, the cold weather which prevented outdoor services, and the very active campaign of 1864, all tended to interrupt the regular services, the interest by no means ceased, and there was no time at which there was not a precious revival in some of the commands.

"CHARLESTON, December 28.

"I am glad to inform you that the good work commenced in the Twenty-sixth Virginia Regiment at Burton's farm still continues. Brother Wiatt (chaplain) has baptized fifteen since they reached Charleston, and others are waiting to be baptized, and still others are concerned about their souls. They have nightly prayer-meetings, and after the meeting is over singing and other devotional exercises are continued in the different messes until bedtime. One of the most interesting features in this revival is, that the young converts, almost without an exception, take hold of the work, and pray, and frequently exhort in public, and may often be seen *conversing* with the *unconverted privately* about the *precious Saviour they have found.* The troops around here (though much scattered), like those in Virginia, all seem anxious to hear the Gospel. I preached last night to one company, and I suppose there were from seventy-five to 100 present.

"G. F. BAGBY."

Even after the weather became cold enough to keep people from attending their comfortable Churches at home, and before we could have any chapels built, these soldiers would come in crowds, many of them barefooted, to our outdoor meetings, and we rarely gave an invitation that there were not some to publicly manifest their interest.

CHAPTER XII.

THERE were some peculiar difficulties in the way of our work during the period embraced in this chapter. The severe weather of the winter and early spring made outdoor services rarely possible, and the skies had scarcely begun to smile upon us when General Grant crossed the Rapidan. Lee at once advanced and attacked him, and there ensued the death-grapple from "the Wilderness" to Petersburg, when we marched or fought, or were busy entrenching nearly every day. And then followed the siege of Petersburg and defence of Richmond, when our little army (reduced at last to 33,000 men to guard forty miles of entrenchments) was on starvation rations, and was yet forced to do an amount of marching, fighting, digging and watching that would have exhausted much sooner any other troops of which history gives any account, and all of which was very decidedly unfavorable to religious services, or any evangelical work among the soldiers.

And yet the good work went graciously on, there were precious seasons along the line of the Rapidan up to the very opening of the campaign. Many were converted on the march, in the trenches, on the battle-field, in the hospital—and the Richmond and Petersburg lines, despite their scenes of carnage and blood, were made glorious by the presence of *Christ in the trenches.*

I remember that the very day on which our line was broken below Petersburg, necessitating the evacuation of Richmond and Petersburg, and that sad march which terminated at Appomattox Court House, I had an appointment to preach and to baptize at the very point at which the lines were broken, and had been laboring there for some days in one of the most interesting revivals which I witnessed.

Indeed, the revivals along the forty miles of Confederate entrenchments, where there were about sixty chapels, during the winter of 1864-65 were as general and as powerful as any we had at all, and only ceased when the army was disbanded. Really they did not cease then, for in the great revivals with which our Churches in Virginia and the South were blessed during the summer and autumn of 1865 a very large proportion of the converts were from among our returned soldiers. I witnessed myself a large number of professions of conversion among them, and in the meetings in which I preached (acting as an independent evangelist from the mountains to the seaboard after I had "laid by", the corn and threshed the wheat, for I took off my coat and went into the field to work on my return from the army), I always found our returned soldiers the most tender and impressible part of the congregations.

Not as claiming by any means any special activity or special success, but merely as illustrating how God helped us in our labors, and blessed our poor efforts during this period, I give the following report of one of the missionaries for the year beginning October 1, 1863, and ending September 30, 1864. It may be proper to say that on October 1, 1864, I accepted an appointment from the Virginia Baptist Sunday-school and Publication Board as missionary-chaplain to A. P. Hill's Corps, and that this report only embraces my labors for the year named:

HEAD-QUARTERS, THIRD CORPS, A. N. VA.,
NEAR PETERSBURG, October 1, 1864.
REV. A. E. DICKINSON, General Superintendent:

Dear Brother: I have given you from time to time informal reports of my work, but now that a year has elapsed since I entered the service of your board, it is perhaps expected that I should send you a more formal report of my labors.

I have confined myself chiefly to those regiments and brigades most destitute of ministerial labor; but would take occasion to say that I have been treated by the chaplains of all denominations with uniform courtesy and kindness, and have invariably found both officers and men ready to afford me every assistance in the prosecution of my work.

In the past year I have preached 161 sermons—generally to large and attentive congregations. I have baptized 222. I have no means of knowing the number of Bibles, Testaments, tracts, religious papers, etc., I have distributed, but I have given large attention to this most important work, have tried always to keep a supply on hand, and have seldom gone to the hos-

"STONEWALL" JACKSON AND STAFF.

(Facing page 355.)

pitals or among the troops without scattering tracts or papers; nor have I the means of knowing definitely the number of prayer-meetings I have conducted. An important part of my work has been to endeavor to secure chaplains for the vacant regiments. I have been instrumental in securing the appointment of twelve chaplains. I could have secured the appointment of a number of others could I have found suitable brethren to take the places. Several excellent men could be gotten from the ranks, but for the refusal of the present secretary of war to make such appointments. I trust that I have also been of some service in assisting ministers coming to labor for a short time in the army, with information as to the most suitable places for them to labor, etc.

The past six months have been very unfavorable to preaching in the army, owing to the unceasing activity which has prevailed, but when denied an opportunity of preaching I have found an abundant work in the hospitals, in pointing the sick and wounded to the great Physician. I might relate many incidents illustrating the eagerness of the soldiers to hear the Gospel, and its abundant success amongst them, but many such statements have been made in the papers, and I deem it unnecessary at present to do more than give this brief summary of my labors.

In reviewing the past, I am constrained to "thank God and take courage."

Yours in the Gospel,
J. Wm. Jones, Army Evangelist.

But, having made this general statement of the work during this period, I must now give some of the details.

The extracts which follow from army letters and newspaper reports will show at the same time the religious status of the army and the spirit of our workers and of the soldiers:

" The religious condition of our army at present is both healthful and hopeful. Now that the weather has become unfavorable for frequent outdoor services, many of the regiments have neatly constructed log chapels, and many other chaplains, in lieu of this convenience, substitute the social prayer-meeting from hut to hut, Bible-classes, tract distribution, private conversation, etc., for the more public ministrations of the word.

There is very great demand for good reading of all sorts, and the friends of the soldier can do nothing more acceptable to him than to send good books, papers, magazines, etc., to Brother Fry, at our depository, who will see them properly distributed. By the way, our depository, under Brother Fry's effective management, is proving a complete success and a great blessing to the army. Not only are chaplains supplied, but pious men in many of the regiments without chaplains, get from it packages of tracts and papers, and go as colporters to their comrades.

" The work of supplying the vacant regiments with chaplains proceeds rather slowly, but *something* is being done. The offer of our board to assist brethren who cannot make a support from the governmental salary, has had already a happy effect. Brethren who may have any intention of entering the chaplaincy ought to make application at once, as there is a great work to be done this winter. By the way, I wonder if the receipts of our board are commensurate with their increased expense in aiding chaplains? They certainly ought to be, for surely, if ever a board deserved to have a warm place in the hearts of the people, and be liberally sustained, the 'Virginia Baptist Sunday-School and Publication Board' is that one. I mean no disparagement of others, when I say, that, in the wide circulation and excellency of its publications, the number and efficiency of its colporters and evangelists, and its success in the great work in which it stood alone the first year of the war, our board, under the energetic management of its superintendent, has had no equal. It needs funds for the prosecution of its great work, and has claims upon the brotherhood which will not be disregarded. Brother, whom the Lord has blessed with plenty in these troublesome times, send on at once to Brother Dickinson a liberal New Year's offering for your brave defenders.

" OCCASIONAL.

" CAMP NEAR ORANGE COURT HOUSE, January 4, 1864."

" CAMP TWENTY-SIXTH VIRGINIA, General Wise's Brigade,
" NEAR CHARLESTON, S. C., January 6.

" It gives me great pleasure to inform you and the friends of our regiment, through the *Herald,* that the Lord continues to pour out His Spirit upon us. During the three months and a half of our camping here, about twenty-five of our officers and men have professed Christ. I have already baptized fifteen, and several more will follow. Conversions are reported almost every week. Prayer-meetings are held in all of the companies nightly, except when some providential circumstance prevents. A great deal of zeal and love for Christ are exhibited by both old and young professors. We have a flourishing Christian Association, composed of some two hundred or more members, whose stated meetings are once in two weeks. We have preaching every Sabbath. We get a goodly number of copies of several religious papers, which are very eagerly read by converted and unconverted. We receive thirty copies of the *Herald*, which is far too small a number. Will not the liberality of our Virginia brethren increase it to fifty or seventy-five? Our officers and men are nearly all supplied with Bibles and Testaments. We are enjoying excellent health, well fixed and in good spirits. We don't cease to remember our Churches in our prayers. Do they remember us?

"WM. E. WIATT,
"Chaplain Twenty-Sixth Virginia Regiment."

"There is a company in one of our Virginia regiments which numbers eighty men, all of whom, except ten, are now connected with some evangelical denomination. Bible-classes have been formed, embracing the entire company, and the little handful who are yet 'out of Christ' give manifest tokens of deep religious impressions.

"There is a Bible-class in every company of Doles's Brigade, Army of Northern Virginia."

"CHARLESTON, SOUTH CAROLINA.

"It gives me great pleasure to report, that our meeting continues with unabated interest. About seventy-five have been hopefully converted. Last night was truly a refreshing time with us. It was difficult to get away from Church. Many of the inquirers refused to leave after the benediction, and of course we stayed with them. We had three or four additional prayers, and before we left the house (which was about half-past nine), several others professed. I do not think I have ever seen such interest manifested on the part of the unconverted. Men may sometimes be seen an *hour before services, running to the house,* in order that they may procure seats. They come from regiments two miles off. I do not think I could consent to leave here now, but I leave those behind who have promised to carry on the meeting indefinitely. I have been engaged in this meeting for nearly four weeks. I do not believe such extensive revivals as we are now having through our beloved country have ever been heard of since the days of Pentecost.

"G. F. BAGBY."

CAMP LETTER, No. 15.

"*Dear Brethren:* At our chaplains' meeting, the other day, I was enabled very nearly to complete my list of chaplains in the *Infantry and Artillery* of the army. The statistics you publish from the *Central Presbyterian*, are incomplete, and I give you the following as *about* the correct statement: Total number of chaplains in Ewell's and Hill's Corps, 86; Methodists, 36; Baptists, 20; Presbyterians, 20; Episcopalians, 6; Roman Catholics, 3; Lutherans, 1. There are still fifty regiments and battalions without chaplains, but it will be remembered that when our Chaplains' Association sent out, just a year ago, an appeal to the Churches for more laborers in the army, *over half* the regiments were without chaplains. The large increase will be gratifying not only to the Christian public, but to all who rightly estimate the *military power* of religion in the army. A year ago there were whole brigades without chaplains, and regiments which had had scarcely a sermon, but this has ceased to be. There is not a brigade which has not one or more chaplains, and the supply of missionary labor has been far greater than during any previous year. Indeed, but for the fact that a large number of chaplains have resigned, the supply would nearly equal the demand. The labors of these messengers of salvation have been wonderfully blessed during the past year, and in contemplating what has been done, we may well ' thank God and take courage.' But there is one thought which strikes me painfully in looking over these statistics—the proportion of Baptist chaplains to those of our Methodist and Presbyterian brethren is *so small*, when we consider the relative membership of each Church. I suppose that there are about as many Baptists as Methodists, and over twice as many as Presbyterians in the army—and yet our Presbyterian brethren have as many chaplains as we, and our Methodist brethren almost twice as many. I rejoice that the ministry of these denominations have awakened to some appreciation of what they owe to the army. I mourn that our

Baptist ministry seem *behind them* in this respect. Brethren of the ministry, there is still an open door to this widespread field of usefulness; and I call upon you to consider whether it is not *your* duty to enter it. And by the way, I would respectfully ask of our older brethren in the ministry, if it is necessary for Congress (according to the law passed by the Senate) to extend the conscript age to fifty-five, does not this call upon some of them to give themselves to the work of army evangelization? If the age of those who are *to do the fighting* is to be extended, ought not the age of those who are *to do the preaching* in the army be also extended? Is it right that our chaplaincies should be filled almost entirely by *young* men—many of them with no experience as preachers? True, most of our useful ministers have families whom they would have to leave, and separation from loved ones is a bitter trial, but then our soldiers have to endure this, besides risking their lives, and it would seem right that they should be willing to make a like sacrifice in preaching to them the glad tidings. . . . 'All quiet along the lines' is the stereotyped phrase which will probably express our military status for weeks to come. The Yankees made a cavalry raid to Madison Court House, the other day, in which they made a few captures and returned the same evening. The spirits of our army were never better. The men are re-enlisting for the war, wherever an effort is made to get them to do so, and there is withal a spirit of content and hopefulness which the people at home would do well to imitate. The rations now issued are better than they were some time ago, and are likely still to improve. General Lee has issued a beautiful address upon the temporary scarcity of rations, and gives example as well as precept. At a dinner to which he was invited the other day, he refused the rich viands with which the table was loaded, and made his dinner off of *beef and bread—remarking that he could not consent to be feasting, while there was a scarcity of rations among his men.* If a similar spirit existed amongst the good people at home, the scarcity of provisions in the army would indeed be temporary. If, instead of constantly croaking about the dangers of starvation, the people would *reduce their rations* in order to feed the army, this goblin would soon disappear. The soldiers are grateful for the sympathies bestowed upon them so lavishly, but they say that they can't live on *sympathy*—they must have meat and bread as well. Wright's Georgia Brigade is now being blessed with a revival, and I trust that other brigades will soon experience like blessings.   I have heard of upwards of thirty chapels in the different camps, and there are doubtless others.   Brethren who can get off would find this a most favorable time to visit and preach for the regiments and brigades which have chapels—especially those of them which are without chaplains.

"OCCASIONAL.

"ARMY NORTHERN VIRGINIA, February 3, 1864."

It is due to the denomination which, as a member of it, I claimed the right to censure in the above letter for failure to send their proportion of *chaplains* to the army to say that they, in some measure at least, redeemed themselves by taking the lead in colportage work, and in employing a large number of army missionaries and evangelists.

The Domestic Mission Board of the Southern Baptist Convention had at work at this period seventy-eight missionaries to the soldiers, and supplemented the salaries of eleven chaplains, while the Virginia Baptist Publication Board had in its employ over 100 colporters and army evangelists, and other State boards of the denomination were doing similar work.

We have seen that the Presbyterian Board appointed eighty missionaries, including some of their ablest men.

Rev. Dr. Bennett in his " Great Revival," gives the following as to the appointments of the great denomination with which he is connected, and which fully redeemed its well-known reputation for missionary zeal by its " abundant labors " in this great harvest-field:

" The earnest purpose of the home Churches to promote the army revival was manifested by the number of ministers sent among the soldiers.   We give a list of those who are sent by the Mission Board of the Methodist Episcopal Church South :

" Revs. Leo. Rosserand J. C. Granberry in the Army of Northern Virginia; J. B. McFerrin, C. W. Miller, W. Mooney, B. P. Ransom, and W. Burr in the Army of Tennessee; J. S. Lane and E. B. Duncan in the Department of Florida; J. J. Wheat and H. J. Harris in Mississippi ; W. C. Johnson to General S. D. Lee's Corps, North Mississippi ; J. J. Hutchinson to army about Mobile ; and beyond the Mississippi river, J. C. Keener to Louisiana troops, and B. T. Kavanaugh and E. M. Marvin to Missouri and Arkansas troops.

" Besides these, and others probably whose names have escaped us, the Conferences of the Methodist Episcopal Church South emulated other Churches in sending forth laborers into the great harvest.

" Rev. Dr. Myers, of the *Southern Christian Advocate*, in noticing these facts, says:

"'The Mississippi Conference appointed one missionary and two chaplains to the army; Memphis, one missionary and six chaplains; Alabama, four missionaries and twelve chaplains; Florida, one missionary and two chaplains; Georgia, eight missionaries and eight chaplains; South Carolina, thirteen chaplains; North Carolina, two missionaries and eight chaplains; Virginia, two missionaries and twenty chaplains. Here are nineteen missionaries and seventy-one chaplains from these eight Conferences. Of course, the Conferences beyond our lines furnish a number also; but except in the case of the general missionaries, sent out by the parent board, we can give no guess even as to their numbers.'

" The Georgia Conference determined, if possible, to furnish one missionary to each Georgia Brigade, and at the session of 1863 the work was begun by sending seven ministers: " R. B. Lester to Jackson's Brigade, Army of Tennessee; A. M. Thigpen to Colquitt's Brigade, near Charleston; J. W. Turner to the troops in and around Savannah, and on the coast below there; G. W. Yarbrough to Wofford's Brigade, General Longstreet's army; T. H. Stewart to Thomas's Brigade, and P. O. Harper to Gordon's Brigade, Army of Virginia; and L. B. Payne temporarily to visit the hospitals between Atlanta and Guyton C. Railroad, until a brigade is selected for him. Another, T. F. Pierce, is now in the State military service, and will receive his appointment to a brigade when his term expires."

But, to return from this digression, I give the following extracts from letters which I wrote to the *Christian Index*, Macon, Georgia:

CAMP, NEAR ORANGE COURT HOUSE, VIRGINIA,
February 10, 1864.

We held, on yesterday, a very pleasant meeting of our Chaplains' Association. A large number of chaplains were present, and the reports elicited showed a very healthful religious feeling throughout the army. A revival was reported as in progress in Davis's Mississippi Brigade, in which nine had professed conversion, and seventy were inquiring the way to life. There is also an interesting state of things in Kirkland's North Carolina Brigade, and in the First North Carolina Regiment. The good work commenced in Wilcox's (old) Brigade last summer seems to be reviving. In one of the regiments there I have heard of men going out in the snow barefooted to attend the nightly prayer-meeting, which was held out of doors for want of a chapel. We had no report from Wright's Georgia Brigade, but I trust that the revival reported there is still in progress. In a number of other regiments and brigades increased interest in the prayer-meetings, Bible-classes, etc., was reported. A committee appointed at the last meeting to visit General Lee with a view to see if something could not be done for the better observance of the Sabbath, reported that they were received with the utmost cordiality, and presented an order on the subject just issued from head-quarters. General Lee was present at this meeting and seemed deeply interested in the proceedings. He is a fast friend of the chaplains, and manifests a lively interest in their work.

There was an interesting statement made of the increase of laborers in the army since February, 1863. Then, over half of the regiments were unsupplied with chaplains, and there were whole brigades without a single chaplain ; now, over two-thirds of the regiments have chaplains, and the number of missionaries is much larger than ever before. Still, there is need of more chaplains—and especially of more Baptist chaplains, as we have nothing like our proportion. The only thing that would palliate the conscription of ministers would be that it would fill up all the vacant chaplaincies.

I learn, from a private source, that Rev. L. W. Allen, of Virginia (widely known and loved), who was captured while serving as captain of a cavalry company, is engaged at Fort Johnson in carrying on a very interesting revival, in which a number of our officers have professed conversion and been baptized in the lake. How wonderful are the ways of Providence!

ARMY NORTHERN VIRGINIA, March 1, 1864.

Perhaps I can give a better idea of our work in the army by a few quotations from my diary. Saturday, February 20. Preached to a large and very attentive congregation in Davis's Mississippi Brigade, and after preaching received five for baptism. They are having a most precious revival in this brigade, and Rev. Mr. Witherspoon, the efficient chaplain of the Forty-second Mississippi, is alone, very much broken down, and calling loudly for help. Already they have had a large number to profess conversion, and the number of inquirers is daily increasing.

Sunday, February 21. Preached this morning at Mahone's Virginia Brigade. Their large chapel was densely crowded, and I have rarely preached to a more attentive congregation. There are only two chaplains in this brigade of five regiments, but they are working men and the lay brethren are earnestly aiding them in their good work. Besides their chapel services, they have regular Bible-classes and prayer-meetings in nearly every company in the brigade, and classes in spelling, reading, writing, English grammar, geography, astronomy, mathematics, Latin, Greek, etc. There are a number of men who did not know their alphabet, but who are now reading very well. There are men coming forward every week to make a public profession of religion, and the genuineness of the glorious revival they had last fall is attested by the almost uniform consistency and activity of the young converts. After a substantial camp dinner, I rode over to Wright's Georgia Brigade and got there just as their Sunday-school was being opened. They had a large attendance of deeply interested young men, and I felt that it was good to be there. I taught a class of some twenty, and have rarely spent a more pleasant, or (to me, at least) profitable hour; there was a sharpened attention to the lesson, an eager inquiry after the meaning of particular passages, and an intelligent expression of opinion which is rarely found in the best regulated Sabbath-schools in the Churches at home. I turned away feeling that if I had been unable to interest or profit the class, they had certainly done both for me. At night the chapel was filled with eager listeners, as I tried to point them to the " friend that sticketh closer than a brother." After preaching, I received five for baptism, and went to my quarters (four miles off), enjoying the moonlight ride and meditating on the great work to be done in our army.

[I may add here, as likely to interest your Georgia readers especially, that there have been recently some *twenty* professions of religion in Wright's Brigade, and there are still a number of inquirers. They have only two chaplains, Rev. Messrs. Cook and Stokes (Methodist), and while they are zealous and efficient they cannot do all the work to be done. They say that they would like to have a Baptist chaplain in the brigade, as a large proportion of the men are Baptists. Cannot the Baptists of

Georgia send on some earnest, working man of God to labor as chaplain or missionary among these noble men?]

Monday, February 22. I went to Davis's Brigade this morning to hear a lecture from the Rev. B. T. Lacy on " The Life and Christian Character of General T. J. Jackson." The lecturer was well prepared for his task by his intimate association with the lamented hero, and for two hours he enchained the audience which, far too large for the chapel, assembled out in the open air. It was a fit and eloquent tribute to a great and good man. After the lecture I received three others from Davis's Brigade and one from Wright's, and we repaired to a mill-pond near by, where some of the brethren had cut off the ice from a space sufficient for our purpose. We sang an appropriate hymn, earnest prayer was offered, and appropriate passages of Scripture read, and, in the presence of a large and solemn congregation, I " went down into the water " and " buried with Christ in baptism " the fourteen young brethren whom I had received.

Tuesday, February 23. We had to-day a very interesting meeting of our Chaplains' Association. After an earnest and practical sermon from Rev. D. B. Ewing, we had a very interesting report on the religious condition of the army, showing revivals in several of the brigades, and a hopeful state of religion in all. Nearly every regiment has its Bible-classes and prayer-meetings, thousands of pages of religious reading, and all the copies of the word of God that can be obtained, are regularly distributed, and great attention is being given to the primary schools, in which many poor fellows are being taught to read and write. These reports clearly indicate that *now* is the time for preachers to come to the army either as temporary missionaries or permanent chaplains. A committee was appointed to prepare an address setting forth the religious condition and wants of the army, and one to devise (if possible) some plans to increase the number of Bibles and Testaments for circulation among the soldiers. Various other matters of interest claimed the attention of the meeting, and we adjourned feeling that our meeting had been profitable as well as pleasant.

Wednesday, February 24. Preached this morning to Kirkland's North Carolina Brigade, which is on picket near " Rapidan Station." As they had lost the use of their chapel by coming on picket, the services had to be held out of doors, but there was a large and attentive congregation present, despite the blustering day. After preaching, I received and baptized in the Rapidan nine hopeful converts. At night I preached in Scales's North Carolina Brigade to a very large congregation, and when at the close of the service an invitation was given for all Christians and all who desired the special prayers of God's people to kneel, *the entire congregation* promptly knelt.

And thus I might go on, but these quotations must suffice for my purpose, which is to show our brethren at home the great work *daily* claiming our attention in the army, and to earnestly send them the Macedonian cry, " Come over and help us." For several days past I have been laboring with the artillery of Ewell's Corps, amongst whom there is a good deal of religious interest. Rev. Dr. Burrows, of Richmond, has been laboring with them for a week, with his usual success. He has also delivered his admirable lecture (which I am glad to say will soon be published) on " Colonel Lewis Minor Coleman, the Christian Scholar and Soldier," and as Colonel Coleman was attached to this command at the time of his death, there was the deepest interest in the lecture, and great good must have been accomplished by its delivery.

.   .   .   .

I have been on the " sick list " for the past week and have not, therefore, been able to visit the camps to much extent, but learn that there is a great deal of religious interest in many of the brigades, and deeply interesting revivals in several of them. I have engagements to baptize in several of the regiments as soon as I am well enough to do so. These candidates professed conversion under the labors of a Methodist and two Presbyterian chaplains, and desiring to join Baptist Churches these brethren promptly requested me to baptize them. I have had since I have been in the army a large number of requests of this sort. And it gives me pleasure to testify to the courtesy and kindness with which I have been treated by the chaplains of the different denominations, all of whom know that I am a decided Baptist. Indeed, there seems to be in the army a truce to denominational bickerings—there are no sectarian sermons preached and no sectarian tracts circulated, but all seem to work together to make men Christians, and then leave it to their consciences and their Bible with what denomination they will connect themselves.

J. W. J.

"I have spent a few days of late with the artillery of Hill's Corps, only one battalion of which, I believe, has a chaplain. Brother M. D. Anderson, our colporter, is laboring very faithfully in this field. A few days since one of the battalions, in which his efforts have been blessed to the good of many souls, sent him $100, and a letter expressive of their high appreciation of his work. Brother J. M. Hart, of the Crenshaw Battery, gave me the following account of a work of grace with which his battalion had been blessed: 'Last summer, while we were in Orange, one of your colporters (Brother Clopton) visited us. He conversed with the men, supplied them with reading matter, and from day to day held prayer-meetings with us. The Divine Spirit was bestowed upon the effort and almost every man was more or less concerned about his soul. Many professed conversion and united with God's people.' . . . .

"A. E. D."

Brother Geo. F. Bagby, South Carolina, writes:
"Since I last wrote. you I have visited portions of Wise's Brigade, preached several times on James' Island (the number of hopeful conversions during our meeting there reached one hundred), and have also visited several points for collecting purposes."

"Quite a revival is in progress in Colonel Carter's command. Night before last six came forward to ask for the prayers of God's people, while last night *four* made a public profession of faith in Christ, and *seven* presented themselves as inquirers. Rev. A. B. Brown is greatly encouraged and delighted that he has found such an inviting field. The Secretary of War has promised to assign him to Carter's and Braxton's Battalions. Major Braxton's command is erecting a chapel, and as soon as it is completed a protracted meeting will be commenced there. Major Braxton, whose gallantry has been conspicuous on many memorable battle-fields, is a Baptist, and is deeply interested in all that pertains to the spiritual good of his men. He gives a cordial welcome to missionaries and colporters, and greatly aids them in gaining access to those under his command. Colonel Carter, too, is a Christian gentleman who has done great good by the efforts he has made in this direction, as well as by his own consistent example. I expect to spend several days with

Brother Brown and then visit other portions of the army, where I have promised to aid in protracted meetings. Beyond all doubt this is the best season for such meetings.

"A. E. D."

March 3, 1864.

Now is the time to preach in the army. There is a half formed intention on the part of many of our brethren that they will come to the army *when the weather opens*, and spend a while in preaching to the soldiers. Let me urge that they *come at once*. There are comfortable houses of worship (*thirty-seven* in all) scattered throughout our camps; there is a good prospect of weeks of uninterrupted labor, and there is an eagerness to hear the Gospel seldom witnessed in camp. Many of our chaplains are now absent, taking a needed respite from their labors, and there are now comparatively few missionaries in the camps; so that, at a time when there is *special demand* for ministerial labors, the *supply* is unusually limited. I appeal, then, to our brethren in the ministry (*especially to our most useful pastors*) to come at once, if only for a short time, and give us a helping hand in reaping the precious sheaves now "white unto the harvest." It will cost some trouble and sacrifice—but ought we not to be willing to endure these for the good of the noble fellows who *risk their all for us?* And do not delay your coming, brethren, for there is many a poor fellow whom you might reach *now*, who will fill a soldier's grave in the early spring campaign. Take your roll of blankets and a box of provisions (if convenient) to help the "mess" with which you may stay, and *come right along.*

J. WM. JONES, Army Evangelist.

I give other extracts from my letters to the *Christian Index:*

The weather has interfered very much with religious services of late, but when denied the more public ministrations of the word the men have often met in their company and held mess prayer-meetings, and thus the good work has gone on. If we shall have a week or two of pleasant weather before the campaign opens, there will be a glorious harvest to be reaped by the faithful laborer. I received on yesterday a note from a Baptist captain in a brigade which has been on picket and deprived of the services of a minister for two weeks or more, telling me that the revival which they enjoyed before leaving their camp is still in progress, and that there are a number of candidates awaiting baptism. I expect to go down in a day or two and baptize them in sight of the Yankee pickets. I preached on yesterday to one of the largest congregations I ever addressed, and received *five* for baptism. The good work goes on, and I feel like calling, in every letter I write, for *more men.*

Harris's Mississippi Brigade has recently given an evidence of self-sacrifice, which deserves to be written in letters of gold on one of the brightest pages of the history of this war. They have resolved to deny themselves one day's rations every ten days and give it to the poor of the city of Richmond. There is nothing in the history of the war more sublime than to see these noble men, cut off from supplies from home, thus offering a portion of their scant allowance to the poor of the city they have so long defended. If the people at home would " go and do likewise" the much agitated question, " How are the army and the poor to be fed?", would be speedily solved. Well may our people " sit at the feet of the camp" to learn lessons of self-denial. Our noble boys have not only given up the comforts of home, and borne cheerfully the privations and hardships of soldier-life, but they are willing to make still further sacrifices to aid the needy. Reader, think of these noble men as you gather around your wellspread board, imitate their example towards the needy in your midst and *reduce your rations* that you may help to increase their scant fare.

. . . . . .

Happening in Lynchburg the other day I visited the " Soldiers' Library," established by the efficient post chaplain (Brother J. L. Johnson), and was very much pleased with its arrangement and management. It is supplied with about eight hundred volumes of religious and miscellaneous books, a large number of pamphlets, weekly issues of all the religious papers published in the South, a number of secular papers, etc. It has a claim for contributions of money and books upon the friends of the soldier in every State since *State lines* are not thought of in distributing its benefits.

I met also Brother A. Broadus, who is widely known in Georgia as one of the most efficient agents to be found. He was busily and successfully prosecuting his work—going from house to house to plead the claims of the soldier. I met him when our army was drawn up in line of battle at " Mine Run," just in rear of our lines, and in reply to our exclamation of surprise at seeing him there, he said that he was " collecting money for army colportage." A bad " time and place," most persons would have thought, but he was succeeding very well.

Our Virginia board has recently appointed Rev. E. J. Willis "General Evangelist in Ewell's Corps." It would have been hard to find a better man for the place. Brother Willis's life has been a checkered but useful one. Graduating in his literary course at a Northern college, and in law at the University of Virginia, he practised his profession for awhile in his native State, and then emigrated to California about the beginning of the " gold fever." He was successful in his profession, and soon elevated to the position of judge, with a prospect of still higher honors; but seeing the great need of preachers in that rising State he left the bench for the pulpit, and was widely useful in proclaiming the glad tidings. Returning to Virginia he was pastor of " Leigh Street Baptist Church," Richmond, and at the beginning of the war was building up a new interest at "Clay Street Chapel." He raised a company " for the war " and has distinguished himself on many a bloody field, especially at Sharpsburg, where in command of his regiment (Forty-fifth Virginia Infantry) he bore its colors in the front, and when the flag-staff was shot away, wrapped them around his sword and still led the charge. I predict for him equal success in the new field upon which he is just entering.

"All quiet along the lines." There is an increase of religious interest, but I defer particulars until after our chaplains meeting to-morrow.

J. W. J.

CAMP NEAR ORANGE COURT HOUSE, VA., March 20, 1864.

March 24, 1864.

Rev. J. D. Chambers, missionary of the Virginia Baptist Sunday-School and Publication Board, reports a very extensive and powerful revival in progress in Bryant's Georgia Brigade, under the labors of Chaplains C. H. Toy, W. L. Curry and J. C. Camp (all three Baptists), and the brigade missionary, Rev. Mr. Haygood (a Methodist minister). There is a fine state of religious feeling throughout that army, but a great lack of chaplains; and both officers and men are very anxious to fill the vacancies.

24

The supply of religious literature—books, tracts and papers—by no means equals the demand.

Rev. Andrew B. Cross, in an account of a visit to Fort Delaware, states that, while our prisoners were eating dinner, he proposed to preach for them. " They readily assented, and circulated the notice among their companions. I went out and selected a spot in the barrack yard, which was protected from the wind and where the sun shone very warm. Here were gathered in a few minutes almost one thousand men, who stood listening attentively for over half an hour that I talked to them, and then seemed unwilling to depart, begging me to come and preach to them again, or send some one else."

"*Messrs. Editors :* You reminded me when I saw you of 'an old and unfulfilled promise.' I will now pay you one instalment. Shortly before we started on the Peninsular campaign, a soldier of my regiment called on me, telling me that J—— wanted to see me. J——, a youth of perhaps seventeen years, was one of the most profane persons I ever heard speak. I walked with the messenger a few hundred yards from camp, where we found J—— sitting alone. 'Oh, sir,' said he, ' I am a lost sinner!' I told him yes, but the Son of man came to seek and to save that which was lost. After some conversation, in which he expressed a very deep sense of his sinfulness, I asked him : ' Did you expect me to come when you sent for me ? ' ' Yes.' 'And why? I had never promised to do anything for you.' ' Because you always do anything for us you can.' ' If, then, you could trust me to come to you without any promise, can you not trust Christ with a promise ? Kneel right here, and right now accept the invitation to come, and humbly, yet confidently, ask—nay, *claim*— the fulfilment of his promise, " I will give you rest." ' We knelt together, and he prayed aloud one of the most earnest, childlike prayers I ever heard. When we rose, I saw by the clear light of the moon a most remarkable change in the expression of his face. The anxious sadness had given way to the most joyful expression. ' Well, sir,' said I, 'how now? Has Jesus repudiated His promise or kept it ? ' ' He has *kept* it ; He has given me rest,' was the reply. Further conversation thoroughly satisfied me that Jesus had indeed fulfilled His promise. I more than once called on him to lead in prayer. His prayers were characterized by a childlike simplicity and confidence rarely to be found. On the march he told some of his friends that he was certain to be killed in the first battle. He was killed dead on the field on the first of July at Gettysburg. Thus fell as brave a soldier as has been sacrificed in his country's cause, and 'a babe in Christ' was taken away from evil to come.

"W. B. CARSON."

The *Southern Christian Advocate* judges, from intelligence from the Southern armies, that "the great revival," commenced last year, still continues.

Revivals are reported in General B. R. Johnson's Brigade (a part of Longstreet's army), near Dandridge, Tennessee, in the camp church at Galveston, Texas, and in the Twenty-third Georgia Regiment, Colquitt's Brigade, near Charleston, South Carolina.

"Of the 111 professors of religion in the Fifty-fifth North Carolina Regiment, Davis's Brigade, 3 are Lutherans, 4 Presbyterians, 8 unconnected with any Church, 32 Methodists, 64 Baptists."

"CAMP OF GORDON'S GEORGIA BRIGADE, March 21.

"The Lord is with us. For about two weeks past we have been rejoicing in His presence and His blessing. There is a deep religious interest pervading this whole brigade. *Scores* are nightly inquiring the way of life, and a goodly number profess to have found it. It was my happy privilege on yesterday, in the presence of a large congregation, 'to bury' sixteen 'by baptism.' Oh, may this interest not subside while the war lasts—nay, may it continue even when it shall have *closed ;* and may these Christ-loving soldiers go home to be as holy firebrands in our Churches!

"A. B. WOODFIN,
"Chaplain Sixty-first Georgia."

"An entire congregation in Scales's (North Carolina) Brigade promptly knelt, a short while since, on an invitation for all Christians, and all who desired the special prayers of God's people to kneel."

"BATH COURT HOUSE, VIRGINIA, March 10.

"The chaplains of this (Colonel Jackson's) brigade have recently closed a very interesting meeting of nineteen days. There were twenty-five or thirty conversions. I baptized nine, and five others are received for baptism. Seven united with the Southern

Methodists. Many penitents are inquiring the way of salvation. We hope the good work thus commenced will continue. We had the assistance of several ministers at different times during the meeting.

"J. D. LEACHMAN,
"Chaplain Twentieth Virginia Regiment Cavalry."

"Captain A. W. Poindexter, Twenty-sixth Virginia Regiment, Wise's Brigade : Enclosed you will please find $101 contributed by my company (K, Twenty-sixth Virginia Infantry) for army colportage. May God bless it to the good of our soldiers! The religious feeling in our regiment is very deep. Prayer-meetings are held in every company every night, and we have reason to believe that they have done much good, and to hope that they will continue to do much. Many who, a year ago, were groping their way in darkness, are now the humble followers of the 'Lamb of God.' The change in the morals of the men has been frequently remarked upon by some of the officers to me. Our chaplain, Rev. William E. Wiatt, is untiring in his efforts among us, and is constantly working for the spiritual welfare of the men. He is greatly beloved by all, and may his labors among us be blessed more abundantly, and all of us be made to rejoice by seeing all of our regiment converted to God! Pray for us, my dear brother."

"PETERSBURG, VIRGINIA, April 17.

"There is quite an interesting meeting in progress in the South Carolina hospital. It commenced some five weeks since. The chaplain is assisted by Rev. Dr. Pryor, who was providentially detained here from his field of labor in the army. His services were very acceptable, and I trust greatly blessed."

"TAYLORSVILLE, VIRGINIA, April 3.

"I trust the Lord has commenced a gracious revival in Johnson's Brigade, now stationed at this place. Notwithstanding the weather has been very unfavorable, the work still progresses. I preached to large and attentive congregations during the past week. As many as twenty-five at one time came forward for prayer. Some have professed faith in Christ. We worship in the Baptist meeting-house.

"GEORGE W. GRIFFIN."

"CHAPLAINS' ASSOCIATION, A. N. VA., ORANGE COURT HOUSE.

"March 23.

. . . "In Davis's Brigade, of Heth's Division, seventy-one have professed conversion in the past six weeks. Although the brigade is now on picket, where, owing to scarcity of timber, there is no chapel, yet seats for outdoor preaching are arranged, and the religious interest is unabated. During the week are held many prayer-meetings, brigade, regimental, company and private; and *prayer-meetings to prepare for prayer-meetings.* Jesus is walking in His garden, and the myrrh, and aloes, and sweet spices breathe forth their richest fragrance. In Mahone's Brigade, of Anderson's Division, since our last meeting twenty have united with various Churches, and a number have professed satisfaction as to the pardon of their sins. Out of 428 professors in three regiments in this brigade, 140 professed conversion since the war begun. During a series of meetings for several weeks in Scales's Brigade, eighteen have been received into the Church; thirty had entrusted their souls to Jesus for salvation. The work of grace was still going on. There were 600 professors out of 2,400 men in four regiments. Alas! 800 *men were destitute of the Scriptures.* Many Bible-classes are held, and personal instruction given by the chaplain to the teachers. In the Twenty-second North Carolina Infantry, in this brigade, there is an alarming deficiency of God's word. But here God is working, and blessing means used to win souls to Christ. Kirkland's, McGowan's and Stonewall Brigades all report an encouraging state of religion in their midst. In all, some are joining the army of the living God, and some are fleeing from the wrath to come towards the shelter of the Cross. This is also true of portions of the artillery of both corps. A protracted meeting of unabated interest was reported from Gordon's Brigade, in Early's Division. Thirty were praising God's free grace that snatched them from the jaws of death, and made them cling to and rejoice in the Cross, and large numbers were pressing forward and asking to see Jesus. How good is God! How blessed are such reports from men soon to march with martial tread to deal and receive fatal shot on the bloody field! How cheering is the thought that our liberties are defended by such soldiers!

"After devotional exercises we adjourned, to meet at the same place in two weeks at 11 o'clock, A. M.

"L. C. VASS, Permanent Clerk."

"CAMP, THIRD VIRGINIA INFANTRY,
"GREENVILLE, NORTH CAROLINA, April 7.
. . . "Already eighteen souls have been happily converted and brought to realize the inestimable value of a Saviour's love. And still the good work continues. Many are inquiring 'What must we do to be saved ? ' And we believe it will increase and extend its influence until many more are convinced of their lost and ruined condition and persuaded to fly for safety to Him who alone can save. Sinners have been convicted in their tents and compelled, as it were, to attend our meetings. Even the vilest sinners—some of whom almost denied the existence of a God, and who never blanched in the presence of the foe—have been made to tremble under the sense of guilt, and here, in the forest, are being converted to God under our feeble but *assiduous* efforts." . . .

"CAMP OF GORDON'S GEORGIA BRIGADE, April 23.
"Under date of March 21, I wrote you that we were enjoying a season of revival from the presence of the Lord. I write again, to say that since that time the gracious work has been steadily progressing among us. Our nightly meetings are still kept up, with most encouraging results. Almost every day witnesses the joyful conversion of some precious souls, and many are still anxiously asking, 'What must I do to be saved?' Since our meeting commenced we have baptized *fifty*, and on to-morrow we expect to baptize about *ten* others. About *one hundred* of the brigade have professed faith in Christ. We would render all the praise unto Him to whom belongeth salvation.

"A. B. WOODFIN,
" Chaplain Sixty-First Georgia Regiment."

"ORANGE COURT HOUSE, Tuesday, April 19.
. . . "In the past month God has been very gracious to our soldiers. He is pouring out in glorious copiousness His Holy Spirit upon them. It is not deemed prudent, at this time, to state with minuteness, the character and extent of this work of grace in different brigades, by name. Let it suffice to be known that in more than one-half of our brigades a mighty moral new organization is going on. Multitudes flock to the ministrations of the sanctuary; large numbers are declaring that sin is to them a burden, both heavy and hateful, and are crying out in

Rev. J. C. Hiden, D. D., of Virginia, entered the army as Chaplain in Wise's Legion, and afterwards became the efficient Post-Chaplain at Charlottesville. Since the war he has been Pastor of Baptist Churches at Portsmouth, Virginia, Wilmington, N. C., Greenville, S. C., Charlottesville, Va., Lexington, Ky., and New Bedford, Mass., and is regarded as one of the most scholarly men, effective preachers, graceful writers, and popular platform speakers in his denomination.

Rev. J. J. Hyman, Chaplain of the 49th Georgia Regiment, was one of the most laborious, self-denying, and successful Chaplains in the army, and he probably preached as many sermons, baptized as many men, and accomplished as much good as any other chaplain during his period of service. Since the war he has been the devoted and useful Pastor of Baptist Churches in Georgia.

Rev. T. Hume, Jr., D. D., after serving for a time in the field was the indefatigable, judicious, able, and very efficient Post-Chaplain at Petersburg where he stuck to his post to the end, and faithfully discharged his duties, despite shot and shell. He has been Pastor of the Baptist Church in Danville, Va., and of the Cumberland Street Church, Norfolk, has been Professor in the Roanoke Female College and the Norfolk Female College, and now, as Professor of English in the University of N. C., has made a reputation in his department second to no other in the country. He is also a chaste, tender, and effective preacher.

Rev. Dr. W. F. Broaddus was Post-Chaplain at Charlottesville, and one of the most efficient workers among the soldiers. Just after the war he did a grand work as Agent for the Education of Soldiers' Children. He was at different periods Pastor of Baptist Churches in Northern Virginia, Lexington, Ky., Charlottesville, Va., and Fredericksburg, Va., was the successful Principal of Female Colleges, was widely known as a most efficient agent, a popular preacher, and a noble man; and died universally lamented, and everywhere recognized as one of the most useful ministers of the Gospel whom God ever gave to the world.

Rev. J. B. Taylor, Sr., D. D., was Post-Chaplain at Richmond and threw into his work the zeal, wisdom, and consecrated tact which ever distinguished him. In early life he was Pastor of the Second Baptist Church of Richmond, Chaplain of the University of Virginia, and organizer and Pastor of the Grace Street Church, Richmond. But for forty years and up to his death, he was the able and efficient Corresponding Secretary of the Foreign Mission Board of the Southern Baptist Convention, while he was a leader in every enterprise of his denomination or of evangelical Christians.

Rev. R. Ryland, D. D., LL. D., was from its origin to the breaking out of the war the able and successful President of Richmond College, Va. He promptly began work in the Confederate hospitals as colporter, was afterwards made Post-Chaplain, and carried into his work the zeal of youth, combined with the ripened experience and wisdom of age. No laborer was more faithful or efficient. He was in active service up to his death and blessed the world with his clear thought, consecrated zeal, and pre-eminent common sense. For many years he was the devoted and beloved Pastor of the First African Church, Richmond, and no man ever did a nobler work among the negroes.

Rev. J. C. Hiden, D. D.,
Post Chap. at Charlottesville and
"Wise Legion."

Rev. J. J. Hyman,
Post Chap. 49th Ga. Regt.

Rev. T. Hume, Jr., D. D.,
Post Chaplain, Petersburg, Va.

Rev. W. F. Broaddus, D. D.,
Post Chaplain, Charlottesville, Va.

Rev. J. B. Taylor, Sr., D. D.,
Post Chaplain, Richmond, Va.

Rev. R. Ryland, D. D.,
Post Chaplain, Richmond, Va.

(Facing page 575.)

the depth of their sorrow and shame, 'God be merciful to me, a sinner.' Many are rejoicing in hope. Considerably over three hundred have professed conversion since we last assembled together. Neither men nor officers seem ashamed to stop their chaplain and tell him they want to talk about their soul's salvation. They are easily approached by the chaplain, and seem thankful for a tender word. One chaplain reported that in his brigade, the Christian officers would rise and publicly invite members of their commands to come and talk with them about their spiritual interests. In another brigade, a captain said to his company while they were on drill, 'I have led you in battle, and in paths of sin. Now I have given my heart to Christ, and I want to lead you, brave men, to this same Saviour. *Who is willing to follow me?*' Every man said he would try! The good work is progressing in our artillery. Such is the power of the Gospel of our Lord Jesus Christ. Thanks be unto God! After hearing such glad tidings, the meeting, led by the chairman, returned hearty thanks unto God for His signal mercy unto us. An interesting conversation arose as to the Church's prospect of a supply from the army for her ministry. More than twenty men, from the rank of colonel to that of private, were known to chaplains—then present—to have the ministry in view, and some were steadily prosecuting their studies. One man, who, twelve months ago, had no prospect of being of any value in the world, had been rescued from his death in sin through God's grace, had learned to read, and was working with much aptness for his Master's cause. Some of these persons possess very high abilities. The attention of all the chaplains was directed to the importance of seeking out among professors of religion, suitable men for the great work of preaching the Gospel.

" L. C. VASS, Permanent Clerk."

Brother J. A. Gresham, Wise's Brigade : "Our good meetings are still going on, with increased interest. Since their commencement, some eight or nine have professed religion—among them our captain; and others are asking the prayers of God's people. We have had no minister to aid us, except our chaplain. He has preached for us several times. He can't be with us often, on account of the scattered condition of our regiment. We have a large barn to hold our meetings in. We have three

Bible-classes, which meet every Sunday. After the school is over, we have prayer-meeting, and then again at night. We have also formed a Christian Association, which meets every Wednesday evening, at 7 o'clock. I cannot inform you of the condition of the regiment, on account of its being so scattered. There are no two companies together."

[Extracts from my letters to the *Christian Index:*]

On Friday last, I preached for Davis's Mississippi Brigade, now on picket at "Peyton's Ford," and in the afternoon led down into the "liquid grave" *twelve* young men who had given me the most satisfactory evidence of "repentance toward God and faith in the Lord Jesus Christ." The large congregation which lined the banks of the "Rapidan" was greatly moved, and I trust that the ordinance was blessed to the good of souls. The stream was very rapid (owing to the recent rains) and the whole scene vividly reminded me of those occasions upon which the great "forerunner" baptized soldiers in the rapid stream of Jordan. I was told by an old citizen, that about fifty years ago Mrs. General Madison (sister-in-law to the President) was baptized in the same place in the presence of a large crowd, of which the President was one. What would have been the feelings of the great expounder of the Constitution if he could have looked into the future and seen that at the same place, in fifty years, the ordinance of baptism would be administered to *Southern soldiers* in sight of the hostile lines of their "Northern brethren?"

The good work which I reported in this brigade some time ago still goes graciously on, though they have been temporarily deprived of their chapel and the services of their efficient chaplain. The private Christians are working and praying, and the Lord is abundantly blessing their efforts. And all through the army there are revivals—the chaplains and missionaries (alas! there are now but few of the latter) seem to appreciate the importance of getting as large a number as possible to accept the glad tidings ere the opening of the campaign. It adds materially to the solemn responsibilities of our preaching to remember, that in every congregation we probably address those who will fall in the impending battle. Everything portends an early move, if the protracted rains shall cease. Exactly *what* the move will be, I, of course, have no means of knowing, and would not say if I did. But this much I may say—recent preparations do not indicate on the part of "Marse Robert" any design of accommodating the Northern press by "evacuating Virginia." General Lee issued an order the other day, intimating that all lady visitors in the neighborhood of camp had best go to the rear as soon as practicable, and in accordance with the order every train is loaded with the wives of officers and soldiers who have been spending happy days with their loved ones. I have witnessed at the cars several parting scenes which touched me deeply. At the signal for the cars to start, manly frames choke with emotion, and helpless womanhood weeps bitter tears, at what may prove a final parting. Mrs. General —— veils her face that she may conceal from rude gazes the bitter anguish of a parting which may know no meeting again—while on the next seat the wife of some rough private sobs aloud as she parts from *her all* who may leave her and her little ones to the cold charities of the world.

Yesterday was the anniversary of the secession of Virginia and the first moving of the Virginia troops to the capture of Harper's Ferry, Norfolk, etc. Three years of carnage have passed by, many hearthstones of the "Old Dominion" have been polluted, her fields have been laid waste, blackened ruins mark where some of her proudest mansions stood, her sons have been slain, and her people draped in mourning; but thus far she has borne herself proudly amidst the battle-storm, and she now enters upon the fourth year of the war with the same stern resolve as when her "*Sic semper tyrannis*" first rung out defiance to the foe. What shall be the end of this year? Shall it terminate, or serve to indefinitely protract, the war? For myself, I have but one fear. I do not doubt the valor or the patient endurance of the army or the people at home. I only fear that we may "trust in an arm of flesh"—may look to Lee and Johnston instead of to the "Lord of hosts."

.   .   .   .   .   .

Our chaplains' meeting on last Tuesday was of more than usual interest, since the report elicited showed a very general revival throughout the army. Extensive revivals were reported in Kirkland's, Davis's, Cooke's, Harris's, Wright's, Perrin's, Scales's, Lane's, Stonewall, J. M. Jones's, Steuart's, Gordon's, Battle's and Daniels's Brigades and portions of the Artillery of both Corps, while in all of the brigades there was a very hopeful state of things. The Lord is evidently with us in these camps, and if we remain here for some days longer, there is every prospect of an even more glorious work than we had last summer and fall. A brother told of a captain in a Georgia regiment who had been a very wicked man, but who, on making a profession of religion, recently, called his company together and told them that they had followed him into many hard-fought battles—that he had also led them into sin, and that he now called upon them to follow him into the service in which he had just enlisted. A large proportion of that company have since professed conversion, and are following their brave captain as he follows Christ.

Another brother mentioned a fact, confirmed by others, that the gambling and profanity in his brigade was almost entirely confined to the *new recruits* fresh from home. This is but one of the many proofs that might be given to show that the usual demoralization incident to camp life is very greatly counteracted in our noble army.

And one of the most interesting facts elicited was, that in almost every brigade there are young brethren (many of them among the young converts) who have decided that, if the Lord spares them to the end of the war, they will devote themselves to the work of the Gospel ministry. Many of these are highly educated, and, before the war, were preparing themselves for, or actively engaged in, some secular calling. These young men should be remembered in the prayers of God's people all over the land, that the Lord would shield them in the hour of danger and prepare them by His Spirit for the glorious work of preaching the " glad tidings " of salvation—and earnest prayer should be made to the " Lord of the harvest" that He would raise up yet many more who, coming from this school of self-denial and privation, shall form a ministry more worthy than we to follow in the footsteps of the " people's preacher."

I had the privilege of baptizing *eleven* candidates again on yesterday—making *sixty-seven* that I have baptized within the past month. Rev. Dr. Burrows is again laboring in our camp, Rev. A. Broaddus, Sr., arrived on yesterday, and I learn that Rev. Dr. Jeter (who has recently spent several weeks of very successful labor in the artillery), and Rev. H. W. Dodge (pastor of our Church in Lynchburg, and one of the brightest ornaments of the Virginia Baptist pulpit), will be on in a few days to remain some time with us.

Can't you send us some of your best Georgia Baptist preachers? Brethren may think that I always "harp on one string," but I mean to harp on it until they remove the cause by coming up to our help in this great work.

We are having beautiful weather now, and the indications of an early move grow stronger daily. I saw a large number of ambulances this morning at the Medical Purveyor's office, loading with "stretchers," bandages, etc., to distribute amongst the brigades. Alas! that we should have need for so many of these!

J. W. J.

CAMP NEAR ORANGE COURT HOUSE, VIRGINIA, April 22, 1864.

From the date of the above letter to the opening of the campaign I was engaged in preaching every day in various commands, and witnessed many manifestations of God's presence and power. I met afterwards, in our field hospitals, several wounded men who told me that they had found Jesus in connection with my preaching just before the opening of the campaign, and some of the other chaplains told me of others who said the same, and some of the most triumphant deaths of which I heard were of those who found "Christ in the camp" along the Rapidan.

I was on a visit to my old seminary friends, Revs. Crawford H. Toy and W. L. Curry—having promised to aid them in a series of meetings—in their camp near Gordonsville, and I was just beginning a sermon to a large crowd of gallant Georgians when "the long roll" beat, the veterans fell in, and Longstreet's Corps was on the march for the battle of the Wilderness.

Omitting such letters as describe the battles and comment on army movements, I append several other extracts from my letters to the *Christian Index.*

· · · · · · ·

In my previous letters I have not said as much as I desired with reference to our hospital work. Of course, the frequent witnessing of such scenes has a tendency to blunt one's sensibilities, and yet it would be indeed a heart of steel that could remain untouched at the succession of woes constantly presented at our field hospitals. I have seen the old gray-haired sire anxiously pace to and fro as ambulance after ambulance brings in its mangled freight, and at last, perchance, his noble boy is borne in, or he learns that he has fallen on the gory field. I saw wounded the other day the last son of five noble boys, which a widowed mother had sent to the defence of the country. And then the groans of the poor fellows, as they bleed and die on the hard ground, with no mother, sister, or other loved one near to soothe their dying moments. But I turn from this part of the sad picture. I am glad to be able to say, that the arrangements for the comfort of our wounded are now much more complete than they have hitherto been. There are a larger number of ambulances, and a much better supply of hospital stores of every kind. And I bear willing testimony to the zeal and efficiency of most of our surgeons.

The "Richmond Ambulance Committee" has been near the army for over three weeks, rendering invaluable assistance to the wounded of every State. They are thoroughly organized, and a set of real working men who do not mind taking off their coats and pitching right into anything which can promote the comfort of our poor wounded fellows. Rev. Dr. Burrows is one of the most efficient members of the organization, and may be seen any day, with coat off and sleeves rolled up, carrying a bucket of soup or lifting a wounded man.

The results of the glorious revivals with which our army has been visited, have been manifested in the very large proportion of the wounded who express a calm confidence in Christ which renders them happy in their affliction. I have talked with poor fellows, dreadfully mangled and about to die, who were as composed and happy as if about to fall asleep under the parental roof. I met a noble young Georgia officer who, too badly wounded to talk, yet wrote me on a slip of paper, in answer to my inquiries: "My whole trust is in Christ, and I feel perfectly resigned to God's will. I am deeply grateful that it is no worse with me." Another noble boy, while breathing out his life, repeated over and over again, with childlike simplicity, "Jesus says, 'him that cometh unto me I will in no wise cast out,' and I have gone to Him, and know that He will be true to His word." But, alas! there are others who die as they have lived, "without God and without hope"—some of them in great agony of mind, but others with stoical indifference. But I must close, and follow our brave boys to other scenes of carnage and, I trust, to glorious victory.

.   .   .   .

I learned of another incident, strikingly illustrating the *military power of religion.* In a brigade of five regiments, where there has recently been a glorious revival, two of the regiments, which had not shared in the revival, broke, while the three which had been thus blessed stood firm, and changed a threatened disaster into a victory, which elicited the commendation of the higher officers, and will secure the promotion of the colonel commanding.

.   .   .   .

Despite unfavorable surroundings the men do not neglect their little prayer-meetings, and thus the good work goes on. On a large part of the line, however, we have regular preaching, and a good deal of interest is manifested in the services. In Bryan's and Wofford's Georgia, Kershaw's South Carolina, and several other brigades, there are revivals of deep interest. Indeed, we might look for a very general revival throughout the army if the position of all the troops would admit of regular labor amongst them, and we had laborers to enter the glorious harvest.

.   .   .   .   .

The past few weeks have been very unfavorable for religious services, as the weather has been too cold for outdoor exercises, and but few chapels have been completed, owing to scarcity of timber and transportation. I refer in this remark to the lines south of the Appomattox. Between the Appomattox and the James, and north of the James too (I believe), every brigade have one or more chapels, and there have been very decided manifestations of the revival spirit. In some of the brigades they are enjoying precious seasons of revival. A number of chapels have been completed on our part of the lines, others are in process of erection, and we are hoping for a like visitation of God's Spirit. Indeed, we have not been without manifestations of His goodness, but every week there have been a few to find peace in believing—the first droppings, we trust, of the copious shower in store for us. The prayer-meetings, Bible-classes, schools, etc., of last winter have been revived, and bid fair to be as interesting and profitable as then. Alas! it is sad to miss so many of those who last winter were the leaders in these enterprises; but it is sweet to think of them as now engaged in more blest employ, away from the sufferings of earth, and free from "war's rude alarms." We shall need now larger supplies of religious reading matter, and it is hoped that the good brethren of Georgia will offer freely of what Sherman has not taken, to send the *Index* to our brave soldiers. Our Virginia Baptist Colportage Board, now that our Southern communications are so liable to interruption, and the railroads are impressed by the Government, will have to supply a larger proportion than ever of the religious reading and the preachers of this army; and as the funds of the board are running low it is to be hoped that our Georgia brethren will give liberally, of their means to help it send the Gospel to their sons and brothers in this army. I am sure that Brother Boykin (while Brother Wharton is in Virginia) will gladly receive and forward any contributions that may be sent him for this object. Brethren, whose homes have not been molested by the enemy, should send large *thank offerings*, and those who have lost, or are liable to lose by the enemy, should imitate the example of a good brother, who, after the enemy had robbed him of nearly everything he had, sent Brother Dickinson one hundred dollars for the soldiers, with the request that he would at least make a safe investment of that.

.   .   .   .

The religious interest in the army has been on the increase for the past few weeks, and many of the brigades are enjoying revivals. I had the pleasure of baptizing, the other day, in a pond between our line of battle and our picket line, and in full view of the enemy. The ceremony was solemn and impressive, and I trust that it was blessed to the good of the congregation.

The Rev. Dr. Armstrong, who was so long a victim of "Beast" Butler's cruelty in Norfolk, has come to this army as Presbyterian minister to A. P. Hill's Corps. He has been regarded as one of the ablest men in the denomination, and will yet find in the army an ample field for his talents.

.   .   .   .

There have been certain changes in our lines within the past week which have lessened the opportunites for preaching (or rather the number of regiments that may be assembled for preaching), and the details for picket duty, work on our fortifications, mining, etc., are very heavy; but the prayer-meetings are regularly kept up in most of the regiments, and in those brigades where it is practicable to have preaching the chaplains are working faithfully.

I say *chaplains*, for I know of but *two* missionaries now present in this whole army. Those good brethren who resolved at the Georgia Baptist Convention that governmental chaplaincies were wrong, and they would do the work of army evangelization as voluntary missionaries, must all have gone to General Hood's army. I have seen none of them here, though I constantly hear as I go amongst Georgia troops, "you are the only Baptist preacher I have seen in a long time."

There are very interesting revivals in Bryan's, Wofford's Thomas's, and Wright's Georgia Brigades, as also in several brigades from other States. I wish that some of the good Baptist brethren of Georgia, who are preaching two or three times per month to small congregations, could witness such a scene as I witnessed at Wright's Georgia Brigade last night. Assembled on the ramparts and on the outside of the trenches, was an immense congregation whose upturned faces showed in the moonbeams, listening eagerly to the truth as the preacher urged an immediate attention to the claims of the Gospel, and when he ceased, and the usual invitation was given, an old familiar hymn rose clear and strong from the great *heart* of the congregation, and about one hundred young men came forward for prayer, as calmly, but as determinedly as if they were marching to meet their country's foe. And then there rose the voice of prayer in which the whole congregation seemed to join in heart. Some words of counsel were spoken, a parting hymn sung, and the congregation dismissed, only to crowd around the preacher, who had papers, tracts and Testaments to distribute, with as much eagerness to get the little treasures as if they were diamonds, rubies, or gold. This is a scene of nightly occurrence. And yet this brigade, from the heart of Georgia, and so largely Baptistic in sentiment, that a large mass of its converts (I learn) desire to connect themselves with Baptist Churches, has never had a Baptist chaplain or permanent missionary. Is there no earnest, working brother among the large Baptist ministry of Georgia who is willing to come and labor among these brave men? The chaplains connected with the brigade are faithful men, but they themselves join in the general wish that there should also be a Baptist laborer among them.

Brother Curry, of Bryan's Brigade, and Brother Hyman, of Thomas's Brigade, have baptized a number recently, and I expect to baptize a number in Wright's Brigade in a few days.

. . . .

A large part of our army is so situated now that religious services are entirely practicable, and the brethren are improving the opportunity. In riding along the trenches about sundown, one sees, almost every hundred yards, a company of worshippers, met either to hear a sermon or to engage in the prayer-meeting.

While preaching the other evening, I heard from where I stood the voice of three other ministers, and the songs of several prayer-meetings. But then in other parts of the line there is an eager desire to have preaching, but no preacher to meet the demand. A number of the brigades are enjoying interesting revivals. Brother Hyman, of the Forty-ninth Georgia, has recently baptized thirty in Thomas's Brigade. I have baptized eight in Wright's Brigade, and other brethren have baptized a number. A number of others have connected themselves with other denominations. The cry is still for more earnest, permanent preachers—men who can and will stick to their posts in cloud as well as sunshine.

 . . . .

The religious interest in the army is on the increase, and only an opportunity for regular and uninterrupted services and more faithful laborers are wanted, that the glorious scenes witnessed on the Rapidan may be re-enacted here. Even amid the adverse circumstances which surround us, the revival spirit is kept alive and many souls are being "born again" in the trenches. It is of nightly occurrence to see a large crowd assembled in the trenches for preaching, and I have not within the past two months seen an invitation for inquirers to come forward for prayer, that there were not at least a few and often large numbers to avail themselves of it. I witnessed, last Sunday afternoon, a beautiful baptismal scene. Assembled on the bank of a little pond just in the rear of the trenches was a large crowd of bronzed veterans from Virginia, South Carolina and North Carolina. The great heart of the congregation united in singing, "People of the living God;" some passages of Scripture bearing on the ordinance were read, and prayer offered for the presence and blessing of the Master, and then, as "Am I a soldier of the Cross?" was sung "with the spirit and understanding," Brother W. B. Carson, chaplain of the Fourteenth South Carolina, led the willing converts "down into the water" and "buried" them with Christ in baptism. Brother J. J. D. Renfroe, of the Tenth Alabama Regiment, has baptized a number recently in his own brigade and in Law's. Other brethren are frequently doing the same, and numbers of young converts are uniting with other denominations. I have not heard from Thomas's or Wright's Georgia Brigade recently, but presume that the good work still goes on in these brigades.

Rev. J. C. Granberry, Methodist missionary to Hill's Corps (and, by the way, one of the ablest preachers and most efficient workers I know), has, within the past two Sabbaths, preached on army missions and taken up collections at Washington street and Market street Methodist Churches, Petersburg. At the former he secured five thousand and at the latter seven thousand dollars—a liberal contribution, when we remember the circumstances which surround these churches; and some of our more highly-favored brethren who " eat the bread of quietness," would do well to imitate this noble example in sending the Gospel to our brave soldiers. Our Virginia Baptist Colportage Board is in need of funds to carry on its work, and, as it has never regarded State lines in the prosecution of its work in the army, but has sent its colporters and missionaries and distributed its publications amongst the troops of all States alike, it has claims upon the brethren of Georgia which have not been and will not be disregarded.

. . . .

The people of Petersburg are bearing themselves nobly in this crisis in their history; there is nothing like a panic, but the men have shouldered their muskets determined to defend their homes to the last, and the women (God bless them) are devoting themselves nobly to the relief of our sick and wounded. I was at a hospital the other day from which the wounded were being removed because of the shelling, and saw a number of ladies bearing delicacies to our poor fellows and ministering with the utmost tenderness to their wants, regardless of the missiles of death which the foe was hurling at them. On yesterday (Saturday) most of the churches were opened, and Yankee shells mingled their discordant notes with the songs of praise. Save this continued shelling all was quiet along the lines on yesterday, and it was my privilege to spend the day in the trenches " breaking the bread of life" to our brave boys who crowded to hear the Gospel, and receive the large number of *Indexes* which I fortunately had for distribution. As I passed through the hospital the other day a gallant Georgia officer recognized the *Index* in my hand, called to me for one, and seemed as glad to get it as if he had just met a friend from home.

25   J. W. J.

The following is an extract from a letter of an officer of the Eighteenth Virginia Cavalry, Imboden's Brigade. It refers to the fight of General Imboden, before the main battle near New Market: "Before the charge, and while we were in line, the command to dismount was given, when our noble chaplain sang a hymn and then prayed, the whole regiment kneeling. It was a solemn and impressive sight just on the eve of battle, and God blessed our arms with victory. The chaplain prayed that if it should please God we might scatter our enemies, but oh! preserve the lives of those dear ones, and prolong them for Thy glory. Truly did God answer the prayer of the devout old man—they were scattered to the four winds, and we lost not a man."

A writer from the Army of Northern Virginia, when the present campaign had been in progress twenty-one days, said: "Frequent prayer-meetings have been held in the trenches; and even on the advance skirmish line, within easy musket range of the enemy, the song of praise and the voice of supplication have been heard. Sermons have also been preached in the trenches—albeit, they have sometimes been cut short by the bursting of the shell or the whistling of the minnie."

"Rev. Dr. Burrows baptized twenty-two soldiers at Chaffin's Bluff, a week or two since."

"RICHMOND, VIRGINIA, Jan. 1, 1865.

"We are receiving some very refreshing accounts of the work of grace in the army from our missionaries:

"Rev. P. H. Fontaine reports the baptism of fifty soldiers.

"Rev. Harvey Hatcher has held several very interesting meetings, in which some seventy souls professed faith in Christ. Brother Hatcher is employed by the board to visit destitute regiments and battalions. He is eminently adapted to army work.

Brother R. W. Cridlin, of the Thirty-eighth Virginia, has been greatly blessed. A large proportion of his regiment have made a profession of faith in Christ since Brother Cridlin has been connected with it.

"Rev. A. Broaddus has recently spent two weeks in protracted meetings in Charlottesville, in which forty persons professed conversion. Rev. J. Wm. Jones has baptized within twelve months *two hundred and twenty-two soldiers.*

"Rev. T. Hume, of Petersburg, writes as follows: I have baptized here, and in adjacent parts, during the past six months, fifty-four—mostly young men of great promise. Some now are awaiting baptism, and not a few scattered about in the trenches and hospitals are earnest seekers after salvation.'

"A. E. D."

CAMP NEAR PETERSBURG, January 2.

. . . The very active campaign in which the "Army of the Valley" has been engaged has been very unfavorable to religious services, and, I regret to add, a number of chaplains have resigned; but, as we were blessed with fine weather during my stay, I found every day large and attentive congregations, and witnessed some indications that the revival spirit had not died out, but only wanted favorable influences to fan the spark into a flame. The Second Corps has now gone into winter-quarters (no matter where), and, under the encouragement of their Christian commander (General John B. Gordon), chapels are being built in most of the camps, and it is to be hoped that a very decided religious influence will prevail this winter. But they greatly need more preachers. I was indebted for transportation, from Staunton to the army and back, to Brother C. F. Fry, one of the most efficient colporters of our Virginia Baptist Board. Brother Fry has a little covered wagon admirably arranged for carrying his tracts, books, rations, forage, etc., in which he kindly took me. For several days in Staunton I enjoyed the hospitality of Brother Geo. B. Taylor. Besides the duties of his pastorate, Brother Taylor is doing a great work in the Staunton hospitals.

OCCASIONAL.

"APPLEWOOD, December 31, 1864.

"To-day closes the eventful year 1864! Reflections crowd the memory almost to stupefaction. Faith and patience have their amplest verge, piety and patriotism their widest scope, in our present condition. Not unlike the Israelites, we are passing through 'darkness drear' to better and brighter prospects beyond. Among the memories of the past my mind rests upon the close of 1863. Then in prison on Johnston's Island we thought it not unfitting to spend the day in religious observances. The 103d Psalm was read and briefly commented on. Officers, *not preachers*, spoke gratefully of the mercy of God to them in blessing their imprisonment. Fifteen had professed faith in Christ. Twenty others gave the hand in pledge of a new life. It was a holy, blessed day to the souls of many, though the body was shut up in close imprisonment. We could all thank God for the freedom of the soul, and for *soul religion*. Among the converts was Lieutenant Wm. J. Read, of Tennessee, son of Dr. Read, missionary of the Baptist Central Foreign Missions to Siam. From this time the work spread till there was a great revival among the officers imprisoned there. There were many religious men among the officers. There were 13 preachers among them—6 Baptist, 6 Methodist and 1 Episcopalian. There were 102 Baptists, 95 Methodists, 45 Presbyterians, 37 Episcopalians, a few Catholics, Lutherans, Jews, and others who had a religion of some sort, among the prisoners, and over 100 professed during the winter, spring and summer. Thus God sanctifies sufferings and overrules the wrath of man. There is a pleasant state of religious feeling in the Twenty-fourth Regiment, Virginia Cavalry. We have occasional preaching and frequent prayer-meetings among the young men. They conduct them almost exclusively. We have several who exercise a public gift in speaking. When our chapel is completed we hope to have a protracted meeting. We have seen a good deal of hard service this summer; and since the 7th of October my squadron has been engaged in five severe battles and three or four skirmishes. I got four men slightly wounded, but not one killed. The regiment, in the same engagement, got four killed and six wounded. Considering how hard the fighting has been, the imminent perils through which we have passed, the many narrow escapes we have had, I most freely and gladly acknowledge the good hand of the Lord was with us. In the future it is easy to foresee the path of peril and blood before us. My speech to my men, in the presence of the enemy, is, '*There are the Yankees, boys—our cause is just—trust in God, and charge them.*' This has been my motto, and I expect it to be so long as I find the Yankees the avowed enemies of my country's freedom.

" L. W. ALLEN."

A correspondent of the *Biblical Recorder* mentions a Confederate captain, who in his company, composed of volunteers and conscripts from different section of the country, has had no man charged with stealing and no deserter since the war began—a fact due to his instruction that "pressing" is stealing, and "running blockade" equivalent to desertion; while, because of his discountenance of the vices of gambling, drunkenness and profanity, not one plays cards or ever gets intoxicated, and only two swear and they very seldom. When not on duty they spend their time in prayer-meetings, in singing and innocent amusements; and a large majority have become church-members.

"CAMP NEAR PETERSBURG, February 5, 1865.
"God has bestowed on my regiment a rich blessing. Sixteen converts have been added to the different religious denominations, several backsliders have been reclaimed, and many are still inquiring with mournful hearts the way to heaven. The prospect is good and the people of God are in the harness laboring for the salvation of souls. Our meeting is still in progress. Pray for us.
"E. B. BARRETT, Chaplain Forty-fifth Georgia Regiment."

How the memories of those days crowd upon me, as I sit in my quiet study twenty-three years after those stirring scenes. Those bright days before the opening of the campaign, when our camps were vocal with God's praises and hundreds of our brave boys were turning to the Lord—those days of constant battle, carnage, death, when Lee withstood Grant's overwhelming force from the Wilderness to Cold Harbor, and from Cold Harbor to Petersburg, and left *hors de combat* more of "General Grant's people" than he himself had—those long, weary days in forty miles of entrenchments, when the "men in gray" were "worn away by attrition," and "the thin line was stretched until it broke"—and amid it all the precious seasons of worship, the realization of the presence and blessing of Jesus, and the assurance that God's Spirit was ever present in His convicting, converting, sanctifying power. I try to forget the "bitter memories of a stormy past," but the hallowed associations that cluster around "Christ in the camp," on the march, in the bivouac, on the battle-field, in the trenches, in the hospital, in life, in death—*these* linger forever, "a sweet savor" in my memory. God be praised for what our eyes saw, our ears heard, and our hearts felt of His presence and power during that memorable campaign of 1864–65.

CHAPTER XIII.

FROM the minutes of our Chaplains' Association (now in my possession, by the kind courtesy of the accomplished secretary and chaplain, Rev. L. C. Vass), the estimate of other chaplains and missionaries in position to know, and a very careful compilation of facts and figures from files of religious newspapers, and hundreds of letters and narratives from chaplains, missionaries, and colporters, I make the following estimate of the number of men in the Army of Northern Virginia who professed faith in Christ during the four years of its existence. During the fall and winter of 1862–63, and spring of 1863, there were at least 1,500 professions. From August, 1863, to the 1st of January, 1864, at least 5,000 found peace in believing. From January, 1864, to the opening of the Wilderness campaign, at least 2,000 more were added to this number. And from May, 1864, to April, 1865, it is a low estimate to put the number of converts at 4,000.

Add to these figures at least 2,500 who, during the war, found Jesus in the hospitals, at home, or in Northern prisons (for Christ was in the prisons, and there were some precious revivals at Point Lookout, Fort Delaware, Elmira, Johnson's Island, and other points), and we have a grand total of at least 15,000 soldiers of Lee's army who professed faith in Jesus during the four years of the war.

Rev. Dr. Bennett ("Great Revival in the Southern Armies," page 413) makes the following estimate of the number of conversions in all of the Confederate armies :

"Up to January, 1865, it was estimated that nearly *one hundred and fifty thousand* soldiers had been converted during the progress of the war, and it was believed that fully one-third of all the soldiers in the field were praying men, and members of some branch of the Christian Church. A large proportion of the higher officers were men of faith and prayer, and many others, though not professedly religious, were moral and respectful to all the religious services, and confessed the value of the revival in promoting the efficiency of the army."

If these figures are correct, then the estimate for Lee's army ought to be increased to at least 50,000, as fully one-third of the converts were in that army. I am fully satisfied that my own estimate is too low (there were, of course, many professions of conversion which were never reported at all, but "whose record is on high,") but I have been very anxious in all of the statements I have made about this great work *not to exaggerate in the least*, and I have, therefore, preferred to *underestimate* rather than to risk *overestimating* these grand results.

What a noble band of recruits for the army of the Lord! Was not "Christ in the camp" a vital, real power; and was not our camp indeed "a school of Christ?"

But figures cannot, of course, give a tithe of the results of a great revival. The bringing back of backsliders, the quickening of the zeal, and faith, and general consecration of God's people, the comfort, the joy, the peace, the strength for hardships, privations, sufferings, trials, temptations—*these* cannot be *counted*, but are really of far more value than mere numbers of professed converts. Add to all this, the joy and gladness which these revivals carried to "loved ones at home" who were wont to spend sleepless nights thinking of, and praying for the soldier boy at the front, and the reflex influence upon the Churches, many of which were blessed with great revivals, directly traceable to our army work, and eternity alone will be able to estimate the glorious results of these army revivals.

But I will be asked—have been asked—"Was this a *genuine* and *permanent* work of grace? Was it not a mere animal excitement produced by the dangers to which the men were exposed, and liable to pass off when those dangers were removed? Are not the accounts of this army work exaggerated? Was not there an abounding wickedness in the army, even to the close of the war?"

Most certainly there was. I have been very unfortunate if, in endeavoring to portray vividly the power of religion in Lee's army, I have been understood as representing that the millennium dawned upon us, or that wickedness and vice were entirely banished from our camps. Far from it.

It was not uncommon, even during our most powerful revivals, to see a party playing cards not far from where the preacher stood, and to hear the profane oath or the vulgar jest as you came from the place of prayer, and visitors would be, naturally, greatly shocked at this state of things.

But I suspect that during the most powerful revivals in our towns and cities, now, precisely the same state of things constantly exists, only green blinds or stained glass hide the view, and church walls obstruct the sound. In the camps all was open, and could be seen and heard.

There is no doubt that many of the professions of religion in the army were spurious. This has been true in every revival—from the days of Judas Iscariot and Simon Magus—and it was not to be expected that our army work would prove an exception.

And yet I do not hesitate to affirm—and think that I can abundantly prove—that the revivals in our camps were as genuine works of grace as any that occur in our churches at home—that as large a proportion of the converts proved the reality of their professions as in any revivals which the world ever saw. I content myself with this calm statement, though I believe that the facts would justify my putting it much more strongly.

The very material of which our congregations were composed was a safeguard against undue animal excitement in the meetings.

We had not women and children, but *men* to deal with—men who were accustomed to go into the "leaden and iron hail of battle," and to face death every day, and who could not have been "scared into religion," even if the preachers had tried to do so.

Besides, there were ministers of every denomination and of different temperaments co-operating together, and if one were disposed to get up any undue excitement, or to use improper "machinery," another would have restrained him.

The Old School Synod of Virginia, in its "Narrative of the State of Religion," says: "The history of the world and of the Church presents few things more extraordinary than the work of God in the army. An army has generally been considered a school of vice. It is the very profession of a soldier to kill and destroy. How can the sensibilities fail to be hardened, and the moral perceptions to be blunted? Removed from the happy influences of the Church, and from the refining, sustaining, elevating society of wife, mother, sister, at home; living a life now of great excitement, and now of dangerous leisure, the soldier, it was supposed, had little chance of being saved. It was fully as much as could be reasonably expected, if those who professed the name of Christ did not fall away, and make shipwreck of their profession. But the extraordinary spectacle is now presented to us, of an army in which there is more zeal, apparently, for God and the salvation of sinners, than there is in the Church at home. Making all due allowance for unconscious exaggeration in the statements which come to us, and discounting not a few cases of spurious conversions, there can be no doubt that the valley of Achor has become a door of hope to our brethren in the field, and that a very large number of them have been turned unto God."

The Southern Baptist Convention, at its session for 1863, adopted the following resolutions:

"*Resolved*, That it is the sense of this body, that the field opened in the army for pious labor is one of the most important that can be opened at present; and that the providence of God calls loudly on His people to make prompt and vigorous efforts to secure the services of chaplains, and to send forth missionaries and colporters into the field.

"*Resolved*, That the pastors of our churches be, and are hereby, earnestly requested to bring this subject prominently and frequently to the attention of their people; and also the duty of constant supplication of the Divine blessing upon such labors among our soldiers, that we may be obedient to the sacred command, 'Whatsoever thy hand findeth to do, do it with thy might.'"

The Virginia Baptist General Association, the Virginia Methodist Conference, the Virginia Episcopal Council, and other religious bodies bore testimony even more emphatic, and I might quote from some of the most distinguished ministers of all of the evangelical denominations as to the extent, power and genuineness of this great work.

Rev. B. T. Lacy, missionary chaplain in Jackson's Corps, in an address before his Synod, said, in speaking of the genuineness of the revival work in the army:

" In this matter there is one safeguard in the camp. They are all grown *men;* even the sick are away in the hospitals. Most of the elements are absent upon which mere enthusiasm operates.

He was satisfied the ordinary evil results from religious excitements are less in the army than at home."

Rev. Dr. Theodorick Pryor, of the Presbyterian Church, who labored in the army with great ability and a burning zeal which younger men might covet, thus gives his impressions of the work:

"Whilst with the army (a period of about two years) my impressions were most favorable as to the influence and effect of religious truth. It appeared to me that during a career of ministerial experience extending through thirty-four years I had never witnessed more precious seasons of grace, or more signal displays of Divine mercy, than it was my privilege to witness in the army. . . . Never before was it my privilege to preach to as large congregations, or to congregations more respectful in deportment, more serious, and upon whom the truth of God seemed to have more marked power and effect."

I might quote pages of testimony to the same effect from leading representatives of all of the evangelical denominations.

But, after all, the best evidence of the genuineness of the revival is to be found in the *after lives* of professed Christians, and of the young converts.

That revival which does not result in more consecration on the part of Christians, and a "godly walk and conversation" on the part of the new converts, is not worth calling a revival.

I might cite hundreds of cases that came under my own observation where lukewarm, careless Christians were stirred up to their duty, and made more zealous and efficient workers for Christ than ever before.

I recall the case of a young lawyer who had borne an outwardly consistent character since he had united with the Church some years before the war, but who (although a ready speaker at the bar or on the hustings) could never be induced to lead a prayer-meeting, open a Sunday-school, or conduct family worship—fluent and eloquent for client or party, but dumb when asked to speak for Christ.

For some time after joining the army his chaplain urged him in vain to take an active part in the meetings. But after his heart was touched by the power of one of the revivals, and just after a great battle, he came to the chaplain and said: "I wish you would call on me to lead in prayer at the meeting to-night. I have been persuading myself that it was not my duty, but I have been recently led to think that I might be wrong, and as I saw my men fall around me to-day (he was captain of one of the companies) I was made to feel keenly that I had not exerted over them the influence which I ought to have done, and to register a solemn vow that if God would spare me I would be more faithful in the future."

He became henceforth one of the most active, useful Christian officers in the army, was spared through the war, and is to-day one of the most efficient laymen in Virginia.

I recall a captain from one of the Southern States who became one of the leading workers in his brigade, and who since the war has been one of the most actively useful and one of the most liberal contributors to every good object of all of the laymen in his State. And yet I learn he was of so little account to his Church, so careless in meeting his Church duties, before he entered the army, that the Church was thinking seriously of excluding him from her fellowship.

The *Southern Presbyterian* gives the following concerning Colonel Lewis Minor Coleman, of whom I have already had an extended notice.

" The following statement by the Richmond correspondent of the *Christian Index* is only one instance of what may be many times repeated, if we but have faith in God and do not stint our prayers. Out of the army and from the bloody battle-field God will raise up faithful servants and able preachers of the precious Gospel.

" This recalls a fact of which I had designed to speak some time since. The Christian character of Lieutenant-Colonel L. M. Coleman, formerly professor of Latin in the University of Virginia, was wonderfully developed by the war. Before going into the field, notwithstanding his rare mental gifts, he was undemonstrative and retiring in religious matters, shrinking even from public prayer, and scarcely, if ever, rising to the boldness of an exhortation. But thrown among his men, under circumstances which would have left them without the means of grace if he had not broken the thrall of this silence, he rose to the height of the occasion; and in the camp, on the march, whatever the weather, he was found at reveille in front of his company, with eloquent prayer invoking the blessing and aid of Almighty God on them and their undertaking. He became a minister in everything except the accidents of the office—licensure and ordination—and he had decided, if his life were spared until the return of peace, to take his place among the 'legates of the skies' in the Baptist pulpit. Here, then, was one *educated by the Holy Spirit, for the ministry, in the school of this war.* Why may we not look with hopeful eyes to the army, therefore, as a sphere of triumph for the Gospel, where believers may be edified in the faith, and faith, the gift of God, may be imparted to sinners?"

General C. A. Evans, of Georgia (the gallant and accomplished soldier who succeeded General Gordon in his brigade and then in his division), was a leading lawyer before the war, but became very active as a Christian in the army, and was gradually led to decide that he would become a preacher of the Gospel if spared to see the close of the war.

When on a visit to Athens, Georgia, in 1869, it was my privilege to find him pastor of the Methodist Church there, to fill his pulpit, to renew at his hospitable board the Christian friendship formed in the camp, and to learn from him that three others of his military family had consecrated themselves to the work of preaching the Gospel. General Evans is now one of the leading preachers in his Church.

There were reported at one of our chaplains' meetings *twenty* soldiers—from the rank of colonel down—who had determined to preach. I received from our colleges and theological seminaries in 1866 some very striking statistics as to the large number of soldiers who were entering the ministry—and I have strong reasons for the statement that a very large proportion of our evangelical preachers, under sixty and over thirty-five, at the South, learned in the army to "endure hardness as good soldiers of Jesus Christ."

And certainly a very large proportion of our most efficient church-members within the past twenty years have been those who found " Christ in the camp," or had the pure gold of their Christian character refined and purified by the fiery trials through which they were called to pass. Rev. Dr. Richard Hugh Bagby, of Bruington, Virginia, told me that of twenty-seven members of his Church, who returned at the close of the war, *all save two came back more earnest Christians and more efficient church-members than they had ever been,* and many other pastors have borne similar testimony.

A recent letter from a gallant soldier and active Christian worker in the noble little State of South Carolina tells me of the two most active and useful laymen in his section, who found "Christ in the camp," and in travelling all over the South I have found illustrations of this in well-nigh every community which I have visited.

And certainly the young converts, while in camp, met admirably all of the tests of genuine conversion. Let me cull only a few illustrations from a large mass of material in my possession. I remember one night in Hays's Louisiana Brigade one of the most gallant, popular and influential captains in the command professed conversion, and a few minutes afterwards I whispered to him, while we were singing, that I should call on him to lead in prayer as soon as we finished the hymn. He at once replied : "It would be a great trial for me to do so before this vast crowd of my old comrades, but if you think I ought to lead in prayer, I will do the best I can." I have rarely heard a more appropriate, tender and every way effective prayer than he made. As I have before remarked, I heard hundreds of these young converts called on to lead in prayer and never knew of one who refused.

And I have heard a number of chaplains bear emphatic testimony to the same effect. Indeed our army converts seemed to take it for granted that instead of being *dumb* Christians, they were to take up their cross at once in leading in prayer, and in speaking for Christ in the meetings.

They used to have brigade prayer-meetings, regiment prayer-meetings, company prayer-meetings and mess prayer-meetings, and prayer-meetings to prepare for prayer-meetings, until one of our missionaries (Rev. J. E. Chambliss) reported to our Chaplains' Association that he could find no time in Davis's Mississippi Brigade to preach without conflicting with some prayer-meeting.

I have incidentally illustrated the earnestness with which these young converts went to work to lead their comrades to Christ, and have space here for only one more illustration of this point.

In Gordon's Georgia Brigade (in a meeting conducted by my friend and brother, Dr. A. B. Woodfin, who was one of our most efficient chaplains and was greatly blessed in his work) there professed conversion one night a captain, who was known as one of "the bravest of the brave" in that brigade of heroes, and at the same time as one of the most wicked men in the army. After the meeting was over he went back to his quarters rejoicing in his new-found hope, called his company around him, and with deep emotion made them a little talk to this effect: "Men, I have led you into many a battle, and you have followed me like men. Alas! I have led you into all manner of wickedness and vice, and you have followed me in this too. I have now resolved to change my course. I have gone to Christ in sincere repentance and simple faith. I have enlisted under the banner of the Cross, and mean, by God's help, to prove a faithful soldier of Jesus as I have been a true soldier of my country.

"I call upon you, my brave boys, to follow me as I shall try to follow 'the Captain of our salvation,' and I want all who are willing to do so to come, here and now, and give me their hands and let me pray for them."

It is hardly necessary to add that the effect was electrical. The men crowded around their loved captain, tears flowed freely, earnest prayers were offered, and the brave fellow continued his personal efforts until nearly every member of his company had found Jesus, and those former ringleaders in every species of vice had become a centre of powerful influence for the religious good of their regiment and brigade.

One of the most potent instrumentalities in our work was the *personal activity* of the young converts, and I could easily fill pages with illustrations of this.

I believe that a willingness to give of one's substance for the good of others is a test of genuine conversion, and that we should doubt the reality of that man's religion who (if properly instructed in his duty) always has money to squander on himself and never a dime for the cause of benevolence or God's suffering poor. I have never seen more princely liberality than among these Christian soldiers. I have some old subscription papers—for regimental library, for tracts, Bibles and religious newspapers, for the Fredericksburg sufferers, and other benevolent objects—which show on the part of these men a self-sacrificing liberality which would put to shame any Church in the land to-day.

In the winter of 1863–64 the Young Men's Christian Association of Posey's (afterwards Harris's) Mississippi Brigade led off in a movement which was followed by a number of other brigades, and deserves to be written in letters of gold on one of the brightest pages of our country's history. They solemnly resolved *to fast one day in every week in order that they might send that day's rations to the suffering poor of the city of Richmond.* Think of it, church-members, who, in these days of plenty, plead poverty as an excuse for giving nothing to the cause of Christ; here were these poor soldiers (away from home, and many of them cut off from all communication with home), receiving only eleven dollars per month *in Confederate currency*, never getting more than half rations, and very frequently not that, voluntarily *fasting one day in the week* (poor fellows, they were often compelled to fast) in order to send that day's rations to God's poor in the city, for whose defence they were so freely and so heroically offering and sacrificing their lives.

How easily church edifices could be built, pastors supported, missionaries sustained, colleges endowed, and every good cause pushed forward, if we had in our Churches to-day anything like the spirit of these Christian soldiers.

How often have I seen these brave fellows, after they had won a hardly contested field, despite their almost complete exhaustion, going over the ground to hunt up and care for the wounded of the enemy—binding up their wounds as best they could, carrying them to the field-hospitals, and providing surgical attendance, sharing with them their scant rations, bringing them water, building brush shelters to protect them from the sun, and proving " good Samaritans " indeed to men whom they had so lately met in the shock of battle.

I might give scores of illustrations of this point, but must content myself now with the story of *Richard Kirkland,* " *the humane hero of Fredericksburg,*" as it is told by the gallant soldier and able jurist, General J. B. Kershaw, of South Carolina (now Judge Kershaw), who commanded the brigade at the time. I will only premise that Kirkland had professed conversion but a short time before, and will give the incident in General Kershaw's own eloquent words:

" CAMDEN, SOUTH CAROLINA, January 29, 1880.

"*To the Editor of the News and Courier:* Your Columbia correspondent referred to the incident narrated here, telling the story as 'twas told to him, and inviting corrections. As such a deed should be recorded in the rigid simplicity of actual truth, I take the liberty of sending you for publication an accurate account of a transaction every feature of which is indelibly impressed upon my memory. Very truly yours,
" J. B. KERSHAW."

"Richard Kirkland was the son of John Kirkland, an estimable citizen of Kershaw county, a plain, substantial farmer of the olden time. In 1861 he entered, as a private, Captain J. D. Kennedy's Company (E) of the Second South Carolina Volunteers, in which company he was a sergeant in December, 1862.

"The day after the sanguinary battle of Fredericksburg, Kershaw's Brigade occupied the road at the foot of Marye's hill and the ground about Marye's house, the scene of their desperate defence of the day before. One hundred and fifty yards in front of the road, the stone-facing of which constituted the famous stone wall, lay Syke's Division of Regulars, United States Army, between whom and our troops a murderous skirmish occupied the whole day, fatal to many who heedlessly exposed themselves, even for a moment. The ground between the lines was bridged with the wounded, dead, and dying Federals, victims of the many desperate and gallant assaults of that column of 30,000 brave men hurled vainly against that impregnable position.

"All that day those wounded men rent the air with their groans and their agonizing cries of 'Water! water!' In the afternoon the general sat in the north room, up-stairs, of Mrs. Stevens's house, in front of the road, surveying the field, when Kirkland came up. With an expression of indignant remonstrance pervading his person, his manner, and the tone of his voice, he said: 'General! I can't stand this.'

"'What is the matter, sergeant?' asked the general.

"He replied: 'All night and all day I have heard those poor people crying for water, and I can stand it no longer. I come to ask permission to go and give them water.'

"The general regarded him for a moment with feelings of profound admiration, and said: 'Kirkland, don't you know that you would get a bullet through your head the moment you stepped over the wall?'

"'Yes, sir,' he said, 'I know that; but if you will let me, I am willing to try it.'

"After a pause the general said: 'Kirkland, I ought not to allow you to run such a risk, but the sentiment which actuates you is so noble that I will not refuse your request, trusting that God may protect you. You may go.'

"The sergeant's eye lighted up with pleasure. He said, 'Thank you, sir,' and ran rapidly down-stairs. The general heard him pause for a moment, and then return, bounding two

"RICHARD KIRKLAND, THE HUMANE HERO."
(See page 400.)

steps at a time. He thought the sergeant's heart had failed him. He was mistaken. The sergeant stopped at the door and said: 'General, can I show a white handkerchief?' The general slowly shook his head, saying emphatically, 'No, Kirkland, you can't do that.' 'All right,' he said, 'I'll take the chances,' and ran down with a bright smile on his handsome countenance.

"With profound anxiety he was watched as he stepped over the wall on his errand of mercy—Christ-like mercy. Unharmed he reached the nearest sufferer. He knelt beside him, tenderly raised the drooping head, rested it gently upon his own noble breast, and poured the precious life-giving fluid down the fever-scorched throat. This done, he laid him tenderly down, placed his knapsack under his head, straightened out his broken limb, spread his overcoat over him, replaced his empty canteen with a full one, and turned to another sufferer. By this time his purpose was well understood on both sides, and all danger was over. From all parts of the field arose fresh cries of 'water, water; for God's sake, water!' More piteous still the mute appeal of some who could only feebly lift a hand to say there, too, was life and suffering.

"For an hour and a half did this ministering angel pursue his labor of mercy, nor ceased to go and return until he relieved all the wounded on that part of the field. He returned to his post wholly unhurt. Who shall say how sweet his rest that winter's night beneath the cold stars!

"Little remains to be told. Sergeant Kirkland distinguished himself in battle at Gettysburg, and was promoted lieutenant. At Chickamauga he fell on the field of battle, in the hour of victory. He was but a youth when called away, and had never formed those ties from which might have resulted a posterity to enjoy his fame and bless his country; but he has bequeathed to the American youth—yea, to the world—an example which dignifies our common humanity."

Want of space compels me to pass by altogether other illustrations of the genuineness of these revivals, and to cull only a few of the hundreds of incidents I have, showing how these men met "the king of terrors."

A noble fellow who fell at Gaines's Mill, the 27th of June, 1862, said to comrades who offered to bear him to the rear: "No! I die. Tell my parents I die happy. On! on to victory! Jesus is with me, and will give me all the help I need."

26

John Anderson, of Company C, Thirteenth Virginia **Regiment,** who was mortally wounded at Second Manassas, gave me, when I told him that the surgeons said that he could only live an hour, many messages to loved ones, which they have cherished as a precious legacy, and among others sent this to his father: " Tell father that it would be very hard to die here on the roadside, away from home and loved ones, but for the fact that I have with me the Friend that sticketh closer than a brother, and He makes it all peace and joy with me."

A Georgia captain, who was shot in the mouth and unable to speak, wrote in my diary, when I visited him in the field-hospital at the Wilderness : " I do not know how it will be with me, whether I shall die or recover, but my full trust is in Christ, and I am perfectly resigned to God's will. I am ready still to serve Him on earth or to ' go up higher,' just as *He* may see fit to direct."

When I asked a soldier named Wayland, who had professed conversion in one of our revivals a short time before, and was mortally wounded in " the bloody angle " at Spottsylvania Court House : " Now that you are about to die, what is the ground of your hope ? " He replied, with a sweet smile : " Jesus says, ' Him that cometh unto me I will in no wise cast out.' I have gone to Him, and I do not think that He will deceive me. I believe that He will be true to His word."

And repeating this over several times, his face brightening into something like ecstatic radiance, he went to realize the preciousness of the Saviour's promise.

Major Augustus M. Gordon, who fell at Chancellorsville, said —they were his last words—" Lay me down now, captain, for I am dying. I am not afraid to die, for I *know* I am going to be with Jesus."

We read, in one of the Georgia papers, of a Georgia soldier who, at Chancellorsville, had his left leg shattered from the ankle to the knee, but who, hearing that a comrade was wounded, said to those who were about to bear him to the rear, " He is worse wounded than I am : carry him off—I can wait here ! " Before the ambulance-corps could get back, a minnie-ball had passed through his unselfish, generous heart.

The chaplain of the Ninth Louisiana Regiment (Rev. F. McCarthy) relates the following :

" A young man named Winn, of the Eighth Louisiana, was

killed during the shelling on the Rapidan, on the 14th ult., whose death was a triumph of grace. He lived an hour after receiving his wound, and was borne to a retired place, where he died the 'death of the righteous.' Being an orphan, he sent noble messages to his sisters, informing them with pride that he fell in the front rank. As his end drew near, he said the angels in great numbers were collecting about him, ready to take him to heaven. His comrades were much affected, and one of them at least has, in consequence, given his heart to Jesus. This young man professed religion about two months ago. Likely enough he was brought into the fold during Brother J. Wm. Jones's meetings at Mt. Pisgah church. I think it worth a lifetime of hardship to prepare, under God, one of our dear defenders thus to die."

I find Winn's name on the list of converts in that great revival in Hays's Brigade, of which I have spoken, and he is but one of many who went from those precious seasons to enter upon more glorious service in the brighter, better land, " beyond the smiling and the weeping."

A writer who visited our wounded on a field of blood says: "As you pass from one to another, washing their wounds and administering some cordial or food, you will hear such petitions as these: ' Will you write to my mother that I trust in Jesus, *her* Jesus?' 'Oh, sir, can you get one brief message to my wife in Virginia? Tell her to train up the children for heaven.' Here is a soldier just breathing his last. You kneel and whisper in his ear, ' Jesus, Saviour.' He smiles, and ceases to breathe."

We find in our exchanges accounts of two soldiers at the point of death. With the first the following conversation occurred: "Are you willing to die here among strangers?" "Perfectly." "Have you a wife?" "Yes." "Are you willing to die without seeing her?" "If God wills it, I am." "Have you children, and if so, how many?" "Five." "Can you trust them in the hands of Jesus?" "Yes. He is all my trust." His countenance was the impersonation of resignation and peace. The second said, in answer to the inquiry whether he loved the Saviour: "Oh, yes, sir, I love Him with all my heart. He is *so* precious to my soul. I know that I am dying, and that I will soon be in heaven, to reign with Jesus forever. Oh, how sweet heaven is! There will be no sorrow there. I do want everybody to serve the Lord."

I have quoted a letter from Captain Abram Poindexter (son

of Rev. Dr. A. M. Poindexter, of Virginia) showing his deep interest in the salvation of his comrades, and his readiness to work for that end.

Rev. Dr. J. A. Broadus, in a memorial address on Dr. Poindexter, thus described the heroic death of this young soldier, and the influence he exerted on his men:

"The older son, *Abram Wimbish Poindexter*, at the age of twenty-one, volunteered before his brother's death in an infantry company which he materially assisted in raising, and was elected first lieutenant. Afterwards, by the death of Captain Easley, he became captain; it was Company K, Forty-sixth Virginia. The young man had made a public profession of religion the previous year, was a graduate of Wake Forest College, and principal of Talladega Academy, in Alabama. As teacher and as officer he showed superior talents and great force and charm of character. He was exceedingly beloved by his men; some were converted through his recognized instrumentality, and his letters, for months previous to his death, showed deep and growing devotion. Obituaries which remain from different friends present discriminating and exalted eulogy. What a joy he must have been to father and mother and sister! Before Petersburg, July 30, 1864, the enemy exploded their now famous mine, and poured through the great gap in the works, enfilading with deadly fire the thin Confederate lines on either side. Captain Poindexter's company was especially exposed, and stood its ground amid heavy loss. Every officer but himself was borne away severely wounded. Addressing the little remnant of his company, the young captain said: 'Boys, we must hold this position, or die in our places, for the salvation of the town depends upon the enemy's not carrying these works.' Presently an officer rode by, and seeing the little handful of a company standing firm he asked who was their commander. They replied, pointing to a dead body, 'There's our captain; he told us we must hold these works, or die in their defence, and we mean to do it.' And they did. Without an officer, the little fragment of a company obeyed their dead captain's commands, and stood firm before the enfilading fire and the rush of the foe. The story was told to Dr. Poindexter by one of the men. Truly that was a captain! truly those were men!"

"I am aware," said a Christian soldier, "that I have many hardships, trials and dangers to meet; but they will not hurt me, if I only do my duty. All these privations and perils tend to humble me, and if I can, by their means, more successfully mortify the deeds of the body—if, by their means, I can uproot pride, vanity, covetousness and all their kindred passions—I shall have occasion to thank God that duty called me to be a soldier."

An officer, of high position and of consistent character, remarked to a minister as they were passing through his command, " That man," pointing to a noble-looking soldier, " was once the worst soldier we had. He is now about the best. A minister preached for us on one occasion and his sermon was blessed to the conversion of this man. His whole character was revolutionized; and, though months have since passed away, his life has been blameless. From being a disobedient, worthless fellow, he has become a gentleman, a gallant soldier, and a true Christian."

Dr. Bennett relates the following incident of the battle of Bethel :

" Captain John Stewart Walker, of the company known as the 'Virginia Life Guard,' was ordered by the commanding general to take his men from the front, where they were doing good service, to the flank to hold in check a heavy force of the enemy supposed to be moving in that direction. On reaching his new post of danger, Captain Walker drew up his company and addressed them in a few stirring words. He reminded them that God had mercifully preserved them in the heat of battle, and that they were now called to face the enemy in greater numbers ; that, as Christians and patriots, they should resolve to do their whole duty to their country ; then kneeling down, he called upon a minister, who was a private in the ranks, to offer prayer. When they arose, nearly every eye was suffused with tears, and God was felt to be present. During that day of battle it is said that three of this company sought and obtained the pardon of their sins."

Rev. Dr. J. C. Granberry, then chaplain of the Eleventh Virginia Regiment, thus speaks of Major Carter Harrison, a brother of Captain Dabney Carr Harrison (of whom an extended sketch is given in a previous chapter): " I shall never cease to remember with admiration one of the earliest victims of this war, Major Carter Harrison, of the Eleventh Virginia. He was an earnest servant of Christ ; modest, firm, unostentatious, zealous. He seized at once the hearts of the regiment by his many virtues, by his courtesy to all and his kind visits to the sick, to whom he bore a word not only of sympathy, but also of pious exhortation. On the lovely morning of July 18, as we awaited the advance of the enemy and the opening of our first battle, our conversation was on sacred things. In a few hours he was mortally wounded, and until midnight endured untold agony; but in his soul was the peace of God, and all was patiently borne for the sake of God and country. He was ready to be offered up, and to leave even his loved family, at the call of duty. I had a conversation with him; he spoke of his faith in Providence, and the answers to prayer which he daily received. I questioned him concerning the state of his mind at the time. He replied that it did not rest on any subject, but now thought of a military order, and then of a Scriptural promise; now of his country, and then of his family; and often arose in a holy ejaculation to God. His flesh rests in hope; his spirit rose to God."

"I recall," says Dr. Granberry, "an interview with the sweet-spirited and gallant Captain James K. Lee, of Richmond, Virginia. 'How glad I am,' said he, as he gave me a cordial grasp, 'to shake the hand of a brother in Christ!' I referred with sympathy to his intense sufferings. With emphasis he answered, 'Oh, they are nothing to the sufferings which Jesus bore for me!' In a few days he too was in the bosom of his Father."

Rev. John W. Miller, whose faithful ministrations many of the soldiers will remember, and whose death some years after the war was widely lamented, thus wrote of some of his hospital work:

"We have had some to die peacefully and happily. One poor fellow who had long been sick with typhoid fever died last week. When I questioned him about his preparation for death, his answer was scarcely articulate, but in his thick mutterings I could distinguish these blessed words of trust in the Saviour, '*He will not let me perish.*'

"Upon asking another why he was not afraid to die, he said: 'Because I am going home to heaven, through Christ.' Another, a little while before he died, said: 'I love God.'

"I find a number of them are members of the Church. Testaments are greatly coveted, and you can scarcely walk through the wards at any time without seeing some of them engaged in reading the sacred word. Divine service has been held several times for the convalescents—and we frequently assemble them for evening prayer."

" It was just after a battle, where hundreds of brave men had fallen," writes another chaplain, "and where hundreds more were wounded, that a soldier came to my tent and said: ' Chaplain, one of our boys is badly wounded, and wants to see you right away.' Immediately following the soldier, I was taken to the hospital and led to a bed, where lay a noble young man, pale and blood-stained from a terrible wound above the temple. I saw at a glance that he had but a few hours to live. Taking his hand, I said: 'Well, my brother, what can I do for you? He looked up in my face, and placing his finger where his hair was stained with blood, he said: ' Chaplain, cut a big lock from here for mother—for *mother*, mind, chaplain.' I hesitated to do it. ' Don't be afraid, chaplain, to disfigure my hair. It's for mother, and nobody will come to see me in the dead-house to-morrow.' I did as he requested me. ' Now, chaplain,' said the dying man, ' I want you to kneel down by me and return thanks to God.' ' For what?' I asked. ' For giving me such a mother. Oh, chaplain, she is a good mother; her teachings comfort and console me now. And, chaplain, thank God that by His grace I am a Christian. Oh, what would I do now if I was not a Christian! I know that my Redeemer liveth. I feel that His finished work has saved me. And, chaplain, thank God for giving me dying grace. He has made my bed feel " soft as downy pillows are." Thank him for the promised home in glory. I'll soon be there—there, where there is no more war, nor sorrow, nor desolation, nor death—where I'll see Jesus and be forever with the Lord.' I kneeled by him, and thanked God for the blessings he had bestowed upon him—a good mother, a Christian hope, and dying grace to bear testimony to God's faithfulness. Shortly after the prayer, he said: ' Good-bye, chaplain; if you see mother, tell her it was all well.'

"A young soldier, while dying very happily, broke out in singing the following stanza:

> " ' Great Jehovah, we adore thee,
> God the Father, God the Son,
> God the Spirit, joined in glory
> On the same eternal throne:
> Endless praises
> To Jehovah, three in one.'

" The chaplain then asked if he had any message to send to his friends. ' Yes,' said he. ' Tell my father that I have tried to eat my meals with thanksgiving.' 'Tell him that I have tried to pray as we used to do at home.' 'Tell him that Christ is now all my hope, all my trust, and that He is precious to my soul.' 'Tell him that I am not afraid to die—all is calm.' 'Tell him that I believe Christ will take me to Himself, and to my dear sister who is in heaven.' The voice of the dying boy faltered in the intervals between these precious sentences. When the hymn commencing, ' Nearer, my God, to thee,' was read to him, at the end of each stanza he exclaimed, with striking energy, 'O Lord Jesus, thou art coming *nearer to me.*' Also, at the end of each stanza of the hymn (which was also read to him) commencing,

> ' Just as I am—without one plea,
> But that thy blood was shed for me,
> And that thou bid'st me come to thee,
> O Lamb of God, I come,'

he exclaimed, '*I come! O Lamb of God, I come!*' Speaking again of his friends, he said, ' Tell my father that I *died happy.*' His last words were, ' Father, I'm coming to Thee!' Then the Christian soldier sweetly and calmly ' fell asleep in Jesus.'

" This was witnessed by about twenty fellow-soldiers, and the effect upon the feelings of all was very marked. Said a Roman Catholic who lay near the dying one, with tears in his eyes, and strong emotion, ' I never want to die happier than that man did.' Said another, ' I never prayed until last night; but when I saw that man die so happy, I determined to seek religion too.' "

Rev. J. W. Talley, of Georgia, thus describes the death of his son at Leesburg, from wounds received at Sharpsburg (Antietam):

" My son, after he had lain in a storehouse from Monday to Tuesday evening on a blanket and a handful of straw, was furnished by a kind lady with a straw mattress, on which he is now dying. May God remember her in mercy ' in that day.'

" The night of the 29th was a night of pain, anxiety, deep, unutterable emotion. We sat or kneeled by his couch, and poured out our souls in prayer for the sufferer. He wanted me to pray for him, and, almost suffocated with emotion, silent prayer yielded to sobs and prayers. At the close, I asked him if he loved Jesus. He answered, 'Yes.' I asked him if he was going to heaven; he said : ' I hope so ; ' and wanted us all to meet him in heaven. He then threw his arms around his mother's neck, and returned her fond embrace and kisses, sent by her a kiss to each of his sisters, and one by me to his brother Willie, now in General Bragg's army. The struggle lasted until Tuesday, September 30, at 2 o'clock P. M., when the tranquil, happy spirit was released from its clay prison. The casket was broken and the jewel was gone."

Dr. Bennett thus describes scenes which occurred at Second Manassas, and at Sharpsburg:

"'Give my love to parents and friends,' said a young soldier, dying of his wounds; 'tell them all is well; I am not afraid to die, for I know they are praying for me.' Another, the son of a faithful clergyman, fell mortally wounded by a shell. A friend near by gave him water, for which he thanked him, saying, 'I am a dying patriot,' and then added, 'Tell my father I died like a man and a hero.' A brave young Christian, when told by the surgeon that he could not live, sent home his last message: 'Tell my relations, father and mother, sisters and brothers, that I trust I am prepared to meet my God. Farewell, one and all, I bid you a long farewell; I hope to meet you all in heaven.' Another gallant soldier, who was killed as the line of battle was being formed, left a pleasing testimony. Just before leaving to join the army, he wrote: 'I wish only to know my duty; it then remains for me to perform it. It was a great trial to part with my family; I seemed to realize that the parting was final; but my country calls, and I cheerfully go forward to death.' It was soon after that he went from the carnage of battle to the peaceful home of the blessed."

J. W. Mills, chaplain of a Florida regiment, gives a graphic picture of the havoc of war:

"Many of our regiment fell in the terrible battle of Sharpsburg. We occupied the centre, where the enemy made his fiercest attack, hoping to break our lines in that vital part of the field, and so win the day. The enemy were formed in a semicircle on the side of a hill. Our brave men marched up to the attack until they could see the heads and shoulders of their adversaries over the summit of the hill, when firing commenced. From the two wings and the centre of this semicircle they poured upon us a murderous fire for about one hour. Five times our colors fell, but as often our men rushed to the spot and raised them to the breeze. Finally, a retreat was ordered— at that moment the colors fell and were left. The enemy had suffered too much, notwithstanding his advantages, to pursue, and our gallant lieutenant-colonel, already wounded in the arm, went back and brought them away under a shower of bullets.

"In the midst of this carnage many a heart turned to the God of battles for refuge and comfort." Mr. Mills again writes:

"A young man said to me after the battle: 'When I was going into the battle, I put my trust in God, and He has brought me through untouched, and I am grateful to Him.' And the tears stood in his eyes as he spoke. He was an unconverted man when he went into the fight. Last night at preaching, while referring to the incidents of the battle and how God had preserved them, many tears fell, and many countenances spoke louder than words undying gratitude to the God of all grace.

"The instances of calm Christian courage exhibited on the field of Sharpsburg have never been surpassed. Here, with thousands of other heroes, Captain James G. Rogers, of Macon, Georgia, offered his life on the altar of his country. He was a worthy citizen and a most useful Christian. As a minister and a Sabbath-school superintendent, he exerted a happy influence wherever he labored to do good. He entered the service a captain of the Central City Blues, of the renowned Twelfth Georgia, and endured cheerfully all the hardships of the soldier's life. He passed unharmed through seventeen desperate battles, and fell gloriously on this bloody field. Wearied and almost worn out by the investment of Harper's Ferry and the march to the battle-field, his men lay on their arms awaiting the attack which was to be made at dawn of day. The assault was terrible, and for an hour Captain Rogers, in command of the regiment, passed up and down the line encouraging his men. While thus exposed, all the fingers of his left hand were shot off, and he was severely wounded in the thigh, but he remained with his men until forced to leave by sheer exhaustion. As he was moving off, supported by some of his men, a bullet struck him in the back of the head, killing him instantly. 'Thus fell,' says the friend from whom we take this account, 'one of the purest, bravest men of our immortalized Confederate army.' When he bade adieu to his family, he said: 'If we meet no more on earth, let us meet in heaven.' In his letters home he often said: 'I never go into battle without feeling prepared to meet my God.' On the morning of his last battle he arranged for the disposal of his effects as if he fully expected to fall. 'Blessed are the dead who die in the Lord.'

" On the same field fell Major James Harvey Dingle, of South Carolina. He was a true Christian soldier. His colonel said of him : ' He was one of the bravest men I ever saw. He did not know what fear was. He was killed near me, and I took the flag from his hand as he was dying; he died without a groan, and looked as if he was sleeping. He was blessed by the men and officers, and was a kind, courteous, efficient and accomplished officer; his loss to the Legion (Hampton) is great. His name will be cherished by the sons of Carolina so long as the good, patriotic and brave are appreciated.'

" Such cases were not isolated ones in the Southern armies; there were hundreds, yea, thousands, of such earnest, faithful, godly men, who endured hardships, poured out their blood, and died in peace amid the rage and carnage of the battle. The dying words of our Christian soldiers, their messages of love, whispered, amid the roar of cannon and the rattle of musketry, in the ear of some comrade who bent over them and gave a cooling draught from his canteen, would fill volumes if they could be collected. It is only by fragments, however, that we can gather up their precious sentences that sparkle with a heavenly light in the midst of the gloomy horrors of war. Many of the best and purest were left scattered over the wide, blood-soaked fields, and languished and died away from home and friends in hospitals and prisons; and not until the coming of their comrades who survived and returned home did their friends and families receive the sweet messages of love that were laid like healing balm on their bleeding hearts.

" Never were stronger proofs given of the sustaining and comforting power of religion than during this terrible war, which stripped our homes of loved ones, our land of plenty, our hearts of joy, and left us nothing to fall back upon in our sufferings and humiliation but the promises of God, who poured out His Spirit so richly upon our soldiers in all the hardships of the march and in all the unutterable anguish that followed our great battles."

Rev. Wm. M. Crumley, of Georgia, whose labors in connection with the " Georgia Relief Association " were so widely useful and so warmly appreciated, published during the war a tract, entitled, "*A Soldier's Bible,*" of which I circulated in the camps a great many copies. I am glad to be able to reproduce it here, as I find it preserved in Dr. Bennett's " Great Revival." It is as follows :

"Among the multiplicity of knapsacks, haversacks, bundles, and old clothes, stored in one of the baggage-rooms of a hospital in Richmond, I found a *Soldier's Bible*. It was a neat London edition, with a silver clasp, on which were engraven the initials A. L. C. On the fly-leaf was written, in a neat and delicate hand, 'A present to my dear son on his fifteenth birthday, from his mother, M. A. C.' Below was written, in the same hand, 'Search the Scriptures; for in them ye think ye have eternal life, and they are they which testify of me.' 'Remember now thy Creator in the days of thy youth.' 'If sinners entice thee, consent thou not.'

"The book had the appearance of having been carefully read, there being many chapters and verses marked with pencil, as though they had strongly impressed themselves on the mind of the young reader. Among them were the chapters which describe the heroic daring of the youthful David, the saintly purity of Joseph, and the unflinching fidelity of the three captive boys at the court of Babylon. The First, Twenty-third and Fifty-first Psalms bore marks of an interested reader. In the New Testament, such Scriptures as speak of the love of God to sinners were carefully noted: 'God *so* loved the world that he gave His only-begotten Son, that *whosoever* believeth in Him should not perish, but have everlasting life.'—John iii. 16. 'Though your sins be as scarlet, they shall be as white as snow; though they be red like crimson, they shall be as wool.'—Isaiah i. 18. At this remarkably encouraging promise was a large blood-stain, as though gory fingers had been tracing out every word; also at John xiv. 1, 2— 'Let not your heart be troubled: ye believe in God, believe also in me.' 'In my Father's house are many mansions'—were the same stains of still broader and deeper dye.

"Albert was the only son of a pious and wealthy planter of the South. Most of his time during his childhood was spent in the country on his father's plantation. The little white cottage was half-buried in evergreens, and richly festooned with fragrant vines, among which the wild birds nestled, and sang with their sweetest melody. On the hill, at the end of a long avenue, stood the quiet country church, where little Albert, accompanied by his parents, sister and aged grandmother, met the families of the neighborhood to spend an hour in Sabbath-school, and then listen to the reverend man of God, who preached to them the precious word of the Lord. Here, and around the family altar,

Albert received that moral training which laid a deep and broad foundation for a character, in many respects, worthy of the imitation of all who may read this simple narrative.

" In the Sabbath-school Albert first formed the acquaintance of little Jennie, neatly dressed in a white muslin with a blue sash, who afterwards became the beautiful and accomplished Miss S——, whose daguerrotype we found in the soldier's coat-pocket. She was the intimate friend of his sister Hattie, and often his successful competitor for prizes offered by the superintendent of the Sabbath-school.

" In the year 1856 Albert was sent to college to complete his education, and Jennie went to a ladies' college of high grade to complete her studies.

"A few notes that ran the college blockade, and vacation meetings, sufficed to keep up their acquaintance and friendship. In the summer of 1860 they both graduated with honors highly creditable to them and gratifying to their friends. On their return home, early attachments ripened into something more than friendship; but scarcely had the bright vision of hope dawned when it was overcast by the dark cloud of war that suddenly rose upon our horizon. The country called the brave young men from every quarter to rally in Southern prowess, and with battle-shock roll back the invading foe. Albert was one of the first to respond. He took his place in the ranks as a common soldier, feeling it was honor enough to be a private, defending his country, his home, and his beloved Jennie; and all the more, as he had her approving smile to encourage him.

"Albert's departure and transfer to Virginia by rail are scenes so common to soldiers that they can be imagined or remembered far better than I could describe them.

" There is one incident, however, which I will mention. Just before he took leave, they were all called around the old family altar. Jennie was there. Maum Patty, the nurse of his childhood, was there, with snow-white kerchief about her ebon brow and silver locks. Many were the bitter sobs, while the deep, earnest voice of the father in solemn prayer, like the patriarch Abraham, bound his son, his only son, a sacrifice on his country's altar. When the amen was pronounced, there was in every heart a feeling too deep for utterance. In this moment of silence, a mother's hand placed the Soldier's Bible in a pocket near his heart. Albert moved slowly down the avenue, the embodiment of youthful chivalry and manly beauty. The spectators stood like breathless statues, fearing most of all that they should see his face no more. Just as he turned the corner at the end of the avenue, he cast one glance back to the scenes of his childhood, which never seemed half so dear.

"After a long and uncomfortable transit by rail and forced marches, with weary limbs and blistered feet, he was thrown into the battle of Manassas, on the 21st of July, 1861, with scarcely time to kneel by an apple-tree in battle-line, over which the shells were howling furiously. Here in prayer he hastily committed his soul and body to his faithful Keeper, then rose calm and serene, with an assurance that no weapon of the enemy would harm him.

"When the battle was over and victory perched upon our banner, Albert found himself surrounded with the dead and dying, among whom were some of his particular friends. He was strongly and strangely exercised with a mingled feeling of joy and grief, a sort of hysteric paroxysm of laughing and crying, weeping for the slain, and rejoicing that he had escaped unharmed, with a deep consciousness that God had been his shield and hiding-place in the hour of danger. Albert endured all the sufferings of fatigue, cold and hunger incident to a winter campaign; none murmured less, none were more faithful in the discharge of duty than he. The demoralizing effects of the camp, with almost the entire absence of religious privileges, produced a coldness in his state; and although he did not compromise his moral character by profanity, gambling and drunkenness, as many others did, yet he failed to enjoy the close communion and clear sense of the Divine presence which he had done in former days. In this state of mind, he entered upon the seven days' battles before Richmond. The solemnities of the occasion aroused him to a sense of his danger, causing him to cleave more closely to his Bible and its precious promises. With his hand on this blessed book pressed to his heart, he called on God to be his shield and support in the hour of battle. He passed the terrible ordeal of Gaines's Mill on Friday and Malvern Hill on Tuesday, where the men fell around him like grain before the reapers and covered the ground thick as autumn leaves. A degree of joy and gratitude swelled his heart as he surveyed the field of death, in view of his own wonderful escape, but not so deep and warm as on a former occasion, when his faith and piety were more earnest and simple. Albert continued at times to read his Bible, but it was evidently more as a task than a pleasant duty; his keen relish for Divine things had abated very much; the excuses of camp-life, long marches, and the general indifference of officers and men upon the subject of religion, offered his conscience the consolation of a temporary opiate. Sometimes, however, on the reception of letters from home, and sometimes, when alone on his midnight round of picket-duty, he would shed a penitential tear and resolve to double his diligence and regain his lost ground as a Christian; but a plant so tender and unprotected by the pale of the Church, unwatered by the dews of the sanctuary, persecuted and scathed by the lightnings of contempt, nipped and browsed upon by every wild beast of the forest, necessarily became greatly dwarfed in life and growth; a feeling of self-security, a trust in fate or chance, impressed him more than a simple faith in the ever-present God. In this spiritually demoralized condition he entered the Sharpsburg fight, without even asking God to protect him and save him from danger and death. Soon after the battle opened he was struck by a ball and carried back to the rear a wounded man; from profuse hemorrhage, a sick, dreamy sensation stole over him; the light faded from his eyes, while a thousand mingled sounds filled his ears, and a faint vision of home, friends, green turf, battle-fields and graveyards flitted by like phantoms of the night. With returning consciousness, there came a sense of shame and sorrow for having declined in his religious state, and a conviction that his wound was the chastening of the Lord to rebuke his wanderings and check his self-reliance.

"As soon as he was sufficiently restored, he drew from his pocket his neglected Bible, kissing it many times over and bathing it in tears as truly penitential as Peter's when he wept at the feet of Jesus. His bloody fingers searched out the old-cherished promises of God, leaving many a gory stain on the blessed pages of inspiration. The law of the Lord again became his meat and drink, on which he feasted by day and by night; a new life was infused into his soul, which enabled him to bear his sufferings with true Christian heroism.

" In this condition I found him in the old Academy Hospital in Winchester, lying on the dirty floor, with a blanket for his bed and a wisp of straw to pillow up his wounded limb. While sitting by his side, trying to minister to his soul and body, I received from him this narrative, substantially as I have given it to you. After much severe suffering, when our army fell back, he was sent to Staunton and thence to Richmond, where I again met him just in time to witness his last triumphant conflict with suffering and death. He was in a hospital, reclining on a clean, comfortable bed, his head resting on a soft, white pillow, on which the familiar name of a distinguished lady of Georgia was marked—she having contributed it from her own bed for the benefit of the suffering soldiers. Near him sat the matron of the hospital, rendering every possible comfort that the sympathy of a woman could suggest, intensely sharpened by the recent loss of a promising son, who fell in a late battle. Reduced by a secondary hemorrhage and amputation, Albert, with a calm, steady faith, came down to the cold waters of Jordan, where he lingered for a short time and dictated a letter to his mother, which I wrote for him, in which he gave an appropriate word to each one of the family, not even forgetting Maum Patty, his old nurse, and reserving a postscript, the last and best, for Jennie. I would like very much to give my readers a copy of this letter, but it is the exclusive treasure of the bereaved and afflicted ones, whose grief is too sacred for the intermeddling of any save the most intimate friends.

"After pausing a few moments at the close of the letter, he seemed self-absorbed, and soliloquized thus: 'I die for my country and the cause of humanity, and, with many others, have thrown my bleeding body into the horrid chasm of revolution to bridge the way for the triumphal car of Liberty which will roll over me, bearing in its long train the happy millions of future generations, rejoicing in all the grandeur of peace and prosperity. I wonder if they will ever pause as they pass to think of the poor soldiers whose bones lie at the foundation of their security and happiness? Or will the soul be permitted from some Pisgah summit to take a look at the future glory of the country I died to reclaim from fanatical thraldom? Will the soul ever visit at evening twilight the scenes of my childhood, and listen to the sweet hymn of praise that goes up from the paternal altar at which I was consecrated to God? Though unseen, may it not be the guardian angel of my loved ones?' Checking himself, he said: 'These are earthly desires, which I feel gradually giving way to a purer, heavenly sympathy.' Then, in a low, sweet voice, he repeated:

" ' Give joy or grief, give ease or pain,
  Take life or friends away,
I come to find them all again
  In that eternal day.'

" He repeated the last line with an emphasis that threw a beauty and force into it which I never saw or felt before. Seeing that he was communing with his own soul, and that spiritual things in the opening light of eternity were rising in bold relief before his vision of faith, I withdrew a short space from him, feeling it was holy ground, ' where the good man meets his fate, quite on the verge of heaven.' He then gently laid his hand on his Bible and the daguerrotype that lay near his side, and amid this profound stillness, surrounded by a halo of more than earthly glory, gently as the evening shadows the curtain dropped, leaving nothing visible to us but the cold and lifeless clay, on which a sweet smile rested, as though it had seen the happy soul enter the pearly gates of the New Jerusalem. Thus, far from home and friends, this noble youth fell asleep in Jesus, swelling the long list of the honored dead; but, ' though dead, he yet speaketh.' The precious treasure, '*The Soldier's Bible*,' has been returned to the family, and is now one of those valued relics that bind many sad hearts with links of gold to bygone days."

T. S. Chandler, of the Sixth South Carolina Regiment, said, when he realized that he was dying : " Tell my mother that I am lying without hope of recovery. I have stood before the enemy fighting in a great and glorious cause and have fallen. My hope is in Christ, for whose sake I hope to be saved. Tell her that she and my brother cannot see me again on earth, but they can meet me in heaven." A little before bedtime of his last night he called to his surgeon and said : " Write to mother, and tell her she must meet me in heaven. I know I am going there."

When Captain John F. Vinson, of Crawford county, Georgia, came to die, he exclaimed : " All is well—my way is clear—not a cloud intervenes." As Lieutenant Ezekiel Pickens Miller, of the Seventeenth Mississippi Regiment, fell mortally wounded on the field of Fredericksburg, he exclaimed : " Tell my father and mother not to grieve for me, for I am going to a better world than this."

" Can I do anything for you ? " said the missionary, kneeling by the side of a private shot through the neck. " Yes, write to

27

my poor wife." "What shall I write?" "Say to my dear wife, it's all right." This was written. "What else shall I write?" "Nothing else, all's right"—and thus he died. He was a convert of the camp.

"Passing through a large stable where the wounded lay," says Mr. Redding, "I noticed a man whose head was frosted with age. After giving him wine and food, I said, 'My friend, you are an old man. Do you enjoy the comforts of religion?' 'Oh, yes!' he exclaimed, 'I have been a member of the Church for twenty-five years. Often in our little church at home our minister told us that religion was good under all circumstances, and now I have found it true; for even here in this old stable, with my leg amputated, and surrounded by the dead and dying, I am just as happy as I can be. It is good even here. I want you to tell the people so when you preach to them.' I left him rejoicing."

"Said a poor fellow, who was suffering greatly from two painful wounds: 'When I was at home, I was wild and wicked, but since I have been in the army I have tried to change my life, and since I have been wounded I have been able to trust my soul in the hands of God, and I feel that if He should call me to die, all will be well.' He spoke with deep feeling, and the big tears filled his eyes and rolled down his pale face. Another from Georgia, who was dying of his wounds far away from home and friends gave a like testimony, and, with tears of joy, praised God in full hope of heaven. Whether dying in hospital or on the battle-field, the testimony of the Christian soldier was the same." "Francis M. Bobo, of Spartansburg, South Carolina, exclaimed when dying: 'I would not take ten thousand worlds for my prospect of heaven!' 'If I die in the hospital or fall in battle,' said a young Georgia soldier, 'weep not for me— all will be well.' These are a few testimonies out of hundreds that might be recorded. They show the deep and joyous piety of thousands of the Southern soldiery."

I quote again from the same source from which I have drawn so many incidents:

"The experiences of soldiers are so full of childlike simplicity that one never tires of reading them.

"A soldier converted on the march was met by his chaplain, who knew that he was under conviction, and asked by him if he had given himself to Christ:

"'Yes,' said the stalwart warrior, with a glowing countenance,

' I have found Him.   Why, sir, when we set off on that march I felt such a weight upon my soul that I could scarcely drag myself along, but after a while God heard my prayers; and then the burden was gone and I felt as if marching was no trouble at all.'

" Good men that work for God faithfully die well even in war, on the field or in the hospital.   Captain Thomas O. Byrd, of the Fourth Mississippi Regiment, was a zealous Christian among his comrades.   He says, writing to his friends at home :

" ' I have prayers in my tent every night with the boys, and assist others to take up the Cross.   I have just had prayers with some wild young men, who are now engaged in singing with much zest and feeling.   Oh, what a field is open here !   Fare is rough, but gladly would I live thus for life for Christ's sake and the good of man.   I have gained a great victory to-day.   I believe God will bless this work.   I feel His love burn in my heart while I write.   I know God will bless my labors if you and Sister ——— and the children will pray for me.'

"Again : ' I find I lack courage to speak out for the cause of our holy religion more than ever, and you know full well that I have always been more or less lacking in this particular ; yet I trust through faith and prayer to come out safe at last, though it may be as through fire.'

" He sickened and died in the army.   A kind lady approached him as he was nearing the verge of eternity.   Said he :

" ' God bless you, sister ; this is the way Jesus went '—meaning perhaps alone, among enemies.   ' Tell my wife farewell—all is right—to meet me in heaven.'

"Another Christian, dying in the hospital, wrote to his wife :

" ' I don't want you to be uneasy about me, but do not forget to pray for me.   I still have strong confidence in the Lord, and endeavor to put my trust in Him in all cases.   I hope the Lord may take care of you ; and if we should not meet again on earth, may we meet in heaven, where wars and sorrows are forever gone.   God helping, we'll meet you there.'

" The death of Colonel Peyton H. Colquitt was that of a true Christian hero.   He had served at Norfolk, Virginia, and as colonel of the Forty-sixth Georgia at Charleston and in Mississippi.   On the field of Chickamauga he was in command of a brigade.   It was ordered to charge a battery ; and while riding up and down the line in front of his men, speaking to them words of encouragement, he was struck in the breast by a ball and fell from his horse.

" His friend, Hon. W. F. Sanford, wrote a touching memorial of the gallant soldier, from which we extract the following account of his last moments:

" ' He was carried to a shade, and there the chaplain of his regiment, Rev. Thomas Stanley, attended him. I give the account of the closing scene in his words: " When I found the colonel he thought his wound was mortal, and though he had not recovered from the shock he seemed calm and collected. I talked with him very freely on the subject of religion. He constantly expressed a spirit of resignation to the Providence of God, and that he had no apprehensions whatever in regard to the future; that he had tried to do his duty, and felt in the last hour that he was accepted of his Saviour. In this hour his faith never wavered—he said he was 'going to the land of light and peace, where he should meet his many loved ones who had gone before;' and again: 'Tell my dear wife I go to meet our angel child, and to come to us.' At one time he said: 'The Providence of God is inscrutable, but I submit in hope.' He died without a struggle. It is comfortable to know that all his wants were supplied during his sufferings. He experienced no pain, and was conscious to the last moment. As soon as he was wounded General Forrest sent his surgeon to him; the poor people, who had been bereft of all their worldly substance, went to see him from miles around." '

" The following touching scene is described by Rev. J. A. Parker, who labored as an army chaplain. He was conveying a number of wounded soldiers by water to the hospitals at Mobile:

" ' At two o'clock in the morning we started in a skiff for the city. The wind was high and the water rough. Poor wounded men, how they suffered the pangs of thirst, with no water save that from the bay! A young soldier, whom I had promised to convey to the city, lay senseless the most of the morning. About midday he roused up and asked: " How far?" " In sight of the city," said I. After lying quiet awhile, he asked why it was so dark. I told him it was not dark—that it was light and I could see the city, and that we would soon relieve him of the rough sailing and make him comfortable. I then left him and went to the other end of the boat to use an oar, for we were drifting. He soon asked for the preacher, and I returned to him. He called for water, which I dipped in a tin-cup from the bay and gave him. After drinking he asked to be sheltered from the sun. This we could not do, but we encouraged him by our approach to the city. "Yes," he replied, "shut my eyes and let me go to the city. I am going home—almost there." He closed his eyes and died.'

"A writer in the *Christian Sun* gives a touching scene in which a Christian soldier met his death :

"'On the lines near Petersburg, Virginia, on a beautiful morning in the last days of summer, a young soldier, connected with a Georgia regiment, might have been seen seated in a ravine, and at the mouth of a bomb-proof which had been made in the side of the hill, reading carefully the word of God. This young man had come to be regarded the model man of the regiment for morality and devout piety. He entered the army at the commencement of the war a Christian, and maintained his reputation untarnished through all the immoralities of camp-life, daily becoming more devout and more Christ-like in his spirit and conversation. He was, in person, well formed, yet not very robust; his hair rather dark, and his eyes a deep blue, with a very light beard. In manners he was as gentle as a woman, yet his comrades assured me that in battle he was as bold as a lion and as brave as the bravest. The Bible from which he was reading on the morning referred to was the gift of a pious mother on entering the service. He had carefully preserved it through all the weary marches and hard fought battles in which his regiment had participated, and a mother's prayers had followed with it wherever he went. While intently reading, and so absorbed as not even to hear for the moment the bursting mortar-shells around him, a comrade came running to tell him that a special friend of his own company had been killed in the trenches by the bursting of a shell among them. He closed his Bible and, clenching it in his hand, ran to the place where his friend lay dead. Just as he arrived at the spot and his eyes rested on the mangled form, a parrot-shell came whizzing, and, exploding in the immediate vicinity, he was struck on the head and instantly killed. He fell on the body of his lifeless comrade, still clasping his Bible, even in death holding on to the Word of Life.'

"Lieutenant J. P. Duncan fell at his post near Petersburg, Virginia. 'His last noble act was to distribute a package of tracts to his men on the subject of heaven. He stepped on a log in rear of his guns to look at the enemy's movements and was instantly killed.' William Smith Patterson, of the Palmetto Sharpshooters, was a noble soldier of Christ and of his country. Colonel Walker, his commander, wrote to his mother:

"'Your son was a gallant young man, and fell bravely doing his duty in the foremost ranks while engaging the enemy. He was never found lacking in his duty either as a soldier or Christian. He was shot through the body and died almost instantly.'

"'When I told her,' says Dr. Whiteford Smith, 'the sad tidings, her first words were: "Glory! glory! glory! The Lord gave, and the Lord hath taken away; blessed be the name of the Lord. I know he is safe, and I would not have him back if I could by asking."'

"Such were the mothers whose sons upheld the banner of the South.

"Sergeant Alfred L. Robertson, of the Twelfth Georgia Regiment, fell in one of the battles in the Valley of Virginia. He was a Christian from childhood. 'He told me,' says a friend, 'as he lay dying upon the battle-field, that he knew his time had come and he was willing to go, feeling that all was bright, desiring only something to alleviate his suffering until his spirit should wing its way to the realms of the blessed.'

"Captain Henry F. Parks and Captain Wesley F. Parks were sons of Rev. W. J. Parks, of Georgia. The former was converted at eight years, the latter at thirteen; both entered the Confederate army and fought gallantly. Wesley died of disease—Henry by the bullet.

"'When he was stricken down upon the battle-field he begged his comrades to leave him and to take care of themselves, for he felt sure that he had received his "last furlough." Said he: "Tell my father and friends that I died praying."' They were buried on the same day.

"Andrew J. Peed, of the Fifty-ninth Georgia, received four wounds in a charge; he lived five hours and then fell asleep in Jesus. Just before his death he said: 'Farewell, boys;' and he requested a fellow-soldier to tell his wife that he was ready to die, and happily ended earth's toilsome journey.

"The Rev. Thomas A. Ware, of the Methodist Episcopal Church, South, who labored with untiring zeal as a chaplain in the Army of Northern Virginia, gives a vivid picture of a scene after a day of blood. In the midst of the surgeon's work, as he spoke to the sufferers stretched upon the ground, his ear caught the soft murmur of prayer.

"'I turned,' he says, 'to catch the words. I saw one form bent over another, prostrate on the grass, until the lips of the suppliant nearly touched the pale face of the sufferer. "Oh, precious Redeemer!" he said, "we thank Thee for Thy *abounding grace*, which of late brought him from the ways of folly and sin to know and love Thee, and that now makes this dark hour the brightest of his life. Be Thou graciously with him to the end. Mercifully pour into the hearts of his dear ones at home the balm of Thy love and, sweetly resigning them to Thy will, bring them all at last to meet him in heaven." The prayer was ended. "Amen," murmured the faded lips. The chaplain recognized me and gave me an introduction to the dying man. "I trust you are a Christian, my friend," said I, "and that even now you are resigned and happy." "Oh, yes," he said, "I entered the army a wicked man, but I must tell you now of the influence of a good sister. Will you please unroll my knapsack, sir, and get me a letter lying on my clothes? I wish you to read it to me. I have often read it, but *you* will be so kind as to read it to me now." I obeyed. The touching appeal for patriotism and piety, especially the *entreaties* for the latter, couched in all the tender sentiments of a sister's love, evoked frequent ejaculations of prayer that "God would reward and bless her forever." "Oh, sir," he said, "her precious letters have proven my salvation. Thank God for such a sister." Soon after the manly form lay cold and stiff on the ground, and the spirit, leaving the impress of its rapture on the upturned face, went with the angels to heaven to await the coming of its best beloved.'

"Not only the veterans, but the boys, died in faith and glorious hope.

"'As I walked over a battle-field,' says a writer, 'I found an interesting boy, who was rolled in his blanket and resting his head against a stump. He had been fearfully wounded through the lungs; his breath came painfully, and his broken arm hung helplessly at his side. His lips were pallid from loss of blood, and it seemed as though such pain and exhaustion would quickly wear his life away. I said:

"'"My dear boy, you are severely wounded."

"'"Yes; I am going to die."

"'"Would'nt you like to have me write to your mother?"

"'"O, yes! do," he eagerly said; "you will write to her,

wont you? Tell my mother I have read my Testament and put all my trust in the Lord. Tell her to meet me in heaven, and my brother Charlie, too. I am not afraid to die."

"'And then, exhausted by the effort, the head fell back and the eyes closed again. Several soldiers had gathered about, attracted by the patient heroism of the boy; and that sermon from those white lips was a swift witness to them of the power of the religion of Jesus. Strong men turned away to hide their tears as they saw that young soul strengthened and cheered in its agony by the hopes of the Gospel. It was not hard to assure him of Christ's love and remembrance, and lead him still closer to the Cross. At length the eyes opened again:

"'"Tell my mother that I was brave; that I never flinched a bit."'"

I have before quoted from the admirable book of Dr. John L. Johnson—the "University of Virginia Memorial"—and I shall now cull from it some of the many dying utterances of "Our Fallen Alumni," which beautifully and touchingly show the reality of the profession of faith in Christ which so large a proportion of these noble men made.

Holmes and Tucker Conrad, of Martinsburg, were my friends at the university, and I could add my emphatic testimony to their humble, earnest, Christian character. They fell in the thickest of the fight at First Manassas, fighting side by side and behaving with most conspicuous gallantry, and were afterwards found clasped in each other's arms. The appropriate epitaph on their tomb tells the touching story of their lives and death:

"HOLMES ADDISON CONRAD   HENRY TUCKER CONRAD

"CHRISTIAN BROTHERS,

"Lie buried here, side by side, as they fell in battle,

"JULY 21, 1861.

"Brothers in blood, in faith;
    Brothers in youthful bloom;
Brothers in life, brothers in death,
    Brothers in one same tomb.
Well fought they 'the good fight;'
    In death their victory won;
Sprung at one bound to heaven's light,
    And God's eternal Son."

James Camp Turner, of Alabama, thus fell at this same battle of First Manassas :

"On the night of the arrival of the regiment on the battle-field, lights being forbidden, because of the close vicinity of the enemy, he read aloud, by the light of the moon, two chapters in the New Testament to the officers of his company. He then lay down to rest for the last time in life, observing as he was about to do so, 'I think, from the signals, there will be hot work to-morrow.' The heroism of the Fourth Alabama, illustrated in the fierce struggle on that 'morrow,' has been heralded to the world, and is now historic. In the thick of the fight, at about 11 o'clock, Lieutenant James Camp Turner fell, pierced through the breast. 'Tell my sister,' said he, 'I die happy on the battle-field, in defence of my country ;' and with these words on his lips—his dying message to his idolized, only sister—his pure spirit ascended to God."

James Chalmers, of Halifax county, who fell on the outpost and died several days after at Fairfax Court House, is thus spoken of by an intimate friend :

"He possessed all the higher attributes of a Christian warrior, with hand on hilt and eye on heaven, fighting at once under the banner of his country and the Cross of his Saviour.

"He had been for many years a most consistent member of the Episcopal Church, and he carried his piety with him into every relation of life. At home he was a working Christian ; around the fireside, in the Sunday-school, or in the hut of the poor, he ever did his duty as a faithful worker in God's cause. In camp his example and precept were most potent for good, and none of those who enjoyed the privilege of nightly kneeling beside him in prayer will soon forget the earnest appeals that arose from his tent to the throne of grace. Upon his death-bed he drew his captain to him, and in whispered accents sent his love to the members of his company, and an earnest appeal to them to put their trust in that Saviour who enabled him joyfully to welcome death as a passport to a land of bliss. . . . . Would that we had some consolation to offer the stricken hearts he left behind him ! Except in the belief that God disposes all things for the best, there is no balm for the hearts that bleed for the loss of such a husband, such a father, such a brother, such a son. It is, however, an inexpressible comfort to know that he has 'fought his last battle,' and has gone to that long home 'where the wicked cease from troubling and the weary are at rest.' His reward, as a faithful soldier of his country, will be meted to him by a grateful posterity. As a soldier of the Cross he now enjoys the perpetual bliss promised the good and faithful, and, in the very presence of God, wears the victor's crown of immortal glory."

Colonel John Baker Thompson, of Staunton, Virginia, one of the most gifted alumni ever sent out from the university, thus wrote his father—the venerable Judge Thompson—on the eve of his gallant death at the head of his regiment:

" NEAR MONTEREY, TENNESSEE., night of April 4, 1862.
"My Dear Father : I write by the light of our bivouac fire. We expect, by God's help, a glorious victory to-morrow. If I should not see you again, take the assurance that I trust in God to be prepared for all. Day after to-morrow is my birthday. Love to all.   Your devoted son,
                    " JOHN B. THOMPSON."

John Thomas Jones, of the Fifth Alabama Regiment, I knew as a consistent Christian at the university, and his character in the army is thus described:

" His letters to his parents and sister during that period are full of affection. He spoke often of death, but with the fullest assurance of a happy eternity. Nor did he ever write despondingly of the cause in which he was engaged. In one of his letters to his father he said: ' Do not be uneasy about me. Even if it should come to the worst, remember me, but do not regret me. Death can be but a temporary separation at most, and I had rather go before than survive you or my dear mother. I do not write thus to make you sad, but I cannot write otherwise than I feel. Our parting on that memorable morning in Pickensville is vividly before me, and your last words are yet ringing in my ears. I have as far as possible kept your parting injunctions. Father, if this should be my last letter, I implore your forgiveness for the coldness or ingratitude with which I may at any time have returned your love.'

"Again he wrote:

"'*Dear Parents :* Do not be uneasy about me, for, sinful as I am and have been, I have put my trust in Christ. Whether I shall live or die, I believe all will be ordered for the best. It is a great consolation to believe you always remember me in your prayers.'

"This same religious constancy followed him through the trials of the soldier's life. As illustrative of this, the following, related by a reliable comrade in arms, is pertinent: 'While we were at Mechanicsville, awaiting Jackson's signal-gun, an officer indulged pretty freely in remarks which smacked strongly of infidelity. He had silenced those whom he had been more directly addressing, and appeared to be "master of the field." Jones, who had been an attentive but silent listener, modestly asked permission to say something in defence of Christianity. He began in a low, conversational tone to answer all that had been said. As he progressed he became more and more interested in his subject, until his whole soul was aroused, and quite a crowd had gathered around and were eagerly listening. The result was that the officer was astonished and silenced, and they who had not previously known the speaker were inquiring who the little fellow was that had made such a defence of Christianity.'

"This incident illustrates not only his moral and religious character, but also that of his mind. One is ready to infer from it that he must have possessed superior mental powers. Such was the fact; though a boyish, yet not undignified, reserve hid from the superficial observer or transient acquaintance the intellectual worth of this young man. In him the mental and the moral were happily blended. The quick and retentive memory, the correct judgment, the delicate taste, susceptible of the highest degree of refinement, all characteristic of his vigorous and grasping mind, were sweetly harmonized by the spirit of fervid but unpretentious piety of this Christian soldier.

"A short time after the incident related above the signal-gun was heard, and the command to march forward was given. The champion of the Christian religion went bravely forth to the defence of his country.

"The result is known. He fell in the forefront of the battle. In accordance with his frequently expressed wishes his remains have never been removed. His couch was spread on the field of battle, and the soldier still 'rests in a land hallowed by his efforts in the cause of liberty.'"

Lieutenant Charles Ellis Munford, of Richmond, fought his

guns of the Letcher Battery with a heroic courage worthy of his long lineage of illustrious sires, and his own reputation as a noble Christian soldier. His death is thus described:

" ' The Letcher Battery still held its ground,' and, according to the "Annual Report of the Board of Visitors of the Virginia Military Institute "—to which some of its guns were afterwards donated—' was in action one hour and twenty minutes, in a position which, from a subsequent survey of the havoc made by the enemy, would appear to have been utterly untenable for a much shorter time.' It had indeed fought with heroic valor; a caisson had exploded in their midst, yet they continued their fire as if giving a holiday salute.

" But did the fame it won compensate for the loss it suffered ? Twenty-two, killed and wounded, lay around their guns; among the killed, Lieutenant Charles Ellis Munford.

" When ordered into battle that young officer had waved an adieu to friends who stood by him with so sweet a smile that none would have supposed him conscious of the danger he was plunging into. Absorbed at once by the duties of his position his eye ran rapidly over the men under his command. Among them were some who were very difficult to discipline; one, especially, seemed thoroughly hardened, not hesitating even to resist the authority of his officers. Lieutenant Munford, almost in despair of making a soldier of him, had recently put him under arrest for some grave offence. But during the fight this man displayed a most extraordinary courage: wherever the dead fell fastest there he seemed to find his duty. Noticing his gallant conduct Munford dashed up to him, seized his hand, and said : ' I have come to ask you to forget what I did to you. You have shown yourself a *hero* to-day; you cannot again be what you have been. Hereafter, be not the hero of a day, but of all time.'

" These were almost his last words before he fell; but they were 'apples of gold in pictures of silver.' As by magic they thrilled the soul of the degraded man, and seemed to transform his very being. A few moments more, and the lips that uttered them were silent forever, and the countenance just now glowing with the inspiration of battle was resuming its pleasant smile and settling into the repose of death. The soldier sought and obtained permission to bear the body from the field. When he delivered his charge to the friends of the dead lieutenant, his rough face was wet with tears, and he said to them, as with the promptings of a new life, '*He was the first who ever saw any good in me, or thought me capable of better things. I shall never forget him.*' Happy the man who is remembered thus !

"The family of Ellis Munford had the mournful pleasure—denied, alas ! to so many others under like bereavement—of following his remains to the grave. He was buried in Hollywood Cemetery, near Richmond, his pastor, the Rev. Dr. Charles Minnegerode, conducting the funeral services."

H. Everard Meade, of Petersburg, died at home, July 10, 1862, of disease contracted while serving in the Twelfth Virginia Regiment, and his death is thus recorded:

"Conscious that the end was near, and that the hour of his departure was at hand, he calmly kissed each member of his family and bade them good-bye, with the parting words to each, ' Meet me in heaven.' Then turning and clasping the hand of his physican, who was also his friend and kinsman, he said to him : ' I am dying, Hugh. Fight Christ's battles, as we are now fighting those of our country. Take Him as your great example, remembering that there is no happiness save in a life of virtue.' With these beautiful words trembling on his lips, he closed his eyes, and the brave young spirit was gone."

Captain Patrick H. Clark, of Halifax county, fell at the post of duty, stricken by disease after passing unscathed through shot and shell; and the venerable Bishop Johns, of the Episcopal Church, thus spoke of him :

" Other appropriate obituaries have borne truthful testimony to the manly virtues, social refinement and accomplished education of this patriotic youth, which endeared him to all who knew him, and rendered his early death a costly sacrifice in the cause of his country, and a deep and enduring affliction to his devoted family and friends.

" It is to record for their solace and support the clear and decided assurance of their dying relative and associate that this notice is penned.

" To the estimable lady who, during his short and severe illness, ministered to him with maternal tenderness, and who had expressed to him her hope of his recovery, he replied—' I am very ill; but do not think I am alarmed. I am not afraid to meet my God. If He spares my life, well. If otherwise, *I am perfectly resigned. My trust is in Jesus.*'

"In the battle of Manassas and before Richmond, his brave heart manifested itself in distinguished deeds of gallant bearing; and in the silence and solemnity of his chamber, when all causes of animal excitement were absent, and he was conscious of the pressure of the cold hand of death, he was calm, collected, and hopeful. Death had no fears to him. He who had nobly laid his worldly wealth, and all he hoped for, even life itself, on the altar of his country, was himself reposing in the arms of Jesus, and could confidently say, 'It is well'—'well' if spared; 'well' if removed; 'well' for time and eternity.

"We may thus, amidst the merited wreaths which his admiring and grateful survivors shower on his honored grave, discern an unearthly and incorruptible bloom bestowed by the invisible hand of grace, to refresh with its fragrance those who mourn him, and hereafter to bear the precious fruit of eternal life."

Major Hugh Mortimer Nelson, of Clark county, Virginia, who was one of the ablest of the "union men" of the Virginia Convention of 1861, but who, like most of his party, buckled on his sword when all of Virginia's efforts at pacification had failed, and did gallant service on the staff of General Ewell, died August 8, 1862.

A faithful friend who was with him wrote thus, immediately after his death: "Truly, I felt it a privilege to listen to him, to hear his testimony to the glorious salvation of which he was assured. 'Saved by grace,' he repeated again and again. 'I am safe, safe in the Lord Jesus.' All his views were bright; no cloud obscured his hope of heaven."

Another, who joined him soon after, wrote of his wonderful serenity and his triumphant trust in his Saviour. "I am in sweet hands—safe in the arms of the Lord Jesus," were his words. A little after, he exclaimed, "Glorious brightness!" One who sat close by, asked, "Where does it come from?" "Straight from my Saviour's countenance," he replied immediately.

His message to his wife and children was "to stand still and wait on the Lord for salvation."

On the 8th day of August, 1862, his brave spirit winged its way to the bosom of its God. And we add, reverently and trustfully, "Let me die the death the righteous, and let my last end be like his."

Lieutenant Cotesworth Pinckney Seabrook, of South Carolina, fell on the field of Chancellorsville. His splendid career and happy end have been worthily written in a sketch by the graceful pen of Captain W. Gordon McCabe, which concludes as follows :

" The following letter, the last he ever penned, reflects the soldierly spirit which animated him and the rest of the army on the eve of that great campaign :

" ' IN THE TRENCHES, FOUR MILES FROM FREDERICKSBURG,
" 'April 30, 1863.

" '*My Dear Mother :* The battle of Fredericksburg, to all appearances, is, like Manassas, to have a duplicate. At ten o'clock yesterday morning, without any previous notice, or the least expectation on our part of an advance by the enemy, a courier, in a desperate hurry, brought the order to be ready to move at a moment's notice, which was soon followed by the final one, and at 10.30 our winter-quarters were broken up, camp deserted, and the " Light Division " was wending its way towards the old battle-field. There are soldiers for you ! After being in camp six months, where a great many little comforts had been collected, to be on the march in half an hour from the time they were told to prepare to leave ! Of course there was no time for cooking, so we had to do without food until this morning, when hard crackers and raw salt beef was served to the thousands of hungry men anxiously expecting something. It rained from the time we arrived yesterday evening until noon to-day, but we were so tired and hungry that sleep was not to be driven off by any circumstances, however disadvantageous, and I for one slept like a top. Our brigade occupies exactly the same position it did in the last battle, and there is not much danger of the Yanks flanking us again. The men are in splendid spirits, ready to yell on the least provocation. " Old Jack " and Lee both caught it mercilessly this morning while making the rounds. We just know that we can thrash Hooker " out of sight," and the beauty of the thing is that he and his men know it too. From the top of the hill, behind our lines, their long lines can be plainly seen. Our skirmishers are only a few hundred yards apart. *The batteries have opened and the men are falling in, so good-bye ; have no fear for me, for I fear nothing for myself. My trust in God is always strong enough in such times as these to keep me cool and confident.'*

"Long before this letter met the loving eyes for which it was

intended, tidings had sped to the mother that her boy, while
leading his men to victory, had fallen in front of the works at
Chancellorsville. He had followed the great leader of his corps
in countless earthly triumphs, and now shared with him a victory
before which paled all the glories of Richmond and Manassas.
He had fought the good fight, he had endured hardness as a
good soldier of Christ; he had won the crown of life promised
to those who are faithful unto death.

"It would be well-nigh impossible to picture the gloom cast
by his death upon his regiment, his brigade, upon all who knew
him. The old brigade he loved so well paid his memory the
unusual honor of attending almost in a body the rude obsequies
accorded the young subaltern. Like the hero of Coruña, he was
buried at night, wrapped in his simple soldier's blanket, on the
field made glorious for all time by his own valor and that of his
comrades. No useless coffin, no farewell shot—only the struggling moonbeams shining on the hero's grave.

"He now sleeps among his own kindred in the far-off Southern land.

"The hold which he had taken on all hearts is evidenced by
the countless letters which came to his family voluntarily, and at
once, from those who knew him. Some had been his companions at college, some on Morris Island, some in the campaigns
in Virginia; but in all cases the testimony was the same to that
most rare union of gentle and soldierly virtues, to his humble
piety, splendid courage, gentleness, purity, self-abnegation. His
captain, a distinguished university man and a tried soldier, who
in the next general action yielded up his noble life, writes to
his mother: 'Of his nobleness and piety I need not tell you.
Though so long absent, his heart, I know, was ever open to his
parents in all things; and I have never known anything of him,
but his praises and his merits, that he might not tell you. Always mindful of his religious duties, he was of late especially
devout, constantly reading his Bible, and often singing hymns
with the men, whose affectionate regard for him caused them to
take every occasion to be with and about him. His cheerful,
bright humor never flagged, even on the battle-field, where his
smile seemed more radiant than ever, while his voice and command gave life and courage to those about him.'

"His lieutenant-colonel, long before death had hallowed his
memory to his friends, described him as 'in battle splendid, in

private life exceedingly beloved—in short, the model of a Christian soldier.'

"Many knew him only on the field of battle. These were impressed by his person and bearing, by his fine soldierly instinct, by the coolness in desperate events which shone clear of all affectation. But to those who possessed the privilege of his friendship, no mere words, nothing but his simple name, '*Pinckney Seabrook,*' can bring back a semblance of the man they loved. Selfish sorrow dares not raise its wail in contemplating that Christian life, so rounded with the sleep which He giveth His beloved; while, as a soldier, his name shall go down upon the lips of comrades eager to speak the biography of one who, to their mind, filled the measure of perfect knighthood—'chaste in his thoughts, modest in his words, liberal and valiant in deeds.'"

Dr. John H. Cowin, of Alabama, left the practice of his noble profession to enlist as a private soldier in the Fifth Alabama Regiment, was made orderly sergeant of his company, and fell in the forefront of the battle at Chancellorsville, his last words being: "*I am sinking very fast, I think. If I die, tell my father that I fell near the colors, and in the discharge of my duty.*"

Lieutenant Francis Pendleton Jones, of Louisa county, Virginia, left the university to enlist as a private in Company D, Thirteenth Virginia Infantry (in the ranks of which he had two brothers), was promoted to a position on the staff of his uncle, General John M. Jones (who was killed at the Wilderness), fell leading a charge on the heights of Gettysburg, got home to die, and thus yielded up his noble, young life:

"He was perfectly conscious that his end was at hand, expressed his entire willingness to die, if it was God's will that he should do so, and said that his hope of salvation was in Christ alone. The day of his death, a friend read to him the fourteenth chapter of John, and at its conclusion he said, with a sweet smile, 'I always loved those words. That chapter was a great favorite with my dear mother, and she used frequently to read it to me when I was a boy. I know its meaning now. Yes! and I will soon meet her, and dear Ed.* too, in one of those bright mansions which Jesus went to prepare for us.' Thus on the 2d day of September, 1863, Francis Pendleton Jones passed from the earth."

---

* A younger brother, who had fallen at Gaines's Mill, June 27, 1862.

28

The death of *Lieutenant William Fauntleroy Cocke*, of Cumberland county, Virginia, has been thus touchingly described by
the facile pen of Mrs. Margaret J. Preston:

"Captain Carter Harrison, in a letter to his brother, thus
speaks of him:

"'My intimate acquaintance with your noble brother, William,
dates from the commencement of the war, when I had the honor
to command the company in which he served; for it was an honor
even to belong to that glorious army in which such men enlisted
as privates.

"'His modest and retiring disposition rendered it necessary to
know him long and well to properly appreciate his great worth,
that rare union of literary and cultivated tastes with sturdy manliness which so remarkably characterized him. Over and above
all this were the Christian faith and sense of duty which rounded
and completed his character. These were daily illustrated in
the cheerfulness and alacrity with which he discharged any duty
assigned him by his military superior. I remember that soon
after going into the service, he was detailed with a large party
on fatigue duty, involving severe labor—a service at that time
peculiarly obnoxious to men unused to labor, for the most part,
and strangers to the requirements of military rule. The officer
in command of the party, entirely unacquainted with your brother,
remarked that "if all the men worked like *that* man "—pointing
to him—" the task would be quickly finished." What an example to the rank and file of our volunteer army! A man
reared in wealth and luxury setting himself to work with such
will and alacrity as to make himself conspicuous among
his fellow-soldiers and call forth such commendation, doing
"with all his might whatsoever his hand found to do" at the
call of duty.

"'At the battle Manassas, while charging the enemy, he be-
thought him that his ammunition was expended; and stooping
over a dead soldier, he gathered from his belt a handful of car-
tridges and transferred them to his own box with such quickness
and dexterity as not to be thrown out of his place in the ranks—
a remarkable instance of coolness in a young volunteer for the
first time under fire. When I related this to Colonel Robert
Preston, of the Twenty-eighth, "God bless the boy," said the
gallant old soldier.

"'You were not present on the night when we contemplated

a surprise of the enemy's outposts near Washington.   When the temper of the men had become such that it was thought necessary to call for volunteers, company by company, and to take only such as were willing to go, at the call, *three* men from Company E stepped to my side without hesitation or a moment's deliberation; one of the three was William Cocke.   Any one who knew him would have counted on him at such a time; *he was always where duty called.*

"'On the march, bivouac, outpost, fatigue duty, anywhere, he was cheerful, uncomplaining, patient and obedient, never seeking or caring for promotion, but only solicitous to do well his part "in that station to which it pleased God to call him."   He was a noble pattern and example of the Christian soldier and gentleman; and so I ever found him to the close.   It was not my fortune to be with him when his well-earned promotion came unsought, nor to be present on that day when his bright career was ended.   But I am persuaded that as he lived, so he died; that the faith which had sustained him in life did not fail him in death.   Your friend and mine, Sergeant Jackson (now gone to his rest), a short time before his death, speaking of your brother in most touching and affecting terms, told me he was always associated in his memory with *the little Greek Testament* he loved so well and read so constantly.   Could a comrade well give a nobler eulogy?   Who would not say, "Let me be thus remembered?"'

"When Lieutenant Cocke passed from under the bare branches of his ancestral oaks, that bleak January morning, 1863, it was to see them no more forever.   Although still lame from his wound, he persisted in returning to his post.   This furlough, which the nursing of his wounded leg necessitated, was his last. In all the rapid, eager, deadly struggles of the next six months, he was a constant participator; marching, fighting, watching, he bore on with the same quenchless endurance and heroic fortitude, even to the end.

"As he passed with Lee's Army through Frederick City, on its march to Pennsylvania, a young female friend—who in the happy days gone by had been accustomed for months together to share, with other joyous summer guests, the hospitalities of Lieutenant Cocke's beautiful home—stood upon the pavement's edge, and with streaming tears of wonder and pride, gazed on him incredulously as he presented himself before her.   It was not strange that, in the bronzed, roughened, hungry soldier, she could with difficulty find a trace of the gay companion of many a well-remembered gala-day of old.   Alas, for the ravages of death!   Both have passed away, to meet in that beautiful city whose streets are ' like a jasper stone, clear as crystal.'

"The hurry and confusion, the fearful rapidity with which event trod upon the heels of event, in those after-crowded weeks, prevent us from knowing much of the closing scenes of this fair and well-wrought life, which did not quite reach twenty-eight years.

"On the fatal morning of July 3, 1863, William Cocke stood facing the enemy's guns before Gettysburg, ready for that terrible onset which was to send a wail of agony through the entire land. ' Never,' writes Captain Cocke, ' do I remember to have seen William more calm, quiet or collected, than he was on that morning, as I had my last sight of him standing within seventy or eighty feet of the enemy's breastworks.'   He had looked death too often and too steadily in the eye to quail now; and we may feel well assured that if it had been announced to him then and there that the next volley was to be the messenger to sum-mon him from the ghastly awfulness of the battle-field into the pure presence of God, not a muscle of that genial and pleasant countenance would have quivered, not a pulsation of that stead-fast heart quickened.   He knew 'in whom he had believed.' We feel sure that the 'little Greek Testament' was turned to for strength and solace in that hour of fearful crisis.   'Let not your heart be troubled;' 'where I am, there shall my servant be.' ' Whosoever believeth in me shall never die.'   And thus com-forted and fortified, would he not hide in his bosom again the dear and well-used volume, and with a supreme faith, uncon-scious of fear, step gloriously forth to his doom?

"All we can know is, that when the deadly onset was made, Lieutenant Cocke rushed upon the batteries: clouds of smoke veiled the carnage that followed; cannon belched their fire, the earth shook with the tread of contending armies, the grass grew sodden with blood; and when the rage of battle ceased, and the broken bands fell back exhausted, William Cocke *was not among them.*   No one had seen him fall, none could give any tidings of him.   All who had closely surrounded him had doubtless sunk beneath the same charge; and the silence that came back upon the souls of those who questioned of his fate was the only answer. Right under the muzzles of the murderous guns he had heard the Voice which said, '*Come up hither.*'

"Captain Cocke was slightly wounded by a ball passing between his ear and his head, which grooved a course for itself in the flesh ; so narrow was the dividing-line between life and death ! Yet he was instant in laborious search for the beloved, missing brother ; but it was all in vain ; ' he saw him no more.'

"We pass over the record of the six torturing months of suspense, in which it remained a question whether he might not be a helpless and wounded captive in some distant fort.   We dwell not on the deferred hope that sickened and at length died utterly away ; while the hearts that had nursed and clung to it, and kept it alive so long, sank down into silent and acquiescent sorrow. ' None knoweth the place of his sepulchre unto this day.'

"Thus meagrely, and with scant materials at hand, has the writer of this sketch endeavored to outline the character of William Fauntleroy Cocke, who, it will be allowed, belonged to that class of men

> " ' Who, living, are but dimly guessed,
>   But show their length in graves.' "

Among the cherished friends of my university days I counted *Wm. T. Haskell*, of South Carolina, one of the purest, truest, noblest, Christian gentlemen whom I ever knew. I remember meeting him on the march to Gettysburg, in command of the battalion of sharpshooters of his division, and for miles we revived hallowed memories of our university days, talked of the hopes of the future, and expressed our confidence that the impending battle would result in another splendid victory for the Army of Northern Virginia, which we hoped would establish the independence of the Confederacy.   I remember he spoke calmly of the probability that he might fall, and expressed his full trust in Christ and entire resignation to God's will.   Alas ! I never saw him again, and the story of his death is thus told in the " University Memorial : "

"We have been kindly favored with the following extract from the unpublished report of Pender's Division in the battle of Gettysburg :

" ' During a successful charge made to drive the enemy from a road in front of Cemetery Hill, Captain William T. Haskell, First South Carolina Volunteers, in charge of a select battalion of sharpshooters, received a wound from which he died in a few moments, on the field. " This brave and worthy young officer," says Colonel Perrin, in his official report of this transaction, "fell while nobly walking along the front line of his command, encouraging his men and selecting favorable positions for them to defend. He was educated and accomplished, possessing in a high degree every virtuous quality of the true gentleman and Christian. He was an officer of most excellent judgment, and a soldier of the coolest and most chivalrous daring." '

" Colonel Perrin, whose tribute is given in this extract, was at the time in command of the brigade, and was made brigadier-general for his conduct in this battle. No higher testimony could be given than that of this distinguished officer who, after a brilliant career, subsequently surrendered his own life in defence of his country.

" The following is the conclusion of an obituary written soon after, by a superior officer of his own regiment; ' Captain Haskell, at the time of his death, was one of but three officers who had been through every engagement in which his regiment had participated, in none of which did he fail to distinguish himself. At Cold Harbor, Manassas, and Chancellorsville his conduct was most strikingly conspicuous.

" ' Such a character as Captain Haskell's deserves far more than the limits of such a notice as this allows. His was indeed no ordinary character. Would that a fitter position had afforded a larger sphere for the happy effects of its influence ! Fortunate indeed were those who had such an example before them—the example of a Christian soldier ! A courteous gentleman, a rigid disciplinarian, a careful observer, constantly attending to the wants and comfort of his men, a brave and heroic leader in battle—prejudice against his discipline, at first new, misunderstood, and not appreciated, melted away before his conspicuous discharge of duty. He who would most rigidly enforce discipline, who knew no compromise in the enforcement of orders, was found to be the first at the bedside of the sick, bringing with him into the dreary hospital the tenderness of a woman, and with a touch like hers softening the hard pallet to the sick or wounded. Requiring an implicit obedience to his own orders, he yielded a like obedience to the orders of his superiors. Sharing whatever hardships his men were called upon to endure, he repressed all murmuring by his cheerfulness under them. He had no rule for his men which did not apply to himself. Every action, every word, seemed to be measured by his duty to his God and his country. Hardships were to be borne cheerfully, not complained of. He lay in his single blanket in the snow and ate his simple ration with the same cheerfulness as if he were enjoying the luxuries of home. While carefully taking every precaution, he could bear no foreboding of evil.

"'Of his conduct in battle, no fitter description can be found than his own language, in writing of his friend, Lieutenant Seabrook, after his death: "He was a brave man—nobly brave! brave as a man can be who has committed his soul to God and given his life to his country." True words of himself. He, too, had committed his soul to his God, and, in his readiness to meet his Saviour, death had no terrors for him. Whatever ties there were to life, he was ready to sacrifice them to his country. That life, which he had freely offered on so many battle-fields, was at last taken in the bloody battle of Gettysburg. The loss is his friends', his fellow-soldiers', his country's—the gain his own! Few have served their country so well; none, we trust, rest more happily from their labors.'

"The same mail brought to Mrs. Haskell the intelligence of the death of Captains Langdon Cheves, Charles T. Haskell, and William T. Haskell, a brother and two sons, one in the vigor of maturity, the others in the prime of youthful manhood. 'These men,' in the language of a public journal which, in this instance at least, gave utterance to the public sentiment—' these men were all of the stuff of which heroes are made. They all did the duties of life with earnestness; all died the death of martyrs in a cause to which they had devoted themselves without stint; and of each of them, it is no exaggeration to say, the anxious inquiry has gone forth, Who can fill his place?'

"In November, 1866, the remains of William Thompson Haskell were raised from the field of Gettysburg by the hands of his comrades, and brought to his native town. At the depot they were met by the survivors of the old company with which he had originally entered the service, and escorted to the Episcopal Church, when, with solemn services and amid deep emotion, they were interred in the adjacent cemetery.

"We have spoken of his rare gifts, of his heroic qualities, of his unselfish patriotism, and his devotion unto death. Let us add, in conclusion, that all these were animated by Christian principle and illuminated by Christian faith. The spirit of apostles, prophets, and martyrs, and of Him who is Head over all, had made its abode in him. A Divine Power had tempered into harmony, and had exalted into heroism the natural qualities of the man. That Power has raised him to a glory infinitely transcending the glory of earthly success or human applause."

Burditt W. Ashton, of King George county, Virginia, private in Company C, Ninth Virginia Cavalry, was killed on the 3d day of July, at Gettysburg, and a friend thus closes a sketch of his noble young life:

"But these accomplishments and these fine points of character which adorn the outer man, are as nothing when compared with the jewel which he wore in his heart, and which was his confidence in the hour of death. The crown of his life was his trust in God. At the early age of fourteen, under the training of his pious parents, he had committed his soul to the Saviour; soon afterwards he was confirmed at the Old Fork Church, in Hanover county, by the Right Rev. Bishop Johns, and thenceforth his life was eminently Christian. Had his life been spared, it was his purpose, after making the needful preparation, to preach the Gospel. A gentleman who formed his acquaintance and friendship while a school-boy at Hanover Academy, and afterwards roomed with him at the university, uses the following strong language in regard to him:

"'I never saw a more beautiful Christian in my life. Truly pious and conscientious, he was prompted in every act by duty and principle. By close application he was storing his strong and vigorous mind with knowledge, to be used in the Master's cause. Uninfluenced by any worldly or personal consideration, and with an eye to the glory of God, he had dedicated himself to His work and service. Had he lived, he would have entered the ministry as an Episcopal clergyman.'

"'It is well,' then, with him. His ministry has only been transferred to a higher sphere. Up there, away beyond the stars, they that wait for the Lord shall meet him 'in the morning.'"

Colonel William Welford Randolph, of Clark county, Virginia, fell at the Wilderness, on the 5th of May, 1864, heroically leading the old Second Virginia Infantry, Stonewall Brigade.

Colonel John Esten Cooke writes, for the "University Memorial," a graceful sketch of this noble soldier, from which I make the following extracts:

"Such is the unadorned record of the career of the noble young Virginian. Such a recital, necessarily brief, and touching upon the mere dates and leading events, must always be unsatisfactory, especially to those who personally knew the original. For behind the naked statement, the dry and incomplete record, is the living, breathing individual, whose face and form and character survive in memory. These lines can give no adequate idea of William Randolph. It was one of the bravest of the brave who thus followed Jackson in all his hard campaigns; marching, musket on shoulder, in the ranks; who mounted the works at Gettysburg, and faced the fire unmoved; who was everywhere in the fore-front of battle, leading, cheering, and inspiring all; and who fell at last on the bloody field of the Wilderness, soon after uttering the grand words: 'Jesus can receive the soul of the warrior on the battle-field as well as on the softest couch.'

"Of the mere attribute of courage we could give, if necessary, a hundred instances. It is the amount of this testimony which excludes it, and we present but a paragraph or two: the first from a letter of General Terry, the last commander of the Stonewall Brigade, to Dr. Randolph, after the death at Cedar Creek, in October, 1864, of Captain Robert Randolph, a younger brother of our subject:

"'I knew your sons, William and Robert, well;' writes General Terry. 'I am proud to say they were my intimate, personal friends. They possessed my unbounded confidence as friends, as gentlemen, and as soldiers. No man has given to the Confederate cause two better soldiers and more gallant gentlemen. As the brigade commander, I feel their loss; and deeply have I to regret the fall of Lieutenant-Colonel William W. Randolph, so soon after his promotion to a position which, I feel assured, he would have filled with distinguished credit to himself and the service. I was looking forward to the day when still further honors awaited your sons. While you have cause to sorrow over their early graves, yet you have reason to be proud to know that they fell where duty called, at the head of their commands. They fell by no random shot, but where the fire was the hottest.'

"'As an officer,' says Major R. W. Hunter, in an eloquent eulogy delivered upon the character of his dead friend and associate, in the Virginia Legislature, 'as an officer, Colonel Randolph possessed the entire confidence of those above and below him. With my own ears I have heard the great Jackson speak in his praise, and his name and daring deeds are still themes around the camp-fire of his regiment.' To this we add the eloquent words of another friend: 'The very soul of the Confederacy was in him.'

"Such was the character, most briefly depicted, of Colonel Randolph, the soldier. He was brave among the bravest; shrunk from nothing in his path; but this mere courage of the soldier was the least beautiful of his traits. Beneath the gray coat which defined the simple outer man, if we may so express it, was the human being of heart, so warm, true, generous, and noble, that those who knew him best may almost be said to have thought least of him as a mere soldier; valuing more the character of the man in his private life than the faculties and fame of the officer. Of this private and unofficial character, the writer of this page had ample knowledge; and, going back to-day in memory to the past, can recall no human being, among all encountered in this world, endowed with qualities more calculated to endear one to his species. Firm in his loves and friendships, utterly true and reliable, so that you could always count upon his word; making no professions which he did not feel; cool, resolute, determined to find what was *right*, and to pursue it careless of consequences; giving his heart with his hand, scorning falsehood, and hating it with a perfect hatred; he was a true man in the fullest sense of that word.

"Of the mere intellectual faculties, those who knew him had a very high estimate. His mind was one of extraordinary vigor, and he saw clearly into every subject, possessing in no ordinary degree that 'judicial intellect' which makes great lawyers and celebrated judges. At the bar he must have taken a very high rank.

"Of Colonel Randolph in his private character, too, much might be said. A friend writes: 'He had the most untiring and dauntless energy I ever saw, the clearest views of complicated questions, and withal, such a grand and noble simplicity of character and total freedom from guile, that it brings tears to my dim eyes to think of him as I saw him last, so hopeful, so self-reliant, so brave, so tender, so true.' A hundred such passages might be quoted, referring to the individual at every period of his life, from the time when, at Hanover Academy, Mr. Lewis Coleman spoke of him to his old pastor as 'a magnificent boy,' to the moment when over his lifeless body strong men wept, saluting him as one of the great commonwealth which gave him birth; but for these details we have no space.

"We shall terminate this sketch by some quotations from his letters to his mother and another person very dear to him, which display in an unmistakable light that crowning grace of manhood—perfect reliance upon God, and a sure realization of the only source from which he could expect hope and happiness. We present these passages without comment. Let the careless reader not omit a perusal of them. In every line a pure spirit speaks and shows the loveliness of trust and humility.

"From 'Newtown, *March* 23, 1862. Tell Ma that I thought of her and her teachings; and that if she does hear of my fall, she must not think of me as one who died without hope.'

"'*April* 10, 1862. In the thickest of the fight I know that God can hear the silent prayer of the greatest sinner, and, through the blood of Him who saved the dying thief upon the Cross, can in like manner translate the soul of the warrior from the battle-field to a sinless, happy home in heaven.'

"'*December* 11, 1862. We are on the verge of a great battle or a retreat. . . . I trust that, if I fall, the great Father of Spirits will take me to Himself, sinner though I am, through the merits of a Saviour whose love I have so often slighted.'

"'*March* 14, 1863. You must pray for me, as I know you do. I feel, somehow, a need which cannot be supplied in this world. . . . Yes, it may be the first whisperings of that mysterious voice whose power can yet turn my heart from its stubborn sinfulness, and to that Power I go, with humbler heart and deeper prayer than ever before.'

"'*March* 31, 1863. These days in camp seem very dreary to me, separated from you. . . . You must redouble your prayers for me, that I may be drawn to Christ. I feel more on this subject than ever before in my life. It is a hard struggle to me, and you cannot know fully the hopeless feeling of one who has been for years so sinful as I have been. But the promise of our Saviour is to the vilest of sinners, and I feel that I am one of them. I have been and am so wicked that I feel as if it is almost impious in me to approach the throne of grace and hope for mercy. I trust to be spared to atone, in some measure, in the future for the past; but if God in His wisdom takes me from you, we will hope to meet in that bright world for which you are so well fitted, and for which atoning grace may prepare me.'

"'*May* 2, 1864. The sweet bright days are gone, and now the stern work of war is to begin. . . . You must not be more uneasy than you can possibly help, . . . but, *above all*, remember that in any event I humbly hope and believe that we will meet again in heaven.'

"'*May* 3, 1864. We have everything to be thankful for since this time last year; let us trust Him for the future. I intend to try and live so that if I am taken we may meet as we must do in that world where there is no more parting, and where sin and sorrow are unknown.'

"The spirit of trustfulness in the living Redeemer—that spirit whose gradual development may be traced, if we mistake not, in these touching words—is the crowning grace of a noble character.

"Do we exaggerate when we say that the death of such a man was a sore and bitter loss, not only to his friends and family, but to his native land as well? The brain to conceive, the heart to dare, the hand to execute—all these went down with him and are lost to us to-day. The great old Commonwealth has not yet lost, it may be, the 'breed of noble minds;' but none of her living sons possess a grander organization than the young soldier whose great qualities we have here so inadequately depicted."

Colonel J. Thompson Brown, of the First Virginia Artillery, who fell at the battle of the Wilderness, was thus spoken of at the close of a memorial sketch by Hon. B. Johnson Barbour:

"'Colonel Brown united in his character in a remarkable degree the excellencies of a soldier, the qualities of a gentleman, and the virtues of a Christian. To a cultivated intellect he joined judgment, energy, and promptitude, and was conspicuous for his gallantry in all the battles of the war in which he was engaged. He possessed the love of his soldiers, the esteem of his commanders, and the admiration of his native State.'

"And thus we close the record of this brave young soldier, painfully conscious of the imperfect manner in which our portion of the duty has been performed, but finding compensation in the reflection that his truest and best epitaph is declared in the multiplied evidences we have given of the unusual and universal grief which his death brought to all his companions in arms, from the great commander to the humblest private; and in the unrecorded sorrow of that other host of friends, who, standing as it were by his tomb, would with one consent inscribe upon it in imperishable characters the declaration, that in the long and mournful catalogue of the victims of the late war, Virginia finds the name of no truer, braver, or better son than John Thompson Brown."

A few days later, at Spottsylvania Court House, fell the accomplished *Major David Watson*, of the same artillery regiment with Colonel Brown, and of whom it was said:

"Major Watson was borne from the field and carried to a neighboring house, where he received all the aid that kindness and sympathy could give. Happily, he retained his faculties long, enough to recognize the presence of that heart-broken mother; she who had leaned forward with throbbing heart to catch the first tidings from every battle-field on which her darling was endangered, and on whose prophetic face for three long, anxious years had been prefigured this coming agony. She came in time to receive the last pressure of that 'dear hand,' and to hear from his own lips this solemn declaration, 'I have never believed in a deathbed repentance; so for three years I have, every night, before retiring to rest, *earnestly prayed to God, not so much that He would spare my life as that He would prepare me for this day, and save my soul.*' Comforting words! welling up from a brave, honest, sincere heart, and recalling the kindred declarations of Jackson and of Havelock."

George Washington Stuart, of Fairfax county, Virginia, private in the Rockbridge Artillery, fell at Chancellorsville and needs no fitter epitaph than the following extract from a letter from General R. E. Lee to his sister, dated "Camp Fredericksburg, May 11, 1863:"

"I grieve greatly on my own account. I am deprived of one whom I loved and admired, and whose presence always brought me pleasure. His gentleness, his manliness, his goodness won the affection of all, and all sorrow at his death. But think what he has gained, what peace he enjoys; what suffering, toil and hardship he may have been spared. God, in His mercy, be assured, has taken him at the right time and right place for him. May He give to his mother and his friends that strength and that support they require! On learning the sad news, I went to Mrs. Marye's the evening I returned from Chancellorsville, where I knew that he had been properly appreciated and kindly received, and learned that he was interred in their family cemetery, where I thought he had better rest. Mrs. P—— told me everything had been done that could be, and that she had written to your mother. Peace to his ashes and honor to his memory, and may God comfort and support us all!

> "'He needs no tears who lived a noble life;
> We will not weep for him who died so well,
> But we will gather round the hearth, and tell
> The story of his strife.
> Such homage suits him well—
> Better than funeral pomp and passing bell.'"

Lieutenant French Strother Bibb, of Charlottesville, Virginia, who fell at Chancellorsville bravely doing his duty in command of his guns of the Charlottesville Artillery, was my pupil when a boy, and I watched with deepest interest his development into the heroic man he proved himself to be, but above all I rejoiced that his simple trust in Christ grew stronger as the years went on. In a sketch of him it is said:

"From Richmond the battery followed the fortunes of the field again until after the battle of Fredericksburg, when it settled down in winter-quarters at Bowling Green, Caroline county, Virginia. Here opportunity was afforded for the display of both the officer and the man. In the former capacity he was faithful, energetic, even ambitious, in the discharge of duty; in the latter he was genial and companionable, and by his good fellowship won the hearts of those under his authority, until, such was his popularity, scarcely a word of complaint was ever uttered against him.

"In illustration of his Christian temper the following incident may be related: Visiting the guard-house, on one occasion, as officer of the day, he found imprisoned there a former schoolfellow and friend of his father. The man had known better days, but was now utterly degraded by long years of dissipation. Moved by the spirit of Him who came to 'proclaim liberty to the captives, and the opening of the prison to them that are bound,' Lieutenant Bibb sat down by him, spoke kindly to him —'The first kind words,' said the poor fellow afterwards, 'that I had heard for many, many long years'—gave him some tracts to read, and proposed his release on condition he would promise to make an effort to reform. The promise was given, and the soldier left the guard-house, and went forth to duty.

"The war was near its close—the young officer had long since filled an honorable grave—when the bereaved father chanced, in passing through a hospital, to find this friend of his youth, who had come thither to die. But he was no longer a debauchee, for his eye kindled as he told of the solemn promise he had made and, by the grace of God, kept until then; of the sustaining trust in the merits of the Redeemer, which filled him with peace and fitted him for the hour of death, now so near. All this he attributed, so far as human agency is concerned, to the labors and kindness of French Bibb, who, boy though he was, ' talked to me,' said he, ' like a father.'

"As he was borne from the field he said calmly to one of his comrades: '*I am willing to die for my country; and I think it had better be myself than you.*' Lingering for some days in the hospital, he bore his sufferings with Christian fortitude, and gave indubitable proof that he died in the full assurance of the Christian faith.

" His company, in formal meeting, gave expression to their feeling at the death of one, who—to use their own words—' distinguished for the mild firmness of his bearing, the courtesy of all his intercourse, his attentiveness to every duty, his conspicuous gallantry in action, had secured, to a rare extent for one so young, the admiration, the esteem, the love of the whole company.' The Sunday-school in which he had both been pupil and teacher, added its tribute to his memory, and thanked God that ' there was so much to mitigate the bitterness of the sorrow in the hope of reunion in heaven.' And when the body was carried home to be buried, and the solemn toll of the church bell, whose gladder tones he had loved so well in life, summoned his friends to the funeral ceremonies, ' every place of business in the town was closed,' and the whole community united in giving honor to their young townsman, who, dying in his country's service, was no less a true soldier of the Cross. The funeral services were conducted by his pastor, Rev. Wm. F. Broaddus, D. D. On his coffin were laid the following lines, written by a lady friend for the burial hour:

> " ' Strew flowers on his coffin'd breast,
> His noble heart is now at rest;
> The young, the beautiful, the brave,
> We will not mourn his early grave.
> Faithfully his duty done,
> On earth a noble name he won;
> But, nobler far than earthly fame,

He bore his Saviour's holy name.
His early days to God were given,
His record in the Books of Heaven.
Then let him rest, till that glad sound
Which calls the nations from the ground
Full on his raptured ear is pour'd—
'Come forth, ye blessed of the Lord.' "

As French Bibb was borne from the field of Chancellorsville he was met by his most intimate friend, *Willie M. Abell* (son of A. Pope Abell, Esq., of Charlottesville), who belonged to the Fifth Virginia Cavalry. The two friends had not met before since they entered the army, and their meeting under the circumstances was so tender and touching that bronzed veterans who stood by with uncovered heads could not restrain their tears. But the two Christian boys could only grasp hands and exchange a few words of tender affection, as French Bibb was carried on to a few days of suffering, followed by his glorious end, and Willie Abell galloped on in the discharge of the soldier's stern duty. But these loving friends, who grew up in the same Sunday-school, were members of the same Church, and had so much in common, were not long divided.

Willie Abell gallantly rode with his regiment, the Fifth Virginia Cavalry, through the stirring campaigns which followed, proved himself a very hero in the fight, and at the same time illustrated the power and influence of the Gospel in his intercourse with his fellows, until he fell in the discharge of a delicate and important duty, and left behind the name of a hero who, though a beardless boy, was as true to country and to duty as any plumed knight who figures in the world's history.

The *Charlottesville Chronicle* thus told the story of his death, and Rev. Dr. J. C. Hiden, then post chaplain at Charlottesville, founded on it the following poem.

" We heard a day or two since an incident related which we think should be published, as not only illustrating a fine trait of character in our young townsman, William M. Abell, who fell on the battle-field near Luray just a week ago, but as illustrating also the spirit of devotion to duty which actuates so widely all of our young men.

" Mr. Abell, who was acting-adjutant of his regiment (Fifth Virginia Cavalry), had gone forward to reconnoitre in advance of the skirmish line, and discovered that a squadron belonging to his regiment was in a position where it was about to be cut off, of which it was unconscious.   He started immediately to inform the colonel, that it might be withdrawn, and just at this moment he received the fatal shot through the body; but in this condition he galloped on, gave the information, saved the squadron, and then lay down to die.   Such are the young men we are losing."

> " The ball has pierced his vitals,
>   But still he grasps the rein;
> *The squadron* is in danger,
>   And he takes no note of pain;
> He bore up in the saddle,
>   Warm blood his body laved;
> But he spurs his faithful charger—
>   The squadron *must be saved.*
>
> ' He gallops through the carnage,
>   No wavering—no pause;
> And he pours his very lifeblood
>   In Freedom's holy cause.
> His life is swiftly ebbing;
>   His strength is waning fast;
> But courage and *his message*
>   Sustain him to the last.
>
> " The *body* may surrender,
>   The 'mortal coil' may fail,
> But his dauntless, untamed *spirit*
>   Has never learned to quail;
> His voice is raised; he utters
>   One piercing, eager cry:
> 'Oh! colonel, SAVE THE SQUADRON!'
>   Then lays him down to die.
>
> " Time-honored Old Dominion!
>   What heroes hast thou borne!
> Thy mother's eye is weeping,
>   Thy lovely bosom torn;
> But still thy grand 'Sic Semper'
>   Defiantly shall wave;
> Thy sons will bear it proudly
>   To freedom or—the grave.

"J. C. H.

"CHARLOTTESVILLE, October 5, 1864."

A few days before *Captain W. Willoughby Tebbs,* of Company K, Second Virginia Regiment, was stricken down he wrote: " Providence still protects me, and if He sees fit, will carry me through safely; if not, what better death could a man die, or

29

could his friends wish for him, than to die in defence of such a cause ? "

Louis Magoon Rogers, of Accomac county, was one of the gentlest, purest men I ever knew, and proved himself one of the most heroic soldiers the war produced. In letters from camp to his mother he said :

" Do not be uneasy about me or the issue of the contest, which is evidently to be tremendous. God will care for me as well as for the issue of the approaching battle. He sees all things, past, present, future. Trust Him.

.   .   .   .

" Soon after breakfast it is my custom to repair from head-quarters to my regiment, where we have a chaplain. He some-times preaches at a neighboring church. On such occasions, being left to my own resources, I go into the woods, to some secluded spot, where I read my Testament without interruption. Alone, I try to commend myself and you to the Creator. By meditation and study I try to withdraw my mind from the vex-ations of the world, and to concentrate my thoughts upon the vasty future, whose portals of joy or despair are so near to all of us.

.   .   .   .

" Let us never forget, my dearest mother, that our Father above is not willing to do His children any harm ; and even if the body seems to suffer here in this world, may not the soul be happier in heaven on account of that very suffering ? Oh, mother, let us trust Jesus. I pray to Him to enable me to do my duty in His name. I find, thank God, that I am useful as a Christian. By holding prayer-meetings and Bible-class in my company the boys who are religious have greatly improved. They are much more thoughtful and attentive than they were when I first returned to my company."

He fell in the heroic effort to save Petersburg in June, 1864 ; lingered until the 24th of August, and calmly passed away, mur-muring with his dying breath : " Father, into Thy hands I commit my spirit."

The noble death of Louis Rogers was but the fulfilment of the prophecy of his noble life when I knew him at the univer-sity.

General Henry A. Wise, in a letter to his father, pays this young soldier the following glowing tribute ·

"RICHMOND, VIRGINIA, July 5, 1869.

"*My Dear Sir:* . . . I first noticed Louis in a shady retreat from the camp at Chaffin, in the year 1862, reading his Bible to a comrade in the woods. His quiet, earnest manner in his pious work struck me. I had before noticed him passingly, as your son, for your sake; but now that I saw his character, I began to notice him for his sake and mine too. I found that he had an exemplary influence with all the young men of his company. He could keep them orderly and obedient and on duty, while his officers could not. I soon found him not only moral, but intellectual; not merely gifted with animal, but with the highest Christian courage. Humble, unpretending, modest in his demeanor, he was too high to do wrong himself, and too firm to be tempted or misled by others. These qualities caused me in 1863 to make him chief clerk of the adjutant-general's office of my staff. He thus was drawn near and made intimate with me. His whole life and conduct were those of duty to God and his command in the army. His company did never so well as when he was with it. He was the fittest man in it for its captaincy, and repeatedly urged me to send him back to the ranks. For months I could not spare him. When I left head-quarters of camp I took him with me. He was a daily example of goodness and usefulness, and I never knew him to blunder, even, much less be guilty of a fault. His companionship as a Christian was a blessing to me. He never obtruded a homily, yet his soft, meek, deprecatory look would often allay a passion or stay a profane word. He was as quick as lightning to perceive, yet so conscientious thàt he never assumed to act without full intelligence of what he was to do. I could trust him as well absent as present, and he never failed me.

"At last he could not be withheld longer from his company, and especially after being promoted to the post of honor—color-bearer of his regiment, with rank of lieutenant. He fell at that post, flag in hand, on the 17th of June, 1864, gloriously, while his regiment was forced back and his gallant major, Hill, lost an arm in saving his person and his flag from the enemy. He lingered feebly in the hospital until his colonel took him to his house in Goochland, where he was fondly nursed as by a father and mother. Alas! he was too feeble when struck to recover from the blow. A brighter, braver, better soul never took flight from earth to heaven, from time to eternity. I would write on the tablet of his tomb:

"LIEUTENANT LOUIS ROGERS, JR.

" His example taught that the best soldier of the Captain of Salvation made the best soldier of the Confederate camps. His eternal parole is that of the Prince of Peace.

" Your friend,

" HENRY A. WISE.

" To GEORGE S. ROGERS, Esq."

Hon. D. B. Lucas has written a deeply interesting sketch of *John Y. Beall*, Acting Master of the Confederate Navy, who was hung under sentence of a court-martial February 24, 1865, and whose execution, Mr. Lucas clearly shows, was without the shadow of law or justice. Mr. Lucas thus describes his death:

" Thus we find Beall in Fort Columbus, face to face with his doom, all hope extinguished, every avenue of mercy or escape closed. His friends told him there was still a slight gleam of hope. He responded that he himself entertained none, nor would exchange, he declared, the penalty of death for the living death of perpetual or indefinite imprisonment; he preferred an open grave to a vault.

" General Dix allowed his friends to visit him freely. Ministers of his own Church brought him the holy unction of their message, and those of other denominations called on similar errands. The Rev. Joshua Van Dyke visited him on the day before his execution and writes: ' I found him to be all that you had described him, and much more. He was confined in a narrow and gloomy cell, with a lamp burning at mid-day; but he received me with as much ease as if he were in his own parlor, and his conversation revealed at every turn the gentleman, the scholar and the Christian. There was no bravado, no strained heroism, no excitement in his words or manner, but a quiet trust in God, and a composure in view of death such as I have read of, but never beheld to the same degree before. He introduced the subject of his approaching end himself, saying that while he did not pretend to be indifferent to life, the mode in which he was to leave it had no terrors or ignominy for him; he could go to heaven through the grace of Christ as well from the gallows as from the battle-field, or his own bed; he died in defence of what he believed to be right; and so far as the particular things for which he was to be executed were concerned, he had no confession to make or repentance to exercise. He did not use one bitter or angry expression towards his enemies, but calmly declared his conviction that he was to be executed contrary to the laws of civilized warfare. He accepted his doom as the will of God.'

" Dr. Weston, chaplain of the Seventh New York Regiment, visited him on the 18th of February, the day whence a respite deferred his execution to the 24th of the same month, and Beall received him 'with marked courtesy.' He found him provided with a Bible, but without a prayer-book. Yet (as he tells us in his diary), as early as the 29th of December, the doorman of the police head-quarters had bought him 'a Book of Common Prayer, for $1.00.' What, then, had become of it, that on the morning first appointed for his execution he had no prayer-book? It is almost too sadly sacred to relate. He had sent it, a gift of life from the hands of death, to his betrothed!

" His Bible had been obtained in prison; upon opening it at random his eyes fell first upon these sublime verses: 'For our light affliction, which is but for the moment, worketh for us a far more exceeding and eternal weight of glory, while we look not at the things which are seen, but at the things which are not seen: for the things which are seen are temporal, while the things which are not seen are eternal.' He had written on the margin several hymns—old hymns, which stand in relation to the prayer-book collection as the essential oil to the remainder of the plant.

" The morning of the 24th of February opened fairly. Mr. Ritchie had spent the preceding night in the fort, and until mid-night had remained in the cell with Beall. On Wednesday night he had slept soundly, and happy dreams of home and childhood had visited him. But on Thursday night the toothache, to which he was subject, and with which he was suffering when arrested, attacked him again, and to some extent robbed him of his last night on earth. He would have liked some laudanum, he said, to still the pain, but declined to ask for it for fear of being misunderstood. Nothing, however, disturbed the tran-quillity of his soul.

" The execution was ordered between twelve and two. Messrs. McClure and Ritchie were left in the cell with the prisoner alone uninterruptedly for about an hour. This time was spent in calm, quiet, pleasant conversation. Old friends were inquired after, old scenes recalled, and the circumstances connected with his own participation in the raid on Lake Erie, and on the Dunkirk and

Buffalo Railway, gone over.   He spoke of his approaching death, and gave directions for the disposition of his body.   He dictated his own epitaph, which was to be : ' Died in defence of his country.'

"As the hour waned, McClure looked at his watch.   Beall noticed the movement, smiled, and inquired the hour.   It was twelve o'clock.   The execution, by the order, was to take place between twelve and two.   His voyage was, therefore, drawing rapidly to a close.   The sails could be seen in heaven coming up from the under-world.   Destiny was making the last entry in the log-book of life.   The harbor and the steeples of the city were in sight.

" Very soon Major Coggswell came in to bid his prisoner farewell.   This officer himself had once been held in Richmond as a hostage, with the sword of Damocles above him, and he could, therefore, sympathize with a soldier under similarly trying circumstances.   Like all around him, also, he had been drawn into the magnetic circle of Beall's friendship.

"After partaking of some nourishment, which Dr. Weston and Mr. McClure shared with him, Beall was left alone with his spiritual adviser.   After him, the officers of the law entered to make the customary preparations.   While the officers were performing their mournful duty, Beall addressed them : 'All I ask,' said he, ' is that there be no unnecessary consumption of time in the execution ; for, after all, it will be to me but a mere muscular effort.'

" His friends returned to find him hooded, and a black mantle thrown over his shoulders.   Mr. McClure, not observing that his hands were fastened behind him, offered his hand.   ' I cannot shake hands,' said he, smiling ; ' I am pinioned.'

" He had dressed himself, upon this morning, with unusual neatness.   His linen was white and clean, and his black silk cravat was gracefully tied beneath a rolling collar.   He wore a new pair of dog-skin gloves of saffron color.   Just the extremities of his fingers protruded from the blue military cloth cape thrown over his shoulders, which entirely concealed the manacles on his wrists, and the noose about his neck.   Upon his head was placed the fatal cap, the blackness of which heightened by contrast the whiteness of the martyr-face beneath it.   This face, naturally colorless, was blanched by long and solitary confinement.   It was smooth, white, and almost transparently clear.

The eyes, whose dulness or suffusion always betrays weeping, nervous agitation, or a sleepless night, were as clear, bright, and calm as an infant's. As he stepped from the threshold of his cell they began to beam, until they shone with an unusual and unearthly splendor.

"As he passed out, he turned to Messrs. McClure and Ritchie and said: ' Good-bye, boys ; I die in the hope of a resurrection, and in defence of my country ! ' . . . .

" Again the march is resumed, and the victim passes into the hollow square around the scaffold. Before stepping upon it, he turns with a smile to Dr. Weston, and remarks : 'As some author has said, we may be as near God on the scaffold as elsewhere.' He may be thinking of the sainted Abbot of Aquila, ' who wished to be buried under a gallows, and it was done.'

" Mounting to the platform, the prisoner takes his seat upon the chair immediately under the fatal rope. The adjutant of the post commences to read the charges, specifications, and the orders of General Dix for his execution. Beall, little dreaming of the test to which he is to be subjected, rises respectfully when the reading is commenced. But finding that, instead of the *last* and briefest order for his execution, the whole prolix and unsoldierly pronunciamento of General Dix is to be gone through with, he deliberately draws up a chair with his foot, and resumes his seat. When he hears himself designated as a citizen of the ' insurgent State of Virginia,' his smile grows intensely sad and significant. He sees now the men before him no longer as his own executioners only, but as the executioners of a sovereign State—his own beloved Virginia ; and he smiles not in derision, but in protest and remonstrance. At the point where the general denounces his heroic attempt to rescue three thousand fellow-soldiers as ' piracy,' he again smiles ; but when he is accused, as a ' guerilla,' of attempting ' to destroy the lives and property of peaceable and unoffending inhabitants,' he mournfully shakes his head in denial. Finally, when the adjutant reaches the concluding passage of the order, in which General Dix descants thus : ' The major-general commanding feels that a want of firmness and inflexibility on his part, in executing the sentence of death in such a case, would be an offence against the outraged civilization and humanity of the age,' the reporters declare that ' the prisoner seems to be reminded of some amusing incident in his military experience.' The truth is, Beall hears in the hypocritical cant of General Dix that officer's self-condemnation, and knows that every breath which the commanding general draws is in default of the penalty which he himself attaches to the violation of the laws of civilized warfare. Even the executioner grows impatient, and cannot endure this ordeal: 'Cut it short! cut it short!' cries he; 'the captain wishes to be swung off quick!' The crowd murmurs, and the reporters call his eagerness to perform his office 'brutality.' They mistake—he means it in kindness.

"The reading over, Beall promptly rises and announces his readiness. Then, reverently turning to Dr. Weston, he bows his head, while over him falls from the lips of the minister, like a spotless mantle, the benediction of the Church's ritual: 'The grace of our Lord Jesus Christ, the love of God, and the fellowship of the Holy Spirit be with you and sustain you!'

" His manner throughout has been one of respectful attention. But when he mounts the scaffold, and sits down under the fatal coil, he turns his back upon the adjutant while he is reading, and faces in the opposite direction. This attitude he does not change. What does it mean? His face is turned upon his own beloved South. Far over waters, mountains, valleys, and intervening hills, through the deep azure sky travel his thoughts to the land of chivalrous deeds and political ideas which, rightly understood, gather in their scope the eternal years of God's own truth, and for which no man should hesitate to die. As the martyr sets his face towards Jerusalem, so this hero, dying for the faith of his fathers, turns his face upon the South. Thus he faces when the last duty save that of the executioner is performed. The provos. marshal asks him whether he has anything to say. Turning upon the officer of the day, he speaks in a calm, firm voice: 'I protest against the execution of this sentence. It is a murder! I die in the service and defence of my country! I have nothing more to say.'

"A moment after a sword-flash is seen behind him, which is the signal to the executioner, and the hero's soul is free.

" Thus died, in the thirty-first year of his age, on the scaffold, John Yates Beall.

" His body, after death, was given to his two faithful friends, whose devotion had halted at no sacrifice in their efforts to save his life, and they laid it privately to rest in Greenwood Cemetery, near New York city.

" His death-scene, as described not alone by his friends who were present, and by the letters to his family and myself of James T. Brady, Esq., and Dr. Weston, but as reported by his enemies, was one of the sublimest spectacles in history. It exhibited courage without bravado, tenderness without weakness, resignation without stoicism, a protest against what he considered a murder without resentment against the murderers. It united to ease, dignity; to manliness, a sense of responsibility; composure to freedom. It combined at once firmness, self-possession, inflexibility, patience, intellectuality, fortitude, and cheerfulness. It was all that his friends could hope, or Christianity demand; all that his country could be proud of in chivalry, or his enemies dread in the example of martyrdom."

I have spoken of *General J. E. B. Stuart,* "the flower of cavaliers," who said to President Davis, who stood at his dying bedside: "If it were God's will, I should like to live longer and serve my country. If I must die, I should like to see my wife first; but if it is His will that I die now, I am ready and willing to go if God and my country think that I have fulfilled my destiny and done my duty."

Colonel Wm. Johnson Pegram—"Willie Pegram, the boy artillerist," we used to call him—left the University of Virginia in April, 1861, at the age of nineteen, and enlisted as a private in an artillery company, but, by superb courage and splendid skill, rose to be colonel of artillery and the idol of the whole army, when he fell on that ill-fated day at Five Forks which caused the breaking of Lee's lines and the fall of the Confederacy.

In an every way admirable sketch of him, written by his adjutant and intimate friend, Captain W. Gordon McCabe, it is said of. him, while in winter-quarters near Fredericksburg in 1862–63 :

" He spent the winter much as he had done the last, attending to the administration of affairs in camp and busying himself in promoting the comfort of his men. His letters to his family at this time breathe the constant prayer that he may be enabled to do his duty by his men as a Christian and a good officer. One of his first cares in winter-quarters was to assemble the men and say a few words to them concerning the importance of building a chapel and holding regular prayer-meetings. All these services he himself attended with earnest pleasure; and it was a common sight to see him sitting among his men in the rude log-chapel, bowing his young head reverently in prayer, or singing from the same hymn-book with some weather-beaten private from whom he had ever exacted strictest military obedience. His discipline, indeed, was that which belongs to long-estabished armies. He justly considered that it was mercy in the end to punish every violation of duty, and he knew that men do not grow restive under discipline the sternest at the hands of officers who lead well in action. He performed with soldierly exactness every duty pertaining to his own position, and held officers and men to a rigid accountability. His closest personal friends ceased to look for any deviation in their favor from his strict enforcement of the regulations. For four years he maintained such discipline, and with notable results. Not only in his lifetime were his men ever ready, nay eager, to meet the enemy, but when he himself had fallen in action, the old battalion followed its officers, some through their very homes, to the plains of Appomattox, with ranks intact, save from casualties of fight.

"When he had been recommended for promotion to the command of an infantry brigade (which General Lee declined to do, on the ground that he ' could not be spared from the artillery,' and made him instead colonel of artillery, which is recognized as really a higher rank than brigadier of infantry), he thus wrote to his mother:

"'Now, my dear mother, you must not think that I am conceited, and that I rely on my own ability, if I get this position and take it. I would not accept the position, but I believe the maxim given me by General Dabney Maury to be the proper one for a soldier to follow : " Never to seek promotion, and never to refuse it, but leave it to your superiors to judge of you." . . . . If I felt that it was from my own merit, I should be afraid to go again on the battle-field. I hope sincerely that before I am promoted to that grade, if it is to be done, brother will be made major-general; for, otherwise, I shall not believe that they ever promote according to merit. Do not be disappointed if General Lee refuses to have me promoted. He will do whatever is for the good of the service, and I had rather be in the ranks than have him do otherwise. Besides, I believe that God rules in small affairs as in great. He orders all things for the best. If I do get it, I will take it with fear and trembling, trusting to God's guidance and mercy, and constantly praying to Him for help who has been so merciful to me a sinner.'

"On the death of his gallant brother, General John Pegram, who fell in the battle of Hatcher's Run, he thus wrote to a comrade in the army:

"'" Words cannot express the grief this blow has brought upon us all. We can only thank God that He did not take him from this world until he had learned to look above it. While we who are left behind can never cease to mourn for one who was so dear to us, we cannot but feel grateful that his death came to him in such a manner—the manner in which he always wished to die; and above all we cannot but feel grateful for the belief that he is enjoying eternal rest and happiness now, and for the hope that we may be united with him hereafter.' The next week he returned to the army.

"The days grew darker and still more dark for 'the cause,' and like a true soldier he put aside his own grief to speak cheering words to those about him. In Richmond he had heard much talk in regard to the necessity of withdrawing from Virginia. His love for his State was such as God has implanted in the hearts of all true Virginians; and it was a pang to him even to contemplate surrendering the battle-scarred bosom of the 'Old Mother' to the petty tyrannies of those who hated and feared her. 'I would rather die,' he said slowly, 'than see Virginia given up, even for three months; but we'll all follow the battle-flag *anywhere*.'

"On the 1st day of April, just as the earth was beginning once more to grow glad with flowers, came to him the last of many fights. The brilliant artillerist, the pride of his corps, who during four years of active service had never lost a gun, was to fall at 'Five Forks,' with all his wounds in front, fighting such odds as had never yet confronted him. For two days previous to the battle he had undergone immense fatigue: in the saddle day and night, with slight intermission, for forty-eight hours; wet, hungry, no blankets; engaging almost continually the cavalry of the enemy. On the very morning of the fight his breakfast consisted of a handful of parched corn, which he generously shared with a comrade. In the centre of the line of battle were posted one gun from his own battalion, commanded by Lieutenant Hollis (Ellett's Battery), and a section from Braxton's Battalion, commanded by Lieutenant Early. Further to the right, sweeping the Gilliam field, were the remaining three guns of Ellett's Battery.

"There had been during the morning some sharp skirmishing with the enemy, but everything had grown quiet towards mid-day, and old soldiers doubted whether there would be any general engagement. Pegram, wearied down by fatigue, was sleeping soundly among the guns on the right, when sudden, ripping volleys of musketry from the centre told him that the enemy were charging his batteries. He instantly jumped into his saddle, and rode at full speed down the line of battle to his guns. Lieutenants Hollis and Early were using double canister at close range, and their cannoneers were serving their pieces in a manner beyond all praise. Within *thirty yards* of the guns the dense columns of the enemy were staggering under their rapid fire. Pegram rode in, speaking cheerily to the men, a sweet serenity on his boyish face, but the old light of battle shining in his eyes. 'Fire your canister low, men!' he shouted, as the blue lines surged still nearer to the heated guns. It was his last order on a field of battle. Suddenly he reeled and fell from his saddle. Small wonder that he was first to fall. The infantry were lying down, by order, firing over a low 'curtain' which they had hastily thrown up; he was sitting on his white horse in the front line of battle, cheering and encouraging his men. He had received his mortal wound, and knew it. 'Tell my mother and sisters,' he said firmly, 'that I commend them to God's protection. It will be a great blow to them at home to lose me so soon after "brother;" but for myself, I am ready. I have done my duty and now I turn to my Saviour.' He knew nothing of the bitter defeat. When victory no longer perched on the battle-flag of his old battalion, he had received his last promotion at the hands of the great Captain. He met a soldier's death, and had but a soldier's burial. Wrapped carefully in a coarse blanket he was laid to rest in the bosom of his mother State, Virginia.

"Brief as was his life, he had been for six years a devoted member of the Episcopal Church; and a comrade read at his grave her grand and solemn ritual for the dead.

"He now sleeps at Hollywood, beside his knightly brother, on a spot sloping to the ever-murmuring James, and overlooking that beautiful city in whose defence both of them so often went forth to battle, counting their lives a worthless thing.

"Thus passed away 'this incomparable young man,' in the

"DEATH OF WILLIE PEGRAM."

"I have done my duty, and now I turn to my Saviour."

(See page 460.)

twenty-fourth year of his age. It was his lot to be tried in great events, and his fortune to be equal to the trial. In his boyhood he had nourished noble ambitions, in his young manhood he had won a fame greater than his modest nature ever dreamed, and, at last, there was accorded him on the field of battle the death counted sweet and honorable."

And thus I might go on and quote by the page the dying words of these dying heroes which are indeed " apples of gold in pictures of silver," and show that they were taught by God's Spirit how to live and how to die. But these must now suffice.

But I would cheerfully leave this whole question of the permanent moral and religious influence of our army revivals to the conduct of the "men who wore the gray" *since* the war; for while thousands slept in soldiers' graves, many came back to resume their old places, or rather to make for themselves *new* places in business and social circles. These men were exposed to some peculiar temptations at the close of the war, and it would not have been strange if they had entered upon a career of lawlessness which would have made the condition of our unhappy South far worse than it was.

After four years' absence from any industrial pursuit, with fondly cherished hopes all blighted, plans all frustrated, fortunes swept away, and avenues of business all closed, they returned to their desolated homes. Alas! in many instances blackened ruins marked the spot of their once happy homes, and there were loved ones to tell tales of outrage and wrong which men of Anglo-Saxon blood have not been wont to hear unmoved.

To make matters worse (under the then avowed purpose of Andrew Johnson to " make treason odious ") there were stationed in every county squads of "blue coats," provost marshals and freedman's bureau agents, who were not always discreet, and not unfrequently did or said things well calculated to provoke serious collisions between these returned soldiers and themselves, or the newly emancipated negroes. Then followed the " carpet-bag " and " negro rule " of the Southern States, which is a blot upon our history, at which every true American should blush, and concerning which Dr. John A. Broadus so well said at an educational banquet in Brooklyn four years after the war: " You brethren at the North think that you have a great deal for which to forgive the South for the four years of war. I will not discuss that. But I tell you, brethren, we of the South have a great deal for which to forgive the North *for the four years since the war.*"

And yet, despite all of these temptations to a different course, I affirm (from a full knowledge of the facts, for important duties have required me to travel extensively in all of the Southern States and to see and know the Confederate soldiers), that, as a a rule, these men, instead of idly sitting down to rake in the ashes of destroyed hopes and ruined fortunes, have taken off their coats and gone to work in the corn, cotton and tobacco fields; in the offices, shops, stores, founderies and factories; on the railways, in the mines, and in every place where honest toil can earn a support. I know scores of young men who were raised in the lap of affluence, and had hardly ever done a day's work, whom the war found idling their time in dressing-gown and velvet slippers, the pets of "society," but who made brave, patient soldiers, and who since the war have shown their manhood by honest, manly work.

A great deal has been written about "the New South" and its wonderful prosperity, and surely it is a cause of devout thankfulness to know that at last large sections of our once desolated Southern land are beginning to "bloom and blossom as the rose." But it is due alike to the truth of history and to these men to say that this prosperity has been brought about, not so much by foreign immigration or foreign capital (though we cheerfully acknowledge what these have done), as by the pluck, energy, skill and patient industry—the brains and brawn—of the "Men in Gray" and the boys they have reared. The men who have managed our railways, mines, furnaces, founderies, factories and great business enterprises—who have filled our offices, State and Federal, since they have been allowed to do so—who have been our leading lawyers, physicians, professors, engineers, editors, preachers, mechanics, etc., etc.—have been the "men who wore the gray." There are eighty-three Confederate soldiers in the United States Senate and House of Representatives to-day, and every gubernatorial chair from Maryland to Texas, and from Virginia to Missouri, has been, as a rule, filled by a Confederate soldier. I have been struck with the fact that, in attending Confederate reunions in all of the States of the late Confederacy, I have found these men the leaders of the States in politics, business, social and religious movements.

It is a significant fact that not only the leading pulpits of the

South, in all of the denominations, are filled by Confederate soldiers, but that this is true of quite a number of prominent pulpits at the North.

In 1867 I addressed letters to all of the college presidents, and many of the leading pastors at the South, in order to ascertain how far our returned soldiers were maintaining their Christian profession, and what proportion of them were preparing for the Gospel ministry.

The replies were in the highest degree satisfactory and gratifying, showing that about four-fifths of the Christian students of our colleges had been in the army, and that a large proportion of them had found Christ in the camp—that nine-tenths of the candidates for the ministry had determined to preach while in the army—and nearly all of the army converts were maintaining their profession, many of them pillars in the Churches.

If the personal allusion may be pardoned, I will say that I have taken especial pains—by correspondence, by inquiries of pastors, and by personal interviews with many of them, as I have travelled in every State from Maryland to Texas—to ascertain the after-lives of the four hundred and ten soldiers whom I baptized in the army, and I have heard of *only three* (there were doubtless others) who have gone back to the world.

One pastor of a leading Church in the south-west said to me: "I am indebted to you for baptizing in the army the best and most efficient men in my Church."

I had a tender meeting several years ago with a delegate from Texas to the Southern Baptist Convention at Baltimore, whom I had baptized on the Rapidan in August, 1863, and I might give a number of touching incidents concerning these men whom I meet all over the South.

In the summer of 1865 I was travelling one day along a country road in Virginia, when I saw a young man plowing in the field, guiding the plow with one hand, while an empty sleeve hung at his side. I know not how others may feel about it, but for myself I never see the empty sleeve or halting gait of the true Confederate soldier that I do not instinctively take off my hat in profound respect for the man—I never pass his "vocal grave" without desiring to pause and cast at least one little violet upon it—and I hope never to see the day when I shall not count it a privilege to share with him, or with his widow or orphan, the last crust of bread that a good Providence shall give me.   And so I said to the friend who was with me: "We must stop.   I must speak to that young man."

When he drew near, singing merrily at his work, I recognized him as a young man whom I had baptized in the army.   I knew his history.   Raised in the lap of luxury he had resisted its temptations, and when the war broke out he was about to bear off the highest honors of one of our colleges, and seemed destined to shine in his chosen profession, for which his tastes and talents fitted him.   He was one of the first to step to the front when Virginia called on her sons to rally to her defence, and was one of the best of her noble soldiers.

To see him thus, then, his hopes blighted, his fortune wrecked, and his body maimed for life, deeply touched my heart, and my words of greeting and sympathy were right warm.   I shall never forget how the noble fellow, straightening himself up, replied, with a proud smile: "Oh, Brother Jones, that is all right.   *I thank God that I have one arm left and an opportunity to use it for the support of those I love.*"   If my voice could reach all the young men of the South to-day, I would ring in their ears the words of that maimed hero, and would beg them to imitate the example of our returned Confederate soldiers, who, as a rule, went to work with an energy and patient industry which have made them a real power in the land to-day.

I recollect that when, several months after, I met General Lee in Lexington, when he came to take charge of Washington College, and he asked me, as he frequently did: "How are our old soldiers getting on these hard times?"   I related to him, among others, the above incident.   The old chieftain's face flushed, his eyes filled with tears, and he said: "It is just like them, sir!   It is just like my poor boys!   They were the noblest fellows that the sun ever shone upon."   And so I believe they were.

And now my task is done.   If my readers have derived half the pleasure from the perusal of this narrative that I have done in reviving these hallowed scenes and recalling these precious memories—in living over again the days when the dark clouds of war were illumined with the sunshine of the Redeemer's smile— then I shall be more than satisfied.

And surely Christian men of every section and of every creed will unite in thanking God that Christ *was* in the camps of Lee's army with such wonderful power to save, and that out of that terrible war God brought such rich blessings.

THE RAVAGES OF WAR AND THE NEW SOUTH

APPENDIX.

LETTERS FROM OUR ARMY WORKERS.

FROM a large number of letters received, in response to circulars sent out soon after the war, I select the following as either containing new matter, or as supplementing and corroborating statements made in the body of the book. They were personal letters not intended for publication, and yet I beg that the writers will excuse the liberty I take in publishing them in the form in which they were written, as I can thus give a clearer view of the interesting and important matters of which they treat. I give them without comment of my own.

[*From Rev. A. C. Hopkins, of the Presbyterian Church, Chaplain Second Virginia Infantry, and Missionary Chaplain to Gordon's Division.*]

"CHARLESTOWN, WEST VIRGINIA, March 22, 1867.

"*Dear Brother Jones:* Upon reflection I find myself so often the theme of my remark that I have determined to waive modesty with you and write a memorial of my own operations as my part of the history of religion in the 'Stonewall Brigade'—as these notes are only for your eyes, I may be more pardonable, and more candid.

"My commission as chaplain Second Virginia Infantry dates from May 3, 1862. Exiled voluntarily from my home in Martinsburg, I sought an entrance into the army; but the low repute in which I had discovered the chaplaincy was held, deterred me from seeking an appointment for some time. The field-officers of Second Virginia directed Adjutant R. W. Hunter to invite me to their command, which I overtook between McDowell and Franklin. I then learned that application had been forwarded for my commission, which resulted as above-mentioned.

"The brigade under Brigadier-General Charles S. Winder was composed of five Virginia regiments, viz.: Second, Fourth, Fifth, Twenty-seventh and Thirty-third. The field-officers of the Second were Colonel J. W. Allen, Lieutenant-Colonel Lawson Botts and Major Frank Jones, all useful members of the Episcopal Church—one of whom had, by letter, authorized me, as I came through Richmond, to invest for him $50 in religious reading-matter for use of the regiments.

"Rev. E. P. Walton (Baptist) was chaplain to Fifth, and Rev. J. M. Grandin (Methodist) to Thirty-third Regiment. Rev. McVeigh (now for some time a prisoner) had been chaplain to Second, but his term of commission having expired under the previous organization of the command, the regiment, as organized in April preceding, was declared vacant; hence my assignment.

"The spring campaign, characterized by rapidity, fighting and fatigue, deprived chaplains of much opportunity for ministerial work, except for the wounded on the battle-field. By the prompt invitations of our field-officers, I held nightly meetings of prayer for the regiment at our head-quarters; and, whenever campaigning did not prevent, preached once or more on Sabbath. The number of professing Christians in the regiment was distressingly small; the prevailing religious sentiment was Episcopal. Besides the field-officers, and adjutant, who was Presbyterian, I could find but three officers, commissioned or non-commissioned, who belonged to any Church. One of these was a captain, and one was lieutenant, both Episcopal, and one a sergeant (Baptist). There were some communicants, of course, among the men of the regiment, whose strength was something upwards of four hundred, I think.

"One thing soon struck me; there seemed to be no affiliation among chaplains. It was more than three months after my attachment to the brigade before I met one of its chaplains, and then almost as per force a non-professing colonel called one up, and introduced us, saying emphatically, 'If you don't know each other, you should.'

"I commenced with the determination of sharing the sufferings, marches and perils of those for whose good I labored. This soon discovered itself to be the proper course; for mingling with men under all conditions gave me soon their friendship and pointed my preaching; while opportunities for extending acquaintance beyond my own command were gained and improved. An illustration of this occurred at the battle of Malvern Hill, when the colonel and lieutenant-colonel of another regiment came to mine (saying they knew they would find *me*) to get me to go and minister to one of their command who was badly wounded, although they had a chaplain.

"The campaign below Richmond was very fatiguing; marching all day in the hot sun and up all night caring for the wounded, with our faithful surgeons, I became exhausted. Attempting to preach in the hot shade of some pines as all lay in line of battle under the gunboats at Harrison's Landing, I fainted, but continued with the troops till our return to vicinity of Mechanicsville, when I obtained a sick-leave for ten days. During these the corps moved back to the vicinity of Gordonsville, and the other chaplains instituted some daily public services. On my return I held frequent services; but was greatly discouraged by the loss at Cold Harbor of our colonel and major.

"At this point Rev. Mr. Tebbs (Methodist) joined the Fourth Regiment as chaplain; but camp was soon broken up for the fall campaign. There was no general religious interest in the brigade, and I felt discouraged. We had not more than begun to realize the magnitude or opportunity of our work.

"The great Second Manassas battle came. It was joined on Thursday evening, when many of our noblest men fell, killed or wounded. Among the mortally wounded was my own loved Colonel Botts, who had become to me almost as a brother. After spending Thursday night sleeplessly in ministering to sick, and that anxious Friday which none will forget, August 29, I repaired to the regiment for some rest Friday night. Colonel Baylor, of the Fifth, now commanding brigade, exhausted by fatigue and care, was stretched on the ground near a tree, and I threw myself upon the earth near another, and was falling to sleep. But the colonel called and inquired if I felt too tired to conduct a prayer-meeting—said that he felt desirous of expressing his gratitude to God for sparing his life, and he wished the brigade to join him in their behalf. Two nights before he had requested the chaplains to summon their regiments to worship, during a brief halt; and, notwithstanding all this, he was not a member of the Church. Of course I acceded to this touching appeal; I could not be too weary for *such* a service. Notice was given, and many poor fellows left their cooking to unite in the solemn service. Poague's and Carpenter's Batteries, who hitherto belonged to the brigade, were largely represented. Captain Hugh A. White, of the Fourth, and others led in prayer at my request, and a most solemn meeting we all enjoyed—for the last time it proved to many. The next evening's sun set upon the corpses of the two noble and generous men, Baylor and White, as they lay not far apart upon that gory field. I would express the hope that their mingled service is continued in heaven. When we left Frederick City for the movement against Harper's Ferry, our regiment being at the head of column, I saw General Jackson and mentioned to him this among other circumstances in Colonel Baylor's last weeks; he seemed greatly delighted, and said: ' I am glad of it; I hope he died a Christian; he needed only Christianity to make him a model man; he was a fine officer too, as was seen by his keeping up his regiment.'

"While we lay about Bunker Hill in the fall of 1862, a work of grace was begun in the army; but our brigade seemed still unblest. Dr. Stiles visited us and preached. A good many began to awaken. Our division was now frequently shifted from position to position previous to crossing the mountains. Still the doctor preached, as he had opportunity, to large and interested audiences, and finally a goodly number made hopeful profession of conversion. But the greatest benefit that I have ever felt from those associations and instructions of our venerable brother, was the impulse imparted to *chaplains*. That earnest man of God made us *ashamed of ourselves*. I fairly felt ashamed to give him an opportunity at me; he talked so plainly of my responsibility; showed me so clearly how many opportunities I was thoughtlessly despising; what great responsibility rested on me. I shook the dust from my feet and went to work with new zeal. This seemed to be the case with us all.

"Colonel ————, of the ———— Regiment, was now commanding the brigade. His notorious profanity made him rather a terror to chaplains; but he was really generous and kind-hearted. After becoming acquainted he gave me the honorable title of ' my elder,' and was always ready to grant any facilities I ever requested for furthering my discharge of duties. At this time he cheerfully exempted men from military duty for erecting our earthen candlesticks, beautifying our native church, and attendance upon worship. We hoped much good was done; but a season of rest had engendered also many vices, and robbery had become common in the vicinity of the army. In one instance a soldier had been murdered by another between the spring and the camp of the Thirty-third Virginia for a small sum of money.

"While we lay near Winchester in the latter part of November, I received a message from General Jackson, through Lieutenant James P. Smith, his adjutant, requesting me to prepare and send him a list of chaplains, their regiments, etc., in his old division; the number and name of destitute regiments; their disposition towards having chaplains and other preferences as to denomination, etc., and to do what I could in this command for securing acceptable chaplains to every destitute regiment.

"About 20th of November Brigadier-General Paxton assumed command of the brigade. Chaplains had been hitherto held under no military responsibility; but Paxton soon indicated that they must not leave without proper furloughs. November 21 we broke camp and marched for Fredericksburg. On that march a chaplain went to General Paxton with oral request for leave of absence; Paxton refused it unless written and endorsed by regimental commander. He went to General Jackson, but the general gave him the same reply, and informed him that such license would degrade the chaplaincy in the eyes of soldiers, and he wished it regarded as important as any other office in the army.

"Opportunities were furnished me on that march for testing the results of our recent interest. I found it quite general and abiding. A young friend (assistant adjutant-general to Paxton) had made profession of faith and attributed it in great degree to the influence and friendship of the lamented Baylor. With a sergeant I had much conversation, who received impressions which led to his hopeful profession of faith. With a high-toned but unconverted officer I had a discussion, protracted through that long march, on certain doctrinal questions; and when he fell in the battle of the Wilderness, I hope he died a Christian. Many other incidents I might relate, but these will suffice to show the power of personal approach and interviews with men, which we are so slow to use.

"General Paxton, who had been represented as a hard-hearted man, I soon found a wise and earnest coadjutor of all chaplains in the faithful discharge of their duties, and interested in knowing what they were doing. He agreed fully with General Jackson in his regard for the office, though at this time he made no profession of religion. When we reached our destination near Guinea Station, I handed my report for General Jackson to him through Lieutenant Smith, and asked and obtained a furlough. My regimental commander (Colonel Nadenbousch), himself not a professor of religion, told me he should have a chapel built for me on my return.

"When my furlough expired, I found the brigade in winter-quarters, near Moss Neck, and some steps had been taken towards having a brigade-chapel erected; but the work had come to a pause. As this had been done, I was told, by the military authority, I awaited their completion of it. At length General Paxton, to whom I had not been introduced, sent for me to his quarters, requested me to hasten the chapel's erection, saying he did not feel authorized to detail men on it, but that, if I would obtain volunteers, he would exempt them from military duties, 'provided they would *work.*' The foundation had been laid in this shape.

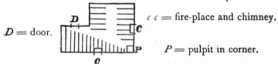

D = door.
$c\ c$ = fire-place and chimney.
P = pulpit in corner.

"The work was put into the hands of a man in the Fourth Regiment. The building was about the centre of the brigade; and the work was soon completed. And if the master-workman (a self-styled 'corporal') did desert the army immediately after his work was done, he left behind a monument which deserves in your book a much more honorable association than with his name.

"Rev. L. C. Vass visited us just at the completion of our 'first temple' and preached the first sermon in it. He became chaplain of the Twenty-seventh Regiment. His appointment supplied all five regiments of the brigade with the living ministry. We seemed now ready, under a favorable Providence, for hard work. All the army was quiet; General Paxton urged us on; General Jackson, near by, encouraged us by frequent attendance at service; regimental officers upheld our hands. But for awhile all seemed spiritually dead. A number of prisoners were under sentence of death for desertion, although not one from my regiment. I was in daily attendance upon them in the guard-house. As most of our chaplains were absent from camp much of that time, this painful service devolved on me, even to announcing their sentences and accompanying them to the stake. Their expressions of hope and gratitude must be my sufficient reward in this life.

"Brother Tebbs having returned from furlough, he and I began frequent services. I also organized a Bible-class in the brigade court-martial room, which, designed primarily for my own regiment, was opened also to any persons. We commenced with about thirty members, and met twice a week at night. In the course of time I had the joy of welcoming nearly every member of that class into a profession of Christ. By the latter part of February a very general interest in religion had spread throughout the brigade. Chaplains were more devoted; congregations larger; but not many taking decided stand for the Lord in public. Chaplains of the brigade, and indeed of the division, began to grow acquainted, interested in each other and co-operative. We discussed the idea of holding stated meetings for mutual prayer and conference. Some of us visited our honored corps-commander and conversed with him regarding such measures, and were gratified to learn that he approved them.

"Sunday morning, 29th of February, 1863, I went to chapel expecting to preach on Revelation iii. 2, to Christians. After I had commenced service Brother Walton introduced you, and with some reluctance, I confess, I yielded the pulpit and invited you to preach. But my reluctance was soon dispelled, for you preached almost my sermon, upon some other text. This seemed to persuade me that that was the message which the Lord wished urged; so I preached *my* sermon that afternoon, having introduced it by that strange providence which I hoped was indicative of good. The next day it reached me that the Lord had impressed His truth upon Christians and they were growing ashamed of themselves. They went to praying, and from that day Christ's people began to work in earnest, as they had not done before. It pleased the Lord also just in that week to send Rev. B. T. Lacy to see us. We consulted about the proposition General Jackson had made him. He preached for us with encouraging results. Rev. Wm. J. Hoge was also sent by the good Lord; he preached; and the wave of interest rolled on. Soon sinners began to inquire the way to God; Christians began to make unusual efforts in winning souls; solemnity characterized the command, and congregations began to exceed the capacity of our primitive house of worship. Be it remembered that up to this time the casualties of war had left my regiment almost unrepresented in Christian profession. But many were now gathered into the fold, and many more from the brigade. I kept no record of numbers. But the greatest work was among the troops of the Fourth Regiment. Cold professors were revived; and sinners were converted; yet the work was silent, quiet and deep. I can recall but a single instance of excitement, and verily do I believe that was the genuine product of deep conviction. For the strong young man had backslidden, and under the physical excitement of his returning conviction, he swooned away into my arms as I talked with him; but when consciousness returned he was calm. Interested men crowded us after service, and we were compelled to hold meetings for praying and conversing with them whenever public services were ended. This work continued till I was laid aside from it on the last day of March. Others may continue the narrative of the communion and ingathering; but I am sure all who found peace did not make public profession, because it had yet not been determined what was best to be done about such cases.

"While this work went on my regiment subscribed $140.00 for reading-matter. I obtained about seventy copies of papers of all denominations, besides a monthly instalment of tracts through the soldiers' true friend, Mrs. E. H. Brown. The regiment, which was from the Valley, and which had known the evil power of the enemy, generously contributed to suffering citizens of Fredericksburg the creditable sum of $505.25; the Fourth Regiment also contributed $349.75, both of which sums were forwarded through me to the injured city. Contributions were also made by other regiments; but the amounts I cannot state. Two tracts which I had requested Rev. R. L. Dabney, D.D., to write, one on ' Profane Swearing,' and one on ' Christ our Substitute,' were published, and I found them of great efficacy. Increased interest had also been manifested in Brigadier-General J. M. Jones's Brigade, near us, and with it increased association between the chaplains of the two commands. This gave more definite shape to our idea of a chaplains' meeting, and we were just reaching the conclusion to invite the other chaplains to meet us. While we were waiting to ascertain a central place, and suitable time, Brother Lacy effected his arrangements for joining the army, and came among us. We talked over the matter with him; ascertained that Round Oak Baptist Church could be used; and determined to call a meeting of the chaplains of the corps for March 16. My own hand wrote the circular; all the chaplains of our brigade and Jones's, I believe, signed it. Brother Vass and I took it to corps head-quarters, and Colonel Faulkner promised to issue it officially. (General Jackson was busy; we did not see him just then; but he had advised us to this course.) Hence the first chaplains' meeting; but I doubt not many other brethren had felt the same need of some such thing.

"Brother Tebbs was compelled to resign in the latter part of March on account of ill health, having taken violent cold in our beloved chapel, where our labors had become so interesting, but which was very damp. I was stricken down in the middle of a sermon on Psalm li. 10, on the night of March 30, and disappointed of a communion which we had appointed for an early day. Henceforth Brothers Vass, Walton and Grandin conducted the meetings.

"Many interesting incidents, of course, occurred in that revival; but only such as every minister meets at such times. But one whose interest culminated after my extreme illness and removal to the hospitable roof of Mr. Buckner (Geo. Washington), some two miles from camp, deserves my notice. A youth of handsome, but pensive face, was seen awaiting every night the ministrations of chaplains. For some nights, however, I did not speak with him. Finally I did, and found him an orphan boy from Shenandoah. Long did he remain in darkness; but nothing daunted. At length he found peace; but after I was removed. And one night, when too sick to read, I received two letters from men in camp; one from him, thanking me for the counsel I had given, and especially for the sermon I had preached the last night I attempted it. It was my privilege to observe the beautiful consistency of little Solomon H——— in a trying military career in subsequent days, and I trust he may long add evidence to evidence, showing that his heart was created anew and his spirit rectified.

"In frequent personal interviews with General Paxton he expressed a growing interest in the Saviour, until he gave evidence of true conversion, and wrote home requesting to be regarded as a member of the Church. In one of these interviews he said with emphasis: 'Ah! how inconsistent men are about religion; persuade the business man that anything is necessary for his interest, and he will do it *at once;* but you may persuade men of their interest in religion, and still they will procrastinate—in many cases till too late.' Having ridden over to visit me while I was ill, he told me that he felt that he would soon be killed, and he wished not to go unprepared. And so it was; he had just issued orders for his maiden charge, which terminated in brilliant success, when he was killed by a ball from the enemy.

"With sadness must I make the confession that not one officer of my own regiment was added to the Church this winter; yet their friendship was warm and even touching, as will be evinced by this incident: One had been visiting me while I was sick, and upon going out of the room he slipped an envelope into my hand bearing some such superscription: 'From the officers, Second Virginia, as a token of our regard.' Opening it I found the sum of $500.00. After the brigade had reached the vicinity of Chancellorsville for that battle, Colonel Nadenbousch, learning that I was exposed to capture at Mr. Buckner's, sent back an express to remove me if my strength would permit it. This was done, and on the day of that memorable battle I was transferred to Richmond. So obstinate was my typhoid pneumonia that I could not rejoin the army till July following, after its return from Gettysburg.

"The spiritual interests of the command suffered no little by the campaign, and I doubt not that the restraints of enlightened consciences saved much of that retribution upon the enemy's country which the world would have justified. Brigadier General J. A. Walker was now commanding the brigade. Its numbers and aspect had greatly changed under the rigors of that demoralizing and arduous campaign.

"On 22d July we set in motion for the eastern side of the Blue Ridge. While resting a day in Madison county I embraced an opportunity for calling together the Christians of my regiment, procuring a roll of some fifty of them who remained; temporarily arranged them in clubs for 'family prayer,' nights after tattoo, and mornings after first roll-call. When we halted longer in Orange, we threw all these clubs into one regimental prayer-meeting, to be conducted exclusively by the professors of religion in alphabetical order, and at the same hours, I announced my purpose of attending them seldom, in order that they might *feel* that they bore all the responsibility. This was found a most delightful service; increasing numbers attended; other regiments followed the example; and these meetings were perpetuated until the casualties of battle literally annihilated the number who composed it! I preached in conjunction with Brother Vass every night or day; or held prayer-meeting at regimental head-quarters for the regiment. I had also a large Bible-class reorganized, which met under a hill, protected from the hot sun by the shade of a poplar and some artificial covering of brush.

"Our brigade reorganized its Christian Association, which had just been formed at the opening of the Chancellorsville Campaign. Considerable interest began to be manifested in my regiment, and many of our most interesting men made public profession of faith. Rev. Wm. R. McNeer, who had for some time been acting chaplain of the Fourth Regiment, now received appointment; and Rev. C. S. M. See was made chaplain of the Fifth Regiment, *vice* Walton resigned. So the brigade was once more supplied with ministers; although Brother Grandin, of the Thirty-third, was a prisoner, having been captured in Jefferson county, visiting his wife, and had not been released. The spirituality of Christians seemed restored to a comfortable state, and a goodly number were gathered into the fold of professors.

"The entire fall was spent in shifting from place to place; and the feverish movements of troops prevented any systematic labor by chaplains. All my regimental meetings were kept up, however, and the Brigade Association held regular meetings and flourished. About Christmas we went into winter-quarters near Pisgah Church, in Orange county. Details of men and teams were so very heavy that it was late before we could proceed to work on chapels. Timber was so far off that an unusually large force of both were necessary. General Walker most generously consented to exempt from military duty all who would work on chapels. The division pioneer corps near by agreed to assist; and Major-General Ed. Johnson courteously offered them inducements to do so. We determined to erect two chapels, one for Fourth and Fifth Regiments, and one for Second, Twenty-seventh and Thirty-third and pioneer corps, according to their positions in camp. Owing to the great difficulty of getting teams, the work progressed slowly; but was finally accomplished, and ready for use on Sunday, January 31, 1864. (This refers to *our own ;* the other was ready *about* the same time.) We adopted in both instances a different form from the preceding one; both were rectangular parallelograms, thus:

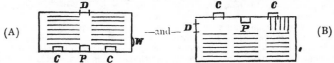

"(A) = chapel of Second, Twenty-seventh and Thirty-third, situated on a beautiful southern exposure slanting downward from door, *D*, to chimneys = *c c*, and pulpit, *P*, with window, *w*, at south-east corner and near the eaves of the house, made by sawing a long piece of one big log out and tacking a piece of cotton over it. Here Vass and I served; Grandin returned from prison, but resigned or was transferred on account of ill health, etc.

"(B) = chapel of Fourth and Fifth, situated on western exposure, with pulpit, *P*, fire-places, *c c*, on either side of pulpit, at lower side of building. Door in one end and near corner, at *D*. Brother See served in B. These were both very comfortable houses, and great improvements upon our first chapel. Nor did *their* architects find relief in desertion.

"Congregations were good; association flourished much; at A we had daily prayer-meeting at noon, besides the forementioned prayer-meetings. Interest increased, services were multiplied and sinners became penitent. But Satan was also very busy; sutlers were trading in liquor; men and officers were gambling, and there was much profanity. The sale of liquor in my regiment became so intolerable to me that I reported the fact to General Walker and urged him to restrain it. After a most courteous hearing he agreed to do so, and by the time I could reach my camp, his adjutant-general waited upon Mr. Sutler to lay down the ultimatum to him. This checked liquor-drinking greatly, but of course not entirely. What was noteworthy in that interview was, that General Walker (himself an ungodly man) gave me clearly to understand that he regarded me in reality the *spiritual* officer of the regiment; that he *expected* me to preserve the moral efficiency of the command by correcting and reporting such violations of morals and orders.

" The Christian Association, meeting alternately in chapels A and B, infused much life into its proceedings by proposing at one meeting practical questions for discussions at the next. At leisure hours I frequently engaged with the young men of my regiment in a game of base-ball, for exercise in part, but principally to effect what it was ever my purpose to do, viz., to draw men out from their tents into the light of day, where evil practices are discouraged or corrected.

" Let me here bear testimony, which both gratitude and justice require me to do. Some chaplains were wont to complain of disrespectful and unsympathetic officers with whom they were thrown. I shall not deny *their* statements of experience. But justice requires that from a singularly fortunate experience *I* should bear conflicting testimony. It seemed a strange dispensation which threw me so habitually with officers who made no profession of religion, and singular discouragement that the Lord never enabled me to do them more good. When the failures of my general work for my men, however, are recited in the great day, I shall hardly be able to find any of these to share my burden of mortification and grief. All with whom I was thrown by the vicissitudes of war, and they were not a few, were ever as ready to grant whatever was for the good of my work as I was to ask; and often has their promptness to confer rebuked my timidity in asking co-operation. Allow me also to testify in behalf of the surgeons of that old command. In my judgment, and surely I had the best opportunities for reaching a true one, there was no class of officers or men who discharged their vexatious duties more faithfully, more diligently, more cheerfully or more skilfully than did the medical corps of that brigade. As a class their efficient services merit the gratitude and admiration of the members of the Stonewall Brigade. There may have been some faults and some neglects; but what other officer.is free from similar accusation? If it was generally known how little favor Government bestowed upon this department, or at least how little Government was able to equip it; how many whining skulks sought to convert the surgeons into escape-valves from military duty; how fatiguing, engrossing and distracting their vocation just at the critical hour when men are most querulous; their occasional demonstrations of temper, indifference or even unkindness will seem pardonable. This honorable profession has suffered too much traduction at the hands of men who were arrested in their ill purposes of escaping duty.

" May 4, 1864, we broke camp and went forth to meet the enemy in the wilderness of Orange and Spottsylvania. Ministrations to the wounded and dying were all that chaplains could render up to the time that I was detached from the regiment, immediately after the disaster at Spottsylvania Court House on 12th of May, and ordered to the field-hospital (permanent) of our corps, by a written order from General Ewell, through Chief-Surgeon McGuire. That disaster, in fact, terminated the separate existence of the Stonewall Brigade; and here properly this history might end. General Walker, having been badly wounded in that battle, was borne off to take command of it no more; but left an express farewell, saying they had his gratitude and admiration for their handsome resistance on that ill-fated morning. The fragments of this and other Virginia brigades of Johnson's Division were thrown into one brigade under Brigadier-General William Terry, and from that time the conglomeration was styled Terry's Brigade.

"When General Lee moved from Spottsylvania Court House towards Hanover Junction, he left the worst wounded men of the Third Corps *d'armie* in permanent hospitals near the field of battle on the farm of Mr. Stuart. Dr. Kemper was left in charge of *all;* and Dr. Bushrod Taylor, Surgeon Forty-eighth Virginia, was left in charge of Second Corps Hospital. The army having moved sooner than it was hoped, we were left without supplies, in a wasted, impoverished, but kind community; exposedto the enemy; and, of course, in great straits. Our Corps Hospital had some 320 badly wounded, who required and had nearly 200 attendants, making in all about 500 men. Of this nmmber there were about fifty of the enemy's wounded, some of whom had been rescued from the merciless flames of that wood which the enemy retreating, beaten by Early, had fired for eluding his pressing column. For about twenty days we lost an average of five per day; and as the wounded died, and the hospital became better organized under the judicious management of Dr. Taylor, the nurses were reduced in number and dismissed to rejoin their commands. We had many reports of the enemy's approach; but for some time they did not appear. In my ministrations I endeavored daily to visit every man, irrespective of his army, and knew no man after the flesh. So large was the number that at first it took me two days to pass entirely around the hospital. On June 10, about 2 P. M., while I was in a Yankee's tent praying and reading with him, at the corner of the hospital, a clatter of sabers was heard, and looking up we saw a detachment of Federal cavalry surrounding the hospital. They fired on one or two men running across the fields, and at first some courageous assaults were made upon our meagre commissary tent; but Colonel Anderson soon rode up, arrested very promptly this robbery of stores, and soon showed that he at least had the instincts of humanity. When the squadron were making their gallant charge, their sergeant, a rude, red-headed Pennsylvanian, dashed with drawn pistol through the middle of the camp. While thus displaying his heroism, a large, fierce-looking sergeant of a Maine regiment, whose arm had been very badly fractured, staggered out of his tent, and in indignant style belabored his cavalry friend, saying: 'Put up your pistol; put up your pistol! What are you flourishing that about here for? Nobody here but one-armed and one-legged and dying men; you needn't be afraid of them.' The only misconduct of which we had a right to complain was that they took off half our nurses; and when Colonel Anderson told us the rigid orders from Torbert, which he refused complying with, we felt assured he did all that he dared to do. This was the Seventeenth Pennsylvania Regiment, and had been detached from Sheridan's raiding party upon Trevillian's Station, with orders to break up our hospital. The Yankee inmates of our hospital behaved gratefully and honorably. They interceded for our men, and none equalled them in their ridicule of the 'gallant charge' and their 'successful assault upon a fortified camp.' I can fairly hear Pat Irishman, of a New Jersey regiment, now, laughing at the flaming heading of some Yankee paper telling of the 'handsome affair,' 'the number of prisoners taken by the Seventeenth Pennsylvania,' etc. It was my pleasure to hear many men in that memorable hospital make profession of faith in Christ. I conversed with every man on the subject of religion, and after the number was reduced by death, I held almost daily service in every tent. Among those who made profession of faith in Christ were several of the Federal wounded, who ever seemed as deeply interested in my ministrations as our own men. One of these became converted from Unitarianism, and wrote through me a long letter telling his sister of it. Some of these were very interesting cases; two I recall particularly, from Boston, who were Congregationalists. One of these was named after Rev. Dr. Channing; another, when he had found peace in Christ, said to me one day: 'Chaplain, I think you all will be victorious.' I asked why. Said he: 'Because I believe your army is composed of better men than ours; during the whole time that I have lain in this hospital I have heard but one oath, and that just seemed to have slipped from a Louisianian in the adjoining tent. In our hospitals you would hear them every moment.'

"Among our own men I met some cases full of interest among both men and officers—so many, in fact, I can hardly begin to relate them. I will, however, give two which interested me much. One was Captain Williams, of North Carolina troops. He was a young man of great modesty, youthful in appearance, tender-looking and generous. Gallantry had won him early promotion. He was the cherished son of a pious mother, towards whom his heart seemed ever turning. For a long time he lingered, his mind ever clear, but he foresaw his end. Under the dissipations of camp he had too far forgotten the pious counsels of his mother, and the regret of this became very harrowing to his heart. He constantly spoke of his mother, and longed for her presence before death. A long time he had great difficulty in understanding how Christ could be his substitute; but finally the Spirit opened his heart. He grew more bright and contented, and finally seemed to rejoice greatly that he could leave his dear mother some comfort in his death. He clung to me and was always begging me to read to him and pray with him; and whereas he seemed to gain no benefit for a long time, he learned eventually to enjoy the word as I have seldom seen men do, making good and touching comments on it as I read verse after verse. One day when I approached him he called me affectionately to him, and most touchingly said, in childlike simplicity: 'Oh, sir, you are an *angel* sent to me, in answer to the prayers of my dear, dear mother, who cannot be with me.' He ultimately died full of hope.

"Another was a young man named Wilson, also from that good old State of North Carolina. His thigh was fractured in 'the upper third,' but his strong constitution long induced hope of his recovery; for several months he was silent, indifferent and even grum-looking, without being sour. When he had passed the crisis, as was hoped, I asked him if his thoughts had not been turned upon death and need of preparation for it. 'No, sir. I never had a serious thought of death or religion.' Astonished, I inquired if he was raised in a Christian family, and if he had any conscious antipathy to the matter of religion. 'None,' said he; 'my mother is a member of the Baptist Church, and the most prayerful woman I ever knew; she raised me most piously, prayed with me, and is praying for me *all the time*. I admire religion; I have a desire to obtain it, and to bear or do what is necessary to get it; but I have never felt one really deep or serious impression in my heart in health or sickness.' For weeks I daily visited him and sought to instruct, to induce, and finally to alarm him, but all seemed hopeless. I was lost in wonder. One night about bedtime he sent for me; he had been taken suddenly ill, and death sat upon his countenance. When I entered the room, like one shaken over the flames of hell he said, with an emphasis which I cannot command: 'I am dying, sir; I am dying; and I am dying in my sins; my mother, oh, my mother!' I talked with him; I prayed; I left him wrapped in grief and wonder. Surgeons said he must die in a few hours, but he lived longer; I remained with him a great deal. A few nights after, at 2 P. M., I was summoned to his tent. Again he saluted me: 'I am dying, sir; I am dying;' but now with changed expression he added: 'I am dying happy; I am going to my Saviour; and you must write to mother that you saw me go into glory.' Again the surgeons pronounced him *in articulo mortis;* but, as if to confirm his testimony and make it reliable, the Lord spared him some time longer, and he gave goodly tokens of recovery. During that time his tongue, so habitually silent hitherto, spoke freely of Jesus' pardoning blood, and his face, hitherto grum, became radiant with sunny hope, while the previous murmuring of his heart gave place to contentment. He wondered at himself, and greatly rejoiced

GENERAL CLEMENT A. EVANS, C. S. A.
(From photograph during the war.)

(Facing page 465.)

every hour that the Lord had prepared such blessed testimony for his dear mother to rest upon in her bereavement. His brother Joseph, who nursed him, received his benedictions, his prayers and his good counsel to meet him in heaven; and he and I informed the afflicted mother of her oldest son's triumphant death. How wonderful are God's ways! Very little faith have I in deathbed repentances; but verily do I believe this was a genuine case of conversion in immediate prospect of death, and an answer, though long deferred, to the faithful prayers of affection.

" On September 27, there seeming no further absolute need of my remaining at the hospital, and not being able to communicate with my old command, I asked and obtained from the surgeon in charge orders to report to the War Department. I reached Richmond the night of the day on which Fort Harrison fell, found all excitement, and after some difficulty obtained a pass out of the city to a friend near town. Next day I visited the War Department, found notice of its close, and instructions to all officers to report to General Barton. About noon an order was issued exempting ministers and chaplains from service in the trenches; but as danger was imminent, I went out and remained there (promoted to the high dignity of lieutenant) for nearly a week. Reporting to the Secretary of War at the end of that time, I was advised of the dismemberment of my old command, or rather its consolidation, and given orders to report for duty to Major-General J. B. Gordon in the Valley, which I accordingly did.

" I overtook the Army of the Valley near New Market, reported to General Gordon, whom I had never seen before, and received from him a temporary assignment to Terry's Brigade, of which my old regiment—now reduced to almost nothing—was a constituent part. In a few days Major R. W. Hunter, assistant adjutaht-general to Gordon, bore me a message from the general asking how I would like to make his head-quarters my home and his *division* my field of labor. Sunday, 22d of October, General Gordon attended my preaching in Terry's Brigade, and invited me to his quarters next day. On the 24th he assigned me to his division, which was now composed of Terry's, Evans's and the Louisiana Brigades. Brothers See, Booker, Gilmore and Williams were in Terry's Brigade; Brother Smith, of the Sixtieth Georgia, in Evans's; and in the Louisiana Brigade there was no chaplain—not even a priest. My labors were therefore directed principally to the last named brigade, to the pioneer corps and the guard-house of the division, which furnished me a considerable measure of work, if some of it was not very interesting. General Gordon gave as a reason for having me with him a sense of temptation to forget the claims of religion upon his own heart in the midst of pressing cares. Nothing worthy of special note occurred during the fall. Religion seemed rather cold under the temptations and distractions of the active campaigns through which the army had passed, a large proportion of the most pious men had been killed or wounded, and the *morale* of the army in the Valley under the discouraging defeats of that memorable campaign had deteriorated. In the remnant of my old regiment, when I rejoined the army, only *two* professing Christians could be found, and one of these was slain immediately afterwards at Cedar Creek. Yet there was also some encouragement. But drunkenness was fearfully prevalent all through the army; so much so that our Chaplains' Association appointed a committee (of which I was one) to memorialize General Early on the subject, which resulted in an order from him prohibiting the liquor traffic. If anything noteworthy occurred during the summer, Brother See can give it to you, for he remained faithfully with his command on foot all that summer.

" Near the last of November General Gordon received orders to take his own and Pegram's Division to the vicinity of Petersburg. For some time after reaching the lines on Hatcher's Run we were shifting about, skirmishing and fighting, and nothing could be done towards building chapels till late in the winter. In that time I obtained a furlough. Visiting the Louisiana Brigade, I remarked to them that I was sure they would build a theatre as usual, and as timber was very scarce, and there were so few interested about religious matters, I feared they would not build a chapel; but I bespoke the use of their theatre for my preaching! On my return from furlough they had nearly completed one of the best arranged, neatest and most comfortable chapels which I ever saw in the army. It was on this plan:

P = pulpit.

c = chimney.

D = door.

"In this house I had many delightful services, of which more anon.

"Terry's Brigade, camped in strict military regularity, had two chapels, one at either wing of the camp. That erected at left wing for use of Brothers Booker, Gilmore and Williams was large, and thus:

d = door fronting upon camp eastward; $c\,c$ = chimneys; P = pulpit. This was first completed.

"The one at right wing for See's use was thus:

D = door facing inward, upward upon camp westward; P = pulpit; $c\,c$ = fireplace in centre; two faces, one to each wing, and chimney-stem passing out through top of roof by the ridge pole. This was very comfortable; but just as it was completed we moved into trenches, and left it for Wallace's Brigade.

"Smith's chapel, in Evans's Brigade, was much larger than either of these, but less convenient and *elegant;* as follows:

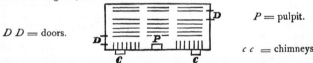

P = pulpit.

$D\,D$ = doors.

$c\,c$ = chimneys.

"These were all built of pine logs and covered with pine slabs, while thick pine slabs or logs made seats. All chapels I have mentioned were made of similar material, and built in same way substantially.

"I devoted myself that winter principally to the Louisiana Brigade, and to the two guard-houses of Gordon's Division and Second Corps. General Gordon, commanding corps, directed me to remain still at his head-quarters. We organized in the Louisiana Brigade a Bible-class and prayer-meeting through the zeal of a lieutenant of the Ninth Regiment and the leader of the band, who was a recently converted educated German atheist, and these two agencies became very operative and interesting. The band, under the generous impulse of its very skilful leader, led or accompanied all our music in public service, and thrilled my soul by many solemn and impressive suggestions as very few church choirs and church organs have ever done. Since our separation how often has my heart longed for the instrumental music of Professor Doll and his accommodating band.

" I gave notice that on the night preceding the national fast (March 9) I should preach to the brigade on profane swearing, and requested that special efforts should be made to secure the attendance of every swearer in the command. When I came out of the pulpit, a bright-faced youth said to me : ' You ought to have pretty near every man in the brigade.' The night appointed arrived, but a hard rain was falling. I got General Gordon to go with me and to make an address at the close of my sermon. A *large* crowd pressed into the chapel, and many stood under the eaves about the door, while many had to retire on account of the rain. I began to think the young man was nearly right. It was evident that the services had made some impression. In a little while I learned that many men and messes had said they felt ashamed of their evil practice, and many messes covenanted, some under fines, to abstain from so vicious a habit.

" On the morning of the 26th, after our assault upon the enemy's lines at Fort Steadman, the following gratifying incident occurred : I was passing through one of our Petersburg hospitals, looking up all the wounded of my own division, when I was attracted by a remark which seemed addressed to no one particularly : ' That's my little chaplain.' I looked around ; saw a young man wounded ; spoke to him, and learned that he belonged to the Louisiana Brigade, and also to that splendid band of soldiers whose conduct on that morning alone deserves celebration in the heart of every Confederate, the Second Corps Sharpshooters ; and that he had received his wound just as he was mounting the enemy's entrenchment. I had hardly spoken to him when he asked, smiling, if I remembered the sermon I preached on swearing in their brigade. ' Yes,' said I. ' Well, sir,' he said, ' I made up my mind that night when you and the general got through that I never would swear again ; and all our mess said the same thing, and we haven't sworn since.' Certainly, in mingling with that gallant command in the vexatious trenches and on the march, I *heard* but little profanity among them from that time.

" This thought suggests a general observation which I had the pleasure of making in the closing trials of our once splendid army. Upon the whole retreat from Petersburg to Appomattox I was passing and meeting our corps time and again every day ; in mud, by day, by night, at every hour of both—hungry, exhausted, fighting, retreating ; mortified, desperate of success, and harassed as I have never seen them— yet, thank God, I can testify that in all this trial and vicissitude I scarcely heard any oaths ! Doubtless *many* were uttered. I can recall one or two, but their utterances were so seldom as to attract my most grateful remark.

" The nature of the campaign, its activity and confusion, up to the very day of our leaving Appomattox, rendered it next to impossible for chaplains to do anything of ministerial work ; so for that period I have nothing special to report. Finding so little opportunity for ministerial labor, I was used by General Gordon in almost constant military service as an aide-de-camp. At Appomattox two chaplains of the Federal army came into our lines after the capitulation to see ' some of the chaplains ' of our army, and to make inquiry as to the regard shown chaplains in our army by officers. They seemed much surprised at learning my testimony as to the kindly regard in which dutiful ministers were held, and spoke of the great contrast which our relation to the army officers bore to their own. They inquired relative to the great work of grace, and the means by which it was promoted. I told them courteously. They then inquired : ' How much salary do you get ? ' Upon learning how small it was, they expressed great surprise, and said they could not live on that ; they were entitled to, I believe, two horses and $130, and that they seemed to think rendered it a speculation of doubtful profit !

"At General Gordon's head-quarters we habitually held ' family worship ' every night, at which all the staff attended.

"And here shall my egotistical memoir end. In your book you will please not insert the one-hundredth part of these *egos*. They are written for *you* alone ; and

I imagine every chaplain who supplies you material in this form *may* make quite as long a list, and will do so unless they undertake your work of writing the history. But I hope you will permit candor and truth to override politeness in pronouncing judgment upon our personal and official defects. Very truly yours,

"A. C. HOPKINS."

[*Copy of a Letter from General T. J. Jackson to Colone. S. Bassett French, Dated*]

"NEAR FREDERICKSBURG, April 15, 1863.

"*Dear Colonel:* Your letter of 13th instant was received yesterday, and your telegram to Mr. Smith was also received; and he, by the signal-line, inquired of Mr. Hopkins's physician respecting his health, and it is improving. This improvement we have known for several days. He is too valuable to us to admit of not being carefully looked after. You will give yourself no concern respecting his being taken care of. He is in a comfortable house, and he will continue to be well cared for.

"Very truly your friend,
[Extract.]
"T. J. JACKSON."

"This will illustrate the general's tender care for his chaplains, and his concern in whatever affects their usefulness. At the same time he sent Captain Smith, his aide-de-camp, to see me, and also Lieutenant Marsden, my wife's cousin, with permission to remain and nurse me if I needed attention. This was during my illness at Mr. Buckner's, 1863.

"With another apology for want of modesty, I am affectionately yours,

"A. C. HOPKINS."

[*From Rev. Dr. Theoderick Pryor, Presbyterian Missionary Chaplain to First Corps.*]

"BRUNSWICK COUNTY, VIRGINIA, FEBRUARY 26, 1867.
"REV. J. WM. JONES:

"*Rev. and Dear Brother:* I have learned through the religious press your purpose, as suggested in your letter. I heartily commend the enterprise and the objects sought to be promoted by it. And most gladly would I contribute, according to my ability, towards the accomplishment of your purpose. Whilst with the army (a period of about two years), my impressions are most favorable as to the influence and effect of religious truth. It appeared to me that during a course of ministerial experience extending through twenty-four years I had never witnessed more precious seasons of grace, or more signal displays of Divine mercy, than it was my privilege to witness in the army. Scores, perhaps I would not err were I to say hundreds, of professed conversions passed under my own observation. Never before was it my privilege to preach to as large congregations or to congregations more respectful in deportment, more serious, and upon whom the truth of God seemed to have more marked power and effect. The *morale* of the army, too, appeared to me to be good. So far as my observation extended, among both officers and privates, there was less profanity than would be found among an equal number of men anywhere else. By officers, from the highest to the lowest grade, in my official capacity as chaplain, I was treated with uniform respect and courtesy, and from the men I received nothing but the utmost kindness and consideration. There were, no doubt, bad men in the army, both officers and privates, but it was my happiness to be thrown with those, for the most part, of an opposite character.

"Whilst many of the severest trials and privations of my life were experienced in the army, it affords me real pleasure to state that many of the happiest seasons of my life were passed with the Army of Northern Virginia. To my dying day shall

I remember those precious meetings, held by day and by night, with that noble army of patriots. In the camp, in the hospital, in the bomb-proof, along the line of toilsome march, I mingled freely with them, and, as best I could, preached to them the Gospel of the grace of God. It is my most cherished hope that the labors of our chaplains, than whom, in my judgment, there was not a body of ministers in the land more worthy of all praise, were largely productive of lasting, nay, eternal good. The last great day alone will develop the full amount of good which, through the mercy of God, that noble body of men were enabled to accomplish. It is with mournful pleasure that in the seclusion of a quiet country charge I revert to those scenes of thrilling interest and excitement, not to say peril, through which you and I and the whole corps of field-chaplains passed with the brave and veteran Army of Northern Virginia.

"May the Lord grant you entire success in your noble enterprise and abundantly bless you in all the work of your hands.

"Your unworthy Brother in Christ,
"THEODERICK PRYOR."

[From Rev. R. W. Cridlin, Baptist, Chaplain Thirty-eighth Virginia.]

"CHESTERFIELD, March 22, 1867.

"*Dear Brother Jones:* Before going into details, allow me to state that I was appointed chaplain of the Thirty-eighth Virginia Infantry June 9, 1863, and remained with it to the surrender.

"(1.) I know very little about the early history of my regiment. We had a history of our regiment (and also one of our brigade) written, but have heard nothing of it since the close of the war. This regiment was composed of men from Pittsylvania, Halifax and Mecklenburg counties, Virginia. It started from Danville in the spring of 1861, under the command of Colonel E. C. Edmunds. It was connected with several brigades. When I joined it, it was attached to Armistead's Brigade, Pickett's Division, First Corps, and it continued in this position to the surrender, under different commanders. General Armistead was killed at Gettysburg. Our next general was Barton; then George H. Steuart, of Maryland, who remained with it till the surrender. I knew very little about the other regiments—viz., Ninth, Fourteenth, Fifty-third and Fifty-seventh. The Rev. Mr. Crocker, of the Methodist Episcopal Church, was at one time chaplain of the Fourteenth; Rev. Mr. Joiner, Methodist Episcopal Church, chaplain of the Fifty-seventh; Rev. W. S. Penick of the Fifty-third, afterwards Brother P. H. Fontaine; Rev. J. W. Walkup, of Rockbridge county, Virginia, was chaplain of the Ninth, afterwards Rev. George W. Easter, of the Episcopal Church. The Rev. Mr. Cosby, now of Petersburg, Virginia (Episcopal), was the first chaplain of the Thirty-eighth Regiment. He remained a short while. Then a Rev. Mr. Colton, of the Methodist Episcopal Church, was appointed, who remained two or three months. I am unable to state how many sermons I preached or prayer-meetings held, Bible-classes conducted, tracts distributed. I have no record and I can't trust my memory. We had a flourishing Brigade Young Men's Christian Association, and when in camp had our Sabbath-schools and Bible-classes. I know I distributed thousands of tracts, and I have reason to believe much good was done. Just here allow me to relate a little incident illustrating the good effects of tracts. While carrying around these little messengers of love, I entered a *tent* and found two young men engaged in a game of cards. At first they seemed ashamed, then they braced up their failing courage (if courage it was) and continued the game. I kindly asked 'if I could take a hand.' Waiting for my turn, I first threw down 'Evils of Gaming;' then 'Mother's Parting Words to her Soldier Boy.' I found that the game was mine. At the sight of the *word* '*mother,*' the *tears* rolled down their cheeks as they both *exclaimed:* 'Parson, I will never play cards again!'

" (2.) My first protracted effort was made soon after the battle of Gettysburg, near Orange Court House.   In this meeting God was with us and His people were revived and more than a hundred converted.   Brother A. Broaddus baptized twenty for me while there.   My next meeting (of much interest) was in the fall of 1864, in which about sixty were turned from ' darkness to light.'   I don't remember any remarkable conversions, or that any means were employed beyond the ordinary means of grace.

" (3.) Most of those who professed were steadfast in their love and devotion to Christ and His cause.   Many of them died in the ' triumphs of faith.'

" (4.) Our first colonel, Colonel Edmunds, was, I think, a member of the Episcopal Church.   His influence was very *beneficial* to his command.   I know nothing of his last moments, as he was killed on the field of Gettysburg.   Our next colonel was the young yet brave and accomplished gentleman and officer, James Cabell, of Danville.   Colonel Cabell was not a member of any Church, but told me a few days before his death ' that he felt prepared.'   He was killed near Drewry's Bluff, May 10, 1864, leaving a young bride and many dear ones to mourn their loss. Colonel George Griggs, of Pittsylvania, was our next colonel.   He was a member of the Baptist Church.   He was ever ready to aid me in my meetings, and was not ashamed to exhort his men publicly to enlist under the banner of Christ.   His life was spared and he has resumed his place at home, where I hope he may be long spared to labor for Christ.   Among my most valuable assistants was Captain J. T. Averett.   Captain John A. Herndon, Captain Jennings, Captain Grubbs, Lieutenant Gardner and others were true soldiers of Jesus.

" General Steuart and his assistant adjutant-general, Captain Darden, were members of the Episcopal Church.   Colonel Phillips, of the Ninth, was a man of more than ordinary talent, and he did all he could for Christ.

" (5.) It was fully and satisfactorily proved in our regiment that true ' *soldiers* of the Cross ' made the best *soldiers* for their country.

" (6.) I don't remember but some four or five who told me that they would devote the rest of their time to the *ministry*.   Captain J. A. Herndon, of Pittsylvania, of the Methodist Episcopal Church, expected to do so.   Brother W. A. Morefield, of Halifax ; Brother Hodges, Methodist Episcopal ; Brother C. Penick, Episcopal Church ; Brother C. F. James (Captain Company F, Eighth Virginia), of Loudon, whom I baptized, is now at Richmond College preparing himself for the *ministry*. No doubt many others will decide to ' go and do *likewise*.'   God grant it.

" (7.) I baptized about forty.   I was not ordained till December, 1863.   I think I can safely put the whole number of conversions in the brigade at 500, as other chaplains had gracious revivals, and have reason to infer they had many conversions.

" My dear brother, you have my best wishes and prayers in your arduous work. We need such a book.   I think it will do much good.. If I can serve you in any way, I am at your service.   May the Lord bless us at an early date with such refreshing showers of grace as we enjoyed in Orange in 1863.

" Yours in Christian love,
" R. W. CRIDLIN.

" CHESTERFIELD COURT HOUSE, VIRGINIA."

[*From Rev. J. K. Hitner, Presbyterian, Private Rockbridge Artillery.*]

" BRIEF COMPEND OF THE RELIGIOUS HISTORY OF THE ROCKBRIDGE ARTILLERY.

" The material of the company from the beginning was composed of men and officers of good moral character, who always exercised a good influence and thus gave a reputation to the company.   I joined the company, Monday, March 22, 1862, and give account from this date.

" Before joining the army, we had heard much about the demoralized condition of the men, their profanity, etc., which no doubt prejudiced my mind somewhat, and I was agreeably surprised to find much of the reverse on joining this company. They were falling back from Kernstown when I joined them; the spirits of the men were good, and all seemed cheerful. I was struck with the absence of strict discipline in our army from the very first, and which, no doubt, contributed in some degree to the inefficiency of the men in circumstances when united and prompt action would have availed much. Whether the men would have submitted to strict discipline, owing to early training, etc., etc., is another question, which I will not discuss. The first Sabbath in the army is marked in my journal as having been 'horribly spent,' being engaged most of the day in cutting wood, cooking, etc., while the rain was pouring down upon us and making us miserable. No doubt the necessary duties of camp-life on the Sabbath, and the fact that many of Jackson's battles were fought on the Sabbath, owing to unavoidable circumstances, made it extremely difficult for professing Christians to improve the ordinary means of grace which otherwise they might have enjoyed. And that many Christians did grow in grace in spite of these depressing circumstances, and that many were led to seek an interest in Christ, not only in this company, but in the army at large, proves that there was a genuine work of the Spirit, though the estimate oft made as to the numbers who were converted men is usually too large.

" Having cleared off in the evening of the Sabbath, enjoyed a prayer-meeting—about thirty present; the singing had a cheering effect. Upon further experience in the company, I found many of the young men to be of high character, good education, and some ten or twelve to be real, active Christians. From the first, great watchfulness and care required lest the reading of the word and use of prayer should be slighted or neglected—which was the experience of many; found need of 'watch and pray.'

" This week so busily engaged in moving about, had no opportunities for prayer-meetings. On the second Sabbath enjoyed two prayer-meetings, and which continued the general rule ever after in the company, when external circumstances would allow of it; and the attendance in our company was always good. And it shall never be forgotten how grandly impressive were those meetings in the open air; a bayonet stuck in the ground for our candlestick, and speakers and hearers seated on the ground or on sticks of wood, while *deep* attention was generally given to the word of God and the supplications to the throne of grace. We often spent the evenings in singing hymns, until the taps gave notice to be quiet.

"About this time (April and May, 1862) we were constantly on the move, so that we had but very few opportunities for holding religious services, even on Sabbath. When possible, General Jackson always insisted on the chaplains taking advantage of the Sabbaths, even when we were near the enemy and were likely to be attacked— as on several occasions—so anxious was he for the spiritual condition of his men. I remember several times when our service was disturbed by shells flying over us and breaking up our meeting. In one of our advances upon the enemy, when we had been on the march during the Sabbath, General Jackson sent down order for the chaplains to have divine service on Monday, and to spend the day in rest. Friday, May 16, 1862, appointed by President as a fast-day, when all extra duties were suspended in the company, but the hard rain prevented our holding the prayer-meetings we had appointed; so on the following Sabbath.

" It seemed that we were to have no Sabbath-day services, for we were either marching or fighting, or the wet weather prevented us from holding any religious meetings. Then, during the day we were continually on the march from early to late, so that when we got to camp we were tired, hungry, worn-out, besides having our rations to cook. Yet I find, on different days of the week and at irregular hours, notices of preaching and prayer-meetings, which were well and eagerly at-

31

tended by the brigade and company, and every notice of such an appointment was always hailed with joy by the men.

"Saturday, June 14, 1862, a day of thanksgiving to God for many mercies and protection, which was much enjoyed throughout this portion of the army; preaching and prayer-meetings in the day. June 15, much to our surprise as to our joy, no orders to move, and we spent the day quietly—preaching in the morning by Dr. Dabney; in the evening enjoyed a communion season, in which many participated and drew near to Jesus.

"Sunday, June 22. Much rejoiced to find we had no marching to perform to-day, but allowed a quiet rest; participated in the usual church privileges of Gordonsville, near which place we have halted. Having made forced marches last week, a rest is very grateful to-day. Monday, up at 3½ A. M., to make up for the rest of yesterday, and pushing on as fast as possible—to what point we were entirely ignorant, though indulging in surmises. (Yet going to Richmond.)

"Sunday, July 6, 1862. Lay under orders all day, expecting to meet or attack the enemy. Men worn down by low rations, marching, heat, and dirt.

"Saturday, August 8. Cedar Mountain.—Incident. A staff officer was struck with a shell and dreadfully wounded. He was a very profane man, yet as he felt his time of life was about ended, he called me to him and gave me his watch and ring to send to his wife. 'But, major, can I do nothing more for you?' 'Tell my wife I die trusting in Christ.' I laid on the ground beside him, praying with him, directing him to Jesus, while the shells were bursting all around us and threatening every moment to send us both into eternity, and the blood flowing from his wound formed a little puddle around him; many, passing by to join in the fierce battle that was then raging, stopped a moment to witness this strange and solemn sight. That man recovered, but never evidenced by his subsequent course that he had ever experienced the great change; far from it; as the dews of death seemed to be gathering over him, he seemed to feel the importance of religion, and doubtless did feel it; but, as he recovered and took a fresh hold on life, he again gave way to the sinfulness of his nature and lived without God—a strange thing. Yet such is the hardening power and deceitfulness of sin.

"During the marches of the fall of 1862 had no regular opportunities for holding prayer-meetings, but had meetings as circumstances would permit, which were comparatively few. Yet the active Christians of the company, among whom were some six seminary students, employed themselves distributing tracts and Testaments and religious papers, which were always eagerly received and carefully read by the men. We oft noticed before going into battle, even as we walked along the road just before engaging, that many of the men drew forth their Testaments and enjoyed the consolations of the Gospel in view of their danger. And from their serious faces we could see they were in earnest and enjoyed the comforting assurances therein provided. The changed, sober countenances of the men on going into battle was very marked, and serious thoughts were occupying their minds.

"In winter of 1862 and 1863, after the first battle of Fredericksburg, we were engaged on picket at Port Royal, some fourteen miles below Fredericksburg, detached from the first regiment in which we had been formed, with several other companies, and we had no preaching throughout this winter, except once or twice by Rev. J. Wm. Jones, of Thirteenth Virginia, who was some three miles from us. Yet the Lord visited us in our prayer-meetings, which we held regularly, generally twice on the Sabbath and twice during the week, in some of the shanties we had erected. These meetings were very well attended. We also distributed tracts, religious papers, and Testaments, and these means of grace were greatly blessed by the Lord to the good of many souls, we trust. The effect was visible in the conduct of the men, and we felt assured from the frequent conversations we had with many that the Lord had been with us to do us good. After we removed to Hamilton's Crossing, in March, near Fredericksburg, we kept up these meetings and tract distributions, and witnessed increased interest among the men. These white-winged messengers of grace, as the tracts have been called, found their way into the hands of very many men of this part of our army. A novel and excellent way was to string a number of tracts and suspend to a tree on the public road, on the Sabbath, inviting all who felt interested to pull off a tract and read it. Oft wagoners stopped their teams, and officers drew near on horseback, and men walking along would turn by to get a tract, and continue on their way reading the good news therein contained, as they went along the road.

"April, 1863. Our company was attached temporarily to Early's Division. During the intervals of repose we enjoyed from fighting, we held two of the most serious and interesting prayer-meetings I ever attended; a deep seriousness prevailed, and the most solemn attention was given while we exhorted sinners to come to Christ. And many conversations were held privately with numbers, from time to time, who appeared to be deeply interested in their souls' salvation. After the second battle of Fredericksburg we continued these meetings, holding them nearly every night, during which time the interest increased. Several ministers of the different denominations visited and addressed us, and some thirty professed a change of heart, at different times. An incident occurred during the progress of the battles around Fredericksburg, while opposing Sedgwick's forces. A member of the company, who had seemed somewhat seriously disposed, was badly wounded and cried out loudly to one who had been taking a prominent part in the prayer-meetings to come and pray with him, as he was dying. He replied he could not leave his post while the battle was going on. Directly we were ordered to 'cease firing,' and he immediately went to the side of the wounded man, who urged him to pray earnestly for him ; he felt he was a great sinner, and had no hope nor comfort at the prospect of death ; that he had slighted religion while in health, and he bitterly regretted, and desired now to find the Saviour in this hour of his extremity. The young brother prayed earnestly for him, but the wounded man could derive no comfort; he tossed in agony, and in a short time afterwards died, as he had lived—without God, and without hope. What a lesson to those in life and health to use well their opportunity !

" The interest in these prayer-meetings continued through the spring, and many professed to have passed from death unto life. The marked changes in the habits and deportment of men and officers were hopeful assurances to us that this was no mere enthusiasm. Some who have since passed away in the storm of battle, or by the influence of disease, gave proof that they had indeed passed from death unto life during this precious season of ingathering of souls, while of others we may only trust that this was truly a seasonable time with them to have trusted in Jesus. And we oft looked back to this period with joyful hearts, when so many professed a change of heart. For, but a short time before, we had but some fourteen professed members of the Church, and now we had over seventy who openly avowed the name of Jesus, and all this in a quiet, regular use of the ordinary means of grace. We felt, truly, the Lord had been gracious to us.

" From this time forward I noticed in the different parts of the army, and more particularly in our own company, what great reverence was paid to the word of God. And, in going around the camps early, how common a thing it was to see the men, while waiting for breakfast, or even on the first halt in an early march, earnestly engaged in reading their Testaments. There was also an increased desire to possess a Testament, and particularly a Bible. At this time, spring of 1863, I think the religious interest was more general and more deeply impressed on the minds of the men than at any other period during the war; at least it was more visible and noticeable in its effects. The spiritual condition of the men in the army, at this time and after, was thought to be deeper and stronger than that of the people at home —commonly said, that all the religion was in the army. I never saw this influence more visibly expressed than at a Sabbath-day service held near Fredericksburg, at the old quarters occupied by General Jackson previous to the second battle of Fredericksburg or Chancellorsville. It was the first quiet Sabbath after the battles—Sabbath, May 10. The services were conducted by Rev. B. T. Lacy, who preached from the text, "All things work together for good to those that love God," etc.: Rom. viii. The attendance was very large—between 2,500 and 3,000—consisting of privates and officers of all grades, from General Lee down. I never witnessed such thoughtfulness and seriousness depicted on the faces of any auditors. The preacher stated this was General Jackson's favorite text—then unfolded the doctrine and the peculiar comfort to be derived from it by those who were truly the children of God. At this time, the condition of General Jackson was very critical, and the men seemed to feel that much depended on his recovery. At the conclusion of the sermon Mr. Lacy stated that it might be God's will to spare his life in answer to our prayers, and called upon all to join him in an earnest petition to the throne of grace that God would be pleased to spare him to us. I heard many broken utterances and ejaculations during that prayer, and some declared they tried to pray then, while they thought they had never tried to pray in earnest before. Deep and solemn earnestness appeared written on every countenance. At the conclusion an impressive pause followed; then the preacher said a few words in application of the text—that it would be all for the best, whatever God would determine in reference to the event; and then the crowd quietly dispersed to their camps, ever to retain in their memories this impressive proceeding. Then, in the evening and on the next morning, the news of his (Jackson's) death was reported in camp, and I was struck with the calm, subdued feeling of resignation among the men of his corps—so different, in contrast, in the spirit and tone manifested by the people at home, when they heard the sad news. The sermon seemed to have wrought its own application in the mind of the army, and the feeling prevailed that it was right and all for the best, though we could not understand it.

"This event was to our minds deeply blessed to the spiritual good of the army. And at this particular time—last of May and first of June, 1863—the deepest religious impressions were most plainly evident in our company, and also general in the Army of Northern Virginia. Many of our company sought to hold religious converse in the day and at night, and very often we talked and prayed with the men while walking our beats on guard. Ministers of the different denominations came and preached for us. There was a marked absence of sectarian feeling, and everything was made to centre on the great and saving truths of the Gospel.

"During the past winter, while in camp, a majority of the messes had family worship, as we termed it, regularly every night, using pine-knots for our lights, by which light we were also enabled to do some reading and chess-playing. Several of the messes kept up the worship even after we moved from camp and were engaged in the spring campaign—simply omitting the singing—alternating in conducting the worship.

"We were now most of the time with the regiment—styled First Virginia Artillery —where we found some earnest Christian men, who zealously joined us in establishing prayer-meetings in the different companies and on different nights, so that we had a prayer-meeting nearly every night in the regiment when we were quiet, and preaching regularly on the Sabbath when not on the march, and when the weather would permit; also, committees to distribute tracts and Testaments, with religious papers, and we had the assurance these means of grace were oft blessed for the good of souls.

"August 23, 1863. While encamped near Gordonsville—Blue Run Church—with the regiment, formed a Christian Association, in order to be more united in our efforts to do good, which association continued in existence throughout the war and did much to improve the moral and religious character of the regiment. Good moral character was the only requisite, while the aim of it was religious; fifty-five names were given in the first meeting, to which list were added others continually. We had in all some 160 members. We also instituted noonday prayer-meetings, which were sustained well at first, but other duties interfered and we changed the meetings into night meetings, which were better attended.

" The religious interest throughout the regiment at this time was very good, and it was visible in the good deportment and attention to religious and military duties by the men. Removed from this place towards the Rapidan, where the enemy were threatening, on the 14th of September, 1863. Now on the march continually, but the prayer-meetings were kept up as often and as regularly as we could find time throughout our active fall campaign, and a good attendance prevailed.

" Went into camp about first of January, 1864, at Frederick's Hall, where nearly all the artillery battalions were encamped, in order to get forage conveniently for the horses, while the main army was encamped near Orange Court House.

" Here, from the first, our prayer-meetings were continued regularly, and our association was reorganized and conducted with renewed interest and zeal. We had lost our previous chaplain, Rev. Mr. T. M. Niven, who was compelled to leave the army on account of an asthmatic affection, early in the fall. His place was now, January 14, supplied by the Rev. H. M. White, who continued with us, ministering in the word and oft sharing our duties, till the end of the war; *all* cheerfully bear testimony to his zeal and efficiency in the Master's cause. He was universally beloved and respected and will ever be most kindly remembered. As we were expecting to remain quiet for some time, the proposition was made in our association that we build a chapel, and the men at once got to work and in a short time, though under great difficulties, we had the pleasure of worshipping God in our new house of worship, which was commodious and pleasant, and which would accommodate nearly 300. And often during this winter were gathered together very many to worship God. The people in the neighborhood supplied us very kindly with candles, and also attended our services on Sabbath and oft on week-days. We invited the ministers of the different denominations to come and preach for us, some of whom came and remained several days preaching to us. These were happy and pleasant days. Yes; the most pleasant I enjoyed while in the army, and this season was blessed to many of our souls. Here we had preaching, Bible-class, meetings of our Christian Association, and prayer-meetings. Many of the men subscribed regularly for the different religious papers; every mess in our company subscribed for some religious paper, and in our company nearly every mess sustained regular evening worship; this was also general in the other companies of the regiment. Committees from the different companies were appointed on the state of religion, who reported from time to time as to the spiritual condition of the men. And oft and over again the active Christians went out by two and three to engage in prayer and seek the Divine aid and blessing in the great work.

" And many times two of the young brethren collected the colored servants in the camps, and communicated to them the knowledge of the Divine truth. And here in this rough log-house we had the pleasure of enjoying one of the most solemn communion seasons that was ever allowed us. Quite a number of the people living near joined with us, and we felt truly we were near to God.

" We moved, April 16, near Barboursville, and up to May 5, 1864, were enabled to enjoy preaching and prayer-meetings, which we held quite often and which were well attended by the regiment, and the religious impression continued among the men.

" The men were always anxious to hear the preaching of the word of God, and a number of times, while near the enemy and expecting orders to move, did we have the word preached to us, while the men gave earnest attention, increased, probably, under the peculiar circumstances in which we were placed.

"And while in position on the fortifications around Spottsylvania Court House, and afterwards around Richmond, we held our prayer-meetings more regularly, and which were very well attended, and much interest was manifested by the men. We had our meetings several times broken up by the sudden call to arms—through the bursting of the shells among us, the rolling of the musketry in our front or on either side—calling us off to more dangerous occupations. Often, here, while awaiting orders to move, did we distribute tracts and religious papers among the men, who read them with avidity—anxious to beguile the weary, anxious hours, and especially when it was concerning a subject of vital importance.

" Kept up our prayer-meetings every night while around Spottsylvania Court House with great interest, joined also by the infantry who were stationed on either side of our pieces for our support. Nor were we alone in our prayer-meetings, for the voice of prayer and praise would oft be heard along our lines in the evening, as far as the ear could hear, from the different prayer-meetings in operation, and nothing made me feel more hopeful that, let the issue of the contest be what it might, many would be benefited by a knowledge of Christ throughout their lives, and would never regret their army life, owing to their having found Christ precious to their souls.

" Our prayer-meetings were kept up and well sustained throughout the campaigns of 1864, while in line of battle around Richmond, the infantry participating with us.

" Often did some of the members retire privately into the woods to enjoy a quiet season of prayer, and even while going into retirement we fell in with others engaged in the same interesting employment, which would only stir up the feeling of devotion that burned in the heart.

" These numerous seasons of prayer were very precious; the company and the regiment enjoyed them. Oft when the circumstances surrounding were deemed unfavorable, some of the men would urge that the prayer-meetings should be held, and those who had recently professed Christ were willing to pray with us in these meetings, which was encouraged, hoping it would prove a means of grace to them.

"As to the results of what seemed to be honest and sincere profession, I am not able to state, though the course of some indicates a declension from the solemn vows made while in the army. Yet I cannot believe that all or much of what I witnessed was mere enthusiasm or hypocrisy. " J. K. H."

[From Rev. Dr. Geo. W. Leyburn, Presbyterian Missionary.]

"Appomattox Court House, February 14, 1867.

" *Rev. and Dear Brother :* I saw some little of the revival at that time, at Fredericksburg; and I had a last interview with General Jackson, which made a considerable impression on me, and of which, with some description of his last camping-place; and the congregation assembled there, the last time that he and many of his brave soldiers ever attended such a service, I gave some account in one of the newspapers.

" I saw besides something of the revivals and of the religious state of our different armies at various times. But I did not see things under circumstances to enable me to contribute to a history with the one exception of Wise's Brigade. Owing to my having a son in this brigade and to the fact of several companies from Bedford, then the county of my residence, being in it, I had more to do with it than any other body of our soldiery. Beside a number of other visits made to it, in Virginia and the South, I spent more than a week, including two Sabbaths, with the regiment, Fourth Heavy Artillery originally (at Gloucester Point) and afterwards Thirty-fourth Infantry, during the summer of 1863, while the brigade enjoyed its quiet time of several months at 'Chapin's Farm,' below Richmond. I preached and held religious services during the time mentioned, which resulted in the hopeful conversion of some eight or ten. At least as many, I think, had been hopefully converted in those Bedford companies before my arrival, part of them in connection with public efforts of ministers in the other regiments and partly through the Divine blessing upon the labors of lay brethren of the regiment, among whom, especially in Company H (to which my son belonged), there were some excellent, working Christian men. I have always thought that, looking at matters 'humanly,' it is probable that we should, at that time, have had a great apparent religious development in the Thirty-fourth except that a great awakening had already manifested itself in two of the regiments (Twenty-sixth and Forty-sixth), whose camps were close by—that of the Forty-sixth within a few hundred yards; and the men of the Thirty-fourth had, many of them, been attending the services held, day and. night, in those neighboring camps, and had become interested in them. The faithful and excellent chaplains of the Twenty-sixth and Forty-sixth, Brothers Wiatt and W. G. Miller, can give you a full history of the work in those regiments. But I may say that it was powerful, and, in the Twenty-sixth especially, enduring. I suppose that few, if any, regiments in all the Confederate armies were more thoroughly pervaded by the influence of religion during the middle and latter periods of the war, than the two just mentioned; and a good deal of the same state of things existed, at the same time, in the Thirty-fourth. The Fifty-ninth, which, with some artillery and a company or two of cavalry, generally detached, filled up the brigade, did not have a chaplain, while I visited the brigade, till the latter part of the war, when they were served by Rev. Lyman Wharton, of Liberty, Bedford county, of the Episcopal Church.

" I shall never forget those bright days and brilliant moonlight nights at Chapin's Farm, the delicious cool water of the camp wells, the full gatherings in the regimental chapel and the sounds of prayer and praise ascending from our encampment, mingling sometimes with similar sounds from those in the vicinity.

" Not being able, for reasons already adverted to, to contribute much of actual detailed history, I will give you the general results of my observations on the religious state of the Confederate armies, especially within the last three years of the war. You, as a more interior man, so to speak, saw some things better than I could do. But it may be of some interest and value to know the impressions, some of them very strong, of one who was a frequent visitor to the army and was in constant intercourse, for years, with our soldiers, on the points following. I shall not, perhaps, follow the order of them very rigidly.

" 1. *The comparative state of different parts of the army*, as respects religion. It struck me everywhere, in my extensive intercourse and observation, that the morality and religious feeling of the soldiers belonging to bodies detached and scattered, in greater or less numbers together, over the country, was much below that of those in more regular service. This was owing, I suppose, to the greater laxity of discipline and exposure to temptation as well as the want of ministerial labor and culture, and the absence, in a great degree, of any public sentiment, even such as we may suppose to have existed in the army, to restrain them. I thought I distinctly saw a great difference also between those parts of the army that enjoyed the labors of chaplains and other means of religious culture and those that did not; indeed the difference struck me as exceedingly great and palpable.

" And these facts, as I suppose, account for the conflicting statements made by persons who visited or belonged to different parts of the army, during the war, as to its moral and spiritual condition. The facts themselves, owing, I suppose, to the causes just indicated, were in exceeding contrast.

" 2. *The attendance on preaching and religious services.* This varied in different regiments and parts of the army, according, I suppose, to the prevalent degree of interest in religion, perhaps a good deal according to the amount of faithful labor employed. And it seemed to me that there were generally, if not always, some careless ones who could not be drawn from their tents to the chapel or place of concourse. But, instituting the comparison, I would think, from my observation, that the attendance in camp, on religious services, was proportionally much larger than in our communities at home, taking our population of all classes who are of sufficient age and have somewhat of ability to attend church. Perhaps, however, the greater convenience of attendance, with the want of employment when 'off duty,' had something to do with this state of facts. Nevertheless it afforded the greater opportunity, to chaplains and ministers, for reaching the masses of the soldiery by the preached word.

"Some of the largest congregations I ever saw in attendance on religious services were in our camps during the war. I shall never forget a Sabbath night that I spent in the spring of 1863, in the then war-battered town of Fredericksburg. The feeling of the great revival there was still up, and the soldiers, beginning at an early hour to crowd in, by nightfall filled the spacious Episcopal church edifice, then used for these convocations, lower floor, galleries, presenting, on a grand scale, the unique spectacle, seen only in camp, of a great religious assembly composed only of males. And when the singing began, what a volume of solemn sound swelled up from the voices of that mighty throng! And when the call was made to prayer, how devoutly did the bodies of those men of war and battle bow before Jehovah, a whole congregation literally 'kneeling before the Lord,' and setting an example well worthy of imitation among us, here at home! After the sermon, a number came forward, some desiring prayer, as awakened persons, others to be admitted to church-fellowship. Brother Owen, whom I learned to admire and love almost as soon as I saw him, and his fellow-laborers there, must have reaped, in those early months of 1863, a glorious harvest indeed!

"But I remember now, with even more interest, so strongly has it been photographed in my memory by events and scenes soon following, the congregation and service, on the morning of that same Sabbath, at General Jackson's head-quarters. You probably have visited and remember that last camping-place of his, near Hamilton's Crossing, where the tents of the general and his staff were pitched in a little valley, between a small stream which ran through it and a wooded ridge which girt the vale on the west. On the slope of this ridge, behind the tents, an area had been formed, in the woods, for a place of religious assemblage, by felling the trees and arranging them for seats. Even an hour before the time for service those seats began to be occupied, and before the service commenced many were standing around in addition to those who could find a place to sit. It was a grand opportunity for tract distribution; and Brother Lacy and myself carried forth a large basketful, which were soon disposed of, as well as some Testaments, in the most rapid manner, and almost without our going into the congregation; you know how; for I have no doubt you have sometimes seen how they would rise and come and help themselves and their comrades, on such occasions.

"Yes! I shall never forget that Sabbath assemblage, at those head-quarters. Mr. Lacy supposed a thousand to be present, and I should have judged the number to be not less. It was one of the most brilliant and noble assemblies of military men ever brought together. Beside Generals Lee and Jackson, I remember that Early and Kershaw were there, and a host of officers of various rank. And then, those masses of men that filled the rude seats and formed the dark margin of those who stood around; they were some of the very *elite* of Jackson's Corps and of the very flower of our Confederate armies. All over the area, till the services opened, the men were seen intently reading the books and tracts. Jackson took his seat between two of the tents, in a position where few could see him. Mr. Lacy preached a solemn and powerful sermon, from the case of the rich man and Lazarus, making it suggestive of the reversed contrasts of this world and the next.

It was the last Sabbath in April, and the day was bright and propitious, except that a breeze was stirring, which created some difficulty to the speaker; but Brother Lacy was able, by the power of his full and strong voice, to overcome this; and he seemed to be listened to with profound attention. That was the last, the very last Sabbath that Jackson ever attended a public service, for it was the one that opened the week of the Chancellorsville fights, and the next one found him torn with the cruel wounds that brought on his death. And often, since that time, have I thought, how many of the brave fellows whom I saw there, that day, reading and listening, were reading and hearing the messages of heaven for the very last time!

"I parted with General Jackson at his tent on the next day, and in the act of parting he was led by the conversation to express himself, in regard to the great struggle in which the country was then engaged, in a manner that was very impressive and interesting. But it has become even more so in the connection of those words with events immediately following and in the light of events now transpiring around us. I communicated the conversation, after his death, to some of the public prints, and do not now repeat it to you because I do not know that it could answer any purpose for your book.

"But, returning to my proper topic, I saw a yet larger, grander concourse of soldiers at a religious service, in General Bragg's army, while it was encamped in Middle Tennessee, near Shelbyville. Bishop Elliott, of Georgia, preached on a Sabbath afternoon, being assisted in the services by Dr. Quintard, the present Episcopal Bishop of Tennessee. The congregation formed a vast circle, filling up with a dense mass a large opening in the woods, many seated on the logs arranged for the purpose, but many standing and forming the outer circumference, and a few, Zaccheus-like, clambering up and seating themselves in the trees to see and hear.

"I have permitted myself, under the impulse of feelings awakened by the recurrence of my memory to those scenes gone by, to enlarge in a degree that I had not expected and hardly consistent with method. If I were preparing this for the press I should detach a good deal of what I have put under this head and print it separately. But, writing to you privately, I have indulged myself somewhat, in writing along as I have done and following my feelings. And now, next, as to

"3. _Good order and attention_, in the attendance on religious services. This, so far as my observation extended, was, with scarce an exception that I remember, most exemplary. I hardly ever saw the idle hanging about outside the building or in the outskirts of the out-door congregations which infests so many of our places of worship at home, and very seldom saw any running in and out or any of the whispering and smiling which are likewise too common among us. And no man who has ever preached to our soldiers, under tolerably favorable circumstances, will fail to say that he seldom ever preached to more attentive hearers.

"And here I may speak of what I observed as to the estimation in which faithful chaplains and ministers were held by the soldiers. True, it was not every chaplain that was held in such esteem. Indeed, it seemed to me that our soldiers were, as a general thing, remarkably correct in their discrimination. They used sometimes to say to me, 'We don't like Mr. ——; he smokes his pipe and enjoys himself with the officers, preaches sometimes and hardly ever comes among us.' And very often I had the pleasure of hearing one and another of them say, 'Our chaplain, sir? ah! he is a good man; he often comes round to see us, is always at work and has done a great deal of good; we all like him.' I wish, in fact, that ministers at home were generally held in as good estimation, 'for their work's sake,' as they were—those at all of the right stamp—on the part of the soldiers. I can testify for myself that I have never, anywhere, as a general thing, been treated with such consideration, on account of my office as a minister, as among the Confederate soldiers; and I shall ever remember the 'pleasant times' that I had among them Next, as to

"4. *The acceptability and value of religious books and tracts* among the soldiers.

"I think I can safely say that I have never seen anything like it in our home communities; and I suppose all chaplains and distributers will render the same testimony, without hesitation. Never, in my view, was there such an opening for evangelism by the press. The word of God in the form of a pocket-Bible or Testament, was the first thing sought after, and the hymn-book came next; but it was generally necessary—this was my experience at least—only to show one's self, with a packet of tracts or religious papers, in the corner of an encampment and begin to give out some of them, and you would be very soon surrounded by an eager crowd, asking for something to read. And as on these and other occasions, a soldier would frequently ask not only for himself, but for some of his mess or of his other comrades; the novel spectacle was sometimes presented of even unconverted men, in camp, acting the part of distributers.

"And, so far as I could see, the matter did not stop with merely receiving the books and tracts. They were generally read, and very promptly. Whether this ready reception and perusal of printed religious matter was due in any great measure or not to the isolation of men in camp and their want of something to occupy their minds, such was the state of facts; and it afforded a great advantage in operating for their spiritual benefit.

"In many cases, as you probably know, the soldiers sent home tracts that pleased them, while, on the other hand, as I know, such publications were in many instances the missives of Christian love and solicitude from those at home to the sons, brothers and husbands in camp. You are also, no doubt, acquainted with the fact that soldiers sometimes learned to read, and even to write, while in the army; and I actually knew of more than one case in which a soldier acquired the ability to correspond with his wife or other friends at home. In the hospitals this work of education was quite considerably carried on. The demand there was great for spelling-books, etc., and my wife at one time prepared a little primer for soldiers (which it was designed to enlarge in another edition), at the request of the Evangelical Tract Society; and I was informed by our secretary, Mr. Miller, that there was a large call for it.

"After saying what I have done under these heads, I would declare my own general experience as to what I may call the susceptibility of our soldiers to religious effort. I have never found any class of men so approachable on the subject of their salvation. I could talk with them about it almost anywhere; often did so on the cars. And here I found one of the admirable uses of religious tracts. A tract almost always afforded an easy way of introducing religious conversation, whilst it also answered the purpose of 'clinching the nail' of what was spoken.

"A word as to

"5. *The character of the piety prevalent in the army.*

"For the first year or so, as a general thing, the transition to camp-life seemed to throw a baleful influence over the morality and the religious character of young men going to the army. But a happy change seemed to take place afterward, owing, perhaps, in a good measure, to the fact that religious effort for our soldiers was so extended and systematized in the after years of the war. But I have always been disposed to think that the character of the chaplaincy improved, after the first year or so; did it not? And I have supposed this to be owing to the fact that some men went into the army as chaplains, at first, under the influence more or less, of the war spirit or other secular motives, who, in time, dropped off. The army lost some excellent ministers by ill health and other causes; but it 'sloughed off' a number of unfit ones after the first enthusiasm of things had worn off; and I suppose that most of those who remained or came in afterwards were men who had their eyes open to the rough realities of the soldier-minister's life and acted under true motives. For my own part, I am free to say that, with the exception of the foreign missionaries that I have had acquaintance with, I have known no such body of faithful, devoted servants of God as the chaplains, in general, of the Confederate army.

"And, as to the prevalent tone of piety, among the soldiers converted in the army or otherwise professing religion, I think it was certainly higher than, as a general thing, it was at home at that time; and I am inclined to believe that it was higher than it is in most of our Churches and communities at home at any time. Almost everybody joined in the psalmody of the camp-services, and the novel example was often to be seen there of fine congregational singing, where most of the parts were well supported, without a female voice. The devoutness of attitude and manner I have already spoken of, and the attention to the preached word.

"And as it seemed to me, so too it seemed to strike almost every minister and Christian that went to camp, that there was a somewhat peculiarly earnest, hearty character about the piety of the soldiers. And I have really feared that our Christian young men from the army would lose something of the warmth and life of their piety in coming home to some of our churches.

"In this connection I would say that, with a very few exceptions, those who professed conversion in the army, within my acquaintance, have stood well, most of them very well. Some of them promise to make valuable church-members.

"I have known of several of the army converts, one of them a distant relative of mine, who have turned their attention to the ministry. I have no doubt that the number would have proved to be a good deal larger but for the fact that the war itself so threw back our young men, that survived, in their education, and the destitution of means, on the part of many of them, for carrying on a course of study.

"On the whole, having, from my relation to it, been familiar with the army, my general impression is, that there has never, in this country, been such a field of evangelistic effort as it presented, and that such effort has never, anywhere among us, produced larger fruits.

"And never, in my opinion, in all the history of religion on this continent, has any body of ministers had the privilege of doing a more enviable, if I might not say glorious, work than that fulfilled by the faithful chaplains of the Confederate armies. How many a poor, brave fellow was cheered in his separation from home and 'the loved ones,' or comforted in the languishings of sickness or wounds; how many a one led to Christ, that went to glory from a hospital bed or a gory battle-field, or that has come back to serve God and the Church, through the self-denying labors of those servants of God! If there has been, in our generation, a ministerial work and crown to be coveted, it seems to me it is that of one of our army chaplains who did his work earnestly.

"And so, in more or less degree, of zealous, active Christian men in the army, especially officers. What a noble work of usefulness did some of them accomplish! The influence, eminently, of Jackson, what was its extent, what its value? In his example, and in that of General Gordon and many officers of every grade, and of untitled men in the ranks, a glorious demonstration has been given to all the world in all time, but especially to our Southern people, that the highest Christian character may be attained and conserved, and the noblest Christian usefulness achieved, under circumstances apparently the most unpropitious for Christian culture; for what outward circumstances could apparently be worse, in this regard, than those of the camp, war and battle?

"I am glad that you have undertaken the history. I am not certain whether you design it to extend to any but the Army of Northern Virginia. But such a chronicle, in regard to all our armies, ought to be executed, and will be, I should think, the most striking and important part of the religious history of our times.

"I do not know whether what I have now written you will furnish you any material for the pages of your book. You are welcome to make any use you choose of my testimony, though I might prefer somewhat to revise it, in case any portion of it should be quoted.

"Believe me very fraternally and truly yours,

"G. W. LEYBURN."

[From Rev. Hugh Roy Scott, Episcopalian.]

"BALTIMORE, January 28, 1867.

"*Dear Sir:* I saw in a paper some days since that you were collecting materials for a book describing the religious history of the Army of Northern Virginia. I send enclosed a tract which I wrote describing a very interesting work of grace that occurred in the division of artillery under General Pendleton.

"I am a Protestant Episcopal clergyman, and during the war had charge of a Church in King George county, Virginia. I made frequent visits to the army, and always found our noble men eager to hear the word of God explained, and on two or three occasions was gratified by seeing the truth take hold of many hearts. But rarely in my life have I seen anything like the awakening at Camp Nineveh.

"The Captain K—— referred to in the tract was Captain Thomas J. Kirkpatrick, a lawyer of Lynchburg, Virginia.

"Praying that your important work, besides preserving a record of God's wonderful dealings with our army, may be a blessing to our deeply afflicted land, I remain,

"Very truly yours,

"HUGH ROY SCOTT."

[From Mrs. Dr. Fairfax, sent me through Mrs. Mary Custis Lee.]

"A private from Mississippi, by the name of Galliard, was brought into the hospital at the University from first battle of Manassas with a terrible wound in the thigh and one in the chest. From his first entrance into the hospital his manners were so polite and he exhibited so much patience that he soon got the name of the old gentleman; not that he was old really, but the sufferings of these poor fellows caused them frequently, when mere boys, to look like men in middle life. Mr. Galliard steadily declined in health, and his attendants were comforted by finding that the prospect before him did not dismay or distress him, but that he was well prepared for it. When his end was approaching, a lady stood by his side, with a clergyman. Being struck with the bright expression on his face, she remarked to the clergyman that she believed Christians frequently experienced a foretaste of heaven before death. He heard but could not speak, and put out his hand, pressing hers most expressively. Soon afterwards, recovering his speech, he said, with a bright look and cheerful voice, 'I'm almost over the river.'

"Another, by the name of Thomas, about whose spiritual condition a good many fears had been expressed, and who had been in an anxious state of mind, just before he expired clapped his hands and looked upwards with such evident joy that no one present doubted but that he had experienced at that moment acceptance with God.

"Rev. Mr. Duncan, of Richmond, told us of his being called up at midnight to see a sick soldier, and finding him full of joy in the prospect of his release. He said: 'The first time I ever prayed was when I knelt on the battle-field of Manassas and thanked God for having spared my life to see my mother again. Now, I shall never see my mother in this life, but I shall soon see a little sister who has gone before me, and when called to my last account I shall make my report just as I would to my commander-in-chief, without fear, because I have an all-sufficient Saviour.' Then he asked a young man who was his attendant to sing 'Jesus, Saviour of my soul,' and when he came to the lines, 'Cover my defenceless head with the shadow of Thy wing,' he repeated them and said, 'O, how sweet!'"

"I AM ALONE IN THE WORLD."

(See page 256.)

[*From Rev. George F. Bagby, Baptist, Chaplain Fortieth Virginia, and Army Evangelist.*]

"ELIZAVILLE, KENTUCKY, March 13, 1867.

"*My Dear Brother:* I enlisted as a private soldier in Company A, Fortieth Virginia, May, 1861. Labored thus, preaching every Sunday, holding prayer-meetings every evening in different commands, and distributing tracts. Soon began to see fruits; several professed conversion, without any extra efforts in way of protracted meetings. Was commissioned chaplain Fortieth Virginia, July 19, and continued to labor as above until March, 1862. Resigned chaplaincy, and soon accepted an appointment as colporter in Wise's Brigade. Held a protracted meeting with one of the commands, afterward of Fourth Virginia, Colonel Goode. Several, say four or five, professed conversion, and several others were revived and reclaimed to the cause. In 1863, I forget what month, together with Brother A. Broaddus and Brother W. E. Wiatt, one of the most faithful men I ever knew, chaplain of the regiment, commenced meeting in Twenty-sixth Virginia. This meeting was exceedingly interesting from first. The work of grace commenced and continued more than a month without abatement. No undue excitement, and nothing extraordinary connected with meeting except that the hardest cases seemed to be reached, and one professed infidel, a sprightly young man, professed conversion. The number who professed conversion at this meeting, including the number who professed subsequently—the revival influence continued several months—probably reached 200. Every company of this regiment was in the habit of holding a prayer-meeting every night after the meeting. I never knew one of these young converts to refuse to pray when called on publicly. After this meeting, held another with a battalion at Chaffin's Bluff; as result of this meeting from twenty to thirty professed conversion.

"When this brigade was sent to South Carolina I went to Army of Northern Virginia. The results, etc., of my labors there you know something of.

"In December, 1863, I followed the brigade (Wise's) to South Carolina; labored much among the troops there, scattered as they were in isolated camps from Charleston to Pocataligo and beyond, a distance of twenty-five or thirty miles. About this time scarcely ever preached a sermon without immediate fruit. Preached to a detached company, said to be very wicked, about eighty in number, about seventy-five present at service. Directly after sermon one of the officers came forward and made an open profession of conversion. About this time visited James Island; commenced a meeting in a deserted Presbyterian meeting-house. Congregation, at first small, gradually grew, and before meeting closed, which lasted one month, soldiers might be seen running an hour before time for service from regiments a mile off in order to obtain seats in the house. About one hundred professed conversion here. The converts belonged mostly to Colquitt's Brigade, which afterward did such good service at Olustee, Florida, and subsequently around Petersburg with Army of Northern Virginia.

"I was then called from my army labors to raise money for Colportage Board. During my labors as agent met with an incident which may prove interesting. While laboring among soldiers about Matthias's Point, in beginning of struggle, was much discouraged by impression which was very prevalent—' chaplains were, if not nuisances, at least, supernumeraries.' But preached on. Upon visiting a certain village in South Carolina, 1863, received a letter from an unknown lady asking that I would call on her, alleging a special reason. I was sick, so my lady friend called on me and said: 'A devoted friend of mine left home for the army, very wicked; *accidentally* heard a Mr. Bagby preach near Matthias's Point, in Virginia. This sermon led him to consider his eternal interests, which resulted in his conversion, and he fell a few days after in the first battle of Manassas.' She wept profusely, while I united my tears of gratitude with hers.

"I think, as near as I can judge, that about 400 professed conversion in connection with my labors during the war. So far as I have been able to ascertain, these converts have been among the most faithful among our church-members. Very few have been the cases of backsliding which have come under my observation; indeed, I can recall *not one*, thank God.

"I have written very roughly and hurriedly; if the above facts will help you I shall be glad. I love you, my dear brother, above all, because you are a faithful laborer in our Master's vineyard. Hope to see you in Memphis. It must, indeed, be a privilege to be near our illustrious general-in-chief. Say to him, if you choose, that a poor Baptist preacher in Kentucky remembers him gratefully and prays for him frequently.

"If I can assist you further with your book call on me. I am truly glad you have thought of this book. It is much needed.

"Yours very sincerely and affectionately,
"G. F. BAGBY."

[From Rev. Harvey Hatcher, Baptist, Army Evangelist.]

"293 HOLLINS STREET, BALTIMORE, MARYLAND, April 8, 1867.

"*Brother Jones:* Your request in the *Herald* for all who preached to the men composing the Army of Northern Virginia to send a detailed account of their labors to you has been noticed, but I thought that my labors were too meagre to deserve a part in your history. After thinking over the matter, I decided to send a few items, which you can use as you deem proper. In May, 1863, I went to the Huguenot Springs (convalescent) Hospital, located in Powhatan county, Virginia, and aided the chaplain, Geo. W. Hyde, for three weeks in a series of meetings. About thirty men professed faith in Christ. I baptized some six or eight. Rev. D. B. Winfree, of Chesterfield, preached five times in the meeting. In June, 1864, by the request of Brother Hyde, I aided him again at the same place for two weeks. Our meeting was suddenly closed by a large number of men coming to the hospital and occupying the chapel. About twenty professed to have a hope in the Gospel. Hyde baptized six or eight while I was there and some after I left.

"In November, 1864, I conducted a meeting of great interest and power near the Howlett House, in a chapel built by the Twenty-eighth and Nineteenth Virginia Regiments, of Pickett's Division. It lasted two weeks and about thirty professed faith, some of whom were killed soon thereafter.

"Good order always prevailed, and the best attention always given to the word preached. I labored in a meeting at Dover Baptist Church, Goochland county, in the fall of 1863, where many from the hospital attended and some were converted, but I forget the number. From there I went to Leigh Street Baptist, Richmond, and aided Rev. J. B. Solomon, where there was considerable interest, confined almost to the soldiers from the surrounding hospitals. Some professed conversion, but I took no note of it and can't give the particulars. I send these items for your inspection, though I doubt their worth for your use.

"God bless you all in Old Virginia.

"Yours fraternally,
"HARVEY HATCHER."

[From Rev. H. M. White, Presbyterian, Chaplain Hardaway's Battalion, Artillery.]

"GLADE SPRING, VIRGINIA, March 20, 1867.

"*Dear Brother:* I am sorry not to be able to give you more statistics. All of my papers, except a pocket note-book, were burned in our head-quarters wagon, on the retreat to Appomattox Court House. I will answer your questions in order, as fully as possible.

"I entered upon my duties as chaplain of Hardaway's Battalion of Artillery, November, 1863. (At that time it was known as the First Regiment, Virginia Artillery, commanded by Colonel J. T. Brown. Soon after my becoming its chaplain, it was reduced in size to four companies, and Colonel R. A. Hardaway ordered to take command.) If my recollection serves me rightly, the four companies (Rockbridge, Captain Graham; Roanoke, Captain Griffin; Powhatan, Captain Dance; Third Howitzer, Captain Smith) did not exceed, all told, five hundred men. Out of these five hundred, nearly two hundred were church-members at the close of the war. I know, certainly, that Rockbridge Battalion had 57; Roanoke Battalion, 37; Powhatan Battalion, 42, = 136, to which add 40 for the fourth (I have lost the list), and make 176, or about one-third of the whole.

"During the eighteen months of my stay among them, exactly *forty* were added to the Church. (This number is a part of the 176 above.) The great revival of 1863 was shared by our battalion, and its fruits reaped not long before I joined it. Those who professed conversion at that time fell under my care and, as far as I know, with but a single exception, kept the faith firm unto the end. And of this exception I must say that, although he fell once by intemperance, yet he deeply repented, confessed his sins, and finally died from wounds, rejoicing in hope. There was no revival in our battalion, in the commonly received sense of the term, during my connection with it, nor do I recollect any incidents of remarkable conversion. Some were converted who did not connect themselves with any Church, not even the 'Camp;' *e. g.*, Lieutenant-Colonel David Watson, for a long time Captain Second Howitzers (Richmond), and lieutenant-colonel of our battalion when killed at Spottsylvania. His life had been irreproachable for a long time, but we did not know, not even his most intimate friends, that he had any hope until on his deathbed he said to his mother, 'I have long since taken Christ as my salvation.' E—— M—— did not connect himself with any Church until his return home. Not a few, I think, held back fearing that their change of views and life were due to the hardships and perils to which they were daily exposed, and might not prove genuine after a return to the luxuries of civil life.

"It was my habit to preach twice a week anyhow, unless prevented by insuperable obstacles, and often I preached four or five times. When our battalion was covering a front of a mile and a half, in the trenches around Richmond (winter of 1864–65), I had religious services in each company separately once a week. Only when in winter-quarters at Frederick Hall (1863–64) did I conduct a Bible-class with my own hand, but there were such in the several companies conducted by some of themselves, and I was told they were *at times* well attended and interesting. Moreover, the men had prayer-meetings among themselves every week, winter and summer, in separate companies. I would sometimes attend these as a listener. I cannot estimate the number of tracts I distributed; one of our men (J. K. Hitner, Rockbridge Battery) always kept them on hand; so did I. One winter I had a library of books, which I gathered from different places, mostly religious; it comprised about fifty volumes. Upwards of one hundred religious papers were received a week; perhaps one hundred and fifty.

"Colonel J. T. Brown (our colonel until January, 1864,) was a sincerely pious member of the Episcopal Church; Colonel R. A. Hardaway, of the Methodist; Captains Smith and Dance, Lieutenants Blair, Read, Cunningham, Bagby, were active Christians. The gallant Colonel R. M. Stribbling experienced a change of heart, I hope, while major of our battalion; soon after he left us to take command of General Dearring's old battalion, he made a public profession of religion. Our officers, without a single exception, upheld my hands in every way possible. Our quarter-master (Captain Christian) used to lend me his wagons to haul logs to build our chapels. We built one each winter of my connection with the battalion. Having come out to extreme south-western Virginia, soon after close of the war, I know but little about the *post bellum* history of our men. I get letters occasionally from some of those who professed conversion while I was chaplain, evincing a very gratifying spirit. I have the first to hear of who has returned to the world, but this is purely negative testimony.

"I will add an anecdote or two about General R. E. Lee, which I received second-hand and cannot, therefore, vouch for. At Mine Run, November, 1863, on Sabbath morning, our army in line of battle confronting the enemy, General Lee and his staff, accompanied by General A. P. Hill and his staff, came riding along the line (the shells now and then bursting in the tree-tops and at points rapidly). On reaching the end of A. P. Hill's line, they came suddenly upon a party of ragged soldiers worshipping God, and notwithstanding the fact that they were expecting the fight to begin at any moment, after the example of General Lee the whole party dismounted and joined in the worship, with cap in hand and reins on the arm, until it was concluded. As our guns were immediately on the left, and some of our boys received it from the infantry present at the time, I believed it.

"At Chapin's Farm, early in spring of 1864, General Lee sent his military carriage to Richmond for Dr. Peterkin. During service Dr. P—— *knelt* to pray; as usual, the men stood up or sat still, for most part; but when General Lee *knelt in the dust*, all dropped down instantly.

" I feel a deep interest in your book, and wish you ' God-speed ' in it.

" Fraternally yours,
" HENRY M. WHITE."

[From Rev. John R. Bagby, Baptist, Lieutenant Powhatan Artillery.]

"POWHATAN COUNTY, VIRGINIA, April, 1867.

"*Dear Brother Jones:* I am glad you have undertaken so noble a work, and am only sorry that I can contribute so little towards it. In giving information like this, I do not know where to begin nor what to say after I have commenced.

" The Powhatan Artillery, of which I was a member, was, in the beginning of the war, a component part of what was known as First Regiment, Virginia Artillery, and afterwards in the command of Colonel J. T. Brown, and finally, after his death, in Hardaway's Battalion of Artillery.

" The first winter of the war, then, you perceive, we were under the Rev. General Pendleton, whose character you know. He preached nearly every Sunday to us during that winter, in a chapel we erected. The services were beneficial in taking the minds of the men back to their old home churches. I think about sixty per cent. of the officers of the regiment were religious at that time, and some of them deeply pious. I might mention the Rev. J. D. Powel, of my company, who had prayers at morning and evening roll-calls, and one or two prayer-meetings during the week, when in camp. He left the army in spring of 1862. Also, my captain, W. J. Dance, had prayers often in his own tent, and engaged publicly in Divine services. His example for good was wonderful with his own men. He maintained his Christian character throughout the war. There was Captain Kirkpatrick, of Lynchburg, too, a noble Christian man, who exerted a happy influence. But I can't specify further. Among the men, there were some devoted men whose religion shone brightly. I might name George W. Baily, of my company, Gilliam, of Amherst Battery, etc. We had no revival during that winter.

" The spring of 1862 was a new era in our history. We left General Pendleton, and were attached to Colonel J. T. Brown's Artillery, where I suppose there might have been about fifty per cent. of religious men among the officers, and something over this among the men. Colonel Brown favored religion and encouraged chaplains, tracts, prayer-meetings, etc. But, coupled with him, we find the indomitable L. M. Coleman, whose whole weight was on the side of Christ, who often sent for me to talk of plans for religious services, etc. He lived a monument of God's grace, and died rejoicing in the faith. This was an active campaign with us, but we kept up religious services as well as possible. All who were really pious before held their ground, but the chaff was sifted out. That winter we were in Caroline county—had no chapel, but had meetings occasionally—grew rather lukewarm. In next campaign was the memorable Pennsylvania disaster, and after our return to the Valley we set more regularly to work for Christ, and later in the season on this side of the mountains we held nightly meetings conducted by *officers* and *men*, which grew in interest till all became more or less under its influence, and many a one dates his conversion to that period. Those were happy times, and long to be remembered. Old Blue Run Church will not soon be forgotten. Some of those men you had the pleasure of immersing in Orange county. These men held out well and went to work for Christ and, when they came home, united with the Church. Among the prominent workers in these meetings were the noble men of Rockbridge Battery, some of the Howitzers, and some of my own men, the most prominent of whom was George W. Baily. Many a telling exhortation and prayer were made by officers and men of our battalion.

"The winter following was one of remarkable interest in our battalion. We erected a commodious chapel near Frederick's Hall, had a regular series of services, formed a Young Men's Christian Association, which worked most delightfully. All the religious men of the battalion were gathered in, and latent energies called forth, and influences exerted, which had a most salutary effect upon the general tone and character of our men. Many religious papers were circulated, and thousands of tracts were scattered. During this winter Dr. Burrows, Dr. Read and many others favored us with visits.

"In the next and closing campaign of the war we were found most of the time in the trenches, yet not forgetful of our obligations to God. Many a prayer-meeting did we hold in hearing of the enemy, and many a soul was made to rejoice. Here we lost George W. Baily (died of disease), in Richmond Hospital, in full assurance of faith. He was as promising a young minister as I ever saw; devoted to the work, and longing to get into the harness. His labors in the army will never be known till eternity reveals them. The men all had implicit confidence in his piety, and his burning appeals were well received. He was a noble Christian soldier and a bright intellect. Colonel Hardaway, our last commander, was a Christian man and a gentleman of high order. He was an advocate of religious services, and humane in his treatment.

"We lost many good men during the war, and we hope they were sustained by their religion. I can't recall any very striking facts in connection with the religious interest of our men, and as I did not keep any *diary*, I have to depend on memory altogether. I suppose during the war our command averaged about fifty per cent. of religious men, and out of these at least forty per cent. held on to their religion, and were worthy examples to those around them; and of those who came home safely, all have, I believe, been more useful Christians than they were *ante bellum*. The restraining and constraining influence of the religious portion of our command upon the rest was untold. There was a moral tone given to our command, which, I suppose, but few others enjoyed. This was a constant thing, not much fluctuation in this power for good. My constant employment, when I could get them, was to scatter tracts, Testaments, hymn-books, etc. These were always *joyously* received, and I hope did much good. You know something of my labors, hence I desist further statements. I wish I had time to deal more in particulars, but can't. I have hurriedly scratched off these facts, which you can use as you think best. May the Lord bless you.

"Your brother, etc.,

"J. R. BAGBY."

498   APPENDIX.

[From Rev. Dr. T. H. Pritchard, Baptist, Army Evangelist.]

" PETERSBURG, VIRGINIA, April 4, 1867.

"Dear Brother Jones: In common with all who love the cause of Christ, and
are devoted to the late Confederacy, I feel a profound interest in, your proposed
work on the religious history of the Army of Northern Virginia. I was in the army
so short a time that I did not imagine my personal experience would be of service
to you. It is true that I never enjoyed the work of preaching the Gospel so much
in my life, and that my labors were not without some fruit. I baptized fifty odd
soldiers, most of them while the army was lying around Orange Court House in the
fall of 1863; but I should not have written you at all on the subject had not a friend
suggested that I should give you an incident of my experience while preaching to
Gordon's and Wright's Brigades, camped under Clark's Mountain to watch the
fords of the Rapidan.

" You remember that Mr. Andrew Broaddus and myself were at the house of old
Brother Brown, and while there the Lord was pleased to bless our efforts to the conversion of some forty or fifty men, most of them in Gordon's Brigade. At that meeting
Colonel John Hill Lamar, who commanded the Sixty-first Georgia Regiment, and
was killed at Monocacy, Maryland, was converted. But it was not that which I sat
down to tell you.

"At the close of our meeting a few of us went down to the river at a ford near
Brother Brown's—I don't remember the name of it—and I baptized some eighteen men
in the Rapidan, in the presence of the enemy's pickets. Several of them sat on a fence
in full view of us, and within range, with their guns across their laps, and witnessed
the ceremony. I don't know that you will find any place in your book for the anecdote; but as the historian should collect many facts, and from them disseminate the
truth and spirit of the times, I send it.

" Our people remember you with affection, and would be glad to see you in our
pulpit again.

" With much regard, I am your brother in Christ,

" T. H. PRITCHARD."

[From Rev. J. W. Walkup, Presbyterian, Chaplain Ninth Virginia Infantry.]

"APPOMATTOX, April 4, 1867.

"Dear Brother: I received your letter a few days since, and am glad that you
have undertaken the work you mentioned, and hope that you may be abundantly
successful. I labored for so short a time in the army (about ten months), and on so
limited a field, that I have but little of interest to narrate. I was chaplain of the
Ninth Virginia Infantry, Barton's Brigade, Pickett's Division, Colonel Phillips commanding.

" I preached to my own regiment every Sabbath when it was in my power; also
often to the whole brigade, and sometimes to other regiments and brigades. Often
also I preached during the week, in the day or at night. I distributed a great many
tracts and religious papers among our men, which were generally very readily, and
sometimes gladly, received.

" I was present a part of the time during the revival in Orange county after
our troops returned from the battle of Gettysburg. There was great interest on the
subject of religion then through our whole division. The preaching of Dr. Pryor,
Rev. J. C. Granberry and others was much blessed. A number, I know not how
many, professed religion in my brigade, some few in my own small regiment. When
we were ordered to march many were still anxious inquirers. Among others who
professed religion there was the assistant surgeon of our regiment, Dr. H——. He
afterwards gave abundant evidence of a change of heart. I saw much of him for

months afterwards, and can say that no subject appeared to have anything like as much interest for him as the subject of religion. Christians and religious books were his chosen companions. On our march from Orange Court House to Richmond I frequently noticed the men reading their Testaments. While we were camped at Petersburg our colonel made a public profession of religion. He hoped that he had been converted some months before. He aided me much in my work, gave me every encouragement. I trust that he is a truly pious man. His Bible was daily read, I believe, and often he sought religious conversation with me. On one occasion, as I was sitting on a log meditating, he came and sat down by me, and said: 'Tell me something good.'

" We had some very good Christians in our regiment. One named Bailey, from Portsmouth, assisted me by his prayers. He fell dead at the battle of Drewry's Bluff, and lay on his back with a sweet, happy smile on his face as it looked heavenward.

" In our brigade there was but one regiment which had no chaplain, and I think there was more open wickedness in that than in all the others combined.

"On one occasion, as I passed through my regiment distributing tracts, Sunday morning before preaching, I found all behaving well, not an oath, no cards nor any open violation of the holy day. I then went to this regiment which had no chaplain for a similar purpose, and to invite them to preaching. I was grieved to find them in many tents playing cards either for amusement or money, and could persuade but five of them to attend preaching.

" I once could have told you much of interest probably, but it has passed from my mind.

" Colonel C——, of the Thirty-eighth Regiment, who fell at the battle of the Half-Way House, between Petersburg and Richmond, interested me much. He was an amiable, noble-hearted man. Several times I conversed with him on the subject of religion while he was well, and I trust that he died a Christian, though he had made no profession publicly. I saw him after he was mortally wounded. He appeared engaged in prayer, and his countenance wore an expression of resignation.

" Yours fraternally,
" J. W. WALKUP."

[*From Rev. J. H. Colton, Presbyterian, Chaplain Fifty-third North Carolina Regiment.*]

" McKENSIE'S BRIDGE, MOORE COUNTY, NORTH CAROLINA, August 1, 1866.
" REV. J. WILLIAM JONES:

"*Dear Brother:* In Daniels's Brigade, afterwards Grimes's, there were four regiments and a battalion—Thirty-second, Forty-third, Forty-fifth, Fifty-third, and Second Battalion—all North Carolina. These all had chaplains, only the Thirty-second and Second Battalion for a time without. The brigade was made up under or in anticipation of the conscription act, consequently there was not that intelligence which was found in the first volunteers.

" I believe, however, the morality of the brigade would compare favorably with any other, but upon this I can speak only with assurance for my own regiment, the Fifty-third North Carolina Infantry. Gambling was not common at any time, drunkenness not prevalent, and swearing not very common.

" We joined the Army of Northern Virginia, June, 1863, but Brother Brooks, of the Second Battalion, and myself were absent from Gettysburg until February, 1864. In the fall of 1863 Brother Thompson, of the Forty-third, had a revival in his regiment.

" Returning, myself, just before the campaign of 1864, I entered earnestly into the work of spiritual preparation for the campaign. We built a neat chapel (in the construction of which I was much indebted to General Rodes for hauling), and Brother Brooks and I joined in worship. We held meetings every night alternately for a month, and part of the time a prayer-meeting at 12 o'clock. There were about ten in my regiment and some two or three in his who joined the Church, most of them the Baptist Church. This was near Orange Court House, and at the time of our marching there was still considerable seriousness in the brigade. Brother Richardson, of the Thirty-second (Methodist), also had a revival at the same time, and some twenty professed Christ.

"I had *generally* prayer or preaching at night when it was practicable. J. W. Bivens, Company O (Baptist), held regularly every night after roll-call prayer in his company, so long as he remained. He lost an arm, June, 1864. Then his brother, J. A. Bivens, a subject of the revival of April, 1864, took his place until he was mortally wounded at Winchester, September, 1864. A. B. West, a licentiate of the Baptist Church, Company K, also rendered me efficient service both by example and conversation. He was not well educated, and did not undertake to preach. He was killed September 19, Winchester, 1864. R. A. Moore, another licentiate of the Baptist Church, Company G, was very active. He was more intelligent and better educated than the others, and as he was generally on the ambulance-corps or nurse in the hospital he did much good.

"April campaign, 1864, we numbered about 300 in camp; about one-fourth were members of some Church—the Baptists in excess, then Methodists, then Presbyterians, with some Lutherans.

"I distributed a great many tracts, and generally received a number of copies of religious newspapers weekly.

"The men were generally supplied with Testaments, as I obtained a supply at two different times. They always seemed particularly anxious to get Testaments. I suppose there was at least a fourth who could not read, and in one company nearly all. The officers of my regiment were generally moral men, and most of them members of the Church, though none were active Christians. The colonel, at his own suggestion towards the close of the war, gave orders for the band to play some sacred music after the roll-call, and prayers by the chaplain, at which he attended.

"It was my privilege to labor in the hospitals at Gettysburg for three months, but I have nothing very remarkable to relate. The wounded were always glad to see the chaplains coming into their tents, and heard gladly the word of God.

"There is one incident which illustrates the power of religion in forgiveness of enemies and the triumph of faith over death. I have thought of dressing it up and giving it publicity, but other duties have interfered. I have not now by me the record of the name of the soldier, but I am pretty sure it was Dunston, of Petersburg, Virginia. His case having become very offensive he was carried to the pest-house, which was an arrangement of tents separate from the rest. This was attended by Federal nurses, and one was a tall fellow by the name of Smith. He was an attentive nurse, as I might remark their nurses were generally, but not so much evidently from Christian principle as from policy, as it kept them out of the field; but he was very profane, and frequently gambling. Dunston lingered several days. The first time I saw him he told me he was a Christian, and I believe had become one in the army. He was quite talkative and very hopeful, and urged me to come again. I called again about the time he began to die. The scene which I witnessed was quite affecting. He was entirely conscious, and was almost in ecstasy. He called Smith to his bedside, and as that tall soldier stooped down he threw his arms around his neck, and said: 'Billy, you have been very kind to me; Billy, you must quit swearing; you are too good to go to hell; quit swearing, Billy.' Then, after manifesting much outward affection towards his nurse, he released him, but continued for some time reaching towards heaven and clasping his hands and saying he saw Jesus, and in this happy frame he died.

"With many wishes for your success in your undertaking, I am, in Christ, yours,
"J. H. COLTON."

[*From Rev. James McDowell, Presbyterian, Chaplain Palmetto Sharpshooters.*]

"MANNING, SOUTH CAROLINA, March 27, 1867.

" REV. J. WM. JONES:

"*Dear Brother:* I was chaplain of the 'Palmetto Sharpshooters,' Jenkins's Brigade; and after he was killed in the battle of the Wilderness, Bratton's Brigade, Longstreet's Corps. I became chaplain in July, 1862, and continued so until the surrender of the army at Appomattox Court House.

" I usually had the following services in my regiment: On Sabbath a prayer-meeting about sunrise, preaching about 11 o'clock, and preaching or prayer-meeting in the afternoon or night. In the week we generally had prayer-meeting about sundown or at night. During the last winter we were in camp the church-members had an interesting prayer-meeting, which some twenty of them conducted in turn. These were held every night. I had a Bible-class for awhile, but it was not very large nor very flourishing.

" I distributed a great many religious papers, tracts, Bibles and Testaments. Number not known.

" We had quite a revival of religion in our brigade at one time while stationed near Petersburg. More of our men joined the Baptist Church than any other denomination. I suppose I received fifteen or twenty into the Presbyterian and Methodist Churches. Means used were preaching, religious conversation and prayer.

" From the after-lives of those professing conversion I have reason to think that that a number of cases were genuine conversion, but some others did not give good evidence afterwards of having been really changed in heart.

" The majority of the officers of my regiment were ungodly men, and their influence was against religion. Those of them highest in rank seldom attended any religious service. Some of our captains and lower officers were pious, and exerted a good influence, but none of higher rank than captain in my regiment. Some of the other regiments were much more blessed in this respect, having pious colonels, who exerted a good influence. General Jenkins (our brigadier) was a professor of religion; General Bratton, who succeeded him, was not.

" I think upon the whole, though there were a great many *very wicked* men, that still religion exerted a considerable power on the general morals and efficiency of the army.

" I think there were several men in the brigade, who were killed, who thought of devoting themselves to the ministry; but none that I know of who survived the war, and none at any time in my regiment.

" Perhaps some of the following incidents may be of some service to you:

" I asked a young man of my regiment, wounded near Lookout Mountain, who afterwards died: 'What would you take for your hope that you are a Christian?' He answered: 'Not ten thousand worlds.'

"A lieutenant in the same hospital, wounded same time, who died after the amputation of a leg, said, in answer to my inquiry as to the cause of his not being a Christian: 'I have often wanted to be a Christian, but I put it off from day to day.'

"Another lieutenant of my regiment, wounded at Spottsylvania, who also died, said: 'I had fixed as a time to attend to my salvation when the war was over and I returned home;' but, poor fellow, death came long before that period. Both cases show the evil of procrastinating.

"A very wicked man in my regiment was shot in battle and died in a few minutes. He used the following, or very similar language, when shot: 'Lord God, have mercy on my miserable soul; I am lost.'

"Another man in my regiment was severely wounded. He said to me in the hospital when it was likely he would die: 'How awful it is for a man to lie down and die in his sins, and not attend to his salvation until it is too late. Lord, have mercy upon me.' And yet he got better and turned back to the world, and continued to neglect his salvation.

"I asked a young man who professed religion in my regiment and joined the Church: 'What are you willing to do for Christ?' He answered: 'To die for him.'

"A noble young man in my regiment, and who had been since before the war a member of the Presbyterian Church, was mortally wounded above Richmond. He lived several days. One day, before praying with him, while I was reading to him the Twenty-third Psalm, when I had read in it as far as the words, 'I will fear no evil,' he exclaimed: 'I fear no evil; Christ is my Friend; O blessed Redeemer!' His death was a triumphant one. He did not seem to fear to die any more than to go to sleep, and a number seemed to be deeply impressed by his calm and happy death.

"Another man in my regiment was mortally wounded. I prayed with him before he died. He was a professor of religion, and I believe a true Christian. As he was sinking in death I asked him: 'Can you still trust in Jesus?' His dying countenance lighted up with a sweet smile, and he answered: 'I can trust in Jesus; I can trust in Jesus.' That name seemed precious to him, and was like music in his dying ears.

"Another young man in my regiment was wounded, and after some time died in Jackson Hospital; but he was no Christian, I fear. I directed him to Jesus as the only Saviour. One day I asked him if he trusted in Christ, or in his prayers and works, to save him. He answered: 'I trust partly in Christ, and partly in my prayers and works.' I fear this is the mistake of many who do not take Christ for their entire and only Saviour. He one day said: 'If my name was only on the Church roll I think all would be right with me.' As if a mere profession of religion would have been sufficient. How many ways Satan has of deceiving men! He said, one day, 'I never was taught the Scriptures. Father is a wicked man. I did badly when a boy, and mother wanted to correct me, and father would not let her, and so I grew up badly.'

"I was requested to visit a young man of the First South Carolina Regiment, mortally wounded at Spottsylvania Court House. I did so, and found him happy, though his sufferings, I think, were great. He said: 'My happiness is inexpressible, it is beyond all expression; tongue cannot express it.' Upon my inquiring as to the ground of his trust, he said: 'I have not a bit of trust in myself. I am a brittle thread: lost, lost, lost, without a Saviour' (or 'but for the Saviour').

"I asked him if he felt the truth of those words—'Jesus can make a dying bed feel soft as downy pillows are.' He answered, 'I know it; I feel it sensibly.' He spoke of his widowed mother, and said, 'I love my mother; but I love my Saviour much more.' He clapped his hands, and blessed the Lord.

"Not far off I witnessed a most triumphant death-bed scene; an experienced Christian of the Third South Carolina Regiment. He said, 'I am weaker, but my way is clearer than ever before. God is my Rock and my Fortress.' He spoke of his great love for Christians, and spoke of this affording him evidence of his being a Christian; for, said he, 'We know that we have passed from death unto life because we love the brethren.' He spoke of his *intense* sufferings, but said, 'Christ is *very precious* to me.' Again he said, 'I hope I will know you in heaven,' and 'I believe in heavenly recognition.' He trusted in Christ *alone*, and said, 'We are not saved by works, but by the unsearchable riches of Christ.' Again he said, 'No denominations are in heaven; loftier thoughts than these will engage our attention there.' It was a privilege to hear his talk, and as I looked on his corpse next day, I thought what a glorious exchange his spirit has made!

"A friend of mine asked a poor young man in a hospital as to his prospects for eternity. He was too far gone to speak, but wrote these words on a strip of paper,

'I've been going the bad way all the time; it is too late, too late.' How dreadful to be without Christ! what a blessed thing it is to have Him for our friend, living and dying.

"With kind regards for you, and best wishes for God's blessing on your enterprise,
"I remain yours very truly, JAMES McDOWELL."

[*From Rev. W. L. Curry, Baptist, Chaplain Fiftieth Georgia Regiment.*]

"NEAR MILFORD, GEORGIA, March 20, 1867.

"*Dear Brother Jones:* . . . I was appointed chaplain of Fiftieth Georgia about September 1, 1862, just as we were entering upon the first Maryland campaign. For several months the army was in such constant motion that little could be done besides occasional preaching.

"Soon after the Fredericksburg battle, December 13, we went into winter-quarters. I then commenced pastoral work—visiting among the tents, holding prayer-meetings, etc. I commenced a sunrise prayer-meeting, which was attended, of course, only by the more earnest of the brethren, who were quite few in number, and kept it up for many weeks. I continued efforts of this kind—preaching, too, quite often for some six months, without any visible fruits of my labors. But about the expiration of this period, I could see serious faces in our little congregations, and we had new attendants at our sunrise meeting, and some who would hardly speak to the chaplain before would now make their way to his tent to inquire what they were to do to be saved. Oh, you can imagine what overflowings of joy I experienced at these tokens of the Divine presence. It was almost the 'first fruits' of all my feeble efforts in the cause of the Master. The number of inquirers increasing, I instituted inquiry-meetings, which were held at same place as the sunrise meeting. Perhaps I should have stated that this place was a certain tree some two or three hundred yards from the camp. We would open the inquiry-meeting with singing and prayer, and while the brethren would keep this up, I would take the anxious out to converse with them. It was not long before I had the privilege of leading a number of noble young fellows into the water, and among them one who afterwards was head and shoulders above all the others in zeal for the cause, in power for usefulness, and in humble, sincere piety. This was Brother Timothy Stallions, who, at his conversion, did not know his letters, though a man of family. He commenced to study, and in a few months, notwithstanding the hindrances and disadvantages of a soldier's life, he was able to read the Bible quite readily, which he often did in our meetings, adding also frequently pointed and earnest remarks. He soon had a name in the whole brigade for courage and piety, which he bore untarnished throughout the war. He is still living, and when I last heard from him was preaching Jesus in his same quiet way—by his devout walk and his fervent exhortations.

"The interest I mentioned above continued almost unabated for some six or eight months. It was a very quiet work, but permanent in its effects. Of course, our regular meetings were broken up when the army left winter-quarters. But all through the summer of 1863 I had the pleasure of baptizing a few at nearly every place where we remained any length of time, beside testifying to the conversion of others who united with other denominations.

"Our corps (Longstreet's) was ordered to Tennessee, you remember, in the fall of 1863, when till late in the winter we were marching and fighting almost without intermission. In the spring of 1864 the work commenced afresh. When I entered my regiment, and for some time afterward, there was no other chaplain present with the brigade, and I had brigade services. This arrangement was continued after the appointment of other chaplains. At Gordonsville, Virginia, in the spring of 1864, our brigade was blessed with a considerable refreshing—about thirty from the different regiments making profession within two weeks. The most of these were baptized at one time, just in front of Dr. Quarles's house, in a beautiful stream that runs by it. The occasion was quite a touching one. The appointment for the baptizing having been circulated, the citizens of the vicinity were present, and among them quite a collection of ladies. Dr. Quarles's female school turned out. The ladies joined in the singing, and the bare sound of female voices brought tears to many a soldier's eye.

"When we left Gordonsville, which we did on the 4th of May, we plunged at once into the severest campaign of the war. The army lived in the trenches, as you know, all that summer. My brigade enjoyed several seasons of respite; that is, they would be relieved from the fatigue and danger of the front line, and would be kept in reserve in the rear. One of these seasons was protracted more than six weeks, during which time we held from three to five meetings a day. It was a precious season. The men were relieved from all duty, even guard-duty and cooking, so that we had nothing to do but hold meetings. A prayer-meeting at sunrise, an inquiry-meeting at 8, preaching at 11, a prayer-meeting at 4 for the success of our (Confederate) cause, preaching again at night, was the usual programme of the day. Our prayer and inquiry-meetings were held under a large, sweet-gum tree, about two hundred yards from the camp. We usually had from fifty to seventy-five brethren at these, not one of whom refused to lead in prayer, and not a few would interest us with remarks and exhortations. The preaching was done in the bivouac (we had no tents except such as the men carried on their backs). The religious interest of the brigade seemed more general than I had ever seen it before. I have looked around over the whole camp during preaching, and failed to see a single loiterer. Some forty or fifty made profession at this time, and I baptized them, or rather the most of them, in a pond, the only one in the vicinity, where we were exposed to the fire of the enemy; but not one of us was hurt on such occasions, though the bullets whistled most unpleasantly around and in the midst. Brother Campbell, of the Tenth Georgia, was my efficient co-laborer.

"I have but few of my army acquaintances near me now. It will always be pleasant for me to testify to their piety and devotion in the army.

"If the above can be of any service whatever to you, you may be assured you are welcome to it, and I send it with strong regret that I could not serve you more efficiently.

"I am sorry I have had to write this in a hurry. As well as I remember, over a hundred made profession of religion in the brigade after I entered it, who continued steadfast during the war and so far as I have heard from them are pious yet.

"Your brother,
"W. L. CURRY."

[From Rev. J. J. Hyman, Baptist, Chaplain Forty-ninth Georgia Regiment.]

"I left my home on the 10th day of March, 1862; joined the Forty-ninth Georgia Regiment as a private soldier on the 1st day of May. I was commissioned chaplain of the Forty-ninth Georgia Regiment. The battles around Richmond prevented us from having regular Divine service. After the battles were over, the Forty-ninth Georgia Regiment was attached to General J. R. Anderson's Brigade, afterwards General E. L. Thomas's. At this time I was the only chaplain in the brigade (four regiments). I, being young, knew but little about the duties of a chaplain, but was willing to do anything in my Master's cause. Being in the command of General Jackson, we had but little time for religious service during the whole of 1862. On the 16th of December, 1862, we went into quarters at Camp Gregg, six miles south of Fredericksburg, Virginia, where I opened regular night service; sometimes in the open air, at other times (when weather was bad) in tents. Congregations were very good; often I have seen large numbers leave the door of the tent, being unable to get in, when the snow was all over the ground. Finding that we had gone into winter-quarters, I commenced preaching regularly three times a week to each regiment in the brigade. About the 1st of February, 1863, the good Lord poured out His Spirit upon us; hundreds were seeking the Lord for pardon of sins; almost daily there were some going down into the water, being buried with Christ in baptism. At this time our brigade was so scattered that I had to preach to each regiment separately; the interest was so great that I preached for weeks from four to six times in a day. Just as I was about to break down, Brother E. B. Barrett came from Georgia as a missionary and gave me much assistance. He joined himself to the Forty-fifth Georgia Regiment as chaplain, and at once entered upon the faithful discharge of his duties; about the same time Brother A. W. Moore came on as chaplain of the Fourteenth Georgia Regiment. The battle of Chancellorsville broke into our service for a few days; when we went back into camp Brother Moore left for Georgia, leaving Brother Barrett and myself in the brigade. We preached night and day, baptizing daily in a pool we prepared for the purpose. In the month of May, 1863, I divided my labors with Thomas's and Wright's Georgia Brigades. I baptized during the month fifteen in Forty-ninth Georgia and sixty-five in Wright's Brigade. The day that the army was ordered to march on the Pennsylvania campaign, yes, while the regiments were being ordered to fall in, I was baptizing near Wright's Brigade. Baptized forty-eight, all in twenty minutes. At another time, near the same place, Brother Marshall and I baptized twenty-six. The long-roll being beat, we left our pleasant camp; was in active campaign until about the 1st of August, when we camped near Orange Court House. Here again we met in Christ's name and He met with us. Never before have I seen the like; often we would meet to worship, having only the dim candle-light; hundreds would be there. When an invitation was given for prayers there would come so many I knew not what to do with them. At this time Brother Barrett was at home, but Brother Moore was present. I did all of the preaching that I could. At this time kept my command supplied with tracts, papers, etc. In August and September I spent some time with General Walker's Virginia Brigade, where souls were being converted. On one occasion, in August, 1863, I went down to Rapidan river with Brother Anderson, chaplain in General Walker's Virginia Brigade, to baptize. We met about 2,000 soldiers, besides many citizens. He (Brother Anderson) went down into the water and baptized twelve. After he came out I opened service in our usual way by singing and prayer. Such music I never before heard. It sounded as though the heavenly host had come down to take part in our earthly worship. I went down into the water and baptized twenty-three. This state of feeling continued with but little change until about the 1st of December, 1863, at which time Thomas's Brigade was ordered to the Valley, below Staunton, Virginia, where we were in active campaign during the whole of winter. While in the Valley, Brother J. H. Taylor became chaplain of Thirty-fifth Georgia Regiment; Brother Moore resigned as chaplain of Fourteenth Georgia Regiment. About the 1st of April, 1864, we left the Valley and returned to Orange Court House. Just as we had arranged for and were having regular Divine service the battle-cry was again heard and we hurried off to meet the enemy. We halted not until we stopped near Petersburg, Virginia. During the months of July and August, 1864, our meetings were truly interesting. I was the only chaplain present in our brigade, preaching both night and day; I visited almost daily Scales's North Carolina Brigade, also Third and Fourth Virginia Regiments, preaching as I went, seemingly with much effect. I preached from three to five times per day all during July and August, besides baptizing almost daily. The labors of these months broke me down and I was forced to leave my command on sick furlough. From this time I was not of much service to the brigade until winter. During my absence the prayer-meetings were kept up by the private members. February, 1865, we built us a large chapel near the line of works around Petersburg. We organized a Sabbath-school of 120 pupils. At this time religious services were truly interesting. We baptized a great many. From here we marched on the 2d of April, 1865, leaving our beautiful camp behind. We halted at Appomattox Court House, Virginia, and 'yielded to overwhelming numbers and resources.' Here I leave the field of blood (ever looking back upon many sacred spots where the Lord blessed us) with mingled grief and joy. I baptized while in the army 238 soldiers. Number professing conversion, 500. Preached about 500 sermons, besides exhortations, lectures, etc.

" Yours fraternally,
" JOHN J. HYMAN."

[From Rev. A. M. Marshall, Baptist, Chaplain Twelfth Georgia Regiment.]

" EATONTON, GEORGIA, March 22, 1867.

"Dear Brother Jones: I was, as you know, chaplain Twelfth Georgia Regiment, Doles's Brigade, but did not get my appointment until just before the battle of Sharpsburg. As soon as the army crossed back on the Virginia side, I commenced a meeting in the regiment, which increased in interest until several regiments and battalions became interested. I called to my assistance Dr. Stiles, Brother Nelson and yourself. The meeting was one of great interest, and promised to result in many conversions, but was suddenly broken up one night by the order to get ready to move. General Jackson attended this meeting several times, and remarked after hearing Dr. Stiles preach one night, that he was ' more convinced than ever, that if sinners had justice they would all be damned.'

" There was no opportunity given for persons to join the Church; but there was every reason to suppose that a number were converted. This was one of the first revivals of religion that I heard of in the army. And I learned at that meeting *how* to conduct services in camp. I was for a long time the only chaplain in Doles's Brigade, and on that account had a great deal to do. I never kept any account of the number of sermons I preached, nor of prayer-meetings. It was our practice to hold prayer-meetings every night when in camp, and frequently of a night when on the march. We had Bible-classes composed, I think, of men in all the regiments of the brigade—Twelfth, Fourth, Twenty-first and Forty-fourth, Georgia. I supplied these regiments as well as I could with Testaments, religious papers and tracts, but have no idea how many were distributed.

" The most remarkable revivals in this brigade were at Guinea's Station, Orange Court House, and Morton's Ford. The first was during the winter of 1862, and the others were during the summer of 1863.

" At Orange Court House we made such arrangements as would accommodate the whole brigade, and I wrote to Brother Geo. B. Taylor, who came and preached very acceptably for several days; other brothers preached frequently, and the meeting increased in interest until we moved to Morton's Ford. I think there were twenty-five or thirty conversions in the meeting. At the ford the meeting was more interesting than before. Here I was assisted by Brother A. T. Spalding, of Alabama, and W. N. Chaudoin, of Georgia. These brethren did most of the preaching, and by the aid of the Spirit they preached with power. There were forty or fifty conversions in this meeting.

" As far as I am able to judge, those who professed religion in the army are as sincere as those who professed at home. Of the officers of the Twelfth Georgia, it affords me pleasure to speak of Colonel Willis, who always rendered me every assistance he could, and gave every encouragement to the men to attend meeting. He was one of the best officers in the army, one of the best friends I ever had, one of the most promising men I ever knew. He was killed while in command of Early's old brigade, at Bethesda Church, in June, 1864. His earnest request was, that if he was ever wounded he wanted the surgeon to tell him his true condition. Dr. Etheridge told him that he was mortally wounded. He said: 'I am no more afraid to die than I am to fight for my country.' Lieutenant-Colonel Hardeman, Major Carson and Dr. Etheridge, were all professors of religion, and were always ready to do all they could for the cause of Christ. There were several captains and subordinate officers of whom I would like to speak if I had time.

"I am yours, etc., A. M. MARSHALL."

[From Rev. C. H. Dobbs, Presbyterian, Chaplain Twelfth Mississippi.]

"KOSCIUSKO, MISSISSIPPI, March, 1867.

"*Dear Brother:* I regret exceedingly that about the close of the war I lost nearly every vestige of information concerning the data you desire, as far as papers, manuscripts, etc. are concerned, hence the impossibility of giving you much in the way of statistics. You can, perhaps, obtain from Mrs. Brown, of Richmond, Virginia, a copy of the by-laws, etc., of the Christian Association in Harris's Brigade, from which you can find the number of church-members, conversions, etc., in the brigade up to that period.

"You will bear in mind the fact that I did not receive my appointment (as chaplain Twelfth Mississippi Regiment) until January, 1863. I then found the brigade camped about eight miles from Fredericksburg, on or near the road leading from Hamilton's Crossing to Chancellorsville. The ground was covered with snow, and as I approached the regiment, unknown to most of the men, having received the appointment at the solicitation of the colonel (Taylor), while on a furlough to Mississippi, I must acknowledge that my heart sank within me. Being a *chaplain* I was viewed with suspicion by many who afterwards became my warmest friends. The situation of affairs was somewhat thus. There had been no regular preaching in the regiment since its organization. Rev. A. A. Lomax, who was a private, had held prayer-meetings and preached now and then, as he could find time. But, all in all, religion was at a low ebb. In every tent was a pack of cards; from every quarter came up blasphemous oaths, not far off was what they called 'hell's half-acre,' or 'the devil's camp-ground,' where keno, chuck-a-luck, etc., were engaged in by hundreds from every part of the army. The daily wickedness exhibited then and there was truly appalling. Yet I knew that many of the best families of Mississippi were represented in this brigade. I knew there were many of the sons of pious parents, and that many a mother's prayer was ascending to God for her beloved son, who was now in the gall of bitterness and in the bonds of iniquity. I knew the arm of God was not shortened, nor His ear closed to the prayers of His people. I took courage; on Sunday numbers came out and stood upon the snow, listening attentively, but as soon as services were over, many of them rejoined their crowds, who were 'playing cards' at arm's length from the pulpit. Things continued thus about one month. Great revivals were in progress in Jackson's Corps, but we were *dead*. About this time I went to Richmond for books, tracts, etc. While in the *Christian Advocate* office some young soldier thrust into my hand a copy of the constitution, by-laws, etc., of the Christian Association of Anderson's Brigade, Hood's Division. I never saw him afterwards, and know not what became of him. It was a simple act on his part, but it put in motion a course of action the results of which will never be known until the judgment. The idea flashed upon my mind, 'just what we need, concert of action. The soldiers of Christ in the army must be brought together and stand breast to breast.'

"I arrived at camp at 4 o'clock next morning. The association was organized with six members; the next night about twenty joined, the next forty, until the number soon reached two or three hundred. A nightly prayer-meeting was organized. On the third night, when an opportunity was afforded for remarks, a man of about forty years of age arose and, trembling with emotion, said he was a backslider; asked us to pray for him. Another said he felt, he knew, he was a sinner, and plead with us to pray. *My heart beat against my ribs with joy.* I saw joy written upon the countenance of every Christian. God was blessing us, and we were encouraged to proceed. A temporary protection was made, and we continued our services day and night. The brigade was now ordered to Morton's Ford, and, owing to the hard service in picket-service, fortifying, etc., the work was somewhat retarded. Brother Duke, chaplain of Nineteenth Mississippi Regiment, returned from a furlough about this time and rendered valuable aid. About this time, however, the battle of Chancellorsville occurred, and we were again stationed near Hamilton's Crossing (three miles from that place and three from Fredericksburg). The work now commenced in earnest again, the sheaves were numbered by hundreds, and the number of inquirers was so great that it was impossible to talk with them all. By this time we had the earnest co-operation of Brothers Lomax and Gordon, privates in the Twelfth Mississippi Regiment, and Brothers Morrison and Leonard, of the Nineteenth. The two former, ministers of the Baptist, and of the latter, the second, Cumberland Presbyterian, and the first, Old School Presbyterian; also of Brother Duke, chaplain Nineteenth, Methodist Episcopal Church, South. Duke at this time received the appointment of captain of scouts, and went to Mississippi. Rev. A. E. Garrison, sergeant of the Forty-eighth Regiment also came forward about this time and co-operated.

" These meetings were now interrupted by the Gettysburg campaign. The men were on picket-duty at the foot of the hills below Fredericksburg, near that creek in the plateau. We had assembled for preaching. While engaged in prayer orders came to move on at once. When I arose from prayer, I found kneeling about me only three or four men; but the others were silently putting on their munitions and paying respectful and earnest attention to the prayer. The meeting was broken up; on the march, however, we continued the meetings as opportunities occurred, and just previous to the battle of Gettysburg we had services, and a number were baptized and received into the faith. When the army returned from this campaign, we were camped on Jones's Farm, near the Rapidan bridge. This was in September. The work now commenced in earnest. Rev. A. A. Lomax received the appointment of chaplain Sixteenth, Rev. A. E. Garrison, Forty-eighth, and G. R. Morrison, Nineteenth. The Sixteenth and Forty-eighth were placed in winter-quarters on the picket-line near the river, and the Nineteenth, with the Twelfth, on Jones's Farm. We remained in this camp from September to spring, when the campaign commenced against General Grant. And here was the scene of our greatest triumphs; cards had given place to the word of life, and the men were all eager in their desire to learn the will of God; and I found many of them prompt and earnest in assisting in the meetings, but more especially in hunting up the anxious, and furnishing me with the data. We had here the young converts' prayer-meeting, the sunrise prayer-meeting, frequently preaching at noon, and always at night, except when providentially hindered. The Christian Association met usually on Saturday.

" The following papers were received weekly and distributed in the Twelfth : *Central Presbyterian,* 50 copies ; *North Carolina Presbyterian,* 20 copies ; *Southern Presbyterian,* 12 copies ; *Religious Herald,* 20 copies ; *Christian Observer,* 8 copies ; *Advocate, Richmond,* 15 copies ; *Advocate, Augusta,* 15 copies ; *Soldier's Visitor and Friend,* each (semi-weekly) 20 copies. Number per week, 160.

" Besides these, about 10,000 pages of tracts and a circulating library of fifteen or twenty volumes.

" For months I often preached once every day, and sometimes twice.

" Two Bible-classes were kept up most of the time, and in almost every regiment there were organizations for reading the Bible aloud at stated periods.

" There was but one revival, which began as above-stated and continued according to our opportunities of using the means until active hostilities commenced with Grant. After, there were but few opportunities of preaching, though prayer-meetings, etc., continued to the close of the war. November, 1864, owing to a chronic dysentery, I was forced to leave the army, having been able to do but little previously for several months.

"A young man opposed to religion, who never attended on the means of grace, looking upon professors of religion with a malignant hatred, was sent to the Corps Hospital, near Spottsylvania (at Stewart's), with pneumonia. I nursed him, procured him medical attention and such luxuries and condiments as could be obtained. There was a good deal of irregularity in the medical department, and it was difficult to obtain proper treatment. Through my endeavors he was relieved, and I attended him carefully. One day he told me he had been under the impression that the Christian religion ' was a humbug,' but my disinterested conduct toward him had undeceived him, and he intended now to lead a different life. He joined the Church, and as long as I knew him he was a zealous Christian.

"As many as twenty or thirty cases might be mentioned of those who acknowledged the instrumentality of a mother's prayers.

"One young man, who had been long anxious, and in doubt, found relief while we were praying, and was afterwards a zealous Christian.

"The regular, earnest, zealous preaching of God's word seems to have been the means most especially blessed. The number of converts, I presume, in the brigade was about five hundred (I can't say for certain, I think it is a very low estimate). One fact under this head : During my first winter in camp, I ' bunked' with six reckless fellows. I had the pleasure of seeing them all members of the Church.

"But few instances came under my observation of ' falling away.' Many died happy ; in their sufferings were supported. I never knew one to regret the step.

"In the brigade fifteen or twenty line-officers were converted, some of whom were very efficient and influential. Our great drawback in the beginning was owing to the ' wickedness in high places.'

"The influence of religion was most excellent. The better the men, the better the soldiers.

"While we were camped near Orange Court House, an invitation was extended to Rev. Mr. Lacy to deliver a lecture on the life, character, etc., of General Jackson. Several neighboring brigades joined with us. General Lee was present, and about one-third of the general officers of our corps. The singing on the occasion was grand, and the effect on the men very beneficial. Dr. Lacy repeated the remark, of which I presume you have heard him speak, that General Jackson made in regard to repentance when suffering as he was. That, unless he had previously made his peace with God, he did not think it would be possible to collect his thoughts to contemplate such a subject then. That remark arrested the attention of several who were subsequently converted.

"About this time we had a communion, when the sacrament of the Lord's Supper was administered. This, I remember, occurred on the day Grant commenced moving. About sixty were received on that occasion into the Church, and there, for the first and last time, commemorated the love of their dying Lord. Never did I enjoy any communion more. Never did I witness one more solemn and impressive than that. I can recall the scene now, and many of the upturned, anxious faces appear as they did then, while our excellent Brother Witherspoon, of Davis's Brigade, presented the truth to them. Their bones for many a long day bleached upon the hard fought fields where they fell. But they fell with the assurance that God was with them.

"It is a little remarkable that very few of our church-members survived the war. Perhaps the explanation is that they were more fearless, but it is true. You know but few, good or bad, returned home; but the proportion is quite remarkable ; *e. g.*, one company: before campaign, 23—17 church-members, 6 not; returned home, 10—5 church-members, 5 not, as near as I remember. This, of course, is to *some extent* an exceptional case; bnt I only know of one company which had a greater proportion of non-professors killed.

"I know, my dear brother, you will consider these meagre facts; but I hope they will be of some service to you. I wish you a hearty God-speed and a splendid success in your work.   Yours fraternally,
                                                   "CHAS. H. DOBBS."

[*From Rev. Dr. Renfroe, Baptist, Chaplain Tenth Alabama Regiment.*]

                                  "TALLADEGA, ALABAMA, January 31, 1867.

"*Dear Brother Jones:* In attempting to give you some account of the religious character of Wilcox's old brigade, in the army of Northern Virginia, I find that I am entirely dependent upon my memory. I loaned my 'notes' of events to a brother, who now informs me that he cannot lay his hand on them, having mislaid them.

"The Tenth Alabama was the regiment of which I was chaplain. The brigade was composed of the Eighth, Ninth, Tenth, Eleventh and Fourteenth Alabama Regiments. I reckon this brigade comprised as noble a body of men as ever served in any army. I reached my post of duty while the army was in winter-quarters at Fredericksburg, in the early part of the year 1863. There were then three other chaplains in that brigade, but they were all then absent but one. Very little preaching had been done in the brigade up to that time. Many Christian soldiers and other good-disposed men told me that I could do no good in preaching to soldiers, but all seemed glad to welcome me among them. I was acquainted with a large number of the regiment before the war. The first Sabbath after I got there I preached twice, and from that time until I left them, I had a large attendance upon worship, and as good order in my congregations as I ever had at home. About that time the Rev. Mr. Bell, of Greenville, Alabama, visited the Eighth, which had no chaplain. He and I preached daily for two weeks. He baptized a Mr. Lee, of Marion, Alabama, the first profession that I saw in the army; though there were many men in the brigade who were Christians before they went to the army, and who maintained their religion. The chaplains of the brigade soon returned. We built arbors, and preached regularly to large and attentive congregations—on through the spring this continued—only interrupted by the battle of Chancellorsville. Then came the campaign to Gettysburg. I preached thirteen sermons on that campaign, but not more than half of them to our own brigade. I preached several sermons in line of battle. After we returned to the south side of the Potomac, at Bunker's Hill, we had several sermons in the brigade. Two of the chaplains (Mr. Rains, of the Fourteenth, and Mr. Whitten, of the Ninth) remained at Gettysburg with the wounded. Up to this time I saw but few signs of the good work—I saw no evidences of revival—I heard of no conversions in our brigade. Then we fell back to Orange Court House. There we at once established arbors— one in the Fourteenth, one in the Tenth, and began to preach. Rev. Mr. Johnson, chaplain of the Eleventh, and Mr. Cumbie, Lieutenant in the Fourteenth, did the preaching at the Fourteenth's preaching place. Their labors were blessed, and many were converted. At the preaching place of the Tenth I did the preaching for the most part. This lasted for about six weeks, in which time I was visited and aided by Rev. A. E. Dickinson, of Richmond, who preached for me a week; then by Rev. J. B. F. Mays, of Alabama, who preached nearly a week for me. God greatly blessed our efforts. I have stood at that place at night and on Sabbaths and preached, as it seemed to me, to a solid acre of men. I think I have seen as many as five or six hundred men, in one way and another, manifest at one time a desire

FATHER RYAN.

(Facing page 511.)

to be prayed for. I have never seen such a time before or since. There were as many evidences of genuine penitence as I ever noticed at home—yes, more. Almost every day there would be a dozen conversions, and there were in the six weeks in the brigade, not less than five hundred who professed conversion. Not all of our brigade, for there was a battalion of artillery camped near us, and other brigades, who attended our preaching, many of whom professed religion. We estimated the conversions then at five hundred and fifty. I baptized about one hundred, Brother Cumbie about fifty, and most of the others joined the Methodists. This work, as you know, prevailed nearly all through the army. But it was partially interrupted by the fall campaign, when we drove Meade back to Bull Run. But the army returned from that campaign to Orange, went into winter-quarters and spent the winter there. Part of this winter I was at home on furlough. But prayer-meetings, Bible-classes and preaching were successfully kept up through the winter. And the revival also, in a less degree, continued. The Young Men's Christian Association was largely attended, many went to exhorting, and a great many prayed in public, some of whom were greatly gifted. A most interesting feature was the large number who would retire after the evening 'roll-call' in groups, to pray. Walk out from camp at that hour in any direction and you would find them, two, three, half-dozen and a dozen, in a place, all bowed in the dark, earnestly praying for themselves and the conversion of their comrades; they nearly always took some unconverted ones with them.

"Through the awful campaign of 1864 there were very limited opportunities to preach to this brigade. It was almost constantly under fire or on the march. From the Wilderness to Petersburg and around Petersburg, this was the case. Though I preached to them as often as I could, yet most of my preaching was to other commands. I have several times preached when shot and shell were flying over our heads, and also several times I had minnie-balls to strike in my congregation while preaching. We often had prayer-meetings in the trenches, where God did greatly bless and comfort our hearts. In the winter-quarters at Petersburg there was much faithful preaching, and regular prayer-meetings kept up in this brigade.

"1. I believe that the conversions were genuine. There were exceptions of course. But I received candidates for baptism just as I do at home, i. e., I assembled the Baptists of the regiment, heard a relation of the applicants' Christian experience, took the vote, etc. All other Baptist ministers, I think, did the same. And their statements of the work of grace were clear and satisfactory.

"2. So far as my knowledge extended, these converts maintained their professions with astonishing faithfulness. Up to the time that I left them, I knew of but two or three exceptions.

"3. The character of the brigade was decidedly moral and religious, compared with what it was before this good work began. The worship of God became a fixed part of the regular duties of the brigade. The religious element was as well defined, as well organized and as constant, as in any congregation to whom I have preached. Christians were recognized as such, ministers were respected and kindly treated and loved. I have never had a congregation at home that seemed to esteem me more, and certainly I never loved a congregation so much. I never was treated disrespectfully by a soldier or officer while I was in the army—not in one instance. They preserved a tender regard for my feelings. None of them ever gambled or swore in my immediate presence; if any did swear in my immediate presence in a moment of unguarded levity or haste or passion, they always followed it with a becoming apology. Card-playing and the like ceased to be public in this brigade, except among the Irish Catholics, of whom there were three companies, who seemed 'neither to fear God nor regard man;' only they were very good soldiers.

"4. The officers of my regiment, to a man, were respectful to me and to my position. They always attended preaching. There was no exception. Some of them were good Christians, while all believed that there was no officer in the regiment worth more to it than a good chaplain, and no part of their daily duties of so much importance as that of religious services. The men who commanded the regiment for the most part of the time that I was with them, were: Colonel W. H. Forney, Episcopalian; Lieutenant-Colonel Shelley, Methodist inclined; Major Joseph Truss, Baptist; Captain Brewster, of seemingly no fixed denominational preference. There never was a time that any one of these noble spirits would not do any and every thing that I desired to further the interests of public worship, preaching, prayer-meetings, etc. They did not allow anything that they could control to interfere with our hours of worship. And Colonel Shelley, who commanded most of the time (Colonel Forney being a prisoner), often said that the work of the chaplain was essential to the welfare of the regiment, essential to its efficiency, etc. The officers of the brigade, nearly all of them, were similar in conduct and disposition to those of my own regiment. And so I found the officers throughout the army, so far as I had opportunity to test the matter. No one of any rank ever treated me other than respectfully and kindly.

" 5. There were some very efficient Christians in the brigade. Lieutenant Cumbie, of the Fourteenth Regiment, was a most useful man. He was pious, devoted and active, a very good preacher, a brave soldier and an efficient officer. Privates E. B. Hardie, of the Tenth, and Jacob Nelson, of the same regiment, were both most excellent young men, faithful and zealous in the service of the Lord, and brave soldiers. Both of them were young ministers. These three men were Baptists, and are pastors at home now, and successful. There were many others who were not preachers, that were in every way faithful and true.

" 6. So far as I have been able to observe, those who professed religion in the army and lived to get home, are as faithful, constant and zealous now, as any other part of the religious community. I am pastor of several of them, and I know many others. Some of them are splendid church-members; but some have made shipwreck of the faith, or never had any faith. Yet I think three-fourths are maintaining a good profession, and proving that they were truly converted.

" 7. I believe it was generally conclusive that religious men made the best soldiers. And I know that officers frequently expressed themselves as believing thus. Religious soldiers complained less at army regulations, hard service and short rations. They did their duty more generally and more willingly, and I never knew one of them to disgrace himself in battle. Many of them died at their posts. They straggled less on marches, and committed fewer depredations on the rights of citizens.

" 8. The religious *status* of this brigade remained firm and decided to the surrender of the army.

" Brother Jones, I am aware that this letter is a very poor and indifferent account of the religious standing of my old brigade. Maybe, however, that you can get something out of it. I baptized about two hundred while I was in the army, two years, but nearly half of them were men of other brigades than my own, and converted under the ministry of other men. The Lord bless you in your good work,

" Yours fraternally,
"J. J. D. Renfroe."

[*From Captain M. M. Jones, United States Army.*]

" City of Utica, New York, January 29, 1867.
" J. Wm. Jones:
"*Dear Sir :* Being a subscriber to the Richmond *Religious Herald*, I read your card of the 17th instant, and for some reason hardly describable am disposed to write you. I have a notion that a religious history of your Army Northern Virginia will be a highly interesting and useful book.

"My personal intercourse with the men (a few of them) who composed that army impressed my mind with the fact that religious interests were much better and more generally attended to than in some armies I have seen. As a prisoner it became a necessity for me to march from Second Bull Run battle-field to Richmond, and, believing that I would gain nothing by keeping *mum* to those whose duty it was, first, to prevent my running away, a matter I was too lame and too much used up to attempt if I had known of any accessible place to escape to; and second to protect us from malignant darkies, cross women and stay-at-home patriots on our route via Culpeper, Gordonsville, etc., etc.; and the result was, barring the starvation rations of green corn we all (guards and prisoners) had for nine days, I had a very pleasant time, being invariably well treated by Confederate officers (we were about one hundred officers) and men. The vast difference in means, food, clothing, etc., in favor of the North was referred to one day in a familiar chat between my personal guard and myself (for I was too lame to keep up on a long march). 'Well,' replied the poor, ragged, coatless, shoeless boy, 'I am sure you do not have as good prayer-meetings as we have.' I was impressed with the reply, and have very often thought of it since.

"Wishing you all success, I am very truly yours, etc.,

"M. M. JONES."

[From a Prisoner at Johnson's Island.]

"The religious history of the prisoners confined during the war on Johnson's Island is worthy of record on several accounts, particularly because it furnishes an excellent illustration of the potency of individual example and effort, even when not under the guidance of an educated mind or extraordinary natural endowments, for the accomplishment of good. Through the labors of a single individual one of the most remarkable moral reformations was effected in this prison that your correspondent ever witnessed. When this Christian gentleman entered this prison, a few days after the great battle of Gettysburg, he found it occupied by about 2,000 prisoners, almost all of whom were officers. These men had been captured at various points in the South, and every Southern State was largely represented; and while it would not be just, probably, to say that there was more impiety manifested by these men than is usually found in such miscellaneous collections, it is nevertheless true that several forms of wickedness, such as profanity, gambling and neglect of the Sabbath, had assumed among them very alarming dimensions; and while there was the greatest need for religious effort, the obstacles in the way of success were so many, and of such a nature, as apparently to render any attempt at a reformation almost hopeless. But, though the impediments to be overcome were so many and so great, God sent us a man bold enough to undertake, and skilful enough to accomplish, the work. He signalized his presence among us by lifting up at once in the view of all the banner of Jesus. At first he had only a few followers. Even many professed disciples of Christ stood aloof from him for awhile, as if doubting to what this movement would come; but he was not discouraged by the day of 'small things;' He persevered in the face of most serious obstacles, exerting his influence at first on single individuals and within the narrow limits of his own prison apartment; then, when his followers had increased in numbers, and he had gained a larger share of the attention of his comrades in bonds, he gradually extended his efforts to other parts of the prison and operated on larger masses. By means of Bible-classes and prayer-meetings a healthful reactionary movement was inaugurated, which subsequently developed itself into almost every scheme that could be devised for the good of the prison. A very large Christian association was organized, under whose superintendence several hundred prisoners were instructed in the truths of God's word, and nightly prayers observed in almost every room of

33

the prison; so that after the lapse of a few months it was no uncommon thing at early twilight to hear ascending from every heart of that 'lone isle in Erie's great water' sweet songs of praise to God. The visible fruit of this movement was a complete reformation in the moral character of the prisoners; so that in many parts of the prison a profane word was scarcely ever heard; the Sabbath was observed with the greatest solemnity, about one hundred made a credible profession of faith in Christ, and God's own children were excited to greater diligence in His service. Your correspondent is acquainted with several young men now preparing for the Gospel ministry, with the prospect of distinguished usefulness, whose attention would probably never have been seriously given to that subject but for that movement, and doubtless many more, whom he does not know, have enlisted in the same glorious service under the influence of that awakening. In addition to the large number actually converted, many left the prison under the most serious religious impressions, and doubtless many of them have already found, and others will yet find, their way into the kingdom. And the chief instrument in this great work was a single individual, who had had few advantages in the way of mental training, and possessed no natural endowments superior to those of the mass of God's people."

I had purposed publishing a roster of the chaplains of the whole army, but find (at the last moment, when it is too late to replace it from other sources) that the roster which I prepared during the war has been lost or mislaid. I very much regret this, and will not attempt now to make a roster lest it should be too incomplete to be of much value. If, however, I shall be able to recover my material, or to secure a full roster, it will be published in a future edition of this book.

I count myself fortunate, however, in being able to publish a large part of the minutes of the Chaplains' Association of the Second and Third Corps, which were preserved by the efficient secretary, Chaplain L. C. Vass, of the Twenty-seventh Virginia Regiment, and have been kindly placed at my disposal. I very much regret that I have not been able to secure the minutes of the Chaplains' Association of the First Corps, which were of deep interest and value, as our brethren in that grand old command were very active and efficient, and were greatly blessed in their work.

I give these minutes in the form in which they were originally written, and am sure that they will be greatly prized by those who were privileged to participate in those precious seasons of Christian counsel and fellowship, and by all who feel an interest in the details of our grand work.

" MINUTES OF CHAPLAINS' ASSOCIATION OF SECOND AND THIRD CORPS, ARMY OF NORTHERN VIRGINIA.

"First Session.

" ROUND OAK CHURCH, VIRGINIA, March 16, 1863.
"According to a previous notice to the chaplains of the Second Army Corps, Army of Northern Virginia, a number of them met at this point this morning. The meeting was called to order by Rev. B. T. Lacy. Rev. A. C. Hopkins was elected Chairman, and Rev. L. C. Vass, Secretary. The meeting was then organized with singing, reading the Scriptures and with prayer. The following were present:
" *Georgia.*—James O. A. Sparks, Fourth Georgia; Alexander M. Thigpen, Sixth Georgia; A. M. Marshall, Twelfth Georgia; J. J. Hyman, Forty-ninth Georgia.
"*North Carolina.*—F. M. Kennedy, Twenty-eighth North Carolina; W. R. Gualtney, First North Carolina; W. C. Power, Fourteenth North Carolina; A. D. Betts, Thirtieth North Carolina.
"*South Carolina.*—George T. T. Williams, First South Carolina.
" *Virginia.*—F. C. Tebbs, Fourth Virginia; E. P. Walton, Fifth Virginia; L. C.

Vass, Twenty-Seventh Virginia; J. M. Grandin, Thirty-third Virginia; A. C. Hopkins, Second Virginia; J. William Jones, Thirteenth Virginia; J. P. Garland, Forty-ninth Virginia; Paul C. Morton, Twenty-third Virginia; James Nelson, Forty-fourth Virginia; Harvey Gilmore, Twenty-first Virginia; B. T. Lacy, acting missionary in corps, Virginia.

"Major Isaac Hardman, Captain O. T. Evans and Rev. T. W. Harris were invited to sit as corresponding members.

"Several important subjects with regard to the chaplain's work were discussed familiarly by those present. Among these was the administration of the Lord's Supper. Its importance as regards Christian growth in grace, and the conversion of sinners, was urged; and touching and profitable remarks on this subject were made by several brethren. All agreed to the necessity, duty and profit of frequent communion seasons in our army.

"Also, brethren considered the nature of the sweeping charges brought against chaplains and chaplaincies generally, in consequence of the deficiencies and delinquencies of some who hold that office. It was agreed that the odium brought upon the office by a *few* must be *lived down* by the rest.

"Also, it was urged upon every chaplain that, in view of the entire destitution of many regiments of religious worship, he should seek to do some missionary work around his own regiment or brigade.

"*Resolved*, That wherever regiments are without chaplains we will, as far as practicable, urge the importance of having a chaplain, and will afford every facility in our power when desired to have such regiments suitably supplied.

"*Resolved*, That a committee be appointed by the chair to draw up an address, urging the imperative duty of humility and penitence on the part of the Church at home under the chastening rod of God, and setting forth also the spiritual wants of our army, and the encouragements and discouragements to chaplains' labors therein.

"The chair appointed on this committee: Rev. James Nelson from Trimble's Division, Rev. J. William Jones from Early's Division, Rev. W. C. Power from D. H. Hill's Division, Rev. F. M. Kennedy from A. P. Hill's Division, and Rev. B. T. Lacy.

"*Resolved*, That this body, after adjournment, meet here on Tuesday, 24th inst., at 11 A. M.

"*Resolved*, That a committee of three be appointed to designate the time and place of meeting in case we cannot assemble as above determined.

"Rev. J. P. Garland and Rev. J. William Jones, of Fourth Brigade, Early's Division, and Rev. B. T. Lacy, were appointed on this committee.

"After singing and prayer, the meeting then adjourned.

"*Second Session.*

"ROUND OAK CHURCH, TUESDAY, March 24, 1863.
"According to previous adjournment, the chaplains met this morning.

"Rev. A. D. Betts, Thirtieth North Carolina Infantry, was chosen Chairman, and Rev. L. C. Vass, Twenty-seventh Virginia Infantry, was continued as Permanent Clerk.

"Rev. George E. Booker, chaplain of the Forty-eighth Virginia Infantry, Rev. A. W. Moore, Fourteenth Georgia, and Rev. A. L. Stough, Thirty-seventh North Carolina Infantry, appeared and gave in their names.

"An invitation was extended to the Christian brethren present to participate in our deliberations.

"The minutes were read and approved.

"The committee to draw up an address to the Churches reported. The address was read, and after some slight changes approved.

"*Resolved*, That the committee that prepared the address, with Rev. George T. T. Williams added, be requested to publish the address in the religious organs of the several Churches.

"*Resolved*, That a committee of two from each division, with Brother Lacy as chairman, be appointed as a committee of correspondence to facilitate the introduction of chaplains into the regiments of our corps.

" The following committee was appointed for this purpose :

" A. P. Hill's Division—F. M. Kennedy and George T. T. Williams.

" Trimble's Division—A. C. Hopkins and James Nelson.

" D. H. Hill's Division—A. M. Marshall and A. D. Betts.

" Early's Division—John McGill and J. William Jones.

" B. T. Lacy as chairman.

" Here the body spent some time in singing and prayer, in thanking God for His goodness to us, and beseeching His blessings on our future labors.

" The proper observance of the day of fasting, humiliation and prayer appointed by President Davis was then discussed. Plans of diffusing our labors were suggested and urged; also, prayer for a wide and deep revival of pure and undefiled religion in our army.

" Then followed a lengthy and interesting conversation about the chaplain's private work in his regiment, by conversation, etc. The great importance of a regular, constant and tender pastoral oversight over the flock under his charge was shown by the statement and experience of many, and was acknowledged by all, and there were resolves made for greater faithfulness in future.

" Here the subject of some further provision for the chaplain's efficiency was discussed, *e. g.*, his need of a tent for study, prayer-meetings, private conversations with inquirers, etc., and of forage for a horse. No resolutions were passed.

" Brother Betts was appointed to preach at the opening of the next meeting.

" The body then adjourned with prayer, to meet at this place on next Tuesday at 11 A. M.

"*Third Session.*

" No regular meeting on last Tuesday because of weather.

" ROUND OAK CHURCH, April 7, 1863.

"According to previous appointment, Brother A. D. Betts, of the Thirtieth North Carolina Infantry, preached the opening sermon from Acts viii. 39, 'And he went on his way rejoicing.'

" The body was called to order, and Brother James Nelson, of the Forty-fourth Virginia Infantry, was elected chairman.

" The minutes of the previous meeting were read and approved.

" In addition to former chaplains present, there appeared J. M. Meredith, of the Forty-seventh Virginia Infantry, J. M. Anderson, of the Fortieth Virginia, John McGill, of the Fifty-second Virginia Infantry, John Paris, of the Fifty-fourth North Carolina Infantry, S. H. Smith, of the Sixtieth Georgia Infantry, William E. Cameron, of the Twenty-sixth Alabama, T. H. Howell, Thirteenth Alabama, and Dr. William M. Strickler, acting chaplain of the Fifth Louisiana.

" Christian brethren present were invited to take part in our discussions.

" Conversation on the progress of religion in the army was made the order of the day. Interesting narratives of God's wondrous work in converting souls were given by several of the brethren. Many souls had been brought to repose in Jesus, and much interest was still prevailing.

" The meeting engaged then in prayer, and in returning thanks to God for His mercies to us and His presence with us.

" The cause of the dear, suffering sick among the soldiers was then taken up.

An interesting letter from Dr. Harvey Black to Dr. McGuire, surgeon in charge of the Corps Hospital, was read, in which he earnestly solicited the appointment of a chaplain for his hospital. The following resolution was adopted with reference to this letter:

"WHEREAS, The labors of a minister in the receiving hospital of Lieutenant-General Jackson's Corps is greatly desired by the sick soldiers; and *whereas,* a gratifying appeal for such services has been made by Dr. H. Black, the surgeon in charge of said hospital; therefore,

"*Resolved,* That we deeply appreciate the importance of such an appointment, and will gladly aid in procuring the services of an efficient chaplain; and that we will endeavor, in the meanwhile, to supply the deficiency by an apportionment of the labors among ourselves.

" Brothers Meredith, Grandin and Vass volunteered their services to labor a portion of the next three weeks in the hospital.

" Brother L. C. Vass, of the Twenty-seventh Virginia Infantry, was temporarily substituted in place of Brother Hopkins (now sick) on the committee for obtaining chaplains for our army.

"After some further conversation and devotional exercises, the meeting adjourned, with the understanding that they would convene again on April 14, 1863, at this place, when Brother Nelson would preach the opening sermon.

"*Fourth Session.*

" ROUND OAK CHURCH, April 14, 1863.
" The chaplains met, according to adjournment, at this place. Brother James Nelson, of the Forty-fourth Virginia Infantry, the last chairman, opened the meeting with a sermon from Romans i. 16, ' For I am not ashamed of the Gospel of Christ,' etc.

" Brother B. T. Lacy, missionary chaplain in the corps, was elected chairman.

" The minutes of the previous meeting were read and approved.

" Rev. A. R. Benick, of the Thirty-fourth North Carolina Infantry, Pender's Brigade, and Rev. E. B. Barrett, of the Forty-fifth Georgia, appeared and gave in their names.

" The progress of religion in our army since our last meeting was the first subject taken up.

" Brother Nelson, of the Forty-fourth Virginia, reported ten conversions in his regiment, among whom was one of its most prominent officers. A number were still concerned deeply. General Trimble had excused the men from drill to attend preaching.

" Brother Gilmore, of the Twenty-first Virginia, reported about fifteen penitents and one convert. Congregation last night large and attentive.

" Brother L. C. Vass, of the Twenty-seventh, reported the work of grace still progressing in the Stonewall Brigade. He held an interesting communion on last Sabbath, admitted a number to the Lord's Supper, and baptized several.

" In Brother Smith's (Sixtieth Georgia) Regiment there had been many conversions since the last meeting.

" Brother Strickler, of the Fifth Louisiana, preached to the Ninth Louisiana on Sabbath. They turned out almost to a man.

"Brother Howell, of the Thirteenth Alabama, had no interest till the past week in his regiment. Church-members were revived. There were many mourners, and a few conversions. No other chaplain in the five regiments in his brigade (Archer's).

"Brother Cameron, of the Twenty-sixth Alabama, reported great interest since the last meeting; several conversions and additions to his Church; men enjoying religion; he is the only chaplain in Rodes's Brigade.

"Brother Meredith, of the Forty-Seventh Virginia, reported on his labors at Dr. Black's Corps Hospital at Guinea's. He spent a profitable time there. Narrated several incidents to show the need of a permanent chaplain there. A Universalist was found who was brought to abandon his false belief (instilled into his mind by an uncle) through reading the Gospel of John, and being pointed to Christ's work. From twenty to thirty are daily passing through the hospital, and from twenty to forty constantly there.

"A Macedonian cry was raised by Captain ——, from the Third Alabama Regiment, for preaching. Their place of worship was filled to overflowing, and their Christian Association on Sunday evening was prospering.

"Brigadier-General William N. Pendleton (Rev. Dr. Pendleton, of Lexington, Virginia) then addressed the body. He said he had come out of his way to meet the chaplains and show his interest in their labors. The ministry was at all times the most blessed of works. How much more now, and here in the army where dangers thicken. Life is uncertain, and therefore there is more solemnity, and a congregation can be gathered at any time.

"He urged upon the chaplains the power of a holy life, and duty and necessity of cultivation of individual piety—that hidden life of God in the soul. Their religion should not be too much in the crowd; too much a matter of feeling, of sympathy; but a matter of experience, of heart. They should improve all opportunities of speaking to soldiers, in knots, by tract, Gospel and prayer.

"They had much to encourage them in prayers for them over the land every day, at 1 P. M., in God's co-operating Spirit and providence, and in the way the religious services of himself and others have been received. He referred to the labors of a captain under him in holding daily prayer with his company, and nearly all were converted.

"He argued that chaplains were a great power in this struggle, and had every motive to stimulate them; for the better Christian a man is, the better soldier he is. 'May the Lord be with you!'

"Rev. Dr. Pendleton was then requested to preach to us, at such time and place as he may name, upon the great work in which we are engaged, our duties and our responsibilities.

"He accepted the invitation, and said he would make known through the chairman the time and place.

"Here the meeting engaged in prayer.

"The meeting then considered the difficulties surrounding chaplains on an active campaign. Was there not too little preaching then?

"Brother J. William Jones, of the Thirteenth Virginia, who introduced the subject, thought there was. He had found soldiers always ready and anxious to hear the Gospel. At Cross Keys a minister was stopped at "*thirdly*" by the colonel forming the line of battle. At Richmond he assembled his own cut-up regiment (Thirteenth Virginia) under the guns of the enemy. Every man and officer was present. A young man remarked to him: 'This is a lesson to me which I shall never forget.' So at Lee's Springs (Fauquier county, Virginia), in crossing the Rappahannock, a shell fell in the midst of the congregation, but fortunately did not explode. They assembled again, and he thanked God for it. Good was accomplished.

"General Pendleton's experience was similar. The largest congregation he ever saw was one Sunday after the army had been drawn up in line of battle all day Saturday. All were disposed to hear. Ministers can do more than they suppose if they have the heart and will. In his two years' service there was not a Sabbath when, if possible, he did not preach once, and often twice.

"Brother Thigpen, of the Sixth Georgia, after consultation with his superior officer, held a prayer-meeting, which was a most precious season, the night after the fight at Malvern Hill. Men never were so tired, or marched so far, as to be unwilling to have prayer. He commenced his prayer-meetings under these peculiar circumstances, and had continued with good results.

" " Brother Lacy, the chairman, said, as God had adapted the Gospel to men in all conditions, so he has rendered its preaching practicable under all circumstances. Unquestionably, if the commissariat neglected its duties because of some derangements in its usual routine, the army would starve, although victorious. Yet even with its deranged system, the army must have bread in the trenches; if not the full supply, yet how invaluable is the dry crust or hard biscuit! Brethren, we are appointed to carry the spiritual bread of life to the men. We draw from a never-failing supply. There is always enough, thank God. If we have some difficulty in getting it to the men in need, let us strive. Difficulties prove their great necessities. In the fight many of these men must fall. One sermon more, brethren, for the love of souls, for the glory of God. Let us *devise* means to get this bread to them.

" Faithful chaplains promote the efficiency of the army. Let every chaplain set an example, like Brother Thigpen, of obedience to military orders. Pray against *blind* zeal. But we must have true *zeal*. If any brother feels he is about as well here as elsewhere, we would say to him, ' You had better go away.' Don't interfere with officers; consult them, and try to *work in* the Gospel. Don't *desert the men because they are in the trenches.* Go, speak a word to them, if you only say, ' I know you were ready to fight for your country; but were you ready to meet your God?' The Gospel hurts no man at any time under any circumstances. Earnest prayer by the camp-fire makes men rest better, and march better.

" Let brevity mark these services. Let the words be few and well chosen. This is the principle : What are the few sentences that will save his soul if I never speak again? A great many useless appendages to sermons will be thus cut off, and we will leave the army better preachers than when we entered it. Long sermons weary and injure your usefulness. Be short and sharp; brief, but brimful of the Gospel.

" Brother Strickler, of Fifth Louisiana, thought the condition of the sick a subject of such importance as to demand immediate consideration : the present plan of supplying the hospital with temporary chaplains was inefficient. He thought there should be a corps of chaplains to attend to the field infirmaries.

" A committee was appointed, consisting of Dr. Strickler, J. P. Garland, Forty-ninth Virginia and B. T. Lacy, to take some action touching this hospital business, and report.

" It was resolved that a committee of three be appointed to report on the subject of a badge for the adoption of the chaplains of our corps. J. Wm. Jones, Thirteenth Virginia, F. M. Kennedy, Twenty-eighth North Carolina, and James Nelson, Forty-fourth Virginia, form this committee.

" After some appropriate remarks by Brother W. C. Power, of Fourteenth North Carolina, the following resolution was unanimously adopted, all the chaplains standing:

" *Resolved*, That we, the chaplains of the Second Army Corps, pledge ourselves to offer prayer—at sunset—every day, for each other and the success of our labors.

" Adjourned with devotional exercises to meet at 11 A. M. next Tuesday, and open with sermon by chairman as usual.

" L. C. VASS, Secretary.
"Fifth Session.

" ROUND OAK CHURCH, April 20, 1863.

" The body met according to adjournment. Brother B. T. Lacy preached the opening sermon from 1 Kings xx. 40, ' And as thy servant was busy here and there, he was gone.' He showed, through the history of this unfaithful soldier, the temptation to which chaplains are exposed; and urged them to faithful discharge of their duties by various arguments.

"Brother F. M. Kennedy, of Twenty-eighth North Carolina, was selected as chairman. Abstract of the minutes of last meeting was read and approved.

"Brother J. N. Bouchelle, of Thirteenth South Carolina Infantry, and Brother Geo. Slaughter, Fifty-eighth Virginia Infantry, appeared and gave their names to the clerk. "Conversation on the state of religion, was, as usual, our first business.

"Brother Kennedy reported that since last week there had been some twenty or thirty penitents in his regiment (Twenty-eighth North Carolina), and several had expressed a desire to join the Church. He has prospect of a gracious work. There was a great improvement in the observance of the Sabbath. He had nearly three hundred members of the Church in his regiment of eight hundred men.

"Brother Nelson, Forty-fourth Virginia, reported the work of grace still in progress: fifteen in his regiment had professed saving faith. He mentioned several incidents showing the change for the better in his regiment, and the power of tracts.

"Brother Power said that, his regiment being absent, he had been preaching for Brother Betts in Thirtieth North Carolina, where a large number were concerned, among them a prominent officer (the colonel), a man of large influence at home, but heretofore unconcerned.

"Brother Vass, of Twenty-seventh Virginia, stated that God was still signally present in the Stonewall (Paxton's) Brigade. Congregations large and many seeking after Jesus. He explained the mode adopted for receiving converts into the Church, viz.: by careful examination, public profession and then sending a certificate home to whatever Church the party wished to join.

"Brother B. T. Lacy, more encouraged than ever, preached on Sabbath morning to a large and important congregation assembled at the corps' head-quarters. Many generals and their staffs were present. There seemed to be deep feeling with some.

"On Sabbath afternoon and on Saturday preached to large and interested assemblies. He also felt encouraged about the little prayer-meeting held at head-quarters, and stated one or two incidents to show his ground of encouragement.

"Brother Grandin, of Thirty-third, had administered, with Brother Booker's aid (Forty-eighth Virginia), the communion on Sabbath to his regiment. He thought there must have been over one hundred communicants. He baptized four. His heart was cheered and he greatly built up.

"Brother Marshall, of Twelfth Georgia Infantry, stated that in his regiment, and in the Forty-fourth Georgia, a very interesting state exists. He holds his services nightly, and at the last meeting there were some twenty-five to thirty inquirers.

"Brother Cameron reported the good work still going on in his (Twenty-sixth Alabama) regiment. Some thirty or forty interested.

"Brother McGill, of Fifty-second Virginia, and Benick, of Thirty-fourth North Carolina, were glad to state that though no marked revolution was going on in their regiments, yet there was a considerable external improvement.

"Brother J. W. Jones, Thirteenth Virginia, had a very pleasant change in his regiment. Several awakened. One most wicked man, deeply concerned. Card-playing and profanity were checked.

"He practised an interchange with brother-chaplains in receiving into the Church. "Several regiments manifested their desire very signally to procure chaplains.

"There were some reports made as to progress in procuring chaplains; correspondence with some, etc.; but nothing of a permanent character to need record.

"The committee on 'badge for chaplains' was continued, with instructions to report at next meeting what sort of badge the chaplains should wear, if any, and its cost.

"The question, 'Where ought chaplains to be in battle?' was somewhat agitated, but left for the next meeting.

"Brother J. N. Bouchelle, of Thirteenth South Carolina, agreed to go to the hospital this week, and Brother Geo. Slaughter, Fifty-eighth Virginia, next week.

"The meeting then adjourned with the benediction, to meet on next Saturday, 25th inst., in this church, to hear Rev. Wm. N. Pendleton, D. D., on the chaplaincy.

"L. C. VASS, Clerk.

"*Sixth Session.*

"ROUND OAK CHURCH, April 25, 1863.

"According to adjournment the chaplains met to-day to hear Rev. Wm. N. Pendleton on the chaplaincy. He did not appear, and Brother F. M. Kennedy, the last chairman, preached from Rom. xiv. 7, 'For none of us liveth to himself.' He presented the law of mutual dependence, which pervades all nature, and is especially seen among intelligent, social beings; and showed how no man could escape influencing others; exhibited to the Christian the manner in which he should live for good to those around him; showed to the impenitent how malign was his example, and urged him to repent and do the works of the Gospel.

"Brother Jno. McGill, of Fifty-second Virginia, was then elected chairman.

"Brother J. M. Anderson, of Twelfth South Carolina, and Brother Robert Hardee, of Second Louisiana, Nichol's Brigade, enrolled their names.

"Brother J. F. Watson, missionary chaplain, gave his name, and Brother Geo. Leyburn, agent of Petersburg Evangelical Tract Society, was invited to participate in our meetings.

"Brother Gilmore suggested that some provision be made to keep the clerk supplied with paper for his duties, minutes, letters, etc.

"The state of religious interest in our army was then considered.

"Brother Anderson, of Fortieth Virginia, had ninety men and officers who were professors of religion in his regiment. He impressed on these the duty of prayer. The first case of conviction was a wild, thoughtless young man, who came forward and audibly asked for prayer for himself. Others had presented themselves since. He was much encouraged. Attendance good, and Christians praying.

"Brother H. Gilmore, of Twenty-first Virginia, said that nine more had professed conversion in his regiment, many of whom were the most profane in it. Others were anxiously inquiring the way of life.

"Brother F. M. Kennedy stated that the interest in Twenty-eighth North Carolina was undiminished. His meetings not interrupted by bad weather.

"Brother Power, of Fourteenth North Carolina, reported a meeting of interest in progress in his regiment; many officers and others were concerned. His lieutenant-colonel, heretofore opposed to chaplains, so far as to think their labors of no consequence, has given himself to Christ, and was working for God. Others, disposed to hide their Church relationship, have come forward and given their names.

"Brother Nelson, of Forty-fourth Virginia, reported about thirty conversions in all in his regiment. One backslider reclaimed in his regiment since our last meeting.

"Brother Kennedy said that Brother Stough, of Thirty-seventh North Carolina, had had about forty conversions in his regiment; and enrolled and baptized a number to-day.

"Brother J. P. Garland said he had a great report to make. One poor trembling soul had been converted to God, and there was joy in heaven. Six or seven were inquiring the way to Jesus.

"Brother J. M. Anderson, Twelfth South Carolina, had been absent some months sick, and just returned. He saw that God was going to bless his regiment before he left. Since he returned, a few days ago, he had preached, and many flocked to preaching. There was a great change in this respect.

"A member of Thirteenth Alabama (its chaplain being away, Brother Howell) stated that they had nightly prayer-meetings, and earnestly besought some minister to come and preach to them. He asked their prayers.

"Brother Smith, of Sixtieth Georgia, remarked that the work goes bravely on in his brigade. Some fifty came forward as penitents on Saturday previous. He had obtained some four or five hundred Testaments for his brigade. On Sunday, thirty odd names were put in hat on slips of paper, asking for prayers. Several who had fallen back into the world had come out and taken their former positions.

"Brother Marshall had much interest in his regiment. Many inquirers. His colonel never lets drills interfere with preaching. His prayer-meeting possessed great interest.

"Brother Jones, of Thirteenth Virginia, had some encouraging circumstances in his regiment. One had decided for Christ, and another was seeking an interest in Him.

"Brother Hardee, of Second Louisiana, mentioned the case of a man condemned to be shot in his regiment, and asked prayers for him.

"We then united in prayer to God; were led by Brother Anderson, of Twelfth South Carolina.

"On Brother Garland's proposition we agreed to pray every afternoon for the sentenced man in Second Louisiana, at the hour of prayer for chaplains, until next Friday morning.

"The subject of the proper position of chaplains in battle was then taken up. Much conversation was had on this topic. Many chaplains stated what had been their habits. Some had gone regularly into battle with a musket. The opinion of many prominent officers was stated; and the general conclusion was as follows: No absolute rule can be laid down. A chaplain shall be wherever duty calls him, irrespective of danger. But ordinarily it is thought wrong for him to take a musket. Some shall be in charge of the ambulances, some at the field infirmaries and some at the point where the litter-bearers meet the ambulances, and where many die. The chaplain should ascertain the *opinion of his regiment* on this subject.

"Brother Geo. Leyburn gave us some information about the Petersburg Evangelical Tract Society. He expressed his gratification with this meeting.

"The committee on the badge was continued, that they might ascertain the cost of several devices.

"Brother Lacy was requested to communicate to General Pendleton our desire to hear him at our next meeting.

"Adjourned with singing and benediction till next Tuesday week, May 5, 1863.
                                              "L. C. VASS, Secretary.
                    "*Seventh Session.*

[The session appointed for May 5 was prevented by the battles of "Second Fredericksburg" and Chancellorsville.]

                            "ROUND OAK CHURCH, Tuesday, May 12.
"At 12 o'clock General Pendleton preached on the duties and responsibilities of the chaplain's work from the text: 'Study to show thyself approved of God, a workman that needeth not to be ashamed, rightly dividing the word of truth.' 2 Timothy ii. 15. He spoke earnestly of the *importance* of our work, and cautioned against a natural tendency to indolence and sloth.

"He urged as essential qualifications for the work, '*personal piety,*' '*an appreciation of the value of the soul,*' and '*a right impression of the dignity and value of our office,*' and gave practical directions for the attainment of these qualifications.

"He then noticed the 'difficulties' and 'encouragements' we meet in the chaplaincy, and in conclusion urged upon chaplains to be 'stirred up to their great work' and especially seek to improve the season of repose which we are now having.

"After a short intermission the chaplains were called to order. On motion, Brother

Jno. McGill, Fifty-second Virginia, was continued moderator, and, Brother Vass being absent, J. Wm. Jones, Thirteenth Virginia, was requested to act as secretary.

" Brother B. T. Lacy made statements with reference to the death of General Jackson, relating many touching incidents connected with his last moments, and paid a feeling tribute to his memory. General Pendleton also made statements illustrative of the humble, earnest piety of the fallen hero. Upon suggestion of the moderator, the meeting then united in prayer that this sad affliction might be sanctified to the good of the army and the country. There was a shadow upon our hearts, for each chaplain felt that he had lost his best friend. On motion, a committee, consisting of Brother B. T. Lacy, Brother A. M. Marshall, Twelfth Georgia, and Brother Garland, Forty-ninth Virginia, were appointed to draw up resolutions expressive of the feeling of the chaplains of the corps on this sad affliction.

" The following ministerial brethren were invited to participate in our deliberations : Miller, Harris, of Carrington's Battery, Lieutenant Bagby and Sergeant Bailey, Powhatan Artillery, Garrison and Robertson, chaplains in General Longstreet's Corps.

" Reports were made on progress in securing chaplains for the vacant regiments. Brother Lacy reported that gratifying arrangements had been made, by which several able ministers would labor for a time as army missionaries. Brother J. Wm. Jones reported that he had secured appointments for three brethren, and had a number of other applications which he hoped soon to dispose of.

" The committee on badges reported progress and asked to be continued— granted. Adjourned with religious exercises to meet again next Tuesday, at the same place, if the army is in its present position.

" J. 'WM. JONES, Secretary *pro tem.*

"Eighth Session.

" ROUND OAK CHURCH, May 19, 1863.

" The chaplains met according to adjournment, and, Brother McGill being sick and absent, Brother J. Wm. Jones preached from Acts x. 38, 'Who went about doing good ?' He held up Christ as our great example in His perfect character; in His tender sympathies; in His spiritual labors; in His earnestness and constancy in labors, and in His sacrifices. He urged hearers to follow Him in their lives.

" After a short recess, Brother W. C. Power, of Methodist Episcopal Church, and of Fourteenth South Carolina, was chosen chairman. The minutes having been accidentally left, a verbal statement was made by the secretary *pro tem.*

" Rev. Jas. M. Sprunt, of Twentieth North Carolina, Iverson's Brigade, Rev. W. B. Carson, Fourteenth South Carolina, McGowan's Brigade, and Rev. Walker Gilmer, of Nelson's Battalion of Artillery, Pendleton's Corps, were present, and their names were recorded as chaplains in this corps. Rev. Wm. J. Hoge, D. D., having come to this corps to labor for awhile, was enrolled among the chaplains.

" Rev. Roy Temple, a member of Carter's Battalion of Artillery, was invited to participate in our deliberations.

" We then heard reports about the progress of religion since our last meeting. Brother Lacy had been preaching to increasing congregations at the 'old headquarters.

" Brother Kennedy, of Twenty-eighth North Carolina, had held very interesting services with his regiment. Deep solemnity marked them. On last Sabbath ten expressed their desire to join the Church, and forty or fifty were penitents. There was no falling off of interest. He asked the prayers of the meeting.

" Brother Grandin, of Thirty-third Virginia, stated that he had talked with many about their souls' interests, and had examined two for church-membership, and that

Brother Vass, of Twenty-seventh Virginia, had on last Sabbath received four into the Church, of whom one was baptized.

"Brother Carson, of Fourteenth South Carolina, had observed a gradual and growing interest for weeks in his regiment, though there had been no revival. He believed that numbers were feeling deeply.

"Brother J. Wm. Jones, of Thirteenth Virginia, had found no diminution of religious interest in his regiment since our active operations. His meetings were largely attended, deep impressions made, and men were deciding for Christ.

"Brother Smith, of Sixtieth Georgia, had now resumed his regular services, which had been somewhat interrupted by our marching. Nine persons had professed to have found pardon for their sins. Nearly the entire congregation will come forward and kneel down for special prayer.

"Brother Hyman's regiment (Forty-ninth Georgia) was blessed with a copious outpouring of God's Spirit. He had baptized eight since the battle, and six are hopefully converted, and expect to profess publicly their faith. About one hundred are anxious about their souls.

"Brother Anderson, of Fortieth Virginia, had several conversions (six) in his regiment. The excitement of battle had exercised a wholesome influence on the men. He needed help, and begged for some.

"Brother Power, of Fourteenth South Carolina, had an interesting state of religion in his regiment when the army moved, and would have regretted the change, had he not remembered that the work was of God. Some twenty-five or thirty had professed conversion. God bore them sweetly onward.

"Brother Betts, of Thirtieth North Carolina, was absent from his regiment during the fight, but found that God had guided him, and he returned in time to render services where they were needed, in the hospital to the wounded. In his regiment great interest had been aroused; several had been baptized and others had made known their feelings.

"Brother Wm. J. Hoge said he had just come; but he had found an opportunity on the cars, as they were detained, to preach Christ.

"His Presbytery had ordered him to report to General Jackson. Now he had gone; but God had opened a way to him in His providence, and he was laboring in General Rodes's Division.

"Brother Marshall, of Twelfth Georgia, had been with his men and held services during the march. The men were tender.

"Brother Slaughter, of Fifty-eighth Virginia, felt encouraged. A good work was beginning in his regiment. He felt his weakness, and begged earnestly for the prayers of the meeting.

"Brother Sprunt expressed his joy at hearing these statements, and hoped to be able to bring similar from his regiment. Now, he too, asked our prayers.

"Brother Wm. J. Hoge then engaged with the brethren in prayer.

"By request, Brother B. T. Lacy gave a statement of the closing scenes of General Jackson's life, which was deeply interesting to all, though it waked anew the troubled fountains of grief.

"The following resolutions [these resolutions have been unfortunately lost] were offered with reference to General Jackson's death, and after a few remarks were adopted unanimously by the members, standing. Thereupon the body adjourned, with their usual exercises, to meet at the same place on this day week.

"L. C. VASS, Secretary."

It is deeply regretted that from this point on there are serious breaks in the minutes of meetings that were held, as many meetings were prevented by active operations.

Rev. L. C. Vass, D. D.,
Chaplain 27th Va. Regt.

Rev. Wm. E. Wiatt,
Chap. of 26th Va. Inf'ty, Wise's Brig.

Rev. Jas. Nelson,
Chaplain 44th Va. Regt.

Rev. J. Powell Garland,
Chaplain 49th Va. Regt.

Rev. Jos. C. Stiles, D. D.,
Army Evangelist.

(Facing page 524.)

Dr. Theo. Pryor, D. D.,
Missionary Chap. 1st Corps, A. N. V.

Rev. L. C. Vass, D. D., was the efficient Chaplain of the 27th Virginia Regiment, Stonewall Brigade, and the accomplished Secretary of the Chaplains' Association. He was one of those Chaplains who was always found at the post of duty, even though it called him to the outpost or the advanced line of battle, or the skirmish line of the army. He was for years the efficient Pastor of the Presbyterian Church at Newberne, N. C.

Rev. James Nelson, D. D., entered the army as a private soldier in the 23rd Virginia Regiment, and afterwards became Chaplain of the 44th Virginia Regiment, making one of the most laborious and efficient Chaplains in the army. Since the war he has had successful pastorates of Baptist Churches in Georgetown, D. C., Farmville, Va., and Staunton, Va.

Rev. Joseph C. Stiles, D. D., was for many years one of the ablest and most effective among the Presbyterian ministers of the country, and occupied prominent pulpits both at the North and in the South. When the war broke out, although over seventy years old, he threw himself into evangelistic labors in the Confederate armies with a zeal, self-denying consecration, and popular power which were absolutely unrivalled by younger men. He was unquestionably one of the ablest preachers, and one of the most successful laborers whom we had in the camps, and it is, perhaps, not too much to say that the beginning of the great revivals which swept through our camps, was due, under God, more to Dr. Stiles than any other man. He lived a life of great usefulness and died greatly lamented by all and especially by our old soldiers.

Rev. Wm. E. Wiatt, of Gloucester County, Va., entered the Confederate army as a private soldier, afterwards became Chaplain of the 26th Virginia Regiment, "when he became Chaplain he did not forget that he was still a soldier," and was one of the most laborious and useful Chaplains in the army. Since the war he has been a successful Pastor of Baptist Churches in Gloucester and Giles Counties, Va.

Rev. J. Powell Garland was the efficient Chaplain of the 49th Virginia Regiment, and was "abundant in labors," and successful in his work ; since the war he has had prominent positions in the M. E. Conference (South) of Virginia, is now Presiding Elder on the Richmond District, and has been popular as a preacher and very successful in his work.

Rev. Dr. Theo. Pryor, D. D. (father of Gen'l Roger A. Pryor), was an able and efficient missionary Chaplain to the 1st Corps A. N. V., has occupied very prominent positions in the Presbyterian Church, and up to 1888, when over eighty years old, he continued to preach the Gospel with wonderful vigor, power and success.

APPENDIX.

"ORANGE COURT HOUSE, August 25, 1863.
"The chaplains of the Second and Third Corps, Army of Northern Virginia, met, according to adjournment, at 10 A. M., in the Baptist church. The former Moderator introduced Rev. J. H. Bocock, D. D., to the meeting, who preached the opening sermon from Song of Solomon iii. 3, 'Saw ye him whom my soul loveth?' The speaker tenderly urged that all Christians, particularly Christ's ministers in the army, should see Christ: (1) In God's word; (2) In His mercies; (3) In the furnace; (4) On the throne, as King of kings and Lord of lords. Devotional services being over, the meeting was organized by electing Rev. J. M. Anderson, Fortieth Virginia, Moderator. Brother Vass, the Permanent Clerk, being absent, Rev. A. C. Hopkins, Second Virginia, was requested to act as Temporary Clerk.

"A free conversation on the subject of religion in the army being engaged in, revealed a general and deep interest in nearly every part of both corps, and also that the last fast-day had been universally and solemnly observed.

"Brother Lacy had preached, Friday morning, at General Ewell's head-quarters, and in the afternoon, in Mahone's Brigade, to large and peculiarly attentive congregations. He thought God's work in the army still progressing.

"Brother Jones reported that in Smith's Brigade religious interest was increasing. Since last meeting, between forty and fifty had been hopefully converted. His daily meetings were large, and he had frequently enjoyed the ministrations of Dr. Broadus.

"In Hayes's Brigade, particularly in the Ninth Louisiana Regiment, he reported that congregations were large and many interested about the salvation of their souls. Christians seemed alive, and had interested themselves to obtain a chaplain.

"Brother Talley stated that in Rodes's Brigade there was a gracious state of things, He had been laboring as chaplain only about two weeks, and had been most warmly received by officers and men. Fast-day had been unusually interesting, having been observed by sunrise prayer-meeting and three other public services during the day. Christians had formed an association in the brigade, which promised well.

"In Mahone's Brigade some thirty or forty conversions had occurred, and seventy-five or eighty were eagerly inquiring what they must do to be saved.

"Brother Booker stated that in Jones's Brigade fast-day had been well observed in four services. Much secret interest was discovered among the command.

"In Wilcox's Brigade the interest continued unabated. There had been seventy-five conversions since we came into camp, near Orange Court House. Brothers Power, Lewis, and others, had been helping the chaplains. Preaching had been suspended and substituted by prayer-meetings, which were thought advisable. Fast-day had been strictly observed by all.

"In Posey's Brigade the work of grace continued, and a great revival was progressing. There had been some fifty or sixty accessions to the Church of Christ, and from forty to fifty persons nightly presented themselves for the prayers of God's people. Fast-day had been observed by everybody in the command.

"Brother Hyman stated that in Thomas's Brigade the Spirit of the Lord still wrought mightily. Fifty persons had joined the Church, and there had been many more conversions. Fast-day had been well observed in brigade and regimental services.

"In Doles's, Daniels's, Scales's, and Stonewall Brigades a good state of religious feeling was existing; congregations good, and services were held daily.

"Brother Hall, from Louisiana, had been in the army a few days; had been preaching in the Washington Artillery to a most attentive congregation. Out of 470 men in the corps, nearly all were out at preaching on fast-day. Israelites, Catholics and Protestants exhibited profound interest on the subject of religion. Brother Hall had come to labor in the army.

"Brother Seay had been preaching, by way of experiment, for two weeks in the army. He was greatly surprised by the great religious spirit of the army, and thought it presented a very happy contrast with the spirit of the community.

"At this period the meeting took a more business turn.

" Brother W. E. Jones, who had been appointed upon the committee to complete the list of chaplains, asked to be excused. Granted; and Brother Dobbs appointed in his place.

" The committee appointed long ago to procure a better supply of chaplains was dissolved, at their request.

" Brother Talley moved that a committee be appointed to bring in an order of business at the next meeting. Carried. Committee—Brothers Lacy, Talley and Hopkins.

"It was moved by Brother Lacy that a committee of three be appointed to report upon the subject of opening a correspondence with other armies in the field. Committee—Brothers Hopkins, Booker and Betts.

" Dr. Bocock exhorted the brethren to go forward and lean upon Jesus Christ for guidance and for strength.

" Rev. Brothers W. A. Hall, James M. Lewis, John S. Grasty, were in attendance throughout the proceedings, and were invited to take part in the proceedings.

" Rev. Henry D. Moore was reported as having become chaplain to the Twelfth Alabama Regiment, Rodes's old Brigade.

"After devotional services, the meeting adjourned, to meet at this place on next Tuesday, at 10 A. M.

"A. C. HOPKINS, Temporary Clerk."

I very much regret to find myself, for want of space, compelled to omit all of the remainder of the minutes of our Chaplains' Association; but the memory of the other sessions at Orange Court House and at Petersburg will never die, at least so long as one who participated in them shall live.

We add to those given in the body of the book two additional proclamations of President Davis.

[Proclamation by the President of the Confederate States of America.]

" The Senate and House of Representatives of the Confederate States of America have signified their desire that a day may be recommended to the people, to be set apart and observed as a day of humiliation, fasting and prayer, in the language following, to wit:

' Reverently recognizing the Providence of God in the affairs of man, and gratefully remembering the guidance, support and deliverance granted to our patriot fathers in the memorable war which resulted in the independence of the American Colonies, and now reposing in Him our supreme confidence and hope in the present struggle for civil and religious freedom, and for the right to live under a government of our own choice, and deeply impressed with the conviction that without Him nothing is strong, nothing wise and nothing enduring; in order that the people of this Confederacy may have the opportunity, at the same time, of offering their adoration to the great Sovereign of the Universe, of penitently confessing their sins and strengthening their vows and purposes of amendment, in humble reliance upon His gracious and almighty power,

' The Congress of the Confederate States of America do *Resolve*, That it be recommended to the people of these States, that Friday, the 8th day of April next, be set apart and observed as a day of humiliation, fasting and prayer that Almighty God would so preside over our public councils and authorities; that He would so inspire our armies and their leaders with wisdom, courage and perseverance, and so manifest Himself in the greatness of His goodness and majesty of His power, that we may be safely and successfully led through the chastening to which we are being subjected, to the attainment of an honorable peace; so that, while we enjoy the blessings of a free and happy government, we may ascribe to Him the honor and the glory of our independence and prosperity.'

" A recommendation so congenial to the feelings of the people will receive their hearty concurrence; and it is a grateful duty to the Executive to unite with their representatives in inviting them to meet in the courts of the Most High. Recent events awaken fresh gratitude to the Supreme Ruler of nations. Our enemies have suffered repeated defeats, and a nefarious scheme to burn and plunder our capital, and to destroy our civil government by putting to death the chosen servants of the people, has been baffled and set at naught. Our armies have been strengthened; our finances promise rapid progress to a satisfactory condition; and our whole country is animated with a hopeful spirit and a fixed determination to achieve independence.

" In these circumstances it becomes us, with thankful hearts, to bow ourselves before the throne of the Most High, and, while gratefully acknowledging so many mercies, confess that our sins as a people have justly exposed us to His chastisement. Let us recognize the sufferings which we have been called upon to endure, as administered by a fatherly hand for our improvement, and with resolute courage and patient endurance let us wait on Him for our deliverance.

" In furtherance of these objects, now, therefore, I, Jefferson Davis, President of the Confederate States of America, do issue this, my proclamation, calling upon the people of the said States, in conformity with the desire expressed by their representatives, to set apart Friday, the 8th day of April, as a day of humiliation, fasting and prayer, and I do hereby invite them on that day to repair to their several places of public worship and beseech Almighty God ' to preside over our public councils and so inspire our armies and leaders with wisdom, courage and perseverance; and so to manifest Himself in the greatness of His goodness and in the majesty of His power, that we may secure the blessings of an honorable peace and of free government; and that we, as a people, may ascribe all to the honor and glory of His name.'

" Given under my hand and the seal of the Confederate States of America, at the city of Richmond, on this 12th day of March, in the year of our Lord one thousand eight hundred and sixty-four.

" JEFFERSON DAVIS.

[L. S.]

" By the President: J. P. BENJAMIN, Secretary of State."

[Proclamation Appointing a Day for Public Worship.]

" It is meet that the people of the Confederate States should, from time to time, assemble to acknowledge their dependence on Almighty God; to render devout thanks for His manifold blessings; to worship His holy name; to bend in prayer at His footstool; and to accept, with reverent submission, the chastening of His all-wise and all-merciful providence.

" Let us, then, in temples and in field, unite our voices in recognizing, with adoring gratitude, the manifestations of His protecting care in the many signal victories with which our arms have been crowned; in the fruitfulness with which our land has been blessed, and in the unimpaired energy and fortitude with which He has inspired our hearts, and strengthened our arms, in resistance to the iniquitous designs of our enemies.

" And let us not forget that, while graciously vouchsafing to us His protection, our sins have merited and received grievous chastisement; that many of our best and bravest have fallen in battle; that many others are still held in foreign prisons; that large districts of our country have been devastated with savage ferocity, the peaceful homes destroyed, and helpless women and children driven away in destitution; and that, with fiendish malignity, the passions of a servile race have been excited by our foes into the commission of atrocities from which death was a welcome escape.

"Now, therefore, I, Jefferson Davis, President of the Confederate States of America, do issue this my proclamation, setting apart Wednesday, the 16th day of November next, as a day to be specially devoted to the worship of Almighty God. And I do invite and invoke all the people of these Confederate States to assemble on the day aforesaid, in their respective places of public worship, there to unite in prayer to our Heavenly Father, that He bestow His favor upon us; that He extend over us the protection of His almighty arm; that He sanctify His chastisement to our improvement, so that we may turn away from evil paths and walk righteously in His sight; and that He may restore peace to our beloved country, healing its bleeding wounds, and securing to us the continued enjoyment of our own right of self-government and independence; and that He will graciously hearken to us, while we ascribe to Him the power and the glory of our deliverance.

"Given under my hand and the seal of the Confederate States, at Richmond, this 26th day of October, in the year of our Lord one thousand eight hundred and sixty-four.

[L. S.]   "JEFFERSON DAVIS.

"By the President: J. P. BENJAMIN, Secretary."

[Letter from Stonewall Jackson.]

"NEAR FREDERICKSBURG, April 10, 1863.

"*My Dear Sir:* Your letter of the 27th ultimo, informing me that, at the recent meeting of the Home Missionary Society of the Baltimore Annual Conference, at Churchville, Augusta county, Virginia, I was 'constituted a life-director of said society,' has been received. I appreciate the honor conferred, and hope that I may yet be privileged to be present at your deliberations for advancing the great missionary cause. The harvest is abundant; and my prayer is, that we may all labor with burning zeal for the glorious cause for which our Redeemer died. The Church has a mighty work before her; and we are assured that, as she advances, her career will become more glorious, until the whole world shall bow before the mild sway of Emmanuel.

"I am greatly gratified at seeing a growing religious interest among our troops here.

"Thanking you for your prayers and good wishes, I remain, very truly and fraternally yours,   "T. J. JACKSON.

"REV. GEORGE V. LEECH, Secretary."

ROSTER OF CHAPLAINS, ARMY OF NORTHERN VIRGINIA.

The following Roster is not as complete as I had hoped to make it, as some of my material has been lost, and I have been disappointed in not finding a Roster in the " War Records Office " in Washington. But even an incomplete Roster will be of wide interest. I shall give the names of all chaplains who were at any time connected with the regiments, so far as I shall be able to ascertain them from lists before me, Minutes of the Chaplains' Association, and other data. I should be grateful for any corrections or additions. It ought to be added that the basis of this Roster is one that I made in February, 1865, so that while the regiments all appear, the corps, divisions, and brigades are different from their organization at an earlier period.

GENERAL LONGSTREET'S CORPS (FIRST CORPS).

KERSHAW'S DIVISION.

Bryan's Brigade.
Tenth Georgia. J. C. Camp.
Fiftieth Georgia. W. L. Curry.
Fifty-first Georgia. C. H. Toy.
Fifty-third Georgia.

Wofford's Brigade.
Sixteenth Georgia.
Eighteenth Georgia.
Twenty-fourth Georgia.
Philip's Legion. Rev. Mr. Flinn.
Cobbs'.
Sharpshooters.

Kershaw's (Old) Brigade.
Brigade at large. W. P. Dubose.

Second South Carolina.
Third South Carolina.
Seventh South Carolina. J. M. Carlisle.
Eighth South Carolina. H. M. Brearley.
Fifteenth South Carolina. H. B. Mc-
    Callum.
James' Battalion.

Humphries' Brigade.
Thirteenth Mississippi. Rev. Mr. West.
Seventeenth Mississippi. W. B. Owen.
Eighteenth Mississippi. J. A. Hackett.
Twenty-first Mississippi. Rev. Mr. Mc-
    Donald.

FIELD'S DIVISION.

Jenkins' (Old) Brigade.
First S. Carolina. Geo. T. T. Williams.
Fifth South Carolina. J. N. Craig.
Sixth South Carolina. W. E. Boggs.
Second Rifles. W. E. Walters.
Sharpshooters. Jas. McDowell.

Anderson's Brigade.
Eighth Georgia. W. C. Dunlap.
Seventh Georgia. Rev. Mr. Stokes.
Ninth Georgia. H. Allen Tupper; J.
    C. Byrnham; A. B. Campbell.
Eleventh Georgia. W. A. Simmons.
Fifty-ninth Georgia.

Benning's brigade.
Fifteenth Georgia. W. F. Robertson.

Second Georgia.
Seventeenth Georgia. Rev. Mr. Hudson.
Twentieth Georgia.

Gregg's Brigade.
First Texas. I. R. Vick.
Fourth Texas.
Fifth Texas.
Third Arkansas. G. E. Butler.

Law's Brigade.
Fourth Alabama. Robt. Frazier.
Fifteenth Alabama.
Forty-fourth Alabama. W. G. Perry.
Forty-eighth Alabama. Rev. Mr. Price.

34

530 APPENDIX.

PICKETT'S DIVISION.

Steuart's Brigade.

Ninth Virginia. J. W. Walkup; G. W. Easter.
Thirty-eighth Virginia. R. W. Cridlin; Rev. Mr. Cosby.
Fifty-third Virginia. W. S. Penick; P. H. Fontaine; Rev. Mr. Colton.
Fifty-seventh Virginia. J. E. Joyner.
Fourteenth Virginia. Rev. Mr. Crocker.

Terry's Brigade.

First Virginia. Rev. Mr. Oldrich.
Third Virginia. Rev. Mr. Hammond; J. W. Ward.
Seventh Virginia. John H. Bocock; F. McCarthy; Rev. Mr. Frayser.
Eleventh Virginia. John C. Granberry; Thos. C. Jennings.

Twenty-fourth Virginia. W. F. Gardiner.

Hunton's Brigade.

Eighth Virginia. T. A. Ware; Geo. W. Harris.
Eighteenth Virginia. J. D. Blackwell.
Nineteenth Virginia. P. Slaughter.
Twenty-eighth Virginia. Rev. Mr. Tinsley.
Fifty-sixth Virginia. Rev. Mr. Robbins.

Corse's Brigade.

Fifteenth Virginia. P. F. August.
Seventeenth Virginia. John L. Johnson; R. M. Baker.
Thirtieth Virginia. W. R. D. Moncure.
Thirty-second Virginia.
Twenty-ninth Virginia. Rev. Mr. Phillippi.

ARTILLERY FIRST CORPS (BRIGADIER-GENERAL ALEXANDER).

Haskell's Battalion. J. A. Chambliss.
Gibbes' Virginia Battalion.
Cabell's Virginia Battalion.
Huger's Virginia Battalion.
Washington Artillery Battalion. Wm. A. Hall.

Missionary Chaplains in the Corps: Rev. Dr. Theodorick Pryor; Rev. Dr. J. C. Granberry; Rev. Harvie Hatcher; Rev. A. B. Woodfin.

SECOND CORPS (MAJOR-GENERAL JOHN B. GORDON COMMANDING).

Chaplains-at-large: Rev. Dr. B. T. Lacy; Rev. Dr. L. Rosser; Rev. E. J. Willis.

GORDON'S DIVISION.

Evans' Brigade.

Sixty-first Georgia. A. B. Woodfin.
Thirty-first Georgia. J. L. Pettigrew.
Thirty-eighth Georgia. J. M. Brittain.
Twenty-sixth Georgia.
Thirteenth Georgia.
Sixtieth Georgia. S. H. Smith.
Twelfth Georgia Battalion.

Louisiana Brigade (Colonel Peck).

Sixth Louisiana.
Seventh Louisiana. Father Hubert.
Fifth Louisiana. Wm. M. Strickler.
Eighth Louisiana. Father Schmilders.
Ninth Louisiana. Rev. F. McCarthy.
First Louisiana. Father Sheran.
Second Louisiana. Robert Hardee.
Tenth Louisiana.
Fourteenth Louisiana.
Fifteenth Louisiana.

Terry's Brigade (Stonewall, J. M. Jones' and Steuart's Virginia Brigades).

Second Virginia. Rev. Mr. McVeigh; A. C. Hopkins.
Fifth Virginia. E. Payson Walton; C. S. M. See.
Fourth Virginia. F. C. Tebbs; Wm. R. McNeer.
Twenty-seventh Virginia. L. C. Vass.
Thirty-third Virginia. J. M. Grandin.
Twenty-third Virginia. Paul C. Morton.
Tenth Virginia. J. P. Hyde; S. S. Lambeth; Rev. Mr. Balthis.
Thirty-seventh Virginia.
Forty-fourth Virginia. Richard I. McIlwaine; James Nelson.
Twenty-fifth Virginia. George B. Taylor; John W. Jones.
Twenty-first Virginia. I. Harvie Gilmore.

GORDON'S DIVISION—*Continued.*

Forty-second Virginia. Thomas Williams.
Forty-eighth Virginia. Geo. E. Booker.
Fiftieth Virginia. J. W. Denny.

First North Carolina. W. R. Gwaltney.
Third North Carolina.
First Maryland. Rev. Mr. Cameron.

PEGRAM'S DIVISION.

Pegram's (Old) Brigade.
Thirteenth Virginia. J. Wm. Jones; Wm. S. Ryland.
Fifty-second Virginia. John Magill.
Forty-ninth Virginia. J. Powel Garland.
Fifty-eighth Virginia. George Slaughter; L. B. Madison.
Thirty-first Virginia. A. D. Lepps.

Fifty-fourth North Carolina.
Sixth North Carolina.
Fifty-seventh North Carolina. John Paris.

Johnson's Brigade.

Lewis's Brigade.
Twenty-first North Carolina.

Fifth North Carolina.
Twelfth North Carolina. J. H. Robbins.
Twentieth North Carolina. L. A. Bickle.
Twenty-third North Carolina.

RODES'S (OLD) DIVISION.

Cook's Brigade.
Twelfth Georgia. A. M. Marshall; Rev. Mr. Poulridge.
Forty-fourth Georgia. H. E. Brookes.
Fourth Georgia. R. F. Evans; James O. A. Sparks.
Twenty-first Georgia.

Second North Carolina.
Fourth North Carolina.

Grymes's Brigade.

Fifty-third North Carolina. J. H. Colton.
Forty-fifth North Carolina. E. H. Harding.
Forty-third North Carolina. E. W. Thompson.
Second Battalion. Rev. Mr. Tennent.
Thirty-second North Carolina. W. B. Richardson.

Battle's Brigade.
Third Alabama. T. J. Rutledge.
Fifth Alabama. W. G. Curry.
Sixth Alabama. G. R. Talley.
Twelfth Alabama. H. G. Moore.
Twenty-sixth Alabama. Wm. E. Cameron.
Sixty-first Alabama.

D. R. Johnson's Brigade.

Fifth North Carolina.
Twelfth North Carolina.
Twentieth North Carolina. James M. Sprunt.
Twenty-third North Carolina.

Cox's Brigade.
Thirtieth North Carolina. A. D. Betts.
Fourteenth North Carolina. W. C. Power.

ARTILLERY SECOND CORPS (COLONEL CARTER).

Cutshaw's Battalion. Rev. Mr. Page.
Nelson's Battalion. T. Walker Gilmer.
Braxton's Battalion. Rev. Dr. A. B. Brown; James Nelson.

Page's Battalion.
Hardaway's Battalion. T. M. Niven; Henry M. White.

THIRD CORPS (GENERAL A. P. HILL).
Missionary Chaplains: Rev. Dr. Geo. D. Armstrong; Rev. J. Wm. Jones.
Fifth Alabama Battalion (Provost Guard).

HETH'S DIVISION.

McRae's Brigade.
Eleventh North Carolina.
Twenty-sixth North Carolina. A. N. Wells.

Forty-fourth North Carolina. R. S. Webb.
Forty-seventh North Carolina. W. S. Lacy.

HETH'S DIVISION—*Continued.*

Fifty-second North Carolina. Rev. Mr. Sanford; J. M. Cline.

Cook's Brigade.

Fifteenth North Carolina. S. W. Howerton.
Twenty-seventh North Carolina.
Forty-sixth North Carolina. A. D. Cohen.
Forty-eighth North Carolina. C. Plyler.

Davis's Brigade.

Second Mississippi.
Eleventh Mississippi.
Forty-second Mississippi. T. D. Witherspoon.
Fifty-fifth North Carolina.
Twenty-sixth Mississippi. M. B. Chapman.

First Battalion.

Archer's (Old) Brigade and Walker's (Old) Brigade.

First Tennessee. W. T. Helm.
Seventh Tennessee. Rev. Mr. Harris.
Fourteenth Tennessee. J. E. King.
Forty-fourth Tennessee.
Twenty-third Tennessee.
Sixty-third Tennessee.
Fortieth Virginia. Geo. F. Bagby; J. M. Anderson.
Forty-seventh Virginia. S. P. Meredith; S. B. Barber.
Fifty-fifth Virginia. R. B. Beadles.
Twenty-second Virginia Battalion.
Thirteenth Alabama. T. H. Howell.

WILCOX'S DIVISION.

Scales's Brigade.

Thirteenth North Carolina.
Sixteenth North Carolina. Rev. Mr. Watson.
Twenty-second North Carolina. F. H. Wood.
Thirty-fourth North Carolina. A. R. Benick.
Thirty-eighth North Carolina. Rev. Mr. McDiarmid.

McGowan's Brigade.

First South Carolina.
Twelfth South Carolina. Rev. Mr. Dixon; J. M. Anderson.
Thirteenth South Carolina. Wallace Duncan; J. N. Bouchelle.
Fourteenth South Carolina. W. B. Carson.

Orr's Rifles. F. P. Mulally.

Thomas's Brigade.

Sixteenth Georgia.
Thirty-fifth Georgia. John H. Taylor.
Forty-fifth Georgia. E. B. Barrett.
Forty-ninth Georgia. J. J. Hyman.

Lane's Brigade.

Seventh North Carolina.
Eighteenth North Carolina.
Twenty-eighth North Carolina. F. Milton Kennedy.
Thirty-third North Carolina. T. J. Eatman.
Thirty-seventh North Carolina. A. L. Stough.

MAHONE'S DIVISION.

Sorrell's Brigade.

Third Georgia. J. M. Stokes.
Twenty-second Georgia. W. H. McAfee.
Forty-eighth Georgia. J. A. Lowry
Second Battalion. J. O. A. Cook.
Sixty-fourth Georgia.
Tenth Battalion.

Forney's (Alabama) Brigade.

Eighth Alabama. W. E. Massie.
Ninth Alabama. E. L. Whitten.

Tenth Alabama. J. J. D. Renfroe; J. M. B. Roach.
Eleventh Alabama. Rev. Mr. Johnson.
Fourteenth Alabama.
Thirteenth Alabama.

Finegan's Brigade.

Second Florida. J. W. Timberlake.
Fifth Florida.
Seventh Florida. J. H. Tomkies.
Eighth Florida.

MAHONE'S DIVISION—*Continued.*

Eleventh Florida. Rev. Mr. Little.
Ninth Florida.
Tenth Florida.
Bonneaco's Battalion.

Harris's Brigade.

Twelfth Mississippi. C. H. Dobbs.
Sixteenth Mississippi. A. A. Lomax.

Nineteenth Mississippi. Rev. Mr. Duke;
 G. R. Morrison.
Forty-eighth Mississippi. A. E. Garrison.

Weisger's Brigade.

Twelfth Virginia. S. V. Hoyle.
Sixth Virginia.
Sixteenth Virginia.
Sixty-first Virginia. Hilary E. Hatcher.
Forty-first Virginia. John W Pugh.

ARTILLERY CORPS (GENERAL WALKER).

Pegram's Battalion. Rev. Mr. Rodman.
Poague's Battalion. James Wheary.
Cutt's Battalion.

Garnett's Battalion.
McIntosh's Battalion.

FOURTH CORPS (GENERAL R. H. ANDERSON).

HOKE'S DIVISION.

Colquitt's Brigade.

Nineteenth Georgia. A. J. Jarrell; W.
 H. C. Cone.
Twenty-third Georgia. W. A. Dodge.

Twenty-seventh Georgia. George S.
 Emory.
Sixth Georgia. A. M. Thigpen.
Twenty-eighth Georgia. A. H. McVay.

Clingman's (North Carolina) Brigade, Martin's (North Carolina) Brigade, and Hagood's (South Carolina) Brigade, which had been attached to Hoke's Division, were at this period (February, 1865) on detached service, and I have been unable to obtain a list of their chaplains.

B. R. JOHNSON'S DIVISION.

Ransom's Brigade.

Twenty-fourth North Carolina. T. B.
 Neil.
Twenty-fifth North Carolina.
Thirty-fifth North Carolina.
Fifty-sixth North Carolina.

Gracie's Brigade.

Forty-first Alabama.
Sixtieth Alabama.
Fortieth Alabama.

Wise's Brigade.

Thirty-fourth Virginia. W. H. Robert.

Twenty-sixth Virginia. W. E. Wiatt.
Fifty-ninth Virginia. L. B. Wharton.
Forty-sixth Virginia. W. Gaines Miller.

Wallace's Brigade.

Seventeenth South Carolina. A. A. Morse.
Eighteenth South Carolina. A. A. James.
Twenty-second South Carolina. E. D.
 Dill.
Twenty-sixth South Carolina. J. L.
 Girardeau.
Holcombe Legion. A. W. Moore.

ARTILLERY CORPS (COLONEL H. P. JONES).

No list obtainable.

POST-CHAPLAINS AT PETERSBURG.

Rev. Thomas Hume, Jr.; Rev. W. M. Young; Rev. J. B. Hardwicke; Rev. T. Hume, Sr.; Rev. L. C. Vass; and the pastors of the different churches, and a number of visiting ministers, missionaries, and colporteurs rendered invaluable service.

POST-CHAPLAINS AT RICHMOND.

These, so far as I can obtain the list, were: Rev. Dr. James B. Taylor, Sr.; Rev. Robert Ryland, D. D.; Rev. Wm. Harrison Williams; Rev. Dr. W. W. Bennett; Rev. J. E. Martin, and Rev. J. T. Carpenter.

The pastors of Richmond were practically chaplains all through the war, and were untiring in their self-sacrificing labors. I recall the following: Rev. Dr. J. L. Burrows, of the First Baptist Church; Rev. Dr. J. B. Jeter, of the Grace Street Baptist Church; Rev. Dr. D. Shaver, and Rev. Dr. L. W. Seeley, of the Second Baptist Church; Rev. Dr. J. B. Solomon, of Leigh Street Baptist Church; Rev. Dr. M. D. Hoge, of the Second Presbyterian Church; Rev. Dr. T. V. Moore, of the First Presbyterian Church; Rev. Dr. C. H. Read, of Grace Street Presbyterian Church; Rev. Dr. J. A. Duncan, Rev. Dr. D. S. Doggett, and Rev. Dr. J. E. Edwards, of the Methodist Churches; and of the Episcopal Churches, Rev. Dr. C. Minnigerode, of St. Paul's; Rev. Dr. G. W. Woodbridge, of Monumental; Rev. Dr. Peterskin, of St. James'; and Rev. Dr. T. G. Dashiells, of St. Mark's.

Among other post-chaplains in the State who did efficient service, I recall the names of Rev. Dr. Geo. B. Taylor, at Staunton; Rev. J. C. Hiden, at the University of Virginia; Rev. Dr. W. F. Broaddus, at Charlottesville; Rev. J. L. Johnson, at Lynchburg; Rev. Geo. W. Hyde, at Huguenot Springs; Rev. Dr. D. B. Ewing, Gordonsville; Rev. A. D. McVeigh, Farmville; and Rev. C. C. Chaplin, at Danville.

I very much regret my inability to procure a Roster of the chaplains in the Cavalry Corps, and that I can only now recall the names of Rev. James B. Taylor, Jr., of the Tenth Virginia Cavalry; Rev. C. H. Boggs, Ninth Virginia Cavalry; and Rev. R. T. Davis, of the Sixth Virginia Cavalry.

Let me say again, that any worthy names that have been omitted from the above list will be inserted with great pleasure if some friend will call my attention to the fact. I should rejoice to be able to preserve in these records the names of *all* of the chaplains, missionaries, colporteurs, and visiting ministers, who at any time labored in the army or hospitals, and contributed in any way to promote the great work of grace among the "Men in Gray."

CAPITOL OF THE CONFEDERATE STATES, MONTGOMERY, ALA.

(Facing page 535.)

APPENDIX No. 2.

THE WORK OF GRACE IN OTHER ARMIES OF THE CONFEDERACY.

In the body of this volume I purposely confined myself to "Religion in *Lee's* Army," not only because I desired to write of what I had personal knowledge, and had far more material than I could possibly use, but because I have been hoping that some competent hand would prepare a companion volume to mine for the other armies of the Confederacy. This I sincerely hope will yet be done. But as there has been a demand on the part of many people for something concerning the other armies, and as the publishers generously propose to give the additional matter without increasing the price of the book, I have consented to compile it. I had hoped to get some chaplain in the Western Army to undertake the work of compilation for me, but as I have failed in my efforts to secure this, I must do the compilation myself, using freely such material as I can command, and the kind help of such brethren as I have been able to induce to help me.

But I shall not be able to observe the same order and consistency of narrative as I could do with more space, and with more time at my disposal to make the compilation. I can only use as I find them newspaper clippings, and extracts from letters of chaplains, colporteurs, and other army workers. I shall have occasion to make free use again of the admirable little volume—"The Great Revival in the Southern Armies,"—of my friend and brother, Dr. W. W. Bennett, whose lamented death last summer has added fresh interest to his very valuable book.

In speaking of helps to the revival, Dr. Bennett says: "A writer, speaking of the religious influence in the Army of Tennessee, says: 'General Cleburne, the hero of many battle-fields, had a place prepared for preaching in the centre of his Division, where himself and most of his officers were present, and where I was assisted by General Lowry, who sat in the pulpit with me and closed the services of the hour with prayer. He is a Baptist preacher, and, like the commander of the Division, is a hero of many well-fought battle-fields. He takes great interest in the soldiers' religious welfare, often preaches to them, and feels that the ministry is still his high and holy calling.' Generals Findly, Bickler, Stewart, with others of the same army, were pious and devoted Christian officers, and gave much assistance to the chaplains and missionaries in the revival that swept so gloriously through the armies in the West. They recommended religion to their soldiers by precept and example. But these men were generals, and their contact with the soldiers was not so close as that of inferior officers. In the companies and regiments the work of pious officers was most effectually done."

Rev. B. B. Ross, of Alabama, writing to Rev. A. E. Dickinson, says: "I am just from a pleasant tour among the hospitals in Mississippi, where I found 3,000 sick. They are greedy, yea, ravenous, in their appetite for something to read. Under the labors of your colporteurs there has been a revival of religion at Quitman, and there is also a revival in progress at Lauderdale Springs. The surgeons have been especially kind f.ɔ me—at times calling my attention to certain cases of the sick, at others making apɼ ointments for me to preach."

Rev. S. A. Creath, Army of Tennessee: "I am still following up the army, trying to be c.f service to them.   At Atlanta I saw 3,000 sick men.   Started to work this morn'ng before sun up, and by 9 A. M. had distributed 20,000 pages of tracts. Several hɪve professed religion, and the Lord's blessing seems to be on us."

Rev. J. A. Hughes thus speaks of his labors at Atlanta: "In going among the thousands in the hospitals, I have met with many things to gladden my heart, and to cause me to love the work.   I find a number of Christians; some tell me that camp-life has had a very unfavorable influence on their religious character; others say it has been of great service to them, that it has bound them closer to the Saviour, made them more acquainted with their own weakness and sins, and afforded them a fine field in which to labor for the souls of their fellow-men.   Some few hesitate to take a Testament, though they will accept a tract.   One man positively refused a Testament but took the tract, 'A Mother's Parting Words to her Soldier Boy,' by the reading of which he was deeply moved and became a true penitent, asked me to pray for him, and finally died in the triumphs of faith.   To a young man who felt himself a sinner I gave 'Motives to Early Piety.'   He was led to Christ, whom he publicly confessed.   A soldier said to me on the street, 'You are the gentleman ʋho gave me a tract the other day.   I had read it before, at home, but never has ʮe reading of that book so affected me as of late; away from home and friends, it t̪s doubly sweet.'   Three have professed conversion from reading, 'Why will ye die?' several from reading 'A Mother's Parting Words.'   A soldier told me 'The Call to Prayer' had roused him to a sense of his duty as a professor of religion."

Lately a colporteur at Lauderdale Springs, Miss., was distributing tracts, and a captain approached him and asked for one.   "Select for yourself, captain," said he. The captain looked over them, and selected "Don't Swear," and began to read it aloud to the soldiers standing around, pausing occasionally to comment on the points made in the tract.   When he had finished, he exclaimed, "I am done swearing. Take this," handing the colporteur a ten-dollar bill, "and send it to aid in bringing out another edition of this tract."

Rev. E. A. Bolles, General Agent of the Bible Societies in South Carolina, said, in speaking of his work in the winter of 1861–62:

"Three months ago I commenced the work of distribution among the soldiers on our coast under the auspices of the Executive Committee of the South Carolina Bible Convention.   During this time several thousand copies of the Scriptures have been given away to needy and grateful soldiers, and thousands of copies are yet needed to meet the demand.   I may safely say that twenty thousand copies are needed for distribution among the soldiers on the coast.   I therefore earnestly appeal to the benevolent for funds to procure the Scriptures, so that the good work so successfully begun may be continued until every destitute soldier is supplied with the Word of Life."

To this gentleman the chaplain of the Fifteenth South Carolina Regiment sent an encouraging report of the state of religion in his regiment:

"The Testaments you sent to me were eagerly sought after by the men, many coming to me long after they were all distributed, and were much disappointed at not receiving one.   Could you send us some more they would be thankfully received and faithfully distributed.   As almost all the men lost their Bibles on Hilton Head, our regiment is perhaps the most destitute on the coast.   I am happy to say there is much religious feeling pervading our regiment, and our nightly prayer-meetings are well attended, and I hope ere long the Lord will bless us with an outpouring of His Holy Spirit."

To the same the Lieutenant-Colonel of the Tenth South Carolina Regiment wrote:

" I would be glad if you will supply the regiment to which I am attached with the Scriptures, as I see by the papers that you are engaged in the work of distribution among the soldiers. We prefer Testaments, as they would be much easier for soldiers to carry in their knapsacks. I have made this application to you because of finding that all our men have not Bibles or Testaments, and I consider a *soldier poorly equipped without one or the other*."

Dr. Bennett gives the following concerning the battle of Shiloh:

" The instances of heroic valor in the battle of Shiloh are abundant. A chaplain, Rev. I. T. Tichenor, of the Seventeenth Alabama Regiment, in a letter to Governor Watts, of that State, who at one time commanded the regiment, says:

" ' During this engagement we were under a cross fire on the left wing from three directions. Under it the boys wavered. I had been wearied, and was sitting down, but seeing them waver, I sprang to my feet, took off my hat, waved it over my head, walked up and down the line, and, as they say, " preached them a sermon." I reminded them that it was Sunday. That at that hour (11½ o'clock) all their home folks were praying for them; that Tom Watts—excuse the familiar way in which I employed so distinguished a name—had told us he would listen with an eager ear to hear from the Seventeenth; and shouting your name loud over the roar of battle, I called upon them to stand there and die, if need be, for their country. The effect was evident. Every man stood to his post, every eye flashed, and every heart beat high with desperate resolve to conquer or die. The regiment lost one-third of the number carried into the field.'

" Among the Christian soldiers that fell was Lieutenant-Colonel Holbrook, of a Kentucky regiment. He was mortally wounded, and fell at the head of his regiment in a victorious charge. After the battle, several of his officers came to see him in the hospital. He was dying fast, but desired to be propped up in bed, and then he talked with them like a Christian soldier: ' Gentlemen, in the course of my official duties with you I have had little or no occasion to speak to you upon the subject of religion, but this is a time when, as fellow-men, we may commune frankly together. And I desire to bear witness to the fact that I am at the present moment deriving all my strength and consolation from the firm reliance which I have upon the blessings of religion. I know I am not prepared for death, as I ought to have been, and as I hope you may be, but I feel safe in reposing upon the strong arm of God, and trusting to Him for my future happiness. Before this war is closed, some of you may be brought upon the threshold of the eternal world, as I have been, and my earnest prayer is that the messenger of death may find you waiting. Throughout my existence, I have found nothing in my experience that has afforded me more substantial happiness than Christianity, and I now, as I lie here conscious that life is waning, desire to bear testimony of a peaceful mind, of a firm faith in the grand scheme of salvation. Farewell, my comrades, may we all meet in a better world.' "

One of the rarest instances of youthful heroism that ever occurred is recorded in connection with this battle. Charlie Jackson, whose brief career as a soldier and whose happy death we place here upon permanent record, was worthy of the great name he bore:

" Some months ago," says a writer, " Charlie's father raised a company of soldiers, in which he was permitted to drill with the privates, and finally became so expert in the manual of arms that, young as he was, he was chosen the drill-master. In due time, marching orders were received. Then the father, consulting the age of his boy, and probably his own paternal feelings, gave him to understand that it was his wish he should remain at home. To this Charlie strenuously demurred, and plainly told his parent that if he could not go with him he would join another company. Yielding to his obstinacy, a sort of silent consent was given, and the lad left Memphis with his comrades. The regiment to which they belonged was detached to Burnsville, several miles distant from Corinth, and here it remained until the Friday or Saturday preceding the battle. Orders were then received that it should repair at once to the field and take its position. Charlie was asleep at the time of the departure, and the father, unwilling that one so young should undergo the fatigue of the long march of twenty miles and the dangers of the coming fight, gave orders that he should not be disturbed. Several hours after the boy awoke of his own accord.

" At a glance, his eye took in the condition of affairs, and his knowledge of coming events satisfied him of the cause. With him, to think was to act. He seized his little gun—a miniature musket which his father had made for him, and alone started on the trail of his absent regiment. Hour after hour he trudged along, and finally, just as they were about halting preparatory to going into battle, he succeeded in joining his company. He had travelled more than fifteen miles. His father chided him, but how could he do otherwise than admire the indomitable spirit of his boy? The battle commenced. Charlie took his place by his father's side, and was soon in the thickest of the fight. A bullet struck him in the body and tore an ugly wound. Still he pressed on, firing, cheering, and charging with the remainder of his regiment. He seemed not to know the sensation of fear, and his youthful example on more than one occasion was the rallying point from which the men took fresh spirit. Suddenly, at a late hour in the day, the little fellow fell shot through the leg a few inches below the hip. He gave a cheer and told his father to go on. ' Don't mind me,' said he, ' but keep on; I'll lie here till you come back.' This of course the feelings of the parent would not permit him to do, and picking him up in his arms, he carried him to the nearest hospital. Within a day or two Charlie was brought to his home in Memphis, feeble, yet full of hope and courage.

" Dr. Keller was called upon to examine the wound and, if necessary, to perform amputation; but at a glance his experienced eye saw that the poor boy was beyond the hope of recovery. Mortification had set in, and an operation would only increase his sufferings without prolonging life. The lad noticed the sober countenance of the physician as he turned away and went to an adjoining room to break the mournful intelligence to the weeping father and mother. Nothing could be done but to relieve him of pain by means of opiates.

" A few moments afterwards he returned to the bedside of the sufferer, when the young hero abruptly met him with the question—

" ' Doctor, will you answer me a straightforward question, and tell me the truth ? '

" The physician paused a moment, and then said :

" ' Yes, Charlie, I will ; but you must prepare for bad news.'

" ' Can I live ? ' was the response.

" ' No ! Nothing can save you now but a miracle from heaven.'

" ' Well, I have thought so myself. I have felt as if I was going to die. Do father and mother know this ? '

" ' Yes,' replied the surgeon. ' I have just told them.'

" ' Please ask them to come in here.'

" When the parents had done so, and taken their places on either side of the bed, Charlie reached out, grasped their hands in his, and said :

" ' Dear father and mother, Dr. Keller says that I can't live. And now I want to ask your forgiveness for all wrong I have done. I have tried to be a good boy in every way but one, and that was when I disobeyed you both and joined the army. I couldn't help that, for I felt as if I ought to be right where you were, father, and to fight as long as I was able. I'm only sorry that I can't fight through the war. If I have said anything wrong or done anything wrong, won't you forgive me ? '

" The afflicted parents could only weep their assent.

" ' Now, father,' continued the boy, ' one thing more. Don't stay here with me, but go back to camp. Mother will take care of me, and your services are more necessary in your company than they are at home. I am not afraid to die, and I wish I had a thousand lives to lose in the same way. And, father, tell the boys when you get back how I died—just as a soldier ought to. Tell them to fight the Yankees as long as there is one left in the country, and *never give up !* Whenever you fill up the company with new men, let them know that besides their country there's a little boy in heaven who will watch them and pray for them as they go into battle.'

" And so is dying one of the bravest spirits that was ever breathed into the human body by its Divine Master. The scene I have described is one of which we sometimes read, but rarely behold, and the surgeon told me that, inured as he was to spectacles of suffering and woe, as he stood by this, a silent spectator, his heart overflowed in tears and he knelt down and sobbed like a child.

" How true are the lines of the poet—

> "'The good die first,
> And they whose hearts are dry as summer's dust,
> Burn to the socket.' "

From this, and other battles, the hospitals were filled with thousands of sick and wounded men, among whom there were the most cheering evidences of true religious feeling. Rev. B. B. Ross, of Alabama, who gladly gave himself to the work of colportage, says of his labors :

" I visited Corinth, the hospitals, and some of the camps, and am glad to report that the soldiers are very greedy for all kinds of religious reading—take the tracts from the agent with delight, and read them with avidity, and, whenever he sees proper to drop a word of admonition or warning, listen to it with patience and respect. But this is especially so in the hospitals."

From Okolona, Mississippi, Rev. J. T. C. Collins wrote to Mr. Ross :

" The soldiers received the books with great eagerness. I never in all my life saw such a desire to get Bibles. Every ward I went into they would beg me for *Bibles and Testaments.* While they gladly received the other books, they wanted *Bibles.* I have been to every man's cot and left either a book or a tract. And when I revisited them, and asked how they liked the books, my heart was greatly cheered by the accounts they gave me. One said he had been improving ever since he had gotten something to interest his mind. Another said, while a friend was reading for him the 14th chapter of John (a chapter to which I had called his attention), he was blessed and made very happy. He is now dead—went safely home."

A chaplain gave this pleasing testimony :

" Religious reading is highly appreciated by the soldiers; and what few tracts we can get are carefully read, and many tears have been seen to run down the soldier's face while reading these friendly visitors. They do not wait for me to go out to distribute them, but come to my tent inquiring, ' Have you any more tracts to spare ? ' There have been two conversions in the regiment. The soldiers were sick at the time, and one of them has since ' gone to his long home,' but felt before he died it was much the best for him to go, that ' he would be in a better world,' where wars and rumors of wars would no more mar his peace."

Dr. Bennett records of the autumn of 1862 :

" The revival, at this period of the war, was undoubtedly greater and more glorious in the army in Virginia than in other portions of the Confederacy, but there were happy signs of spiritual life among the troops in the far South and West. On Sullivan's Island, near Charleston, S. C., there was a blessed work of grace, which powerfully checked the ordinary vices of the camp and brought many souls into the fold of the Good Shepherd. Speaking of this work, in a letter of October 9, Rev. E. J. Meynardie, chaplain of Colonel Keitts's Regiment of South Carolina Volunteers, says :

"'On Thursday evening, 25th ult., the religious interest, which for some time had been quite apparent, became so deep and manifest that I determined to hold a series of meetings, during which, up to last night, *ninety-three* applied for membership in the various branches of the Church, nearly all of whom profess conversion. Every night the church at which we worship was densely crowded, and obvious seriousness pervaded the congregation. To the invitation to approach the altar for prayer prompt and anxious responses were made; and it was indeed an unusual and impressive spectacle to behold the soldiers of the country, ready for battle, and even for death on the battlè-field, bowed in prayer for that blessing which the warrior, of all others, so much needs. God was with us most graciously, and it was a period of profound interest and great joy.'

" The influence of this meeting has pervaded the regiment, and is still operating most beneficially. To what extent it has improved the morals of the soldiers it is impossible to estimate. Suffice it to say, that it has struck at the very root of camp vices, and the great crime which is more frequently committed in the army, against God and common decency, than any other, hides its hideous head—I mean profanity. The testimony of a soldier who writes for the *Southern Lutheran* is: ' When we first came into camp, swearing was a common practice; but now, thank God, an oath is seldom heard. Our men seem to feel as if they ought to be more observant of God's law.'

" The Church of Christ is very strongly represented in the regiment. We have many praying men; and indeed a more quiet, orderly, and religiously-disposed body of troops cannot, I presume, be found in the service; and be assured that when the time for fighting comes, beneath the banner of the Cross and our country's flag, we shall present an unflinching front. It was the religious fanaticism of Cromwell's puritanic army which made it invincible. It is the genuine religious tone of Jackson's which, under a pious commander, has thus far rendered it unconquerable, and we trust that the powerful religious element in this command will inspire sentiments of the highest order of patriotism when the occasion comes for every man to stamp himself a hero!"

Alluding to the battle of Perryville and its incidents, a chaplain writes :

" Many a Christian hero fell in this sanguinary battle, but among them all none offered a purer life on the altar of his country than Thomas Jefferson Koger, of Alabama. He was a pious, zealous, eminently useful minister of the Methodist Episcopal Church, South, and for nearly twenty years had been a member of the Alabama Conference. At the close of his term as Presiding Elder on the Columbus District he entered the army of the South as a private in the ranks, but was afterward appointed chaplain. In reference to his entrance upon a military life, exchanging the quiet round of ministerial duties for the bustle and toil of a soldier's life, we must let him speak in his own vindication, if any be needed.

" In a letter to his dear friend, Rev. O. R. Blue, he says:

"' I go from a deliberate conviction that it is my duty to go. It is under these feelings alone I leave my family. I go, trusting in God to bless and prosper me in the just cause. Pray for me.' To his wife, writing from Bowling Green, he says : ' As to the cause of my absence, I think there need be no apprehension. There is as much need of preachers and preaching here as in any place I have ever been yet; and I try to maintain my place as a Christian minister as earnestly and heartily as I ever did. It is a mistake to suppose that men in arms are beyond the reach and influence of the gospel. They are not; and the gospel is the only refining and elevating influence operating on them. Wife, children, home and its endearments, are only sweet memories here—not actual restraints, as they are when present. And then, the sick are always open to religious impressions.'

" At the expiration of the term of service of the regiment which he served as chaplain, he returned home, and at once set to work to raise a company for the war.

It was his wish to return to the army as chaplain, but the person who was expected to take command of the new company having declined only the day before the election, he was the unanimous choice of the men for captain. Having been mainly instrumental in raising the company, he did not feel at liberty to decline, and thus unexpectedly he found himself regularly enrolled as a soldier. He carried the spirit of his Master with him into the camp; he prayed with his men every night, and preached to them on Sabbath whenever circumstances permitted. He maintained his integrity, and never compromising on any occasion his character as a minister of Christ. His men loved him devotedly, and always showed him the highest respect. The thoughts of this good man have a melancholy interest now after the storm of war is hushed, and we look back on the past as on a horrible dream. From the camp he wrote:

" ' No man leaves wife and children more reluctantly than myself. But I have made up my mind to do it, and must bear it. I am trying to lead a godly life, and do good as best I can in my place as an officer and minister of the gospel. I feel that I am in the way of duty, and can ask God's best blessing on my work. I am a soldier for conscience' sake. I am here because duty calls me, and for no other reason. If it were not the path of duty, I should utterly loath the interminable, never-ceasing confusion of camp life.'

" Again referring to his position as a soldier:

" ' I could not be a soldier unless conscience approved. It is only when my own land is invaded, my wife and children endangered, that I dare bear arms; and then, when interests so vital, so personal, are at stake, it is only by effort I could remain at home.'

" With a cheerful and buoyant spirit he endured the privations and fatigues of military life, sustained by such a noble and chivalric sense of duty. His march to Perryville was his last. After his regiment was drawn up in line of battle, his colonel, passing along the line, observed him writing, and asked what he was doing. He replied, ' Writing to my wife.' This hurried note, written on the edge of battle, was the last message of love to his family. It was cut short by the order ' Forward,' and at the head of his men he plunged into the fight. His sword was shattered in his hand by a ball, and the next moment another pierced his body. He fell and died on the field. After the battle, two of his faithful soldiers, at their own request, were detailed to bury him, and while performing this sad duty were captured by the enemy. One who knew him well and loved him (Rev. J. B. Cottrell, of Alabama) draws his character in a few meaning lines:

" ' T. J. Koger will not again meet in Conference with us. Few of our number would be more missed. A very peculiar man in appearance, and a peculiarly true and earnest soul, he was most highly esteemed by us all. Few men ever loved the Church better, or were more at home in her councils or at her altars. He was popular among his brethren, and popular among the people. Perfectly fearless, he avoided no duty or responsibility. In every respect he was *reliable.* On the battle-field of Perryville he fell, attesting his devotion to his native South. He was one of the few men who could have gone on to any position in the service in which he fell, and afterwards have come back to the work of a Methodist preacher. One bright, sunny spirit less—we'll miss and lament him.' "

Rev. Dr. Joseph Cross, who was with General Bragg's army, thus describes the battle-field after the fight at Murfreesboro:

" Ah! how many expired with the year. Here they lie, friend and foe, in every possible position, a vast promiscuous ruin.

" ' They sleep their last sleep, they have fought their last battle;
No sound can awake them to glory again.'

" After a pretty thorough inspection of the ground in the rear of our lines, from

Stone river to the extreme left, I rode to the front, where the dead lie thick among the cedars, in proportion of five Yankees to one Southron. Here are sights to sicken the bravest hearts—sad lessons for human passion and oppression. Here is a foot, shot off at the ankle—a fine model for a sculptor. Here is an officer's hand, severed from the wrist, the glove still upon it, and the sword in its grasp. Here is an entire brain, perfectly isolated, showing no sign of violence, as if carefully taken from the skull that enclosed it by the hands of a skilful surgeon. Here is a corpse, sitting upon the ground, with its back against a tree, in the most natural position of life, holding before its face the photograph likeness of a good-looking old lady, probably the dead man's mother. Here is a poor fellow, who has crawled into the corner of a fence to read his sister's letter, and expired in the act of its perusal, the precious document still open before him full of affectionate counsel. Here is a handsome young man, with a placid countenance, lying upon his back, his Bible upon his bosom, and his hands folded over it, as if he had gone to sleep saying his evening prayer. Many others present the melancholy contrast of scattered cards, obscene pictures, and filthy ballad books—' miserable comforters' for a dying hour. One lies upon his face literally biting the ground, his rigid fingers fastened firmly into the gory sod; and another, with upturned face, open eyes, knit brow, compressed lips, and clenched fists, displays all the desperation of vengeance imprinted on his clay. Dissevered heads, arms, legs, are scattered everywhere; and the co-agulated pools of blood gleam ghastly in the morning sun. It is a fearful sight for Christian eyes!"

The scenes on the battle-fields and in hospitals are full of incidents showing the power of divine grace to cheer and support the soul in the dark hour of death. "Tell my mother," said a dying soldier, "that I am lying without hope of recovery. I have stood before the enemy fighting in a great and glorious cause, and have fallen. My hope is in Christ, for whose sake I hope to be saved. Tell her that she and my brother cannot see me again on earth, but they can meet me in heaven." A little before bed-time in his last night he called to his surgeon (Dr. Leverett), and said: "Write to mother, and tell her she must meet me in heaven. I know I am going there." Thus died T. S. Chandler, of the Sixth South Carolina regiment.

It was now that the signs of that wonderful revival in the army of the West began to appear. "I shall never forget," says Rev. W. H. Browning, "the look of astonishment in the Association of Chaplains in January, 1863, when Brother Winchester, a chaplain and a minister in the Cumberland Presbyterian Church, announced a conversion in his command, and stated that he believed we were on the eve of one of the most glorious revivals ever witnessed on the American continent! His countenance glowed with an unearthly radiance, and while he spoke ' our hearts burned within us.' He urged us to look for it—pray for it—preach for it. A revival in the army! The thing was incredible. And yet, while we listened to this man of faith, we could almost hear the shouts of redeemed souls that were being born to God. We could but catch the zeal of this good man, and went away resolved to work for a revival.

"This good man was not permitted to participate in the revival which he so feelingly predicted. He was soon called to the spirit world, and from his home among the blessed looked down upon the glorious scenes of salvation among the soldiers whom he loved so ardently, and for whom he prayed with a faith strong and unfaltering.

" A General Association of Chaplains and Missionaries had been formed in this army in August of this year (1863), but the subsequent movements interfered greatly with its complete organization, and it was not until November following that it was properly reorganized and made really efficient. Rev. Dr. McDonald, President of Lebanon University, was the President, and Rev. Welborn Mooney, of the Tennessee Conference, Methodist Episcopal Church, South, was the Secretary. The proceedings of this Association Mr. Browning supposes were lost in the subsequent reverses of the army, and hence we are cut off from most reliable information concerning the progress of the revival.

"The seeds of truth were sown by such faithful laborers as Rev. M. B. DeWitt, chaplain of the Eighth Tennessee, Rev. Mr. Weaver, of the Twenty-eighth Tennessee, Rev. Tilmon Page, of the Fifty-second Tennessee, and Rev. W. H. Browning, chaplain of General Marcus Wright's brigade. In other portions of the army, under the preaching of Rev. S. M. Cherry, Rev. Messrs. Petway, Taylor, Henderson, and scores of other devoted and self-sacrificing ministers, the revival influence became deep and powerful.

"Rev. L. R. Redding, Methodist, of the Georgia Conference, M. E. Church, South, who labored as a missionary in this army, has furnished us an account of the work in his own and other corps during the winter and spring of 1863–'64. Beginning his work in General Gist's brigade, and aided by Rev. F. Auld, Rev. A. J. P. De Pass, and other zealous chaplains, he soon witnessed scenes that filled him with the highest joy. The congregations increased daily, and soon a permanent place of worship was established in the rear of the brigade. The soldiers, eager to hear the Word of Life, soon fell to work and built a rude but commodious chapel, and furnished it with pulpit, seats, and lights. It was dedicated in the presence of the general and his staff by Rev. Dr. J. B. McFerrin, who, with his well-known zeal, had devoted himself to the work of an army missionary. An immense congregation attended, and the 'word ran and was glorified.' From this time until the army marched away in the spring the revival progressed with increasing power. A Christian Association was formed, which met daily at half-past eight in the morning, for the purpose of uniting the members of the various Churches, as well as the new converts, in the work of saving souls, of gathering the results of the night meetings, and of hearing the recitals of religious experience. These meetings were marked by great fervor and power. The young believers were organized into private prayer-meetings, which met at seven o'clock in the morning. 'Sometimes,' says Mr. Redding, 'I would quietly unpeg the door and walk in while the young men were engaged in their delightful meetings, and would find the young convert of the previous night leading in prayer, and earnestly invoking God's blessing upon his impenitent comrades.' In the evening, at the close of dress-parade, the drums would beat the Church call on Chapel Hill. It was a glorious sight, just as the setting sun bathed the mountain tops in his ruddy light, to see those toil-worn veterans gathering in companies and marching to the house of the Lord. From all directions, down from the hills, out of the woods, across the valleys, they came, while the gallant Colonel McCullough, of the Sixteenth South Carolina, himself a godly man, leads his men to the place of worship. Then the Twenty-fourth South Carolina falls into line, led by their chaplain, Mr. Auld, and their brave Colonel Capers, son of the deceased Bishop Capers, of the Southern Methodist Church. The benches and the pulpit have to be removed from the house, and a dense multitude of hearers crown the chapel hill. A clear, strong voice starts a familiar old hymn, soon thousands of voices chime in, and the evening air is burdened with a great song of praise. The preacher now enters the stand, a thousand voices are hushed, a thousand hearts are stilled, to hear the word of the Lord. Perhaps the speaker is Rev. William Burr, of Tennessee. As he rises with his theme, his silvery, trumpet-like voice, clear as a bugle note, rings far out over the mass of men, and hundreds sob with emotion as he reasons with them of righteousness, of temperance, and a judgment to come. At the close of the sermon, hundreds bow in penitence and prayer, many are converted; tattoo beats—the men disperse to their cabins, not to sleep, but to pray and sing with their sorrowing comrades; and far into the night the camps are vocal with the songs of Zion and the rejoicings of new-born souls.

In this revival, described by an eye-witness, one hundred and forty were converted in two weeks, among them Colonel Dunlap, of the Forty-sixth Georgia, who united with the Presbyterian Church. Among the private soldiers that contributed to the success of this work, we are glad to place on record the name of W. J. Brown, of Company I, Forty-sixth Georgia. His influence with his regiment was very great, and he threw it all in favor of religion.

" But soon came the order to march; the chapel and the snug cabins were exchanged for the drenched and dreary bivouac, and the sound of the gospel of peace for the notes of whistling minies and bursting shells. In the battle, and in the hospital, the genuineness of those army conversions was fully tested. In the terrible campaign that followed, whenever the smoke of battle cleared away, and the weary men had a little rest, they gathered their shattered but undaunted cohorts, and, with renewed zeal, and with love tested in the fire of war, repledged their faith to each other and charged again and again the strongholds of Satan. Lying behind the strong barrier of the Chattahoochee River for a few days, these Christian soldiers built a brush arbor, and beneath it many souls were born of God. Dying, those noble men of the South gave testimony to the power of divine grace. 'Can I do anything for you?' said the missionary, kneeling by the side of a private shot through the neck. 'Yes, write to my poor wife.' 'What shall I write?' 'Say to my dear wife, it's all right.' This was written. 'What else shall I write?' 'Nothing else, all's right'—and thus he died. He was a convert of the camp."

" Passing through a large stable where the wounded lay," says Mr. Redding, "I noticed a man whose head was frosted with age. After giving him wine and food, I said, 'My friend, you are an old man. Do you enjoy the comforts of religion?' 'Oh, yes,' he exclaimed, 'I have been a member of the Church for twenty-five years. Often in our little church at home our minister told us that religion was good under all circumstances, and now I have found it true; for even here in this old stable, with my leg amputated, and surrounded by the dead and dying, I am just as happy as I can be. It is good even here. I want you to tell the people so when you preach to them.' I left him rejoicing."

The Rev. P. A. Johnston, chaplain of the Thirty-eighth Mississippi Volunteers, wrote of a revival at Snyder's Bluff:

" The Lord is at work among us. His stately steppings are often heard and his presence felt to the comfort of our souls. We have had for the past week very interesting prayer-meetings. They were well-attended and the very highest interest manifested. Souls are hungry for the 'bread of life.'

"Often in these prayer-meetings there are from twelve to twenty mourners. There have already been two or three conversions, and four have joined the Church. Sinners are being awakened, mourners comforted, and the Christian established in the faith. The camp is a rough, hard life. But, sir, I feel fully compensated for every privation and hardship I have been subjected to.

" And now, one word to state a very important fact. The partitions are well-nigh broken down that have heretofore kept Christians so far apart. We know each other here only as Christian brethren travelling to a better world. Our meeting is still progressing. Pray for us."

"Rev. J. W. Turner, writing from Savannah, Georgia, says: 'Our people seem to have deserted us,' was the language of a sick soldier in one of the hospitals in this city. He was a member of the Twenty-fifth Georgia Regiment, which has been encamped near this place for nearly eighteen months. The Baptists had given fruitful attention to this part of the field, as they did indeed with self-sacrificing zeal to every portion of the army. 'There are three Baptist ministers,' says Mr. Johnston, 'acting as general chaplains, colporteurs, etc., within and around this city. They are giving their whole time to the distribution of Testaments, tracts, and Baptist periodicals, and to the preaching of the word.'"

An officer of the Fifth Georgia Regiment, stationed at Bridgeport, Tennessee, sent back home his appeal:

"Our regiment now numbers about 650, and these men have not heard a sermon in *five months*. What a thought! Who is to blame? The men? I think not. The officers? No. Who then? The ministry or the Christians at home. I have done all in my power to secure the services of some minister to preach for us, but have, so far, entirely failed. Our regiment is composed mostly of young men, many of them, at home, members of the Church—Christians; and shall it be said that any of these have backslidden or have died, and are forever lost, for the want of proper counsel? God forbid."

Dr. Bennett thus continues his narrative of the great revival in the summer of 1863:

"Charleston, South Carolina, was a point of great interest during the whole period of the war, and the fiery temper of the men who opened the fearful drama might be supposed to be unfavorable to the progress of the revival. But it was not so. Among the soldiers that lay for many weary months on the bare sands of the barren islands, and on the borders of the lagoons around that city, the work of grace went steadily forward. Christian Associations were formed, religious books, tracts, and papers were distributed, and earnest sermons preached, which resulted in most blessed scenes. In the Forty-sixth Georgia such an organization was formed, and the soldiers who united in it said: 'Our object is to make it a depository for the names of members of the Church, that they may be known as such, and that thereby we may be the better enabled to watch over each other for good; that each may feel that *he* has something to do in teaching sinners the way of life; and that by a godly walk and pious conversation he ought to honor his profession and glorify the God of his salvation.' One hundred and eighty-four Christian soldiers gave their names to the Association. Of this regiment, Rev. T. C. Stanley was then the chaplain, Lieutenant N. B. Binion was President of the Association, and W. J. Brown, Secretary. These men came out not only to fight, to suffer, to die for their country, but to work for God and the truth in the midst of all the evils and corruptions of the camp."

The signs from other portions of the army in the West and Southwest were equally cheering. Along the lines in East Tennessee the revival began to spread with great power. Rev. W. B. Norris, writing from Loudon, Tennessee, says:

"During the month (April) there has been a deep religious interest among the soldiers here. We have had a series of meetings for about two weeks, which, we hope, resulted in much good. The church in which we met was always crowded to the utmost, and there were always many seekers for the way of eternal life."

In the Fifty-ninth Tennessee Regiment there was a glorious work. Rev. S. Strick, the chaplain, says:

"God is at work among our men. Many are earnestly seeking the pardon of their sins—some have been converted. Our nightly prayer-meetings are well attended by anxious listeners, and my tent is crowded daily by deeply penitent souls. Never have I known such a state of religious feeling in our army as at this time. God's Spirit is moving the hearts of our soldiers."

"Rev. Messrs. McFerrin, Petway, and Ransom, of the M. E. Church, South, went to the help of General Bragg's army; Messrs. Thweat and Harrington, of the same Church, to the army in Mississippi; while Bishop Pierce, Dr. A. L. P. Green, and Rev. J. E. Evans went to General Lee's army in Virginia. Rev. Dr. Kavanaugh was sent to the army of General Price, and Rev. Mr. Marvin (now Bishop) was directed by Bishop Pierce to take position as missionary with any army corps west of the Mississippi. The work of these ministers, with that of other zealous men from sister Churches, gave a great impulse to the revival. In Colonel Colquitt's Forty-sixth Georgia Regiment, camped near Vernon, Mississippi, the work was

35

powerful, and great numbers were converted. 'Last night,' says Rev. T. C. Stanley, 'there were about eighty presented themselves for prayer, kneeling upon the ground. The Christian heart could not but be touched while witnessing such a scene. We were under the tall spreading oaks of the forest, and the moon bathing all with its gentle beams, typical of the Spirit that was in mercy sent down from above, enveloping us as with a garment of love, cheering the heart of the Christian and comforting many a poor penitent.'

"In the ordeal through which Vicksburg passed before the siege closed, the feeling of dependence on God was very marked among the suffering soldiers. We take the following from a chaplain's journal, kept during the siege:

"'Our case is desperate. I hope in God. There is much turning to him now, to recount his promises, and to claim his protection. There is no difficulty now in having religious conversation. Everybody is ready for it. . . . A bright Sabbath morning; but its stillness is broken by the harsh and startling detonations of the engines of destruction. I sigh for the sweet, undisturbed sanctuary. 'As the hart,' etc. Read a sermon to a small company of gentlemen to-day. Got on somewhat of a Sunday feeling. We sit up till a late hour every night, discussing the situation, etc. . . . A furious fire was poured upon us this morning at three o'clock from the batteries beyond the trenches. One shot struck a hospital near me and killed one man; the others were frightened and cried out most piteously. Nothing that I have met is more harrowing to my feelings than scenes like this. Tried to observe to-day as the Sabbath by acts of piety and works of charity.'

"In the army of General Bragg the revival went on despite the sufferings of the troops in their retrograde movement to the vicinity of Chattanooga. Rev. W. H. Browning, writing to the *Southern Christian Advocate* of the work of grace, says:

"'I am truly gratified to state to you that the religious interest in this army, though abated to some extent by the retrograde movement to this place, has again revived, and there is now a general spirit of revival manifest in every part of this army. In this brigade we have been holding meetings each night for more than two weeks. There are generally from thirty to fifty penitents at the altar each night, and about forty conversions. In most of the brigades in this division they are holding similar meetings. Indeed, the same may be said of the entire army.

"'The most careless observer can but notice the marked change that has taken place in the regiments. Instead of oaths, jests, and blackguard songs, we now have the songs of Zion, prayers and praises to God. True, there are yet many profane, wicked, and rude, yet the preponderance is decidedly in favor of Christianity. I verily believe that the morals of the army are now far in advance of those of the country. And instead of the army being the school of vice, as was once supposed, and really was, it is now the place where God is adored, and where many learn to revere the name of Jesus. Many backsliders have recently been reclaimed—the lukewarm have been aroused, and sinners have been converted. Will not our families and friends at home awake to the importance of a deeper work among themselves? This is a time that calls for universal humiliation and prayer.'

"In addition to these extracts we can only give brief, but expressive, records from other parts of the army. Rev. R. G. Porter, chaplain of the Tenth Mississippi Regiment, Bragg's army, says:

"'It makes my very soul happy to witness the manifestations of God's saving power as seen here in the army—from ten to forty at the altar of prayer—have preaching every day when not hindered by the men being called off.'

"The Rev. Dr. Palmer, of New Orleans, preached with power and love, and under his word the revival deepened. Rev. C. W. Miller, army missionary, writes of the work in Georgia, General D., H. Hill's Corps:

"'Since I arrived here as missionary I have been engaged every night in religious services with the soldiers. A revival and extensive awakening have been in progress in General Bate's Brigade for four weeks. Every night the altar is crowded with weeping penitents. Several have been happily converted. To me it is the most interesting sight of my life. You cannot look upon these penitent, weeping men at the altar of prayer without thinking of the bloody fields of Perryville and Murfreesboro, and the victorious veterans rolling up to heaven the shouts of triumph. Here they are. Some sending up the note of a more glorious victory—others charging through the columns of the foe to 'take the kingdom of heaven by force.' "

From the Thirty-eighth Alabama Volunteers Rev. A. D. McVoy sent good tidings :

" We have held nightly meetings almost uninterruptedly, whenever the weather permitted, ever since last October, with large attendance, much interest, and good results. Some conversions and accessions to the Church have gladdened our hearts. While stationed in Mobile we had every convenience for religious worship—a large arbor with seats and stands for fire. Since we have been transferred to Tennessee we have resumed our nightly meetings, either in quarters or upon some neighboring hill, where the shade is good, and where with logs we could construct our rude altar to God. Such a place as this has truly become a little Bethel to our souls. I never saw men more concerned about their soul's salvation. In a little gathering last night, which was greatly interrupted by rain, we had thirty to rise for prayers. The feeling seems to be deep and earnest. The members of the different Churches, who number over two hundred in my regiment, are greatly revived and aroused to duty. I have never found men listen with more profound attention to the word of God. We seem to be upon the eve of a gracious revival and outpouring of the Holy Spirit, for which we are praying, watching, and struggling."

Rev. W. T. Bennett, chaplain of the Twelfth Tennessee Regiment, Polk's corps, wrote :

" Our regiment is being greatly blessed. We meet from night to night for exhortation, instruction, and prayer. Already there have been upwards of thirty conversions. Most of them have joined the Church. There are yet a large number of inquirers. The moral tone of the regiment seems rapidly changing for the better."

" Rev. T. C. Stanley, to whom we have already referred, reported favorably from the Forty-sixth Georgia Regiment. More than two hundred were enrolled in the Association, and the movement was heartily seconded by the field, staff, and line officers. Colonel Colquitt, Major Spears, Quartermaster Leonard, and others, gave aid and counsel to the chaplain.

" Among the troops at Columbus, Mississippi, a work of much interest began, which was interrupted in its progress by their removal to Jackson. The chaplain laboring there, Rev W. H. Smith, sent forth an earnest call to the home churches for help. ' Brethren ! ministers ! are you asleep ? Do you not hear the cries of your countrymen calling to you from every part of the land ? The soldiers feel their need of salvation, and are crying for the gospel ! And will you withhold it from them ? Awake ! arise ! gird yourselves with the whole armor of God, and come forth " to the help of the Lord, to the help of the Lord against the mighty." ' "

From James's Island, near Charleston, a pious captain of a Georgia regiment writes :

" Since our chaplain came we have had a gracious revival. Many souls have been converted, and many added to the Church. And many of those who had grown cold have been revived, and we now have a warm-hearted, worshipping congregation."

Even under the fire of the Federal batteries the work went on. Rev. Mr. Browning, from Chattanooga, says :

" Yesterday evening, about five o'clock, the enemy began to throw shells across the river again, firing slowly for about an hour ; notwithstanding this, at the usual hour (twilight) we had a very large crowd of anxious listeners at the rude arbor the men had erected for the worship of God. A short discourse was delivered, when the penitents were invited to the altar. Fifty or sixty came forward, earnestly inquiring the way of salvation. Ten of this number were converted and enabled to 'testify of a truth' that Christ was their Saviour. The work is still extending. Each night increases the attendance, the interest, and the number of penitents.

"During a ministry of a fourth of a century I have never witnessed a work so deep, so general, and so successful. It pervades all classes of the army (in this brigade), and elicits the co-operation of all denominations. We know no distinction here. Baptists, Cumberlands, Old Presbyterians, Episcopalians, and Methodists, work together, and rejoice together at the success of our cause."

Mr. B. writes again from the same place: "The glorious work of God is still progressing in this brigade. About one hundred and thirty conversions up to this time. The interest is unabated. From sixty to seventy-five penitents at the altar each night. It is wonderful that for nearly five weeks we have been enabled to continue this work, with but one night's interference from rain and one on picket. Surely the Lord has been good to us. We have been too closely confined to ascertain the state of the work in other brigades, further than that a good work is in progress in some of them, perhaps all. The chaplains of this corps have not met for several weeks. To-morrow is the regular time, but as the enemy shell the town every few days it is doubtful whether we will have a quorum."

"The spreading revival called for all the workers that could be supplied from the home work. Bishop Early, of the Methodist Episcopal Church, South, appointed Rev. J. N. Andrews, of the North Carolina Conference, a missionary to the soldiers in North Carolina, and the Rev. Leonidas Rosser, D. D., of the Virginia Conference, to take the place of Rev. Dr. James E. Evans, whose health had failed, in General Ewell's corps in the Army of Northern Virginia."

"In the retreat of our army from Middle Tennessee one of the soldiers," says Dr. W. A. Mulkey, a surgeon in the army, "was struck by an unexploded shell, the ponderous mass sweeping away his right arm and leaving open the abdominal cavity, its contents falling upon his saddle. In a moment he sank from his horse to the ground, but soon revived, and for two hours talked with as much calmness and sagacity as though he were engaged in a business transaction.

"Soon several of his weeping friends gathered around him expressing their sympathy and sorrow. He thanked them for their manifestations of kindness, but told them that instead of weeping for him they ought to weep over their own condition; for, sad to say, if, even among the professors of his company, there was one who lived fully up to the discharge of his Christian duties, he was not aware of it.

"He said, 'I know that my wound is mortal, and that in a very short time I shall be in eternity; but I die as has been my aim for years—prepared to meet my God.' After exhorting those who stood around him to live the life of Christians, he said, 'Tell my wife to educate my two children and train them up in such a way as to meet me in a better world. Before she hears of my death I shall be with our little Mary in heaven.'

"He then observed that in entering the army he was influenced alone by a sense of duty; that he did not regret the step he had taken; and that while dying he felt he had tried to discharge his duties both as a soldier and Christian.

"Thus died an humble private in the ranks of our cavalry, in whose life were most harmoniously blended the characters of patriot, soldier, and Christian."

From General Bragg's army that veteran soldier of the Cross, Dr. J. B. McFerrin, wrote:

"I have the pleasure of saying that notwithstanding the recent numerous movements of the Army of Tennessee the work of God still progresses. Many have been brought to Christ in various brigades, and wherever the troops remain long enough in one place religious services are observed with great effect. The chaplains and missionaries work with zeal, and have much good fruit. Let our friends at home thank God and take courage. Hundreds of soldiers are coming to Jesus. My health is good, though I feel weak with jaundice. We now have at work in this army as missionaries from our Church: Revs. R. P. Ransom, C. W. Miller, Wellborn Mooney, W. Barr, Brother Allen, and your humble servant."

A lieutenant in Buford's Brigade, Army of Mississippi, wrote:

"A glorious revival of religion has just closed in our brigade for want of more laborers. The fruits of the meeting are a large number of conversions, and a still larger number of earnest penitents. I believe all the mourners are in earnest and fully determined to accomplish their salvation. We have in our regiment a very prosperous Christian Association, which meets every Wednesday night, and a prayer-meeting every night, which is always largely attended by an attentive audience. Having no chaplain or preacher in the regiment, we feel that the work of the Lord devolves upon the lay members; and quite a number of them take a lively interest in the great work—stand up boldly before the people as advocates for the cause of Christ; and oh! how beautiful it is to see the 'young beginner,' boldly, yet tremblingly, pleading with God in behalf of his fellow-soldiers! Pray for us, that the Lord may prosper our efforts to advance his kingdom."

Rev. A. D. McVoy, writing to the *Southern Christian Advocate* from Chattanooga, says:

"In the trenches the dull days are passed without improvement. It is true we have splendid scenery, and these huge mountains enclose a magnificent theatre of war. We can climb the rugged sides of Lookout or Missionary Ridge and look down upon two armies watching each other, hesitating to attack each other in their present positions. But for the past two weeks the clouds have gathered thick and low over us and drenched the country with superabundance of rain. The cold, mud, and rain, have produced great suffering and sickness among the troops; for we have been entirely without shelter in very exposed positions. Up to the present very few flies have been furnished—no tents. In our field hospital we have over three hundred and fifty sick from our brigade (Clayton's)."

But in the midst of these hardships the work of salvation steadily progressed.

"I never saw," says Mr. McVoy, "men who were better prepared to receive religious instruction and advice. In fact, they earnestly desired and greatly appreciated the attention of the chaplains and missionaries in this respect. The dying begged for our prayers and our songs. Every evening we would gather around the wounded and sing and pray with them. Many wounded, who had hitherto led wicked lives, became entirely changed, and by their vows and determinations evinced their purpose to devote themselves to God. Most of those who died in a conscious state gave gratifying and satisfactory testimony of the efficacy of the religion of the Lord Jesus Christ in a dying hour. I witnessed some triumphant deaths—prayer and praise from dying lips. One young Tennesseean, James Scott, of the Thirty-second Tennessee, I think, attracted the attention of all. He continually begged us to sing for him and to pray with him. He earnestly desired to see his mother before he died, which was not permitted, as she was in the enemy's lines, and he died rejoicing in the grace of God. We will long remember Jimmie Scott. An attractive countenance, pleasing manners, he endured his intense suffering with great fortitude; not a murmur or complaint was heard from him, and his strong religious faith sustained him to his dying moment.

"I might go on and describe many scenes like the above to show how our wounded boys die. They know how to fight, and many of them know how to die."

The devotion of the ladies of the South to the sick and wounded soldiers was so earnest, unselfish, and untiring, that it will stand forever as an example of true heroism.

The hospital at which Mr. McVoy served was established at the house of a lady who, with a bleeding heart, gave herself to Christian ministrations with sincere love.

"With one son killed and the other severely wounded, and the care of a large family upon her, her place devastated and ruined, her stock killed up, she ceased not to minister to the wants of our wounded and comfort the suffering, distributing all the milk and eggs she could procure. Many a wounded soldier will long remember Mrs. Thedford, for she was truly a mother to them in their hours of distress and pain. The entire family were untiring in providing for the wounded. Mrs. Durrett, from Tuscaloosa, although she arrived some time after the battle, when most of the wounded had been sent off, contributed greatly by her motherly nursing and attention to relieve and comfort. Not much can be done in the army at present by the chaplains and missionaries until the rainy season shall pass. I was glad to meet the Rev. Mr. Miller, from Kentucky Conference, who has just arrived to commence his operations as a missionary. He was mounted on a beautiful Kentucky horse, fully equipped for the contest."

Rev. C. W. Miller writes of a trip through the South :

"Along the railroads the 'tax in kind' is being deposited in such quantities that we imagine if an old Egyptian could raise his head after a sleep of 3,500 years and look upon the corn, etc., in this land, he would think that it was the seventh year of plenty in the days of Joseph.

"And yet hundreds of homes are saddened by hunger and want. The grasp of extortion's mailed hand and marble heart is upon all this abundance; and hungry orphans and penniless mothers starve in a land of plenty! 'I speak that I do know, and testify that I have seen.' 'If the clouds be full of rain they empty themselves upon the earth,' thus teaching men to pour forth the blessings which Heaven has deposited with them for the poor; but they heed not the lesson, and challenge the ascending cries of orphans, widows, and helpless age, to bring down God's vengeance.

. . . .

"On my return I visited the memorable field of Chickamauga. Everywhere may be seen the marks of an awful struggle. Trees are scarred and perforated by balls of all sizes. Solid oaks and pines, in many instances of enormous size, are shivered by cannon-balls. But the saddest sight there is the long array of Confederate graves. All over that bloody field sleep, in their narrow beds, the deathless heroes of the 19th and 20th of September. No hand of affection plants a rose or trains the evergreen over their grave. Side by side they repose upon the field their valor won. The grand old forest above them stands sentinel at their graves, whilst turbid Chickamauga sings their requiem along its banks.

"We are preaching and laboring for the spiritual good of the soldiers as much as the situation will allow. The troops are in line of battle, and we assemble a regiment or two around their camp-fires at night and speak to them the Word of Life. The soldiers receive gladly the truth, and are always anxious to hear preaching. Never was there an ampler field for ministerial labor. May God give success to the efforts of his servants with these brave men."

We have already stated that the Presbyterian Church sent over fifty laborers into the army. At the session of the Synod of Virginia, Dr. J. Leighton Wilson, Secretary of Missions, gave a sketch of the army revival and urged that his Church prosecute its Army Mission work with increased zeal. Dr. Wilson said :

"There is a state of religion in the Army of Tennessee quite as interesting as that in the Army of Northern Virginia. The Rev. Dr. Palmer says he has never before seen so great a movement. Go where you will, and only let it be known that you are to preach—it hardly makes a difference who the preacher is—and crowds will attend to hear. Dr. W. thought it doubtful whether there had been anything since the days of Pentecost equal to this wonderful work of the Holy Spirit of God in our army. If ever there was a mighty, an imperative call upon us, it is now. If we do not rise to the occasion, our Church will degrade herself before the world and before other denominations." Of his work after the battle of Chickamauga Dr. J. B. McFerrin wrote:

" The revival in the army progressed up to the time of the Chickamauga fight; and even since, notwithstanding the condition of the troops moving to and fro, or engaged in erecting fortifications, the good work in some regiments still goes on. The good accomplished by the ministry of the word will never be appreciated by the Church till the light of eternity shall reveal it. Some of the fruits have already ripened; souls converted in the army have gone to the rest that remains to the people of God. The chaplains and missionaries will have many seals to their min‑istry. Oh! how joyful to think of being the honored instruments of bringing brave souls in the tented field to enlist under the banner of the Captain of our salva‑tion.

"Since I last wrote to you I have witnessed much suffering in the army. The terrible fight at Chickamauga sent many to their long homes, and made cripples for life of hundreds who were not mortally wounded; but, my dear brother, to witness the dying triumph of a Christian soldier gives one a more exalted appreciation of our holy Christianity."

A scene at Jackson, Mississippi, when all day long shot and shell were rained upon the city by the enemy, has been thus described by an officer of the Twenty‑sixth South Carolina Regiment, General Evans' brigade:

"As the night shades were covering the wounded, dying, and dead, our zealous and beloved chaplain, Rev. W. S. Black, of the South Carolina Conference, gave notice to the different commanders of companies that he would like to have a word of prayer with and for them, indicating the centre of the line as the most suitable place. It would have made your heart glad to see those brave and half‑starved soldiers (who had had but one meal a day for several days, and at this time were breaking their fast for the first time that day) throwing down their victuals and flocking to the indicated spot. The chaplain gave out his hymn, and then officers and men united in singing the praises of God. Oh! how we felt to praise and adore Him who had been our preserver through the storms of the day; and when it was said 'Let us pray,' I imagine that I (with many others) had never more cheerfully humbled ourselves in the dust, and lifted our hearts to God in believing prayer. It seemed to be (of all others) the time to pray! The missiles of death, the music of the distant cannon, and the sharp, cracking sound of the sharpshooters' guns, were in striking contrast with the hallelujahs and praises of that devoted band of Christian soldiers. At such a sight angels might gaze with astonishment and admiration. Our blessed Saviour, whose ear is always open to the plaintive cry, drew near and comforted our hearts. Some of us felt that all would be well both in life and death."

Rev. Dr. B. T. Kavanaugh, one of the most efficient laborers in Price's com‑mand, wrote to Dr. W. W. Bennett the following account of the revivals in that corps, on both sides of the Mississippi:

"Among those who came out of Missouri with General Price's army were John R. Bennett (your brother), W. M. Patterson, Nathaniel M. Talbott, and myself, be‑sides Brothers Minchell, Harris, Dryden, and McCary. Subsequently we were joined by Brother E. M. Marvin (now Bishop) and others.

"But little visible effects followed our preaching for the first year or two, while the soldier's life was a novelty; but, after two years hard service, the romance of the soldier's life wore off, and a more sober and serious mood seemed to prevail in our camps.

"The first decided revival that occurred under my observation and ministry was in the State of Mississippi, to which State I had followed General Price's army, while we were encamped near Tupelo. Here we kept up nightly meetings for several weeks in our camp, and there were some forty conversions or more. Brothers Bennett, Harris, and myself held a profitable meeting near Granada, Mississippi, where we had some conversions; but for a length of time the army was kept in motion so constantly that we had but little opportunity for religious services.

"When the army retreated from Big Black into Vicksburg Brothers Bennett, Patterson, and myself, rode together into that devoted city. The regiment to which I was then chaplain had been captured at Big Black, and as I had no duties to perform, I told those brethren that I should make my escape from the city before the enemy's lines were thrown around us, and requested them to join me. Brother Bennett refused, saying he should stick to his men; and Patterson refused to leave Bennett alone.

"I obtained leave of absence and made my escape by riding all night alone, and found myself outside of Grant's line the next morning, and went into Selma, Alabama, where I spent the summer. I requested Bishop Paine to give me a commission as a missionary to General Price's army, which was then in Arkansas. I obtained it, and left the house of Robert A. Baker, my cousin, in Alabama, on the 15th of September, 1863. I succeeded in making the trip, crossing the Mississippi just below Bolivar, swimming my horse, and arrived in General Price's camp early in October.

"My first work was to organize all the chaplains and missionaries into an Association for mutual aid and co-operation. When we went into camp at Camp Bragg, thirty miles west of Camden, we there commenced our work in earnest. Through the winter of 1863-'64 we kept up our meetings in camp, had seats and pulpit prepared, and were successful in having more than one hundred conversions.

"After the battles of Mansfield and Pleasant Hill, in Louisiana, our armies returned to Arkansas and made an encampment at a place called Three Creeks, on the southern line of the State of Arkansas. Here I commenced preaching on the 10th of June, 1864, and continued our meetings until the 10th of September. An extensive revival commenced within a few days after our meeting commenced, and grew in interest and power to the close. We had preaching, beginning at early candle-light—or rather pine-knot fires on stands around the preaching-place. After about ten o'clock at night, the preaching and other exercises at the stand closed; but this was but the beginning of the night's work.

"As soon as dismissed, the young converts gathered in groups of tens and twenties, and went off in companies into the adjoining woods; and taking their friends, penitents seeking religion, with them, they spent the whole night in singing, praying, and praising God. I had lodgings close by the camp at Mrs. Tooke's, a sister of General Buckner, from which, night after night, at all hours, until morning, I could hear the shouts of the new-born souls and the rejoicing of those who were laboring with them for their salvation.

"This meeting continued, after this manner, until a large majority of the two brigades were happily converted. Before we had progressed very far, an effort was made by some of the officers to interrupt us by having ' roll-call' observed at nine o'clock. I went to General Parsons, who was the division commander, and requested him to suspend roll-call at night altogether. He said, ' Doctor, I will do anything in my power to promote this great reformation; for I assure you that since your meetings commenced I have not had a complaint entered against a single man in my army, and the people in the country have not been disturbed by a single soldier.' Roll-call was suspended.

"The people in the country around us became interested in our meetings, and attended them. The remark had been made by many, before our revival meetings commenced, that it was very difficult for a man to be religious in the army; but now it was far more common to hear it said that no one could be very religious unless he belonged to the army.

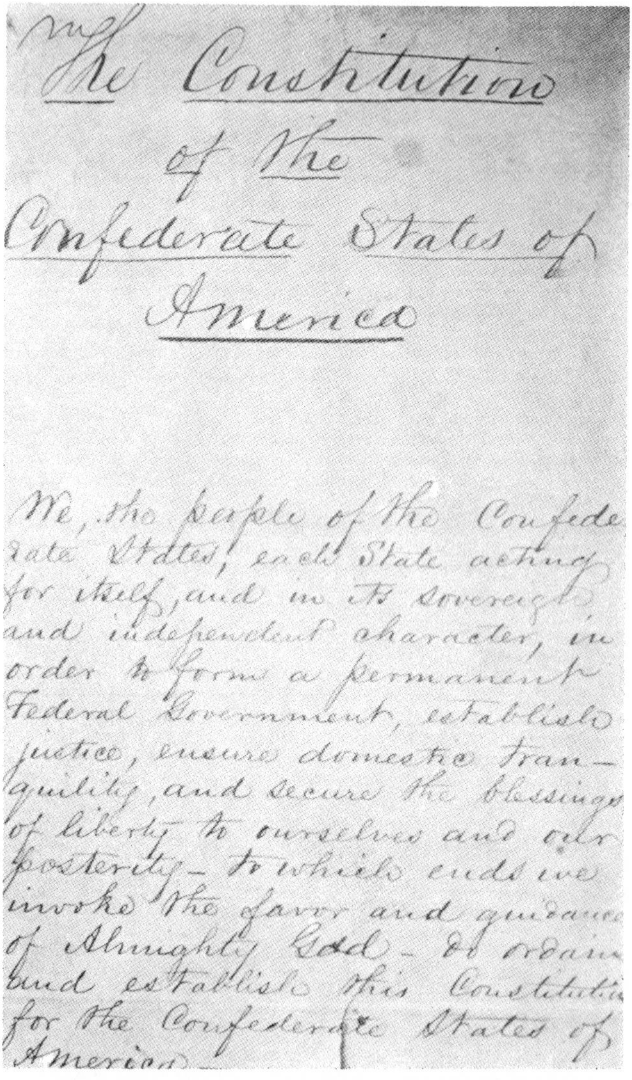

The Constitution
of the
Confederate States of
America

We, the people of the Confede
rate States, each State acting
for itself, and in its sovereign
and independent character, in
order to form a permanent
Federal Government, establish
justice, ensure domestic tran-
quility, and secure the blessings
of liberty to ourselves and our
posterity — to which ends we
invoke the favor and guidance
of Almighty God — do ordain
and establish this Constitution
for the Confederate States of
America —

A FACSIMILE REPRODUCTION OF THE ORIGINAL
DOCUMENT IN THE POSSESSION OF HON.
A. L. HULL, UNIVERSITY OF GEORGIA.

(Facing page 553.)

" Like meetings were held in other camps of the same army at some ten, twenty, and thirty miles from us. Brothers Jewell and Winfield, of Camden, were zealously and constantly engaged in the great work in the encampment near their homes, and were very successful.

" At Three-Creeks I had the efficient aid of Brothers Talbott, Minchell, and Dryden, from Missouri, and a Baptist chaplain from Arkansas, whose name I do not remember.

" To sum up the results of these gracious revivals in the army, we may safely say that at Three-Creeks there were 500 conversions. Under Brothers Winfield and Jewell there were 300. At Camden and Camp Bragg there were 200. Making in all in Arkansas 1,000 souls.

" To show the genuineness of this work of grace upon the lives of these converts, we have to remark that after our camp was broken up, and the army was put upon the march to distant fields, wherever we went into camp but for a night our boys held prayer-meetings every night, greatly to the astonishment of the people in the country who were witnesses of their devotion.

" After the army was disbanded, in riding through the country in Arkansas and Texas, I met with some of our converts, who had returned to their families and parents, and they were still true to their profession and evinced a decidedly firm Christian character.

" The parents of some of those young men have since told me that in place of having the characters and habits of their sons ruined by being in the army they had returned to them as happy Christian men."

Beyond the Mississippi, as Dr. Kavanaugh has already related, his work and that of his co-laborers was greatly blessed of God. In a letter to Bishop Paine, of the Methodist Episcopal Church, South, he gave a report of the revival and its results in two months:

" General Fagan's Arkansas Brigade—Members received into Army church, 209; conversions, 85. General Churchill's Arkansas Brigade—Joined the Army church, 112; converted, 35. General Tappan's Arkansas Brigade—Joined, 245; converted, 40. General Parsons' Mississippi Brigade—Joined, 85; converted, 35. Total members Army church, 651; conversions, 195.

" The Army church was organized before my arrival; gotten up by Brother Marvin (now Bishop Methodist Episcopal Church, South,) aided by others. It has worked well. In Tappan's Brigade the devoted chaplains have built a large log-church, 60 by 30 feet, and are determined to keep up their meetings. I dedicate it next Sunday.

" I am greatly delighted with my work on this side of the river. I have gone into it with all my energy, and indeed over-did my strength the first round; but as the weather is not so favorable for out-door work this round I shall not be able to preach so often. It is truly delightful to see the work prosper in our hands as it has done for the past two months.

" The army here has gone into winter quarters. Every brigade is well provided with log-huts, and with all that is necessary for their comfort while in camp."

The following is the Constitution of the Army church organized by Brother Marvin:

" ARTICLES OF FAITH AND CONSTITUTION OF THE CHURCH OF THE ARMY, TRANS-MISSISSIPPI.

" The Christian men in the army, believing that the habitation of God by his Spirit constitutes the Church, agree, for their edification and for the conversion of their fellow-men, to organize the Church of the Army, with the following articles of faith and constitution :

" I. We believe the Scriptures of the Old and New Testament to be the Word of God, the only rule of faith and obedience.

"II. We believe in one God, the Father, the Son, and the Holy Ghost; the same in substance; equal in power and glory.

"III. We believe in the fall in Adam, the redemption by Christ, and the renewing of the Holy Spirit.

"IV. We believe in justification by faith alone, and therefore receive and rest upon Christ as our only hope.

"V. We believe in the communion of saints, and in the doctrine of eternal rewards and punishments.

"The Christian men who have been baptized, adopting these articles of faith and constitution, in each regiment, shall constitute one church; who shall choose ten officers to take the spiritual oversight of the same.

"Of the officers so elected the chaplain, or one chosen by themselves for that purpose, shall act as Moderator.

"The officers will meet once a month, and oftener if necessary; and in the exercise of discipline will be guided by the direction of Christ. They will keep a record of the names of all the members and the manner in which their ecclesiastical connection with this church is dissolved."

Writing from Kingston, Georgia, February 4, Dr. J. B. McFerrin says:
"We have a good meeting in progress. It has been going forward since Sunday last. Large crowds, mostly soldiers, are in attendance. Many penitents, some conversions, and a few backsliders reclaimed. Last night five asked for membership in the Church of God. We give the applicants choice of churches and receive them into various Christian organizations—different divisions, but one *grand army.*"

From Dalton, February 3, Rev. A. D. McVoy sent good tidings:
"We have a large brigade church built, in which we have been holding services for two weeks. About ten days ago we commenced a series of nightly meetings; at first more on the order of prayer-meetings, but the interest began to increase so rapidly that in three nights we found a revival springing up in our midst. Great crowds gather nightly. We find our church too small. Large numbers are seeking the Lord—forty to fifty every night. The word of God and religious services seem to be better appreciated at present than ever before in this brigade. Men's minds appear to dwell more on religion and the soldiers more concerned about their soul's eternal welfare. The meeting is progressing with increasing interest. Eight joined the different Churches—one, the Presbyterian; two, the Baptist; and five, the Methodist Church. Missionary C. W. Miller is preaching for us at present with great success. A number of ladies from the neighborhood attend, making the scene very home-like.

"The prospect before us is very encouraging. Wickedness and vice seem restrained. Members of the Churches are becoming revived. The Spirit of the Holy One is present and felt. Good resolutions are being formed by many in every regiment. A number are endeavoring to fulfil their promises made to God upon the eve of and during the late battles. We are expecting and praying for great things."

The work of Rev. L. B. Payne in hospitals in Georgia for one month was 27 sermons, distributed 300 papers, 18,000 pages of tracts, and about 32,000 pages of reading matter in books, which he had procured by soliciting donations. Some have been awakened, others professed conversion.

Rev. J. W. Turner, in and near Savannah, Georgia:
"He preached in January 16 sermons, travelled about 400 miles, distributed 177 books, conversed privately with several soldiers on religion, and prayed with 102 soldiers who professed to be seeking Christ."

"Rev. A. M. Thigpen labored in Colquitt's Brigade, near Charleston. In the Twenty-third Georgia, 60 conversions. The meeting was conducted in harmony by Presbyterians, Baptists, and Methodists."

In a letter from General Johnston's army, Rev. J. J. Hutchinson describes a most pleasing scene. He says:

"Ten days ago General Pendleton, a hero of Manassas memory, preached to the soldiers at Dalton. General Johnston and very many other officers were present. On the same day Major-General Stewart, who is an Elder in the Presbyterian Church, assisted in this brigade in the administration of the sacrament of the Lord's Supper. On the same day I preached to General Finley's Brigade, where the general and his staff were present, and where he united audibly with our prayers. General Cleburne, the hero of many battle-fields, treated me with much attention and kindness— had a place prepared for preaching in the centre of his division, where himself and most of his officers were present, and where I was assisted by Brigadier-General Lowry, who sat in the pulpit with me and closed the services of the hour with prayer. I partook of the hospitality of General L. at dinner, and spent several delightful hours in profitable religious conversation. The general is a Baptist preacher, and, like the commander of the division, is a hero of many well-fought battle-fields. He takes great interest in the soldiers' religious welfare, often preaches to them, and feels that the ministry is still his high and holy calling. I wish I had the space to give you more of his interesting life's history, and to speak of this noble and pious officer as he deserves."

The same missionary says: "Never have I seen such a field for preaching the gospel and inculcating religious truth as the Confederate army now presents: ' the fields are white unto the harvest.'"

In many of the hospitals the revival was deep and powerful. The conversion of the sick soldiers and the happy deaths often witnessed made a deep impression on the minds of unbelievers. At one of the large hospitals in Tennessee the following scene was witnessed. At the close of a sermon a call was made for penitents. Among others that came forward and bowed in prayer was a surgeon. At the close of the service he took the chaplain by the hand and said:

"I am a great sinner! I have a pious mother—was brought up in the lap of the Church—studied my profession in N———, travelled and studied in Europe—came home and entered the army a skeptic and scoffer of religion.

"But," said he, "I see such a difference between the death of the believer and the unbeliever, the question has forced itself upon my mind, *What makes the difference?* I took from my trunk the Bible my mother gave me five years ago, making me promise to read it, which, in the excitement of worldly pleasures, I had wholly neglected. The sight of that heavenly book, just as it was when she gave it to me, with the remembrance of her parting kiss, her parting tear, her parting prayer, brought a little fountain of tears from my eyes and a prayer from my swelling heart.

"I read it and found the answer to the question, *What makes the difference?* in that beautiful text, ' Precious in the sight of the Lord is the death *of his saints.*' I came here to-night resolved to accept publicly the invitation of the gospel, which for two days and nights you have so earnestly urged upon this congregation. Oh, that I had submitted my stubborn heart to God years ago! I thank God that I am spared to bear testimony here to-night that Christ is able and willing to save the chief of sinners. Oh," said he, as his eyes filled with tears of joy, "that my dear mother knew that her prodigal son had returned to his Saviour! But she shall know as soon as a letter can reach her. Oh, that I could have told the congregation to-night what a great sinner I am and what a great Saviour I have found."

"Well," said the chaplain, "with your permission I will give a statement of the cause of your awakening, and the state of your feelings of joy and gratitude to-night."

The history of his case was given with thrilling effect.

A writer said of General Johnston's army not long after the opening of the campaign from Dalton to Atlanta:

" It is wonderful to see with what patience our soldiers bear up under trials and hardships. I attribute this in part to the great religious change in our army. Twelve months after this revolution commenced a more ungodly set of men could scarcely be found than the Confederate army. Now the utterance of oaths is seldom, and religious songs and expressions of gratitude to God are heard from every quarter. Our army seems to be impressed with a high sense of an overruling Providence. They have become Christian patriots and have a sacred object to accomplish—an object dearer to them than life."

Rev. L. B. Payne says of the work in General Johnston's army :

" Since my last report, which was for April, we have been in line of battle or on the march nearly every day. Notwithstanding we have had prayer-meetings in the breastworks several times, and I have preached some six or seven times; and, thank God ! the revival still goes on. Souls have been converted every time I have had meetings during our fights. Some twenty-five have joined the Church, and thirty or more have been converted in the last month. Several have professed conversion after they were wounded and come to the infirmary."

Rev. L. R. Redding reported from the lines near Atlanta : "A most gracious revival is in progress in Gist's Brigade. We have built a bush-arbor in rear of our line of battle, where we have services twice a day. Up to the present writing (July 18th) twenty-five have joined the Church, and penitents by the score are found nightly at the altar. In other portions of the army, chaplains and missionaries report sweeping revivals in progress. Thus, notwithstanding the booming of cannon and bursting of shell, the good work goes bravely on."

Rev. J. B. McFerrin wrote from Atlanta to the *Southern Christian Advocate :*

" The other day I rode to the line of battle to see the soldiers as they were resting in a shady wood. To my great joy, a young captain whom I had baptized in his infancy approached me and said : ' I wish to join the Church, and I wish you to give me a certificate ; the Lord has converted me.' I gave him the document with a glad heart. ' Now,' said he, ' if I fall in battle, let my mother know of this transaction. It will afford her great joy.' Oh, it was good to be there and feel that God was in that place.

" Yesterday I baptized Colonel T., of Tennessee. He is a lawyer and a statesman, and has been in the army from the beginning of the struggle. He became interested on the subject of religion months ago, sought Christ, found the pearl of great price, united with the Church, was baptized in the name of the Holy Trinity, and now sends home his letter to have his name recorded with his wife's on the Church register, and I trust it is inscribed in the book of life."

Rev. Neil Gillis, writing to the same paper, from camp on the Chattahoochee, said :

" I never heard or read of anything like the revival at this place. The conversions were powerful, and some of them very remarkable. One man told me that he was converted at the very hour in which his sister was writing him a letter on her knees praying that he might be saved at that moment. Another, who was a backslider, said to me at the altar that his case was hopeless. I tried to encourage him ; discovered hope spring up in his countenance ; then commenced to repeat such promises in the Scriptures as I could remember, and while I repeated : ' Believe on the Lord Jesus Christ, and thou shalt be saved,' he bounded to his feet and began to point others to the Cross with most remarkable success."

Not only in the army at home did our soldiers manifest the deepest interest in religion, but even in the dreary prisons of the North they prayed for and received the Divine blessing. An officer at Johnson's Island writes to the *Southern Presbyterian :*

" This is the last quarter of a long, long twelve-months' confinement. I try to pass my time as profitably as I can. We have preaching regularly every Sabbath, prayer-meetings two or three times a week, and worship in my room every night. We also have a Young Men's Christian Association, Masonic meetings, etc. I attend all of these and fill out the rest of my time by reading the Bible. We have had some precious religious times. There have been about one hundred conversions; colonels, majors, captains, and lieutenants, being among the number."

A lieutenant writes thus: "I am glad to state that I am a better man than when you saw me last. There are about two thousand officers here, and I never have seen so great a change in the morals of any set of men as has been here in the last four months."

The incidents of the campaign for this season are rich in spiritual fruits. In hospital and on the open field the Christian soldiers met death bravely. Said a young Kentuckian to a minister who asked him, "Do you think you will recover?" "No," said he, "tell my brother that I died in a holy cause, and am ready to meet God." It is now, in times of great peace, a matter of wonder how men could calmly worship under the fire of formidable batteries. "Late one afternoon," says Rev. C. W. Miller, writing of the scenes on the retreat from Dalton, "the firing along the line had lulled, and the writer called the brigade together for worship. A chapter from the Holy Book had been read, a song sung, and several fervent prayers offered. Presently, while a soldier was praying, and all were devoutly kneeling before God, a distant report as of the discharge of artillery was heard; then in an instant *whirr, whirr, whirr—boom!* went a 32-pound shell just above our heads, and buried its fragments in the hillside a little beyond us. But the 'devout soldier' prayed on. Another and another shell *shrieked* above us, but the prayer was regularly finished, the preacher pronounced the benediction, and the men went to their *casemates*, as they called their holes in the ground. I have related this incident to show you how indifferent men become to danger under the indurating influence of war."

Dr. Bennett gives this interesting statement:

"Let us now for a moment leave these noble Christian soldiers, in their happy meetings under the fire of musketry and cannon, and look in upon their comrades who languished in Northern prisons. We have before us a letter, written from Fort Delaware to the *Christian Observer*, giving an account of a revival among the Confederate officers there confined. They had in the morning at half-past nine an 'inquirer's prayer-meeting;' at 12 M. 'the professor's prayer-meeting, where the Church-members pray for each other, leading the meeting in turn.'

"It was a new business to me," says the writer, "when my turn came, but you must know I am preparing for the work and must learn. God's help enabled me to get along tolerably well. He always fits the instrument for his work.

"We get a mail daily, morning papers at noon, and boxes of nick-nacks come promptly when our friends start them. All the officers here (and there are about 600) seem to be in good health and spirits. The general health of all on the Island is good, considering the number of privates (6,000) confined here. All seem to enjoy themselves; and, altogether, there are worse prisons than Fort Delaware. We have a large lot to play in. We have here in our barracks three ministers—Rev. Dr. Handy, of the Presbyterian Church of Portsmouth, Virginia; and Captain Harris, of Georgia, and Captain Samford, of Texas, local Methodist preachers. A revival of religion has been in progress for two weeks—17 converts, many backsliders reclaimed, and a refreshing season to old professors, numbering 150 reported names. These are among the results of the revival."

Rev. Dr. Kavanaugh reports over 500 conversions in two brigades in the Southwest. He says in his report:

"Wicked men come into the congregation, or into the outskirts of it, and are suddenly stricken down and fall to the earth, and remain for hours speechless and apparently unconscious. Some of their friends became alarmed for them and spoke of running for the doctor. But old Brother Talbott happened to be experienced enough to know something about such cases, and told the bystanders to give themselves no uneasiness, for it would all come out right' in the end. Generally they would lie about two hours, and then rise shouting the praises of God their Saviour. There have been several cases of this kind.

"All the conversions are sound, clear and powerful. There is no such thing as urging the mourner to believe he 'has received the blessing;' but each is able to tell, for himself, what great things God has done for him. Conversions take place at all hours through the day and night. Many are converted in the woods—sometimes alone, and sometimes with a friend or two. There is no abatement in the work as yet, but our meetings are kept up to a late hour every night. Off at a little distance you can hear singing, praising, and praying, all going on at various points throughout the two brigades, very much resembling a very large camp-meeting in olden times, when there was much more zeal and power manifested than is now known in like meetings."

At Atlanta the Confederates, now commanded by General Hood, held that city against the heavy battalions of General Sherman. The fights along the line were frequent and deadly, but the religious enthusiasm of the soldiers was undiminished. "They are not afraid of death," writes a devoted chaplain, A. D. McVoy, "and are ready to die when God calls them."

Among those brought in wounded from the front lines there were many Christians whose deaths were morally grand.

"I witnessed," says Mr. McVoy, "the passing away of a Louisianian of Gibson's Brigade, Fourth Louisiana, the other day. Seldom have I seen a stronger Christian faith, a firmer reliance on God, and a clearer assurance of salvation in a dying hour. He was cruelly lacerated by a piece of shell that had ploughed deeply across his right side, and his sufferings were intense and unremitted. Still his mind was fixed upon God. 'Chaplain,' said he to me, 'I am dying. I have done my duty. I wish I could be spared to see victory secured to my brave comrades, but it is the will of God, and I cheerfully submit. I am suffering a thousand deaths, but when I think upon the sufferings of my Saviour, that he endured ten thousands more than I for the salvation of my soul, my sufferings are nothing.' Then he would fervently pray, and besought me to pray with him, which I did. This comforted him greatly, so that he almost shouted for joy. 'Chaplain,' said he, 'I have three motherless children in Louisiana, and could I only gaze once more upon them, could I but fold them to my breast, could I but kiss them good-bye, I would die contented; but God's will be done. I commit them into the hands of my Heavenly Father. I want them instructed to know and serve God that they may meet me in heaven.'

"One of his companions, who had brought him out of the trenches, was kneeling over him and weeping bitterly. 'Chaplain,' said the dying soldier, 'this is the best friend I have in the army; pray for him that he may meet me in heaven.'

"When asked what word he desired to leave with his company, he said, 'Tell them to be better boys. Some of them are reckless and wicked. Tell them to repent, serve God, be good soldiers, and meet me in heaven.'

"When asked how he felt in view of death, he said, 'I have no fears; all is clear. Jesus died for me; I know He will save me. Blessed be the Lord.' His colonel passing by, came to his side and said, 'Is this you, Dawson? I am sorry to find you so dreadfully wounded.' 'Yes, Colonel, I am dying, but I am going home to heaven. I have tried to do my duty. It is God's will, and I cheerfully give myself up a sacrifice on the altar of my country.'

"He then committed himself to God and lingered for some hours, continually praying and praising God, when he died the glorious death of a brave Christian soldier."

Writing further of the glorious work the same faithful laborer says:

" Many are joining the Church. While exhorting a large group of soldiers a few nights since to come to Christ a young man rushed forward and threw his arms around my neck, crying out, ' I have found Jesus, I have found Jesus! Oh, how good my Saviour is! Bless the Lord, O my soul!' This was a very affecting scene, and induced many to think seriously concerning their souls.

" Thus the work of God is going on amid the cannon's roar, the fatiguing monotony of the trenches, and the heroic movements of the picket line. Religion is infusing a spirit of fortitude, endurance, and determination, into the hearts of the soldiers that no hardship, no suffering, can undermine or break down."

Bishop Lay, of the P. E. Church, in a letter to a relative in Charleston, South Carolina, describes a scene of the deepest interest in the same army. The Bishop was earnestly laboring as a missionary in the Georgia army. He says:

" Yesterday in Strahl's Brigade, I preached and confirmed nine persons. Last night we had a very solemn service in General Hood's room, some forty persons, chiefly generals and staff officers, being present. I confirmed General Hood and one of his aids, Captain Gordon, of Savannah, and a young lieutenant from Arkansas. The service was animated, the praying good. Shells exploded near by all the time. General Hood, unable to kneel, supported himself on his crutch and staff, and with bowed head received the benediction. Next Sunday I am to administer the communion at head-quarters. To-night ten or twelve are to be confirmed in Clayton's Division. The enemy there are within two hundred and fifty yards of our line, and the firing is very constant. I fear it may be hard to get the men together. I wish that you could have been present last night, and have seen that company down, all upon bended knee. The reverence was so marked that one could not fail to thank God that He has put such a spirit into the hearts of our leaders."

Dr. McFerrin writes from the Georgia army:

" Meetings have been frequently held when the soldiers were in line of battle. The religious interest I think has not at all abated since our great revival in the winter and spring. Hundreds in many parts of the army are seeking the fellowship of Christians by uniting with the Church of the Lord Jesus Christ."

" Asa Hartz," a gallant and gifted Confederate officer, thus writes from the Federal prison on Johnson's Island:

" We vary our monotony with an occasional exchange. May I tell you what I mean by that? Well, it is a simple ceremony. God help us! The 'exchanged' is placed on a small wagon drawn by one horse, his friends form a line in the rear, and the procession moves; then passing through the gate, it winds its way slowly round the prison-walls to a little grove north of the enclosure; the 'exchange' is taken out of the wagon and lowered into the earth—a prayer—an exhortation—a spade—a head-board—a mound of fresh sod—and the friends return to prison again —and that's all of it. Our friend is ' exchanged; ' a grave attests the fact to mortal eyes, and one of God's angels has recorded the 'exchange' in the book above. Time and the elements will soon smooth down the little hillock which marks his lonely bed, but invisible friends will hover around it till the dawn of that great day when all the armies shall be marshalled into line again—when the wars of time shall cease and the great eternity of peace shall commence."

I had hoped to receive letters from a number of chaplains and missionaries who served in the other armies of the Confederacy, and sent letters of request to many of them, but the following are all that I have been able to secure:

Letter from Rev. A. S. Worrell (Baptist Chaplain).

Dr. Worrell was one of the most useful workers in the Army of Tennessee, and I am glad to give even the brief sketch he has been able to send from his sick-bed.

" REV. J. WM. JONES, D. D.

" *My Dear Brother:* With your request to forward to you some reminiscences of the revivals in the Army of Tennessee, during our late civil war, I now attempt to comply. And since you wish me to tell of things that came within my own knowledge, I shall, of necessity, have to speak of matters ' *Quorum pars fui*,' if not '*pars magna*.' Let the charitable reader receive *this* as my apology for any seeming egotism that may crop out in this communication.

" I connected myself with the Army of Tennessee in the summer of 1862, when preparations were being made to march into Kentucky. Up to this time there had been very little religious interest in this army. The war spirit had absorbed well nigh every other interest. Chaplains were few, and not in great demand.

" Early in 1862 I received ' authority ' from the War Department at Richmond, Virginia, to ' raise a regiment for the service.' When this fact became known, a number of companies met at ' Big Shanty,' near Marietta, Georgia, the drill camp for volunteers, and formed on my name and authority. This occurred without any effort on my part. At this point matters began to look serious. What could I do with a regiment of soldiers ? I had never studied military tactics for an hour ; and all my study had been to make men *live*, not to kill them. After earnest prayer, I decided that I was already ' engaged in a great work, and could not come down,' and that others might have all the military honors, while I would be content to preach the gospel. I have never regretted that decision.

" The command to which I was attached belonged to General E. Kirby Smith's Corps, which formed the right wing of General Bragg's invading force. Leaving Knoxville, we crossed the Cumberland Mountain, and entered 'the civilized part of Kentucky ' at ' Big Hill.' Our advance division swept everything before it, so that our brigade and one or two others took no part in the battles, or rather skirmishes, which opened the way to the heart of the famous ' Blue Grass Region' —'the country of Kings,' as I then thought; nor have I materially modified my view of it since.

" The almost continuous marching and countermarching of our troops left little for the chaplains to do save to administer to the wants of the sick, and to keep up with their commands.

" While our commanding general was engaged in inaugurating a governor for the State of Kentucky, the Federal general was massing his troops at different points with the view of cutting off his retreat south. These movements resulted in the battle at Perryville, under auspices singularly unfavorable to our forces. After this battle, General Bragg began his retreat, and within a week or such a matter we were temporarily beyond the enemy's reach ; and our army next concentrated at Murfreesboro, Tennessee.

" During the Kentucky campaign, I conceived the idea of publishing a paper designed especially for the soldiers; repairing to Atlanta, I made arrangements for issuing it, and called it *The Soldier's Friend*. The paper was designed to elevate its readers, and especially to benefit them religiously. Few issues of the paper were made till after the bloody battle of Murfreesboro had been fought, and our army had gone into winter-quarters at and near Tulahoma. Many thousands of the paper were scattered among the troops during this winter of 1863, when for the first time in the history of this army a genuine and very general revival of religion prevailed among our soldiers. In this glorious work the writer was permitted to take part through the instrumentality of his paper only ; his time being occupied in editorial work and in preaching and administering to the sick and wounded in the hospitals in Atlanta. It was greatly to my advantage in my labors for the soldiers that I had a chaplain's commission without ' assignment' to any particular place or command. It served me as a passport to any point within the limits of the Confederacy. This favor was procured through the influence of my highly esteemed friend, General John B. Gordon.

" As the spring of 1863 approached, and the Union forces began to concentrate

GENERAL M. P. LOWRY, C. S. A.
(Of Mississippi.)

(Facing page 560.)

at different points in Tennessee, General Bragg retreated into North Georgia, where, a few months later, the terrible battle of Chickamauga was fought. Speaking of this battle, General James A. Garfield said to the writer, about the winter of 1872, as we were en route to California, that the Confederate victory, in the battle of Chickamauga, was most complete, and that, if a vigorous pursuit had been made by the Confederates, the Union army could have easily been captured. He said, also, that he, though only an adjutant-general, checked a portion of the retreating soldiers, which served to arrest the panic, and make it possible to resist their pursuers. General Bragg was severely censured by some for not pressing the pursuit; but what troops, after such a battle, could be expected to pursue even a vanquished foe!

"Our army having taken position on 'Missionary Ridge' and places in line therewith, our faithful chaplains again began their work. Before the revival spirit became general, however, our army was driven from their position, and went into winter-quarters at Dalton, Georgia. Here it was that General Joseph E. Johnston superseded General Bragg in command of the army. Under their new general the soldiers, much discouraged at their defeat at Missionary Ridge, began to take heart again. It was at Dalton that *the* great revival took place. Chaplains, missionaries, and visiting pastors from the churches seemed intent on preaching the gospel to this entire army; and, no doubt, a large army was here recruited for the service of King Immanuel.

"With the aid of Rev. W. H. Roberts, of Georgia, Dr. Samuel Henderson, of Alabama, and Brigadier-General M. P. Lowry, of Cleburne's Division, the writer held an interesting meeting in the Baptist house of worship in Dalton. General Lowry preached but once, and from the text: 'Behold! I stand at the door, and knock: if any man hear my voice, and open unto me, I will come in, and sup with him, and he with me.' The sermon was clear, pointed, strong, and persuasive; and, at its close, many came forward for prayer and instruction. How many were converted that night I do not know; but I believe there were many. An incident occurred during the after part of the meeting that I shall never forget. I think it was at the close of a prayer, when a young man, with face all radiant, arose, and sang what was to me a new song; seemingly forgetful of all around him, and wholly engaged in loving, adoring praise to his *present* Redeemer. That song echoed and re-echoed in my soul so long, that I believe I could even now sing it.

"I baptized as a result of this series of meetings, in a creek north of Dalton, a large number of professed believers; of whom one, William Jayne, afterwards became a useful minister of the gospel; and is still laboring, I think, in his native State, Kentucky.

"The troops encamped in the town were now ordered to the front; and this left us without a congregation.

"Wishing to find some other troops to whom I might preach before 'the opening of the campaign of 1864,' I went some two or three miles south-east of Dalton, where I found a battalion of artillery, commanded by Major Johnston, a kinsman of our commanding general. This command, if I remember correctly, had been almost entirely neglected; having heard few sermons during their whole previous term of service. I preached to them several times, and much interest was manifested by the large crowds that rushed forward for prayer at the close of each sermon. I hope to meet a number from that command in that blessed region where wars will be known no more.

"An interesting incident occurred at the close of one of our meetings. A soldier informed me that there was a Jew belonging to his command, who desired that I should occupy his bed that night. I excused myself by telling the soldier that I had comfortable lodgings in Major Johnston's tent, and that I could not afford to rob the generous-hearted Jew of his bed. It was insisted, however, that I should accept the offer, as the Jew wished to converse with me on the subject of religion. I

36

yielded, and went into the log-hut which a large mess of soldiers had built for their accommodation; and there I was introduced to Mr. Magnus, of Rome, Georgia, I think. I found him to be a very intelligent and affable gentleman, and intent on making his Gentile guest comfortable that night. His was the most costly as well as the most comfortable bed I ever found in the army.

" The next morning he conducted me aside, and said he wished to talk to me on the subject of religion. ' I believe,' said he, ' in the necessity of *an* atonement. I believe in *a* Messiah who is to make this atonement. Will this suffice?' I told him that this would not answer; that he must believe in *the* Messiah already come, even Jesus of Nazareth; and that he must accept the atonement wrought by Him on the cross.

" 'Ah!' he exclaimed; ' I was taught from childhood to *hate* Jesus of Nazareth, and to regard Him as an impostor! It is so hard to rise above such influences! Yet, if Jesus *is* the Messiah, I wish to know it, that I may believe in Him, and receive the benefit of His death. Have you any special argument that you can give me in proof that Jesus of Nazareth *was* the true Messiah?'

" On hearing this, my heart ascended to God for help, and never were arguments furnished to me so readily. I seemed to remove every objection from his mind, and left him in the hands of Infinite Mercy, strongly impressed that the atonement would avail for him not many days hence.

" Soon after this conversation closed, an order was issued for the battalion to pre-pare to move at once. I learned afterwards that dear Magnus had received a severe wound from which he would probably die. General Sherman, the commander of the Union forces, now began to manœuvre his troops with the view of locating General Johnston's lines; and at this time our general issued an order for the chaplains to make no further appointments for preaching. The opening of this ever memorable campaign put an end to the revival spirit, and chaplains from this time to the fall of Atlanta could do little more than administer, individually, to the wants of the sick and wounded. Prominent among the workers known to me were Revs. G. W. Given, S. C. Hearn, W. H. Roberts, and others.

" The writer meanwhile did what he could in the hospitals and on ' Relief Committees,' noting with painful solicitude the fact that the wily Sherman was gradually manœuvring our forces from every strong position that they had assumed. It appeared to many of General Johnston's most ardent admirers that he should have fought the enemy in detail (as he had opportunity of doing) before they crossed the Ostanaula River, or, at any rate, before they crossed the Etowah. He seemed never to be able to summon the courage to hazard a Waterloo defeat. Possibly this was best, since it may have spared to their families many soldiers who else might have fallen on the field of battle without materially benefiting the cause dear to Southern hearts. Certain it is that my love and unbounded admiration for General Johnston made it difficult for me to see any error in his movements.

" An incident occurred at Marietta, Georgia, when the two armies were a few miles north-west of this city, which I beg the privilege of relating. A young man was brought to the depot very seriously wounded in the head. He was attended by a faithful old body-servant. The poor negro seemed to be almost heart-broken at the calamity that had befallen his young master. I asked him the young man's name. He said it was ' Vincent, from Louisiana.' Looking at the young man, I recognized him as formerly a student in Union University, Murfreesboro, Tennessee, when the writer taught in that institution of learning. Being well acquainted with the surgeon in charge, I managed to have the young man's wound dressed with but little delay, and himself assigned to comfortable quarters. Uncle ' Sam '—for that was the servant's name—stayed by the young man and waited on him with maternal tenderness.

" About this time a strange preacher from North Alabama came into town, having endured many dangers and hardships in his escape through 'the Yankee lines.' This preacher called to see young Vincent, who begged the former to pray for him. Upon this the minister retired from the room in haste, and went up and down the city to borrow a prayer book! This incident caused no little amusement among the chaplains and others present.

"Young Vincent was sent to Atlanta, and thence to other hospitals, and, under the faithful nursing of dear 'Uncle Sam,' he recovered. In August of 1865, when the writer and his family and another gentleman and his wife were travelling from Texas into the interior of Louisiana, about midway between Marshall and Shreveport, we stopped, about 9 o'clock at night, at a respectable farm-house, and asked to stay all night. Especially did we plead for the ladies to have places. The old gentleman said: 'Yes, of course, the *ladies* must have a place, and I will do the best I can for you gentlemen. Uncle Sam, take that baggage into the house, and see that these horses are fed. Come in, gentlemen.'

"'Will you please tell me your name, sir?' said I.

"'Vincent, sir,' was the reply.

"'I once knew a young man in Union University, Tennessee, by that name.

"'My son,' said the old gentleman, 'attended that school at such a time.'

"'I suppose he is dead,' I continued.

"'Oh, no; he is living.'

"'Where,' I asked, 'is Uncle Sam?'

"'He will be here directly.'

"When Uncle Sam came in, and was made to recognize me, we had a joyous meeting indeed! He ascribed the life of his young master to the prompt care I had bestowed upon him when he was wounded, and I ascribed his recovery to the excellent nursing of the faithful old servant. Mr. Vincent's hospitality and cordiality after this knew no bounds.

"With great respect, I am

"Your brother in Christ,

PARIS, TEXAS, February 12, 1888. "A. S. WORRELL."

SKETCH OF THE WORK IN THE ARMY OF TENNESSEE.

By Rev. S. M. Cherry, Chaplain and Distributing Agent of Religious Reading of the Methodist Episcopal Church, South.

I had long known of Rev. S. M. Cherry as one of the most active and efficient workers in the Army of Tennessee, and am glad to present the following from his pen:

"REV. J. WILLIAM JONES, D. D.

"*My Dear Brother:* In response to your request I furnish you such items as I can for your Appendix to 'Christ in the Camp,' from the ARMY OF TENNESSEE.

"I was pastor of the Methodist Church in Winchester, Tennessee, in 1860-61. The First Tennessee Regiment, Confederate States Army, was organized in that place in April, 1861. Colonel Peter Turner, now the senior Supreme Judge of Tennessee, was in command. It was the first regiment from Tennessee to go to Virginia early in May. Many of the soldiers of that gallant command were from the counties where I had preached the first, second and third years, and the sixth year of my itinerant life. I was with the young men much during the few days they remained in Winchester, and as they had no chaplain then, I tendered my services to act in that capacity soon after they reached Virginia. But fighting, not preaching, was the chief concern of our soldiers at that time, and my services were not accepted. The State troops were ordered to rendezvous near Winchester, and I had the privilege of visiting their camps and preaching to the soldiers in May and June, till they were ordered to Kentucky. In July, 1861, I entered the army as a member of an independent company of riflemen from Nashville and other towns of our State. My object was to minister to the soldiers in spiritual things, but I remained a private until the organization of the Fourth Tennessee Regiment, Confederate States Army, some weeks after we went into camp at Knoxville, East Tennessee. I was then elected chaplain. Colonel Wm. M. Churchwell was in command of the regiment, and General F. R. Zollicoffer of the brigade. I began work at once by preaching as often as opportunities offered, and holding prayer meetings from tent to tent, and visiting the sick at the hospitals. Measles prevailed; many soldiers contracted the disease; the hospital provision was very deficient, and the mortality was great.

"Our brigade was composed of the Fifteenth Mississippi, Eleventh and Twentieth Tennessee State troops, and Fourth Tennessee Confederate. I remember no chaplain of the Mississippi regiment, but each of the Tennessee regiments had chaplains —Rev. F. E. Pitts, D. D., Eleventh, Rev. John A. Edmondson, Twentieth; and Rev. P. G. Jamison and Rev. J. G. Bolton were privates in the Eleventh Tennessee, and while doing good service as soldiers, they were 'instant in season and out of season' as soldiers of the Cross, very few in the army proving more faithful throughout the entire war than did John G. Bolton, who won the confidence of his comrades and kept it for four years because of his fidelity to Christ and his country.

"The chaplains of the Eleventh and Twentieth I think concluded the camp was not the place for them as chaplains, and Dr. Pitts returned home and raised a regiment, of which he took the command, and Rev. J. A. Edmondson resigned and returned home. The five preachers mentioned, and Rev. Geo. D. Guiner, Lieutenant Fourth Tennessee, were members of the Tennessee Conference.

"Our brigade marched into Eastern Kentucky under General Zollicoffer, who was unfortunate in both encounters under his command, and the noble-hearted man lost his life the first year of the war at Fishing Creek, Kentucky. The Fourth and Eleventh Tennessee Regiments were ordered to Cumberland Gap, where we established comfortable winter quarters. The soldiers did not take interest enough in religious services to prepare a place of public worship. But whenever the weather was at all favorable we had service for all who were disposed to attend. Very few of the commissioned officers were religious. The large proportion of the soldiers were wicked and many were reckless. For more than a year very few manifested any desire to become Christians save the sick or wounded. So indifferent were the soldiers that many chaplains very naturally concluded that the army was not a field for ministerial success or usefulness, and the second year of the war found many regiments and some brigades in our army without chaplains. I was alone a portion of the time at Cumberland Gap, and my congregations were generally small; yet I preached as regularly as at all practicable to any and all soldiers who came that way, infantry, cavalry and artillery, and looked very carefully after the sick and dying.

"After the battle at Fishing Creek, Kentucky, the Fifteenth Mississippi and Twentieth Tennessee Regiments were transferred from our brigade, which was commanded by General Stevenson, of Virginia. But the Thirty-sixth Tennessee and the Twenty-ninth North Carolina Regiments supplied their place. I was glad to find Rev. E. C. Wexler, of the Holston Conference, a man of ability, chaplain of the latter or the Twenty-ninth North Carolina Regiment. Our association for the ensuing months of 1862 were very intimate, and I found him a very true and faithful servant of God. He died during the war. Colonel Vance, of the Twenty-ninth North Carolina Regiment, was one of the most exemplary Christian soldiers in camp. He took great interest in camp worship and did much to aid his chaplain and others who labored for the salvation of the soldiers. He has served his State in Congress since the war, and has recently published a book of poems. The only time during the war that I knew not that it was Sunday till late in the day was after the battle of Perryville, Kentucky. We were retreating from that State and had crossed Dix's River and encamped for the soldiers to cook their rations. The day was raw and damp. Colonel Robert Vance came to me and asked why we were not arranging for service. I asked him why should we, and he said it was Sunday. Chaplain Wexler and I preached during the day, regardless of the weather.

Rev. Lieutenant Parker, of the North Carolina Conference, was a member of the Twenty-ninth North Carolina Regiment, and a very nice Christian officer, rendering efficient aid to the chaplains. Sergeant Guerra, an exhorter in the Thirty-sixth Tennessee, I found an active, earnest Christian, ready and willing to work for his Lord, at any time, place, and in any way. He was a Spaniard.

"My daily journals for 1862–65 are before me, and I shall give your readers such extracts as I think may be of interest to them.

"Cumberland Gap, February 20, 1862. Frank Wallace, quite a youth, came to my quarters to talk with me about seeking salvation.

"March 22. A severe skirmish west of the Gap. Benjamin Grisham, Thirty-sixth Tennessee Regiment, mortally wounded. As he was carried back to the surgeon, I saw a Testament in his side-pocket, and he was praying earnestly, but said he was not prepared to die, and begged us to write his friends to prepare for death.

"Sunday, March 30. Preached at 11 A. M. to the Fourth, and in the P. M. to Thirty-sixth, and at night to the Eleventh Tennessee Regiments. Congregations larger and more serious than heretofore.

"April 6. Talked to Mr. C., a man of intelligence and varied information, who has done office-work in Washington City, and has the brain for a general, but is a poor private soldier, for he is a great slave to whiskey, and is often in the guard-house for drunkenness. He is recovering from a debauch, and tells me that he is terribly haunted by his wife. I presume his dissipation has broken her heart. Whiskey is a great curse to our soldiers, and especially the officers, who can secure it more readily than the privates. Preached to our regiment in the A. M., and Rain's regiment in the P. M. Soldiers attentive to the word.

"April 8. Visited our sick at the hospital at Tazewell; found forty-two in the wards; preached for them at night.

"April 11. Brother Box, of Company C, Fourth Tennessee, is very low. Will probably die, but he assures me that all is right, and he is not afraid of the future.

"Sunday, April 27. At 11 A. M. preached to the Fourth Tennessee. In the afternoon, by invitation of J. Courtney Brown, went to the top of the mountain peak, and preached for the Third Georgia Battalion.

"Brother Brown was a private soldier of Yeizer's Battery of Artillery, from near Rome, Georgia. A man of superior culture and devout piety; I think one of the noblest Christian gentlemen I met in the army. When the war began he was engaged in teaching near Rome, and was preparing for the ministry of the Baptist Church, if I mistake not. If he yet lives, I doubt not he has attained to eminence and usefulness in his church. We often took sweet counsel together, and I was much benefited by a prayer-meeting he conducted on the mountain spurs at Cumberland Gap. No other man was more helpful to me in army work in 1862 than was the gifted and faithful J. Courtney Brown.

"Sunday, May 4, 1862. Preached to-day on the peak south of the Gap, at the corner-stone of Virginia, Kentucky, and Tennessee. My congregation was seated in the three States: the Georgians in Kentucky, the Alabamians in Tennessee, and the Tennesseeans in Virginia. I used the corner-stone as a book-board for Bible and hymn-book. Text: Psalms xlii. 11.—'Some of us are neither cast down nor disquieted. Our hope is in God, and we praise him on the mountain top.'

"May 11. Preached for the Third Georgia Battalion. Dr. Chapman, the assist-

566   APPENDIX.

ant-surgeon, is quite sick, but he enjoys religion. Had preached on Saturday and Sunday at Willis Chapel, in Lee county, Virginia. Large, serious congregation on Sunday. "May 14. A very pleasant prayer-meeting on the mountain peak with the Georgians at twilight. "May 18. Owing to rain, did not preach to our regiment in A. M., but did in the P. M., but rained us out at Third Georgia at night. "Monday, May 19. Preached to-night for Third Georgia Battalion. "By request of Captain McCullam, Company G, Forty-second Georgia, preached for that regiment on the night of May 22. Much pleased with the captain and that regiment. "June 1. Preached at 8.30 A. M. at the corner-stone, and at 11 A. M. to the Twenty-ninth North Carolina, and in the afternoon heard Chaplain Quigg of the Forty-second Georgia. Secured sixty-seven subscribers for *The Weekly Message*, a holiness paper published by Mrs. Bumpass, of Greensboro, North Carolina. "Wednesday night, June 4. Preached for Third Georgia Battalion. "On the night of the 6th preached for Yeizer's Battery, and received Mr. John D. Baker, of Rome, Georgia, into the church. "Sunday, June 8. Heard a sermon by Chaplain Lane of the Thirtieth Alabama, and then preached for the Eleventh Tennessee. Raised sixty-three subscribers for the *Message* in the two regiments. I desire the circulation of all the religious papers possible in our army. At night I visited our sick at the hospital at Tazewell, and saw a priest adminster the rite of extreme unction to a poor son of Erin, who was evidently near death's door. If the man was truly penitent and trusted in Christ for salvation, who doubts the grace of God was given in the pardon of his sins? I slept with the priest, Father Borgraph, the next night. "June 10. I attended the funeral of General Robert Hatton at the Methodist church in Knoxville. He fell at the front of his command, while charging a battery at the battle of Chickahominy, in Virginia, a few days ago. The general was a member of our Church, and his father I had long known as a worthy minister of the Tennessee Conference. His widow is one of the most devout women I know. She has been abundant in good works. For eight years she was State Librarian. 'Her children rise up and call her blessed.' "Having been sick for some time, I was granted leave of absence for twenty days, and I took advantage of my short furlough to visit the Army of Mississippi, which I found encamped at Tupelo, Mississippi. · There I met the following members of our Conference: Rev. Dr. F. S. Petway, Revs. J. H. Strayhorn, John Goal, J. W. Johnson, J. W. Cullom, J. D. Barbee, John A. Thompson, William H. Browning, J. B. Allison, Charles Dunham, and A. W. Smith, the latter just recovering from a shot through the lungs while bearing a comrade from the field of conflict. He was made major for his gallantry, but he filled the office for a while, and wisely resigned in order to become chaplain of a brigade; and he continued most earnest in his labors of love till the close of the war, and returned to Tennessee, and after several years' service in various stations, he finally died from the effects of his army wound, the most popular pastor ever at Columbia, Tennessee, and served the Church for a longer period there than any member of our Conference. "Lieutenant Charles Dunham, a most worthy young minister, fell in battle during the war. "I also visited Rev. Dr. D. C. Kelley, lieutenant-colonel of Forrest's renowned regiment of cavalry. The doctor was quite sick at Aberdeen. His record for gallantry is known and read of many, and needs no mention. These brethren, and others whose names are not noted here, were all active and abundant in labors for Christ in the camp at Tupelo, Mississippi, in June, 1862. "During my stay with my brethren of the Army of Mississippi I had the privilege

APPENDIX. 567

of preaching to the soldiers, nightly, of the following commands: Fifth, Eighth, Seventeenth, Twenty-fourth, Twenty-fifth, and Thirty-seventh Tennessee, and Sixteenth Alabama Regiments. On the 21st of June, while visiting the sick of the Twenty-fourth Tennessee Regiment, I found a young soldier dying, far from his home. I read the Fifty-first Psalm, and, while telling him of Christ, the Saviour of sinners, he made a happy profession of faith and was baptized, and exhorted his comrades to make ready for death. This army is well supplied now with preachers. I returned as I came, *via* Mobile, Montgomery, Atlanta, and Chattanooga, preaching at the latter place.

"On my return to East Tennessee, July 3, 1862, I found our troops at Bean's Station, having evacuated Cumberland Gap in my absence. I gave our soldiers a talk on the 4th, chiefly incidents of my visit to our friends in the Department of Mississippi. At night preached to a large congregation.

"Sunday, July 6. 9.30 A. M. had a good attendance of the Fourth Tennessee at preaching. At 4 P. M. preached to a large congregation of the Third Georgia. Excellent service. A youth of that command came to speak with me alone. He seemed very serious. He wished to know if one who had been converted fell into sin might hope for pardon and heaven. I offered him the precious promises of God's word for his encouragement. I have reason to hope the word spoken to-day has been as seed sown in good ground.

"July 9. Preached to the Fourth Tennessee at night.

"Bean's Station, East Tennessee, Sunday, July 13. Small congregation at the morning service of the Fourth Tennessee. At 4 P. M. went over the mountain and preached to the Twenty-ninth North Carolina.

"Thorn Hill, East Tennessee, July 20. Chaplain Stricklend, of the Georgia Conference and Fortieth Georgia Regiment, preached us a plain, practical sermon on profanity at 9 A. M. At 11 A. M. I preached for his regiment—good attention. At 4 P. M. we heard Brother Wexler preach to the Twenty-ninth North Carolina on the riches of the grace of the gospel. I held his prayer meeting for him at night.

"July 21. Talked to Sergeant Baker, who resolves to lead a new life.

"July 22. Preached at night for the Eleventh Tennessee Regiment—good attention.

"July 25. Prayer meeting for our regiment at Thorn Hill.

"Sunday, July 27th, preached at 9 A. M. to Fourth Tennessee. At 10½ heard Chaplain Wexler on the First Psalm. I preached at 3 P. M. to the Third Georgia, and at night to the Eleventh Tennessee. Trust that in the three talks some good was accomplished.

"Sunday, August 3. Rev. Allen Tribble came out from Middle Tennessee last week. He preached for us at 9 A. M. At 11 I preached at the guard line to soldiers and citizens in the church. In the afternoon our regiment marched over to Clinch River, and I preached there at night.

"August 6. A severe skirmish on Walden's Ridge. We lost about ten killed and forty wounded. I helped to dress the wounds of the Federal soldiers; captured Sergeant-Major Smith and Mr. Mapps, of the Sixteenth Ohio.

"August 7. I assisted in the burial of Captain Edgar, Sixteenth Ohio Regiment, and a private soldier. Sergeant Tipton, of his company, wept when he saw the face of his dead captain. I talked with the captured prisoners.

"Walden's Ridge, near Tazewell, East Tennessee, Sunday, August 10, 1862. At 9 A. M. preached on the left wing of the Fourth and right wing of the Eleventh Tennessee Regiments. Heard Chaplain Wexler preach to the Twenty-ninth North Carolina at 10½ A. M. on purity of person, thought, purpose, affection, word and action. I preached for Third Georgia in the afternoon and Rains' regiment at night. Talked to the Federal prisoners.

"Tazewell, Tennessee, August 13, 1862. Having served the Fourth Tennessee

Regiment one year as chaplain, and learning that Rev. Allen Tribble, of the Ten-nessee Conference, a most excellent man, would like to enter the army as chaplain, and believing that he would be very acceptable among his friends and kindred in the Fourth Tennessee, and having such a high appreciation of the Georgia soldiers in our brigade who have no chaplain, I petitioned for a transfer to the Third Geor-gia Battalion, which was granted by those in authority. I was glad to receive the following from the colonel in command of our regiment, who was captain of the company in which I served for awhile as an independent private.

"'Rev. S. M. Cherry, being about to be transferred as chaplain from the Fourth Tennessee Regiment, I take great pleasure in recommending him as a chaplain of merit and entirely worthy of commendation. He has served this regiment as chap-lain with zeal and I believe with much usefulness, and besides in other respects he has contributed materially to the comfort and welfare of the regiment.

"'J. H. McMURRAY, Colonel commanding Regiment.'

"This testimonial was very unexpected, as the colonel was no Christian and a man of very few words. He was killed at the battle of Chickamauga, as were many of the officers and soldiers of that regiment. Captain Ross, of Coffee county, Ten-nessee, I found a very true Christian during all his stay in the army. Very few of the officers of that regiment made any profession of piety, but they treated me with due respect during my connection with the regiment.

"The Third Georgia Battalion, which soon after became the Thirty-seventh Georgia Regiment, was one of the noblest bodies of men with whom I came in personal contact during the war. I found the surgeon, Dr. R. B. Gardner, of Barnesville, a most congenial, companionable Christian man of sweet spirit and exemplary character. Dr. Gardner after the war wished to live in Tennes-see, and at my suggestion came to Giles county and taught school at Bethel and elsewhere, and was for some years a minister in the Methodist Church be-fore his death. The assistant surgeon, Dr. Holmes, was also a true Christian of manly deportment. Among others to whom I was strongly attached were Captains Carter, of Barnesville, and Wilson, of Spring Place—the latter a Presbyterian of culture, and the former a warm-hearted Methodist. They and many others whose names I doubt not are now as then in the Lamb's Book of Life were just such Christians as were greatly needed in camp. Among others I remember so well was Lieutenant Amos R. Kendall, now Dr. Kendall, the pastor of the First Meth-odist Church in Macon, Georgia. The lieutenant was not then religious, if I re-member correctly.

"August 15. Visited our sick soldiers at Bean's Station.

"August 16. Took leave of our wounded Federal prisoners of the Sixteenth Ohio, and had a night march from Walden's Ridge through Tazewell to Cumber-land Gap.

"Sunday, August 17. Lay in front of the Gap all day and had to lie low and keep out of the way of the enemy's shells.

"August 18. An interesting talk with young McDuffie, of the "Lula Guards." A pious mother's influence at home now tells well upon her noble boy in camp, who is trying here to live a Christian.

"August 20th. Went with our soldiers on a scout over the Double Mountain south of the Gap. Was in rifle range of the enemy.

"August 22. Had prayers with Captain Phelps' company.

"August 24. Preached valedictory to the Fourth Tennessee at night, and then marched down Powel's Valley the remainder of the night.

"Sunday, August 25. Rested at Rodger's Gap while the cannon were carried over the Cumberland Mountains by hand. Met Chaplains McHan, of the Thirty-sixth, and Kramer, of the Thirty-ninth Georgia Regiments. Crossed the Cumber-land Mountains at Rodger's Gap.

"August 26. Marched seventeen miles and crossed the Pine Mountains; encamped at the Cumberland River in Kentucky.
"August 27. Met Generals Reynolds and Heth.
"August 28. Reached Barboursville to-day. No sympathy for Southern soldiers here.
"August 29. Marched down the Cumberland River and encamped at Laurel Bridge.
"August 30. Went through Loudon.
"Sunday, August 31. Crossed the Rock Castle River and marched through the deep dust and among the towering rocks of Rock Castle county. Soldiers suffering much for water.
"September 1. We descended Big Hill into the Blue Grass Region of Kentucky. When we reached Rodgersville the battle between Rodgersville and Richmond was over, and we saw Salem church and yard full of wounded Federals. General Kirby Smith gained the most complete victory over the Federals here that I knew won during the war. General Pat. Cleburne here gained great renown. Our loss was between four and five hundred killed and wounded—Federals twice as great, and then four thousand prisoners taken. Three-fourths of our wounded were Tennesseeans. Among the number I met was Rev. A. M. Kerr, my preceptor when a youth, and for many years pastor of Pleasant Hill Cumberland Presbyterian Church, in Giles county, Tennessee, near where I was reared.
"September 2. Gave the day to looking after the wounded, Confederate and Federal.
"September 3. Our division entered Lexington, Kentucky, and we were welcomed with more enthusiasm than any place where we have been since the war began. Such marked kindness and cordial greeting were almost overwhelming to those of us who had been a year soldiering in East Tennessee.
"Lexington, Kentucky, September 4. The streets were densely thronged at an early hour by the citizens to witness the entry of General John H. Morgan to his native city. The vast multitude were almost frantic with joy as the long cavalcade swept through the chief street of the city. Such a fluttering and floating of Confederate flags I never saw before. The face of the renowned hero beamed with joy at such a hearty welcome to his home.
"Our battalion remained at Lexington on garrison duty for nearly a month, and we had our regular service on the first, second and third Sundays in September at our handsome encampments in new tents captured from the Federals.
"September 18 was Thanksgiving Day by order of President Davis. A message from the Forty-third Alabama Regiment was received requesting me to hold their thanksgiving service. The First Presbyterian Church was tendered for our use; but when I consulted General Kirby Smith he wisely advised me to decline the offer for good reasons, and we worshipped at the encampment.
"There was more sickness than usual among our soldiers, and the hospitals were filled by the corps. In visiting the sick, by special inquiry, I found several pious praying men, and the majority of the sick and wounded were readers of the Bible.
"The fourth Sunday in September we were at Winchester, Kentucky. Brother Rand preached for the soldiers in the forenoon and I in the afternoon.
"Saturday, October 4. Went to Frankfort, the capital of Kentucky, to witness the inauguration of Governor Hawes. Generals Bragg, Buckner, Buford, Reynolds, Stevenson and Humphrey Marshall and others were in attendance. The newly installed governor and generals left before night.
"Lexington, Kentucky, Sunday, October 5, 1862. Visited our sick for the last time in the hospitals here. All are ordered off. The city is rapidly evacuated, to the sorrow and surprise of many citizens and soldiers—the first scene of the kind I have yet witnessed. Our friends we leave, who have been so abundant in their

hospitality, merit our hearty commiseration. All denominations of Christians have been marked in their kindness to us, notably members of the Reformed Church, who have shown me special favors. In the afternoon we marched to Nicholasville.

"October 6. Crossed the Kentucky River and passed through Pleasant Hill or 'Shakertown'—a lovely place. Peace and prosperity prevail here. Never a marriage or birth in the town. None go to war. Men and women live apart. All property is held for the use of all. At Harrodsburg I met Dr. Joseph Cross, one of our chaplains and member of the Tennessee Conference. Rev. Robert A. Holland, a gifted young minister of Louisville, Kentucky, is going out with us. Met South Carolina soldiers to-day for first time. Marched six miles from Harrodsburg and camped at Eldorado.

"October 7th. Marched to Salt River, then to Salvisa, thence to the Kentucky River and across, and all day and nearly all night marching and manœuvring. Reached Versailles before daylight. Here I met Bishop Kavanaugh again. He and his noble wife showed me no little kindness during our six weeks in their State. We met several times.

"October 8. Marched for Lawrenceburg.

"October 9. At Lawrenceburg saw Morgan's Cavalry dashing through; heard the roar of cannon in our front; saw 400 Federal prisoners of Sill's Division. At night the camp-fires were grand.

"October 10. Aroused at midnight; marched to Harrodsburg, where I visited a great many of the wounded of the Perryville battle, Rev. Lieutenant Ransom among the number; also, William Westmoreland, one of my school-mates; neither of whom ever reached home. Our loss about three thousand killed and wounded. Our troops in battle line near the city and in fine spirits regardless of the steady cold rain. I was glad to find them so cheerful and hopeful. A great battle imminent. Met General Bragg as I returned about dusk.

"October 11. Our army is in full retreat. Regret to leave our wounded. We cross Dix's River and encamp on the eastern bluff.

"Sunday, 12. Rested to-day. Soldiers very attentive to the preaching of Chaplain Wexler and myself.

"Monday, 13. Marched nearly all night *via* Camp Dick Robinson to Lancaster, Ky. Bragg's army took the Crab Orchard Road, while our corps returns *via* Cumberland Gap to East Tennessee.

"Sunday, October 19. Preached for Chaplain Beauman to the Fifty-eighth North Carolina Regiment. Walked up to the Peak above Cumberland Gap, where we so often held our prayer meetings months ago. The enemy did much work here during the three months of their occupancy of this natural stronghold.

"Blain's Cross Roads, East Tennessee, October 26. Snow three inches deep. No preaching. Rev. R. A. Holland and I called on Chaplain Oslin, of Forty-third Georgia, and Rev. Timmons, of Watkins' Regiment.

"October 26. By request of Dr. Gardner I went with our sick soldiers to Strawberry Plains, then to Knoxville, where I met Colonel Reeves, a Baptist minister, whom I found very affable.

"October 27. Visited the sick at the hospital; accommodations for the sick were poor indeed.

"Sunday, November 2. Preached for the Fourth and Eleventh Tennessee and Forty-second Georgia Regiments, at Lenoir's Station, East Tennessee.

"November 23. Met Chaplain Riddle, of a Kentucky regiment, and we went together to the Methodist church, where I preached to a large congregation of soldiers and citizens. Brother Riddle is a Baptist minister, and manifests the charity that a true minister should.

CAMPAIGN IN MIDDLE TENNESSEE.

" The chaplains and other preachers with our corps began a series of meetings at Normandy, on the Chattanooga Railroad.

" November 26. Chaplain Wexler and I were assisted by Bro. J. G. Bolton. But in three days we marched to Manchester. There we had services nightly, regardless of the unfavorable weather.

" On Sunday night, November 30, after sermon by Bro. Wexler and exhortation by Bro. Tribble, six soldiers knelt for prayer; my twenty-seventh birthday.

" December 3. Bro. Bolton preached at night; I followed by exhortation; there were four penitents, and Sergeant-Major E. F. Shropshire, of Thirty-ninth Georgia, Ringgold, Georgia, made a happy profession of faith in Christ. The first public profession of religion I witnessed in the army.

" December 4. I preached at night; 7 penitents, 2 conversions.

" Captain Brady, Thirty-ninth Georgia, preached the last sermon of the Manchester meetings. Snow on the 5th, and Sunday, 7th, the division was marching to McMinnville. Captain Brady, a most excellent Christian, killed in Georgia, 1864.

" From McMinnville we marched to Woodberry, thence to Reedyville, where we encamped on Stone's River. Here I met General Joseph E. Johnston for the first time, with whom I was most favorably impressed. Also met General Bushrod Johnson.

" Reedyville, Tenn., December 13. Preached at night for Eleventh Tennessee Regiment and Third Georgia Battalion.

" Sunday, 14. Preached in the forenoon for Fifty-second Georgia Regiment. Colonel, lieutenant-colonel, and major set the soldiers a good example by attending service. Am much pleased with officers and men of this command. Dined with Rev. Dr. Harpe, a most genial Christian gentleman. Returned to our quarters and preached in the afternoon.

" December 15. Visited the Pisgah Hospital. Many sick of the Forty-third Georgia and Forty-sixth Alabama there.

" On the 19th the Fourth Tennessee left our division to join Cheatham's. I part with my old regiment with regret.

" Sunday, 21. At 10 A. M. preached for the Ninth Georgia Battalion for the first time. A large attendance of officers and privates. God's presence and power manifested in our service. In the afternoon preached for the Eleventh Tennessee Regiment.

" December 25. Rev. William Dow Cherry, pastor of Methodist church, McMinnville, preached for Twenty-ninth North Carolina Regiment. He is my only brother. His command was surrendered at Fort Donelson, but he risked his life and escaped imprisonment.

" December 27. Our division, General McCown's, marched after midnight this morning for Murfreesboro.

" Sunday, 28. We went into line of battle near the city and continued thus till night. No service to-day.

" Murfreesboro, Tenn., December 31, 1862. Our division, which is on the extreme left wing, southwest of Murfreesboro, advanced and attacked the enemy at daylight, and drove back Sill's Division for three miles across the Wilkerson Turnpike, and as far as the Nashville Pike. I rode out with Rev. Dr. F. S. Petway. Ector's Texas brigade of our division charged and captured a battery which annoyed us so yesterday. It belonged to Johnson's Federal brigade. I counted 47 Federals and 10 Confederate dead around the battery. The Federals rallied in a cedar glade near the home of Mrs. Burrus. We were exposed to a fearful fire. Never did I see men fall so rapidly. General James E. Rains, of our brigade, fell dead while cheering on our command. His last reported words were, " Forward, my brave boys, forward." He was a gallant man and had treated me with special courtesy for nearly a year and a half of our army association. His father a venerable Methodist minister of Nashville, Tennessee. Our wounded called to me for help. I took up Lieutenant Beasley and rode out, when the order to retire came. Went back and brought off three more of our boys; got an ambulance for Lieutenant Pryor, who could not sit on my horse—spent awhile with the Federal wounded. Saw Lieutenant Whitecotton, Third Georgia Battalion, wounded in the head. The three named are of our battalion. Two Federals, wounded in the back, asked me to have them carried to our quarters rather than the Federal. Another begged to be carried off. I was struck with the bright hazel eyes of the boy. His wound I thought was mortal. He was a member of the Methodist Church, son of a minister, I think; said his peace was made with God. I had him taken to our hospital. There the scene was shocking. Hundreds with bleeding wounds shivering around the fires patiently waiting their turn for the surgeon's services. The amputating knives were fast removing maimed limbs which were piled promiscuously by the house. Our loss 4,000 killed and wounded; 40 of our battalion. Federal loss three to our one on the left and centre.

"Stone's River, northwest of Murfreesboro, January 1, 1863. Went out to the line to talk with the boys of our brigade; found them very serious; no swearing heard to-day at the front, where the troops are protected by rocks rudely piled up between them and the enemy's lines. Riding over the field of carnage I found many Federal wounded still on the field and had them carried to their hospital. Saw the body of General Sill. He was on the Federal left wing of the army at Perryville, when we came in contact with his division. Here he was on the right and was slain. He was buried near the Chattanooga Railroad. I also saw the body of Colonel Foreman, Fifteenth Kentucky, Federal. Talked for some time with the Federal wounded.

"January 2. Visited our brigade again to-day, where I found them yesterday. Went with Rev. Dr. James L. Coleman to visit his brother. They wept when they met; they lost a brother in battle two days ago. The doctor and I were schoolmates in Athens, Alabama, when I was quite a child. We are members of the same Conference now. General John C. Breckinridge made an attack late in the afternoon to turn the Federals' left flank. His loss was heavy. Among the mortally wounded I saw General Hanson, of Kentucky. His wife and sister were weeping above the dying general.

"January 3. Lieutenant Pryor died to-day. I talked to him of his future hopes. They were not such as he wished. I called on Chaplains W. C. Atmore, Fifteenth Kentucky; J. E. Reed, Thirty-eighth Illinois, and J. C. Thomas, Eighty-eighth Illinois, of the Federal army—an hour's conversation with them.

"Sunday, January 4. Last night General Bragg withdrew his army from Murfreesboro, and all day Sunday we were marching to Shelbyville, Tennessee. We went into camp on Duck River, by a church where I was pastor my second year in the Conference, six years ago.

"The Army of Tennessee remained in camp around Shelbyville, Tennessee, for full five months. Our division changed its camping place several times, but nearly all the time we were either on Duck River or Flat Creek in the bounds of my second pastoral charge, where I found many friends. It was well for me, for I was sick much of this time. The kindness and hospitality of the people were greatly appreciated. I give brief items from my journal of January to July, 1863.

"January 10. Met Rev. Dr. John B. McFerrin, Revs. J. R. McClure, John S. Davis, and W. P. Owen, of our Conference, and we had a charming conversation.

"Sunday, 18. Preached to Third and Ninth Georgia Battalions. Fair attendance.

"January 19. Rev. Dr. Joseph Cross and I spend the night with Rev. J. S. Malone, whose father is with him, a venerable minister of Kentucky, greatly afflicted.

"January 24. The Eleventh Tennessee, so long with our command, is transferred, and we got the Thirty-ninth North Carolina in lieu of the Eleventh, which we give up with real regret.

"Sunday, 25. Heard a short, sensible sermon at the Presbyterian church, from Rev. Dr. Pease, of the Episcopal Church. Congregation composed largely of officers. In the afternoon preached in camp to our own command.

"Shelbyville, Tennessee, Sunday, February 1. Heard Dr. Cross, Methodist, in the forenoon, and Dr. Teasdale, of the Baptist Church, Mississippi, in the afternoon preach to large congregations. At night I preached for Chaplain Bennett to the Twelfth Tennessee Regiment.

"February 7. Met Charles J. Amos, a colporteur of the Tract Society of Richmond, Virginia.

"Sunday, 8. Rev. Dr. Quintard (now bishop) preached at the Presbyterian church. I preached to the Third and Ninth Georgia Battalions, and Twenty-ninth North Carolina Regiment in the afternoon.

"Shelbyville, Tennessee, February 18. The first meeting of our chaplains in this army was at the Presbyterian church to-day. Rev. Dr. Bryson, Presbyterian, in the chair; Rev. Mr. Bowde acting as Secretary. Ten chaplains present.

"A paper was read on regiments destitute of chaplains. Also the destitution of Bibles, Testaments, tracts, etc., and the need of *a Department Agent* to visit the hospitals in the rear and secure post and regimental chaplains, secure donations for religious reading, and otherwise promote the spiritual interests of the army. Rev. Dr. Quintard was recommended to Lieutenant-General Polk for the agency of our corps.

"Sunday, March 1. Heard a very practical sermon at the Presbyterian church by Dr. Quintard. In the afternoon preached to our own command.

"March 7. A tornado visited Shelbyville to-day, unroofing the Baptist church, demolishing other buildings, and yet but one man was killed.

"Sunday, March 8. Rev. A. S. Riggs preached at Wesley chapel and administered the Sacrament of the Lord's Supper—Revs. E. J. Allen, J. B. Stevenson, Wm. Anthony, Thomas Moody and myself, of our Conference, among the communicants. A precious communion.

"Sunday, March 15. Rev. Dr. Bunting, Presbyterian chaplain of Terry's Texas Rangers, preached to a thousand men of Ector's and Vance's brigade. I preached in the afternoon.

"March 16. Dr. Petway went with me to the chaplains' meeting. Eight present. Each gave his own experience and manner of work in the army. Committees were appointed to select a badge to be worn by chaplains, and the best manner of performing their work. My name was on each committee. Chaplain Milliken, Baptist, offered a resolution, with remarks, that we devote ourselves more fully to our peculiar work of saving souls. Also, that half an hour of each meeting be devoted to social prayer. Our meetings are becoming more spiritual.

"March 17. In visiting the brigade hospital I found Mr. Bankston, of our battalion, very low—perhaps will die. Has been serving God for ten years; is not afraid to die, and with faltering voice gave glory to God.

"March 19. General W. B. Bate takes command of our brigade and General A. P. Stewart of our division, the latter an eminent educator of Tennessee and an exemplary member of the Cumberland Presbyterian Church.

"Sunday, March 22. Dr. J. B. McFerrin preached with great power to our brigade on purity. Regret to learn that Chaplain Crouch, of Armstrong's Brigade, was killed at Thompson Station 5th or 6th instant.

"March 24. At an interesting meeting of our chaplains Brother Bennett and I were appointed to wait on Lieutenant-General Polk and see if he could and would dispense with the inspection of arms on Sunday. The general received us with marked courtesy and assured us that there should be no interference with our hours for religious service. He talked at length of his home arrangements for the cleanliness and comfort of his slaves on his plantation, and promised to afford all facilities in his power to aid us in our spiritual services for the soldiers. I was favorably impressed with our bishop-general.

"March 27. At the brigade hospital Sergeant Anderson, Thirty-ninth North Carolina, told me of his happy profession of religion yesterday. This has been appointed by President Davis as a day of fasting and prayer. I preached to the Twenty-ninth and Thirty-ninth North Carolina Regiments, and raised fifty-nine subscribers for *The Message*.

"Shelbyville, Sunday, March 29. Preached for the presiding elder, Rev. A. S. Riggs, at 11 A.M. Among those who took the Sacrament of the Lord's Supper I observed Colonels Armstrong, Bell, and Vance, Rev. Colonel Reed, C. P. Church and Supreme Judge Wright. In the afternoon I preached at the brigade hospital for the sick and wounded.

"March 30. Consultation with Chaplains McDonald and Malloy on our plan of army work. Mr. Ford, of the Third Georgia Battalion, brother of Rev. Mr. Ford, of Georgia, died to-day. A good man ready to go; a member of our church. His brother was with him.

"March 31. Ten chaplains at our meeting to-day.

"Sunday, April 5. Preached in the forenoon to our brigade; in the afternoon to the Ninth, Fourteenth and Fifteenth Regiments of Ector's Texas Brigade. I raised 150 subscriptions for *The Message*. Brothers Morris and Finney organized a 'Christian Association' of between forty and fifty members. I found Colonel Camp, of the Fourteenth Texas, reading his Bible. His banner is inscribed with 'In God we trust.' He is a Methodist and has the appearance of a Christian.

"Shelbyville, Tennessee, May 6. Rev. S. S. Moody, my first presiding elder, and as pure and devout a Christian minister as I ever knew, died in great peace at his home near the city to-day. He leaves a model family—his eldest son a minister, in charge of the churches near our encampment.

"May 7. Rev. Dr. J. B. McFerrin preached at the funeral of Brother Moody to-day. A revival reported in Ector's Texas Brigade—seventeen conversions to date. I began a meeting in our brigade to-night.

"May 8. Prayer meeting under a large beech tree; twenty penitents at the place of prayer.

"May 9. Captain Wilson conducted service to-night; twenty-four penitents. Thos. Scott, Twenty-ninth North Carolina, and Chas. Bruce, Thirty-seventh Georgia, professed conversion.

"Sunday, May 10. I preached to a large congregation at 10 A.M.—several at the camp altar for prayer. At 4 P.M. we organized the 'Soldiers' Religious Association' for our regiment. A number joined. At night Captain Wilson conducted the meeting. Many penitents. The Thirty-ninth North Carolina Regiment built us a rude camp altar of logs and we were ready for a general revival, as we thought, from all the indications in our brigade; but the Twenty-ninth and Thirty-ninth North Carolina Regiments were ordered away, and we had a meeting for three weeks nightly in our regiment. The Third and Ninth Georgia Battalions were consolidated, and our regiment was known as the Thirty-seventh Georgia. Captains Carter and Wilson, and Rev. S. S. Taylor, a worthy primitive Baptist preacher of our regiment, assisted me in the meeting. The number of penitents continued to average ten nightly, but the conversions were not so numerous as the number and earnestness of the seekers indicated that there should be. General Vance was quite sick in Shelbyville in May. He was attended by his faithful wife.

"May 11. Attended the funeral of Dr. R——, who died on yesterday of inebriety, late surgeon in our brigade. The hill where we buried him is red with 250 new-made soldier graves. Heard of the fall of General Stonewall Jackson. What a stroke to our country!

"May 12. At our chaplains' meeting Chaplains C. S. Hearn, Fifth Tennessee, and W. T. Bennett, Twelfth Tennessee, reported eighty-five conversions in Vaughn's and forty-five in Strahl's Brigade. Rev. H. D. Hogan, a private soldier, began a very fine revival in the Twenty-fourth Tennessee Regiment. He is now a presiding elder in Kansas.

"Sunday, May 17. Attended Chaplain Bennett's Sunday school in the Twelfth Tennessee Regiment, which is full of interest. Dr. McFerrin preached for us in the afternoon.

"May 19. At the chaplains' meeting a resolution was discussed and adopted declaring 'that the army is not of necessity a school of vice, but may become of the highest order of virtue.' Another, 'that the best laborers were needed for the great work.' We had a discussion also with regard to 'talent, education and qualification of ministers for the chaplaincy and the preference for men in the ranks.'

"Shelbyville, Tennessee, Sunday, May 24. John P. McFerrin, son of Rev. A. P. McFerrin and nephew of Rev. Dr. J. B. McFerrin, was recommended for license to preach. He has been a gallant soldier for some time. Four months later he was terribly wounded at Chickamauga. He is now pastor of the First Methodist Church in Chattanooga. Dr. John P. McFerrin has been a very successful pastor for more than twenty years. Presiding Elder A. S. Riggs administered the Sacrament of the Lord's Supper for Chaplain Page, of the Fifty-first Tennessee Regiment. What an impressive scene to witness so many stern soldiers weeping while commemorating the death of the great Captain of our salvation!

"May 25. The Christian Association of Thirty-seventh Georgia adopted a constitution and elected officers: Chaplain S. M. Cherry, President; Captain Wilson, Vice-President; Lieutenant Bennett, Secretary; Rev. S. S. Taylor, Treasurer; Captain Carter and Lieutenant Hartsfield, Watchmen. Ninety-nine members enrolled.

"May 29. Our regiment marched from Flat Creek across Duck River through Shelbyville and Wartrace to Fairfield and encamped on Garrison's Creek, near Hoover's Gap.

"Sunday, May 31. Preached for Twentieth Tennessee, Chaplain John A. Ellis, of the Tennessee Conference.

"June 2. We organized a chaplains' meeting at Fairfield: Chairman, S. M. Cherry; Secretary, Dr. F. S. Petway. Present: Chaplains Rush, Third Georgia, H. B. Moore, Seventeenth Tennessee, Jno. A. Ellis, Twentieth Tennessee, McMurray, Forty-fifth Tennessee, and Rev. S. S. Taylor, Thirty-seventh Georgia Regiments.

"The Confederate States Bible Society, or some other association, consigned to me several thousand copies of the New Testament for gratuitous distribution in the Army of Tennessee. Chaplains, preachers and officers very gladly received them at the ratio of about 400 to 500 to each brigade, or 100 or more to each regiment, and they were soon eagerly received and read by our soldiers.

"Near Fairfield, Tennessee, Sunday, June 7, 1863. Dr. McFerrin preached to our brigade in the forenoon. In the afternoon an experience meeting was held by the Christian Association of the Thirty-seventh Georgia Regiment. Several soldiers spoke of God's grace being sufficient to keep them in peace and hope amid all the evils of the camp and field. A gracious season we had as they witnessed for the love and power of Jesus Christ. We now have the Ninth Alabama, Twentieth Tennessee and Thirty-seventh Tennessee, with the Thirty-seventh Georgia in Bates' Brigade, Stewart's Division.

"June 14. Preached funeral of Thos. White. Yesterday he died suddenly on guard duty. He was not well, but would not be excused from duty, his brother offering to take his place. They had not met for six years until they saw each other on guard duty. Neither knew the other was here until the Ninth Alabama came into our camp a day or two ago. How sad and strange, after six years' separation, they should meet here only to be together for a few hours, then to part so suddenly and strangely to meet no more on earth! Heard Rev. Lieutenant Curry, of Ninth Alabama and Alabama Conference, preach to the Twentieth Tennessee. Am pleased with him.

"June 15. Preached at night for Brown's Brigade at Beech Grove. Several penitents; three professing. Dr. McFerrin has been assisting the chaplains of this command, and they have indications of a fine revival.

"Near Fairfield, Tennessee, Sunday, June 21. Chaplain Ellis preached to our brigade in the forenoon, I in the afternoon, and Lieutenant Curry, Ninth Alabama, at night. Some penitents.

"June 23. Protracted meeting continued, with prospects for a good revival.

"June 24. Masonic celebration of St. John's Day at Bell Buckle. The lodge furnished a fine dinner for the fraternity of the army. While I was addressing the brotherhood in the afternoon, there was an assault at Hoover's Gap. The officers of Second, Thirteenth, and Fifteenth Arkansas Regiments were ordered to their commands. I hurried to Fairfield, and found our brigade was engaged. Soon we were busy with the wounded, and sixty were brought to the house of Mr. Fields, among them Captain Carter and Lieutenants Murphy and Hutchison of our regiment. Major Claybrook, Twentieth Tennessee, mortally wounded. Private Waggoner, of Carter's company, Thirty-seventh Georgia, died during the night, saying: 'I am ready.' I aided the surgeons in taking of the arm off young Castleman, Twentieth Tennessee. He is a son of a Methodist preacher. I preached to him before the war. Chaplain Ellis and I ministered to the wounded till after midnight. Visited the wounded, and gave them such temporal and spiritual aid as I thought most needed. Those who are able to go are being sent to Wartrace.

"June 25. We saw the Federals advancing in three columns. Saw the Stars and Stripes floating in the distance. Skirmishing between the pickets. Our army is retiring slowly, in good order.

"From June 27 to 30 we marched *via* Wartrace, Tullahoma, Allisonia to Winchester.

"July 2. We left Winchester to-day. Here our first troops from Tennessee entered camps two years and two months ago. Now we evacuate Middle Tennessee.

"July 3. Our army is climbing the mountain at Sewanee, and pass University Place, where the Episcopalians are founding a school.

"July 4. We have crossed the Cumberland Mountains, and are in the Sequatchie Valley, and pass through Jasper.

"Sunday, July 5. Rest all day in the quiet retreat of the valley on the banks of the Sequatchie River.

"July 6. Crossed the Tennessee River at Kelley's Ford on a pontoon bridge, the first I ever saw. We encamped at Lookout Station — and the campaign in Middle Tennessee is over.

"CHATTANOOGA, CHICKAMAUGA, AND MISSIONARY RIDGE.

"After resting for five days at Lookout Station, on the Tennessee River, west of Chattanooga, our brigade marched to Tyner's Station, east of the city, where we went into camp, and remained for seven weeks. Dr. W. E. Munsey was pastor of the Methodist church in Chattanooga. We renewed our acquaintance formed while he was pastor at Knoxville, where I first entered camp two years ago.

"Sunday, July 12, 1863. Too wet for camp services, and I preached for Dr Munsey.

"July 15. Preached for our brigade; first camp service since we were broken up so suddenly at Fairfield over three weeks ago.

"July 16. Held prayer-meeting for Ninth Alabama.

"July 17. Our chaplains held an informal meeting.

"Sunday, July 19. Preached for our brigade in the forenoon, and for Brown's in the afternoon, and Rev. R. P. Ransom for us at Bates' brigade at night.

"July 22. Attended the meeting of the chaplains of the Army of Tennessee in Chattanooga.

"Sunday, July 26. Preached at Tyner's Station to Bates' brigade in the morning, and Rev. Wellborn Mooney preached for us at night.

"July 27. A letter to-day from Corresponding Secretary A. W. Miller, of the Evangelical Tract Society, and 100 copies of the *Army and Navy Messenger*, and another supply of Testaments for the soldiers. In looking up chaplains to distribute Testaments some weeks ago, I could not find a single chaplain in Churchill's Arkansas Brigade.

"July 28. Rev. R. P. Ransom preached for our brigade at night.

"August 1. Lieutenant-General D. H. Hill has taken command of our corps. When I called to see him he was alone in his quarters, and gave me a cordial greeting. Conversed fully and freely of chaplains and their work. Complimented the Methodist ministry. He is a Presbyterian I think. Expressed his preference for attending camp worship and disapprobation of officers *slinking* off to town to church. I am pleased with our General Hill.

"Our army is now well supplied with evangelists and missionaries of ability, zeal, and fidelity, who seem ready and willing to aid the chaplains in their work. Among the number are Rev. Mr. Wills, Macon, Georgia, and Rev. Mr. Caldwell of the Presbyterian Church. Evangelists, Rev. Dr. J. B. McFerrin, Rev. R. P. Ransom, and Rev. Wellborn Mooney, of the Tennessee Conference, and Rev. C. W. Miller, of Kentucky Conference—four able missionaries—the latter to the Kentucky Brigade.

"Sunday, August 2. Chaplain Ellis and I began a brigade meeting. We were assisted during the three weeks it continued by Messrs. Wills, Caldwell, McFerrin, Ransom, Mooney, Miller, Stevenson, and Rev. Colonel Reed, of the Cumberland Presbyterian Church, and Dr. Bryson, Presbyterian; Rev. R. P. Ransom preaching oftener than any one during the meeting. I was appointed to superintend the erection of an arbor, and the soldiers constructed one that furnished us plenty of logs for seats and a penitent's form, mourner's bench, or anxious seat; and we had mourners at almost every service, which was held nightly and three times on Sunday, and occasionally happy professions of saving faith.

"August 21 had been appointed as a 'Day of Fasting, Humiliation, and Prayer,' by President Davis. Chaplains Willoughby, McVoy, Ellis, and myself consulted with regard to the propriety of a general service of the entire division. We agreed that a service for each brigade would be better. General Stewart acquiesced in the arrangement. In the forenoon Rev. R. P. Ransom preached on 'The Lord God Omnipotent reigneth;' Rev. Mr. Bryson in the afternoon, and young John P. Mc-Ferrin at night. Four Tennessee soldiers professed religion that night, and we had a shout in the camp.

"Dr. B. M. Palmer, of New Orleans, Presbyterian, preached us two grand sermons at the close of the meeting. His themes were: 'Unbelief,' night of August 22, and 'Retribution,' Sunday, 23d, A. M., and he made a profound impression. Colonel Reed was announced for afternoon service and Dr. Palmer for night, but lo! the 'Long Roll' at 2 P. M., and our brigade was on the march, manœuvre, picket, or battle line for four weeks before we could encamp near the same place in quiet again. And they were memorable weeks of dust, conflict, carnage, and death to thousands of both armies.

37

"I have no record of the extent of the revival in the Army of Tennessee around Chattanooga in July and August, 1863. I have no doubt that it was general, as chaplains and missionaries were all busy so far as I can recall. "August 24. Visited the sick at Ringgold, and then to Catoosa Springs, where there were a large number of convalescents, the most pleasant place for the sick to rest and recuperate that I have seen. I preached to them day and night during my stay, and there were penitents, professions, and profuse praise by the pardoned and happy Christian soldiers. Then I was at Spring Place, Dalton, The Rock, Thomaston, Barnesville, and a camp-meeting in Upson county, Georgia. Then to La Fayette, and on to Chickamauga.

"Could not preach on Sunday, September 13, our division was marching; but preached on the night of 15th, and Dr. McFerrin preached the night of the 16th. "September 17. We marched from La Fayette, Georgia, in the direction of Chattanooga; passed Rock Spring Church and Pea-Vine, near which we bivouacked. While resting on my blanket in the shade, Lem. Robins, of our Thirty-seventh Georgia, came near me, and I asked him to take a seat on my blanket. He sat down, and began to talk cheerfully about his religious enjoyment; handed his hymn-book and an ambrotype of his wife to me to keep and return with messages of love to wife, father, and mother, spoke of his mother's prayers and her solicitude for his salvation, and her great satisfaction on hearing of his Christian conduct in camp. He was confident that he would not survive the coming conflict. But he was ready to die, and fully resigned to God's will. Was it a premonition? Two or three days after he was killed at Chickamauga.

"Our division suffered severely on the 19th and 20th of September, on the north side of the Chickamauga, west of Tedford's Ford. I was looking after our wounded on the field and at the field-hospitals on the 19th, 20th, and 21st. I was glad to see so many of our preachers with the wounded and dying on the field. Among others, the following names are on my journal: Dr. Joseph Cross, Dr. F. S. Petway, Revs. William Burr, W. H. Browning, C. W. Miller, and W. Mooney. I have no desire to write of the fearful conflict and terrible carnage on the Chickamauga Saturday and Sunday. Our loss was great; the Federal much greater.

"On the 22d I was with our brigade in front of Chattanooga, and we had prayers with the regiment, to thank God that so many of us were still alive. "Sunday, September 27. *Base of Missionary Ridge.* Preached to our brigade (116 Psa., 12–15). At the close of the service several soldiers stood or knelt, in token of their purpose to pay their vows unto the Lord for all his benefits unto them. Among the number was Dr. Childs, adjutant of our regiment, killed in the battle of Missionary Ridge, November 25.

"The Army of Tennessee remained encamped on the south and east of Chattanooga, from Lookout Mountain to the base and crest of Missionary Ridge near two months, or until the 25th of November, 1863. Rev. Mr. Stacey, of Newnan, Georgia, a Presbyterian minister, preached for us here, and I preached for the Kentucky Brigade, exchanging places occasionally with Professor Pickett, of Bethany College, Christian Church, who was with the Kentucky Brigade. He was a gentleman of culture and Christian charity. He was defective in hearing.

"Early in October I returned to the rear to look after our wounded. At Spring Place I found Captain Wilson and others improving; those at Dalton convalescing. But at Atlanta I found many in a critical condition. Rev. John P. McFerrin was there, terribly mangled; lamed for life. Mr. Parnell, of the Fifty-eighth Alabama, destined to die. I read the word to him, and, while kneeling by his bunk and praying for his salvation, he joined heartily in the prayer, trying to repeat each petition. Then he said to me: 'Tell my father I never deserted my post, but fell a brave soldier, and am now trying to get religion.'

"We continued to have regular camp service in front of Chattanooga, whenever the weather was at all favorable, in October and November. During that time Dr. Petway and Rev. William Burr preached two or three times each, and Dr. McFerrin and Rev. W. Mooney once each for our brigade. Chaplain Ellis was with us much of the time, and was faithful and modest in his work. I had occasion to visit nearly all the regiments in the army, and I found many of the chaplains at the post of duty.

"November 3 and 4. The chaplains of the army met in a two days' council on Lookout Mountain, and held two sessions each day. Rev. B. W. McDonald, D. D., of the Cumberland Presbyterian Church, was Chairman; Chaplain A. D. McVoy, Fifty-eighth Alabama, Secretary. I clip report from *The Army and Navy Herald:*

" ' LOOKOUT HOTEL, *On Lookout Mountain*, November 3, 1863.

" 'A meeting of the chaplains and missionaries of the Army of the Tennessee convened at the above place this day.

" 'After preliminary religious exercises, B. W. McDonald was chosen President, and A. D. McVoy, Secretary.

" 'After a discussion relative to general meetings, the next general meeting was appointed to be held on the first Wednesday in December.

" ' The chaplains of each corps were requested to hold regular meetings for consultation.

" 'A committee was appointed to draft a constitution and by-laws.

" ' The chaplains of each division were requested to furnish the Chairman with the roll of chaplains and the regiments destitute.

" ' *Afternoon Session.*

" 'An inquiry was made relative to obtaining supplies of tracts, papers, Bibles, and Testaments.

" 'An inquiry was made in regard to Christian Associations. After the nature, operations, and success of such associations were explained, a committee was appointed to consider the subject, and report at the next meeting.

" *Second Day.*

" ' W. T. Hall offered the following resolutions, which were approved :

" ' *Whereas*, experience teaches that the religious wants of the army are most efficiently met by chaplains ;

" ' *And whereas*, it is exceedingly desirable that the most efficient clergymen of the Church be dedicated to this work ;

" ' *And whereas again*, it has come to our knowledge that several excellent chaplains have already resigned, and many others are known to be on the point of resigning their positions as chaplains, because of incompetent support ;

" ' *And whereas again,* frequent changes of this kind are very detrimental to the cause of religion in the army, and greatly to be deprecated ; therefore—

" ' *Resolved*, by the chaplains and missionaries in General Bragg's army, That we recommend to the various religious denominations in the Confederate States of America that they institute an inquiry into the support of their ministers in the army, and prevent the resignation and suffering of any for want of competent support.

" ' Ordered to be published in the religious papers.

" ' J. M. Craig offered a memorial to Congress, through the general officers of this army, for the privilege of drawing forage for one horse. Approved.

" ' W. E. Walters offered a preamble and resolutions, which were approved, in reference to the destitute and suffering families on Lookout Mountain and in the vicinity of this army. Ordered to be forwarded to General Bragg by the Secretary.

" ' B. W. McDonald offered the following :

" ' *Resolved*, That we earnestly pray and toil for the evangelization of the army, and that we make a special business to pray for each other and assist each other in our work.

"'The other resolutions were in reference to the preparation of business, and a request to the chaplains to send up a narrative of the state of religion in their respective commands.

"'After religious exercises the meeting adjourned.

"'A. D. McVoy, Secretary.'

"*The Army and Navy Herald* was established in Macon, Georgia, October, 1883, and the agent, Rev. Dr. Camp, came to Missionary Ridge, late in November, to get General Bragg to designate some one to act as 'Distributing Agent of the Soldiers' Tract Association for the Army of Tennessee.' After consulting with Dr. McFerrin, and chaplains and others in the army, I was appointed to that work and took leave of my regiment, the Thirty-seventh Georgia, on Sunday, November 22, 1863, after a most happy association of fifteen months, and a brigade acquaintance of nearly two years. The treatment of the officers and privates of that regiment during all of that time was remarkably kind and respectful, for which I entertain a very high and Christian appreciation.

"The battle of Missionary Ridge was fought the same week of my assignment to duty for the entire army. Among the victims of that battle, from our Thirty-seventh Georgia, were Captain McMullen, a true and tried Christian I dearly loved, and Dr. Childs, my messmate, to whom I was strongly and tenderly attached. He was trying to do his duty to God and his country.

"The Army of Tennessee encamped around Dalton, Georgia, the entire winter of 1863-64, and until May, in the spring—over five months. The post quartermaster furnished me with room No. 1, at the Chester House, close to the square and depot, the day after my arrival at Dalton, and I fixed a lock on the door with my army knife, and soon had a counter arranged for my army papers, tracts, Bibles, Testaments, hymn books, and other religious literature. This became at once the head-quarters of chaplains, missionaries, evangelists, preachers, and all who sought religious reading from my hands. I tried to share my bunk, which was rough, with any and all who might seek shelter for a night or longer, and I had pens, ink, and stationery for those who wished to write. I had no lack of company day nor night from December till May. How earnest and eager the preachers were to secure religious reading of all kinds, and how hungry the soldiers to secure the same, may be slightly indicated by extracts from *The Army and Navy Herald*, which I clip, every number of which I have bound and now mutilate for the first time for the benefit of the readers of 'Christ in the Camp.' The citizens who remained in Dalton tendered us the different church edifices for the use of the soldiers, and we had a protracted meeting lasting for five months in them, only equalled in duration by colored congregations since the war.

"During the months of December, January, February, and March, Dr. J. B. McFerrin preached nine times in Dalton, and I preached as often. Rev. Dr. Stiles, of Virginia, a Presbyterian minister, preached several times with great power and much profit to the soldiers and preachers. Rev. Mr. Caldwell, of the same Church, preached three or four times with good success. Rev. Mr. Flynn preached more than once. He, too, was a Presbyterian; also, Rev. Mr. Wood. Missionary Mooney five times, Miller three times, and R. P. Ransom, H. H. Kavanaugh, and Captain Sutherland, Twenty-third Alabama, and Alabama Conference; Chaplain W. A. Parks, Fifty-second Georgia, and Georgia Conference, each preached once or oftener, and others may have preached in my absence that I did not hear, besides these named. I only mention such as I heard. Nearly every time there was preaching penitents were called, and we would have from two to fifteen to come forward and from one to four professions nightly. I went to the front two or three Sundays, at Tilton,

ARLINGTON — HOME OF GEN. R. E. LEE, C. S. A.

(Facing page 580.)

where I found Brother J. G. Bolton with a fine Sunday-school. The Brinsfields there took an active part in that work. I found in March a revival prevailing in Finley's Florida Brigade. General Finley, an Episcopalian, encouraging Chaplains Wiggins and Tomkins in the good work.

" General Manigault, an Episcopalian, attended camp service when I visited his brigade. Colonel Jones, a Methodist, in Walthall's Brigade, active in camp service. Also, a good revival in Dea's Brigade, in March.

" I give here some of the names of preachers in the army around Dalton : J. H. Willoughby, Eighteenth Alabama; Elbert West, Twenty-fifth Alabama; W. W. Graham, Twenty-eighth Alabama; J. S. Holt, Thirty-fourth Alabama; C. M. Hutton, Thirty-sixth Alabama; A. D. McVoy, Thirty-eighth or Fifty-eighth Alabama; W. F. Norton, Thirty-ninth Alabama; Dr. B. W. McDonald, Fiftieth Alabama; R. W. Norton, —— ——; J. P. McMullen, Mississippi, Alabama Brigade; Revs. Lieutenant Curry and Jones, Thirty-second and Fifty-eighth Alabama.

" R. L. Wiggins, Fourth Florida; J. H. Tomkins, Seventh Florida; J. G. Richards, Tenth South Carolina; W. T. Hall, J. H. Myers, Forty-second Georgia; —— Thompson, Fortieth Georgia; Dr. Rosser, Forty-first Georgia; W. A. Parks, Fifty-second Georgia; L. B. Payne, Missionary, Cummings' Georgia Brigade; H. H. Kavanaugh, Sixth Kentucky; C. W. Miller, Missionary, Kentucky Brigade; T. H. Davenport, Third Tennessee; C. S. Hearn, Fifth Tennessee; —— Swearer, ——, Tennessee; P. G. Jamison, Eleventh Tennessee; W. T. Bennett, Twelfth Tennessee; L. H. Milliken, Thirteenth Tennessee; J. A. Ellis, Twentieth Tennessee; J. F. McCutchen, Twenty-fourth Tennessee; —— Harris, Twenty-sixth Tennessee; M. B. Chapman, Thirty-second Tennessee; J. H. McNeilly, Forty-ninth Tennessee; J. B. Mack, Fiftieth Tennessee; S. A. Kelley, Missionary to Strahls' Tennessee Brigade; R. G. Porter, Tenth Mississippi.

" J G. Long, Dr. J. H. Gibbs, D. C. Boggs, J. C. Kennedy, H. McCann, G. L. Petrie, —— Henderson. The above met with the Chaplains' Association of Hood's Corps—chiefly chaplains.

" Dr. J. B. McFerrin, Revs. R. P. Ransom, W. Mooney, and William Burr, acted as missionaries to different commands from Tennessee.

" Thus far I have confined myself to my own journals and the records of the Chaplains' Association of Hood's Corps, at Dalton. The material after this is largely taken from the *Army and Navy Herald*, 1864–65."

[*From Army and Navy Herald*, December 1, 1863.]

" REV. S. M. CHERRY.—This gentleman, through the courtesy and by order of General Braxton Bragg, has been detailed as Agent for the Soldiers' Tract Association of the Methodist Episcopal Church, South, in the Army of Tennessee. He will distribute the publications of this Association, and all other religious matter placed in his hands. All the chaplains, therefore, in that army, will report to him when in want of any of our publications, as he will be constantly supplied from this point."

REPORTS OF REV. S. M. CHERRY, CENTRAL DISTRIBUTING AGENT, ARMY OF TENNESSEE.

" DEPOSITORY, DALTON, April 30, 1864.

" The following report of operations and labors in the Army of Tennessee for the present month is respectfully submitted :

" I have visited the Brigades of Generals Brown, Bate, Reynolds, Walthal, Finley, Tucker, Lowry, Gist, Stephens, Wright and Roddy. I have universally met with warm welcomes and kindly greetings by the officers and soldiers of each command. Three of the above-named generals are consistent members of the Church, and are wielding their influence for the spread of morality and piety among the soldiers, affording much help and encouragement to chaplains and missionaries laboring in their brigades; and each of their commands are now blessed with gracious revivals —the most extensive in the army—with congregations large, serious and attentive. I have preached in each of the brigades visited, and am pleased to report interesting revivals in most of them.

"I have preached several times during the month at the Methodist church in Dalton. The revival there is increasing in interest all the while. In two weeks a large number have professed faith, and 53 have joined the Church.—The Baptist and Presbyterian churches are densely crowded every night, and both report excellent meetings with many awakenings and conversions.

"Brown's Brigade has enjoyed a precious revival for two months. Last week 101 conversions and 78 accessions to the Church were reported in the brigade; and a very large Christian Association has been organized, which is doing much good.

"Recently a chapel has been erected in Bate's Brigade for camp service, and a number have been converted at their late protracted meeting.

"Walthal's Brigade has no chaplain at present, but I learn that preachers, who are private soldiers, are conducting a good meeting—many penitents and conversions.

"Tucker's Mississippi Brigade has been favored with a revival meeting for several weeks. Over one hundred have been converted, 90 have joined the Church, and two nights ago there were 140 penitents at the altar.

"Finley's Florida Brigade reports 130 accessions to the Church, and as many conversions this spring; and 70 penitents still seeking salvation.

"A protracted meeting began in Lowry's Brigade of Alabama and Mississippi troops twenty days ago. Last night about 140 penitents came forward for prayer. 53 have joined the Church; the general assists in the labors of the pulpit and altar, and has baptized a dozen of his own soldiers.

"Gist's Georgia and South Carolina Brigade is just entering upon a wonderful work of grace. 60 have recently joined the Church (40 in the past five days).

"A fine meeting is progressing in Wright's Tennessee Brigade. There are a number of earnest inquirers and some happy conversions.

"The following are the reports from brigades which I have not been able to visit this month.

"Cummings' Georgia Brigade has a remarkably fine meeting in progress—45 professions of faith and 38 accessions to the Church in a very few days.

"In Stovall's Georgia Brigade a meeting has been in progress eighteen days. 75 have joined the Church, and as many are converted.

"Gibson's Louisiana Brigade has neither chaplain nor missionary, but ministers from other commands have commenced a protracted meeting which promises great good. 40 have professed faith and asked for Church membership within the last twelve days.

"A meeting is being held by different chaplains and other ministers in General Granberry's Texas Brigade which has no chaplain. There are crowds of penitents at the altar—35 conversions and 42 accessions to the Church within a few days; and a large number are interested on the subject of salvation.

"In General Dea's Alabama Brigade during two months 50 or 60 have joined the Church, and perhaps as many have been converted; while 125 penitents are still seeking God.

"General Govan's Arkansas Brigade and General Polk's Arkansas and Tennessee Brigade are both blessed with very gracious and promising revivals.

"General Clayton's Alabama Brigade reports 49 recent accessions to the Church.

"A few conversions and accessions are reported in General Strahls' Tennessee Brigade.

"There may be religious interest manifested in commands that I have not mentioned; and there is a very fine work progressing in Hotchkiss' Battalion of artillery. Ten joined the Church one night this week, and 50 were still at the altar.

"The wonderful work of grace is spreading all over the army. Over one thousand of our soldiers are now publicly seeking salvation, and two or three hundred have joined the Church in this army during the past week—more than any month prior to the present.

"I have distributed for your society 130 Bibles, 8,000 copies of the *Herald*, 400 copies of the Soldiers' Paper, and 850,000 pages of tracts; preached 30 sermons, furnished every regiment and brigade in this army with religious literature which can be reached through our very efficient chaplains, missionaries, pious officers and soldiers.

"I never saw our soldiers more healthy and hopeful of success; and the spiritual field is now truly white unto the harvest.

"Your co-laborer in the cause of Christ and our country,

"S. M. CHERRY,
"CENTRAL DISTRICT AGENT ARMY OF TENNESSEE.

"To Rev. Robert J. Harp, Superintendent Southwestern Department Soldiers' Tract Association Methodist Church, South."

REPORT FOR MAY, 1864.

"RECEIVING AND DISTRIBUTING HOSPITAL,
"MARIETTA, GEORGIA, May 31, 1864.

"*Dear Brother:* The month of May has been less favorable for distributing religious reading than the several months preceding it. The army was in the midst of a most extensive revival at the beginning of the month. Protracted meetings were being held in almost every brigade; thousands of our soldiers were thronging our rude camp altars, hundreds were giving their hearts to God, and scores were nightly asking for certificates of Church membership. About 300 were baptized on the first day of May, and the great work seemed to be growing in depth and interest all the while. Officers and privates were unusually serious and much impressed by the preaching of the word, and bowed together at the place of prayer. The Lieutenant-Colonel of the 1st Arkansas Regiment professed religion at the camp altar the night before the command went into line of battle. Not less than five hundred professed to find peace in believing the first week of the month, and two thousand were publicly seeking salvation. But these interesting meetings have been interrupted by the advance of the enemy, who has despoiled our country and desecrated our arbors and altars consecrated to the worship of God. About the 5th instant the soldiers were called from their camps to meet the enemy in the vicinity of Dalton—they literally went from the altar to their entrenchments—from their knees to the battle with their foes—still singing the songs of Zion and supplicating the throne of grace as they surrounded the fires of the bivouac, or waited to receive the fire of the foe. Some of them have since fallen, full of faith and hope.—Our army having been in line of battle, on the march, in bivouac or in conflict with the enemy for more than three weeks, our chaplains and missionaries have had but little opportunity of preaching, holding prayer meetings or distributing, but they are generally at their posts ministering to the wounded and dying soldiers.

"Several ministers who aided us in our distributions to the soldiers have been killed or wounded, among which are the following: Rev. McMullen of the Presbyterian Church, Missionary to Baker's Alabama Brigade; Rev. John W. Brady of the Georgia Conference, Captain of the Thirty-fifth Georgia Regiment, were killed instantly at Resacca on the 15th instant. Rev. B. L. Selmon of the Alabama Conference, and Captain in the Twenty-third Alabama Regiment, was severely wounded. Rev. Mr. Curry of the Alabama Conference, and Lieutenant in the Twenty-eighth

Alabama Regiment, shot through the arm. Rev. Mr. Ransom, Lieutenant in First Tennessee Regiment, severely mangled by a cannon ball—but calm and resigned to the will of God, rejoices that he sought God in his youth and urges young men who feel it their duty to preach to enter upon the great work without delay. I fear his wounds are fatal, and that we will lose this noble soldier of the cross and of his country.* Many of our Christian soldiers have been slain; those of them who survive long enough to speak of the future died very triumphantly.—Major Roberts, of the Twenty-third Alabama, when dying, said to me, 'Tell my mother I expect to meet her in heaven.' But alas! another dying by his side similarly wounded said: 'I am not ready to die.'

"When our army after a week's resistance fell back from Dalton on the night of the 12th, I succeeded in obtaining transportation through the kindness of Major John L. Bransford, for all the supplies in our Depository at Dalton, which I shipped safely to Atlanta, where they are deposited at the Wayside Home in care of Captain Davis, who kindly assisted me. Subsequently I have been ministering to the wounded, in co-operation with the various Battle-field Relief Committees and at the General Receiving and Distributing Hospital. Have distributed 5,000 copies of the *Herald*, 20,000 pages of tracts, and preached only three sermons during the month Have made arrangements to furnish all who wish sacred literature either at Marietta or Atlanta for the present.—Soldiers are in fine spirits, cheerful and confident of success in the decisive conflict.

"Yours truly, S. M. Cherry."

REPORT FOR JUNE, 1864.

"Our army has been in battle line in the vicinity of Marietta and New Hope Church the entire month. While the soldiers are in the trenches and subject to the fire of the foe almost daily the facilities for preaching are few, and the missionaries and chaplains are more efficient at the field-hospitals than they would be along the lines. The soldiers are very eager for suitable reading while confined so closely to the trenches, and I have spared no pains in furnishing all that I could reach through the missionaries, chaplains, officers, and soldiers, with papers and tracts. The cavalry especially have been better supplied than heretofore, as they have been more convenient to my quarters than formerly.

"The distribution for the month has amounted to 11,000 copies of the *Army and Navy Herald* and 84,000 pages of tracts.

"My labors have been confined principally to the Receiving and Distributing Hospital, Marietta, Georgia, where the wounded are brought from the field-hospitals for attention, and, after a few hours' rest, are shipped to the rear, if able to be removed. Here I have had the privilege of ministering to the wounded and dying soldiers of the different commands of our army that have been engaged with the enemy during the month.

"I am glad to report that a large majority of the severely and mortally wounded with whom I have conversed in reference to their hopes of future happiness have given strong testimony of their preparation for death and eternity. Some of the mangled and gory have died praising God for His presence and power, enabling them to die triumphing over their last enemy. I have witnessed the peaceful and happy exit of many of our noble brave from the earth, who sent sweet messages to their far-distant mothers, wives, and sisters to meet them in heaven, for they were ready to die, and were going home.

"The revival interest in the army has not waned; whenever the chaplains or missionaries have an opportunity to preach to the soldiers, and penitents are invited forward for prayer, a large number come quietly and signify their penitence and

---

* He afterwards died of his wounds.

desire to lead a new life; and many are still making applications for church membership.

"I have preached twice during the month: once at Walker's Division Hospital, where the disabled soldiers were very serious and attentive, and quite a number were forward for prayer; once in Marietta, but few soldiers present.

"Our soldiers seem remarkably cheerful and very hopeful of success.

"S. M. CHERRY, Distributing Agent.

"Marietta, Ga., June 30, 1864."

REPORT FOR JULY, 1864.

"Since my last report from Marietta, made June 30. I have been quartered with the Savannah Relief Committee, and devoting what time I could spare from the duties of my office to ministering with that efficient Battle-field Relief Committee to the wounded at Dr. Bateman's. Several receiving and distributing hospitals, which had been located near the Chattahoochee and in Atlanta, are now three miles south of the city.

"I have not been able to furnish reading material for all the commands of the army with that system, promptness, and regularity as when the troops were in camp or quarters. Yet all the papers and other reading I can procure are distributed judiciously to the soldiers, and demands are made for more.

"The distribution for the month of July amounts to 1,917 Testaments, 17,890 *Heralds*, and 60,000 pages of tracts for the Soldiers' Tract Association; 225 Bibles and 1,600 Testaments for the Confederate States Bible Society; and 100,000 pages of tracts of the Evangelical Tract Society, besides a few packages of miscellaneous reading. In short, all the supplies on hand at the Wayside Home in Atlanta have been exhausted.

"The great revival interest is still prevailing in the army. There were a large number of penitents, professions of piety, candidates for church membership, and baptisms reported at the late meeting of the Association of Chaplains and Missionaries. Wherever and whenever an opportunity is offered for preaching or for prayer-meeting, the ministers are ready to labor for the salvation of souls, and many are seeking and securing the pearl of great price.

"Rev. Mr. Smith, a Presbyterian missionary, of Jackson's Brigade, died recently in Atlanta. He was very efficient in furnishing the troops with religious reading— a zealous laborer in the vineyard of Christ.

"Rev. Captain Charles H. Dunham, formerly of the Tennessee Conference, but a gallant officer in the Forty-eighth Tennessee Regiment for three years, and Rev. Lieutenant Cornelius Hardin, Thirty-fifth Mississippi Regiment, recently ordained by Bishop Paine, were both mortally wounded on Kenesaw Mountain, and died full of faith and the Holy Ghost, in Marietta.

"Rev. Mr. Hudson, chaplain Sixth Texas Cavalry, a faithful and useful man in the army, and much beloved by his soldiers, was mortally wounded near Newnan, July 30, while in the discharge of his duty as chaplain.

"I have preached but few times during the month, as the soldiers are either moving or confronting the enemy in the trenches almost daily. While General Roddy's command remained here I preached nightly to his soldiers, who seemed very eager to hear the words of life. The attendance and attention were good at each hour's service, and a large number of penitents were forward for prayer.

"The soldiers are always glad to receive the publications of our society, and eagerly read the same.

"It is difficult to supply the increased demand for the Scriptures, tracts, and papers, the circulation of which, in the army, is accomplishing much good.

"S. M. CHERRY, Distributing Agent.

"Near Atlanta, July 31, 1864."

REPORT FOR AUGUST, 1864.

"Our army has been closely confined to the trenches around Atlanta the entire month, and exposed to a continuous fire of artillery, and frequent picket skirmishes, and a few assaults from the enemy; but notwithstanding the proximity of the foe and the exposed position of our troops, the soldiers seemed very eager for religious services at various points along the lines, and even sat quietly listening to the preaching of the word amid the flying and falling missiles of death, seeming to feel secure while engaged in the worship of God. I preached three nights in succession to General Roddy's Division of cavalry. The command had but one chaplain present for duty, and there are many more professors of piety, but the soldiers seemed very eager to have preaching, and were attentive and serious; twenty-eight came forward for prayer, and there were very favorable indications for an extensive revival of religion among them; but the general was ordered elsewhere, and the meeting closed. I was treated with much courtesy and kindness by General Roddy and his officers, who expressed a desire to have the soldiers attend preaching. An efficient chaplain or missionary might accomplish much good in that excellent division; and the soldiers were very solicitous to secure the services of a zealous, faithful minister.

"The first Sabbath in the month I visited General French's division, of Stewart's corps, and preached in the morning to Ector's Texas, Reynolds' Arkansas, and Gholson's Mississippi brigades. The congregation was large and serious, and sat for an hour upon the ground in the open field, without any protection from the burning sun, and listened gladly to the words spoken, which I trust accomplished some good. One wounded soldier since testified that he was a changed man from that hour. All were eager to get papers and Testaments. I regret much that I had so few of the latter to distribute. Gholson's and Reynolds' brigades are both without chaplains. I have preached once since to the latter. They were having meetings every night. Five joined the church, and there were a number of penitents and professions of piety. At 2 P. M. I preached for Sears' Mississippi brigade. The interest there was very good; two joined the M. E. Church at the close of service. A fine revival has been carried on for some time by their faithful chaplains, and a large number have been converted and joined the Church during the month. I was received by Colonel Barry, commanding brigade, and staff officers, with marked respect. They attended preaching. A shower of rain fell before the close of the sermon, but the soldiers only crowded the closer to the preaching place. Again, at four in the afternoon, I preached for Cockrill's Missouri brigade, where a fine revival was in progress; above one hundred of those gallant Missourians, far away from their homes, have sought and secured a title to a home in the many mansioned house of our Father in heaven. Among the number, a noble young officer, of fine intellect, joined the Church one day, and was killed on the post of duty the day following.

"In Scott's Alabama and Louisiana brigade I have preached four times. Quite an interesting revival; seventy at the altar for prayer. I received fourteen applications for church membership. Some very pious and zealous young officers in that command have charge of large Bible classes, and are wielding a fine influence for the cause of Christ.

"At Adams' Mississippi brigade preached once; attentive audience. Seventy-five men were seeking salvation, and many professed conversion. I baptized four young soldiers.

"Featherston's Mississippi brigade has been blessed with a very gracious revival for two or three weeks; over one hundred have joined the Church recently. I have preached for them once. Colonel Stehpens, commanding brigade, and other officers, gave me a cordial reception.

"I preached one night for Quarles's Tennessee and Alabama brigade—preaching

APPENDIX. 587

the same evening in another part of the brigade. Both places were thronged with serious soldiers, and many came forward for prayer; quite a number of conversions.

"I have also preached once each for Mercer's (Georgia) and Govan's (Arkansas) Brigades, Cleburne's Division; and for Wright's and Gordon's Brigades, of Cheatham's Division, together; and once at Griffin, where a revival was progressing, principally among the soldiers.

"Total sermons preached, ... 18
"Testaments distributed, ... 1,400 copies.
"*Army and Navy Herald,* . . . . . 13,000 "
"Soldiers' Paper, ... 600 "
"Tracts, ... 20,000 pages.

"I am under many obligations to the Savannah Relief Committee for special favors and material aid bestowed. I have been quartered with those affable and kind-hearted gentlemen the past month, and all the members of the committee have assisted me in this work of distribution.

"S. M. Cherry.
"Near Atlanta, Ga., August 31, 1864."

REPORT FOR OCTOBER, 1864.
"Rev. Robert J. Harp, Superintendent:

"*Dear Brother:* The army has been in motion the entire month, moving from Palmetto, Georgia, to North Alabama; hence it has not been in my power to preach to the soldiers, and furnish the chaplains and missionaries with papers, tracts, etc., as promptly as heretofore; but, under all the circumstances, I have been trying to labor to the best advantage. A week was spent in Newnan, Georgia, the first of the month, during which time that place was the base of supplies for our main army. Soldiers returning to their commands stopped at the Camp of Direction, while the sick, going to the rear, stopped at the General Receiving and Distributing Hospital, and several cavalry commands were still remaining in the vicinity. I preached here several times to good congregations, representing almost every regiment in the Army of Tennessee; many came forward as seekers of salvation, while the officers in command at Palmetto showed marked respect for the cause. I also preached at the reserve camp of the First, Third, Fifth, Eighth, and Tenth Confederate Cavalry, and once in Newnan, distributing each day hymn-books, Testaments, and papers to the soldiers en route for the main army, and those in the hospitals and camps.

"When our General Hospital, Transportation Office, and Military Post-office were ordered to Blue Mountain (as a temporary base of supplies), I shipped the supplies of the Association to Selma, Alabama. . . . As the army continued to march northwest, our stay at Blue Mountain was short; we found it necessary again to change our base of supplies. During our stay in this vicinity I preached six times to some soldiers of the Second Regiment Engineer Corps, and other troops which I found at Oxford, Alabama (six miles below Blue Mountain), and to the citizens who attended the Methodist church. The soldiers, with but few exceptions, were serious and attentive, but very few seemed inclined to seek religion (fewer than at any meeting which I had attended for a long time, where so many soldiers were present); but it is a noticeable fact that the soldiers who remain in departments where they are less exposed to conflicts with the enemy, are not so much inclined to be religious as those who face the enemy in mortal combat. Those who expect to expose themselves to danger and death feel the need of God's protection to cover their heads in the day of battle, and when the battle is over and they have escaped the missiles of death, gratitude prompts the noble and brave heart to surrender itself to God. I have scarcely known a surgeon, quarter-master, commissary, ordnance officer, or one of their clerks, or a teamster, or a permanently detailed soldier in the various departments, to make a profession of religion; while generals, colonels, majors, captains, lieutenants, and privates in the ranks, by the score, the hundred and the thousand have sought and secured the pearl of great price in the army. Exposure to danger and providential escapes have a great tendency to drive the shelterless soul to Christ for refuge.

"I preached several times at Montevallo, and once at Talladega, Alabama; at the latter place I raised a collection amounting to $143, for the Association, and at the former place $116, to furnish the soldiers with Testaments, $100 of which was from Mr. Sharp.

"During the month I have distributed of the

"*Army and Navy Herald*,	10,000 copies.
"Soldiers' hymn books,	2,000 "
"Soldiers' papers,	600 "

"3,000 copies of the *Herald* on hand.

"Our thanks are due to Major Bransford, Chief of Transportation for the Army of Tennessee, and his affable clerks, for the assistance they have given me in the discharge of my duties; also to the citizens and ministers at the different places visited, for their assistance, encouragement and hospitalities during my sojourn with them.

"S. M. CHERRY,
"General Distributing Agent, Army of Tennessee.
"Selma, Ala., en route for North Alabama."

REPORT FOR NOVEMBER AND DECEMBER, 1864.

"REV. ROBERT J. HARP, Superintendent:

"*Dear Brother:* In November I brought the supplies of the Association in my possession to Cherokee, Alabama, the nearest point of railroad transportation to our army, then at Florence, Alabama, preparing for the continuation of the fall campaign into Middle Tennessee.

"It was not practicable or advisable for me to carry supplies and follow the army, and the time was spent in distributing *Heralds*, hymn-books, and Testaments on the railroads from Selma to Demopolis, Alabama, and thence to Meridian and Corinth, Mississippi, and from Corinth to Cherokee, Alabama, and on the steamboats from Selma to Montgomery, Alabama. I also furnished reading for the hospitals at Lauderdale Springs, Corinth and Iuka, Mississippi.

"I visited and preached twice for Patterson's Brigade of Roddy's Division of Cavalry. The officers and soldiers took much interest in preaching and were glad to be furnished with 500 copies of the *Herald*. I supplied a portion of Forrest's corps of cavalry also with *Heralds* and hymn-books on their return from Middle Tennessee.

"I visited the Wayside Home at Okalona, Mississippi, preaching twice to the soldiers who stop over at night either in going to or from the front, several of whom came forward for prayer. At Corinth I had the privilege of preaching to a portion of the Second Regiment Engineer Corps, and the sick and wounded soldiers several times—interest was manifested by a number of them, who gave evidence of a desire to seek religion. I also enjoyed the privilege of attending the session of the Memphis Conference, held at Aberdeen, Mississippi, November 9-14; and the Montgomery Conference at Tuskegee, Alabama, December 7-13. At both places I was treated with great courtesy and true kindness by the members of the Conferences and the citizens, and secured many assurances of aid and encouragement in my mission. All seemed eager to learn of the good results of the work of your association among the soldiers.

"I met the army beyond the Tennessee River on its return from Middle Tennessee. The soldiers were very eager indeed to see the *Herald* again, and they greeted the copies furnished them as a familiar friend of other and happier days. I regretted that the supply on hand was not sufficient to satisfy the pressing demands of the entire army. Many of the readers and some of the distributors of your publications have fallen during the past bloody campaign.

"It has been exceedingly difficult to get supplies from Macon to this point, thus far. No Southern Express Office this side of Meridian, near 200 miles distant. I have had to bring all in person that I have gotten through with much toil and trouble. But we hope to have better facilities for furnishing the army during the winter. The demand for religious reading is now very great. Let the association do all it can for the soldiers of this army.

"The distribution for the months of November and December amount to
"12,000 copies *Army and Navy Herald*.
"2,000 hymn-books.
"600 copies Soldiers' paper.
"13 Sermons preached.

"S. M. CHERRY.

"Corinth, Miss., December 31, 1864."

REPORT FOR JANUARY, 1865.

"REV. ROBERT J. HARP, Superintendent:

"*Dear Brother:* New Year's Day General Cheatham's Corps reached Corinth, Mississippi, from the campaign into Middle Tennessee, and as the troops of that command passed through to their camps I had an opportunity of distributing to them papers, tracts and hymn-books. In the evening I visited Cleburne's Division and preached for the soldiers of Govans' Arkansas and Gransbury's Texas Brigades, and furnished them with a supply of books, which were gladly received and well used in our evening service. Captain Brown, commanding Gransbury's Brigade, and Brother Hudson, of Division Headquarters, gave me a very kind reception. During a stay of one week at Corinth I had the privilege of preaching twice at night at the quarters of a portion of the Engineer Corps and the Distributing Hospital. The soldiers took an interest in preaching, and some of the sick, wounded and frost-bitten came forward as penitents.

"The army rested for several days at Tupelo, and there I visited most of the commands of Lee's Corps, furnishing them with hymn-books and papers; preached for Brantly's Mississippi Brigade at night by request of Chaplain Hall. The night was cool, but the soldiers around the log fire were quite attentive. The next Sabbath morning preached for Sharpe's Mississippi Brigade, and in the afternoon for Lowry's Alabama and Mississippi Brigades; kindly received by Colonel Abecrombie, Forty-fifth Alabama, and Chaplain McBride, Fifth Mississippi Regiment, and by General Sharp and Chaplain Archer. The soldiers in each command came out in the smoke and wind to hear preaching. The troops began to leave Tupelo on the 19th and all were gone by the 28th. I remained until the last command left in order to distribute all supplies that might arrive. On Sunday, 29th, I preached for Quarles's Tennessee and Alabama Brigades, West Point, Mississippi, and furnished hymn-books and papers for them and Ector's Texas Brigade. All papers, tracts and hymn-books in my possession were distributed before I left Mississippi.

"I regret to report that I hear much more profanity among the troops since the return of the army from Tennessee than we were accustomed to hear last summer, yet many of the soldiers are still living consistent Christians, and are not spiritually demoralized by defeat and great hardships. The faithful services of efficient chaplains and missionaries are much needed by the soldiers now. Many of the chaplains and some of the missionaries have shared all the rigors of the winter campaign, preaching whenever an opportunity offered; others have resigned and returned to their homes.

"The labors for the month; 2,000 copies *Army and Navy Herald;* 300 soldiers'
papers; 1,500 hymn-books; 8 sermons preached.   "S. M. CHERRY.
" Meridian, Mississippi, January 31, 1865."

REPORT FOR FEBRUARY, 1865.

" REV. ROBERT J. HARP, Superintendent :

"Dear Brother: The second day of the month I reached Montgomery, where I
was kindly entertained by Brother S. S. Sikes, chaplain on post duty.   With him
visited the ' Stonewall Hospital,' and was glad to see the soldiers all recognize the
' parson,' who visits each ward promptly three or four times each week, and holds
service on the Sabbath.   At night, by request of Brother Brown, an earnest, zealous
young preacher, an inmate of the hospital, I preached at the ' Concert Hall Hospital '
to the sick and convalescent soldiers; they were quite attentive and serious, and
took much interest in singing.   Brother Brown was holding meetings nightly, with
good interest manifested by the soldiers.

"At Macon, the second Sabbath in the month, by request of Miss Goulding, one
of the matrons of the ' Ocmulgee Hospital,' I preached in one of the wards to a
number of soldiers, who seemed desirous of hearing the word.

" With 15,000 copies of the *Army and Navy Herald* I started for Augusta on the
13th and furnished papers to the soldiers on the trains and those we met on the
roads.

" On Sunday, the 19th, preached in the morning to a portion of Lowry's Brigade
and Loring's Division at Camp Direction, in Edgefield District, South Carolina;
in the afternoon to the Forty-sixth Georgia Regiment.   I found the chaplain,
Brother Brown, at his post; two chaplains of Loring's Division at the morning service.   Papers were distributed freely to the soldiers at both places.   Several days
were spent in Augusta furnishing papers for the soldiers who were passing through
the city.

" Instead of proceeding to Columbia with the army, as was intended, by your
request and the advice of the treasurer, Brother Burke, I remained in Augusta to aid
in shipping a large supply of paper for the publications of the association, and
returned to Mayfield, where I continued to supply with papers the large number of
Confederate soldiers who were returning from furlough to their commands, and the
militia of Georgia going on furlough to their homes.

" We are under special obligations to Major W. F. Ayer, Chief Quartermaster,
Major Jno. S. Bransford, Chief of Transportation, and Major Throckmorton, of the
Transportation Department, all of the Army of Tennessee, for the invaluable services they rendered the association in securing an early shipment of the paper, and
saving several thousand dollars for the benefit of the soldiers and the association.

" Our thanks are also due Mr. Jones and Honeycut for assistance given me.   I
am glad to report that the trains are thronged daily with the soldiers who were fur-
loughed home, now returning to our army in South Carolina.

" Receipts for the month: Mr. Thompson, Mrs. Morton, B. Banks, Gainsville,
Georgia, $20 each; Mrs. M. E. Hundley, Mrs. Dr. Jas. Jones, $10 each, Thomp-
son, Georgia.   Distributions: 7,000 copies of the *Army and Navy Herald;* 112
Bibles; 300 Testaments; 200 gospels, and 9 sermons preached.

" Milledgeville, March 1, 1865."   " S. M. CHERRY.

REPORT FOR MARCH, 1865.

" REV. ROBERT J. HARP, Superintendent:

"Dear Brother: The 4th of March I received at Milledgeville 15,000 copies of
the *Army and Navy Herald* of the issues of February 16 and 23, and March 2.
The day following I succeeded in getting the entire supply on Captain Clark's supply train.   Through the kindness of the wagon-master and teamsters the papers

were carried free of charge to Warrenton, thence by the favor of Major Hall to Camak. Learning that Lieutenant-General S. D. Lee would leave Augusta on the 18th for Charlotte, North Carolina, I collected all my supplies together for shipment to our soldiers in North Carolina. After furnishing General S. D. Lee's command, at 'Camp Organization,' with a liberal supply, and other troops around Augusta and on the railroads, I had 16,000 papers to bring through on the wagon train of the dates November 15, 1864, January 5, 12, 19, 26, February 2, 9, 16, 23, and March 2, 1865.

"Through much difficulty I succeeded in getting the papers on the ordnance train, the teamsters kindly taking a package of one thousand papers on each wagon after being heavily loaded with ammunition. Owing to the high water, and the bridges having been washed away on the Enoree, Tyger and Little Rivers, our route was rather circuitous, and the bad condition of the roads rendered our progress slow. We came through the Districts of Edgefield, Newberry, Laurens, Spartanburg, Union, York and Chester, to Chesterville, South Carolina, by the wagon train, a distance of one hundred and fifty miles. Two weeks were consumed in the trip. At Chesterville we took the train for Raleigh, North Carolina. The *Heralds* now on hand have been brought two hundred miles by Government wagons free of charge.

"The first Sabbath in the month I spent in Milledgeville, Georgia, and preached for Brother George Yarbrough, who gave me the welcome of a brother.

"The second Sunday I was in Thomson, Georgia, where I took up a collection of $206 for your association, preached there twice, and once at night in Warrenton, Georgia, when our wagon train was passing through.

"At Camp Organization, near Augusta, I preached twice on fast day to very large, attentive audiences; also at the same place the night preceding the march to Chesterville,

"The chaplains at Camp Organization, Brothers Hanks and Gregory, held a protracted meeting for several days with good results—a number of penitents, and about twelve professions of faith and applications for church membership.

"The distribution of the *Army and Navy Herald* for the month was 12,000 copies; 15,000 copies now on hand. I also preached nine sermons.

"I shall go directly to the army and distribute the papers in my possession. We may still encounter difficulties in furnishing our soldiers in North Carolina and Virginia with the publications of your association; but, regardless of the obstacles and difficulties to overcome, the soldiers must and shall have all the papers and tracts you can furnish. Let the home population continue their contributions for this purpose: I know of no other source of supply of religious reading for our soldiers now accessible.					"S. M. CHERRY.

"Chesterville, South Carolina, March 31, 1865."

DYING WORDS.

"Marietta, Georgia, June 9, 1864. Thomas F. Folks, of Jackson's head-quarters' scouts, Twenty-eighth Mississippi Regiment, from Warren county, Mississippi, died of his wounds in great peace to-day. He was of fine form and handsome face with beautiful black hair and flowing beard. He talked so calmly of death and so tenderly of his mother. All was well with the noble young man. How I sympathized with his brother when he leaned so fondly over the dying form and caressed him as if he were a child, saying so pathetically and touchingly: 'Tom, you are dying; speak to me, boy, poor fellow!'

"June 10. T. M. Holland, Company D, Fifty-fourth Tennessee—home Randolph, Tipton county, Tennessee—was resigned to the will of God, but from the nature of his wound could say but little, but declared himself ready and willing to go.

"June 11. Lieutenant Rankin, Twenty-ninth Mississippi, when wounded was placed in my charge, and I carried him to the Medical College Hospital. While in the ambulance with him he said he believed the wound was mortal. He had grown cold by neglecting his duty, but had tried to be a Christian and lead a better life, and had hope of heaven.

"June 17. When I began speaking to Mr. White, of the Sixteenth Alabama, to-day, who was a penitent at the altar during the revival in Lowry's Brigade last month, he said he feared his wound was mortal, and he felt like he was almost lost, but I began to read him selections of Scripture suitable to encourage the penitent, and his faith took right hold of God's promises, and he began to thank God, and to say very softly, 'Sweet Jesus.' Then turning his dying eyes on me, he said, 'Tell my mother I am prepared to meet my God in peace.'

"June 22. To-day talked with Brother Coffee, who is dying of his wounds, brother of Rev. Mr. Coffee, Cumberland Presbyterian Church—he is ready for his discharge. To-day General Hooker's Corps attacked General Hood's, and was handsomely repulsed, but Stevenson's Division lost heavily, especially Brown's Brigade and Fifty-fourth Virginia Regiment. I stayed with Rev. Atticus G. Haygood, who has been with us at Marietta for some time.

"June 23. Chaplain Porter and I leave together. The Court-House is Stevenson's Division Hospital. The wounded cover the floor, which is wet with human gore. I spoke to C. L. Langston, Company D, Twentieth Alabama Regiment, shot through the breast. He said, 'If I die I feel that I will go home to heaven.' Went to the hall of the Griffin, Georgia, Relief Committee; some one said a minister had just died. I found out directly that it was Lieutenant Cornelius Hardin, Thirty-fifth Mississippi Regiment. He and his brother were sitting side by side eating their dinner together in the trenches when the same shell severed the leg of one and the arm of the other. The young preacher, who had been very recently ordained by Bishop Paine, if I mistake not, while on furlough to his home in North Mississippi, said in dying, 'God has always been with me, and is with me now.' Perry, his brother, was hopeful of recovery, and said to me, 'Pray for me specially that I may get well to support my poor widowed mother and sisters.' But he was not afraid to die. He wished all his mother's family to live so that they should finally live in heaven. Cornelius and Perry Hardin 'were lovely and pleasant in their lives and in death they were not divided.' We buried them side by side in their soldier blankets in a beautiful grove of oaks near where they left earth for heaven. I wrote their mother and sisters of their last hours and resting place, dreading to receive a reply. But when the missive came it breathed so much 'sweetness out of woe' and faith and hope in God and the reunion in heaven that I thanked God that there are such noble mothers to testify that God's grace is sufficient to sustain in the greatest trials on earth.

"The same day I looked upon Colonel Cook, Thirty-second Tennessee, who lay alone under a fly with a mortal wound. Colonel Walker, Third Tennessee, also is dying. Both of these brave men testify that they are resigned to death. How much good grew out of the great revival in their brigade a few weeks ago God only knows.

"Atlanta, July 20. Heavy artillery firing. Severe loss in the brigades of Featherston, Scott, Reynolds' Arkansas and Stephens' Georgia. General Stephens severely wounded. I talked with a soldier, Fifty-third Alabama Cavalry, horribly mangled. His parents not religious, and he has made no profession, but is praying, and says he trusts in God for salvation. How hard to instruct those in religious truth that have had no home training!

"Ed. Stafford, a nice, bright-eyed boy of nineteen years of age, from Springfield, Arkansas, mortally wounded, confessed that he had been a wild boy, but he said, 'Pray for me, and write to my mother that I was a faithful soldier to the last.' He praised God after I read the Fifty-first Psalm, and prayed for his salvation.

"East Point, near Atlanta, Georgia, July 25, at 3 P. M. I was called to see Lieutenant G. P. Dean, Fifteenth Texas Regiment. His wound was slight but had gangrened. Chaplain Kramer and Rev. W. H. Potter, of Georgia, were with me. Brother Kramer prayed, and the lieutenant said he was trying to trust in God, and prayed for God to help him to believe, and then with feeble, fast failing voice said, 'I hope to meet you all in heaven.' While I read, 'Let not your heart be troubled, ye believe in God, believe also in me. In my Father's house are many mansions,' etc., he whispered, 'How glorious,' and was gone while I read to him of Christ's coming to receive unto himself all who come unto him and believe on him. He left with me a letter for his betrothed in C——, Alabama.

"July 28. Generals Stewart and Loring were among the wounded to-day. I was with each of them. Talked to Colonel Crook, who is terribly wounded. He testifies that he has been trying to be a true Christian in the army, and all is right living or dying. This gallant young Tennesseean talks like a true Christian—a member of the Methodist Church, Twenty-eighth Tennessee Regiment.

"East Point, August 8, 1864. S. W. Jenkins, Company E, Fifty-eighth Alabama, is fearfully riddled with balls, but as he lay beneath a little fly dying this hot dusty day his eye was very bright. I grasped his hand and said, 'How is it now with you, my dear boy?' He pressed my hand closely, and said, 'I am all right, parson; have not seen a dark day for two years; can't doubt now, and I thank God for it. Write my mother that I am mortally wounded, but I will meet her in heaven.' He had attracted my attention by his eager interest in our camp worship from the time his regiment entered our brigade a year or more ago. He delighted to do what he could to help us in the camp service. He was but a boy, the son of a widow, but had been a member of the Methodist Church for four years, and a most consistent Christian in camp, and there he lay dying upon the ground the most glorious, triumphant death I witnessed during the war, if not in all my life.

"These ten dying men I heard testify in two months. They were from Alabama, Arkansas, Tennessee, Texas, and Mississippi. That has been more than twenty-three years ago. Little thought had I then in noting their last words in my journal that I should pen them now for the purpose I do. But these being dead yet speak by the words spoken in death. Colonel Crook recovered and preached for years.

CHRISTIAN LOVE AND UNITY.

"Our Chaplains' Association and all of our army acquaintance and work together had a wonderful power in breaking down barriers and removing denominational prejudices that may have existed before we met among the soldiers. I remember the first day of May, 1864. I went out to Cumming's Georgia Brigade and witnessed a baptismal service. Chaplain Thompson, Baptist, led fifteen soldiers into the water and baptized them, and was followed by Chaplain Rosser, Methodist Protestant, with four others who were baptized in the same way—only one service on the water's edge for the two chaplains. Five others were baptized on the land by Chaplain Rosser. The same day I saw Chaplain W. A. Parkes, Methodist South, administer the sacrament of the Lord's Supper to Stewart's Division, and among them, between two soldier communicants, kneeling on the rough logs on the bare ground, was Major-General Stewart, an elder in the Cumberland Presbyterian Church. Major Hatcher, one of his staff, kneeled by his side. Dr. McFerrin and many of the chaplains were in the habit of offering the soldiers the privilege of joining the Church by asking all that wished to join the Church to come forward, and their names would be taken and the denomination of their choice and preachers of their own faith and order would be looked up by the preachers, and they would receive baptism at the hands of such ministers as they preferred, and their names could be forwarded wherever they wished or certificates furnished them of their baptism or reception into the Church.

"On one occasion a soldier came among others to be received into the Church,

38

and when Dr. McFerrin asked him what Church or denomination of Christians, he replied : ' The Roman Catholic, sir; I know no better.' I scarce need add that he was a son of Erin's Isle. Such was the brotherly love and fraternal friendship existing between the chaplains in the army that in reading my journal now there are many familiar names that I find which recall faces once very dear to me, and yet I cannot remember the denominations of the faithful servants of Christ. Rev. S. S. Taylor, Thirty-seventh Georgia, with whom I was so long intimately associated, who was killed at Franklin, Tenn., December, 1864, was a Primitive Baptist, a private soldier, yet an humble, devout soldier of Christ.

PREACHING PLACES.

" The first winter of the war our brigade did not take interest enough in religious services to prepare a place of worship. The second winter our heavy battles were in December and January, and we were much on the march in these months and changed our camping places frequently, and we had preaching and prayer-meeting when the weather would permit as often as practical at such places as we thought most suitable. But at Dalton, Georgia, rude chapels were built by the soldiers of different brigades. I remember distinctly, in Brown's Brigade, Chaplains Chapman, Davenport and Harris had a very convenient and comfortable house built, large enough to accommodate all who would attend, as they supposed. But when the great revival began, soon the chapel was so crowded that they enlarged it by taking out the logs on one side, which doubled the seating capacity. But still the eager hearers could not find room, and the end logs were removed. But, when roll-call was over of an evening, there would be a rush of the soldiers to get as near as possible to the preachers, and it finally became necessary to remove the logs of the other side, only leaving those at the end by the preaching place remaining.

" At Tyner's Station, near Chattanooga, the summer of 1863, we had arbors prepared of pine, or black-jack poles, covered with brush, and for lights we had there and at Fairfield small scaffolds a few feet high and two or three feet across the top, covered with earth and torch-light fires upon them.

" But soldiers were not particular about places. What they preferred were men who would be with them at any time or any place where duty called the soldiers, willing to endure hardship and exposure and their perils, if need be, to preach Christ to them.

" Many sermons were preached in the trenches, and soldiers there heard the word which was blessed to their salvation. Any place where the preacher could stand and the soldiers could sit, stand or recline was suitable for the true worshippers of God in the army who sought to worship the Father in spirit and in truth. Rock, stump or moss-covered log would answer the chaplain well enough for pulpit or book-board, and logs or rails were just suited for the soldiers to sit upon or kneel beside in the true worship of God. God was with us in our service, and that was all we asked or desired.

" Since writing the above on *preaching places* I find by reference to my journal that on Sunday, August 7, 1864, I preached for French's Division, Ector's, McNair's and a part of Gholson's Brigades in the trenches near Atlanta, and that a caisson was used for a pulpit, and there was no screen from the burning sun. Preached for Seer's Brigade in afternoon and heard the experience of soldiers to Chaplain Lattimore, Baptist, and saw him and Chaplain —— baptize fifteen soldiers in a pond in which the Federals threw three shells the day before, none, however. during the baptizing.

CHAPLAIN'S BADGE.

" The badge adopted by the Chaplains' Association of the Army of Tennessee was the Maltese cross, worn on the collar or lappel of their coats.

LAST DAYS WITH THE ARMY OF TENNESSEE.

"In March, 1865, we were at Camp Direction, at Hamburg, S. C., across the river from Augusta, Georgia. There I met Chaplains Brown, Forty-sixth Georgia, and Daniel, Fifty-seventh Georgia, Gregory and Hanks and Rev. J. P. McFerrin, who had recovered of his wounds sufficiently to preach to the soldiers. We had frequent camp services there until our march through South Carolina, via Edgefield and Laurens' Court-House and Spartanburg and Union Districts and across the Saluda, Enoree and Broad Rivers to Chesterville. This march across the State we made March 18 to 31. I was in company with Chaplains M. B. Dewitt, Eighth Tennessee, R. G. Porter, Tenth Mississippi, and Gregory and Tatum. Dr. Dewitt was one of our most efficient chaplains in the army. I saw much of him during the war. He was ready all the time for all good work. He is now pastor of the Second Cumberland Presbyterian Church in Nashville and is deservedly popular. He has been a leader among his people for years as editor, pastor, etc., and has just been offered the presidency of a leading school of his Church.

"R. G. Porter is the 'Gilderoy' of our Church papers and has been a popular writer in the Methodist press for many years, also presiding elder and pastor for many years in North Mississippi.

"Sunday, April 2. Heard Dr. J. B. McFerrin preach at 11 A. M. and 7 P. M. at the Methodist church in Charlotte, N. C. I preached at 9 A. M. and 4 P. M. to the sick and wounded in the hospitals and at 3 P. M. to the colored people. Post Chaplain Kennedy received me very kindly.

"The march across South Carolina was under General S. D. Lee. From Charlotte we went to Smithfield, North Carolina, via Raleigh, on the railroad. There had been some fighting about Averysboro, near Smithfield, during our march by the Army of Tennessee. At Smithfield I was kept busy during the week distributing religious reading to the chaplains and preaching. A few hours after my arrival, Chaplain Hill, of Kirkland's Brigade, carried me out to the camps, and I preached to a large audience at night, April 4.

"April 5. Preached at night for Chaplains McBride and Moore, Cleburne's old division; 18 penitents forward for prayer.

"April 6. Preached at night for Loring's Division; 14 seeking religion.

"April 8. Supper with Chaplain M. B. Chapman, Thirty-second Tennessee, one of the true and tried men of the war, a true blue Presbyterian in fidelity, but full of charity, very successful as a modest chaplain, and equally so for many years after the war, in building up a good church at Smyrna, Tennessee. No better man in the army or Presbyterian Church, I think. He died some years ago. Preached for Cumming's and Pettus's Brigades at night.

"Smithfield, North Carolina, April 9, 1865. Breakfast with Chaplain Harris, Twenty-sixth Tennessee. Rode his mule to head-quarters of Lieutenant-General Stewart, now in command. Met Brothers Ransom, Burr, and Mooney, and a number of chaplains. At 11 A. M. preached to Palmer's Brigade of Tennessee troops. Dined with Chaplain Chapman and Colonel McGuire; preached in afternoon for Chaplain Porter to Sharp's Mississippi Brigade. Brother R. P. Ransom preached from 'The Righteous Scarcely Saved.' Slept with Chaplains Tomkies and Giles of Florida Brigade.

"April 10. Smithfield evacuated; went to Raleigh and assisted Brother Crowder till nearly midnight in packing Testaments, psalms, tracts, and hymns.

"Raleigh, North Carolina, April 11. Got my literature on a soldiers' train, and a seat on the top of a box-car, and left Raleigh at 4 P. M.

"April 12. Greensboro', North Carolina, was reached in time for breakfast. We came slowly and stopped often on account of Stoneman's raid. Paid $20 for breakfast and begged the colored door-keeper to let me in the dining-room. President Davis and Cabinet at the hotel where I eat. General Lee's surrender confirmed; met many of our preachers. Called on Sister Bumpass, who edits *The Message*, for which I have been writing and securing subscribers for several years. She and her son and daughters gave me a warm welcome. At 5 P. M. a pleasant prayer meeting at her home. Her prayer and that of Miss Alla Clary impressed me by the simplicity and sincerity of their earnest supplications.

"April 13. Met Chaplains A. D. McVoy and Moses L. Whitten, the latter my Conference class-mate. I begin to realize the war is over, but I thank God that I have been with the Southern Army as a chaplain, and am not willing to leave it yet.

"April 14. Brought my Testaments, hymn-books, etc., from the depot to the store of Sterling and Campbell; met General Beauregard.

"April 15. Secured an old government horse.

"Greensboro', North Carolina, Sunday, April 16. Breakfast before day-light. When Sister Bumpass bid me good-bye her hearty words, 'Brother Cherry, I don't believe the Yankees will get you,' did my soul great good. I overtook Dibbrell's Division of Tennessee and Kentucky soldiers acting as escort to President Davis five miles from Greensboro'. I saw Secretary of State J. P. Benjamin and Adjutant-General S. Cooper.

"April 17. Saw President Davis again at Lexington. At Jersey Church dined with Mr. G. S. He was much troubled, but said he was trying to live for heaven. I paid him $5 for my dinner, and promised to pray for him. While at the railroad bridge of the Yadkin River, President Davis rode up and looked across the river with apparent anxiety. I responded to his inquiry for Quarter-master General Lawton. He talked for awhile and rode away. I pity him in the day of his misfortune. We crossed the classic Yadkin by getting the wheels of our wagons astride of the rails on the cross-ties of the railroad which was on the roof on top of the bridge. Stoneman had burnt the other bridge. The picture of the President, cabinet, and escort, crossing the river in such romantic style at sunset would have afforded an artist a splendid sketch.

"April 18. Passed through Salisbury to-day, the early home of President Andrew Jackson; marched all night, going through Concord at midnight.

"April 19. Charlotte, North Carolina, was reached early in the morning. Stoneman has burnt the bridge across the Catawba River before us to-day. Heard of President Lincoln's assassination, which we much regret.

"April 20. Marched to the Tuckasage Ford on the Catawba River.

"April 21. Preached at night for Colonel McLemore's Brigade. Slept for the last night in the army with Chaplain Austin W. Smith, at General Dibbrell's headquarters. I have been much with Brother Smith this week and during the war. He is one of God's noble and faithful men. He has been very true to me, and tender as a woman with sick and wounded soldiers.

"Mecklenburg County, North Carolina, April 22. Took leave of my army friends in Dibbrell's Division of McLemore's and Breckenridge's Brigades, Cavalry. General Dibbrell is an exemplary member of the Methodist Church, and has treated us kindly this week. Crossed the Catawba on the pontoon, near the burnt bridge, and reached Rock Hill, South Carolina, and stopped with Brother Bennick, a nice Dutchman, who preached to the soldiers at night; met Chaplains Monk and Mc-Cheever, of Ferguson's Brigade.

"Rock Hill, South Carolina, Sunday, April 23. Sick to-day, but preached at 11 A. M. to a crowded congregation, chiefly soldiers, from Ex. xxxiii. 18; dined on cold biscuit, ham, and syrup. Heard Chaplain Williams, Third South Carolina Cavalry, preach at 3 P. M. Took supper with Mrs. Roddy, an Associate Reformed Presbyterian. She and her nephew sang a psalm at sunset, a custom of her family at that hour wherever they are.

"At night preached for Ferguson's Cavalry Brigade and administered the Sacrament of the Lord's Supper to the soldiers by request of the chaplains, and thus ended my work in the army. I knew not then that the Army of the Tennessee had been surrendered. Dr. McFerrin preached in Greensboro', North Carolina, that morning to the Army of Tennessee a valedictory sermon for the soldiers. I preached my first sermon to the soldiers, I think, at Winchester, late in April, 1861, and my last at Rock Hill, South Carolina, Sunday night, April 23, 1865.

"I spent a couple of weeks with Chaplain Whitten with his kindred in Newberry, South Carolina. Came alone on horseback to Macon, Georgia, where I was paroled, May 23, just a month after the surrender of the army; met some of the escort there of President Davis, who were with him at his capture at Irvington, Georgia. Of course, it was a hoax about the President having on his wife's clothing when captured. Those who took the President at night I presume did not know the difference between a gentleman's *robe de chambre* and a lady's apparel. Some time was spent with Chaplain Bolton, of Tennessee, with our true, tried army friends at their homes in Barnesville and Thomaston, and elsewhere in Pike and Upson Counties, Georgia, and I mounted my faithful gray horse, which brought me from North Carolina through South Carolina into Georgia, and I started home *via* Columbus, Georgia; Auburn and Tuscaloosa, Alabama; Aberdeen, Mississippi; and Moulton, Alabama, and home again to Tennessee, July 13, after an absence in the army of four years and four days since I first left my charge at Winchester, Tennessee, August 9, 1861. Never before or since did I have such a broad and inviting field for constant work and great usefulness as I did in the Army of Tennessee.

"My appreciation of Southern manhood and true chivalry and consistent Christianity was increased and intensified by my army acquaintance and association.

"Christ was in the Camp of the Southern States' Army; to me there is no doubt on that point. All Christian virtues had a full test in army life. Thousands of boys, young men, and men in middle life stood the test and they were more than conquerors over all the temptations, trials, and troubles of the camp and conflict through Christ the great Captain of their salvation. And now, after nearly twenty-three years since the surrender and thirty-three years of active itinerant life, like Dr. McNeilly, a Presbyterian pastor of Nashville, and a faithful chaplain in the Army of Tennessee, I thank God that he gave me the privilege of preaching to the soldiers of the South and of taking part in the great revival around Dalton.

"Yours, fraternally,

"S. M. CHERRY.

"Home near Vanderbilt University,
"Nashville, Tennessee, March 8, 1888."

It is due to Mr. Cherry to say, that he prepared the above deeply interesting sketch of his work on very short notice, and under the interruption of severe sickness. Is not he the man to give us a full History of Religion in the Army of Tennessee? All who read the above sketch will want the *full work*. Shall we not have it?

Brother Cherry has not only prepared the sketch of work in the Army of Tennessee, but has also sent me a large number of valuable clippings from the *Army and Navy Herald*, from which the following are selected:

REPORT OF THE DEPARTMENT OF SOUTHWESTERN SOLDIERS' TRACT ASSOCIATION, METHODIST EPISCOPAL CHURCH, SOUTH.

"MACON, November 10, 1863.

"To THE REV. W. W. BENNETT,
GENERAL SUPERINTENDENT, RICHMOND, VA.:

"By the blessings of God I am enabled to submit the accompanying report of the financial condition of this department. Much time during the quarter has been spent in the necessary business connected with the establishment of a publishing house in this city and the issue of the *Army and Navy Herald*, hence you will see by report I have only taken five collections during the quarter (making an aggregate subscription of $12,343.70, of which $10,894.20 has been paid), while eight weeks of the quarter have passed without my being able to leave other business to reach suitable places for that purpose; this, in connection with the fact that it was necessary for Dr. Camp to go to the army in Mississippi, which almost entirely suspended his collections, accounts for the small amounts of the receipts of the quarter. Rev. S. S. Sweet has been pushing forward our operations at this place with zeal and energy, and I think we shall soon be able, if we continue to get paper, to issue a large amount of printed matter. We have already issued

Hymn books.. 15,000 copies.
Tracts...528,000 pages.
Army and Navy Herald.................................. 20,000 copies.

Distributed during quarter.

Scriptures.. 3,122 copies.
Tracts..370,000 pages.
Hymn books.. 1,087 copies.

Stock in hand at sundry places.

Paper to value of................................... $1,560 00
Rags, etc.. 2,140 00
Presses, type, and fixtures of printing office, valued at.... 4,000 00

Report of gross amount of subscriptions and collections for quarter.

	Subscriptions.	Due on subscriptions.	Received on subscriptions.
Bethel Camp Meeting................$3,722 00		$669 34	$3,052 66
Houston " 4,015 75		445 73	3,560 00
Mount Zion " 2,487 50		337 00	2,150 00
Spring Hill "		......	378 45
Liberty " 1,100 00		42 60	1,057 50
Mt. Zion Q. M...................... 801 65		20 00	781 65
Buena Vista Camp Meeting........... 1,028 75		25 00	1,903 75
Tabernacle "		......	2,123 50
Lumpkin " 1,740 00		193 00	1,517 00
Upson "		......	800 00
Fort Valley........................		......	180 00
Milledgeville		......	540 00
Atlanta Depot......................		......	317 00
To treasurer.......................		......	182 00

Due on subscription............... $1,732 59
Total collected per quarter...... ....$17,673 85
Collected on subscriptions of last quarter.......................... 869 00
Receipts on sales.. 391 00

Gross receipts per quarter..................................... 18,290 85
Gross receipts per last quarter................................. 13,905 49
Gross receipts from Louisiana.............................. 5,337 00

$37,533 25

Contributions in stock (not less)................................. $ 500 00
Due on subscriptions, mostly good............................... 2,100 25

$40,133 50

" Disposed of as per reports submitted the 10th of August and the 10th of November, 1863.
" I herewith transmit the accompanying reports of the treasurer and agents.
" Yours fraternally,
" ROBERT J. HARP, *Superintendent Department Southwest.*"

" DALTON, GA., February 17, 1864.
" At a meeting of the Chaplains' Association of the Army of Tennessee the following reports, motions and resolutions were adopted, which may be interesting to the public.
" Communications from Hardee's and Hindman's Corps presented a very encouraging report of the state of religion in the above corps.
" B. W. McDonald, on committee to receive Bibles from the enemy, if practicable, reported a communication from the Secretary of War, stating that there was no commerce allowed between us and the enemy, and therefore the Bibles could not be procured in that way.
" W. H. Browning, on committee to supply destitute regiments with religious privileges, reported that every regiment in Hardee's Corps, except Cleburn's Division, had been visited and furnished with religious services.
" W. T. Bennett, on committee to publish the tract on ' Depredations on Private Property,' reported that the publishers at Macon, Ga., were willing to adopt and publish the tract as their own.
" J. G. Richards introduced the following :
"*Resolved*, That the General Association recommend to the chaplains and missionaries of the several brigades to furnish to the Corps Associations statistical tables, stating the amount of reading matter distributed, the number of prayer meetings held, sermons preached, the number of Christian Associations and their membership, and that the Corps Associations report the same to this association.
" J. B. McFerrin moved that the secretary be requested to notify those concerned of the above, and he takes this method of doing so.
"A committee was appointed to overture the President C. S. A. to appoint an early day of fasting, humiliation and prayer.
" M. B. DeWitt introduced the following :
"*Resolved*, That we, the chaplains and missionaries of the Army of Tennessee, in association assembled, do most earnestly, yet respectfully, petition the Congress of the Confederate States to so alter or amend the army regulations as to forbid all reviews, inspections, other parades and all other work not essentially necessary to the security of the army on the Sabbath day. God has commanded us to ' keep this day holy,' which cannot be done under the present regulations.
" The following substitute for the above was adopted :
"*Resolved*, That we, chaplains and missionaries of this army, move a memorial from the army to Congress to remove existing regulations affecting the sanctity of the Sabbath.
"Association adjourned with prayer.
"A. D. McVOY, *Secretary.*"

{ " CAVALRY BIVOUAC,
{ " LEFT WING, ARMY OF TENNESSEE, October 15, 1864.
" EDITOR *Army and Navy Herald :*
"A few copies of your paper have, from time to time, since the connection of my

600 APPENDIX.

regiment (Twenty-eighth Mississippi Volunteers, Armstrong's Brigade) with this army, fallen into my hands. I found it superior to any religious paper which I had ever seen, in soundness of doctrine, perspicuity of argument and versatility of thought. Its absence I have often regretted; its Christian, strengthening advice I have often missed around my bivouac fires. I ask, in the name of many, can it not come oftener?

"Without complaining, I would also ask why is the cavalry forgotten by the religious associations of the country? A fact is but stated to you when I say that my brigade is totally bereft of all religious instruction. There is not a chaplain—no, not one, among us. Since the first of February last three sermons have been preached to us, two by itinerant ministers, one by a soldier, a professor of religion in my regiment. By little prayer meetings held by a few members (of different churches) in the regiment, evidences have been given of a willingness to submit to the Divine Will. Each regiment composing the brigade has lost upwards of one hundred men in battle since May 17. Many of these souls might have been prepared. I know that outside the abuse heaped upon us, my arm of the service is supposed to be the most godless and reckless: thus the greater need for God's word. It matters not of what denomination he be, we only ask for a sensible man, who preaches the Gospel of Christ; let the road be called by any name, so it lead to the True Portal. One active minister in the brigade would do. For his maintenance several have *expressed their willingness to contribute one day's rations per week*—thus seven can maintain a preacher. I appeal to you, who have the most influence, to send us aid speedily, for what soldier can count on the rising of another sun?

"A Young Episcopalian."

ANECDOTES OF GENERAL FORREST.*

(*By a Colonel.*)

"*God our Helper.*"—FORREST.

An incident occurring the night ensuing the recent battle of "Tishamingo Creek" illustrates alike the desperate character of the contest and the feelings of the general commanding, in an hour of excessive trial.

At a late hour of the night he ceased for a few hours the pursuit of the enemy, and we found him seated in earnest thought, in a log hut on the side of the road—his exhausted staff asleep all around him. A staff officer of General S. D. Lee had just arrived, to inquire after the fate of the day. General Forrest was dictating a despatch in answer to his inquiry, and closed it with the expression: "By the help of Almighty God we have won one of the most complete victories of the war." Some one present hinted that hard fighting had a good deal to do with the victory. After a style usual to the general, when deeply in earnest, he brought his clenched fist down on his thigh, exclaiming, "I say by the help of God, and it *was* by His help; for without it we never could have whipped in the fight with the odds against us."

The Avenue to a Brave Man's Heart.

Wearied and exhausted, yet pondering the work of the next day, General Forrest sat in a hovel by the roadside on the night which closed in the brilliant victory of Tishamingo Creek. Ever and anon some remark was made descriptive of special

---

* This article is supposed to have been written by Colonel Kelly, who has since the war become a distinguished Methodist minister. General Forrest became a devout and active Christian some years before his death, carrying into the work of his Church (the Cumberland Presbyterian) something of the energy and zeal which helped to win his high reputation as "The Wizard of the Saddle."

acts of bravery during the day, till the general, aroused from his thoughtfulness, exclaimed: " Yes! not one, but all the boys did well to-day," and then, with a voice trembling with the depth of his emotion, added : " The boys sometimes fret me, and I am provoked into saying hard things to them, but when they do as they did to-day, I can forgive them for everything else." Such sympathy as this is what binds his men so strongly to him. They are sure, when they have done their duty, to find his *heart* in the right place.

Forrest and Providence.

Such are the number of anecdotes current in camp and the press illustrating the self-dependent energy and recklessness of General Forrest's character, that there is liable to be generated thereby a belief that he is as thoughtless of God and Providence as he is reckless of danger. No greater mistake could be made. Napoleon never believed more fully in destiny than does General Forrest in a personal Providence ; and in his quieter moments, especially after the perils of battle, often refers to it with great earnestness. Four men were shot down at his side, at the taking of Fort Pillow; a few days after Major Strange, Assistant Adjutant-General, was wounded at his side in a skirmish near Bolivar, Tennessee; on referring to it afterwards he asked " if any man could account, on the mere principles of reasoning or accident, for his escape."

The following order, published the Sunday after his return from the West Tennessee expedition, is illustrative of his private feelings :

" Head-quarters Forrest's Cavalry Department, Tupelo, May 14, 1864.

General Order, No. 44.

" The Major-General Commanding, devoutly grateful to the Providence of Almighty God, so signally vouchsafed to his command during the recent campaign in West Tennessee, and deeply penetrated with a sense of dependence on the mercy of God in the present crisis of our beloved country, requests that military duties be so far suspended that divine service may be attended at 10 o'clock A. M., to-morrow, by the whole command.

" Divine service will be held at these head-quarters, at which all soldiers who are disposed to do so are kindly invited to attend. Come one, come all.

" Chaplains, in the ministrations of the gospel, are requested to remember our personal preservation with thanksgiving, and especially to beseech a throne of grace for aid in this our country's hour of need.

" By command of Major-General Forrest."

The general is far from being a Christian, it is true, in many of his moments of excitement, but no man is more truly a believer in the God of the Bible and Providence, or more ready to acknowledge his wrongs and his faith.

Revival Intelligence.

" Rev. S. M. Cherry writes (March 10th), that there is a general revival at Dalton—the church in town crowded every night. About fifty had joined the Church in town, and the work is progressing in several brigades outside of town—especially Clayton's and Dean's, Alabama; Finley's Florida, Brown's Tennessee, and Reynolds' Virginia troops. He writes again on the 25th that 'the revival interest is undiminished.' "

A Bequest.

" Brother Harp—I hand to Rev. J. W. Burke, Treasurer, ninety-five dollars ; a part of a bequest from Wm. E. Howard, deceased. Mr. Howard was a Texan soldier in the Army of Tennessee, brave and patriotic. He belonged to Douglass' battery. Was converted during our revivals in the army. Mortally wounded and left a request that his effects should be appropriated to the cause of Christianity in the Army of Tennessee; especially in the distribution of religious reading. I have received from Lieutenant Ben Hardin a portion of his bequest and hand over the above-mentioned sum to the Soldiers' Tract Association. Here is work of genuine conversion to Christ. When realized the bequest will amount to some $800 or $1,000. This I shall divide among the Benevolent Institutions working for the salvation of the soldiers.

"Respectfully,　　　J. B. McFERRIN."

LETTERS FROM THE ARMY.

Lieutenant W. M. Davis, Company A, 12th Louisiana Regiment, near Montavalo, Alabama, in a private letter, says: "The Bible Class which I organized in the regiment last July, with fourteen members, has continued to deepen and widen in its influence, interest and numbers, until it now has 160 intelligent and promising men belonging to it, who not only read the Bible, but who study it diligently and closely, and take a deep interest in the subject before the class. We recite a chapter three times a week—Wednesdays, Fridays and Sundays.

"The Association which I organized about the same time with fifteen members, and reorganized at Canton, Mississippi, January 12, 1864, under the name of 'The Soldiers' Christian Union Association,' now numbers 175 members, about fifteen of whom are earnest seekers—the others have been truly and happily converted to God. About 100 of these have been converted since the organization of the Bible Class and Association. These classes are anxious to get the *Herald*.

"We are encamped near town, where there are three large churches. There is preaching in each of them every night, with large and attentive congregations, and a deep feeling manifested. In fact, there is a considerable revival going on among the soldiers. Rev. Mr. Shelton, together with the different chaplains of the army, are laboring with great zeal and God is blessing their labors abundantly. Sinners are being convicted, mourners happily converted, backsliders reclaimed, with a general revival of religion in the church. I think I could distribute 500 copies of the *Herald* to great advantage among the soldiers, for all who read it are anxious to procure more of them."

Rev. E. B. Barrett, chaplain Forty-fifth Regiment Georgia Volunteers, writes as follows: "We are having a deep and widespread work of grace in our brigade. Scores sit with us on the anxious seat; but there are few as yet who profess conversion. In God we put our trust for the final consummation of this great work. We have as a co-laborer Rev. W. H. Stuart (Methodist), of the Georgia Conference. He is a whole-souled man, and appears all the time to be overwhelmed with the responsibility of the work. Before long I trust you will hear of our great success and great rejoicing in the gospel."

Rev. J. L. Lattimore reports a revival of religion in Sears' (Mississippi) Brigade, at Selma, Alabama.

"DALTON, GA., April 12, 1864.

"ROBERT J. HARP, *Editor of the Army and Navy Herald:*

"*Dear Sir:*—At a meeting of the 'Stonewall Association' of Baker's Brigade a resolution was passed to forward a copy of the constitution and by-laws of the association to your valuable journal for publication. The objects of the society being so plainly set forth in the articles, it is unnecessary to add further remarks. Suffice it to say the objects sought after by the society commend it to the favorable consideration of all true Christians and every lover of religious and civil liberty. No patriot, much less Christian, can look at the vice and immorality following the footprints of our armies without expressing a heartfelt regret for the deplorable condition of their morals; one of our objects is to encourage virtue and morality and

frown on vice and immorality wherever exhibited.   Much good has resulted from
the efforts of organizations of this kind throughout the country, and we are
desirous of throwing our mite, though small it be, on the side of virtue, truth and
religion.

"We earnestly desire the co-operation of all those who favor the enterprise.
Truly, the field is white 'unto the harvest.' I am happy to state that the society
numbers 300 members, and is still increasing both in numbers and interest.

"All journals favorable to the objects of the Stonewall Association will confer a
favor by giving publication to our constitution and regulations, and all favors and
contributions will be thankfully received, appreciated and duly acknowledged.

"JOHN A. BILLUPS,
"Corresponding Secretary Stonewall Association.

"P. S.—All religious papers, tracts, hymn books and Testaments will be valuable
auxiliaries to our enterprise and are heartily desired.   Anything of the above order
directed to John A. Billups, Forty-second Regiment Alabama Volunteers, Baker's
Brigade, Dalton, Georgia, will be delivered to the society or disposed of according
to request."

CONSTITUTION OF THE "STONEWALL ASSOCIATION" OF BAKER'S BRIGADE.

Whereas, We observe with regret the existence of vice and immorality, in its
various forms, spreading a degrading and demoralizing influence among the soldiers;
and, *whereas,* the reverses visited upon us at different points are traceable to the prevalence of intemperance and other vices of the army; and, *whereas,* the spread of
true religion—humble trust in God as the Ruler of Nations as well as men—and
healthful moral discipline is necessary to obtain God's favor and achieve our independence; and, *whereas,* it is the duty of every soldier to use his best efforts to promote good morals and excite dependence upon and trust in God as the means of
safety in this our national chastisement:

Now, therefore, to effect these objects, we, the undersigned soldiers of Baker's
Brigade, hereby form ourselves into an association, to be known as the "Stonewall
Association," and we most heartily subscribe to the following articles, which are
hereby adopted for the government of this association:

Article 1. The objects of this association are hereby declared to be the moral,
social, intellectual and religious good of the soldiers of this brigade; the cultivation
of a social and brotherly feeling, attention to the sick and wounded, as far as may
be possible, to perpetuate the memory of those members who may sacrifice their
lives on their country's altar in this struggle for civil and religious freedom—in
short, to do our utmost to aid and assist each other in our efforts to bear hardships
and to perform the duties of the complete soldier.

Art. 2. The officers of this association shall consist of one president, three vice-
presidents, one secretary, one assistant secretary, one corresponding secretary, one
assistant corresponding secretary, one treasurer, one assistant treasurer—whose
term of office will be three months.

The president shall open and close the meetings with prayer, preside over its deliberations, preserve order and decorum, call extra sessions if necessary, and perform generally all the duties of president of deliberative bodies.   He will appoint
monthly a committee whose duty it shall be to make arrangements for all meetings
for divine service and of this association.

The vice-presidents will be designated as first, second and third, the duties of
whom will be to assist the president when necessary and perform such duties as the
president may direct.   In the absence of the president the senior vice-president
present will occupy the chair and perform the duties assigned to the president.

The secretary will keep correct minutes of the proceedings of each meeting,
which minutes will be read and submitted for correction and approval at the

ensuing session. The assistant secretary will perform the duties of the secretary in his absence.

The corresponding secretary will carry on in behalf of the association all its correspondence. It will be his duty to notify all persons who may be elected to honorary membership and receive, read and preserve the correspondence of the association.

The treasurer will receive and keep all funds contributed to the association, and disburse such amounts as may be necessary to defray its expenses, and use the funds for such other objects as the association may direct. On retiring from office, he will submit a report of all funds that have come into his possession, amounts disbursed, for what objects, and the balance in the treasury.

Art. 3. Church membership or a profession of religion will not be made prerequisites to membership, and all persons desirous of promoting virtue and a high tone of morality are eligible to membership. No tax is imposed upon the members of the association; all necessary funds will be raised by contributions.

Art. 4. The regular meetings of the association while in camp will be held on Monday night of each week, and in bivouac or on the march as often as the president may deem practicable.

Art. 5. The sick and wounded of this brigade are justly entitled to our warmest sympathies, and the association proffers its aid to alleviate, as far as circumstances will permit, the sufferings of brother countrymen in arms in a common cause. The president will appoint, monthly, a committee of one from each regiment to visit the sick of our brigade and report their condition and see that suitable arrangements may be made for their comfort and assistance. A suitable tribute of respect will be paid to the memory of those members whose lives may be sacrificed upon the altar of their country.

Art. 6. Punctual attendance upon the meetings of the association is heartily enjoined; every member is expected to attend all its sessions, unless prevented by sickness or military duties.

Art. 7. The association will take strict cognizance of the deportment of its members; and conduct grossly immoral, persisted in regardless of friendly admonition, may be visited with expulsion.

Art. 8. Ministers visiting this brigade are cordially invited to seats in the association.

Art. 9. Honorary membership will be conferred, by a unanimous vote, upon nomination by any member present.

Art. 10. A subject for discussion will be announced by the president for the ensuing meeting, and all members are invited to participate. No subject calculated to produce jars or schisms will be discussed, and only such as are of a moral or religious character.

Art. 11. An essay will be read immediately after discussion, by a member previously designated by the president, upon some subject promotive of the interest of the association. Ten minutes will be allowed for the reading of such essay.

Art. 12. The utmost decorum will be observed by every member of the association, while in session, and language of a disrespectful or unbecoming character will never be indulged in.

Only one member is entitled to the floor at a time, and if two members rise at the same time to speak, the president will decide who has a right to the floor. No member will be allowed to speak more than five minutes at once, nor more than twice upon the same subject. A plurality of the votes cast is necessary to elect officers, and in the approval and adoption of reports and resolutions.

ATLANTA REDIVIVUS—PAROLED PRISONERS—HOW GOD TAKES CARE OF HIS WORK.

"ATLANTA, April 13, 1865.

"*Dear Brother Harp:* The ensign of tyranny, the modern 'abomination that maketh desolate,' has for a while, at least—God grant that it may be forever!—passed away from us. Nearly all of our noble houses of business have been destroyed : many, very many of our 'pleasant places' have had the beauty, and music, and life, crushed and burnt out of them, but for an old resident like myself, I assure you 'it is good to be here.'

"Except the few who found special friends and near relatives, Atlanta refugees and exiles were not specially overwhelmed with kindness. But, my good friend, we forget all the sorrows of the way in our joy that we have got back home, or to the place where home was. The attachment of the old citizens of our war-scathed city to this place of former business and happiness is almost romantic. Women and children cry for joy when they get back, and the men are not proof against tender and grateful emotions. Our people have the quick, springy step of the olden time; nearly everybody is cheerful and hopeful, and I do not know a single reconstructionist among us. If such an one should visit us, these sad ruins would shame him out of his cowardice. Of course we cannot build fine houses, but we are building shanties, that will serve, in the want of something better, for shelter and for trade.

"As to our churches, we are getting along better than any despondent man can believe. I have alluded to the energy of our people. Why, our negro Methodists set themselves to the work (as zealously as the returned Jews at Jerusalem), of rebuilding their temple. They have rebuilt their church, and are having regular services.

"Rev. A. M. Thigpen, an old Army Chaplain and Missionary, is at Wesley Chapel, doing good work. Rev. Mr. Hornady serves the Baptist, and the venerable Dr. Wilson the Presbyterian congregation. Your correspondent 'holds forth' at Trinity, his 'nursing mother.' Fathers O'Reilley and O'Neal minister to the Catholic membership. Sunday-schools are flourishing, congregations steadily improving. We have an 'itinerant' weekly union prayer-meeting. We devoutly hope for a glorious revival of religion.

"Our first communion was a blessed time we will never forget. 'Brethren, pray for us!'

"A constant stream of paroled prisoners flows through our city daily. 'Still they come.' These from Missouri, those from Arkansas, others from Louisiana, and from all the States west of the Savannah. No reconstructionists among *them*. And there will be no such monstrous growths among them so long as they remember Rock Island, Point Lookout, Elmira, and those other places of torture, and hunger, and oppression.

"God bless these brave fighters, these long-enduring sufferers! Let the people receive them as such heroic sons of the South deserve to be received.

"We sigh and weep over the evils of war, and we wonder what is to become of the country and the Church. The All-Seeing Eye is upon us, and all will be well.

"Hundreds of these brave boys have been born again, even in so dreary a place as a prison. Hundreds have learned to read and to write, have added to their stock of information, and are preparing under a strange tuition to do good service to their country and race. When Stephen was stoned, the Church wept one of her strongest pillars broken. She saw no good in that fierce Saul of Tarsus standing by. But the Master did. I am informed by reliable Christian men, among them Rev. Robert W. Ayres, of the Memphis Conference, that a large number of young men in those dreary prisons have been '*studying for the ministry.*' We read about God's making the 'wrath of man to praise Him.' Now, here is an instance. 'He that keepeth Israel neither slumbereth nor sleepeth.' What earnest preachers these theological students of the army and the prison will make.

"The Church and the country will need them every one. 'Pray ye therefore the Lord of the harvest.'

"Very truly yours in the faith, etc.,
"ATTICUS G. HAYGOOD."

APPENDIX.

[Letter from Rev. W. H. Robert, Baptist Missionary.]

"DENISON, TEXAS, October 25, 1880.

" REV. J. W. JONES, D. D., RICHMOND, VIRGINIA:

"My Dear Brother : On my sick-bed yesterday, my pastor, Rev. W. E. Tynes, handed me a copy of the old *Herald* of date October 21, and in looking it over I was entranced by your article on revivals of religion in our Virginia army. I read it over again and again and remembered many things similar in connection with our army in Georgia and Tennessee, especially in winter-quarters about Dalton, in 1864 and 1865, our chapels there and *' the army church of Finley's Florida Brigade,'* etc., my acquaintance with Dr. J. L. M. Curry and his first sermon I induced him to preach. I was then living at La Grange, Georgia, had just sold out the Southern Female College of which I was President, to Professor I. F. Cox, now there. Dr. Sumner at once sent me a commission to labor in the Army of Tennessee and the hospitals in Atlanta and La Grange, and soon gave me general charge of the work about Dalton, when our men were in winter-quarters. I made my head-quarters at Dalton, with Major Sibley, in charge of Georgia relief stores, etc.

" Many things of interest I could record of those scenes and incidents about Dalton and Atlanta. I always signed myself W. H. R. of La Grange, Georgia, Army Mississippi. I baptized 110 in five or six weeks. I circulated thousands of tracts, Testaments, and hymns, and preached to thousands of our noble boys.

" If you have it, I would be very glad to have one copy of ' A Mother's Parting Words to her Soldier Boy,' and a copy of ' Soldier's Hymns.' I want the one called ' My Mother's Bible,' and would like to see ' the Confederate New Testament.'

" I am now waiting the summons to cross the river. My health is feeble, my wife is also old and infirm, and we must live in the past, and *standing still* to see the salvation of God, look to, live upon, and enjoy the hopes of the future; the Lord bless and save us.

" Fraternally yours,

"W. H. ROBERT."

[Letter from Rev. Dr. D. C. Kelley.]

The following is from Dr. Kelley, now missionary treasurer of the Methodist Episcopal Church, South, who was one of the most accomplished and gallant colonels who rode with Bedford Forrest, " the wizard of the saddle : "

" NASHVILLE, TENNESSEE, February 9, 1888.

" REV. J. WILLIAM JONES, D. D., DALLAS, TEXAS :

"Dear Brother : Yours of January 25 received, and answer somewhat delayed. . . I was in the cavalry, and General Forrest was ever on the go. We were with the infantry very little. I preached myself, from two to three times every week, often at night after long rides ; and conducted two revivals, to one of which the following extract from a letter recently received refers :

" ' I very often think of the time in Mississippi, when we were camped near where a protracted meeting was going on in a little log-house, and you went over at night and preached for them, and what a revival of religion they had.'

" I should be glad to do all in my power to aid you in your enterprise, but my time is very much occupied, and I think Brother Cherry will be of more real service to you than I could be, along this line.

" With best wishes for your success,

" Yours truly,

" D. C. KELLEY."

[Letter from Rev. Dr. T. R. Markham, Presbyterian Chaplain.]

" NEW ORLEANS, February 23, 1888.

" *Dear Doctor :* Your former letter found me in the busiest season of the year.

That letter not indicating haste and my work in the army being altogether in camp, in the field, and on the march, our milder section not demanding winter-quarters, there is really so little of importance to communicate that it would add scarce anything to the interesting and valuable materials gathered with such care and arranged with such skill in your admirable work. A meeting of thirty successive days preceding the fall of Atlanta, in which one hundred and forty men made profession of faith in my brigade (Featherstone's), is about the only one of any duration that I was able to hold in our shifting experience. We were literally campaigners in the Army of Tennessee, always on the move, and my work was a round of itinerating, largely fragmentary and mostly through personal interviews in hospitals and around camp-fires and in the trenches.

"Drs. Bryson and McNeeley ought to be able to give you something, but probably they have. Sorry so little is at hand with me.

"Yours truly and fraternally,

"Thomas R. Markham."

"In July, 1863, Rev. Dr. E. H. Myers, of the *Southern Christian Advocate*, thus urged all to lift their hearts to God:

"There is great necessity," he said, "for us to cultivate our intercourse with Heaven. Our temporal condition looks none the brightest. God is trying us in a fiery furnace of war; and for the present, the battle seems to go against us. The high hopes for our country and of a speedy peace, which we entertained a few weeks since, have been in a measure disappointed, and we may be doomed to yet greater disappointment. But there is a refuge for the soul in every storm. God's peace and love, the joys and hopes of salvation, the sanctifying and comforting influences of the Holy Ghost, are not subject to human circumstances; and they may be ours amid every variety of calamity. But these are the fruits of the cultivation of personal religion; and, independent of every other consideration, the uncertainty of all other sources of comfort alone should be an inducement to us to betake ourselves to that refuge, to watch closely, pray much, believe with all our heart, and to cleave the closer to God, the louder the storm swells, and the more furiously the billows dash upon the wreck of earthly hopes.

"He who, in the dark hour, feels that he grows in grace and maintains soul-communion with God, stands upon a rock. He shall never be moved."

[Letter from Bishop Andrew.]

"Summerfield, Alabama, September 9, 1863.

"*Dear Brother Bennett:* I have received two or three numbers of *The Soldiers' Paper*, and in token of my high appreciation of the paper, and especially of the cause it is intended to serve, I send the enclosed $20, which I hope you will receive in due course, and be enabled by it to send out a few more messengers of love to instruct, awaken, and comfort the gallant men who for our sakes are daily breasting difficulty, privation, sickness, and even death, in camp, and hospital, and battle-field. Surely they deserve all that we can do for them; and especially do they deserve at our hands the words of eternal life. This is certainly the richest boon which we can bestow upon them. I have heard with deep concern the earnest and oft-repeated appeals for more faithful laborers in the army vineyard. Surely these calls ought not to be so long unheeded. Are there not preachers enough at command if they would become willing to take up the cross and enter upon this glorious work? Where are all the refugee preachers? It seems to me they might, many of them, go into these opening fields, and certainly it will be better than being idle. Let no man of God keep back in this great work. Were I not so old I should have been there long before now; but age is upon me; my eyes are dim and my limbs grow stiff, so that I am now unable to go in and out as in other days; but God will accept the will for the deed. I wish my offering was greater, but such as it is, accept it in the name of the Great Shepherd. God bless you, my brother, in your soul and body, and aid you mightily in your glorious work.

"Yours, very affectionately,
"JAS. O. ANDREW."

[General Bragg's Order to his Troops.]

"HEAD-QUARTERS ARMY OF TENNESSEE,
"Field of Chickamauga, September 22, 1863.

"It has pleased Almighty God to reward the valor and endurance of our troops by giving to our arms a complete victory over the enemy's superior numbers.

"Homage is due and is rendered unto Him who giveth not the battle to the strong.

"Soldiers, after two days of severe battle, preceded by heavy and important out-post affairs, you have stormed the barricades and breastworks of the enemy, and driven before you, in confusion and disorder, an army largely superior in numbers, and whose constant theme was your demoralization, and whose constant boast was your defeat.

"Your patient endurance under privations, your fortitude and your valor, displayed at all times, and under all trials, have been meetly rewarded.

"Your commander acknowledges his obligations, and promises to you, in advance, the country's gratitude.

"But your task is not ended. We must drop a soldier's tear upon the graves of the noble men who have fallen by our sides, and move forward.

"Much has been accomplished. More remains to be done, before you can enjoy the blessings of peace and freedom.

"(Signed) BRAXTON BRAGG.
"Official: *George Wm. Brent*, A. A. G."

[General Lee's Order on the Chickamauga Victory.]

General Lee issued the following congratulatory order to the Army of Northern Virginia, announcing the victory at Chickamauga by General Bragg:

"HEAD-QUARTERS A. N. VA., September 24, 1863.
"*General Orders No. 89:*

"The commanding General announces to the army, with profound gratitude to Almighty God, the victory achieved at Chickamauga by the army of General Braxton Bragg.

"After a fierce and sanguinary conflict of two days, the Federal force, under General Rosecranz, were driven with heavy loss from their strong positions, and leaving their dead and wounded on the field, retreated, under cover of night, on Chattanooga, pursued by our cavalry.

"Rendering to the Great Giver of victory, as is most justly due, our praise and thanksgiving for this signal token of His favor, let us extend to the army that has so nobly upheld the honor of our country, the tribute of our admiration for its valor, and sympathy for its suffering and loss.

"Invoking the continued assistance of heaven upon our efforts, let us resolve to emulate the heroic example of our brethren in the South, until the enemy shall be expelled from our borders, and peace and independence be secured to our country.

"R. E. LEE, General."

[*Address of Bishop Andrew.*]

"TO THE CHAPLAINS IN THE ARMY:

"*Dear Brethren :* Permit an aged minister, a fellow-laborer in the kingdom and patience of Jesus, to address a few words of advice to you. It is to be presumed that before you volunteered for the service in which you are now engaged you took time patiently and deliberately to consider the work upon which you were about to enter, soberly and in the fear of God; made up your minds to take the work as that which God designed you to do; you assumed it with all its responsibility, crosses, sacrifices, and labors; you entered not from any mere patriotic impulse or romantic notions, nor that you might acquiesce in any lost fame or notoriety, but you loved the souls of our soldiers, and you believed that God, in His providence, indicated the army mission as your allotted providential field of labor. If you have entered on your work with such feelings, you have consecrated yourself, soul and body, to the accomplishment of this great work to which God and the Church have set you, and will not be driven from it by any mortifications or difficulties to which it may expose you; these you may expect—they will be sure to meet you. You will be opposed by the devil, your own wicked hearts, and frequently by ungodly officers, who, instead of setting proper examples before their men, do everything they can, so far as example goes, to corrupt them, and hinder their success. By this class of officers you will probably be contemned, and treated with no very great degree of respect. Make up your account to this, and be not thrown off your balance when it occurs; let it not move you from your great business. It may sometimes happen that even when such officers make no open opposition to your religious operations among their men, yet there are a thousand ways in which they can throw obstacles in your way, and thwart your efforts for the soldier's salvation; nor is this strange, when you reflect that very seldom exhortation and prayer which you deliver is a standing reproof to them, but it is your business to overcome all these difficulties by patient, persevering, and pious efforts. Remember, Christian faith, and meekness, and love, shall triumph over all hindrances. But ungodly officers are not the only difficulties which you must encounter. Among the soldiers you will find much opposition, secret or open. Your patience may be taxed in consequence of the careless recklessness of some of these—the utter indifference of others—the professed infidelity of others—but that all can be overcome by Christian patience and persevering effort; and that it was through many or all these phases of experience that you were brought at last to the cross of Christ, don't give up a poor fellow because in these respects his case would seem to be hopeless. But while from many, both officers and soldiers, you meet with small encouragement, from a large number of both officers and men you will meet a cordial greeting and cheering encouragement. Be thou faithful in the ministry of the word—preach the truth always, and indorse it with your life, and God will not let you labor in vain; some seed will fall into good ground, though much of it may seem to have fallen on thorny ground, or by the highway. It may be that the circumstances which surround you may offer but few facilities for public preaching, but remember that the pulpit is not the only place where the faithful pastor will preach—in private, by the wayside, in the tent, in the hospitals by the bedside of the sick or wounded soldier; there especially is your place. Be much with the sick, wounded, and dying—there, while life is ebbing out, when the past is painfully remembered, and the future looms up gloomily before the vision of the dying patriot, when he thinks of home and loved ones there, and feels that his earthly mission is almost ended, then preach Jesus to him, talk to him of the cross and pardon, and of heaven, and kneel beside him, and in the language of pleading, earnest faith, commend his departing spirit to the God who made him, and the exalted Redeemer who died for him, rose again, and ever liveth to intercede for him, and then, when the vital spark is extinct, give him Christian burial. Remember,

39

if you would succeed in your work, you must be the soldier's *friend*—no affective and repulsive dignity must drive him from you.   You must convince him that you are his friend, and that you seek his good; he must *feel* that you are his friend, and that he can safely and fully confide in you, and then you may hope to do him good.

"My dear brethren, do you work with all your heart!   Don't you forget that to the souls of the soldiers is your great work, for this you were sent to your present field by God and the Church.   This is work enough to engage all your powers, and when you have done all you will feel that you have done too little, and will then have great cause of humiliation before God.   You must have no secondary work to occupy your head and heart.   One of our generals remarked to Bishop Paine, in reference to a certain missionary, who had been unusually successful, said he, he is the best man I have known, he is obliged to do good, for he thinks and talks of nothing else, he aims at nothing else.   Now here is a proper pattern for army missionaries.   If you would do good in the army, let that be your paramount object in all your conduct, and all your plans must be subordinate to this one object.   I once knew a very respectable clergyman who went into the army as chaplain to a regiment; though full of zeal to go, he stayed but a few months, when he returned to easier work, saying that he believed the army presented the finest field for usefulness with which he was acquainted, but that he could not remain in it without losing his self-respect.   No wonder this man left, and there have been a good many such, who were zealous to go, but they have soon left the field to return to more comfortable quarters; and these have caused the chaplaincy to stink in the nostrils of officers and men, and done great injury to the cause of God in the army.   Dear brethren, do not you follow this example, but do the work of God faithfully, and leave your good name in His hands.

"James O. Andrew."

[Cheering Indications.]

"*Dear Herald:* It is interesting, in these times of trouble, to mark the tokens of the Divine favor.   'The Lord of hosts is with us; the God of Jacob is our refuge.'   The horizon is brightening; the last clouds of the storm are glorified with the bow of promise.   What are our late victories, east and west, north and south, but so many proofs of a Heavenly Providence in our behalf?   'When mine enemies came upon me to eat up my flesh, they stumbled and fell.'   And they are still stumbling and falling; and after the campaign they are now projecting, it is confidently hoped, they will never be able to rise.

"Among all the indications of the times, there is none more cheering than the great revival now going on in our army.   Instead of dying out, it seems to be increasing in power.   Hundreds of Confederate soldiers are daily rallying to the standard of Christ.   Nothing like this has occurred in the Yankee army.

> 'Our foes, like Gideon's fleece, are found,
> Unwatered still, and dry.'

"Never before, in any war, was the Spirit of God poured out so gloriously upon camp and field.   Surely, 'He hath not given us over unto our enemies.'   This is the Divine pledge of our final success.   Heaven does not bless in this manner those whom he is about to abandon.   You, Mr. Editor, ought to be greatly encouraged in your evangelical labor of love.   The chaplains and missionaries in the field ought to gird up their loins and press the battle of the Lord with redoubled vigor and resolution.   How wonderfully their Master is rewarding their work!   Meanwhile, let our brethren at home lift the voice of supplication for their country.   Let pastors everywhere urge this duty upon their people.   Since the recent fast, a number of our churches are enjoying delightful visitations of grace. In Americus and Cuthbert, from which I have just returned, many souls have recently been converted. Arriving here, I find the Baptist church and one of the Methodist churches receiving crowds of penitents every night at their altars. 'Save now, we beseech thee, O Lord! O Lord, we beseech thee, send now prosperity. Praise ye the Lord.'

" JOSEPH CROSS.

" Macon, April 8, 1864.

Extracts from a letter written by one of our correspondents in the Navy :

" FLAG SHIP, ———, C. S. N., July 29, 1864.

"*Mr. Editor:* Having a few moments leisure, I spend them in penning a few statements, to show you how your paper is received in the navy, and the good which it has accomplished. The sailors and mariners are composed mostly of foreigners, from different parts of the world. They are not of the lowest class of men, most of them having a good education, but they have been very wicked. When a few months ago I became connected with this branch of the navy, I saw several copies of your paper come on board this vessel ; but few of the crew at that time would read or seemed to take any interest in them ; but it is quite different now—they are eagerly sought after and thoroughly read by every man on board, and I have noticed that several, after reading them through, send them to their families and friends at home to read ; but this is not all the good it has done. I have noticed quite a change in the men. They are far from being as wicked as they were. A good many are leaving off swearing, and say they are determined to become better men. My firm belief is, that your paper is the means of effecting this gratifying change. . . Hoping the knowledge that your paper is doing so much good in this branch of the service will encourage you in your labors, I close by assuring you that we hope and pray that it may be the means of saving many souls, and that you may reap your reward in heaven.

" Very respectfully,

" A. O. BASS.

" P. S.—If you can spare us a larger number, they will be thankfully received, as the demand for them is greatly increased.

"August, 1864."

[*Report of Operations of the Soldiers' Tract Association for the past year, submitted to the Council in May,* 1864, *taken from the Minutes of the Proceedings.*]

" W. W. Bennett, Superintendent of the Soldiers' Tract Association, offered his report, which was read, received, and ordered to be filed and published in the Church papers :

"TO THE COUNCIL OF BISHOPS AND BRETHREN, ASSEMBLED AT MONTGOMERY, ALABAMA :

"*Dear Brethren :* The Soldiers' Tract Association having been adopted by the Bishops at their meeting in May last as a Church enterprise, it is proper that we should present to this body a brief statement of its operations.

"At the annual meeting of the association in November last, it was remodelled so as to conform as nearly as possible to the organizations of other benevolent enterprises of the Church.

" The object of the association is to supply the soldiers of our armies with religious literature, from the Holy Scriptures down to the simple and unpretending but often powerful little tract.

"All our own publications, and all we have been able to purchase, are supplied gratuitously to the soldiers. We allow them to pay for nothing that comes from the shelves of our depositories.

" We are enabled to pursue this plan by the very liberal donations which have flowed into our treasury from the friends of the enterprise, both in and out of the army. The soldiers themselves have been among our most liberal patrons. Even some of the privates in the ranks have sent one-tenth of their monthly pay to aid in this good work.

" For the sake of convenience in reaching all our widely scattered troops, we have found it necessary to establish centres of operations at Richmond, Virginia; Macon, Georgia; and beyond the Mississippi, at Marshall, Texas, or Shreveport, Louisiana; it is yet uncertain which place has been selected as the most suitable. From these points we can easily reach all our armies with such reading matter as our means and the facilities for publishing will enable us to furnish.

" Connected with these depositories the association has twenty-five ministers and laymen actively engaged in carrying forward our work. Besides these, regular agents and colporteurs, there are scores of chaplains and pious laymen in the army who are constantly engaged in circulating religious reading among their comrades in arms.

" The association has not been without encouragement in its work. Hundreds of letters from all portions of our armies assure us that the fruit in this truly inviting field of Christian effort has been abundant. As an auxiliary to the preaching of the gospel, the first and great instrument in the conversion of men, the Soldiers' Tract Association has striven to do its part of the work of saving our soldiers from the vices of the field and camp. The powerful and stirring gospel sermon has been followed by the earnest appeals of the hortatory, or the touching story of the narrative tract, and thus under these combined influences many a gallant soldier has been enrolled under the banner of Immanuel.

" Many persons, judging by the lessons of past history, have learned to regard the camp as the great school of vice, and of almost all other wars this is true, but ours will ever stand as a grand exception on the page of history. To thousands it has already become the school of virtue, of salvation. And, unlikely as it may seem, this war has, amid all its bitter trials, shown to many the path of learning. Many men who entered the service without the knowledge of a single letter of the alphabet, have, in a comparatively brief period, learned to read and write. In a recent address from the president of one of the Christian associations in the army, it was stated that, through the faithful labors of the pious members of the association, many soldiers had been taught in regular classes the elementary principles of education, and could read for themselves the word of God, and write cheerful letters to their friends at home. In after years, amid the prosperity of our dear native land, not a few chosen leaders of a free, happy, Christian people may say, ' We learned to read while in the army;' and many thousands will say, ' We learned to serve God in the army.' From the army spring the hopes of the Church and the country.

" The association has issued for army circulation, up to the first of the present month,

" Of Tracts—4, 8, 12, and 16 pages—17,000,000 pages.

" Of Soldiers' Hymn-Books, 70,000 copies.

" Of the Holy Scriptures, Bibles, Testaments, Gospels separately bound, 20,000 copies.

" Of Bible reading for soldiers in tract form, composed of selections from the New Testament and Psalms, 15,000.

" Of the Soldiers' Paper, published at Richmond semi-monthly, 150,000.

" Of the *Army and Navy Herald,* published at Macon, Georgia, semi-monthly, 142,000.

" In response to the request of the bishops, at their last meeting, the association has published 5,000 of the Southern Methodist Primer, and 5,000 each of the Infant

SERGEANT COLLIER'S BRAVE ACT.

(Facing page 613.)

Manual, Caper's Catechism (first part), and Nos. 1 and 2 of the Wesleyan Cate-
chisms. These have been furnished to Sunday-schools at cost prices. And many
of them are in use in the Bible classes and Sunday-schools in the army.

"It is the desire of the association to add to its list of publications tracts of larger
volume than those heretofore published. The call in the army is very urgent for
large tracts, and for books on practical piety. And we take occasion here to say
that now is the time for those among us who wield the pen of the ready writer to
lay out their strength in this direction. Thousands are imploring us to teach them
the way of life, both by speaking and writing. Oh, let us not be found lacking in
duty, especially to the brave men who face all the perils and bear all the trials of
this war for our country's sake.

"The contributions to the funds of the association have reached the sum of
$174,659.47; and the expenditures have amounted to $128,067.30, leaving a balance
in the treasury of $46,552.17.

"All of which is respectfully submitted.

"(Signed) W. W. Bennett, ⎫
R. J. Harp,   ⎬ Agents."
W. F. Camp,   ⎭

[*A Gallant Son of Georgia.*]

(*From the Macon Telegraph.*)

The public have already learned from the papers the fearless and noble act of
Sergeant Isaac P. Collier, which is the subject of the annexed correspondence.
They will now learn that he is as unambitious as brave. He declines promotion
properly tendered him for the heroic act:

"Camp Fifth Georgia Regiment, June 24, 1864.

"*Editor Telegraph:* I send you a copy of an order promoting Sergeant Collier,
Company K, and his declination. It is characteristic of the man—brave and gallant,
but quiet and unassuming, It speaks for itself:

"'Head-quarters Jackson's Brigade,
"'Walker's Division, Hardee's Corps, Army of Tennessee.
"'In the Field, three miles west of Marietta.

"'*General Orders No. —:*

"'On the 21st instant, while this brigade was in line of battle behind breastworks,
and under a heavy fire from the enemy's artillery, a shrapnel shot with a Roman
fuse struck the works, passed under the top log, and fell among the men in the
ditch.

"'While the fuse was still smoking, and the men were flying from the danger of
the apprehended explosion, Sergeant Isaac P. Collier, of Company K, Fifth Regiment, Georgia Volunteers, seized the projectile and threw it out of the ditch.

"'In the judgment of the brigade commander, this is a case which calls for the
exercise of the power of appointment for "acts of distinguished valor," which is
vested in the President. The witnesses of the bravery of Sergeant Collier are Lieutenant A. H. Hightower; Corporal E. V. Burkett, Privates E. P. Simpson, W. D.
K. Talley, J. T. Backus, Company K, Fifth Georgia Regiment, Privates John All-
bright and J. A. Shettleworth, of Beauregard's Battery. As there is a vacancy of
second lieutenant in Company E, Fifth Georgia Regiment, Sergeant Isaac P. Collier
is hereby promoted to the rank of second lieutenant, and is assigned to duty as such
in Company E, Fifth Georgia Regiment, to take rank from the 21st day of June,
1864. He will report to the commanding officer of the company for duty. This
order is subject to the approval and ratification of the President.

"'By command of Brigadier-General John K. Jackson.

"'S. A. Moreno, A. A. General.'

"'COMPANY K, FIFTH GEORGIA REGIMENT, June 24, 1864.

"'*Captain :* I have the honor to most respectfully decline the above promotion. In throwing the shell from the ditch, I am conscious of having done nothing but my duty in attempting to save my life and the lives of the men around me. I prefer to remain in my company with my comrades, whom I left home with on the 7th day of May, 1861.

"'ISAAC P. COLLIER, Third Sergeant, Company K.

"'CAPTAIN T. A. MORENO, A. A. General.'

"No casualties in the regiment the past two days. Please give the above a place in your columns, and oblige,

"Very respectfully,

"SID. CHEATHAM, Lieutenant and Adjutant."

[*From the Southern Christian Advocate.*]

THE DYING SOLDIER.

BY G. Y. V.

" Bear me quickly from the Legion—
    I am wounded in the strife,
They have pierced the vital region,
    See! how ebbs the tide of life!
I am dying! yes! I'm dying!
    Soon you'll miss me, comrades brave;
My poor form will soon be lying
    In a far-off soldier's grave.

" Well you know, when I enlisted,
    'Twas to gain my country's right,
And I've faithfully assisted—
    Standing in the hottest fight.
Yes, amid the cannon's rattle,
    Where the Northerns pour'd their fire,
I have stood the awful battle,
    Facing all the dreadful ire.

" Oh, my country! how I love her,
    Land of all my hopes most dear;
God of battles, smile above her,
    Guard her coasts both far and near.
Grant to all our men direction,
    (Thee we thank for mercies past.)
With thy favor and protection,
    We shall win the goal at last.

" Long our foes have violated
    Every right our fathers gave,
Much we bore and long we waited,
    Hoping still the land to save;

But at length their deeds exceeded
All that freemen could endure,
And we only then seceded,
But to make our rights secure.

" Hark ! I thought the Legion shouted,
What is that which greets my ear ?
'Oh, they fly ! the foe is routed.'
These my dying moments cheer.
Comrades, triumph springs from trouble,
Bravely, firmly, nobly stand.
Heaven will grant you more than double,
Soon shall freedom crown the land."

Ceasing then, 'mid pains of dying,
Tow'rd his friends his eyes he mov'd,
And while on their arms still lying,
Kindly spoke of those he loved—
Then, as if new strength were given,
Nerving him for death's dark tide—
Said, " My home is yon bright heaven,
* * * Trust is in the Crucified."

If our space allowed it would be of interest, to old soldiers at least, to give a number of the "songs of the camp" with which our brave fellows cheered the camp, the march, the bivouac, and even the battle-field. I give the following, however, not only for its rare beauty, but because it was sung in our Confederate armies more generally, perhaps, than any other except some of the old hymns :

THE SONG OF THE CAMP.

A Crimean Incident—By Bayard Taylor.

The subjoined touchingly beautiful poem—for it is a poem in the fullest sense and meaning of the term—was written by Bayard Taylor while the fortress of Sebastopol was beleaguered by the allied armies. To a full understanding and appreciation of it, let it be remembered that "Annie Laurie" is the song of the British camp, and wherever there is a British regiment—whether in Canada or India, England or China—whenever the simple Scotch air that accompanies

Maxwelton's banks are bonny,
When early falls the dew ;
And 'twas there that Annie Laurie
Gave me her promise true—
Gave me her promise true ;
And ne'er forget will I,
But for bonny Annie Laurie
I'll lay me down and die,

is struck up, the heart and voice of every soldier responds as promptly as would their hands if the order were given to charge the enemy :

The Incident.

" Give us a song !" the soldierscried,
The outer trenches guarding,
When the heated guns of the camp allied
Grew weary of bombarding.

The dark Redan in silent scoff
  Lay grim and threatening under;
And the tawny mound of the Malakof.
  No longer belched its thunder.

There was a pause. The guard then said
  " We storm the forts to-morrow !
Sing while we may, another day
  Will bring enough of sorrow."

They lay along the battery's side,
  Below the smoking cannon—
Brave hearts from Severn and from Clyoe,
  And from the banks of Shannon.

They sing of love and not of fame;
  Forgot was Britain's glory—
Each heart recalled a different name,
  But all, sang "Annie Laurie."

Voice after voice caught up the song,
  Until its tender passion
Rose like an anthem rich and strong
  Their battle-eve confession.

Dear girl, her name he dared not speak
  Yet, as the song grew louder,
Something upon the soldier's cheek
  Washed off the stains of powder.

Beyond the darkened ocean burned
  The bloody sunset's embers,
While the Crimean valleys learned,
  How English love remembers.

And once again a fire of hell
  Rained on Russian quarters,
With scream of shot and burst of shell,
  And bellowing of the mortars.

And Irish Nora's eyes are dim
  For a singer dumb and gory;
And English Mary mourns for him
  Who sung of "Annie Laurie."

Ah, soldiers! to your honored rest
  Your truth and valor bearing,
The bravest are the tenderest—
  The loving are the daring.

We are indebted to Rev. S. M. Cherry for the following clippings from the *Army and Navy Herald,* which was so widely circulated and so eagerly read, and which accomplished so much good in all of the Confederate armies:

" Mr. R. H. L. Crosthwait, Secretary of the Christian Association, Third Engineer Troops, Army Tennessee, writes under date of September 16: 'For a week or so before we left the front our command being nearly all together, we had the services of Revs. Jones and Turner, and during what few opportunities there were for divine worship there was an accession to the church of thirteen members. I never saw a better prospect for a revival than there is in our regiment at this time.' "

"October, 1864.

"We have received several communications lately from chaplains, missionaries, and privates in the Armies of Tennessee and Northern Virginia, conveying the glad and soul-inspiring information that the religious feeling in the army has not abated in the least since the commencement of the stirring campaign through which they have passed; and in many regiments in which there are no chaplains, or where the services of chaplains have been to a great extent impracticable, on account of the presence of the enemy, the prayer meetings have been marked with solemn interest."

"January, 1865.

A correspondent of the Knoxville *Register*, in a recent letter from Camp Watauga River, calls for more chaplains, and says:

"To the glory and honor of our young Republic, our armies are not yet devoid of that Christian zeal that characterized them when civilians. However strange it may seem to those who see so many defects in the conduct of the soldiers—so much corruption in the army—there is a strong religious sentiment among the troops of the Confederacy, which is being developed more and more daily; and but an effort, on the part of the ministerial fraternity, would kindle a flame that would change the entire morals and character of our soldiers, and which would be contagious—society catching the spirit, would become ignited, when one mighty altar of prayer and Christian worship would mark the boundary of the Confederacy.

"Not a meeting is held by the chaplains of the different commands but what they have large assemblies of soldiers in attendance; and when the invitation is extended to those who desire an interest in the prayers of the Christian, many are seen pressing through the crowded throng and bowing humbly on the cold, damp ground, with but the broad blue sky for a covering. What scenes—which contrast strongly to the great revival periods of the early pioneer settlements. The eloquent voice of the minister, the heavy sighing of the penitent, and the deep melancholy spirit of the soldier audience, is a scene for the artist, and one of no small moment. Not an evening passes by but what there can be seen here and there gathered together, small clumps of soldiers, singing sacred songs, and occasionally sending up an humble prayer to heaven. The idle jester, and he who would make light of their romantic worship, stand in awe, and refrain from saying anything that would tend to mortify or molest their feelings. How often do we hear the expression, not alone from the young but the aged soldier, as the crowded throng disperses, and they go winding their way to their respective commands, that 'I am determined to live a better life, and move in conformity with the Christian church,' etc.

"What a field for the minister, a harvest for the church, and a monument for God! The soldiers have at length learned that in this great harvest of death, they are the material reaped.

"We should have more chaplains, more agents for the Tract Society, and more ministers who are true and devoted to the religious welfare of the soldiers. Tracts, religious papers, and small religious books should be distributed through the army. There is a great demand for such reading, and but little energy seemingly manifested on the part of the chaplains to supply the deficiency, although of so great importance. The security of our nationality and the well-being of society is wholly dependent on the redemption of the morals of the soldiery."

"DALTON, GEORGIA, April 4, 1864.

"*Brother Burke:* It does my heart good to write you this letter. If you only could have been in our brigade last night, to see the lost sheep of Israel flocking to their shepherd. There were at least one hundred and twenty or more under deep penitence, and six converted. We have three ministers—two Methodists and one Baptist—all preaching from one stand. I call it a Methodist and Baptist revival, as there were nine baptized yesterday, in a creek near our camp. I am glad to say that God is in our midst.

"Let this be read out to the congregation of our church, and tell Brother Christian that he must let his church know what our blessed Saviour is doing for the poor soldiers.

"If the revival keeps up much longer, thank God, we will have a brigade of Christian soldiers, fighting for Christ and their country. I understand that the revival influence is spreading all over Johnston's army. Our men seem to be in good spirits. I hope and trust in God that this army will be converted into a Christian army before this war is over.

"I now bid you good-bye, and hope to be remembered in all your prayers. God bless you all as ministers of our Church and congregations, is my prayer, for Christ's sake.

"Your Christian brother,

"L. L. DEMILLY,

"*First Florida Brigade and Regiment.*"

"At Fort Sumter, a revival has been in progress, ' about two hundred have joined the Church, and a still larger number have been converted.' In the Eleventh Georgia Regiment, eighty members have been added to the Society as the fruits of a recent meeting, but space fails us."

"CAMP McLAWS' DIVISION, April 28, 1864.

"*Dear Brother Harp:* I write you this hasty note to let your readers know that we are in the midst of a glorious revival. The men have fixed up good preaching places, with logs placed parallel for seats; and for our night services, we manage it exactly as they do at camp-meetings—huge pine knot fires are the appropriate lights for our chapel in the woods.

"In every brigade of this grand old division there is a deep and wide-spread religious interest. I have seen more excitement; but profounder feeling, as manifested in the great crowds that flock to every service, the reverent attention given to the preaching of the word, the large number of earnest penitents that crowd our rude altars, I have not seen, at home or in the army. Old soldiers say that they have not seen such a state of things in this army before. Large numbers are being daily added to the churches. Here are Baptists, Methodists, and Presbyterians working together in the utmost harmony of feeling. Anything looking like controversy would be considered an intolerable impertinence in the army. I think that the unity and brotherly love among the Christians of our noble armies will, when those armies return home, effectually rebuke the intolerant bigotry that has so often reared its foul crest close by the altars of God.

"I have attended meetings in three brigades in this division of Longstreet's Corps: in my own (General Bryan's); in General Wofford's (Rev. George W. Yarbrough, of the Georgia Conference, the missionary), and in General Humphrey's (Barksdale's old brigade), and in all I have found the most remarkable religious awakening.

"I am giving out the papers and tracts to the various chaplains and missionaries. I carried nearly one hundred to meeting in my brigade a few nights back. After service when I announced that I had soldiers' papers for distribution, there rushed up two or three hundred men, and the papers were gone in less than two minutes. I have already told you how to secure transportation for all the religious literature you can spare me.

"Tell the people at home that all the men in this brave army are in the very highest spirits. It is better than the excitement of 1861. There is more faith in it. What a revival of religion and of patriotic feeling we have in the army! how much encouraged are the people at home! General Bryan, who is a man of prayer and faith, accounts for this double awakening as an answer to the prayers of God's people. He is right. Prayer and faith are stronger than the sword, and will overcome our cruel and fanatical foes.

"Yours in the faith of Christ,

"ATTICUS G. HAYGOOD,
"*Missionary to Bryan's Brigade in East Tennessee.*"

JOHNSON'S ISLAND.

"Through the kindness of Rev. F. M. Haygood, we are permitted to copy the following paragraph from a letter just received from his brother, Captain W. B. Haygood, Company C, Forty-fourth Georgia Regiment, written from Johnson's Island, March 31:

"God has blessed us with a gracious revival of religion for the last two months. Many have found Him as a sin-pardoning God. We have a Young Men's Christian Association and quite a number of Bible classes in full operation on the island. The Confederate Fast Day will be strictly observed by many of us on the 8th of April."

[*For the Army and Navy Herald.*]

"*Brother Harp:* A few days ago I went to the front, on a visit to my old friends of the Thirty-fifth Alabama Regiment, whom I served as chaplain for twelve months, and who, until recently, were in the Mississippi department. I found them in the ditches, ready for the fight, and confident of victory in case of an attack. The boys seemed glad to see me, and I am sure that I have never made a visit which afforded me more real pleasure and gratification.

"About a year ago, while encamped at Canton, Mississippi, a wonderful revival of religion began in the regiment, through the instrumentality of a few earnest laymen, who, a few months previous, had united themselves into a Christian Association—the first organization of the kind in the whole south-western army. The revival rapidly communicated itself to the whole brigade. The Association was resolved into a Brigade Association, and soon a brigade church was erected, which was more signally honored by the presence of the Lord than many gorgeous temples, whose costliness and magnificence have been the wonder of all beholders.

"When ordered to other points, no sooner had they settled in camp than they went to work to erect a place of worship; when the woods would become vocal with the voice of prayer, songs of praise, and the glad shouts of the newly converted.

"Brother McCutcheon, chaplain of the Seventh Kentucky, was untiring in his efforts to save souls, and his name is still held in grateful remembrance by the brethren. I was told that from the time of the commencement of the work until the present it has been one continuous revival.

"Except when the regiment is actually on the move their Bible class meets every afternoon at half-past two o'clock, and at four they have a meeting for prayer, or preaching, whenever the services of a preacher can be obtained. Upon my arrival, I was promptly notified that I was impressed into service during my stay. They have a little black horn, which they have carried through the whole of their arduous campaign, and which is held as sacred as were the rams' horns of the olden service. The sounding of this, which, by the way, forcibly reminds one of the good old days of camp-meetings, is the signal for divine service.

"The hour for preaching having arrived, the horn was sounded, when from up and down the line such crowds came pouring in, that in a few minutes I had around me a larger congregation than I had seen for years.

"As I endeavored to preach to them the word of life, although an occasional shell would go screaming past, they listened with the most earnest and undivided attention. I felt that it was a privilege, indeed, to preach to such men; and while I beheld their devout demeanor, and contrasted it with that of former days, I could but exclaim: 'What hath God wrought!'

"Gambling, once the prevailing vice in the regiment, had given place to the reading of God's word, and oaths and obscene jests to prayer and praise. Said an officer to me: 'Almost all of our boys are religious.' Another remarked that he had not seen a deck of cards in the regiment for twelve months, and that an oath was seldom heard. Even those who have made no profession of religion have become much reformed in their habits. A spirit of *religiousness* (if you will allow the expression) seems to be resting upon every one.

"I was conversing to-day with a wounded officer, a member of General Clayton's staff, who, though a polished gentleman and a ripe scholar, is unfortunately not a Christian. Said he, in remarking upon the deep religious spirit of the army: 'I am not astonished at this, when I see the example which so many of our generals set before their men. A few days ago,' he continued, 'I was present at a communion service near the quarters of Lieutenant-General Stewart, during which the general, who is an elder in the Cumberland Presbyterian Church, both assisted in the distribution of the elements and led in prayer. The effect upon the congregation was perfectly electrical.'

"The second afternoon of my stay I preached to a still larger congregation. Everything being comparatively quiet along that part of our lines, the men thronged the tops of the breastworks and the adjacent fort, the sides of the ditches, and the ground on every side. So great was the crowd, that it was with the utmost difficulty I could make myself heard by those who were on the outskirts.

"Movements being on foot, and duty calling me elsewhere, I reluctantly took leave of the brethren. God may keep us yet longer in the crucible of affliction; he may have in reservation for us still fiercer fires; but the dross is already being consumed, and the day is not far distant when we shall come forth as a refined gold —a people that 'fear God and work righteousness'—a people favored of the Lord.

"Before closing this already too lengthy communication, I will state that I was beset with the urgent requests: 'Send us something good to read;' 'Send us religious papers;' 'Send us tracts.' 'Oh,' said the brethren, 'eternity alone will reveal the great good which these little messengers have accomplished among us.'

"God bless you, my brother, in your work of love! Take courage, for your labor is not in vain in the Lord.   "R. A. WILSON.

"Atlanta, July 5, 1864."

[*Extracts from a letter received from Rev. E. B. Duncan, Army Missionary.*]

"TALLAHASSEE, June 27, 1864.

"REV. ROBERT J. HARP:

"I have just returned from East Florida, where I have been for the last week, actively engaged, day and night, preaching, praying, and talking in camps and hospitals. There is certainly a good work going on. Men and officers are seriously concerned—easy of access. I found a kind reception everywhere. In fact my acquaintance has settled down into a pleasant familiarity that makes my mission pleasant, and were it not for my excessive labors, would be highly agreeable. Preaching nearly every night, and generally three services on Sabbath, and going through the camp consecutively, is quite a privilege as well as duty. With no class of men does religious conversation pay better than with soldiers. It is the work of an apostle, and an apostle's reward.

"I spent a week at Camp Milton, in front—here were our principal cavalry, near Jacksonville. Our force here has been keeping back the Yankees for months. A short time ago they made an advance to Camp Milton. Our cavalry fell back to Baldwin, seven miles, with sick men and horses and camp equipage, then returned and drove back the whole Yankee force, and (as they say) killed fifteen men, while Lieutenant Hart alone was slightly wounded on our side.

"Our Soldiers' Christian Association, formed when here last, in Scott's Battalion, is working finely—officers and men meeting on a great moral basis : as it ought to be. I arrived the night of their meeting. Some ten or twelve joined. I found the camp serious. Some had been converted to God. One young man stated, that while sitting on his horse, on picket, he was turning over the leaves of our little Soldiers' Hymn Book, when at the forty-fourth page, the words were applied to his heart, 'How firm a foundation ye saints of the Lord,' etc. How easy it is to find when we seek! One converted in camp, and another (quite a youth) stated that he was very much dissatisfied in camp—wanted to get home—commenced seeking religion. God pardoned his sins—says he is now perfectly satisfied. How religion makes every burden easy! I joined these, and another excellent man in the church, and gave them certificates to read to their churches at home.

"We have here what is called the rainy season. It rains every day, and we are in the mud and water yet, but we have kept up our meetings. Sabbath, I preached to the battalion on holiness. The rain held up till I was through, then fell in torrents. Went down to the Second Florida Cavalry to preach at 4 o'clock, and found it submerged in mud. The officers and men in bad plight, and some in rather bad humor. I remained in a close camp, unknown, that I might learn the moral status of the camp, while intermittent showers were falling. I thought I should be thwarted in my purpose. I went out, like Noah's dove, to find a dry place to set my foot upon to preach once, and again all looked hopeless, but at 4 o'clock the clouds parted—a little light in the horizon indicated a chance from that quarter, but the ground seemed to forbid it. The earth was covered, except here and there an island.

"I took a stool, and on a little high ground, sung, 'How firm a foundation,' etc. They flocked around until we had a large company, who stood in the mud and water while I told them of God's love, in giving His Son, 'that whosoever believeth in Him might not perish, but have everlasting life.' Many felt its force; many confessed judgment, who will have the debt cancelled by the suretyship of the Son of God, I hope. Camps being moved to a dry place, Monday, I preached at night. It was pleasant to see the large attendance seated on the ground, in earnest attention. Afterwards formed a Soldiers' Christian Association in the regiment that promises much. Thus closed a pleasant, profitable week, at Camp Milton.

"The Yankees are leaving Jacksonville (at least some of them).

"I preached at Baldwin, Columbus and Suwannee bridge, on my way to this place.

"My work was quite interesting on the coast."

[*June*, 1864.]

"During one of the series of engagements which have recently come off at the front, as a body of our cavalry was being hotly pursued by the enemy's infantry and artillery, a cannon ball came whizzing just over the head of one of our boys, and passed between the legs of a brave fellow of the infantry, who was just in the rear of the cavalry, and in the act of stepping across a branch. Both legs of his pants were almost torn off, but no damage was done to the soldier further than the loss of a finger. He stood perfectly amazed at his almost miraculous escape. While standing thus, the young cavalryman, near whose head the ball had passed—and by the way as brave a boy as ever bestrode a horse—rode up and remarked : ' That is the answer to a pious mother's prayers.' The soldier was touched to the heart ; and bursting into tears, said, Yes, he had a pious, good mother. He felt that in answer to her prayers he had escaped almost unharmed from the deadly missile. Mothers ! let your boys in the army know that you pray for them, and they will be braver soldiers and better boys. A mother's prayer is a safer shield for her boy than bomb-proof fortifications."—*Atlanta Confederacy.*

[1864.]

An Atlanta correspondent says : " We have learned of a very touching and affect-ing incident, which occurred in this army on the battle-field of the 23d of July, and which is worthy of being engraved in letters of gold commemorating the magnan-imity and true Christian spirit of the two noble heroes concerned. The preparations for battle were being made. A corps commander rode up to one of his division gen-erals, and finding some confusion, reprimanded him with some severity. The tone and manner were calculated to wound, and they soon parted with feelings of evident bitterness towards each other. The corps commander felt, after the excitement was over, that he had probably spoken too harshly to a brother officer, and as they both were about entering the danger of the battle-field, he felt it to be a duty he not only owed himself, but a former friend, to render an apology. He, therefore, dis-patched a staff officer after the battle had opened, through a storm of fire, to com-municate with him, and express his regrets, and ask forgiveness. The division commander replied that he had been deeply wounded by the language of his supe-rior officer, but the apology was satisfactory, and he freely forgave. In a few min-utes after, a fatal bullet pierced the division commander, and his soul winged its flight to another world. How beautiful and touching was this evidence of mutual forgiveness, enacted by two distinguished soldiers, in the day of battle, and in the hour of danger and death.'

[*A Religious Army.*]

" P. W. A.," writing to the *Savannah Republican*, on Sunday, 25th of May, 1864, says :

" I rode along the lines to-day, and found the men resting after their many marches and hard battles. Some were reading their well-thumbed Bibles ; some were indicting letters to the loved ones at home, to assure them of their safety ; some were sleeping—perchance dreaming of the bloody work still remaining to be done ; others were enjoying the music of the brigade bands, as they rehearsed those solemn and touching airs which the grand old masters of the art divine, in their most holy and impassioned moods, have given to the world ; and others again were sitting under the trees, with their arms stacked near at hand, listening to the Word of Life, as preached by those faithful servants of God, the hardy, zealous, self-denying chaplains of the army. As the army thus rested—its great heart quiet, its huge arms unstrung, its fleet feet still—I could but reflect, and wonder as I reflected, that this vast machine, this mighty giant, this great, unmeasured, and immeasurable power should be so terrible in battle, and yet so calm, and gentle, and devout in the hour of peace."

The following tribute to the Army of Tennessee is from the pen of a correspond-ent of the *Atlanta Register*, who writes from Marietta, June 1st :

" It is wonderful to see with what patience our soldiers bear up under trials and hardships. I attribute this in part to the great religious change in our army. Twelve months after this Revolution commenced, a more ungodly set of men could scarcely be found than the Confederate Army. Now the utterance of an oath is seldom, and religious songs and expressions of gratitude to God are heard from every quarter.

"GOD BLESS THAT YOUNG LADY!"
(See page 623.)

Our army seems to be impressed with a high sense of overruling Providence. They have become Christian patriots, and have a sacred object to accomplish— an object dearer to them than life. They have also perfect confidence in their commanders. Such an army may be temporarily overpowered by vastly superior numbers, but they never can be conquered.—Our armies, God being with us, are invincible."

[July, 1864.]

An army correspondent of the *Augusta Constitutionalist* relates the following incident as a fact:

"A soldier on the mountain was struck, a few days ago, by a minie ball in the breast. The ball penetrated a pocket Bible, which saved his life. But the most singular part of the incident is, that the tip of the ball indented the following line, and penetrated no further: 'Thou shalt not fall in the pit.' This is vouched for by a member of the Savannah Relief Committee, who saw the Bible."

[Americus, Georgia, October, 1863.]

Passing down the S. W. Railroad a few weeks ago, we witnessed a scene which brought tears unbidden to the eye. As the train stopped at Americus, a bright-eyed girl of some fifteen summers entered the car with cup in hand, followed by two servants. She approached an emaciated soldier who had long been an inmate of a Yankee hospital, "Will you have something to eat, sir?" The poor man, scarcely able to raise his head, looking up in wonder and astonishment, to see if his hearing had not deceived him, replied: "Yes, ma'am." A waiter covered with clean white table-linen and crowded with boiled ham, and biscuit, and butter, was placed before him and permission given to take what he wished. After he had supplied himself, this "angel of mercy" passed on to others who were anxiously awaiting their turn. But as the poor fellow commenced eating, tears of gratitude commenced trickling down his cheek. He observed that we were noticing him, and remarked: "Stranger, this is something we poor soldiers do not often enjoy. God bless that young lady." Soon this "messenger of good" returned with a huge demijohn of buttermilk, and in the kindest tone addressed our friend, "Will you have some, sir?" The poor man drank heartily, and with tears glistening in his eyes thanked his benefactress, who sped away to relieve some other thirsty soldier. Another prayer went up, "God bless that young lady."

Little did the young lady dream of what an amount of happiness she was conferring upon or what sacred memories she had awakened in that poor soldier's heart. It would have been confined to his own breast, and that little circle that awaited his coming on the banks of the Chattahoochee, had we not intruded and drawn it from him. Away from home—from wife and those little ones whose prattling makes life more sweet—sick and just escaped from prison—almost famished for something to eat, for his purse was empty, he was in a condition to appreciate such kindness as was shown him. And most heartily do we unite in his prayer and say, "God bless Miss Kate Vernon," for this we learned was the young lady's name.

We understand that the ladies of Americus have a regular organization to provide food for soldiers passing on the road. So if any soldier should be travelling in that direction he may rest assured that he will find friends there.

And not only in this matter, fellow-soldier, have the citizens of Americus and vicinity exhibited their appreciation and love for the soldier, but they have contributed nearly six thousand dollars to send to you tracts, the Bible and the *Army Herald.* And so when we say, "God bless the people of Americus," you are ready to respond with a hearty "Amen."

[January, 1865.]

The following letter is from our indefatigable missionary to the Florida Army, Rev. E. B. Duncan:

" *My very dear Brother:*—I am lingering along in my home-bound course to my Flora land; the cold, bleak weather would urge me forward but for *justifiable* circumstances.

"After leaving your room in Macon I visited and at night preached at the Floyd House Hospital, where I came in competition with the theatre across the way, but gained the *ascendancy*. Leaving my kind hostess and friend, Mrs. Campbell, next morning, I reached Andersonville, where I felt at home again amongst my old Florida friends of Captain D.'s artillery company. Though the weather was very cold, I preached two nights, held prayer-meeting the third, visited the messes, and before leaving preached in the stockade to the Yankee prisoners. They stood up round me, while I stood on a box and declared to them the Gospel from the words of the Philippian jailor and the Apostle's advice to him. I had unusual liberty, and they listened with most profound attention. At the close I invited them to seek religion and come to God, when the ground was literally covered with those that prostrated themselves. But few in that vast assembly remained standing, evincing how afflictions tend to bring man to God. They treated me with the greatest respect, thanking me kindly and begging me to return, and followed me when leaving, as if loath to let me go. Many came to shake hands, until, like the Indian, I said, ' I shake hands in my heart.' I visited their hospital and promised to preach to the patients before I left; so, having little time to spare, I preached to them a half hour just before leaving. They were very attentive, and I preached with liberty. I heard no complaint against any one for *mistreatment*—they spoke to the contrary. Several recognized me as having preached to them last August, and urged me to prevail upon the preachers to visit the stockade. I left, feeling that I had done the work of my Master and that I heard the sound of His footsteps behind me. While I have no sympathy with invasion, I feel myself a debtor to preach the Gospel to any soul this side the grave.

" I reached Americus Saturday; took up quarters with our friend and brother H.; an appointment was announced for me to preach, which I filled on the bright, beautiful Sabbath morning of the 12th, to a large audience, from the ' First and Great Commandment.' After visiting my old friends and forming new ones, I reluctantly left. God bless the people of Americus! I stopped at Cotton Hill, where I am *friend bound* till to-morrow morning. Then off for duty.

" Yours very truly, good-bye,   " E. B. DUNCAN."

I have a good deal more material on hand, but the above is all that I can now find space for, and is sufficient to show that Christ *was* in the Camp of the other armies of the Confederacy as well as in Lee's army, and that wherever the

" Jacket in gray
The soldier-boy wore "

was found, there also was manifested the presence and power of " the Captain of our Salvation."